Risdley

Fodor's Affordable France

FOURTH New EDITION

"These books succeed admirably; easy to follow and use, full of cost related information, practical advice and recommendations...maps are clear and easy to use."
—*Travel Books Worldwide*

"Good helpmates for the cost-conscious traveler."
—*Detroit Free Press*

"Concentrates on life's basics...without skimping on literary luxuries."
—*New York Daily News*

"The Fodor's series puts a premium on showing its readers a good time."
—*Philadelphia Inquirer*

Portions of this book appear in
Fodor's France and *Fodor's Paris*

Fodor's Travel Publications, Inc.
New York • Toronto • London • Sydney • Auckland

Fodor's Affordable France

Editors: Lisa Leventer, Conrad Little Paulus
Editorial Contributors: Nancy Coons, William Echikson, Nigel Fisher, Simon Hewitt, Corinne LaBalme, Laura M. Kidder, Alexander Lobrano, Robert Noah, Kristen D. Perrault, M.T. Schwartzman, Mary Ellen Schultz, George Semler, Dinah Spritzer
Creative Director: Fabrizio La Rocca
Cartographers: David Lindroth; Maryland Cartographics
Cover design: Tigist Getachew
Cover Photograph: Peter Scholey/TSW

Design: Vignelli Associates

Special Sales

Fodor's Travel Publications are available at special discounts for bulk purchases for sales promotions or premiums. Special editions, including personalized covers, excerpts of existing guides, and corporate imprints, can be created in large quantities for special needs. For more information, contact your local bookseller or write to Special Markets, Fodor's Travel Publications, 201 East 50th Street, New York, NY 10022. Inquiries from Canada should be directed to your local Canadian bookseller or sent to Random House of Canada, Ltd., Marketing Dept., 1265 Aerowood Dr., Mississauga, Ontario L4W 1B9. Inquiries from the United Kingdom should be sent to: Fodor's Travel Publications, 20 Vauxhall Bridge Rd., London, England SW1V 2SA.

PRINTED IN THE UNITED STATES OF AMERICA
10 9 8 7 6 5 4 3 2 1

Contents

Maps

Contents

Fodor's Choice for Budget Travelers

No two people will agree on what makes a perfect vacation, but it's fun—and can be helpful—to know what others think. We hope you'll have a chance to experience some of Fodor's Choices yourself while you're visiting France. For detailed information about each entry, refer to the appropriate chapters within this guidebook.

Best Budget Hotels

Auberge de la Commanderie, St-Emilion. An unbeatable setting in one of France's prettiest wine towns, a private garden and restaurant, and views of the surrounding vineyards make this 19th-century hotel a top choice. *$*

Esméralda, Paris. Right across from Notre-Dame (and so a little noisy), very cheap—and very charming. *$*

Gutenberg, Strasbourg. A 200-year-old mansion (with modern amenities) steps away from the splendid Cathédrale Notre-Dame and the heart of Strasbourg. *$*

Hôtel de la Cathédrale, Rouen. Rouen's magnificent cathedral, painted so often by Monet, will be your nearest neighbor if you stay in this cozy hotel in a medieval building. *$*

Little Palace, Nice. If the bustle of Nice leaves you craving the country, stay here—a homey, old-fashioned oasis of charm. *$*

Hôtels St-Albert et Montaigne, Sarlat. These comfortable lodgings on the delightful town square share a good regional restaurant and the services of the pleasant Garrigou family. *$*

Vauban, Briançon. Named for the military engineer whose fortifications dominate this old Alps town, the Vauban has a reasonable restaurant specializing in regional cuisine, balconies affording views of the mountains, and gracious hosts. *$*

Best-Value Restaurants

Les Bookinistes, Paris. This Left Bank bistro offers excellent food at reasonable prices, a cheery setting overlooking the Seine, and friendly service. *$$*

Le Blazon, Amboise. The food in this pretty little restaurant (which is also a delightful hotel) behind the château is superior, the menu changing with the seasons. *$$*

Brasserie Georges, Lyon. One of Lyon's oldest and largest brasseries, with hearty food, thirties decor, great prices, and music. *$*

Le Buisson Ardent, Chartres. You'll dine here on imaginative, inexpensive food in a wood-beamed room overlooking Chartres Cathedral. *$*

Café de la Bourse, St-Malo. What this large seafood restaurant lacks in ambience it makes up for in the bounty of its offerings and the friendliness of its staff. *$*

Dar Djerba, Marseille. Marseille has a number of North African restaurants, and this is perhaps the best; cozy and authentic, it specializes in couscous of all kinds. *$*

La Grilladine, Beaune. Good, hearty Burgundian fare at reasonable prices and a cozy setting recommend this restaurant. *$*

Hiély-Lucullus, Avignon. Considered by some to be among France's top 50 restaurants, Hiély-Lucullus offers innovative cuisine in an elegant setting. *$$*

Museums and Works of Art

Bayeux Tapestry, Bayeux (Musée de la Tapisserie)

Chapelle du Rosaire, Vence. A place of worship and a work of art, designed and decorated by Matisse.

Fondation Maeght, St-Paul-de-Vence. A gem of a museum of modern art, blending its stunning holdings (Miró, Matisse, and Kandinsky, among others) with stylish presentation.

Géricault's *The Raft of the Medusa*, Paris (Louvre)

Grünewald's *Isenheim Altarpiece*, Colmar (Musée Unterlinden)

Janmot's *The Poem of the Soul* painting cycle, Lyon (Musée des Beaux-Arts)

Musée des Arts Décoratifs, Lyon. You can see the well-displayed furniture, silverware, ceramics, and objects of early Lyonnaise life in a satisfying couple of hours.

Musée Matisse, Le Cateau-Cambrésis. The Palais Fénelon is now home to paintings, sculpture, and drawings by native son Henri Matisse.

Musée de Peinture et de Sculpture, Grenoble. In addition to an excellent series of 17th-century French and Spanish paintings, this museum houses one of the most exciting modern collections outside Paris, starring Gauguin, Matisse, Modigliani, Miró, Picasso, and others.

Musée Ingres, Montauban. Drawings and paintings by the great French classicist and works from his own collection, housed in the Bishop's Palace.

Musée d'Orsay, Paris. A refurbished Belle Epoque railway station overlooking the Seine is the setting for art from the mid-19th through the early 20th century, including the Impressionist and Post-Impressionist works formerly housed in the Jeu de Paume.

Palais de la Berbie, Albi. Albi's own Henri de Toulouse-Lautrec is honored in this former Bishop's Palace.

Châteaus and Gardens

Chenonceau, Loire Valley. The most romantic of the châteaus, with arched galleries spanning the Cher, this palace owes its gardens to Catherine de Médicis.

Fontainebleau, Ile-de-France. François I, Henri II, Napoléon, and the best artists of their day all contributed to make this quintessential royal château a work of art inside and out.

Monet's garden, Giverny, Ile-de-France. The artist painted his most famous works in and of his gardens here, which include a profusion of flowers and an enchanting water garden, complete with water lilies, paths, and a Japanese footbridge.

Musée Rodin, Paris. The sculpture of Rodin set amid more than 2,000 rosebushes—not to be missed.

Orangerie, Strasbourg. A serene spot, with a lake, flowers, copper beeches, and a nearby rare-bird reserve that's home to a flock of flamingoes.

Pierrefonds, Oise. This huge château, begun in the 12th century, was restored in the 1860s by the fairy-tale imagination of Viollet-le-Duc and the money of Napoléon.

Vaux-le-Vicomte, Ile-de-France. Andre Le Nôtre's gardens, carefully restored, are for many the real reason to visit this château.

Versailles, Ile-de-France. Home to Louis XIV and 20,000 of his best friends (and a few servants), the vastness of Versailles is stunning, the opulence overwhelming; the 250 acres of grounds represent classical French landscaping at its most formal.

Villandry, Loire Valley. The château's remarkable gardens were replanted earlier in this century to evoke their origins in the 16th, the result an extravagant, geometric *jardin à la française*.

How This Guide Will Save You Money

If you're one of the rock-bottom-budget travelers who sleep on park benches to save money and would never, ever dress up for boeuf bourguignon at La Grilladine, then look to another guidebook for your travel information.

But if you're among those who budget some of the finer things into their traveling life, if you would stay home before spending a night in a hostel dormitory with strangers, and if you're willing to pay a little more for crisp sheets, a firm bed, a soft pillow, and a really superb dining experience every now and again, read on. It's for you that Fodor's team of savvy, budget-conscious writers and editors have prepared this book.

We share your traveling style and your champagne tastes, and we know that saving money means making choices. Some of us do that by sticking to public transportation and picnic lunches. Others splurge on a hotel with amenitites but forgo fancy meals. Still others take the hostel route in order to go on a shopping spree.

Here, we've tried to include enough options so that all of you spend time and money in the ways you most enjoy. The hotels we suggest represent good value, and there are no dives, thank you—only clean, friendly places with an acceptable level of comfort, convenience, and charm. We also recommend a wide range of inexpensive and moderately priced restaurants where you can eat well in pleasant surroundings. You'll read about the best budget shopping and how to make the arts and nightlife scene without breaking the bank. And we'll tell you how to get around by public transportation.

As for planning what to see and do, you'll find the same lively writing and authoritative background information available in Fodor's renowned Gold Guides.

Please Write to Us

Everyone who has contributed to *Affordable France* has worked hard to make the text accurate. All prices and opening times are based on material supplied to us at press time, and Fodor's cannot accept responsibility for any errors that may have occurred. The passage of time brings changes, so it's always a good idea to call ahead to confirm information when it matters—particularly if you're making a detour to visit specific sights or attractions. When reserving at a hotel or inn, be sure to mention if you have a disability or are traveling with children, if you prefer a private bath or a certain type of bed, or if you have any other concerns.

Do let us know about your trip. Did you enjoy the restaurants we recommended? Was your hotel comfortable and were the museums you visited worthwhile? Did you happen upon a treasure that we haven't included? We would love to have your feedback, positive and negative. If you do have suggestions or complaints, we'll look into them and revise our entries when it's the right thing to do. So please send us a letter or postcard (we're at 201 East 50th Street, New York, New York 10022). We look forward to hearing from you. In the meantime, have a wonderful trip!

Karen Cure
Editorial Director

France by Rail

ENGLAND

La Manche
(English Channel)

Calais
Boulogne
Cherbourg
Dieppe
Amiens
Le Havre
Caen
Rouen
Be
Seine
Roscoff
Brest
Morlaix
St-Brieuc
St-Malo
Quimper
Rennes
Chartres
Lorient
Vannes
Le Mans
Orléa
Angers
Blois
Nantes
Tours
Loire
La Roche-sur-Yon
Bo
ATLANTIC
OCEAN
Niort
Poitiers
La Rochelle
Royan
Saintes
Limoges
Angoulême
Bay of Biscay
Périgueux
Brive-la-
Gaillarde
Au
Bordeaux
Garonne
Arcachon
Langon
Dordogne
Cahors
Ro
Montauban
Bayonne
Albi
Biarritz
Pau
Tarbes
Toulouse
Lourdes
Carcassonne
N
Rail Lines
SPAIN
ANDORRA
0   50 mi
0   75 km

ENGLAND

Boulogne

NO
DE

*La Manche
(English Channel)*

Cherbourg

Dieppe

Amie

Le Havre

N28

N13

A15

Rouen

Caen

A13

Seine

N175

NORMANDY

Roscoff

N12

St-Malo

Chartres

Brest

Morlaix

A11

St-Brieuc

A10

Quimper

N165

BRITTANY

Rennes

N24

Orle

A81

Le Mans

Lorient

Vannes

Angers

Blois

A11

LOIR
VALLE

Nantes

PAYS-DE-LA
LOIRE

Tours

*ATLANTIC
OCEAN*

N137

Loire

A10

Les Sables
d'Olonne

Poitiers

Niort

N20

La Rochelle

POITOU-
CHARENTES

Royan

Saintes

Limoges

Angoulême

LIMOUSIN

Bay of Biscay

A10

Périgueux

Bordeaux

Brive-la-
Gaillarde

Arcachon

Garonne

Dordogne

Langon

Cahors

N10

AQUITAINE

A62

Montauban

Bayonne

N117

MIDI-PYRENEES

Albi

Biarritz

Pau

Tarbes

Toulouse

LAN
ROU

N113

Carcassonne

N

0   50 mi

0   75 km

S P A I N

ANDORRA

Making Your Vacation Affordable

By William Echikson

The medieval church bells gently ring. A soft morning sun streams into the room, and slowly, luxuriously, you rise. The buttery morning smell of fresh croissants floats in the air. As you sip your café au lait at the corner café, the neighborhood wakes up before your eyes. Working mothers lead toddlers to nursery school, children hurry along, their backpacks full of books.

Not far away, farmers ready their stands—the local produce market will soon open. A dazzling array of delectable pâtés and cheeses, fresh vegetables and fruit, at ridiculously low prices, is on display. With a little finger pointing and some body language, you choose a picnic lunch. And with a fresh baguette and a bottle of wine or mineral water, you're ready to launch another day of exploring.

This is affordable France. Of course, the mere mention of France conjures up images of *haute couture* and *haute cuisine*—luxurious and expensive—and this face of France does demand a full wallet. But the other face of this wonderful country is—like its people—solid, substantial, and thrifty. In Paris or the provinces, budget-minded visitors can join the locals in their special joie de vivre, and the miraculous part of the treat is that it doesn't cost much.

Away from the exclusive haunts of the super-rich, France is Europe's bargain country. Nowhere else is such delicious food available at such reasonable prices, and nowhere else do so many little family-run lodgings dot the countryside. Even in Paris, the budget-traveler can live like a king. The key is choosing carefully.

Start with the stomach. To the rest of the world, French restaurants mean premium prices, and at first you may want to head for a fast food outlet. Stop right there. Though a few McDonald's and Burger Kings are visible in big French cities, you should look, instead, for the many small, family-run restaurants that serve fine three-course meals for $10 to $15. For a little more, say $20, you can have a virtual feast—usually with wine and unlimited bread thrown in. Even fashionable restaurants often offer reasonable fixed-price menus, especially at lunchtime. And, of course, there's the *pique-nique*. On a nice day, the parks and nearby forests are full of families spreading out their blankets.

And as for where to lay your head, France has a multitude of reasonable lodging options. Bargain seekers don't even have to search for youth hostels, where as little as $15 buys a double room with shower, though admittedly not much in the way of comfort or charm. World-class hotels cost the earth here, as anywhere else, but only in such jet-set haunts as Monaco and Cannes is the general range of lodging out of reach. Otherwise, no matter where you go, you should be able to find a double room with bath for under $50. Even in Paris, where prices run about

20% more than elsewhere, there are double rooms with shower for less than $40 a night. In most areas, $70 will let two of you live in some style.

Shoppers must be careful; some basic American staples cost two to three times more in France, while certain luxuries cost that much less. Electronic goods and jeans often go for astronomical prices—Levi's up to $60 a pair, a roll of film $10, alkaline batteries $8. But high fashion can be cheaper than elsewhere. Men's sportscoats in the most modern designs and colors can be bought in Paris for about $180. Chic dresses from boutiques not connected to haute couture salons are a similar bargain. Remember, it costs nothing to window shop, and in France, even ordinary shop windows and newspaper stands are arranged with extraordinary flair.

Getting around without breaking the budget means learning some local tricks. Going by car is the most flexible option, and if there are two or more of you, it can work out to be fairly reasonable. Keep off the toll roads, which are expensive, and stay in country *gîtes*. Be sure to shop around for gasoline; the price per liter varies as much as 25 centimes. Domestic airfares can be a bargain, especially if you travel as a family, but then you miss the scenery. All told, the best way to go is by train. They run on time, crisscross the country, and are comfortable and fast. A 500-kilometer trip (a little more than 300 miles) costs only about $60. Even on the TGV the only extra cost (except a hefty supplement at peak times) is about $3 for the obligatory seat reservation.

One caveat here, though: Most trains run to and from Paris, which means that you won't be able to go easily from one part of the country to another without going through the capital. If you want to visit a region at leisure, you'll have to rent a car—or ride a bike. Here, too, the railroad can help out. Almost every major train station rents bicycles. As much as France is a country of train lovers, so is it also a cyclist's paradise. After all, this is the home of the Tour de France. A common sight on rural Sunday afternoons is bicyclists whizzing by, training for a race. So, imitate the frugal French, who long ago took up cycling as a cheap, healthy way to see the country. It's fun, too.

One last tip about the trains: Near almost every small-town station there's a down-to-earth, inexpensive Hôtel de la Gare, with decent food. In some cases it has gone upscale, as in the grimy industrial town of Roanne, where the station buffet became the three-star (Michelin Guide) restaurant Troisgros. Today, a meal there will take a chunk out of your wallet, but any Frenchman (or woman or child) would say it's worth every penny of the splurge. Gastronomy is the French obsession. This is a country full of bakers who toil through the night to supply your breakfast table, of farmers who patiently age fresh milk into delectable cheese, and of vintners who have guarded their vineyards through centuries, ever improving their wine. For these people, their work is not a job, but a passion, an emotion that lies somewhere between love and religious zeal.

France has undergone an extraordinary renewal in the past generation. Since World War II, its economy has expanded faster than America's and faster than Germany's—at a rate second only to that of Japan. By the start of the 1990s, the country was the world's fourth-largest exporter, and this growth built a new urban society. Before the war almost half the population earned its living from the land; today, that figure is less than 10 percent. Many towns' populations have tripled. Boring old backwaters like Lyon and Strasbourg have become dynamic cities.

Many wonder whether France has lost its Frenchness. But the miracle seems to be how it has managed to thrive and modernize while withstanding homogenization. And few countries combine with such ease modern technology with Old World comfort and class. It's possible to shop in a *hypermarché*, bigger than any American supermarket and to wake up in the morning to the sound of medieval bells. The bullet train speeds through an ageless picture of rolling hills, ancient villages and fairytale châteaus in this unique, and above all, affordable land.

1 Essential Information

Important Contacts

No single travel resource can give you every detail about every topic that might interest or concern you at the various stages of your journey—when you're planning your trip, while you're on the road, and after you get back home. The following organizations, books, and brochures will supplement the information in *Affordable France*. For related information, including both basic tips on visiting France and background information on many of the topics below, study Smart Travel Tips, the section that follows Important Contacts.

Air Travel

The major gateways to France include Paris's **Orly Airport** (tel. 49–75–52–52) and **Charles de Gaulle** (Roissy) Airport (tel. 48–62–22–80). Flying time is 7½ hours from New York, 9 hours from Chicago, and 11 hours from Los Angeles.

Carriers Carriers serving France include **Air France** (tel. 800/237–2747), **American Airlines** (tel. 800/433–7300), **British Airways** (tel. 800/247–9297), **Continental** (tel. 800/231–0856), **Delta** (tel. 800/241–4141), **TWA** (tel. 800/892–4141), **United Airlines** (tel. 800/241–6522), and **USAir** (tel. 800/428–4322).

Carriers from the United Kingdom include **Air France** (tel. 0181/759–2311), **British Airways** (tel. 0181/759–2313), and **Caledonian Airways** (tel. 0293/567100), the charter division of British Airways. Charter flights often offer the best value; contact **Nouvelles Frontières** (11 Blenheim St., London W1Y 0QP, tel. 0171/629–7772), and look into Caledonian Airways' service between Gatwick and Beauvais, north of Paris.

Complaints To register complaints about charter and scheduled airlines, contact the U.S. Department of Transportation's **Office of Consumer Affairs** (400 7th St. NW, Washington, DC 20590, tel. 202/366–2220 or 800/322–7873).

Consolidators Established consolidators selling to the public include **BET World Travel** (841 Blossom Hill Rd., Suite 212-C, San Jose, CA 95123, tel. 408/229–7880 or 800/747–1476); **Euram Tours** (1522 K St. NW, Suite 430, Washington DC, 20005, tel. 800/848–6789); **TFI Tours International** (34 W. 32nd St., New York, NY 10001, tel. 212/736–1140 or 800/745–8000); **UniTravel** (Box 12485, St. Louis, MO 63132, tel. 314/569–0900 or 800/325–2222); **Council Charter** (205 E. 42nd St., New York, NY 10017, tel. 212/661–0311 or 800/800–8222); and **Travac Tours and Charter** (989 6th Ave., 16th Floor, New York, NY 10018, tel. 212/563–3303 or 800/872–8800; 2601 E. Jefferson, Orlando, FL 32803, tel. 407/896–0014 or 800/872–8800).

Publications For general information about charter carriers, ask for the Office of Consumer Affairs' brochure "**Plane Talk: Public Charter Flights.**" The Department of Transportation also publishes a 58-page booklet, "**Fly Rights**" (Consumer Information Center, Dept. 133-B, Pueblo, CO 81009; $1.75).

For other tips and hints, consult the Consumers Union's monthly "**Consumer Reports Travel Letter**" (Box 53629, Boulder CO 80322, tel. 800/234–1970; $39 annually); the newsletter "**Travel Smart**" (40 Beechdale Rd., Dobbs Ferry, NY 10522, tel. 800/327–3633; $37 annually); *The Official Frequent Flyer Guidebook,* by Randy Petersen (4715-C Town Center Dr., Colorado Springs, CO 80916, tel. 719/597–8899 or 800/487–8893; $14.99 plus $3 shipping); *Airfare Secrets Exposed,* by Sharon Tyler and Matthew Wonder (Universal Information Publishing; $16.95 plus $3.75 shipping from Sandcastle Publishing, Box 3070-A, South Pasadena, CA 91031, tel. 213/255–3616 or 800/655–0053); and *202 Tips Even the Best Business Travelers*

May Not Know, by Christopher McGinnis (Irwin Professional Publishing, Box 1333, Burr Ridge Pkwy., Burr Ridge, IL 60521, tel. 708/789–4000 or 800/634–3966; $10 plus $3 shipping).

Within France France's domestic airline service, **Air Inter** (tel. 45–46–90–00), has flights from Paris to all major cities. For long journeys—from Paris to the Riviera, for instance—air travel is a time-saver, though train travel is always much cheaper. Most domestic flights from Paris leave from **Orly Airport.**

Barge Travel

For information on cruising France's inland waterways, contact **Bourgogne Voies Navigables** (1 quai de la République, 89000 Auxerre, tel. 86–52–18–99). For tours of France that travel by barge, *see* Theme Trips *in* Tour Operators, *below.*

Better Business Bureau

For local contacts in the home town of a tour operator you may be considering, consult the **Council of Better Business Bureaus** (4200 Wilson Blvd., Arlington, VA 22203, tel. 703/276–0100).

Bicycling

For information on cycling in France, contact the **Fédération Française de Cyclotourisme** (8 rue Jean-Marie-Jégo, 75013 Paris, tel. 44–16–88–88). The yellow Michelin maps (1:200,000 scale) are fine for roads, but the best large-scale maps are prepared by the **Institut Géographique National** (IGN, 107 rue La Boétie, 75008 Paris, tel. 42–56–06–68). Try their blue series (1:25,000) or orange series (1:50,000). Both indicate elevations and steep grades. Several good bike routes are described in detail in the chapters that follow. Also *see* Theme Trips *in* Tour Operators, below.

Bike Rentals Among firms that rent bikes are **Bicyclub** (8 pl. Porte-de-Champerret, 75017 Paris, tel. 47–66–55–92), at 60 francs per day or 350 francs per week, and **Paris Vélo** (4 rue du Fer-à-Moulin, 75005 Paris, tel. 43–37–59–22), at 80 francs per day or 360 francs per week. Both stores require a 1,000-franc deposit, though they may accept a credit card.

Bus Travel

For service from the United Kingdom, contact **Eurolines** (tel. 0171/730–3499), the international affiliate of **National Express.**

Within France Excursions and bus holidays are organized by the **SNCF** (88 rue St-Lazare, 75009 Paris, tel. 45–82–50–50) and other tourist organizations, such as **Horizons Européens.** Ask for the brochure at any major travel agent, or contact **France-Tourisme** (214 rue de Rivoli, 75001 Paris, tel. 42–60–31–25).

Camping

A guide to the country's equipped campsites and natural camping areas is available for 121 francs (includes shipping) from the **Fédération Française de Camping et de Caravaning** (78 rue de Rivoli, 75004 Paris, tel. 42–72–84–08).

Car Rental

Major car-rental companies represented in France include **Alamo** (tel. 800/327–9633, 0800/272–2000 in the United Kingdom); **Avis** (tel. 800/331–1084, 800/879–2847 in Canada); **Budget** (tel. 800/527–0700,

0800/181–181 in the United Kingdom); **Hertz** (tel. 800/654–3001, 800/263–0600 in Canada, 0181/679–1799 in the United Kingdom); and **National** (sometimes known as Europcar InterRent outside North America; tel. 800/227–3876, 0181/950–5050 in the United Kingdom). Rates for an economy car in Paris begin at $27 a day and $180 a week, with unlimited mileage. This does not include VAT, which in France is 18.6%.

Local car-rental firms in Paris include **Rent-A-Car** (79 rue de Bercy, 75012, tel. 46–82–60–60), which offers small Fiat Pandas or larger Rover 214s. Other outfits include **Dergi** (60 blvd. St-Marcel, 75005, tel. 45–87–27–04); **Locabest** (104 blvd. Magenta, 75010, tel. 44–72–08–05); and **ACAR** (99 blvd. Auguste-Blanqui, 75013, tel. 45–88–28–38), with economy cars and Renault Espace minivans.

Rental Wholesalers Contact **Auto Europe** (Box 7006, Portland, ME 04112, tel. 207/828–2525 or 800/223–5555); **Europe by Car** in New York City (write 1 Rockefeller Plaza, 10020; visit 14 W. 49th St.; or call 212/581–3040, 212/245–1713, or 800/223–1516) or Los Angeles (9000 Sunset Blvd., 90069, tel. 800/252–9401 or 213/272–0424 in CA); **Foremost Euro-Car** (5658 Sepulveda Blvd., Suite 201, Van Nuys, CA 91411, tel. 818/786–1960 or 800/272–3299); or the **Kemwel Group** (106 Calvert St., Harrison, NY 10528, tel. 914/835–5555 or 800/678–0678).

The Channel Tunnel

For information, contact **Le Shuttle** (tel. 01345/353535 in the United Kingdom, 800/388–3876 in the United States), which transports cars, or **Eurostar** (tel. 0171/922–4486 in the United Kingdom, 800/942–4866 in the United States), the high-speed train service between London (Waterloo) and Paris (Gare du Nord). Eurostar tickets are available in the United Kingdom through **InterCity Europe,** the international wing of BritRail (London's Victoria Station, tel. 0171/834–2345 or 0171/828–8092 for credit-card bookings), and in the United States through **Rail Europe** (tel. 800/942–4866) and **BritRail Travel** (1500 Broadway, New York, NY 10036, tel. 800/677–8585).

Children and Travel

Baby-Sitting Paris agencies include the **American University of Paris** (31 av. Bosquet, 75007 Paris, tel. 40–62–06–00, fax 47–05–33–49, only during school year); **Bébé Cool Services** (4 rue Faustin-Hélie, 75016 Paris, tel. 45–04–27–14); **Home Service** (2 rue Pierre-Semard, 75009 Paris, tel. 42–82–05–04); **Institut Catholique** (21 rue d'Assas, 75006 Paris, tel. 44–39–52–00, only during school year).

Discount Rail Passes The SNCF allows children under 4 to travel free (provided they don't occupy a seat) and children 4 to 11 to travel at half fare. The Carte Kiwi (280 francs) allows children under 16 and as many as four accompanying adults to make four journeys at half fare.

Flying Look into **"Flying with Baby"** (Third Street Press, Box 261250, Littleton, CO 80126, tel. 303/595–5959; $5.95 plus $1 shipping), cowritten by a flight attendant. **"Kids and Teens in Flight,"** free from the U.S. Department of Transportation's Office of Consumer Affairs, offers tips for children flying alone. Every two years the February issue of *Family Travel Times* (*see* Know-How, *below*) details children's services on three dozen airlines.

Games The gamemeister, Milton Bradley, has games to help keep little (and not so little) children from getting fidgety while riding in planes, trains, and automobiles. Try packing the Travel Battleship sea battle game ($7), Travel Connect Four, a vertical strategy game ($8), the Travel Yahtzee dice game ($6), the Travel Trouble dice and board game ($7), and the Travel Guess Who mystery game ($8).

Know-How *Family Travel Times,* published four times a year by Travel with Your Children (TWYCH, 45 W. 18th St., New York, NY 10011, tel. 212/206–0688; annual subscription $40), covers destinations, types of vacations, and modes of travel.

The *Family Travel Guides* catalogue (Carousel Press, P.O. Box 6061, Albany, CA 94706, tel. 510/527–5849; $1 postage and handling lists about 200 books and articles on family travel. *Traveling with Children—And Enjoying It,* by Arlene K. Butler (Globe Pequot Press, Box 833, 6 Business Park Rd., Old Saybrook, CT 06475, tel. 203/395–0440 or 800/243–0495, 800/962–0973 in CT; $11.95 plus $3 shipping), helps you to plan your trip with children, from toddlers to teens. Also check *Take Your Baby and Go! A Guide for Traveling with Babies, Toddlers and Young Children,* by Sheri Andrews, Judy Bordeaux, and Vivian Vasquez (Bear Creek Publications, 2507 Minor Ave., Seattle, WA 98102, tel. 206/322–7604 or 800/326–6566; $5.95 plus $1.50 shipping). *Innocents Abroad: Traveling with Kids in Europe,* by Valerie Wolf Deutsch and Laura Sutherland (Penguin USA, 120 Woodbine St., Bergenfield, NJ 07621, tel. 201/387–0600 or 800/253–6476; $15.95 or $4.95 paperback), covers child- and teen-friendly activities, food, and transportation.

Lodging Novotel (tel. 800/221–4542) and Sofitel hotels (tel. 800/221–4542) offer discounts for families; some properties have special programs for children. Club Med (40 W. 57th St., New York, NY 10019, tel. 800/258–2633) has a "Baby Club" (from age four months) at its resort in Chamonix, "Mini Clubs" (for ages four to six or eight, depending on the resort), and "Kids Clubs" (for ages eight and up during school holidays) at all its resort villages in France except in Val d'Isère. Some clubs are only French-speaking, so check first.

Tour Operators Contact Grandtravel (6900 Wisconsin Ave., Suite 706, Chevy Chase, MD 20815, tel. 301/986–0790 or 800/247–7651), which has tours for people traveling with grandchildren ages 7 to 17; Families Welcome! (21 W. Colony Pl., Suite 140, Durham, NC 27705, tel. 919/489–2555 or 800/326–0724); or Rascals in Paradise (650 5th St., Suite 505, San Francisco, CA 94107, tel. 415/978–9800 or 800/872–7225).

Customs

U.S. Citizens The U.S. Customs Service (Box 7407, Washington, DC 20044, tel. 202/927–6724) can answer questions on duty-free limits and publishes a helpful brochure, "Know Before You Go." For information on registering foreign-made articles, call 202/927–0540.

Canadians Contact Revenue Canada (2265 St. Laurent Blvd. S, Ottawa, Ontario, K1G 4K3, tel. 613/993–0534) for a copy of the free brochure "I Declare/Je Déclare" and for details on duties that exceed the standard duty-free limit.

U.K. Citizens HM Customs and Excise (Dorset House, Stamford St., London SE1 9NG, tel. 0171/202–4227) can answer questions about U.K. customs regulations and publishes "A Guide for Travellers," detailing standard procedures and import rules.

For Travelers with Disabilities

Complaints To register complaints under the provisions of the Americans With Disabilities Act, contact the U.S. Department of Justice's Public Access Section (Box 66738, Washington, DC 20035, tel. 202/514–0301, fax 202/307–1198, TTY 202/514–0383).

In the U.S.
Hearing Impairments Contact the American Academy of Otolaryngology (1 Prince St., Alexandria, VA 22314, tel. 703/836–4444, fax 703/683–5100, TTY 703/519–1585).

Mobility Impairments Contact the **Information Center for Individuals with Disabilities** (Fort Point Pl., 27–43 Wormwood St., Boston, MA 02210, tel. 617/ 727–5540, 800/462–5015 in MA, TTY 617/345–9743); **Mobility International USA** (Box 10767, Eugene, OR 97440, tel. and TTY 503/343– 1284; fax 503/343–6812), the U.S. branch of an international organization based in Belgium (*see below*) that has affiliates in 30 countries; **MossRehab Hospital Travel Information Service** (1200 W. Tabor Rd., Philadelphia, PA 19141, tel. 215/456–9603, TTY 215/ 456–9602); the **Society for the Advancement of Travel for the Handicapped** (SATH, 347 5th Ave., Suite 610, New York, NY 10016, tel. 212/447–7284, fax 212/725–8253); the **Travel Industry and Disabled Exchange** (TIDE, 5435 Donna Ave., Tarzana, CA 91356, tel. 818/ 344–3640, fax 818/344–0078); and **Travelin' Talk** (Box 3534, Clarksville, TN 37043, tel. 615/552–6670, fax 615/552–1182).

Vision Impairments Contact the **American Council of the Blind** (1155 15th St. NW, Suite 720, Washington, DC 20005, tel. 202/467–5081, fax 202/467–5085) or the **American Foundation for the Blind** (15 W. 16th St., New York, NY 10011, tel. 212/620–2000, TTY 212/620–2158).

European Organizations Contact the **Comité Nationale Français de Liaison pour la Réadaptation des Handicapés** (38 blvd. Raspail, 75007 Paris, tel. 53–80–66–*France* 66) or the **Association des Paralysés de France** (17 blvd. Auguste-Blanqui, 75013 Paris, tel. 40–78–69–00), which publishes a useful Paris hotel list.

U.K. Contact the **Royal Association for Disability and Rehabilitation** (RADAR, 12 City Forum, 250 City Rd., London EC1V 8AF, tel. 0171/ 250-3222).

Belgium Contact **Mobility International** (Rue de Manchester 25, B1070 Brussels, Belgium, tel. 00–322–410–6297), an international clearinghouse of travel information for people with disabilities.

Publications Several free publications are available from the U.S. Information Center (Box 100, Pueblo, CO 81009, tel. 719/948–3334): **"New Horizons for the Air Traveler with a Disability"** (address to Dept. 355A), describing legally mandated changes; the pocket-size **"Fly Smart"** (Dept. 575B), good on flight safety; and the Airport Operators Council's worldwide **"Access Travel: Airports"** (Dept. 575A).

The 500-page ***Travelin' Talk Directory*** (Box 3534, Clarksville, TN 37043, tel. 615/552–6670; $35) lists people and organizations who help travelers with disabilities. For specialist travel agents worldwide, consult the ***Directory of Travel Agencies for the Disabled*** (Twin Peaks Press, Box 129, Vancouver, WA 98666, tel. 206/694– 2462 or 800/637–2256; $19.95 plus $2 shipping).

Travel Agencies and Tour Operators The Americans with Disabilities Act requires that travel firms serve the needs of all travelers. However, some agencies and operators specialize in making group and individual arrangements for travelers with disabilities, among them **Access Adventures** (206 Chestnut Ridge Rd., Rochester, NY 14624, tel. 716/889–9096), run by a former physical-rehab counselor. In addition, many general-interest operators and agencies (*see* Tour Operators, *below*) can also arrange vacations for travelers with disabilities.

Hearing Impairments One agency is **International Express** (7319-B Baltimore Ave., College Park, MD 20740, tel. and TTY 301/699–8836, fax 301/699– 8836), which arranges group and independent trips.

Mobility Impairments A number of operators specialize in working with travelers with mobility impairments: **Flying Wheels Travel** (143 W. Bridge St., Box 382, Owatonna, MN 55060, tel. 507/451–5005 or 800/535–6790), a travel agency that specializes in European cruises and tours; **Hinsdale Travel Service** (201 E. Ogden Ave., Suite 100, Hinsdale, IL 60521, tel. 708/325–1335 or 800/303–5521), a travel agency that will give you access to the services of wheelchair traveler Janice Perkins;

Nautilus Tours (5435 Donna Ave., Tarzana, CA 91356, tel. 818/344–3640 or 800/345–4654); and **Wheelchair Journeys** (16979 Redmond Way, Redmond, WA 98052, tel.206/885–2210), which can handle arrangements worldwide.

Developmental Contact the nonprofit **New Directions** (5276 Hollister Ave., Suite
Disabilities 207, Santa Barbara, CA 93111, tel. 805/967–2841).

Discounts

Options include **Entertainment Travel Editions** (Box 1068, Trumbull, CT 06611, tel. 800/445–4137; $28–$53, depending on destination); **Great American Traveler** (Box 27965, Salt Lake City, UT 84127, tel. 800/548–2812; $49.95 annually); **Moment's Notice Discount Travel Club** (163 Amsterdam Ave., Suite 137, New York, NY 10023, tel. 212/486–0500; $25 annually, single or family); **Privilege Card** (3391 Peachtree Rd. NE, Suite 110, Atlanta GA 30326, tel. 404/262–0222 or 800/236–9732; $74.95 annually); **Travelers Advantage** (CUC Travel Service, 49 Music Sq. W, Nashville, TN 37203, tel. 800/548–1116 or 800/648–4037; $49 annually, single or family); and **Worldwide Discount Travel Club** (1674 Meridian Ave., Miami Beach, FL 33139, tel. 305/534–2082; $50 annually for family, $40 single).

Electricity

Send a SASE to the **Franzus Company** (Customer Service, Dept. B50, Murtha Industrial Park, Box 142, Beacon Falls, CT 06403, tel. 203/723–6664) for a copy of the free brochure "Foreign Electricity Is No Deep Dark Secret."

Ferry Travel

Dover–Calais Contact **P&O European Ferries** (Channel House, Channel View Rd., Dover, Kent CT17 9TJ, tel. 0181/575–8555); **Sealink** (Charter House, Park St., Ashford, Kent TN24 8EX, tel. 01233/646801); or **Hoverspeed** (International Hoverport, Marine Parade, Dover CT17 9TG, tel. 01304/240241).

Other Folkestone–Boulogne crossings are available from Hoverspeed.
Crossings Newhaven–Dieppe crossings are available from Sealink. The Portsmouth–Le Havre crossing is offered by P&O. For Ramsgate–Dunkerque crossings, contact **Sally Line** (Argyle Centre, York St., Ramsgate, Kent CT11 9DS, tel. 01843/595522).

Driving distances from the French ports to Paris are as follows: from Calais, 290 kilometers (180 miles); from Boulogne, 243 kilometers (151 miles); from Dieppe, 193 kilometers (120 miles); from Dunkerque, 257 kilometers (160 miles). The fastest routes to Paris from each port are via the N43, A26, and A1 from Calais and the Channel Tunnel; via the N1 from Boulogne; via the N15 from Le Havre; via the D915 and N1 from Dieppe; and via the A25 and A1 from Dunkerque.

Gay and Lesbian Travel

Organizations The **International Gay Travel Association** (Box 4974, Key West, FL 33041, tel. 800/448–8550), a consortium of 800 businesses, can supply names of travel agents and tour operators.

Publications The premiere international travel magazine for gays and lesbians is **"Our World"** (1104 N. Nova Rd., Suite 251, Daytona Beach, FL 32117, tel. 904/441–5367; $35 for 10 issues). The 16-page monthly **"Out & About"** (tel. 212/645–6922 or 800/929–2268; $49 for 10 issues) covers gay-friendly resorts, hotels, cruise lines, and airlines.

Tour **Toto Tours** (1326 W. Albion, Suite 3W, Chicago, IL 60626, tel. 312/
Operators 274–8686 or 800/565–1241) has group tours worldwide.

Travel The largest agencies serving gay travelers are **Advance Travel**
Agencies (10700 Northwest Freeway, Suite 160, Houston, TX 77092, tel. 713/
682–2002 or 800/695–0880); **Islanders/Kennedy Travel** (183 W. 10th
St., New York, NY 10014, tel. 212/242–3222 or 800/988–1181); **Now
Voyager** (4406 18th St., San Francisco, CA 94114, tel. 415/626–1169
or 800/255–6951); and **Yellowbrick Road** (1500 W. Balmoral Ave.,
Chicago, IL 60640, tel. 312/561–1800 or 800/642–2488). **Skylink
Women's Travel** (746 Ashland Ave., Santa Monica, CA 90405, tel.
310/452–0506 or 800/225–5759) works with lesbians.

Health Issues

Finding a The best bet is to ask the **American Hospital** (63 blvd. Victor-Hugo,
Doctor Neuilly-sur-Seine, just outside Paris, tel. 46–41–25–25, fax 46–24–
49–38) to recommend an English-speaking doctor. A midnight visit
to a local public hospital could be frightening and confusing, as the
interns on duty often speak little English.

For members, the **International Association for Medical Assistance
to Travellers** (IAMAT, 417 Center St., Lewiston, NY 14092, tel. 716/
754–4883; 40 Regal Rd., Guelph, Ontario, Canada N1K 1B5, tel.
519/836–0102; 1287 St. Clair Ave., Toronto, Ontario, Canada M6E
1B8, tel. 416/652–0137; 57 Voirets, 1212 Grand-Lancy, Geneva,
Switzerland; membership free) publishes a worldwide directory of
English-speaking physicians meeting IAMAT standards.

Medical- Contact **International SOS Assistance** (Box 11568, Philadelphia, PA
Assistance 19116, tel. 215/244–1500 or 800/523–8930; Box 466, Pl. Bonaventure,
Companies Montréal, Québec, Canada H5A 1C1, tel. 514/874–7674 or 800/363–
0263); **Medex Assistance Corporation** (Box 10623, Baltimore, MD
21285, tel. 410/296–2530 or 800/573-2029); **Near Services** (Box 1339,
Calumet City, IL 60409, tel. 708/868–6700 or 800/654–6700); and
Travel Assistance International (1133 15th St. NW, Suite 400, Washington, DC 20005, tel. 202/331–1609 or 800/821–2828). Because
these companies also sell death-and-dismemberment, trip-cancellation, and other insurance coverage, there is some overlap with the
travel-insurance policies sold by the companies listed under Insurance, *below.*

Hiking

For details on hiking in France, contact the **Club Alpin Français** (24
av. Laumière, 75019 Paris, tel. 42–02–68–64) or the **Fédération
Française de la Randonnée Pédestre** (64 rue de Gergovie, 75014 Paris, tel. 45–45–31–02), which publishes good topographical maps and
guides. The IGN maps sold in many bookshops are also invaluable
(*see* Bicycling, *above*).

Insurance

Travel insurance covering baggage, health, and trip cancellation or
interruptions is available from **Access America** (Box 90315, Richmond, VA 23286, tel. 804/285–3300 or 800/284–8300); **Carefree Travel
Insurance** (Box 9366, 100 Garden City Plaza, Garden City, NY
11530, tel. 516/294–0220 or 800/323–3149); **Near Services** (Box 1339,
Calumet City, IL 60409, tel. 708/868–6700 or 800/654–6700); **Tele-
Trip** (Mutual of Omaha Plaza, Box 31716, Omaha, NE 68131, tel. 800/
228–9792); **Travel Insured International** (Box 280568, East Hart-
ford, CT 06128, tel. 203/528–7663 or 800/243-3174); **Travel Guard International** (1145 Clark St., Stevens Point, WI 54481, tel. 715/345–
0505 or 800/826–1300); and **Wallach & Company** (107 W. Federal St.,
Box 480, Middleburg, VA 22117, tel. 703/687–3166 or 800/237–6615).

In the U.K. The **Association of British Insurers** (51 Gresham St., London EC2V 7HQ, tel. 0171/600–3333; 30 Gordon St., Glasgow G1 3PU, tel. 0141/226–3905; Scottish Provident Bldg., Donegall Sq. W, Belfast BT1 6JE, tel. 01232/249176; call for other locations) gives advice by phone and publishes the free **"Holiday Insurance,"** which sets out typical policy provisions and costs.

Lodging

Apartment and Villa Rental Among the companies to contact are **At Home Abroad** (405 E. 56th St., Suite 6H, New York, NY 10022, tel. 212/421–9165); **Europa-Let** (92 N. Main St., Ashland, OR 97520, tel. 503/482–5806 or 800/462–4486); **Hometours International** (Box 11503, Knoxville, TN 37939, tel. 615/588–8722 or 800/367–4668); **Interhome** (124 Little Falls Rd., Fairfield, NJ 07004, tel. 201/882–6864); **Property Rentals International** (1008 Mansfield Crossing Rd., Richmond, VA 23236, tel. 804/378–6054 or 800/220–3332); **Rental Directories International** (2044 Rittenhouse Sq., Philadelphia, PA 19103, tel. 215/985–4001); **Rent-a-Home International** (7200 34th Ave. NW, Seattle, WA 98117, tel. 206/789–9377 or 800/488–7368); **Vacation Home Rentals Worldwide** (235 Kensington Ave., Norwood, NJ 07648, tel. 201/767–9393 or 800/633–3284); **Villas and Apartments Abroad** (420 Madison Ave., Suite 1105, New York, NY 10017, tel. 212/759–1025 or 800/433–3020); and **Villas International** (605 Market St., Suite 510, San Francisco, CA 94105, tel. 415/281–0910 or 800/221–2260). Members of the travel club **Hideaways International** (767 Islington St., Portsmouth, NH 03801, tel. 603/430–4433 or 800/843–4433; $99 annually) receive two annual guides plus quarterly newsletters, and arrange rentals among themselves.

Home Exchange Principal clearinghouses include **HomeLink International/Vacation Exchange Club** (Box 650, Key West, FL 33041, tel. 305/294–1448 or 800/638–3841; $60 annually), which gives members four annual directories, with a listing in one, plus updates; **Intervac International** (Box 590504, San Francisco, CA 94159, tel. 415/435–3497; $65 annually), which has three annual directories; and **Loan-a-Home** (2 Park La., Apt. 6E, Mount Vernon, NY 10552-3443, tel. 914/664–7640; $35–$45 annually), which specializes in long-term exchanges.

Hotels A directory to small, inexpensive hotels can be obtained from **Logis de France** (83 av. d'Italie, 75013 Paris, tel. 45–84–83–84, fax 44–24–08–74; 75 francs).

A few French-based subbudget hotel chains offer clean, very basic, very small accommodations often for less than $30 a night. The following chains publish directories with locations and rates (none has a U.S. reservation number): **Accor** (in Paris, tel. 43–04–10–22); **Hotels & Compagnie** (in Paris, tel. 64–46–49–00); and **Groupe Envergure** (in Paris, tel. 64–62–46–46).

Housekeeping and Self-Catering Best bets are the **Gîtes Ruraux,** which offer low-cost housekeeping/self-catering vacations in a furnished cottage, chalet, or apartment in the country; rentals are by the week or month. For details, contact the **Maison des Gîtes de France** (35 rue Godot-de-Mauroy, 75009 Paris, tel. 49–70–75–75, fax 49–70–75–76), naming which region interests you, or send away for the *French Farm and Village Holiday Guide* (Hunter Publishing, 300 Raritan Center Pkwy., Box 7816, Edison, NJ 08818, tel. 908/225–1900; $17.95 plus $3 shipping and handling).

Money Matters

ATMs For specific foreign **Cirrus** locations, call 800/424–7787; for foreign Plus locations, consult the **Plus** directory at your local bank.

Currency Exchange If your bank doesn't exchange currency, contact **Thomas Cook Currency Services** (41 E. 42nd St., New York, NY 10017 or 511 Madison Ave., New York, NY 10022, tel. 212/757–6915 or 800/223–7373 for locations) or **Ruesch International** (tel. 800/424–2923 for locations).

Wiring Funds Funds can be wired via **American Express MoneyGram**ˢᴹ (tel. 800/926–9400 from the United States and Canada for locations and information) or **Western Union** (tel. 800/325–6000 for agent locations or to send using MasterCard or Visa, 800/321–2923 in Canada).

Passports and Visas

U.S. Citizens For fees, documentation requirements, and other information, call the **Office of Passport Services** information line (tel. 202/647–0518).

Canadians For fees, documentation requirements, and other information, call the Ministry of Foreign Affairs and International Trade's **Passport Office** (tel. 819/994–3500 or 800/567–6868).

U.K. Citizens For fees, documentation requirements, and to get an emergency passport, call the **London Passport Office** (tel. 0171/271–3000).

Photo Help

The **Kodak Information Center** (tel. 800/242–2424) answers consumer questions about film and photography. An informative book on taking expert-quality travel photographs is *Kodak Guide to Shooting Great Travel Pictures* (Fodor's Travel Publications, 800/533–6478 or from bookstores; $16.50).

Rail Travel

Train-ferry travel from the United Kingdom is provided by **Sealink** (tel. 0233/647047) and **British Rail International** (tel. 0171/834–2345).

For information on rail travel within France, contact the **SNCF** (88 rue St-Lazare, 75009 Paris, tel. 45–82–50–50).

Discount Passes Buying a rail pass can save you money if you plan to do a lot of traveling by train. The French Flexipass allows you unlimited train travel on any three days within a one-month period, in addition to which the France Rail 'n' Drive Pass buys you the use of an Avis car for two days. With both passes, you can buy up to six additional days of train travel. The BritFrance Rail Pass covers both France and Britain in packages of 5 or 10 days. All these passes must be purchased stateside and are sold by travel agents as well as by **Rail Europe** (226–230 Westchester Ave., White Plains, NY 10604, tel. 914/682–7456 for group reservations [10 people or more] or 800/438–7245; 2087 Dundas E, Suite 105, Mississauga, Ontario, Canada, L4X 1M2, tel. 905/602–4195 or 800/361–7245).

France is also one of 17 countries in which you can use Eurail Passes, which provide unlimited rail travel during their period of validity. Passes are available in 5-, 15-, or 21-day, or one- or two-month packages. Another option is the Europass, offering unlimited rail travel in your choice of three, four, or all five of the participating countries (France, Germany, Italy, Spain, and Switzerland) for a minimum of 5 and a maximum of 15 days (within a two month period). For all of the above, apply through your travel agent or **Rail Europe** (*see above*); **DER Tours** (Box 1606, Des Plaines, IL, 60017, tel. 800/782–2424); or **CIT Tours Corp.** (342 Madison Ave., Suite 207, New York, NY 10173, tel. 212/697–2100 or 800/248–8687; 310/670–4269 or 800/248–7245 in western United States).

Senior Citizens and Students Senior citizens (over 60) and young people (under 26) are eligible for reduced fares with the Carte Vermeil and Carrissimo, respectively, which carry up to 50% discounts on travel within France. They can be purchased at SNCF stations (140 francs for four trips or 260 francs for unlimited discount travel for Carte Vermeil; 190 francs or 295 francs, for 4 or 8 trips respectively, for Carrissimo) with proof of identity and two passport photos. The reductions are 50% during "blue" periods (most of the time) and 20% during "white" periods. Every station can give you a calendar of white/blue periods and sell you the appropriate tickets. Note that there is no reduction for buying an *aller-retour* (round-trip) ticket rather than an *aller simple* (one-way) ticket, with one exception: Rail travelers get a 25% discount for a return ticket (ask for a *billet de séjour*) between stations at least 500 kilometers apart, providing journeys do not take place at peak times and include at least part of a Sunday. For further information contact the SNCF (88 rue St-Lazare, 75009 Paris, tel. 45–82–50–50).

Senior Citizens

Educational Travel

The nonprofit **Elderhostel** (75 Federal St., 3rd Floor, Boston, MA 02110, tel. 617/426–7788), for people 60 and older, has offered inexpensive study programs since 1975. The nearly 2,000 courses cover everything from marine science to Greek myths and cowboy poetry. Fees for two- to three-week international trips—including room, board, and transportation from the United States—range from $1,800 to $4,500.

For people 50 and over and their children and grandchildren, **Interhostel** (University of New Hampshire, 6 Garrison Ave., Durham, NH 03824, tel. 603/862–1147 or 800/733–9753) runs 10-day summer programs involving lectures, field trips, and sightseeing. Most last two weeks and cost $2,125–$3,100, including airfare.

Organizations

Contact the **American Association of Retired Persons** (AARP, 601 E St. NW, Washington, DC 20049, tel. 202/434–2277; $8 per person or couple annually). Its Purchase Privilege Program gets members discounts on lodging, car rentals, and sightseeing.

For other discounts on lodgings, car rentals, and other travel products, along with magazines and newsletters, contact the **National Council of Senior Citizens** (1331 F St. NW, Washington, DC 20004, tel. 202/347–8800; membership $12 annually) and *Mature Outlook* (6001 N. Clark St., Chicago, IL 60660, tel. 312/465–6466 or 800/336–6330; subscription $9.95 annually).

Publications

The 50+ Traveler's Guidebook: Where to Go, Where to Stay, What to Do, by Anita Williams and Merrimac Dillon (St. Martin's Press, 175 5th Ave., New York, NY 10010, tel. 212/674–5151 or 800/288–2131; $12.95), offers many useful tips. "The Mature Traveler" (Box 50400, Reno, NV 89513, tel. 702/786–7419; $29.95), a monthly newsletter, covers travel deals.

Students

Groups

Major tour operators include **Contiki Holidays** (300 Plaza Alicante, Suite 900, Garden Grove, CA 92640, tel. 714/740–0808 or 800/466–0610) and **AESU Travel** (2 Hamill Rd., Suite 248, Baltimore, MD 21210-1807, tel. 410/323–4416 or 800/638–7640).

Hosteling

Contact **Hostelling International–American Youth Hostels** (733 15th St. NW, Suite 840, Washington, DC 20005, tel. 202/783–6161) in the United States, **Hostelling International–Canada** (205 Catherine St., Suite 400, Ottawa, Ontario K2P 1C3, tel. 613/237–7884) in Canada, and the **Youth Hostel Association of England and Wales** (Trevelyan House, 8 St. Stephen's Hill, St. Albans, Hertfordshire AL1 2DY, tel. 01727/855215 and 01727/845047) in the United Kingdom. Membership ($25 in the United States, C$26.75 in Canada, and £9 in the

United Kingdom) gets you access to 5,000 hostels worldwide that charge $7–$20 nightly per person.

Information is also available from the French headquarters, **Fédération Unie des Auberges de Jeunesse** (27 rue Pajol, 75018 Paris, tel. 44–89–87–28, fax 44–89–87–10).

ID Cards To get discounts on transportation and admissions, get the **International Student Identity Card** (ISIC) if you're a bona fide student or the **International Youth Card** (IYC) if you're under 26. In the United States, the ISIC and IYC cards cost $16 each and include basic travel accident and illness coverage, plus a toll-free travel hot line. Apply through the Council on International Educational Exchange (*see* Organizations, *below*). Cards are available for $15 each in Canada from **Travel Cuts** (187 College St., Toronto, Ontario M5T 1P7, tel. 416/979–2406 or 800/667–2887) and in the United Kingdom for £5 each at student unions and student travel companies.

Organizations A major contact is the **Council on International Educational Exchange** (CIEE, 205 E. 42nd St., 16th Floor, New York, NY 10017, tel. 212/661–1450) with locations in Boston (729 Boylston St., 02116, tel. 617/266–1926); Miami (9100 S. Dadeland Blvd., 33156, tel. 305/670–9261); Los Angeles (1093 Broxton Ave., 90024, tel. 310/208–3551); 43 other college towns nationwide; and the United Kingdom (28A Poland St., London W1V 3DB, tel. 0171/437–7767). Twice a year, it publishes *Student Travels* magazine. The CIEE's Council Travel Service is the exclusive U.S. agent for several student-discount cards.

Campus Connections (325 Chestnut St., Suite 1101, Philadelphia, PA 19106, tel. 215/625–8585 or 800/428–3235) specializes in discounted accommodations and airfares for students. The **Educational Travel Centre** (438 N. Frances St., Madison, WI 53703, tel. 608/256–5551) offers rail passes and low-cost airline tickets, mostly for flights departing from Chicago. For air travel only, contact **TMI Student Travel** (100 W. 33rd St., Suite 813, New York, NY 10001, tel. 800/245–3672).

In Canada, also contact **Travel Cuts** (*see* ID cards, *above*).

Publications See the ***Berkeley Guide to France*** (Fodor's Travel Publications, 800/533–6478 or from bookstores; $17.50).

Tour Operators

Group tours and independent vacation packages can turn out to be a bargain depending on what they include. Among the companies selling tours and packages to France, the following have a proven reputation, are nationally known, and offer plenty of options from which to choose.

Group Tours For deluxe programs, try **Tauck Tours** (11 Wilton Rd., Westport, CT 06881, tel. 203/226–6911 or 800/468–2825) or **Maupintour** (Box 807, Lawrence, KS 66044, tel. 913/843–1211 or 800/255–4266). Another operator falling between deluxe and first-class is **Globus** (5301 S. Federal Circle, Littleton, CO 80123, tel. 303/797–2800 or 800/221–0090). For first-class and first-class superior tours, try **Trafalgar Tours** (21 E. 26th St., New York, NY 10010, tel. 212/689–8977 or 800/854–0103); **Brendan Tours** (15137 Califa St., Van Nuys, CA 91411, tel. 818/785–9696 or 800/421–8446); and **Insight International** (745 Atlantic Ave., Boston MA 02111, tel. 617/482–2000 or 800/582–8380).

Packages **The French Experience** (370 Lexington Ave., Suite 812, New York, NY 10017, tel. 212/986–1115) has the greatest variety of packages, from canal barging to stays in countryside cottages. Just about every airline that flies to France sells packages that include round-trip airfare and hotel accommodations. Among U.S. carriers, contact

American Airlines Fly AAway Vacations (tel. 800/321–2121), **Continental Airlines Grand Destinations** (tel. 800/634–5555), **Delta Dream Vacations** (tel. 800/872–7786), and **United Airlines Vacation Planning Center** (tel. 800/328–6877). Other packagers include: Brendan Tours (*see* Group Tours, *above*); **Alek's Travel** (103 N.W. 2nd Ave., Fort Lauderdale, FL 33311, tel. 305/462–6757 or 800/ 929–7768); **Five Star Touring** (60 E. 42nd St., Suite 612, New York, NY 10165, tel. 212/818–9140 or 800/792–7827); **DER Tours** (11933 Wilshire Blvd., Los Angeles, CA 90025, tel. 310/479–4140 or 800/782–2424); and **Jet Vacations** (1775 Broadway, New York, NY 10019, tel. 212/ 474–8740 or 800/538–2762).

Theme Trips Theme trips are, by their nature, more expensive than a general-interest tour or package, but they still may be a better deal than arranging everything on your own.

Travel Contacts (45 Idmiston Rd., London SE27 9HL, England, tel. 011/44–81766–7868, fax 011/44–81766–6123), with 135 member operators, can satisfy virtually any special interest in France.

Adventure **All Adventure Travel** (5589 Arapahoe, No. 208, Boulder, CO 80303, tel. 800/537–4025) can book biking, hiking, kayaking, diving, rafting, and many other adventures in France. **Uniquely Europe** (2819 1st Ave., No. 280, Seattle, WA 98121, tel. 206/441–8682 or 800/426–3610) has hiking, walking, biking, and skiing tours.

Archaeology **4th Dimension Tours** (1150 N.W. 72nd Ave., Suite 250, Miami, FL 33126, tel. 305/477–1525 or 800/343–0020) will lead you to France's Roman ruins.

Art and **Esplanade Tours** (581 Boylston St., Boston, MA 02116, tel. 617/266–
Architecture 7465 or 800/426–5492) has art-treasure and nature tours of Romanesque France, Champagne, Burgundy and the upper Loire, the Côte d'Azur, and the Dordogne.

Ballooning **Bombard European Balloon Adventures** (855 Donald Ross Rd., Juno Beach, FL 33408, tel. 800/862–8537 or 407/775–0039) is the leader in hot-air balloon tours of France.

Barge Travel **Barge & Voyage Associates** (140 E. 56th St., Suite 4C, New York, NY 10022, tel. 800/546–4777) represents 13 barges that carry 6 to 12 passengers; hot-air ballooning and bicycling are available from most barges. For barges with room for up to 50 passengers in Burgundy, Alsace-Lorraine, Bordeaux, and the south of France, try the **Kemwel Group** (106 Calvert St., Harrison, NY 10528, tel. 800/234–4000). **Le Boat** (215 Union St., Hackensack, NJ 07601, tel. 201/342–1838 or 800/992–0291) has one of France's most diverse barge fleets and runs theme tours around food and wine, gardens, golf, horseback riding, and sketching and art. **Fenwick & Lang** (900 4th Ave., Suite 1201, Seattle, WA 98164, 206/382–1384 or 800/243–6244) has more than 35 years experience in booking barge tours of France.

Bicycling Bike tours of the French countryside are available for five days to two weeks. Contact **Backroads** (1516 5th St., Suite L101, Berkeley, CA 94710, tel. 510/527–1555 or 800/462–2848); **Châteaux Bike Tours** (Box 5706, Denver, CO 80217, tel. 303/393–6910 or 800/678–2453); **Bridges Tours** (2855 Capital Dr., Eugene, OR 97403, tel. 503/484–1196); **Euro-Bike Tours** (Box 990, De Kalb, IL 60115, tel. 800/321–6060); and **Progressive Tours** (224 W. Galer, Suite C, Seattle, WA 98119, 206/285–1987 or 800/245–2229). *See also* Bicycling, *above.*

Food and Wine Culinary theme tours are available from **Annemarie Victory Organization** (136 E. 64th St., New York, NY 10021, tel. 212/486–0353); **Avalon Wine Tours** (Box 473, Jamestown, RI 02835, tel. 401/423–3730 or 800/662–2628); and **European Culinary Adventures** (5 Ledgewood Way, Apt. 6, Peabody, MA 01960, tel. 508/535–5738 or 800/852–2625). If you want to learn French cooking, **Le Cordon Bleu** (404 Irvington St., Pleasantville, NY 10570, tel. 800/457–2433 in U.S.), one of the world's best-known cooking schools, has courses for beginners and connoisseurs. The prestigious **Ritz-Escoffier** cooking school in Paris's Ritz hotel (800/966–5758) schedules 1- to 12-week courses in cooking and bread- and pastry making.

Golf **ITC Golf Tours** (4134 Atlantic Ave., Long Beach, CA 90807, 310/595–6905 or 800/257–4981) custom designs golf itineraries in France.

Horseback For weeklong tours through Beaujolais, the Dordogne, Brittany, *Riding* and the Loire Valley, contact **FITS Equestrian** (685 Lateen Rd., Solvang, CA 93463, tel. 805/688–9494 or 800/666–3487).

Learning **Earthwatch** (680 Mt. Auburn St., Watertown, MA 02272, tel. 617/ *Vacations* 926–8200) recruits volunteers to serve in its EarthCorps as short-term assistants to scientists on research expeditions.

Music **Dailey-Thorp Travel** (330 W. 58th St., New York, NY 10019, tel. 212/307–1555; book through travel agents) specializes in classical music and opera programs throughout France; its packages include tickets that are otherwise very hard to get. Also try **Keith Prowse Tours** (234 W. 34th St., Suite 1000, New York, NY 10036, tel. 212/398–1430 or 800/669–8687).

Tennis **Steve Furgal's International Tennis Tours** (11828 Rancho Bernardo Rd., San Diego, CA 92128, tel. 619/487–7777 or 800/258–3664) can take you to the French Open and arrange a variety of accommodations and activities in Paris.

Organizations The **National Tour Association** (546 E. Main St., Lexington, KY 40508, tel. 606/226–4444 or 800/682–8886) and **United States Tour Operators Association** (USTOA, 211 E. 51st St., Suite 12B, New York, NY 10022, tel. 212/750–7371) can provide lists of member operators and information on booking tours.

Publications Consult the brochure **On Tour** and ask for a current list of member operators from the National Tour Association (*see* Organizations, *above*). Also get a copy of the **"Worldwide Tour & Vacation Package Finder"** from the USTOA (*see* Organizations, *above*) and the Better Business Bureau's **"Tips on Travel Packages"** (Publication No. 24-195, 4200 Wilson Blvd., Arlington, VA 22203; $2).

Travel Agencies

For names of reputable agencies in your area, contact the **American Society of Travel Agents** (1101 King St., Suite 200, Alexandria, VA 22314, tel. 703/739–2782).

U.S. Government Travel Briefings

The U.S. Department of State's Overseas Citizens Emergency Center (Room 4811, Washington, DC 20520; enclose SASE) issues **Consular Information Sheets,** which cover crime, security, political climate, and health risks as well as embassy locations, entry requirements, currency regulations, and other routine matters. For the latest information, stop in at any U.S. passport office, consulate, or embassy; call the interactive hot line (tel. 202/647–5225 or fax 202/647-3000); or, with your PC's modem, tap into the Bureau of Consular Affairs' computer bulletin board (tel. 202/647–9225).

Visitor Information

Contact the **French Government Tourist Office** in the United States at 610 5th Ave., New York, NY 10020 (tel. 212/315–0888 for travel professionals or 900/990–0040 [50¢ per minute] to reach an operator who can send you information and itineraries for your specific destination); 676 N. Michigan Ave., Chicago, IL 60611, tel. 312/751–

7800; 2305 Cedar Springs Rd., Dallas, TX 75201, tel. 214/720–4010; 9454 Wilshire Blvd., Suite 303, Beverly Hills, CA 90212, tel. 310/ 271–2358; in Canada at 1981 McGill College, Suite 490, Montréal, Québec H3A 2W9 (tel. 514/288–4264); 30 St. Patrick St., Suite 700, Toronto, Ontario M5T 3A3 (tel. 416/593–4723); or in the United Kingdom at 178 Piccadilly, London WIV OAL, England (tel. 0891/ 244–123 [39p per minute cheap rate and 49p per minute at other times]).

Weather

For current weather and forecasts, plus the local time and helpful travel tips, call the **Weather Channel Connection** (tel. 900/932–8437; 95¢ per minute) from a Touch-Tone phone.

Smart Travel Tips

The more you travel, the more you know about how to make trips run like clockwork. To help make your travels hassle-free, Fodor's editors have rounded up dozens of tips from our contributors and travel experts all over the world, as well as basic information on visiting France. For names of organizations to contact and publications that can give you more information, *see* Important Contacts, *above.*

Air Travel

If time is an issue, **always look for nonstop flights,** which require no change of plane. If possible, **avoid connecting flights,** which stop at least once and can involve a change of plane, although the flight number remains the same; if the first leg is late, the second waits.

Aloft
Airline Food If you hate airline food, **ask for special meals when booking.** These can be vegetarian, low-cholesterol, or kosher, for example; commonly prepared to order in smaller quantities than standard catered fare, they can be tastier.

Jet Lag To avoid this syndrome, which occurs when travel disrupts your body's natural cycles, try to maintain a normal routine. At night, **get some sleep.** By day, move about the cabin to **stretch your legs, eat light meals, and drink water—not alcohol.**

Smoking Smoking is banned on all flights within the United States of less than six hours' duration and on all Canadian flights; the ban also applies to domestic segments of international flights aboard U.S. and foreign carriers. Delta has banned smoking system-wide. On U.S. carriers flying to France and other destinations abroad, a seat in a no-smoking section must be provided for every passenger who requests one, and the section must be enlarged to accommodate such passengers if necessary as long as they have complied with the airline's deadline for check-in and seat assignment. If smoking bothers you, request a seat far from the smoking section.

Foreign airlines are exempt from these rules but do provide no-smoking sections. British Airways has banned smoking; some nations have banned smoking on all domestic flights, and others may ban smoking on some flights. Talks continue on the feasibility of broadening no-smoking policies.

Cutting Costs The Sunday travel section of most newspapers is a good source of deals.

Charter Flights Charters usually have the lowest fares and the most restrictions. Departures are limited and seldom on time, and you can lose all or most of your money if you cancel. (The closer to departure you cancel, the more you lose, although sometimes you will be charged only a small fee if you supply a substitute passenger.) The flight may be canceled for any reason up to 10 days before departure (after that, only if it is physically impossible to operate). The charterer may also revise the itinerary or increase the price after you have bought the ticket, but only if the new arrangement constitutes a "major change" do you have the right to a refund.

Before buying a charter ticket, **read the fine print** about the company's refund policies. Money for charter flights is usually paid into a bank escrow account, the name of which should be on the contract. If you don't pay by credit card, **make your check payable to the carrier's escrow account** (unles you're dealing with a travel agent, in which case, his or her check should be payable to the escrow account). The U.S. Department of Transportation's Office of Consumer Affairs has jurisdiction.

Charter operators may offer flights alone or with ground arrangements that constitute a charter package. You typically must book charters through your travel agent.

Consolidators Consolidators, who buy tickets at reduced rates from scheduled airlines, sell them at prices below the lowest available from the airlines directly—usually without advance restrictions. Sometimes you can even get your money back if you need to return the ticket. Carefully read the fine print detailing penalties for changes and cancellations. If you doubt the reliability of a consolidator, **confirm your reservation with the airline.**

Major Airlines The least-expensive airfares from the major airlines are priced for round-trip travel and are subject to restrictions. You must usually **book in advance and buy the ticket within 24 hours** to get cheaper fares, and you may have to **stay over a Saturday night.** The lowest fare is subject to availability, and only a small percentage of the plane's total seats are sold at that price. It's good to **call a number of airlines**—and **when you are quoted a good price, book it on the spot**—the same fare on the same flight may not be available the next day. Airlines generally allow you to change your return date for a $25 to $50 fee, but most low-fare tickets are nonrefundable. However, if you don't use it, you can apply the cost toward the purchase price of a new ticket, again for a small charge.

Travel Passes You can save on air travel within Europe if you **travel to and from Paris aboard Air France.** As part of its Euro Flyer program, you can then buy between three and nine flight coupons, which are valid on Air France flights to more than 100 European cities. At $120 each, these coupons are a good deal, and the fine print still allows you plenty of freedom.

From the U.K. The route from London to Paris is the busiest in Europe, with up to 17 flights making the hour-long trip daily from Heathrow and four or five from Gatwick, all to Charles de Gaulle. There are also regular flights from the new London City Airport in the Dockland and several regional airports, including Manchester, Birmingham, Glasgow, Edinburgh, and Southampton; and flights from London to Nice, Lyon, Bordeaux, Marseille, Clermont-Ferrand, Caen, Quimper, Nantes, Montpellier, and Toulouse, as well as from Manchester to Nice. Flying to France is much cheaper than it used to be, and lower prices on scheduled flights have elbowed out most of the charters, but **look for charter flights to the south of France in the summer.**

Arts and Entertainment

Find out about the arts for free. Reading local newspapers and magazines is a good way to find out what's being offered for free. While theater and concert tickets are expensive, performances in churches are often free–as are some of the *son-et-lumière* (sound-and-light) shows staged outdoors at historic sights in summer.

Movies are cut-rate in Paris for Wednesday shows and sometimes for the 6 PM show. Half-price theater tickets for same-day performances can be bought at the booth near Madeleine Church. Note that museum admission fees are often reduced on Sunday and occasionally Wednesday.

Barge Travel

France has Europe's densest inland waterway system, and canal and river vacation trips are popular. You can take an all-inclusive organized cruise or simply rent a boat and plan your own leisurely route. Some of the most picturesque waterways are in Brittany, Burgundy, and the Midi. The Canal du Midi between Toulouse and Sète, constructed in the 17th century, is a historic marvel. For further information, contact a travel agent; ask for a "Tourisme Fluvial" brochure in any French tourist office; or contact Bourgogne Voies Navigables. *See also* Tour Operators *in* Important Contacts, above.

Beaches

When your prime concern is inexpensive accommodations and perhaps a few quiet moments on the sand, you'll **skip the beach scene in July and August** in favor of June or September.

You'll also **steer clear of the Riviera.** It's as crowded as it is pricey, and, anyway, sand is in shorter supply than pebbles. Better beaches, with vast stretches of sand, face north toward the Channel and west toward the Atlantic. The most picturesque beaches are those in Brittany.

Prices are highest at the popular resorts such as Biarritz, Arcachon, Les Sables d'Olonne, La Baule, Dinard, St-Malo, Cabourg, Deauville, and Le Touquet—though even here the careful traveler can find good values. Price levels are lower at St-Raphael on the Mediterranean, at St-Georges de Didonne and St-Jean-de-Luz on the Atlantic, and Etretat, Trouville, and Houlgate on the Channel.

Between October and May, prices are rock bottom—at the sprinkling of hotels that remain open. At Breton beaches, the nation's most picturesque, there's a great deal to be said for the eerie solitude of a beach town in blustery weather, or in sunniest springtime just before the hordes descend.

Bicycling

There is no shortage of wide, empty roads and flat or rolling countryside in France suitable for biking. The French themselves are great bicycling enthusiasts. Bikes can be hired from many train stations for around 44 francs a day (ask for a list at any station); you need to show your passport and leave a deposit of 500 francs (unless you have Visa or MasterCard). In general, you must return the bike to a station within the same *département* (county or region). Bikes may be sent as accompanied luggage from any station in France; some trains in rural areas transport them without any extra charge. *See also* Bicycling *in* Important Contacts, *above.*

Boules

The sport that is closest to French hearts is *boules* or *pétanque*–an easy-to-grasp version of bowling, traditionally played beneath plane trees with a glass of *pastis* (similar to anisette) at hand. The local *boulodrome* is a social focal point in southern France.

Bus Travel

France's excellent train service means that long-distance buses are rare; regional buses are found mainly where the train service is spotty. Excursions and bus holidays are organized by the SNCF and other tourist organizations.

From the U.K. Unless you're eligible for rail travel with a special discount pass (*see* Rail Travel *in* Important Contacts, *above*), buses offer you the lowest fares of all. A London-to-Paris bus journey can be a rewarding experience (and typically costs only a little more than £60 round-trip). Eurolines (*see* Bus Travel *in* Important Contacts, *above*), the international affiliate of National Express, runs four daily Citysprint buses in summer from Victoria Coach Station to the rue LaFayette in Paris near the Gare du Nord; these buses use the Hovercraft crossing, and the journey time is around 7½ hours. Three daily buses from Victoria to Porte de Bagnolet (métro Gallieni) on the outskirts of Paris use traditional ferries for the Channel crossing and take a bit longer (9 to 10 hours).

Eurolines has buses to the Riviera, leaving Victoria three times a week for such resorts as Nice and Cannes. The round-trip fare to Cannes starts at £109 in low season. The Atlantic coast is also served by Eurolines, with two buses a week to Bordeaux and Biarritz in mid-summer (journey time 24 hours; price approximately £99 round-trip); the Bordeaux service can be extended to Lourdes via Tarbes. There is also regular service from London to Chamonix and the Alps (22½ hours; from around £97 round-trip).

In addition, Eurolines operates an express bus that runs overnight to Grenoble, where there are connecting buses to Nice and Marseille (round-trip to Nice costs about £109); as well as a fast bus to Lyon six days a week in summer, leaving London mid-evening and reaching Lyon the following afternoon (about £85 round-trip).

Business Hours

Banks Banks are open weekdays but have no strict pattern regarding times. In general, though, hours are from 9:30 to 4:30. Most banks, but not all, take a one-hour, or even a 90-minute, lunch break. Note that many 24-hour exchange offices have sprung up around Paris (particularly along the rue de Rivoli) and the larger French cities.

Museums Most are closed one day a week (usually Tuesday) and on national holidays. Usual opening times are from 9:30 to 5 or 6. Many museums close for lunch (noon–2); many are open only afternoons on Sunday.

Shops Large stores in big towns are open from 9 or 9:30 until 7 or 8 (without a lunch break). Smaller shops often open earlier (8 AM) and close later (8 PM) but take a lengthy lunch break (1–4). This siesta-type schedule is routine in the south of France. Corner groceries, often run by immigrants ("*l'Arabe du coin*"), frequently stay open until around 10 PM. Many Paris stores (small and large alike) are beginning to open on Sundays.

Cameras, Camcorders, and Computers

Laptops Before you depart, **check your portable computer's battery,** because you may be asked at security to turn on the computer to prove that it is what it appears to be. At the airport, you may prefer to **request a manual inspection,** although security X-rays do not harm hard-disk or floppy-disk storage. Also, **register your foreign-made laptop with U.S. Customs.** If your laptop is U.S.-made, call the consulate of the country you'll be visiting to find out whether or not it should be registered with local customs upon arrival. You may want to **find out about repair facilities at your destination** in case you need them.

Photography If your camera is new or if you haven't used it for a while, **shoot and develop a few rolls of film** before you leave. Always **store film in a cool, dry place**—never in the car's glove compartment or on the shelf under the rear window.

Every pass through an X-ray machine increases film's chance of clouding. To protect it, carry it in a clear plastic bag and **ask for hand inspection at security.** Such requests are virtually always honored at U.S. airports, and usually are accommodated abroad. Don't depend on a lead-lined bag to protect film in checked luggage—the airline may increase the radiation to see what's inside.

Video Before your trip, **test your camcorder, invest in a skylight filter to protect the lens, and charge the batteries.** (Airport security personnel may ask you to turn on the camcorder to prove that it's what it appears to be). The batteries of most newer camcorders can be recharged with a universal or worldwide AC adapter charger (or multivoltage converter), usable whether the voltage is 110 or 220. All that's needed is the appropriate plug.

Videotape is not damaged by X-rays, but it may be harmed by the magnetic field of a walk-through metal detector, so **ask that videotapes be hand-checked.** Videotape sold in France is based on the SECAM standard, which is different than the one used in the United States. You will not be able to view your tapes through the local TV set or view movies bought there in your home VCR. Blank tapes bought in France can be used for camcorder taping, but they are pricey. Some U.S. audiovisual shops convert foreign tapes to U.S. standards; contact an electronics dealer to find the nearest.

Car Rental

Renting cars in France is expensive—usually at least twice the cost of renting in the United States. In addition, the price doesn't usually take into account the whopping 18.6% VAT tax. If you are flying into Paris first and are planning to spend time there, pick up your car the day you're leaving. You won't need a car in the capital, and it may be more of a hassle than a convenience.

Cutting Costs To get the best deal, **book through a travel agent and shop around.** When pricing cars, **ask where the rental lot is located.** Some off-airport locations offer lower rates—even though their lots are only minutes away from the terminal via complimentary shuttle. You may also want to **price local car-rental companies,** whose rates may be lower still, although service and maintenance standards may not be up to those of a national firm. Also **ask your travel agent about a company's customer-service record.** How has it responded to late plane arrivals and vehicle mishaps? Are there often lines at the rental counter, and, if you're traveling during a holiday period, does a confirmed reservation guarantee you a car?

Always **find out what equipment is standard** at your destination before specifying what you want; **do without automatic transmission or air-conditioning** if they're optional. In Europe, manual transmissions are standard and air-conditioning is rare and often unnecessary.

Also in Europe, **look into wholesalers**—companies that do not own their own fleets but rent in bulk from those that do and often offer better rates than traditional car-rental operations. Prices are best during low travel periods, and rentals booked through wholesalers must be paid for before you leave the United States. If you use a wholesaler, **know whether the prices are guaranteed** in U.S. dollars or foreign currency, and if unlimited mileage is available; find out about required deposits, cancellation penalties, and drop-off charges; and confirm the cost of any required insurance coverage.

Insurance When you drive a rented car, you are generally responsible for any damage or personal injury that you cause as well as damage to the vehicle. Before you rent, **see what coverage you already have** through your personal auto-insurance policy and credit cards. For about $14 a day, rental companies sell insurance, known as a collision damage waiver (CDW), that eliminates your liability for damage to the car; it's always optional and should never be automatically added to your bill.

Requirements In France your own driver's license is acceptable; an International Driver's Permit, available from the American or Canadian Automobile Association, is a good idea.

Surcharges Before picking up the car in one city and leaving it in another, **ask about drop-off charges or one-way service fees,** which can be substantial. Note, too, that some rental agencies charge extra if you return the car before the time specified on your contract. To avoid a hefty refueling fee, **fill the tank just before you turn in the car.**

The Channel Tunnel

The Channel Tunnel provides the fastest route across the Channel—25 minutes from Folkestone to Coquelles (near Calais), 60 minutes from motorway to motorway. It consists of two large, 50-kilometer-long (31-mile-long) tunnels for trains, one in each direction, linked by a smaller service tunnel running between them.

Le Shuttle, a special car, bus, and truck train, operates continuously, with trains departing every 15 minutes at peak times and at least once an hour through the night. No reservations are necessary, although tickets may be purchased in advance from travel agents. Most passengers travel in their own car, staying with the vehicle throughout the "crossing," with progress updates via radio and display screens. Motorcyclists park their bikes in a separate section with its own passenger compartment, while those on foot must book passage by coach.

Eurostar high-speed train service whisks passenger-only trains between stations in Paris (Gare du Nord) and London (Waterloo) in 3 hours and between London and Brussels (Midi) in 3¼ hours. At press time, fares were $154 for a one-way, first-class ticket and $123 for an economy fare.

The Tunnel is reached from exit 11a of the M20/A20. Tickets for either Tunnel service can be purchased in advance (*see* Important Contacts, *above.*)

Children and Travel

The easiest way to break down any Gallic arrogance is to show up with a child. Normally stiff salesmen go ga-ga and become immediately helpful. Bakers are often known to give young children free sweets, and children are accepted in both fancy and informal restaurants with little fuss. Changing compartments for infants are available on all TGVs. In short, don't worry about bringing a child to France.

Baby-Sitting For recommended local sitters, **check with your hotel desk.** *See also* Children and Travel *in* Important Contacts, *above.*

Driving If you are renting a car, **arrange for a car seat when you reserve.** Sometimes they're free.

Flying Always **ask about discounted children's fares.** On international flights, the fare for infants under age 2 not occupying a seat is generally either free or 10% of the accompanying adult's fare; children ages 2 through 11 usually pay half to two-thirds of the adult fare. On domestic flights, children under 2 not occupying a seat travel free, and older children currently travel on the "lowest applicable" adult fare.

Baggage   In general, the adult baggage allowance applies for children paying half or more of the adult fare. Before departure, **ask about carry-on allowances** if you are traveling with an infant. In general, those paying 10% of the adult fare are allowed one carry-on bag, not to exceed 70 pounds or 45 inches (length + width + height), and a collapsible stroller; you may be allowed less if the flight is full.

Facilities   When making your reservation, **ask for children's meals and a free-standing bassinet** if you need them; the latter are available only to those with seats at the bulkhead, where there's enough legroom. If you don't need the bassinet, **think twice before requesting bulkhead seats**—the only storage for in-flight necessities is in inconveniently distant overhead bins.

Safety Seats   According to the Federal Aviation Administration (FAA), it's a good idea to **use safety seats aloft.** Airline policy varies. U.S. carriers allow FAA-approved models, but airlines usually require that you buy a ticket, even if your child would otherwise ride free, because the seats must be strapped into regular passenger seats. Foreign carriers may not allow infant seats, may charge the child's rather than the infant's fare for their use, or may require you to hold your baby during takeoff and landing, thus defeating the seat's purpose.

Lodging   Most hotels allow children under a certain age to stay in their parents' room at no extra charge, while others charge them as extra adults; be sure to **ask about the cutoff age.**

Customs and Duties

In France   There are two levels of duty-free allowance for travelers entering France: one for goods obtained (tax paid) within another European Union (EU) country and the other for goods obtained anywhere outside the EU or for goods purchased in a duty-free shop within the EU.

In the first category, you may import duty-free: 300 cigarettes or 150 cigarillos or 75 cigars or 400 grams of tobacco; 5 liters of table wine and (1) 1½ liters of alcohol over 22% volume (most spirits), (2) 3 liters of alcohol under 22% by volume (fortified or sparkling wine), or (3) 3 more liters of table wine; 90 milliliters of perfume; 375 milliliters of toilet water; and other goods to the value of 2,400 francs (620 francs for those under 15).

In the second category, you may import duty-free: 200 cigarettes or 100 cigarillos or 50 cigars or 250 grams of tobacco (these allowances are doubled if you live outside Europe); 2 liters of wine and (1) 1 liter of alcohol over 22% volume (most spirits), (2) two liters of alcohol under 22% volume (fortified or sparkling wine), or (3) 2 more liters of table wine; 60 milliliters of perfume; 250 milliliters of toilet water; and other goods to the value of 300 francs (150 francs for those under 15).

Back Home
In the U.S.   You may bring home $400 worth of foreign goods duty-free if you've been out of the country for at least 48 hours and haven't already used the $400 exemption, or any part of it, in the past 30 days.

Travelers 21 or older may bring back 1 liter of alcohol duty-free, provided the beverage laws of the state through which they reenter the United States allow it. In addition, 100 non-Cuban cigars and 200 cigarettes are allowed, regardless of your age. Antiques and works of art more than 100 years old are duty-free.

Duty-free, travelers may mail packages valued at up to $200 to themselves and up to $100 to others, with a limit of one parcel per addressee per day (and no alcohol or tobacco products or perfume

valued at more than $5); outside, identify the package as being for
personal use or an unsolicited gift, specifying the contents and their
retail value. Mailed items do not count as part of your exemption.

In Canada   Once per calendar year, when you've been out of Canada for at least
seven days, you may bring in C$300 worth of goods duty-free. If
you've been away less than seven days but more than 48 hours, the
duty-free exemption drops to C$100 but can be claimed any number
of times (as can a C$20 duty-free exemption for absences of 24 hours
or more). You cannot combine the yearly and 48-hour exemptions,
use the C$300 exemption only partially (to save the balance for a lat-
er trip), or pool exemptions with family members. Goods claimed
under the C$300 exemption may follow you by mail; those claimed
under the lesser exemptions must accompany you.

Alcohol and tobacco products may be included in the yearly and 48-
hour exemptions but not in the 24-hour exemption. If you meet the
age requirements of the province through which you reenter Canada, you may bring in, duty-free, 1.14 liters (40 imperial ounces) of
wine or liquor *or* 24 12-ounce cans or bottles of beer or ale. If you are
16 or older, you may bring in, duty-free, 200 cigarettes, 50 cigars or
cigarillos, and 400 tobacco sticks or 400 grams of manufactured tobacco. Alcohol and tobacco must accompany you on your return.

An unlimited number of gifts valued up to C$60 each may be mailed
to Canada duty-free. These do not count as part of your exemption.
Label the package "Unsolicited Gift—Value Under $60." Alcohol
and tobacco are excluded.

In the U.K.   If your journey was wholly within EU countries, you no longer need
to pass through customs when you return to the United Kingdom. If
you plan to bring large quantities of alcohol or tobacco, check in advance on EU limits.

Dining

Few countries match France's reputation for good food, and eating
in France can be a memorable experience whatever your budget.
The simple pleasures of a picnic lunch with baguette, camembert,
and local *jambon* (ham), purchased at local boulangeries,
fromageries, and charcuteries, can be as enjoyable as haute cuisine.
But the prime feature of French dining is the plethora of restaurants
where you can eat out without digging too far into your finances. Although takeout places are mushrooming in the larger towns, most
locals balk at eating french fries with anything other than a juicy
steak, and their notion of "fast food" is gobbling down a three-course
lunch in a brasserie in less than 90 minutes.

Many French spend a lot of the evening eating, too, but unless your
own appetite is equally gargantuan we suggest you **make lunch the
main meal of your day.** The best values can be had in bars or
brasseries that specialize in drinks the rest of the day, and many
"serious" restaurants also offer a good-value lunchtime menu. Go
for the *plat du jour* if there is one: It will usually be the freshest and
best prepared main course available, and often sells out quickly (often before 12:30). Note that you will be charged the full cost of the
fixed-price menu whether or not you eat everything on it.

Many restaurants also offer fixed-price menus in the evening, although they are pricier than their lunchtime offerings. Be wary of
ones that don't, as eating à la carte is nearly always more expensive.
Remember that the cost of a fixed-price meal rises significantly as
you add extras—aperitifs, coffee, bottled wine. Go for a carafe of
house wine if possible, and if you want coffee to finish your meal, get
it at the counter in a café, where it will cost you significantly less.

There is no shortage of possibilities for snacks—from pâtisseries (pastry shops) to street vendors hawking roast chestnuts or thin pancakes known as crêpes.

French breakfasts are relatively skimpy: good coffee, fruit juice if you request it, bread, butter, and croissants. You can "breakfast" in cafés as well as hotels. If you're in the mood for bacon and eggs, you're in trouble.

Dinner, the main meal, usually begins at 8 PM. Lunch, which can be as copious as you care to make it, starts at 12:30 or 1.

Tap water is safe, though not always appetizing (least of all in Paris). The more palatable alternative is mineral water—there is a vast choice of both *eau plate* (still) and *eau gazeuse* (fizzy).

Ratings   Highly recommended restaurants are indicated by a star ★.

The following price categories are used throughout the book, based on the cheapest fixed-price menu or on a main course, salad, and dessert chosen à la carte:

Category	Paris, Ile-de-France, and the Riviera	Less Expensive Regions
$$	175 frs–300 frs	125 frs–250 frs 25-50
$	100 frs–175 frs	75 frs–125 frs 15-25
¢	under 100 frs	under 75 frs

For Travelers with Disabilities

The French government is doing much to ensure that public facilities provide for visitors with disabilities. A number of monuments, hotels, and museums—especially those constructed within the past decade—are equipped with ramps, elevators, and special toilet facilities. Lists of regional hotels include a symbol to indicate which hotels have rooms that are accessible to people using wheelchairs. Similarly, the SNCF has special cars on some trains that have been reserved exclusively for people using wheelchairs and can arrange for those passengers to be escorted on and off trains and assisted in making connections (the latter service must be requested in advance).

When discussing accessibility with an operator or reservationist, **ask hard questions.** Are there any stairs, inside *or* out? Are there grab bars next to the toilet *and* in the shower/tub? How wide is the doorway to the room? To the bathroom? For the most extensive facilities, meeting the latest legal specifications, **opt for newer properties,** which more often have been designed with access in mind. Older properties or ships must usually be retrofitted and may offer more limited facilities as a result. Be sure to **discuss your needs before booking.**

Discount Clubs

Travel clubs offer members unsold space on airplanes, cruise ships, and package tours at as much as 50% below regular prices. Membership may include a regular bulletin or access to a toll-free hot line giving details of available trips departing from three or four days to several months in the future. Most also offer 50% discounts off hotel rack rates. Before booking with a club, **make sure the hotel or other supplier isn't offering a better deal.**

Driving

Roads marked *A*, for *autoroutes*, are expressways. There are excellent links between Paris and most other French cities, but poor ones between the provinces (principal exceptions: the A62 between Bordeaux and Toulouse, and the A9/A8 that runs the length of the Mediterranean). It is often difficult to avoid Paris when crossing France; this need not cause too many problems if you steer clear of rush hours (7–9:30 AM and 4:30–7:30 PM). Most expressways require you to pay a *péage* (toll); the rates vary and can be steep. The *N*, or *Route Nationale*, roads and the *D*, *Route Départementale*, roads are usually wide, unencumbered, and fast (you can average 80 kph/50 mph with luck). The cheap, informative, and well-presented regional yellow Michelin maps are an invaluable navigational aid. You can find them in most bookshops and newsagents.

Breakdowns If you break down on an expressway, go to the nearest roadside emergency telephone and call the breakdown service. If you break down anywhere else, find the nearest garage or, failing all else, contact the police (dial 17).

Fuel Availability and Costs Gas is more expensive on expressways, cheaper in rural areas. Don't let your tank get too low, as you can go for many miles in the country without hitting a gas station. Keep an eye on pump prices, which vary enormously: anything between 5.50 and 6.30 francs per liter. At the pumps, opt for "super" (high-grade/four-star) rather than "essence" (low-grade/two-star).

Parking Parking is a nightmare in Paris and is often difficult in large towns. Meters and ticket machines (pay and display) are commonplace (be sure to have a supply of 1-franc coins). As a summer gift, parking is free during August in most of Paris, but be sure to check the signs. In smaller towns, parking may be permitted on one side of the street only, alternating every two weeks: Pay attention to signs. The French park as anarchically as they drive, but don't follow their example: If you're caught out of bounds, you could be subject to a hefty fine and your vehicle may be unceremoniously towed away to the dread compound (at least 500 francs to retrieve it).

Rules of the Road In France, you **drive on the right.** Be aware of the erratically followed French tradition of giving way to drivers coming from the right, unless there is an international stop sign. Seat belts are obligatory, and children under 12 may not travel in the front seat. Speed limits: 130 kph (81 mph) on expressways; 110 kph (68 mph) on major highways; 90 kph (56 mph) on minor rural roads; 50 kph (31 mph) in towns. French drivers break these limits and police dish out hefty on-the-spot fines with equal abandon. You may use your home driver's license in France.

Electricity

To use your U.S.-purchased electric-powered equipment, **bring a converter and an adapter.** The electrical current in France is 220 volts, 50 cycles alternating current (AC); wall outlets take Continental-type plugs, with two round prongs.

If your appliances are dual voltage, you'll need only an adapter. Hotels sometimes have 110-volt outlets for low-wattage appliances marked "For Shavers Only" near the sink; don't use them for high-wattage appliances like blow-dryers. If your laptop computer is older, carry a converter; new laptops operate equally well on 110 and 220 volts, so you need only an adapter.

Gay and Lesbian Travel

The French are relatively open-minded about sex, and their liberal attitudes are reflected in their outlook toward homosexuals. The largest gay and lesbian communities, which are in cosmopolitan Paris, are low-key and reserved in public, although active and easily accessible to visitors. Discos and nightclubs are numerous and popular; it takes a serious *couche-tard* (night owl) to keep up with the hip scene (*see also* Arts and Nightlife *in* Chapter 2, Paris).

Hiking

France has a huge network of footpaths—some 40,000 kilometers (25,000 miles). The most popular are in such hilly regions as the Vosges, Massif Central, Pyrénées, Alps, Ardennes, Jura, Beaujjolais, and Champagne. Other good bets include windswept Brittany, the picturesque Dordogne Valley, and forested areas of the Ile-de-France (Fontainebleau, St-Germain, Rambouillet).

Insurance

Travel insurance can protect your investment, replace your luggage and its contents, or provide for medical coverage should you fall ill during your trip. Most tour operators, travel agents, and insurance agents sell specialized health-and-accident, flight, trip-cancellation, and luggage insurance as well as comprehensive policies with some or all of these features. Before you make any purchase, **review your existing health and homeowner's policies** to find out whether they cover expenses incurred while traveling.

Baggage
Airline liability for your baggage is limited to $1,250 per person on domestic flights. On international flights, the airlines' liability is $9.07 per pound or $20 per kilogram for checked baggage (roughly $640 per 70-pound bag) and $400 per passenger for unchecked baggage. However, this excludes valuable items such as jewelry and cameras that are listed in your ticket's fine print. You can buy additional insurance from the airline at check-in, but first **see if your homeowner's policy covers lost luggage.**

Flight
You should **think twice before buying flight insurance.** Often purchased as a last-minute impulse at the airport, it pays a lump sum when a plane crashes, either to a beneficiary if the insured dies or sometimes to a surviving passenger who loses eyesight or a limb. Supplementing the airlines' coverage described in the limits-of-liability paragraphs on your ticket, it's expensive and basically unnecessary. Charging an airline ticket to a major credit card often automatically entitles you to coverage and may also embrace travel by bus, train, and ship.

Health
If your own health insurance policy does not cover you outside the United States, **consider buying supplemental medical coverage.** It can reimburse from $1,000 to $150,000 worth of medical and/or dental expenses incurred as a result of an accident or illness during a trip. These policies also may include a personal-accident, or death-and-dismemberment, provision, which pays a lump sum ranging from $15,000 to $500,000 to your beneficiaries if you die or to you if you lose one or more limbs or your eyesight, and a medical-assistance provision, which may either reimburse you for the cost of referrals, evacuation, or repatriation and other services, or may automatically enroll you as a member of a particular medical-assistance company. (*See* Health Issues *in* Important Contacts, *above*.)

For U.K.
Travelers
You can buy an annual travel-insurance policy valid for most vacations during the year in which it's purchased. If you go this route, make sure it covers you if you have a preexisting medical condition or are pregnant.

Trip Without insurance, you will lose all or most of your money if you must cancel your trip due to illness or any other reason. Especially if your airline ticket, cruise, or package tour is nonrefundable and cannot be changed, it's essential that you **buy trip-cancellation-and-interruption insurance.** When considering how much coverage you need, look for a policy that will cover the cost of your trip plus the nondiscounted price of a one-way airline ticket should you need to return home early. Read the fine print carefully, especially sections defining "family member" and "preexisting medical conditions." Also **consider default or bankruptcy insurance,** which protects you against a supplier's failure to deliver. However, such policies often do not cover default by a travel agency, tour operator, airline, or cruise line if you bought your tour and the coverage directly from the firm in question.

Language

The French study English at school for a minimum of four years (often longer) but to little general effect. However, English is widely understood in major tourist areas, and no matter what the area, at least one person in most hotels can explain things to you. Young people usually speak more than their parents' generation. Be patient, and speak slowly.

The French may appear prickly at first to English-speaking visitors, but they usually will try to help out, especially when you at least make an effort to speak their language. So even if your own French is terrible, try to master a few words. *See* the French Vocabulary and Menu Guide at the back of the book.

Lodging

France has a wide range of accommodations, ranging from rambling old village inns that cost next to nothing to stylish converted châteaus that cost the earth. Prices must, by law, be posted at the hotel entrance and should include taxes and service. Prices are always by room, not per person, and you should always check what bathroom facilities that includes, if any. Because replumbing drains is often prohibitive, if not impossible, old hotels may have added bathrooms—often with showers, not tubs—to the guest rooms, but not toilets. Breakfast is not always included in the price, but you are usually expected to have it and are often charged for it regardless. In smaller rural hotels you may be expected to have your evening meal at the hotel, too. Ask for a *grand lit* if you want a double bed. Negotiating rates has become acceptable in Paris and the provinces. Although you may not be able to reduce the price, you might get an upgrade to a newly redecorated, larger, or deluxe room.

Apartment and Villa Rentals If you want a home base that's roomy enough for a family and comes with cooking facilities, **consider a furnished rental.** It's generally cost-wise, too, although not always—some rentals are luxury properties (economical only when your party is large). Home-exchange directories do list rentals—often second homes owned by prospective house swappers—and some services search for a house or apartment for you (even a castle if that's your fancy) and handle the paperwork. Some send an illustrated catalogue and others send photographs of specific properties, sometimes at a charge; up-front registration fees may apply.

Bed-and-Breakfasts B&Bs, known in France as *chambres d'hôte*, are increasingly popular, especially in rural areas. Check local tourist offices for details.

Camping French campsites have a high reputation for organization and amenities, but they tend to be jam-packed in July and August. More and more campsites now welcome advance reservations; if you're traveling in summer, it makes good sense to **book ahead.**

Home If you would like to find a house, an apartment, or other vacation
Exchange property to exchange for your own while on vacation, **become a
member of a home-exchange organization,** which will send you its
annual directories listing available exchanges and will include your
own listing in at least one of them. Arrangements for the actual exchange are made by the two parties to it, not by the organization.

Ratings Highly recommended hotels are indicated by a star ★.

The following price categories are used throughout the book, based
on a standard double room including tax and service charge:

Category	Paris, Ile-de-France, and the Riviera	Less Expensive Regions
$$	500 frs–800 frs	300 frs–400 frs *60-80*
$	300 frs–500 frs	150 frs–300 frs *30-60*
¢	under 300 frs	under 150 frs

Credit Cards The following credit card abbreviations are used: AE, American Express; DC, Diners Club; MC, MasterCard; and V, Visa.

Mail

Airmail letters to the United States and Canada cost 4.30 francs for
20 grams, 7.90 francs for up to 40 grams, and 12.50 francs for up to 60
grams. Letters to the United Kingdom cost 2.80 francs for up to 20
grams. Letters cost 2.80 francs within France; postcards cost 2.80
francs within France and if sent to Canada, the United States, the
United Kingdom, and EU countries; 4.30 francs if sent airmail to
North America. Stamps can be bought in post offices and TABACS.

Receiving If you're uncertain where you'll be staying, **have mail sent to the lo-
Mail cal post office,** addressed as "poste restante," or to American Express, but remember that during peak seasons, American Express
may refuse to accept mail.

Medical Assistance

No one plans to get sick while traveling, but it happens, so **consider
signing up with a medical assistance company.** These outfits provide
referrals, emergency evacuation or repatriation, 24-hour telephone
hot lines for medical consultation, dispatch of medical personnel, relay of medical records, cash for emergencies, and other personal and
legal assistance. (*See also* Health Issues *in* Important Contacts,
above.)

Money and Expenses

The units of currency in France are the franc (fr) and the centime.
Bills are in denominations of 500, 200, 100, 50, and 20 francs. Coins
are 20, 10, 5, 2, and 1 francs and 50, 20, 10, and 5 centimes. Note that
the old 10 franc coin has been changed and replaced by a smaller,
two-tone version. At press time (spring 1995), the exchange rate
was about 4.7 francs to the U.S. dollar, 3.75 to the Canadian dollar,
and 8.35 to the pound sterling.

ATMs Cirrus, Plus, and many other networks connecting automated-teller
machines operate internationally. Chances are that you can **use your
bank card at ATMs** to withdraw money from an account and get cash
advances on a credit-card account if your card has been programmed
with a personal identification number, or PIN. Before leaving
home, **check on frequency limits** for withdrawals and cash advances.
Also **ask whether your card's PIN must be reprogrammed** for

use in France. Four digits are commonly used overseas. Note that Discover is accepted only in the United States.

On cash advances you are charged interest from the day you receive the money, whether from a teller or an ATM. Although transaction fees for ATM withdrawals abroad may be higher than fees for withdrawals at home, Cirrus and Plus exchange rates are excellent because they are based on wholesale rates only offered by major banks.

Costs The following prices are for Paris; other cities and areas are often cheaper. Coffee in a bar: 5 francs (standing), 10 francs (seated); beer in a bar: 10 francs (standing), 13 francs (seated); Coca-Cola: 6–10 francs a can; ham sandwich: 14–29 francs; one-mile taxi ride: 35 francs; movie-theater seat: 45 francs (20%–30% cheaper on Monday and Wednesday); foreign newspaper: 9–12 francs.

Exchanging Currency For the most favorable rates, **change money at banks.** You won't do as well at exchange booths in airports, rail, and bus stations, or in hotels, restaurants, and stores, although you may find their hours more convenient. To avoid lines at airport exchange booths, **get a small amount of currency before you leave home.**

Taxes All taxes must be included in posted prices in France. The initials TTC (*toutes taxes comprises*—taxes included) sometimes appear on price lists but, strictly speaking, are superfluous. By law, restaurant and hotel prices must include 18.6% taxes and a service charge. If you discover that these have rematerialized as additional items on your bill, kick up a fuss.

VAT A number of shops, particularly large stores and shops in holiday resorts, offer VAT refunds to foreign shoppers. You are entitled to an Export Discount of 18.6%, depending on the item purchased, but it is often applicable only if your purchases in the same store reach a minimum of 2,800 francs (for U.K. and EU residents) or 1,200 francs (other residents, including U.S. and Canadian). Remember to ask for the refund, as some stores–especially larger ones–offer the service only upon request.

Traveler's Checks Whether or not to buy traveler's checks depends on where you are headed; **take cash to rural areas and small towns, traveler's checks to cities.** The most widely recognized are American Express, Citicorp, Thomas Cook, and Visa, which are sold by major commercial banks for 1% to 3% of the checks' face value—it pays to **shop around.** Both American Express and Thomas Cook issue checks that can be countersigned and used by you or your traveling companion, and they both provide checks, at no extra charge, denominated in francs. Note that **traveler's checks, whether in dollars or francs, are almost never accepted outside banks that process that credit card;** look for a CHANGE sign and the logo that represents your particular brand of check.

So you won't be left with excess foreign currency, **buy a few checks in small denominations** to cash toward the end of your trip. Record the numbers of the checks, cross them off as you spend them, and keep this information separate from your checks.

Wiring Money You don't have to be a cardholder to send or receive funds through MoneyGram[SM] from American Express. Just go to a MoneyGram[SM] agent, located in retail and convenience stores and in American Express Travel Offices. Pay up to $1,000 with cash or a credit card, anything over that in cash. The money can be picked up within 10 minutes in the form of U.S. dollar traveler's checks or local currency at the nearest MoneyGram[SM] agent, or, abroad, the nearest American Express Travel Office. There's no limit, and the recipient need only present photo identification. The cost runs from 3% to 10%, depending on the amount sent, the destination, and how you pay.

You can also send money using Western Union. Money sent from the United States or Canada will be available for pickup at agent locations in 100 countries within 15 minutes. Once the money is in the system, it can be picked up at any one of 25,000 locations. Fees range from 4% to 10%, depending on the amount you send.

Packages and Tours

A package or tour to France can make your vacation less expensive and more convenient. Firms that sell tours and packages purchase airline seats, hotel rooms, and rental cars in bulk and pass some of the savings on to you. In addition, the best operators have local representatives to help you out at your destination.

A Good Deal? The more your package or tour includes, the better you can predict the ultimate cost of your vacation. Make sure you know exactly what is included, and **beware of hidden costs.** Are taxes, tips, and service charges included? Transfers and baggage handling? Entertainment and excursions? These can add up.

Most packages and tours are rated deluxe, first-class superior, first class, tourist, or budget. The key difference is usually accommodations. If the package or tour you are considering is priced lower than in your wildest dreams, **be skeptical.** Also, **make sure your travel agent knows the hotels** and other services. Ask about location, room size, beds, and whether the facility has a pool, room service, or programs for children, if you care about these. Has your agent been there or sent others you can contact?

Big vs. Small An operator that handles several hundred thousand travelers annually can use its purchasing power to give you a good price. Its high volume may also indicate financial stability. But some small companies provide more personalized service; because they tend to specialize, they may also be experts on an area.

Buyer Beware Each year consumers are stranded or lose their money when operators go out of business—even very large ones with excellent reputations. If you can't afford a loss, take the time to **check out the operator**—find out how long the company has been in business, and ask several agents about its reputation. Next, **don't book unless the firm has a consumer-protection program.** Members of the United States Tour Operators Association and the National Tour Association are required to set aside funds exclusively to cover your payments and travel arrangements in case of default. Nonmember operators may instead carry insurance; look for the details in the operator's brochure—and the name of an underwriter with a solid reputation. Note: When it comes to tour operators, **don't trust escrow accounts.** Although there are laws governing those of charter-flight operators, no governmental body prevents tour operators from raiding the till.

Next, **contact your local Better Business Bureau and the attorney general's office** in both your own state and the operator's; have any complaints been filed? Last, **pay with a major credit card.** Then you can cancel payment, provided that you can document your complaint. Always **consider trip-cancellation insurance** (*see* Insurance, *above*).

Single Travelers Prices are usually quoted per person, based on two sharing a room. If traveling solo, you may be required to pay the full double occupancy rate. Some operators eliminate this surcharge if you agree to be matched up with a roommate of the same sex, even if one is not found by departure time.

Using an Agent Travel agents are an excellent resource. In fact, large operators accept bookings only through travel agents. But it's good to **collect brochures from several agencies,** because some agents' suggestions may be skewed by promotional relationships with tour and package firms that reward them for volume sales. If you have a special interest, **find an agent with expertise in that area;** the American Society of Travel Agents can give you leads in the United States. (Don't rely solely on your agent, though; agents may be unaware of small-niche operators, and some special-interest travel companies only sell direct).

Packing for France

Pack light: Baggage carts are scarce in airports and railroad stations, and luggage restrictions on international flights are tight.

Over the past few years, the French have become less formal in their dress. Paris is still the world's fashion capital and both men and women spend a lot on clothes. But there is no need to wear a tie and jacket at most of even the fanciest restaurants, and jeans are de rigueur at the new Bastille Opéra. However, sneakers are seldom worn in cities, even with casual clothing; the same goes for shorts, which are seen as vulgar. Men who wear them will probably be denied admission to churches and cathedrals, as will women (though they no longer need to cover their heads and arms to enter).

For beach resorts, take a cover-up, as wearing bathing suits on the street is frowned upon. Most casinos and nightclubs along the Riviera require jackets and ties. If you like to dress formally, take a cocktail dress or tuxedo.

Most of France is hot in the summer, cool in the winter—and rainy year-round. Do not forget a raincoat and umbrella. You'll need a sweater or warm jacket for the Mediterranean in winter.

If you are staying in budget hotels, take along small bars of soap; many either do not provide it or limit guests to one tiny bar per room. Zip-closure bags, a pocket calculator, and a small flashlight are also indispensable.

Bring an extra pair of eyeglasses or contact lenses in your carry-on luggage, and if you have a health problem, **pack enough medication** to last the trip or have your doctor write a prescription using the drug's generic name, because brand names vary from country to country (you'll then need a prescription from a doctor in the country you're visiting). **Don't put prescription drugs or valuables in luggage to be checked,** for it could go astray. To avoid problems with customs officials, carry medications in original packaging. Also, don't forget the addresses of offices that handle refunds of lost traveler's checks.

Luggage Free airline baggage allowances depend on the airline, the route, and the class of your ticket; ask in advance. In general, on domestic flights and on international flights between the United States and foreign destinations, you are entitled to check two bags—neither exceeding 62 inches, or 158 centimeters (length + width + height), or weighing more than 70 pounds (32 kilograms). A third piece may be brought aboard; its total dimensions are generally limited to less than 45 inches (114 centimeters), so it will fit easily under the seat in front of you or in the overhead compartment. In the United States, the FAA gives airlines broad latitude to limit carry-on allowances and tailor them to different aircraft and operational conditions. Charges for excess, oversize, or overweight pieces vary.

If you are flying between two foreign destinations, note that baggage allowances may be determined not by piece but by weight—generally 88 pounds (40 kilograms) in first class, 66 pounds (30 kilograms) in business class, and 44 pounds (20 kilograms) in economy. If your flight between two cities abroad *connects* with your transatlantic or transpacific flight, the piece method still applies.

Safeguarding   Before leaving home, **itemize your bags' contents** and their worth,
Your Luggage   and label them with your name, address, and phone number. (If you
use your home address, cover it so that potential burglars can't see
it.) Inside your bag, **pack a copy of your itinerary.** At check-in, **make
sure that your bag is correctly tagged** with the airport's three-letter
destination code. If your bags arrive damaged or not at all, file a
written report with the airline before leaving the airport.

Passports and Visas

If you don't already have one, **get a passport.** While traveling, **keep
one photocopy of the data page** separate from your wallet and leave
another copy with someone at home. If you lose your passport,
promptly call the nearest embassy or consulate, and the local police;
having the data page can speed replacement.

U.S. Citizens   All U.S. citizens, even infants, need a valid passport to enter France
for stays of up to 90 days. New and renewal application forms are
available at any of the 13 U.S. Passport Agency offices and at some
post offices and courthouses. Passports, which are valid for 10
years, are usually mailed within four weeks; allow five weeks or
more in spring and summer.

Canadians   You need a valid passport to enter France for stays of up to 90 days.
Application forms are available at 28 regional passport offices as
well as post offices and travel agencies. Whether for a first or a renewal passport, you must apply in person. Children under 16 may be
included on a parent's passport but must have their own to travel
alone. Passports are valid for five years and are usually mailed within two to three weeks of application.

U.K. Citizens   Citizens of the United Kingdom need a valid passport to enter
France for stays of up to 90 days. Applications for new and renewal
passports are available from main post offices as well as at the passport offices located in Belfast, Glasgow, Liverpool, London, New-
port, and Peterborough. You may apply in person at all passport
offices, or by mail to all except the London office. Children under 16
may travel on an accompanying parent's passport. All passports are
valid for 10 years. Allow a month for processing.

Rail Travel

To save money, **look into rail passes** (*see* Important Contacts, *above*).
But be aware that if you don't plan to cover many miles, you may
come out ahead by buying individual tickets.

Many travelers assume that rail passes guarantee them seats on the
trains they wish to ride. Not so. You need to **book seats ahead even if
you are using a rail pass;** seat reservations are required on some European trains, particularly high-speed trains, and are a good idea on
trains that may be crowded—particularly in summer on popular
routes. You will also need a reservation if you purchase overnight
sleeping accommodations.

The SNCF is generally recognized as Europe's best national rail
service: It's fast, punctual, comfortable, and comprehensive. The
high-speed TGVs, or Trains à Grande Vitesse (average 255 kph/160
mph on the Lyon/southeast line, 300 kph/190 mph on the Lille and
Bordeaux/southwest lines), are the best domestic trains. They operate between Paris and Lille, Paris and Brussels, Paris and Lyon/
Switzerland/the Riviera, and Angers/Nantes, and Tours/Poitiers/
Bordeaux. As with other main-line trains, a small supplement may
be assessed at peak hours. You must **always make a seat reservation
for the TGV**—easily obtained at the ticket window or from an automatic machine. Seat reservations are reassuring but seldom neces-

sary on other main-line French trains, except at certain busy holiday times.

If you know what station you'll depart from, you can get a free schedule there (while supplies last), or you can access the new multilingual computerized schedule information network at any Paris station and many provincial ones. You can also make reservations and buy your ticket while at the computer.

If you are traveling from Paris (or any other terminus), **get to the station half an hour before departure** to ensure that you'll have a good seat. The majority of intercity trains in France consist of open-plan cars and are known as Corail trains. They are clean and extremely comfortable, even in second class. Trains on regional branch lines are currently being spruced up but lag behind in style and quality. The food in French trains can be good, but it's poor value for the money.

Before boarding, you must punch your ticket (but not EurailPass) in one of the orange machines at the entrance to the platforms, or else the ticket collector will fine you 100 francs on the spot.

It is possible to get from one end of France to the other without traveling overnight. Otherwise you have the choice between high-priced wagons-lits (sleeping cars) and affordable *couchettes* (bunks, six to a compartment in second class, four to a compartment in first, with sheet and pillow provided, priced at around 89 francs). Special summer night trains from Paris to Spain and the Riviera, geared to young people, are equipped with disco and bar.

Senior-Citizen Discounts

Older travelers to France can take advantage of many discounts, such as reduced admissions of 20%–50% to museums and movie theaters. Seniors 60 and older should **buy a Carte Vermeil,** which entitles the bearer to discounts on the French domestic airline (Air Inter), rail travel outside Paris, the bus and Métro, and reduced admission prices for films and many cultural events. Cards are available at any rail station in France (cost: 140 francs). *See also* Rail Travel *in* Important Contacts, *above.*

To qualify for age-related discounts, **mention your senior-citizen status up front** when booking hotel reservations, not when checking out, and before you're seated in restaurants, not when paying your bill. Note that discounts may be limited to certain menus, days, or hours. When renting a car, **ask about promotional car-rental discounts**—they can net lower costs than your senior-citizen discount.

Shopping

Though Paris is the fashion capital, good clothes can be bought everywhere and are invariably cheaper outside the capital; the presence of numerous clothing manufacturers just outside Troyes, in southern Champagne, makes prices there up to 50% lower than elsewhere in France. Local wines and brandies such as cognac, Armagnac, calvados, and marc come in great variety. Hand-crafted items are abundant: olive-wood bowls and utensils and the clay figurines known as *santons* in Provence, and local pottery, *faïence,* such as that found in Quimper, Brittany, for instance. Every region has its distinctive food products as well.

Shop prices are clearly marked and bargaining isn't a way of life. Still, at outdoor and flea markets and in antiques stores, you can try your luck. If you're thinking of buying several items, you've nothing to lose by cheerfully suggesting to the proprietor, *"Vous me faites un prix?"* ("How about a discount?").

Hypermarchés, a peculiarly French form of supermarket discount store on the outskirts of most towns, are much cheaper than the small family-run grocery stores and much, much cheaper than France's super-expensive pharmacies. The biggest names are Carrefour, E. Leclerc, Auchan, and Intermarché, and they sell almost everything from film to yogurt, Pampers, stationery, and sporting goods.

Sports

France has no shortage of sports facilities. Many seaside resorts are well equipped for water sports, such as windsurfing and waterskiing, and there are swimming pools in every French town. In winter, the Alps and the somewhat less pricey Pyrénées and Vosges boast excellent skiing facilities—both for *ski alpin* (downhill) and *ski de fond* (cross-country).

Bicycling (*see also* Bicycling, *above and in* Important Contacts) is popular and, like *équitation* (horseback riding), possible in many rural areas. The many rivers of France offer excellent fishing (check locally for authorization rights) and canoeing. Tennis is phenomenally popular in France, and courts are everywhere: Try for a typical *terre battue* (clay court) if you can. Golf and squash have caught on; you may be able to find a course or a court not too far away. The French are not so keen on jogging, but you'll have no difficulty locating a suitable local park or avenue. (*See also* Boules *and* Hiking, *above and in* Important Contacts.)

Students on the Road

For students, France holds special allure, particularly Paris. During the summer, young people from all over Europe congregate in the French capital. During the school year, students dominate the Left Bank. Cheap food and lodging is easy to find throughout the country, so there's little need to scrounge. In addition, there are student bargains almost everywhere, on train and plane fares, and for movie and museum tickets. All you need is an International Student Identity Card (*see* Students *in* Important Contacts).

To save money, **look into deals available through student-oriented travel agencies** to those with a bona fide student ID card, and to members of international student groups. *See* Students *in* Important Contacts, *above*.

Telephones

For the moment, all French phone numbers have eight digits; a prefix is required only when calling the Paris region from the provinces (add 16–1 for Paris) and for calling the provinces from Paris (16, then the number). The number system was changed only in 1985; therefore, you may still come across some seven-digit numbers in Paris and some six-digit ones elsewhere. Add 4 to the beginning of such Paris numbers, and the former two-figure area code to provincial ones.

Because more phone lines are now needed, **in October 1996 all numbers will get a prefix of two new digits.** In Paris and Ile-de-France, 01 will precede the number (replacing the 16–1); in the northwest, 02; in the northeast, 03; in the southeast, 04; and in the southwest, 05.

Long Distance The country code for dialing France is 33.

To make a direct international call from France, dial 19 and wait for the tone, then dial the country code (1 for the United States and Canada; 44 for the United Kingdom), area code (minus any initial 0), and number.

Operators and Information When calling home from France, you can avoid hotel surcharges by using the local access numbers to English-speaking operators provided by AT&T, MCI, and Sprint: **AT&T:** 19–0011; **MCI:** 19–0019, and **Sprint:** 19–0087.

To find a number in France or to request other information, dial 12. For international inquiries, dial 19–33 plus the country code.

Pay Phones The French telephone system is modern and efficient. Telephone booths are plentiful; they can almost always be found at post offices and often in cafés. A local call costs 80 centimes for every three minutes; half-price rates apply weekdays between 9:30 PM and 8 AM, from 1:30 PM Saturday, and all day Sunday.

Most French pay phones are operated by *télécartes* (phone cards), which you can buy from post offices, métro stations, and some tobacco shops (cost: 40 francs for 50 units; 96 francs for 120). Some pay phones accept 1-, 2- and 5-franc coins (1-franc minimum). Lift the receiver, insert the télécarte or coins in the appropriate slots, and dial.

Tipping

The French have a clear idea of when they should be tipped. Bills in bars and restaurants include service, but it is customary to leave some small change unless you're dissatisfied. The amount of this varies: 30 centimes if you've merely bought a beer, or a few francs after a meal. Tip taxi drivers and hairdressers about 10%. Give ushers in theaters and movie theaters 1 or 2 francs. In some theaters and hotels, coat check attendants may expect nothing (if there is a sign saying POURBOIRE INTERDIT—tips forbidden); otherwise give them 5 francs. Washroom attendants usually get 5 francs, though the sum is often posted.

If you stay in a hotel for more than two or three days, it is customary to leave something for the chambermaid—about 10 francs per day. In expensive hotels you may well call on the services of a baggage porter (bell boy) and hotel porter and possibly the telephone receptionist. All expect a tip: Plan on about 10 francs per item for the baggage boy, but the other tips will depend on how much you've used their services—common sense must guide you here. In hotels that provide room service, give 5 francs to the waiter (this does not apply to breakfast served in your room). If the chambermaid does some pressing or laundering for you, give her 5 francs on top of the charge made.

Gas-station attendants get nothing for gas or oil, and 5 or 10 francs for checking tires. Train and airport porters get a fixed 6–10 francs per bag, but you're better off getting your own baggage cart if you can (a 10-franc coin—refundable—is sometimes necessary). Museum guides should get 5–10 francs after a guided tour, and it is standard practice to tip tour guides (and bus drivers) 10 francs or more after an excursion, depending on its length.

When to Go

June and September are the best months to be in France, as both are free of the midsummer crowds. June offers the advantage of long daylight hours, while cheaper prices and frequent Indian summers, often lasting well into October, make September attractive.

July and August in southern France can be stifling. Paris can be hot in August, too, but it is pleasantly deserted. Many restaurants, theaters, and small shops close, but enough stay open these days to make a low-key, unhurried visit a pleasure. **If you want to go to the countryside in summer, stay away from the coast,** where prices will be inflated and hotels and restaurants will be more crowded. Don't travel on or around July 14 and August 1, 14, and 31.

The ski season in the Alps and Pyrénées lasts from Christmas to Easter; if you can, **avoid Christmas and February, when school holidays mean crowds.** Many hotels and restaurants take a winter *congé* (break) in early January. If Paris and the Loire are among your priorities, remember that the weather is unappealing before Easter. If you're dreaming of Paris in the springtime, May is your best bet, not rainy April. But the capital remains a joy during mid-winter, with plenty of things to see and do.

Because people usually begin their vacations on Friday or Saturday, airfares are more expensive on weekends, so try to **travel mid-week.** Also, you may save money by arranging to stop in big cities over the weekend, when the business travelers have left and the rates may be lower.

Climate What follows are average daily maximum and minimum temperatures for Paris and Nice.

Paris								
Jan.	43F	6C	**May**	68F	20C	**Sept.**	70F	21C
	34	1		49	10		53	12
Feb.	45F	7C	**June**	73F	23C	**Oct.**	60F	16C
	34	1		55	13		46	8
Mar.	54F	12C	**July**	76F	25C	**Nov.**	50F	10C
	39	4		58	15		40	5
Apr.	60F	16C	**Aug.**	75F	24C	**Dec.**	44F	7C
	43	6		58	15		36	2

Nice								
Jan.	55F	13C	**May**	68F	20C	**Sept.**	77F	25C
	39	4		55	13		61	16
Feb.	55F	13C	**June**	75F	24C	**Oct.**	70F	21C
	41	5		61	16		54	12
Mar.	59F	15C	**July**	81F	27C	**Nov.**	63F	17C
	45	7		64	18		46	8
Apr.	64F	18C	**Aug.**	81F	27C	**Dec.**	55F	13C
	46	8		64	18		41	5

Seasonal Events Contact the French Government Tourist Office for exact dates and further information on the following events.

January The **International Circus Festival,** featuring top acts from around the world, is held in Monaco. The **St. Vincent Tournament,** a colorful Burgundy wine festival, takes place on the third weekend in a different wine village each year. Visitors buy a cup for about $10 and then drink as much as they like–or just frolic in the decorated streets.

February The **Carnival of Nice** provides an exotic blend of parades and revelry during the weeks leading up to Lent. Other cities and villages also have their own smaller versions.

March In Paris, **Salon de Mars,** a deluxe antiques fair, takes place at the Champs-de-Mars.

The **Monte Carlo Open Tennis Championships** get under way at the ultraswanky Monte Carlo Country Club. From then until September, there are **son-et-lumière shows,** historical pageants featuring special lighting effects, at many châteaus in the Loire Valley. The show at Beaune's Hospice is also very well done.

May The **Cannes Film Festival** sees two weeks of star-studded events. Classical concert festivals get underway throughout the country. At the end of the month, the **French Open Tennis Championships** are held at Roland Garros Stadium in Paris.

June   The **Festival du Marais,** including everything from music to dance to theater, is held in Paris, and the **Tour de France,** the world's most famous bicycle race gets underway.

July   On **July 14,** all of France celebrates Bastille Day, commemorating the Storming of the Bastille in 1789—the start of the French Revolution. Look out for fireworks and street festivities. The three-week **Tour de France,** the world's most famous bicycle race, climaxes on the Champs Elysées in Paris on the fourth Sunday of the month.

September   The **Music Festival of Besançon and Franche-Comté** hosts a series of chamber music concerts in and around Besançon. The **Festival of Autumn,** a major arts festival, opens in Paris and continues until December.

November   **Les Trois Glorieuses,** Burgundy's biggest wine festival, features the year's most important wine auction and related merriment in several Burgundy locations.

December   On the 24th, a Christmas celebration known as the **Shepherd's Festival,** featuring midnight mass and picturesque "living crèches," is held in Les Baux, Provence. From late in the month to early January, **Christmas in Paris** spells celebrations, especially for children, during the school holiday. A giant crèche is set up on the square in front of the Hôtel de Ville (City Hall), and there are automated window displays in the *grands magasins* (department stores) on boulevard Haussmann.

National Holidays   In 1996: January 1, April 7 and 8 (Easter Sunday and Monday), May 1 (Labor Day), May 8 (VE Day), May 16 (Ascension), May 26 and 27 (Whit Sunday and Monday), July 14 (Bastille Day), August 15 (Assumption), November 1 (All Saints' Day), November 11 (Armistice), and December 25. Changing holidays in 1997: March 31 and April 1 (Easter Monday and Tuesday), May 8 (Ascension), May 18 and 19 (Whit Sunday and Monday). If a public holiday falls on a Tuesday or a Thursday, many businesses and shops and some restaurants close on the Monday or Friday.

Great Itineraries for Budget Travelers

A lean travel budget does not mean that you can't savor the best of France. Inexpensive public transportation makes it possible to sightsee in some of the country's most visitable areas without the expense of renting a car. The following tours take in favorite landmarks and popular attractions—and all can be done by bus and/or train.

Great Gothic Cathedrals

Medieval cathedrals are among France's most precious heritage, and some of the best ones are conveniently close to Paris.

After paying homage to Notre-Dame, take the métro (line 13) north to the dowdy suburb of **St-Denis,** where the kings of France are buried in a cathedral-size basilica with a majestic nave and the earliest Gothic choir (1140s). Catch the train at Paris's Gare du Nord and head north to **Beauvais,** whose 13th-century choir is the highest in the world—alas, the nave was never built! Then continue to **Amiens** (by train, via Creil): Its cathedral is almost as high, and the largest completed one in France. Go east from Amiens to **Laon,** where the many-towered cathedral sits atop a mighty hill known as the "crowned mountain." You can make a detour from Laon to **Soissons**—check out its cathedral and the ruined facade of the abbey of St-Jean-des-Vignes—before continuing southeast to **Reims,** where the kings of France were crowned. The richly sculpted facade is the glory of Reims. Disciplined Gothic is on display at the cathedral in nearby **Châlons-sur-Marne,** where the old church of Notre-Dame-en-Vaux also warrants scrutiny.

All these sites are just short distances apart by train. (If you are traveling by car, you can cut across the country—via the cathedral towns of Troyes and Sens—to **Orléans.**) If you are traveling by train, return to Paris (via Meaux, with its own cathedral) and head southwest to visit the majestic cathedrals at Orléans and **Tours;** the facade of the latter contains delicate ornaments by Renaissance craftsmen at work on nearby châteaus. The stained glass at Tours is also outstanding. Head north to **Le Mans,** whose choir—almost as high as that at Beauvais—juts out spectacularly atop a steep mound, then head northeast to **Chartres** and its spires and glass of unparalleled splendor.

Duration	7 days.
Getting Around *By Car*	Amiens is a 148-kilometer (92-mile) drive from Paris (north along the A1 and then northwest on D934). A car enables you to cut from Châlons-sur-Marne to Orléans via Troyes and Sens (265 kilometers/165 miles), without returning to Paris.
By Train	Rail travelers will have to make separate trips from Paris to visit Sens and Troyes.
The Main Route	**One night: Paris.** Visit Notre-Dame and the Basilica of St-Denis.
	One night: Amiens. Visit the cathedrals of Beauvais and Amiens.
	One night: Laon. Explore the cathedrals of Laon, Soissons, and Reims.
	One night: Châlons-sur-Marne. See the Châlons cathedral and the church of Notre-Dame-en-Vaux.
	One night: Orléans. Visit Orléans cathedral (if traveling by car, stop at Troyes and Sens en route).
	One night: Le Mans. Visit the cathedrals of Tours and Le Mans. Return to Paris via Chartres.
Information	*See* Chapter 3, Ile-de-France, and Chapter 7, Champagne and the North.

Burgundy

Burgundy is one of France's best-known wine-making regions. Though the opportunity to try some of the world's most celebrated wines is a major drawing card, visitors will also enjoy the region's irresistible combination of rolling hills, picturesque towns, impressive churches, and outstanding restaurants.

The cathedral town of **Sens** is the gateway to Burgundy as you approach from Paris. The attractive Yonne Valley leads south toward old, pretty **Auxerre,** redolent of the unhurried flavor of Burgundian life. Continue south along the Yonne Valley to historic **Clamecy,** and detour by local excursion bus or by car to nearby **Vézelay,** whose Romanesque basilica counts as one of Europe's leading early medieval buildings. The tiny surrounding village remains unspoiled by tourist crowds, as does the patchwork of meadowland that can be surveyed from the basilica's hilltop site. Veer south through the Morvan Forest to **Autun,** once a major Roman town—several monuments from that period still stand—and home to a powerful cathedral. Then cut east to stylish, historic **Beaune,** where you can sample Burgundy's famous wines and admire the medieval Hôtel Dieu, with its multicolored tile roof. Finally, head north through the vineyards to **Dijon,** Burgundy's capital and the opulent home of the once-mighty grand dukes (their palace now houses an exceptional art museum) and several superb restaurants.

Duration 7 days.

Getting Around *By Car* Sens is 110 kilometers (70 miles) southeast of Paris via A6/N6. Though Burgundy's towns can be visited by public transportation, its charming rural corners can best be appreciated by car.

By Train Trains run from Paris to Sens and Auxerre, where you can change for Clamecy and Autun. To get from Autun to Beaune, change at Etang. Dijon, a 20-minute train trip from Beaune, is 90 minutes from Paris by TGV.

The Main Route One night: Auxerre. See Sens and visit the old town of Auxerre.

One night: Clamecy. Make excursion to Vézelay.

One night: Autun. Admire Roman remnants and cathedral.

One night: Beaune. Sample wines at the Marché aux Vins.

One night: Dijon. Head through vineyards, then visit Dijon's museums, churches, and restaurants.

Information *See* Chapter 9, Burgundy.

Châteaus of the Loire Valley

The Loire Valley provides a fascinating three-dimensional overview of French history, thanks to the hundreds of châteaus that dot its wooded terrain. A cathedral and museum make **Orléans** an interesting place from which to start your tour, but the first château you encounter is farther west at **Chambord**—the largest of all the Loire châteaus and surrounded by an extensive forest. Nearby **Cheverny** was one of the last Loire châteaus to be built, as its formal neoclassicism testifies. The attractive town of **Blois** makes an excellent base for visiting Chambord and Cheverny and has churches and narrow streets, as well as a château that was built over several periods. **Chaumont** and **Amboise** both offer terrific views across the Loire, and at Amboise, you may visit the Clos-Lucé and its display of models based on designs by Leonardo da Vinci (who died here in 1519). **Chenonceau,** built across the River Cher, has an unforgettable setting.

Tours is the principal city of the Loire Valley; despite heavy bombing in 1944, it retains its picturesque old quarter and superb cathedral. It makes a sensible base for exploring such nearby châteaus as **Villandry** (with its formal Renaissance gardens and tree-lined avenues), fortresslike **Langeais,** romantic **Azay-le-Rideau,** and **Ussé** (said to have inspired Perrault's fairy tale *Sleeping Beauty*). **Chinon** is, or was, an authentic castle; its ruined walls tower high above a delightful town. A medieval abbey at **Fontevraud** and a famous riding school at **Saumur** (home of another opulent château) add variety to the tour. **Angers** has a castle and two fine museums—one with the colossal, vividly colored 14th-century *Apocalypse* tapestry, the other showcasing the sculpture of 19th-century local David d'Angers.

Duration 10 days.

Getting Around *By Train* A respectable train service runs down the valley from Orléans to Angers, stopping at Blois, Chaumont, Amboise, Tours, Langeais, and Saumur. Branch lines connect Tours to Chenonceau and Azay-le-Rideau/Chinon. You will need to take a bus from Blois to reach Chambord and Cheverny, and from Saumur to reach Fontevraud. A bike is the best way to reach Villandry (from Azay) and Ussé (from Chinon).

By Car Orléans is a 90-minute drive (120 kilometers/75 miles) south of Paris via A10. Picturesque roads run along both banks of the Loire.

The Main Route **One night: Orléans.** See the cathedral.

Two nights: Blois. See Chaumont, and take a bus to Chambord and Cheverny.

One night: Amboise. See château and Clos-Lucé, then visit Chenonceau.

One night: Tours. You could stay three nights and see Azay and Chinon from here rather than changing hotels.

One night: Azay-le-Rideau. Make excursion to Villandry.

One night: Chinon. Make excursion to Ussé.

One night: Saumur. Stop off at Langeais en route; then see Fontevraud Abbey.

One night: Angers.

Information *See* Chapter 4, The Loire Valley.

Eastern Brittany and Le Mont-St-Michel

Castles, ancient town walls, and spectacular coastal views await you as you venture into Brittany. Start your tour at **Vitré**, with its cobbled streets and venerable hilltop castle, and detour to **Fougères**, site of one of Europe's largest medieval castles (surrounded by a moat!). Lively **Rennes**, the capital of Brittany, provides the intriguing contrast of graceful neoclassical architecture and rickety half-timbered medieval houses.

Head north toward **Le Mont-St-Michel,** a staggering medieval abbey atop a steep offshore crag that becomes inaccessible at high tide. A huge granite cathedral dominates historic **Dol-de-Bretagne,** where nearby Mont Dol emerges from marshy wasteland. With its tumbling alleyways and striped black-and-white timber houses, pretty **Dinan** seems straight out of a Hollywood movie set. A bracing seaside walk along the ramparts of **St-Malo** awaits you farther north, and a short boat trip will bring you to the elegant resort of **Dinard** and its own spectacular coastal promenades.

Duration 6 days.

Getting Around Several mainland trains from Paris (Gare Montparnasse) stop at Vitré on their way to Rennes. All other towns visited are accessible
By Train by train except Fougères (take a bus from Vitré) and Le Mont-St-Michel (catch a bus or taxi from Pontorson station).

By Car The A11/A81 expressway is the fastest way to drive from Paris to Vitré and Rennes.

The Main Route **One night: Vitré.** Visit castle.

One night: Rennes. Visit Fougères castle and old Rennes.

One night: Mont-St-Michel. Explore Dol.

One night: Dinan.

One night: St-Malo. Make boat excursion to Dinard.

Information *See* Chapters 5, Brittany, and (for Le Mont-St-Michel) Chapter 6, Normandy.

Provence

Roman remains and soft, sun-kissed landscapes of vines and olive groves provide the backdrop for a tour of Provence. Start at **Orange**, site of a majestic Roman theater and stately triumphal arch, before continuing on to the bustling nearby town of **Avignon**, famous for a now-decapitated medieval bridge and its role as the 14th-century home-in-exile of the popes, who built the colossal fortress-palace. A short trip west brings you to **Nîmes** and its well-preserved Roman arena, temple, and Maison Carrée; detour to the nearby three-tiered Pont du Gard aqueduct, a major feat of Roman engineering.

The sturdy castle at **Tarascon** sits by the River Rhône. Farther south is the picturesque town of **Arles,** with its own Roman remains. Make excursions from Arles to the cliff-top village of **Les Baux-de-Provence,** with its medieval ruins, and to **St-Rémy-de-Provence,** site of a well-preserved Roman arch and mausoleum. Continue south to the vibrant port of **Marseille,** then head inland to the area's historic capital, **Aix-en-Provence,** a mixture of narrow medieval streets and majestic 18th-century mansions.

Duration 7 days.

Getting Around *By Car* Orange is a six-hour drive (628 kilometers/390 miles) from Paris via the A6/A7 expressway. The expressway continues to Avignon and Marseille.

By Train The TGV runs from Paris (Gare de Lyon) to Avignon, continuing toward either Nîmes or Marseille. Trains serve all other points on this itinerary with two exceptions: You'll need to take a bus from Nîmes to the Pont du Gard and from Arles to Les Baux and St-Rémy.

The Main Route **One night: Avignon.** Visit theater and archway in Orange.

One night: Nîmes. Detour to the Pont du Gard.

Two nights: Arles. Visit Tarascon castle and make excursions to Les Baux and St-Rémy.

One night: Marseille.

One night: Aix-en-Provence.

Information *See* Chapter 12, Provence.

Chronology

Knowing French history will make your tours through the nation's cities, towns, and villages just that much more meaningful.

The Beginnings

ca. 3500 BC	Megalithic stone complexes are erected at Carnac, Brittany.
ca. 1500 BC	Lascaux cave paintings are executed (Dordogne, southwest France).
ca. 600 BC	Greek colonists found Marseille.
after 500 BC	Celts appear in France.
58–51 BC	Julius Caesar conquers Gaul, and writes up the war in *De Bello Gallico.*
52 BC	Lutetia, later to become Paris, is built by the Gallo-Romans.
46 BC	Roman amphitheater is built at Arles.
14 BC	The Pont du Gard, the aqueduct near Nîmes, is erected.
AD 212	Roman citizenship is conferred on all free inhabitants of Gaul.
406	Invasion by the Vandals (Germanic tribes).
451	Attila invades, and is defeated near Troyes.

The Merovingian Dynasty

486–511	Clovis, king of the Franks (481–511), defeats the Roman governor of Gaul and founds the Merovingian Dynasty. Great monasteries, such

as those at Tours, Limoges, and Chartres, become centers of culture.

497 Franks are converted to Christianity.

567 The Frankish kingdom is divided into three parts—the eastern countries (Austrasia), later to become Belgium and Germany; the western countries (Neustria), later to become France; and Burgundy.

732 Arab expansion is checked at the Battle of Poitiers.

The Carolingian Dynasty

768–778 Charlemagne (768–814) becomes king of the Franks (768); conquers northern Italy (774); and is defeated by the Moors at Roncesvalles in Spain, after which he consolidates the Pyrénées border (778).

ca. 780 Carolingian renaissance in art, architecture, and education.

800 The pope crowns Charlemagne Holy Roman Emperor in Rome. Charlemagne expands the kingdom of France far beyond its present borders and establishes a center for learning at his capital, Aix-la-Chapelle (Aachen, in present-day Germany).

814–987 Death of Charlemagne. The Carolingian line continues until 987 through a dozen or so monarchs, with a batch called Charles (the Bald, the Fat, the Simple) and a sprinkling of Louis. Under the Treaty of Verdun (843), the empire is divided in two—the eastern half becoming Germany, the western half France.

The Capetian Dynasty

987 Hugh Capet (987–996) is elected king of France and establishes the principle of hereditary rule for his descendants. Settled conditions and the increased power of the Church see the flowering of the Romanesque style of architecture in the church of Notre-Dame la Grande in Poitiers and the basilica at Vézelay.

1066 Norman conquest of England by William the Conqueror (1066–87).

1067 Work begins on the Bayeux Tapestry, the Romanesque work of art celebrating the Norman Conquest.

ca. 1100 First universities in Europe include Paris. Development of European vernacular verse: *Chanson de Roland*.

1140 The Gothic style of architecture first appears at St-Denis and later becomes fully developed at the cathedrals of Chartres, Reims, Amiens, and Notre-Dame in Paris.

ca. 1150 Struggle between the Anglo-Norman kings (Angevin Empire) and the French; when Eleanor of Aquitaine switches husbands (from Louis VII of France to Henry II of England), her extensive lands pass to English rule.

1194 Chartres Cathedral is begun as Gothic architecture spreads throughout western Europe.

1204 Fourth Crusade: Franks conquer Byzantium and found the Latin Empire.

1257 The Sorbonne university is founded in Paris.

1270 Louis IX (1226–70), the only French king to achieve sainthood, dies in Tunis on the seventh and last Crusade.

1302–07 Philippe IV (1285–1314), the Fair, calls together the first States-General, predecessor to the French Parliament. He disbands the Knights Templars to gain their wealth (1307).

1309   Papacy escapes from a corrupt and disorderly Rome to Avignon in southern France, where it stays for nearly 70 years.

The Valois Dynasty

1337–1453   Hundred Years' War between France and England: episodic fighting for control of those areas of France gained by the English crown following the marriage of Eleanor of Aquitaine and Henry II.

1348–1350   The Black Death rages in France.

1428–31   Joan of Arc (1412–31), the Maid of Orléans, sparks the revival of French fortunes in the Hundred Years' War but is captured by the English and burned at the stake at Rouen.

1434   Johannes Gutenberg invents the printing press in Strasbourg, Alsace.

1453   France finally defeats England, terminating the Hundred Years' War and the English claim to the French throne.

1475   Burgundy at the height of its power under Charles the Bold.

1494   Italian wars: beginning of Franco-Hapsburg struggle for hegemony in Europe.

1515–47   Reign of François I, who imports Italian artists, including Leonardo da Vinci (1452–1519), and brings the Renaissance to France. The palace of Fontainebleau is begun (1528).

1558   France captures Calais, England's last territory on French soil.

1562–98   Wars of Religion (Catholics versus Protestants/Huguenots) within France.

The Bourbon Dynasty

1589   The first Bourbon king, Henri IV (1589–1610), is a Huguenot who converts to Catholicism and achieves peace in France. He signs the Edict of Nantes, giving limited freedom of worship to Protestants. The development of Renaissance Paris gets under way.

ca. 1610   Scientific revolution in Europe begins, marked by the discoveries of mathematician and philosopher René Descartes (1596–1650).

1643–1715   Reign of Louis XIV, the Sun King, an absolute monarch who builds the Baroque power base of Versailles and presents Europe with a glorious view of France. With his first minister, Colbert, Louis makes France, by force of arms, the most powerful nation-state in Europe. He persecutes the Huguenots, who emigrate in great numbers, nearly ruining the French economy.

1660   Classical period of French culture: writers Molière (1622–73), Jean Racine (1639–99), Pierre Corneille (1606–84), and painter Nicolas Poussin (1594–1665).

ca. 1715   Rococo art and decoration develop in Paris boudoirs and salons, typified by the painters Antoine Watteau (1684–1721) and, later, François Boucher (1703–70) and Jean-Honoré Fragonard (1732–1806).

1700 onward   Writer and pedagogue Voltaire (1694–1778) is a central figure in the French Enlightenment, along with Jean-Jacques Rousseau (1712–78) and Denis Diderot (1713–84), who, in 1751, compiles the first modern encyclopedia. The ideals of the Enlightenment—for reason and scientific method and against social and political injustices—pave the way for the French Revolution. In the arts, painter Jacques-Louis David (1748–1825) reinforces revolutionary creeds in his severe neoclassical works.

1756–63 The Seven Years' War results in France's losing most of her overseas possessions and in England's becoming a world power.

1776 The French assist in the American War of Independence. Ideals of liberty cross the Atlantic with the returning troops to reinforce new social concepts.

The French Revolution

1789–1804 The Bastille is stormed on July 14, 1789. Following upon early Republican ideals comes the Terror and the administration of the Directory under Robespierre. There are widespread political executions—Louis XVI and his queen, Marie-Antoinette, are guillotined in 1793. Reaction sets in, and the instigators of the Terror are themselves executed (1794). Napoléon Bonaparte enters the scene as the champion of the Directory (1795–99) and is installed as First Consul during the Consulate (1799–1804).

The First Empire

1804 Napoléon crowns himself Emperor of France at Notre-Dame in the presence of the pope.

1805–12 Napoléon conquers most of Europe. The Napoleonic Age is marked by a neoclassical style in the arts, called Empire, as well as by the rise of Romanticism—characterized by such writers as Chateaubriand (1768–1848) and Stendhal (1783–1842), and the painters Eugène Delacroix (1798–1863) and Théodore Géricault (1791–1824)—which is to dominate the arts of the 19th century.

1812–14 Winter cold and Russian determination defeat Napoléon outside Moscow. The emperor abdicates and is transported to Elba in the Mediterranean (1814).

Restoration of the Bourbons

1814–15 Louis XVIII, brother of the executed Louis XVI, regains the throne after the Congress of Vienna is held to settle peace terms.

1815 The Hundred Days: Napoléon returns from Elba and musters an army on his march to the capital, but lacks national support. He is defeated at Waterloo (June 18) and exiled to the island of St. Helena in the South Atlantic.

1821 Napoléon dies in exile.

1830 Bourbon king Charles X, locked into a prerevolutionary state of mind, abdicates. A brief upheaval (Three Glorious Days) brings Louis-Philippe, the Citizen King, to the throne.

1840 Napoléon's remains are brought back to Paris.

1846–48 Severe industrial and farming depression contribute to Louis-Philippe's abdication (1848).

Second Republic and Second Empire

1848–52 Louis-Napoléon (nephew and step-grandson of Napoléon I) is elected president of the short-lived Second Republic. He makes a successful attempt to assume supreme power and is declared Emperor of France, taking the title Napoléon III.

ca. 1850 The ensuing period is characterized in the arts by the emergence of realist painters—Jean-François Millet (1814–75), Honoré Daumier (1808–79), Gustave Courbet (1819–77)—and late-Romantic writers—Victor Hugo (1802–85), Honoré de Balzac (1799–1850), and Charles Baudelaire (1821–87).

1853 Baron Haussmann (1809–91) re-creates the center of Paris, with great boulevards connecting important squares, or *places*.

1863 Napoléon III inaugurates the Salon des Refusés in response to critical opinion. It includes work by Edouard Manet (1832–83), Claude Monet (1840–1926), and Paul Cézanne (1839–1906) and is commonly regarded as the birthplace of Impressionism and of modern art in general.

The Third Republic

1870–71 The Franco-Prussian War sees Paris besieged, and Paris falls to the Germans. Napoléon III takes refuge in England. The Commune is established, an attempt by the extreme left to seize power. France loses Alsace and Lorraine to Prussia before the peace treaty is signed.

1871–1914 Before World War I, France expands her industries and builds up a vast colonial empire in northwest Africa and Southeast Asia. Sculptor Auguste Rodin (1840–1917), musicians Maurice Ravel (1875–1937) and Claude Debussy (1862–1918), and writers such as Stéphane Mallarmé (1842–98) and Paul Verlaine (1844–96) set the stage for Modernism.

1874 Emergence of the Impressionist school of painting: Monet, Pierre-Auguste Renoir (1841–1919), and Edgar Degas (1834–1917).

1889 The Eiffel Tower is built for the Paris World Exhibition. Centennial of the French Revolution.

1894–1906 Franco-Russian alliance (1894). Dreyfus affair: the spy trial and its anti-Semitic backlash shake France.

1898 Pierre and Marie Curie (1859–1906, 1867–1934) observe radioactivity and isolate radium.

1904 The Entente Cordiale: England and France become firm allies.

1907 Exhibition of Cubist painting in Paris.

1914–18 During World War I, France fights with the Allies, opposing Germany, Austria-Hungary, and Turkey. Germany invades France; most of the big battles (Vimy Ridge, Verdun, Somme, Marne) are fought in trenches in northern France. French casualties exceed 5 million. With the Treaty of Versailles (1919), France regains Alsace and Lorraine and attempts to exact financial and economic reparations from Germany.

1918–39 Between wars, Paris attracts artists and writers, including Americans—Ernest Hemingway (1899–1961) and Gertrude Stein (1874–1946). France nourishes major artistic movements: Constructivism, Dadaism, Surrealism, and Existentialism.

1923 France occupies the Ruhr, a major industrial area in Germany's Rhine valley.

1939–45 At the beginning of World War II, France fights with the Allies until invaded and defeated by Germany in 1940. The French government, under Marshal Pétain (1856–1951), moves to Vichy and cooperates with the Nazis. French overseas colonies split between allegiance to the legal government of Vichy and declaration for the Free French Resistance, led (from London) by General Charles de Gaulle (1890–1970).

1944 D-day, June 6: The Allies land on the beaches of Normandy and successfully invade France. Additional Allied forces land in Provence. Paris is liberated in August 1944, and France declares full allegiance to the Allies.

1944–46 A provisional government takes power under General de Gaulle; American aid assists French recovery.

The Fourth Republic

1946   France adopts a new constitution; French women gain the right to vote.

1946–54   In the Indochinese War, France is unable to regain control of her colonies in Southeast Asia. The 1954 Geneva Agreement establishes two governments in Vietnam: one in the north, under the Communist leader Ho Chi Minh, and one in the south, under the emperor Bao Dai. U.S. involvement eventually leads to French withdrawal.

1954–62   The Algerian Revolution achieves Algeria's independence from France. Thereafter, other French African colonies gain independence.

1957   The Treaty of Rome establishes the European Economic Community (now known as the European Union—EU), with France a founding member.

The Fifth Republic

1958–68   De Gaulle is the first president under a new constitution; he resigns in 1968 after widespread disturbances begun by student riots in Paris.

1976   The first supersonic transatlantic passenger service begins with the Anglo-French Concorde.

1981   François Mitterrand is elected the first Socialist president of France since World War II.

1988   Mitterrand is elected for a second term.

1989   Bicentennial celebration of the French Revolution.

1990   TGV (*train à grande vitesse*, or high-speed train) clocks a world record—515 kph (322 mph)—on a practice run. Channel Tunnel link-up between French and English workers.

1992   Winter Olympics staged in and around Albertville, Savoie. EuroDisney (now known as Disneyland Paris) opens east of Paris.

1994   Channel Tunnel becomes operational—Paris–London train time is slashed to three hours.

1995   Completion of the Très Grande Bibliothèque (Giant National Library) marks the end of President Mitterrand's monumental building program in Paris. Schengen Agreement abolishes border controls between EU countries.

1998   Soccer World Cup to be staged in France.

2 Paris

A city of vast, noble perspectives and winding, hidden streets, Paris remains a combination of the pompous and the intimate. Whether you've come looking for sheer physical beauty, cultural and artistic diversions, world-famous shopping, history, or simply local color, you will find it here in abundance.

The city's 20 districts, or arrondissements, have their own distinctive character, as do the two banks of the Seine, the river that weaves its way through the city's heart. The tone of the *Rive Droite* (Right Bank) is set by spacious boulevards and formal buildings, while the *Rive Gauche* (Left Bank) is more carefree and bohemian.

The French capital is also, for the tourist, a practical city: It's relatively small as capitals go, and its major sites and museums are within walking distance of one another. The city's principal tourist axis is less than 6 kilometers (4 miles) long, running parallel to the north bank of the Seine from the Arc de Triomphe to the Bastille.

There are several "musts" that any first-time visitor to Paris will be loath to miss: the Eiffel Tower, the Champs-Elysées, the Louvre, and Notre-Dame. It is only fair to say, however, that a visit to Paris will never be quite as simple as a quick look at a few landmarks. Every *quartier* has its own treasures, and travelers should adopt the process of discovery—a very pleasant prospect in this most elegant of French cities.

Paris Basics

Arriving and Departing

By Plane
Airports and Airlines

Paris is served by two international airports: **Charles de Gaulle,** also known as Roissy, 26 kilometers (16 miles) northeast of the downtown area, and **Orly,** 16 kilometers (10 miles) south. Major carriers, among them **TWA, American Airlines,** and **Air France,** fly daily from the United States, while **Air France** and **British Airways** between them offer hourly service from London.

Budget Airport The easiest way to get into Paris from **Charles de Gaulle** (Roissy) air-
Transport port is on the **RER-B** line, the suburban express train. A new station opened right beneath Terminal 2 in 1994. Trains to central Paris (Les Halles, St-Michel, Luxembourg) leave every 15 minutes; the fare is 44 francs, and the journey time is 30 minutes. **Air France buses** run every 15 minutes from Charles de Gaulle to the Arc de Triomphe and the Air France air terminal at Porte Maillot. The fare is 48 francs, and the journey time is about 40 minutes, though rush-hour traffic often makes this a slow and frustrating trip. Additional-ly, the **Roissybus**, operated by RATP, runs directly to and from rue Scribe at Paris Opéra and Roissy every 15 minutes and costs 35 francs.

From **Orly** airport, the simplest way to get into Paris is on the **RER-C** line; there's a free shuttle bus from the terminal building to the train station, and trains leave every 15 minutes. The fare is 40 francs, journey time is 28 minutes. Alternatively, take the **Orlyval** shuttle train that runs between Orly and Antony RER station every seven minutes. The fare is 50 francs, and the journey time is about 25 minutes. **Air France buses** run every 12 minutes between Orly air-port and the Air France air terminal at Les Invalides on the Left Bank; the fare is 32 francs, and the trip can take from 30 minutes to an hour.

Avoid taxis unless you are two or more passengers. Taxi rides to central Paris can top 200 francs, with a 6-franc charge per bag to boot.

By Bus Paris has no central bus depot. Long-distance bus journeys within France are rare compared with train travel. The leading Paris-based bus company is **Eurolines** (28 av. du Général-de-Gaulle, Bagnolet, tel. 49–72–51–51).

By Car In a country as highly centralized as France, it is no surprise that expressways converge on the capital from every direction: A1 from the north (England/Belgium); A13 from Normandy/the northwest; A4 from the east; A10 from Spain/the southwest; and A7 from the Alps/Riviera/Italy. Each connects with the *périphérique*, the beltway that encircles Paris. Note that exits from the beltway into the city are named, not numbered.

By Train Paris has six international train stations: **Gare du Nord** (northern France, northern Europe, and England via Calais, the Channel Tunnel, or Boulogne); **Gare St-Lazare** (Normandy and England via Dieppe); **Gare de l'Est** (Strasbourg, Luxembourg, Basel, and central Europe); **Gare de Lyon** (Lyon, Marseille, the Riviera, Geneva, Ita-ly); and **Gare d'Austerlitz** (Loire Valley, southwest France, Spain). **Gare Montparnasse** has taken over as the main terminal for Bor-deaux- and southwest-bound trains since the introduction of TGV-Atlantique service. For information call 45–82–50–50.

Getting Around on the Cheap

Paris is relatively small as capital cities go, and most of its prize monuments and museums are within easy walking distance of one another in any given area. To help you find your way around, we sug-gest that you buy a *Plan de Paris par arrondissement*, a city guide available at most kiosks with separate maps of each district, includ-ing the whereabouts of métro stations and an index of street names.

Maps of the métro/RER network are available free from any métro station and many hotels. They are also posted on every platform, as

Paris Métro

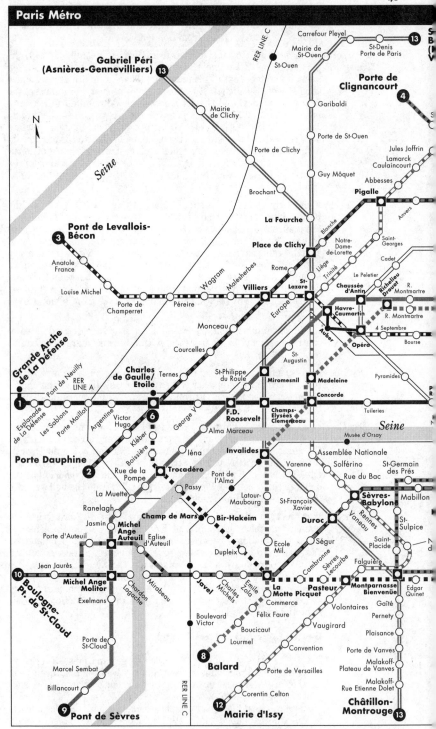

Gabriel Péri
(Asnières-Gennevilliers) 13

Carrefour Pleyel

St-Denis
Porte de Paris 13

S
B

Mairie de
St-Ouen

St-Ouen

Porte de
Clignancourt 4

Garibaldi

S

Mairie
de Clichy

Porte de St-Ouen

Jules Joffrin
Lamarck
Caulaincourt
Abbesses

Porte de Clichy

Guy Môquet

Pigalle

Anvers

Brochant

Blanche

Notre-
Dame-
de-Lorette

Saint-
Georges

La Fourche

Pont de Levallois-
Bécon 3

Place de Clichy

Cadet

Rome

Liège

Le Peletier

R.
Montmartre

Anatole
France

Wagram

Malesherbes

Villiers

St-
Lazare

Trinité

Chaussée
d'Antin

Richelieu
Drouot

Louise Michel

Porte de
Champerret

Péreire

Europe

Havre-
Caumartin

R. Montmartre

4 Septembre

Monceau

Auber

Opéra

Bourse

Grande Arche
de La Défense 1

Courcelles

St-
Augustin

Pyramides

Charles
de Gaulle/
Étoile

Ternes

St-Philippe
du Roule

Miromesnil

Madeleine

P
R

Pont de Neuilly

RER
LINE A

Concorde

Tuileries

Esplanade
de La Défense

Les Sablons

Porte Maillot

Argentine

Victor
Hugo

6

George V

F.D.
Roosevelt

Champs-
Elysées
Clemenceau

Seine

Porte Dauphine

Kléber

Alma Marceau

Musée d'Orsay

N

Boissière

Iéna

Invalides

Assemblée Nationale

2

Rue de
la Pompe

Trocadéro

Pont de
l'Alma

Varenne

Solférino

St-Germain
des Prés

La Muette

Passy

Latour-
Maubourg

St-François
Xavier

Rue du Bac

Mabillon

Ranelagh

Champ de Mars

Bir-Hakeim

Duroc

Sèvres-
Babylone

Jasmin

Michel
Ange
Auteuil

Rennes

St-
Sulpice

Porte d'Auteuil

Eglise
d'Auteuil

Ecole
Mil.

Ségur

Vaneau

Saint-
Placide

N
d

Jean Jaurès

Dupleix

Cambronne

Sèvres
Lecourbe

Falguière

10

Michel Ange
Molitor

Chardon
Lagache

Mirabeau

Javel

Charles
Michels

Emile
Zola

La
Motte Picquet

Pasteur

Montparnasse
Bienvenüe

Edgar
Quinet

Boulogne-
Pt. de St-Cloud

Exelmans

Commerce

Volontaires

Gaîté

Pernety

Boulevard
Victor

Félix Faure

Vaugirard

Plaisance

Porte de
St-Cloud

Boucicaut

Porte de Vanves

Lourmel

Convention

Malakoff-
Plateau de Vanves

Marcel Sembat

8 Balard

Porte de Versailles

Malakoff-
Rue Etienne Dolet

Billancourt

Corentin Celton

Châtillon-
Montrouge 13

9 Pont de Sèvres

RER LINE C

12 Mairie d'Issy

RER LINE C

Seine

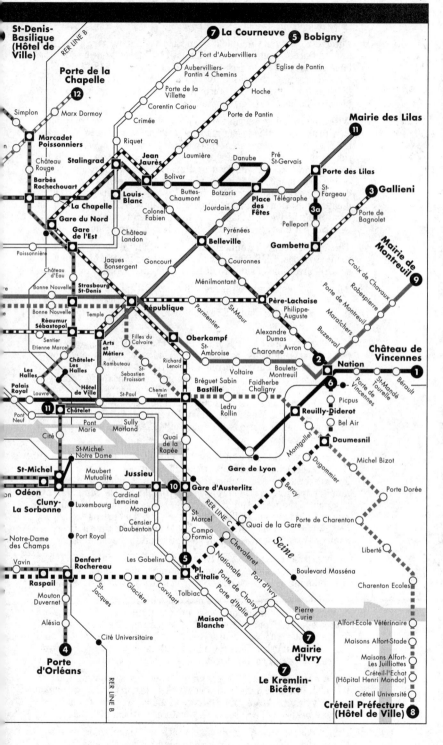

are maps of the bus network. Bus routes are also marked at bus stops and on buses.

By Métro The métro, by far the quickest and most efficient way of getting around the city, runs from 5:30 AM until 1:15 AM (this means that the famous "last métro" can pass your station anytime after 12:30 AM). Stations are recognizable either by a large yellow "M" within a circle, or by their distinctive, green, curly Art Nouveau railings and archway bearing the full title (Métropolitain).

With 13 lines crisscrossing Paris and its environs, the métro is fairly easy to navigate. It is essential to know the name of the last station on the line you take, however, as this name appears on all signs. A connection (you can make as many as you like on one ticket) is called a *correspondance*. At junction stations, illuminated orange signs, bearing the name of the line terminus, appear over the correct corridors for *correspondance*. Illuminated blue signs, marked *sortie*, indicate the station exit. Some lines and stations in the less salubrious parts of Paris are a bit risky at night: lines 2 and 13 in particular. In general, however, the métro is relatively safe throughout.

The métro network connects with the RER network at several points in Paris. RER trains, which race across Paris from suburb to suburb, are a sort of supersonic métro and can be great time savers.

All métro tickets and passes are valid for RER and bus travel within Paris. Tickets cost 7 francs each, though a *carnet* (10 tickets for 41 francs) is a better value. They can be bought in the métro and at most TABAC stands.

If you're staying for a week or more, the best deal is the weekly *(coupon jaune)* or monthly *(carte orange)*, sold according to zone. Zones 1 and 2 cover the entire métro network; tickets cost 63 frs a week or 219 frs a month. If you plan to take suburban trains to visit places in the Ile-de-France, consider a four-zone (Versailles, St-Germain-en-Laye; 113 frs a week) or six-zone (Rambouillet, Fontainebleau; 150 frs a week) ticket. Weekly and monthly passes are available from rail and major métro stations. The monthly pass requires a passport-size photograph.

Alternatively, there are one-day (Formule 1) and three- and five-day (Paris Visite) unlimited travel tickets for the métro, bus, and RER. The advantage is that unlike the coupon jaune, which is good from Monday morning to Sunday evening, the latter are valid starting any day of the week and give you admission discounts to a limited number of museums and tourist attractions. The prices are 38, 95, and 150 frs for Paris only; 95, 210, and 285 frs for the suburbs, including Versailles, St-Germain-en-Laye, and Disneyland Paris.

Access to métro and RER platforms is through an automatic ticket barrier. Slide your ticket in and pick it up as it pops up. Keep your ticket during your journey; you'll need it to leave the RER system.

By Bus Paris buses are green and are marked with the route number and destination in front and major stopping places along the sides. Most routes operate from 6 AM to 8:30 PM; some continue until midnight. Ten night buses operate hourly (1 to 6 AM) between Châtelet and various nearby suburbs. The brown bus shelters, topped by red-and-yellow circular signs, contain timetables and route maps.

You can use your métro tickets on buses, or buy a one-ride ticket on board. If you have individual yellow tickets (as opposed to weekly or monthly tickets), state your destination and be prepared to punch one or more tickets in the red-and-gray machines on board the bus.

By Taxi Paris taxis may not have the charm of their London counterparts—there is no standard vehicle or color—but they're cheaper. Daytime rates (7 AM–7:30 PM) are a standard 2.80 francs per kilometer, and nighttime rates are around 4.50 francs. There is a basic charge of 12 francs for all rides. You are best off asking your hotel or restaurant to call for a taxi; cruising cabs can be hailed but are annoyingly difficult to spot. Otherwise, ask where to find the nearest taxi stand (*station de taxis*). Note that taxis seldom take more than three people at a time.

By Bicycle You can rent bikes in the Bois de Boulogne (Jardin d'Acclimatation), Bois de Vincennes, some RER stations, and from the Bateaux-Mouches embarkation point by place de l'Alma. Or try Paris-Vélo (2 rue du Fer-à-Moulin, 5e, tel. 43–37–59–22). Rental rates vary from about 90 francs to 140 francs per day, 160 francs to 220 francs per weekend, and 420 francs to 500 francs per week. The 1,000-franc deposit per bike can be put on a credit card.

Important Addresses and Numbers

Tourist Information There are the main Paris tourist office (127 av. des Champs-Elysées, 75008 Paris, tel. 49–52–53–54; open daily 9 AM–8 PM; closed Christmas Day and New Year's Day) and branches at all mainline train stations, except Gare St-Lazare. Dial 47–20–88–98 for recorded information (updated weekly) in English.

Embassies U.S. (2 av. Gabriel, 8e, tel. 42–96–12–02), Canada (35 av. Montaigne, 8e, tel. 44–43–29–00), and U.K. (35 rue du Fbg. St-Honoré, 8e, tel. 42–66–91–42).

Emergencies Police (tel. 17), ambulance (tel. 15 or 45–67–50–50), doctor (tel. 43–37–77–77), and dentist (tel. 43–37–51–00).

Hospitals The American Hospital (63 blvd. Victor-Hugo, Neuilly, tel. 47–45–71–00 or 47–45–71–00) has a 24-hour emergency service.

The Hertford British Hospital (3 rue Barbès, Levallois-Perret, tel. 47–58–13–12) also offers a 24-hour service.

Pharmacies Pharmacie des Champs-Elysées (Galerie des Champs, 84 av. des Champs-Elysées, 8e, tel. 45–62–02–41), open 24 hours; Drugstore (corner of blvd. St-Germain and rue de Rennes, 6e), open daily until 2 AM; Pharmacie des Arts (106 blvd. Montparnasse, 14e), open daily until midnight.

English-Language Bookstores W.H. Smith (248 rue de Rivoli, 1er, tel. 42–60–37–97), Galignani (224 rue de Rivoli, 1er, tel. 42–60–76–07), Brentano's (37 av. de l'Opéra, 2e, tel. 42–61–52–50), and Shakespeare and Co. (37 rue de la Bûcherie, 5e).

Travel Agencies American Express (11 rue Scribe, 9e, tel. 47–77–70–00), Air France (119 av. des Champs-Elysées, 8e, tel. 44–08–24–24), and Wagon-Lits (32 rue du Quatre-Septembre, 2e, tel. 42–66–15–80).

Where to Change Money Exchange offices in most of the mainline Paris rail stations (Austerlitz, Lyon, Est, Nord, St-Lazare) are open 7 AM–8 PM. They are convenient but do not offer the best rates. A majority of the banks in central Paris provide exchange facilities at more competitive rates, usually with a fixed commission. Note also: The *Change Automatique* (66 av. des Champs-Elysées), open round the clock, accepts $5, $10, and $20 bills, as does the *Change de Paris* bureau (2 rue de l'Amiral-Coligny) across from the Louvre.

Where to Stay on a Budget

At last count, the Paris tourist office's official (albeit incomplete) hotel guide listed 1,478 hotels in the city's 20 arrondissements. Despite this huge choice, you should always be sure to make reservations well in advance, except, paradoxically, during July and August, when the trade fairs, conventions, and conferences that crowd the city the rest of the year come to a halt.

Our criteria for selecting the hotels reviewed below were cleanliness, friendly management, value for money, and—where possible—character. A few chain hotels are included for their price and/ or convenient location. For the most part, hotels on the Right Bank offer greater luxury—or at any rate formality—than those on the Left Bank, where hotels tend to be smaller but often more charming.

It is possible to find budget hotels even in central Paris, but don't expect spacious rooms or high standards of comfort. Luckily, those parts of Paris in top demand among fat-walleted business travelers (mainly the 7th, 8th, and 17th arrondissements) do not correspond with the preferences of the average visitor, who can find better value in such central locations as the Marais and Latin Quarter. However, there is no reason to despair if you do not find a hotel in the heart of the city: Paris is relatively small, and public transportation so efficient that you are never far from the hub of things. The best way of reserving a hotel room is through the Paris tourist office (127 av. des Champs-Elysées, 8e, tel. 49–52–53–54). You can also book hotels through the tourist offices at Orly and Charles-de-Gaulle airports, and in train stations.

Other than in the largest and most expensive hotels, almost all Parisian hotels have certain idiosyncrasies. Air-conditioning is relatively rare in budget hotels. This can cause difficulties chiefly because of noise in summer, when on stuffy, sultry nights you may have no choice but to open the windows. Ask for a room *sur cour*—overlooking the courtyard (almost all hotels have one)—or, even better, if there is one, *sur le jardin*—overlooking the garden.

The most enduring example of quirkiness is French plumbing, which sometimes looks like avant-garde sculpture. Shared toilets or bathrooms down the hall, though increasingly rare, are still found in many modest establishments. Never assume that what is billed as a bathroom (*salle de bain*) will necessarily contain a tub. Some rooms have toilets (what the French call *w.c.* or *cabinet de toilet*), some have *bidets* only—but no tub or shower. Others have a shower but no toilet, and still others have only washstands. Our reviews indicate the number of rooms with full bath facilities including tub (*baignoire*) or shower (*douche*), and number of rooms with shared baths. Be sure you know what you are getting when you book.

Almost all Paris hotels charge extra for breakfast, with prices ranging from 30 francs to more than 100 francs per person in luxury establishments. Even the cheapest hotels generally assume you will be having breakfast there, and will add the breakfast charge to your bill automatically. If you don't want to have breakfast at the hotel, say so when you check in. For anything more than the standard French breakfast of *café au lait* (coffee with hot milk) and *baguette* (bread) or croissants, the price will be higher. Some hotels have especially pleasant breakfast areas, and we have noted this where applicable.

Unless otherwise stated, the hotels reviewed below have elevators, and English is spoken. Additional facilities, such as restaurants, are listed at the end of each review.

Prices   The lodgings reviewed below are grouped in three price ranges: 500 frs–800 frs ($$), 300 frs–500 frs ($), and under 300 frs (¢). All prices are for a standard double room, including tax and service. (A nominal *séjour* tax—per person, per night—was introduced in 1994 to pay for increased promotion of tourism in Paris.)

Highly recommended lodgings are indicated by a star ★.

1st Arrondissement

$$ Britannique. During WWI the Britannique served as headquarters for a Quaker mission. Today it's a friendly, family-owned hotel in a restored 19th-century building, with a handsome winding staircase and nicely decorated, soundproof rooms (those with shower are significantly cheaper). Ask for a room on one of the top three floors. *20 av. Victoria, 75001, tel. 42–33–74–59, fax 42–33–82–65. 31 rooms with bath, 9 with shower. AE, DC, V. Métro: Châtelet.*

¢ Lille. You won't find a less expensive base for exploring the Louvre than this hotel, a short distance from the Cour Carrée. The facade received a face-lift a few years ago, but the somewhat shabby interior and minimal plumbing down long corridors were not upgraded—hence the very low prices. Still, the Lille is a slice of Old Paris. There's no elevator, and not all rooms have TVs or phones. *8 rue du Pélican, 75001, tel. 42–33–33–42. 6 rooms with shower, 7 with shared bath. No credit cards. Métro: Palais Royal.*

3rd Arrondissement

$ Hôtel Bellevue et Chariot d'Or. A modest hotel with a grandiose name, the Bellevue offers simply decorated, no-frills guest rooms that are slightly larger than average for this price range. The breakfast room is impressive, however, with high molded ceilings and glorious, stained-glass windows. The Bellevue is in Paris's garment district, not far from Beaubourg, Les Halles, and the Marais. Quadruple rooms are bargains for families. *39 rue de Turbigo, 75003, tel. 48–87–45–60, fax 48–87–95–04. 57 rooms with bath, 2 with shower. Facilities: breakfast room. AE, DC, MC, V. Métro: Arts et Métiers, Etienne Marcel.*

4th Arrondissement

$$ Bretonnerie. This lovely small hotel is on a tiny street in the Marais, a few minutes' walk from Beaubourg. The cozy rooms are decorated in Louis XIII style, but vary considerably in size from cramped to spacious. Some have antiques, beamed ceilings, and marble bathrooms. There are a bar and breakfast room in the vaulted cellar. *22 rue Ste-Croix-de-la-Bretonnerie, 75004, tel. 48–87–77–63, fax 42–77–26–78. 30 rooms and 2 suites, all with bath. Facilities: breakfast room, bar. MC, V. Closed Aug. Métro: Hôtel de Ville.*

$ ★ Place des Vosges. A loyal American clientele swears by this small hotel on a charming street just off the exquisite square of the same name. Oak-beam ceilings and rough-hewn stone in public areas and some of the guest rooms add to the atmosphere. Ask for the top-floor room, the hotel's largest, with a view of Marais' rooftops. There's a welcoming little breakfast room. *12 rue de Biraque, 75004, tel. 42–72–60–46, fax 42–72–02–64. 11 rooms with bath, 5 with shower. Facilities: breakfast room. MC, AE, DC, V. Métro: Bastille.*

¢ ★ Castex. This family-run hotel in a 19th-century building is a real find. The decor is strictly functional, but the extremely friendly owners, squeaky-clean rooms, and rock-bottom prices mean the Castex is often fully booked months ahead. There's a large American clientele. The eight least expensive rooms, two per floor, share toilets on the immaculate, well-lighted landings. There's no elevator, and TV is in the lobby only. *5 rue Castex, 75004, tel. 42–72–31–52, fax 42–72–57–91. 4 rooms with bath, 23 with shower. MC, V. Métro: Bastille.*

¢ Le Fauconnier. This youth hostel offers simple, clean beds in rooms for two, four, or six at a bit more than 100 francs per person per night. The building, a lovely 17th-century town house, is on a small, quiet street near the Seine. Breakfast is served in a pleasant ground-floor room or, in summer, on a small patio. Most rooms have a shower or wash basin; the toilet is down the hall. Guests must be

Paris Lodging

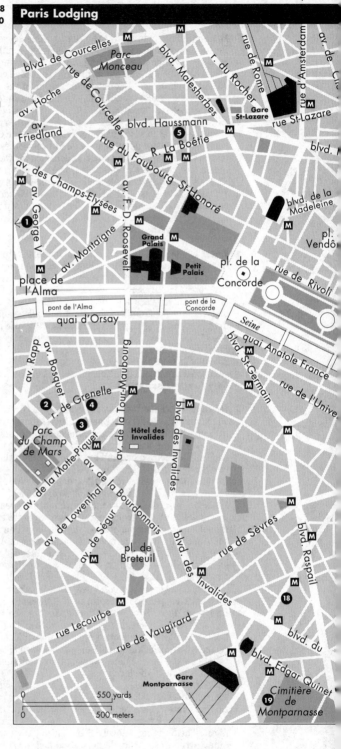

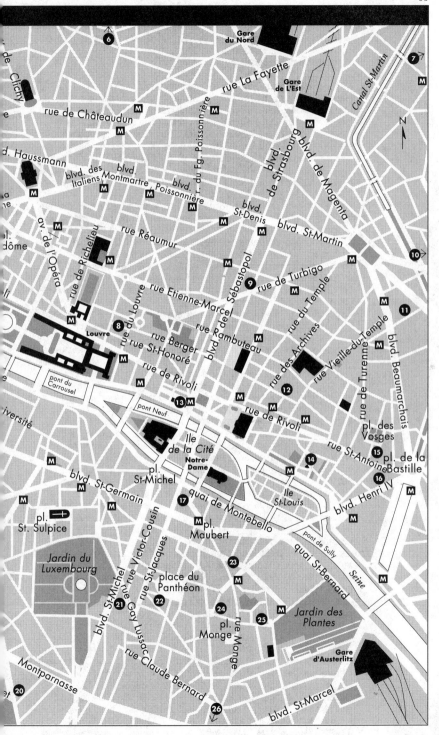

between the ages of 18 and 30. *11 rue du Fauconnier, 75004, tel. 42–74–23–45, fax 40–27–81–64. 28 rooms with shower; toilets on landings. No elevator. No credit cards. No reservations. Métro: St-Paul.*

5th Arrondissement

$$ ★ **Elysa Luxembourg.** The Elysa is what the French call *un hôtel de charme*. Though the building is not large, most rooms are surprisingly spacious, and all are exquisitely maintained and refurbished yearly. Cream-color furniture is set against pale blue or pink fabrics. You'll find a minibar in every room and a breakfast lounge serving Continental or buffet breakfasts. This is one of the rare hotels in the city with a sauna. *6 rue Gay-Lussac, 75005, tel. 43–25–31–74, fax 46–34–56–27. 25 rooms with bath, 5 with shower. Facilities: breakfast room, minibars, sauna. AE, MC, V. Métro: Luxembourg.*

$$ ★ **Panthéon.** In a handsome 18th-century building facing the Panthéon, this excellent hotel has prices that range from moderate to expensive. Some of the charming rooms have exposed beams, balconies, and stunning views that stretch all the way to Sacré-Coeur; a vaulted breakfast room and impressive lobby are added attractions. The desk staff is very helpful. *19 pl. du Panthéon, 75005, tel. 43–54–32–95, fax 43–26–64–65. 34 rooms with bath. Facilities: breakfast room, air-conditioning. AE, DC, V. Métro: RER Luxembourg.*

$ ★ **Esméralda.** You'll either love this hotel or hate it. The Esméralda, in a fusty 17th-century building across from Notre-Dame (request a room with a view), is famed for its cozy, eccentric charm. Some closet-size rooms are nearly overpowered by gaudy imitation antiques, and there's usually an assemblage of dogs and cats snoozing in the (tiny) lobby. Single rooms with showers on the landings are very cheap. *4 rue St-Julien-le-Pauvre, 75005, tel. 43–54–19–20, fax 40–51–00–68. 12 rooms with bath, 4 with shower, 3 with shower on landing. No credit cards. Métro: St-Michel.*

$ ★ **Familia.** The hospitable Gaucheron family runs this comfortable hotel with great panache. A mural painted by a local art student adorns the lobby, and the 30 rooms are clean, neat, and equipped with cable TV (with CNN) and hair dryers in the bathrooms. Rooms overlooking the attractive Left Bank street have double-glazed windows. Seven rooms with balconies are highly prized and must be booked well in advance. *11 rue des Ecoles, 75005, tel. 43–54–55–27, fax 43–29–61–77. 14 rooms with bath, 16 with shower. Facilities: TV, minibars. MC, V. Métro: Jussieu, Maubert-Mutualité, Cardinal Lemoine.*

$ ★ **Grandes-Ecoles.** This delightful hotel in three small old buildings is set far off the street in a beautiful garden. There are parquet floors, antiques, and a (nonworking) piano in the breakfast area. Most rooms have beige carpets and flowery wallpaper. You won't find a quieter, more charming hotel for the price. There's a faithful American clientele, including some backpackers. The rooms with bathroom facilities on the well-lighted landings are especially inexpensive. *75 rue du Cardinal Lemoine, 75005, tel. 43–26–79–23, fax 43–25–28–15. 29 rooms with bath, 10 with shower, 9 with shared bath. MC, V. Métro: Cardinal Lemoine.*

$ ★ **Jardin des Plantes.** Across the street from the lovely Jardin des Plantes on the edge of the Latin Quarter, this pleasant hotel has a botanical-theme decor and low prices for its rooms with shower (those with bath cost more, but are still reasonable). There's a fifth-floor terrace where you can breakfast or sunbathe in summer, and a sauna in the cellar. *5 rue Linné, 75005, tel. 47–07–06–20, fax 47–07–62–74. 29 rooms with bath, 4 with shower. Facilities: sauna, bar-tearoom, terrace. AE, DC, MC, V. Métro: Jussieu.*

6th Arrondissement

$ **Acacias St-Germain.** Housed in a 19th-century building near Montparnasse, this hotel offers spotlessly clean rooms (remodeled in 1995) decorated in summery fabrics and colors, and a small, flower-filled patio. Look into the remarkable low-season and weekend discounts. Expect high-season prices that may be well over 500 francs. All rooms have TV with CNN, and hair dryers. *151 bis rue de Rennes, 75006, tel. 45–48–97–38, fax 45–44–63–57. 24 rooms with bath, 17 with shower. Facilities: room service, TV, baby-sitting, dry cleaning, laundry service, meeting room, travel services, airport shuttle, parking (fee). AE, DC, MC, V. Métro: St-Placide.*

7th Arrondissement

$ **Champ de Mars.** With the money you'll save by staying at this simple, clean hotel with reasonable prices, you'll be able to sample the specialties in the gourmet shops that line this street. Don't expect luxury or atmosphere, just a nondescript room for a very good deal, in a nice neighborhood near the Eiffel Tower and Les Invalides. *7 rue du Champ-de-Mars, 75007, tel. 45–51–52–30. 19 rooms with bath, 6 with shower. MC, V. Closed 2 weeks in mid-Aug. Métro: Ecole Militaire.*

$ **Kensington.** Perhaps the main reason to stay in this small hotel is the superb view of the Eiffel Tower from the top two floors. Rooms, furnished in white Formica, are tiny and uninspiring, but they are always impeccably clean; all have double-glazed windows. There's no restaurant, but limited room service is available. Rooms with no bath are quite inexpensive. *79 av. de la Bourdonnais, 75007, tel. 47–05–74–00, fax 47–05–25–81. 12 rooms with bath, 14 with shower. AE, DC, MC, V. Métro: Ecole Militaire.*

¢ **Grand Hôtel Lévêque.** A superb location near the Ecole-Militaire and a charming welcome are the Lévêque's biggest assets. Many of the airy, high-ceilinged rooms were recently renovated, and although rooms vary in size, all are immaculate, as are the tiled bathrooms. The bright front rooms overlook a pedestrians-only street lined with enticing food shops. Rooms that open onto the back courtyard are a few francs cheaper. If you are burdened with heavy luggage, book a room on a lower floor, as there is no elevator. *29 rue Cler, 75007, tel. 47–05–49–15, fax 45–50–49–36. 35 rooms with shower, 15 with shared bath. Facilities: lounge. MC, V. Métro: Ecole Militaire.*

8th Arrondissement

$ ★ **Argenson.** This friendly, family-run hotel provides what may well be the best value in the swanky 8e. Some of the city's greatest sights are just a 10-minute walk away. Old furniture, molded ceilings, and skillful flower arrangements add to the charm. The best rooms have full bath, but they are pricier; reserve well in advance for one of these. The smallest rooms have shared baths. *15 rue d'Argenson, 75008, tel. 42–65–16–87, fax 47–42–02–06. 27 rooms, 24 with bath or shower. MC, V. Métro: Miromesnil.*

11th Arrondissement

$ ★ **Allegro République.** This eccentric, eclectic neighborhood hosts a mixture of Turkish restaurants and lace-curtained bistros (the famous Astier is across the street from the hotel). The Allegro, which opened in 1994, has small, cheerful rooms with beige floral bedspreads and apple-green tiled bathrooms. The management is exceptionally friendly. *39 rue Jean-Pierre Timbaud, 75011, tel. 48–06–64–97, fax 48–05–03–38. 6 rooms with bath, 36 rooms with shower. AE, MC, V. Métro: République, Parmentier.*

$ **Résidence Alhambra.** The Alhambra's gleaming white exterior, backyard garden, and flower-filled window boxes provide a bright spot in an otherwise drab neighborhood. The hotel is on the edge of the historical Marais quarter, convenient to five métro lines. The smallish guest rooms are painted in fresh pastel or cool ivory shades and have marble-topped breakfast tables; most have color TVs. The lobby is filled with plants and leather armchairs. *11 bis–13 rue de Malte, 75011, tel. 47–00–35–52, fax 43–57–98–75. 10 rooms with bath, 48 with shower. Facilities: TV. MC, V. Métro: République.*

13th Arrondissement

¢ **Hôtel des Beaux-Arts.** A peaceful, casual ambience and low prices compensate for this hotel's out-of-the-way location in a residential area near Paris's Chinatown. Added pluses include a courtyard with gazebo for summer breakfasts and a large, quiet park across the street. Good housekeeping is evident in the (compact) rooms and halls. The most attractive accommodations are on the top floor under the eaves, though they are probably hot in summer. Three métro lines and several bus routes run from the nearby place d'Italie. Proprietress Madame Foutrel advises guests to book well in advance, as she has considerable repeat business. *2 rue Toussaint-Féron, 75013, tel. 44–24–22–60. 11 rooms with shower, 14 with shared bath. No English spoken. AE, MC, V. Métro: Tolbiac.*

14th Arrondissement

$$ **Istria.** An artists' hangout in the 1920s, this small, charming hotel
★ was totally rebuilt in 1988 around a flower-filled courtyard on a quiet street. It is now a family-run establishment with simple, clean, and comfortable rooms decorated in soft, summery colors. *29 rue Campagne-Première, 75014, tel. 43–20–91–82, fax 43–22–48–45. 4 rooms with bath, 22 with shower. AE, MC, V. Métro: Raspail.*

$ **Daguerre.** This sparkling-clean hotel not far from the Montparnasse
★ cemetery opened in 1994. All rooms are equipped with TV (CNN), safes, minibars, and hair dryers. Two ground-floor rooms are set up for wheelchair users. *94 rue Daguerre, 75014, tel. 43–22–43–54, fax 43–20–66–84. 8 rooms with bath, 22 with shower. Facilities: minibars, TV. AE, MC, V. Métro: Gaîté, Denfert Rochereau.*

16th Arrondissement

$ **Keppler.** Well situated on the edge of the 8e and 16e near the Champs-Elysées, this small hotel in a 19th-century building has many of the amenities of a larger hotel—room service, small bar—at extremely reasonable prices. The spacious, airy rooms are simply decorated with modern furnishings. Some rooms with shower are less expensive. *12 rue Keppler, 75016, tel. 47–20–65–05, fax 47–23–02–29. 31 rooms with bath, 18 with shower. Facilities: bar, room service. AE, MC, V. Métro: Kléber, George V.*

18th Arrondissement

$ **Timhôtel Montmartre.** A magnificent location—right in the leafy little square where Picasso lived at the turn of the century—compensates for rather basic rooms decorated with Toulouse-Lautrec posters. Single rooms are well under 500 francs; many doubles are just slightly more. *11 rue Ravignan, 75018, tel. 42–55–74–79, fax 42–55–71–01. 6 rooms with bath, 57 with shower. AE, DC, MC, V. Métro: Abbesses.*

19th Arrondissement

¢ **Le Laumière.** Though it's some distance from downtown, the low rates of this family-run hotel, close to the rambling Buttes-Chaumont park, are hard to resist. Most rooms are strictly functional, but some of the larger ones overlook the garden. The staff is exceptionally helpful. Rooms with bath are a little more than 300 francs, but others are well under. Shared baths (both showers and toilets) are on well-lighted landings. *4 rue Petit, 75019, tel. 42–06–10–77, fax 42–06–72–50. 18 rooms with bath, 28 with shower, 8 with shared bath. MC, V. Métro: Laumière.*

Exploring Paris

Paris for Free—or Almost

Unfortunately, Paris doesn't offer many organized sights that can be enjoyed without first digging deep into your pockets. That said, the city is one of the world's most scenic and exciting capitals, and just strolling along, breathing in its rich, romantic atmosphere, is an occupation in which every visitor will want to indulge.

Museums Except for its modern art museum and those galleries with temporary exhibitions, the vast halls of **Beaubourg** (Pompidou Center) are always open free of charge. Outside, on the plateau Beaubourg, you can be entertained for hours by the fire-eaters, Indian rope tricksters, musicians, mimes, and clowns who gather here during summer months. Similar entertainment can be found on the square in front of St-Germain-des-Prés, on the Left Bank.

Walks A walk along the **Seine** is at the top of the list; although roads have invaded some sections of quays, you can still stroll peacefully along the riverbank between place de la Concorde and the Louvre before crossing the Pont des Arts footbridge and continuing along the **Left Bank,** past Notre-Dame, as far as the Jardin des Plantes; the last section of this walk takes you through the avant-garde statuary of the **Musée de la Sculpture en Plein Air.** The northern banks of the **Ile St-Louis** also make for an idyllic saunter. Other great places to wander are the **Marais,** with its clash of ramshackle streets and stately mansions; **Montmartre,** with its tumbling alleyways and flights of steps; along the banks of the **Canal St-Martin,** with its locks, footbridges, and flavor of Amsterdam; and, of course, down the **Champs-Elysées,** continuing along the arcaded rue du Rivoli to the Louvre.

Parks Paris's many parks and gardens can be enjoyed free of charge. The **Tuileries, Jardin du Luxembourg,** and the **Palais-Royal** are the most central locations, but don't forget the lower reaches of the Champs-Elysées or the landscaped gardens at **Les Halles,** with their ivy-strewn archways and dramatic views of St-Eustache. A short métro ride will take you to **Parc Monceau** (mock ruins), the **Jardin des Plantes** (superb flowers), the **Arènes de Lutèce** (Roman ruins), the **Buttes-Chaumont,** and **Parc Montsouris** (the last two have their own lake). The **Champ de Mars,** stretching away from the Eiffel Tower, has long, straight, uncrowded alleys that make it the best jogging venue in Paris. The **Bois de Boulogne** and **Bois de Vincennes** offer acres of woods and lakes. Gardening enthusiasts should consider paying the small admission charges to admire the outstanding floral displays at the **Serres d'Auteuil, Parc Bagatelle,** or **Parc Floral** at Vincennes. Melancholy charm lurks amid the lush foliage and bombastic sepulchres at the vast, lugubrious **Père Lachaise Cemetery.**

Views Everyone has a favorite Paris view, but here are some of the most dramatic: the **Sacré Coeur** as you emerge from rue de Steinkerque; the **Eiffel Tower** from Trocadéro; the **Arc de Triomphe** from avenue

Foch; **Notre-Dame** from Pont de l'Archevêché; the columns at **place
de la Nation** from cours de Vincennes. The best views of Paris are
from high up the Eiffel Tower or Tour Montparnasse, but cheaper
alternatives are from the dome of the Sacré Coeur, the towers of
Notre-Dame, the elevator at Beaubourg, or from high up rue de
Ménilmontant in northeast Paris. Other picturesque views include
Ile de la Cité from the Pont des Arts footbridge; **rue des Barres** and
the back of St-Gervais church from quai de l'Hôtel de Ville; and the
Tuileries and **Right Bank** from the café terrace at the Musée
d'Orsay.

People-
Watching
The best places include **St-Germain-des-Prés** and **place St-Sulpice**
(6e), **boulevard Montparnasse** (14e), **place de l'Opéra** (9e), **place de la
Contrescarpe** (5e), and **place Victor-Hugo** (16e).

And for the price of a cup of coffee, you're guaranteed a ringside seat
in any of Paris's sidewalk cafés, where you can amuse yourself for
hours watching the world go by.

Concerts
A number of Paris churches give free concerts (especially on Sunday
afternoons), including **St-Sulpice** (6e), the **Madeleine** (8e), **St-
Germain-l'Auxerrois** (1er), **St-Eustache** (1er), **St-Merri** (4e), **Notre-
Dame** (1er), and the **American Church** (7th). You can also attend con-
certs for free at the headquarters of **Radio-France** (116 av. du Prési-
dent-Kennedy, 16e). Check details in *Pariscope* or *L'Officiel des
Spectacles*.

Orientation

The best method of getting to know Paris is on foot. With this in
mind, we've divided our coverage of Paris into six tours. Use our
routes as a base; concentrate on the areas that are of particular interest to you; and, above all, enjoy to the full the sights, sounds, and
smells of this exciting city.

To make your days run more smoothly (not to mention cheaply) you
might want to buy the *Carte Musées et Monuments*, a one-, three-,
or five-day pass (60 frs, 120 frs, or 170 frs) that allows you unlimited
access to the permanent collections of 65 museums and monuments
in Paris and the surrounding area. Not only that, you can say goodbye to the long ticket lines. The pass is sold at any of the participating museums and monuments (many of which are described below),
the main métro and RER stations, the tourist office (127 av. des
Champs-Elysées, 8e), and Musée & Compagnie (49 rue Etienne-
Marcel, 75001), and it comes with an information-packed leaflet and
a métro plan.

Tour 1: The Historic Heart

*Numbers in the margin correspond to points of interest on the Paris
map.*

Of the two islands in the Seine—the Ile St-Louis and Ile de la Cité—
it is Ile de la Cité that forms the historic heart of Paris. It was here
that the earliest inhabitants of Paris, the Gaulish tribe of the Parisii,
settled around 250 BC. Whereas the Ile St-Louis is largely residential, the Ile de la Cité remains deeply historic: It is the site of the
great, brooding cathedral of Notre-Dame. Few of the island's other
medieval buildings have survived, most having fallen victim to Baron Haussmann's ambitious rebuilding of the city in the mid-19th century. Among the rare survivors are the jewellike Sainte-Chapelle, a
vision of shimmering stained glass, and the Conciergerie, the grim
former city prison.

The tour begins at the western tip of the Ile de la Cité, at the sedate
❶ **square du Vert-Galant.** The statue of the *Vert Galant* himself, literally the "vigorous [by which was really meant the amorous] adventur-

er," shows Henri IV sitting sturdily on his horse. Henri, king of France from 1589 until his assassination in 1610, was something of a dashing figure as well as a canny statesman.

Crossing the tip of Ile de la Cité, just east of the Vert Galant, is the oldest bridge in Paris, confusingly called the **Pont Neuf**, or New Bridge. Completed in the early 17th century, it was the first bridge in the city to be built without houses lining either side. Turn left (north) onto it. Once across the river, turn left again and walk down to rue l'Amiral-de-Coligny, opposite the massive eastern facade of the Louvre. Before heading for the museum, however, stay on the right-hand sidewalk and duck into the church of **St-Germain-l'Auxerrois**. This was the French royal family's Paris church in the days before the Revolution, when the Louvre was a palace rather than a museum. The fluid stonework of the facade reveals the influence of 15th-century Flamboyant Gothic, the final, exuberant fling of the Gothic before the classical takeover of the Renaissance. Note the unusual double aisles and the exceptionally wide windows—typical of the style. The triumph of classicism is evident, however, in the 18th-century fluted columns around the choir, the area surrounding the altar.

The Louvre colonnade across the road screens one of Europe's most dazzling courtyards, the **Cour Carré**, a breathtakingly monumental, harmonious, and superbly rhythmic ensemble. In the crypt below, excavated in 1984, sections of the defensive towers of the original, 13th-century fortress can be seen.

Stroll through the courtyard and pass under the **Pavillon de l'Horloge**, the Clock Tower, and you'll come face-to-face with I. M. Pei's **Great Pyramid,** surrounded by three smaller pyramids, in the Cour Napoléon. The pyramid marks the new entrance to the Louvre and houses a large museum shop, café, and restaurant. It is also the terminal point for the most celebrated city view in Europe—a majestic vista stretching through the Arc du Carrousel, the Tuileries Gardens, across place de la Concorde, up the Champs-Elysées to the towering Arc de Triomphe, and ending at the giant modern arch at La Tête Défense, a further 2½ miles away. Needless to say, the architectural collision between classical stone blocks and pseudo-Egyptian glass panels has caused a furor.

The pyramid, unveiled in 1989, marked the first completed objective of former president François Mitterrand's Grand Louvre Project, a plan for the restoration of the museum launched in 1981 and expected to cost $1.3 billion by the time it is finished in 1996. In November 1993, exactly 200 years since the Louvre first opened its doors to the public, Mitterrand cut the ribbon on the completed second phase. This includes the renovation of the **Richelieu Wing**, former home of the Ministry of Finance, which was gutted by Pei and his associates and reopened to house more than 12,000 artworks (a third of them brought out from storage), notably the Islamic and Mesopotamian collections, French painting and sculpture, and the sumptuous Napoléon III apartments. The new wing is characterized by its sunlit exhibition spaces surrounding airy courtyards, a marked contrast to the formal Denon and Sully wings. Also open now is the **Carrousel du Louvre,** a subterranean shopping complex with a wide range of stores, a food court, an auditorium, and a large parking garage. The third and final phase of the project includes improvement of the air-conditioning and lighting, the restoration of the Tuileries Gardens, and a pedestrian bridge that will connect the Tuileries with the Musée d'Orsay.

Today's **Louvre** is the end product of many generations of work. Philippe-Auguste built it in the early 13th century as a fortress to protect the city's western flank. The earliest parts of the current building date from the reign of François I at the beginning of the

Paris Arrondissements

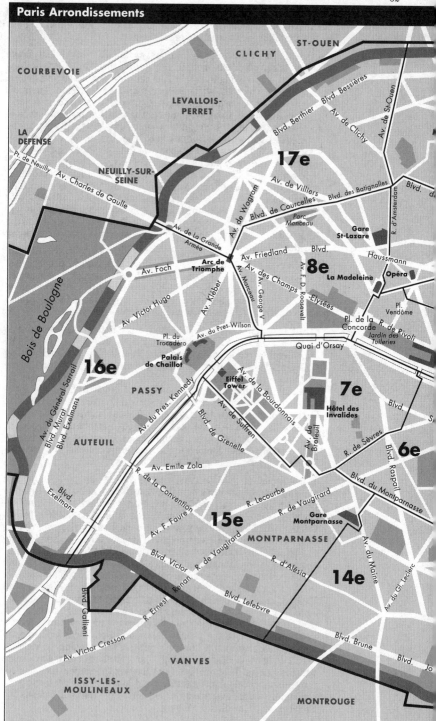

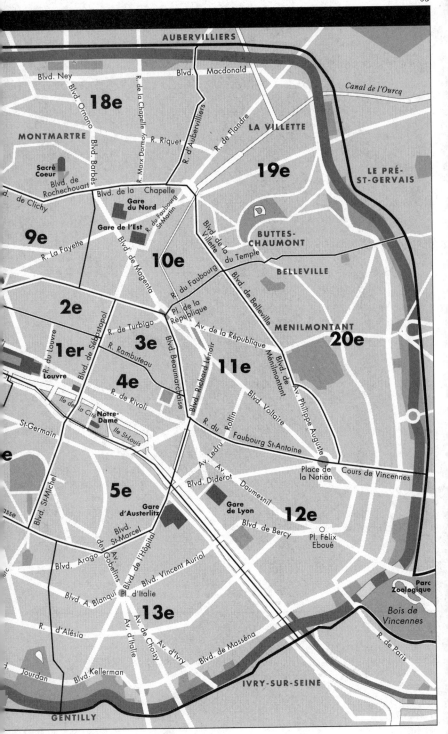

Paris

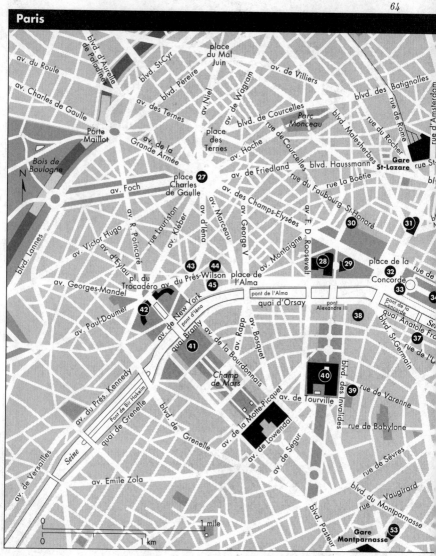

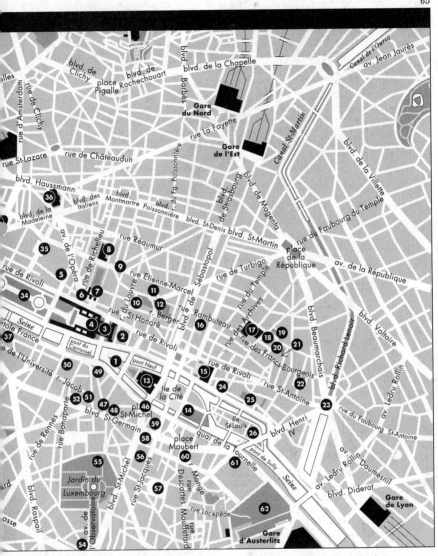

16th century, and subsequent monarchs—Henri IV (1589–1610), Louis XIII (1610–43), Louis XIV (1643–1715), Napoléon (1802–14), and Napoléon III (1851–70)—all contributed to its construction. The open section facing the Tuileries Gardens was once the site of the Palais des Tuileries, the main residence of the royal family in Paris.

Over the centuries, the Louvre has been used as both a royal residence and a home for minor courtiers; at one point, it was taken over by a rabble of artists who set up shop and whose chimneys projected higgledy-piggledy from the otherwise severe lines of the facades. After a stint as headquarters of the French Revolution, the Louvre was finally established, in Napoléon's time, as a museum, though the country's last three monarchs continued to make it their home.

The number-one attraction for most visitors is Leonardo da Vinci's enigmatic *Mona Lisa*, "La Joconde" to the French; be forewarned that you will find it encased in glass and surrounded by a mob of tourists. The collections are divided into seven sections: Oriental antiquities; Egyptian antiquities; Greek and Roman antiquities; sculpture; paintings, prints, and drawings; furniture; and objets d'art. Don't try to see it all at once; try, instead, to make repeat visits—the Louvre is half-price on Sunday. Some highlights of paintings, in addition to the *Mona Lisa*, are *The Inspiration of the Poet*, by Nicolas Poussin (1594–1665); *The Oath of the Horatii*, by Jacques-Louis David (1748–1825); *The Raft of the Medusa*, by Théodore Géricault (1791–1824); and *La Grande Odalisque*, by Jean-Auguste Dominique Ingres (1780–1867). Probably the best-loved bit of sculpture is Michelangelo's pair of *Slaves*, intended for the tomb of Pope Julius II; the French crown jewels (in the objets d'art section) include the mind-boggling 186-carat Regent diamond. *Palais du Louvre, tel. 40–20–53–17. Admission: 40 frs adults, 20 frs ages 18–25, after 3 PM, and on Sun. Open daily 9–6, Mon. and Wed. until 9:45; closed Tues. Métro: Palais Royal.*

Stretching westward from the main entrance to the Louvre and the glass pyramid is an expanse of stately, formal gardens. These are the **Jardins des Tuileries** (*see* Tour 3: From the Arc de Triomphe to the Opéra, *below*).

Running the length of the Louvre's northern side is Napoléon's arcaded rue de Rivoli. Cross it and you're in **place des Pyramides,** face-to-face with its gilded statue of Joan of Arc on horseback. Walk up rue des Pyramides and take the first left, rue St-Honoré, to the ❺ Baroque church of **St-Roch.** The church was completed in the 1730s, the date of the cool, classical facade. It's worth having a look inside to see the bombastically Baroque altarpiece in the circular Lady Chapel.

Return to rue des Pyramides and follow rue St-Honoré to **place André-Malraux,** with its fountains. The Opéra building is visible down the avenue of the same name, and on one corner of the square, at rue ❻ de Richelieu, is the **Comédie-Française,** the time-honored setting for performances of classical French drama. The building dates from 1790, but the Comédie-Française company was created by Louis XIV in 1680. If you understand French and have a taste for the mannered, declamatory style of French acting, you will appreciate an evening here (*see* The Arts and Nightlife, *below*).

To the right of the theater (as you face it from the Louvre) is the unobtrusive entrance to the gardens of the **Palais Royal.** The buildings ❼ of this former palace date from the 1630s and are royal only in that the builder, Cardinal Richelieu (1585–1642), magnanimously bequeathed them to Louis XIII. Today the Palais Royal is home of the French Ministry of Culture and is not open to the public. But don't miss the **gardens,** divided by rows of perfectly trimmed little trees, a surprisingly little-known oasis in the heart of the city. There's not much chance that you'll miss the black-and-white striped columns in the courtyard or the revolving silver spheres that slither around in the two fountains at either end, the controversial early-1980s work of architect Daniel Buren. Walk to the end, away from the main palace, and peek into the opulent, Belle Epoque, glass-lined interior of **Le Grand Véfour,** one of the swankiest and most sumptuously appointed restaurants in the city.

❽ Around the corner, on rue de Richelieu, stands France's national library, the **Bibliothèque Nationale,** containing more than 7 million printed volumes. Visitors can admire Robert de Cotte's 18th-century courtyard and peep into the 19th-century reading room. *58 rue de Richelieu. Open daily 10–8. Métro: Bourse.*

❾ From the library, walk along rue des Petits-Champs to the circular **place des Victoires.** It was laid out by Jules Hardouin-Mansart, a leading proponent of French 17th-century classicism, in 1685, in honor of the military victories of Louis XIV. You'll find some of the city's most upscale fashion shops here and on the surrounding streets.

❿ Head south down rue Croix-des-Petits-Champs. The second street on the left leads to the circular 18th-century **Bourse du Commerce,** or Commercial Exchange. Alongside it is a 100-foot-high fluted column, all that remains of a mansion built here in 1572 for Catherine de Médicis. The column is said to have been used as a platform for stargazing by her astrologer, Ruggieri.

⓫ You can easily spot the bulky outline of the church of **St-Eustache,** away to the left. It is a huge church, the "cathedral" of Les Halles, built, as it were, as the market people's Right Bank reply to Notre-Dame. Under construction from 1532 to 1637 and modified over the centuries, the church is a curious architectural hybrid. Its exterior flying buttresses, for example, are solidly Gothic, yet its column orders, rounded arches, and comparatively simple window tracery are unmistakably classical. Few buildings bear such eloquent witness to stylistic transition. St-Eustache also features occasional organ concerts. *2 rue du Jour, tel. 46–27–89–21. Métro: Les Halles.*

⓬ If Notre-Dame and the Louvre represent Church and State, respectively, Les Halles (pronounced "lay al") stands for the common man. For centuries, this was Paris's central market. Closed in 1969, it was replaced by a striking shopping mall, the **Forum des Halles.** The surrounding streets have since undergone a radical transformation, much like the neighboring Marais, and the shops, cafés, restaurants, and chic apartment buildings make it an example of successful urban redevelopment.

⓭ From place du Châtelet cross back over the Seine on the Pont-au-Change to the Ile de la Cité. To your right looms the imposing **Palais de Justice,** the Courts of Law, built by Baron Haussmann in his characteristically weighty classical style around 1860. The main buildings of interest on the Ile de la Cité, however, are the medieval parts of the complex, spared by Haussmann in his otherwise wholesale destruction.

The **Conciergerie,** the northernmost part of the complex, was originally part of the royal palace on the island. Most people know it, however, as a prison, the grim place of confinement for Danton, Robespierre, and Marie-Antoinette during the French Revolution. Inside you'll see the guardroom (the Salle des Gens d'Armes), a striking example of Gothic monumentality; the cells, including the one in which Marie-Antoinette was held; and the chapel, where objects connected with the ill-fated queen are displayed. *Admission: 26 frs adults, 17 frs children, students, and senior citizens. Joint ticket (with Ste-Chapelle): 40 frs (20 frs). Open daily 9:30–6:30 (10–4:30 in winter). Métro: Cité.*

The other perennial crowd-puller in the Palais de Justice is the
★ **Sainte-Chapelle,** the Holy Chapel, one of the supreme achievements
of the Middle Ages. It was built by the genial and pious Louis IX
(1226–70) to house what he took to be the Crown of Thorns from
Christ's crucifixion and fragments of the True Cross. Architecturally, for all its delicate and ornate exterior decoration, the design of
the building is simplicity itself; in essence, no more than a thin, rectangular box much taller than it is wide. Some clumsy 19th-century
work has added a deadening touch, but the glory of the chapel—the
stained glass—is spectacularly intact: The walls consist of at least
twice as much glass as masonry. Try to attend one of the regular,
candlelit concerts given here. *Tel. 43–54–30–09. Admission: 26 frs
adults, 17 frs children under 18. Open daily 9:30–6:30 (10–5 in winter). Métro: Cité.*

Take rue de Lutèce opposite the Palais de Justice down to place Lou-
is-Lépine and the bustling **Marché aux Fleurs,** the flower market.
Around the corner is the most enduring symbol of Paris, the cathe-
★ dral of **Notre-Dame.** The building was started in 1163, with an army
of stonemasons, carpenters, and sculptors working on a site that had
previously seen a Roman temple, an early Christian basilica, and a
Romanesque church. The chancel and altar were consecrated in
1182, but the magnificent sculptures surrounding the main doors
were not put into position until 1240. The north tower was finished
10 years later. Despite various changes in the 17th century, principally the (temporary) removal of the rose windows, the cathedral remained substantially unaltered until the French Revolution, when
much destruction was wrought, mainly to statuary.

Stand in place du Parvis, in front of the cathedral, to gaze first at the
building's facade, divided neatly into three levels. At the first level
are the three main entrances: the Portal of the Virgin on the left, the
Portal of the Last Judgment in the center, and the Portal of St. Anne
on the right. Above the portals are the restored statues of the kings
of Israel, the Galerie des Rois (which took a beating during the
French Revolution), which complete the first level. A large rose window centers the second level, and at the third level is the Grande
Galerie, a series of pointed double arches at the base of the twin towers. The south tower houses the great bell of Notre-Dame, the one
tolled by Quasimodo, Victor Hugo's fictional hunchback.

The interior of the cathedral, with its vast proportions, soaring
nave, and gentle, multicolored light filtering through the stained-
glass windows, inspires awe, despite the inevitable throngs of tourists. (There is no charge to visit the interior of the cathedral.) On the
south side of the chancel is the **Treasury,** with a collection of garments, reliquaries, and silver and gold plate. *Admission: 15 frs
adults, 10 frs students and senior citizens, 5 frs children. Open
weekdays 9:30–6. Métro: Cité.*

The 387-step climb to the top of the **towers** is worth the effort for the
close-up view of the famous gargoyles and the expansive view over
the city. *Entrance via the north tower. Admission: 31 frs adults, 20
frs students and senior citizens, 7 frs children. Open daily 9:30–
12:15 and 2–6 (5 in winter).*

The **Crypte Archeologique,** the archaeological museum under the
square, contains structural remains unearthed during excavations
here in the 1960s. The foundations of the 3rd-century Gallo-Roman
rampart and of the 6th-century Merovingian church can also be
seen. *Admission: 26 frs adults (40 frs including Notre-Dame towers), 17 frs students and senior citizens, 6 frs children 7–17. Open
daily 10–6:30, 10–5 in winter.*

If your interest in the cathedral is not yet sated, duck into the **Musée
Notre-Dame,** which displays artwork and documents tracing the cathedral's history. *10 rue du Cloître Notre-Dame. Admission: 12 frs,*

*6 frs students and senior citizens, 4 frs children under 14. Open Wed.
and weekends only, 2:30–6.*

Tour 2: The Marais and Ile St-Louis

The history of the Marais (marsh) began when Charles V, king of
France in the 14th century, moved the French court from the Ile de
la Cité. However, it wasn't until Henri IV laid out the place Royale,
today the place des Vosges, in the early 17th century that the Marais
became *the* place to live. Following the French Revolution, however,
the Marais rapidly became one of the most deprived, dissolute areas
in Paris. It was spared the attentions of Baron Haussmann, the man
who rebuilt so much of Paris in the mid-19th century, so that, though
crumbling, its ancient, golden-hued buildings and squares remained
intact. Most of the Marais's spectacular *hôtels particuliers*
(mansions), one-time residences of aristocratic families, have been
restored and transformed into museums. Today's Marais once again
has staked a convincing claim as the city's most desirable district.

15 Begin your tour at the **Hôtel de Ville** (City Hall), overlooking the
Seine. It was in the square on the Hôtel de Ville's south side that
Robespierre, fanatical leader during the period of the French Revolution known as the Reign of Terror, came to suffer the fate of his
many victims when a furious mob sent him to the guillotine in 1794.
Following the accession of Louis-Philippe in 1830, the building became the seat of the French government, a role that came to a sud-
den end with the uprisings in 1848. In the Commune of 1871, the
Hôtel de Ville was burned to the ground. Today's exuberant building, based closely on the Renaissance original, went up between
1874 and 1884.

From the Hôtel de Ville, head north across rue de Rivoli and up rue
du Temple. On your right, you'll pass one of the city's most popular
department stores, the **Bazar de l'Hôtel de Ville,** or BHV as it's commonly known. The first street on your left, rue de la Verrerie, will
take you to the stores, restaurants, and galleries of the rue St-Martin.

★ **16** **Beaubourg**—also known as the **Pompidou Center** for its full name,
Centre National d'Art et de Culture Georges Pompidou—is next.
The center hosts an innovative and challenging series of exhibits, in
addition to housing the world's largest collection of modern art. Its
brash architectural style—it has been likened to a gaudily painted
oil refinery—has caused much controversy, however. Many critics
think it is beginning to show its age (it only opened in 1977) in a particularly cheap manner: Witness the cracked and grimy plastic tub-
ing that encases the exterior elevators, and the peeling, skeletal
interior supports. Probably the most popular thing to do at
Beaubourg is to ride the escalator up to the roof to see the Parisian
skyline unfolding as you are carried through its clear plastic piping.
There's a sizable restaurant and café on the roof. Aside from the art
collection (from which American painters and sculptors are conspic-
uously absent), the building houses a movie theater; a language laboratory; an extensive collection of tapes, videos, and slides; an
industrial design center; and an acoustics and musical research center. *Plateau Beaubourg, tel. 42–77–12–33. Admission free. Admission to art museum: 35 frs Open Wed.–Mon. noon–10 PM, weekends
10–10. Guided tours in English: weekdays 3:30, weekends 11, during
summer and Christmas seasons only. Métro: Rambuteau.*

Don't leave the plateau without stopping for coffee at the **Café
Beaubourg** on the corner of rue St-Merri. A staircase takes you up
from the first floor to a *passerelle*, or foot bridge, linking the two
sides of a mezzanine. Philippe Starck's severe, high-tech design is
lightened by the little glass-top tables, covered with artists' etch-
ings.

Leave plateau Beaubourg by its southwestern corner and head down little rue Ste-Croix de la Bretonnerie to visit the Marais's Jewish quarter. You'll see the more obvious of the area's historical highlights if you take rue Rambuteau, which runs along the north side of the center (to your left as you face the building). The **Quartier de l'Horloge,** the Clock Quarter, opens off the plateau here. An entire city block has been rebuilt, and despite the shops and cafés, it retains a resolutely artificial quality. The mechanical clock around the corner on rue Clairvaux will amuse children, however: St. George defends Time against a dragon, an eagle-beaked bird, or a monstrous crab (symbolizing earth, air, and water, respectively) every hour, on the hour. At noon, 6 PM, and 10 PM, he takes on all three at once.

You are now poised to plunge into the elegant heart of the Marais. The historic homes here are now private residences, but don't be afraid to push through the heavy doors, or *portes-cochère*, to glimpse the discreet courtyards that lurk behind.

From the little market on rue Rambuteau, take the first left, up rue du Temple, to the 17th-century **Hôtel de Montmor,** at No. 79. It was once the scene of an influential literary salon—a part-social, part-literary group—that included the philosopher Descartes (1596–1650) and the playwright Molière (1622–73).

Take rue de Braque (opposite) down to the Hôtel de Soubise, now ❶⓻ the **Archives Nationales** (its collections form part of the **Musée de l'Histoire de France,** whose entrance is at the far end of the courtyard). The museum's highlights are the Edict of Nantes (1598), Louis XIV's and Napoléon's wills, and the Declaration of Human Rights (1789). Louis XVI's diary is also in the collection, containing his sadly ignorant entry for July 14, 1789, the day the Bastille was stormed at the start of the French Revolution: *Rien* (nothing), he wrote. You can also visit the apartments of the Prince and Princess de Soubise: Don't miss them if you have any interest in the lifestyles of 18th-century French aristocrats. The Archives buildings also include the elegant **Hôtel de Rohan,** built for the archbishops of Strasbourg in 1705 (open only during temporary exhibits). *60 rue des Francs-Bourgeois, tel. 40–27–62–18. Admission: 15 frs adults, 10 frs students. Open Wed.–Mon. 1:45–5:45. Métro: Rambuteau.*

Turn right onto rue des Archives, then take the first right onto rue des Quatre-Fils, which becomes rue de la Perle. At No. 1 is the ❶⓼ **Musée Bricard de la Serrure,** the Lock Museum. The museum's sumptuous building is perhaps more interesting than the assembled locks and keys within; it was built in 1685 by Bruand, the architect of Les Invalides. If you have a taste for fine craftsmanship, you will appreciate the intricacy and ingenuity of many of the older locks. One represents an early security system—it would shoot anyone who tried to open it with the wrong key. *Hôtel Bruand, 1 rue de la Perle. Admission: 20 frs adults. Open weekdays 2–5. Métro: St-Sébastien.*

★ ❶⓽ From here it is but a step to the Hôtel Salé, built between 1656 and 1660, and today the popular **Musée Picasso;** be prepared for long lines. The collection encompasses pictures, sculptures, drawings, prints, ceramics, and other assorted works of art given to the French government after the painter's death, in 1973, in lieu of death duties. What's notable about it—other than its being the world's largest collection of works by Picasso—is that these were works that the artist himself owned and especially valued. There are works from every period of his life, as well as paintings by Paul Cézanne, Joan Miró, Pierre Auguste Renoir, Georges Braque, Edgar Degas, Henri Matisse, and others. The palatial surroundings add greatly to the visit. *5 rue de Thorigny, tel. 42–71–25–21. Admission: 26 frs adults. Open Wed.–Mon. 9:30–6. Métro: St-Sébastien.*

Cut across place Thorigny and take rue Elzévir. Halfway down on the left is the **Musée Cognacq-Jay,** transferred here in 1990 from its original home near the Opéra. The museum is devoted to the arts of the 18th century: furniture, porcelain, and paintings (notably Watteau and Boucher). The Hôtel Donon, a 15th-century mansion, was virtually in ruins before its tasteful transformation by the City of Paris. *8 rue Elzévir, tel. 40–27–07–21. Admission: 17 frs adults, 9 frs students and children. Open Tues.–Sun. 10–5:30. Métro: St-Paul.*

Continue down rue Elzévir to rue des Francs-Bourgeois, where the substantial **Hôtel Carnavalet** became the scene, in the late-17th century, of the most brilliant salon in Paris, presided over by Madame de Sévigné. She is best known for the hundreds of letters she wrote to her daughter during her life; they've become one of the most enduring chronicles of French high society in the 17th century. In 1880, the hotel was transformed into the **Musée de l'Histoire de Paris.** To celebrate the bicentennial of the French Revolution in 1989, the museum annexed the neighboring Hôtel Peletier St-Fargeau. Together the two museums chronicle the entire history of the city of Paris. Material dating from the city's origins until 1789 is housed in the Hôtel Carnavalet; objects from that time to the present are in the Hôtel Peletier St-Fargeau. *23 rue de Sévigné, tel. 42–72–21–13. Admission: 27 frs adults, 19 frs children and senior citizens. Open Tues.–Sun. 10–5:30. Métro: St-Paul.*

Now walk a minute or two farther along rue des Francs-Bourgeois to **place des Vosges,** or place Royale as it was originally known, the oldest square in Paris. Laid out by Henri IV at the beginning of the 17th century, it is the model for all the later city squares of most French urban developments. The harmonious balance of the square, with its symmetrical town houses of pale pink stone, makes it a pleasant place in which to spend a hot summer's afternoon. At No. 6 is the **Maison de Victor Hugo,** which commemorates the workaholic French writer. *Admission: 18 frs. Métro: St-Paul.*

From place des Vosges, follow rue du Pas-de-la-Mule and turn right down rue des Tournelles until you reach **place de la Bastille,** site of the infamous prison destroyed in 1789 during the French Revolution. Until 1988, there was little more to see at place de la Bastille than a huge traffic circle and the **Colonne de Juillet,** the July Column. As part of the countrywide celebrations held in July 1989, the bicentennial of the French Revolution, a 3,000-seat **opera house** with five moving stages and a gleaming, curved-glass facade was put up on the south side of the square. Redevelopment projects have changed what was formerly a humdrum neighborhood into one of the city's most chic and attractive.

The **Bastille** was built by Charles V in the late-14th century as a fortress to guard the eastern entrance to the city. By the reign of Louis XIII (1610–43), however, it was used almost exclusively to house political prisoners, including, in the 18th century, Voltaire and the Marquis de Sade. This obviously political role led the "furious mob" (in all probability no more than a largely unarmed rabble) to break into the prison on July 14, 1789, kill the governor, steal what firearms they could find, and set free the seven remaining prisoners. The ground plan of the prison is marked by paving stones set into the modern square.

Return toward the Hôtel de Ville down rue St-Antoine, forking off left down rue François-Miron to the church of **St-Gervais-St-Protais,** named after two Roman soldiers martyred by the Emperor Nero in the 1st century AD. The original church—one of the earliest in Paris; no trace remains of it now—was built in the 7th century. The present building, a riot of Flamboyant decoration, went up between 1494 and 1598, making it one of the last Gothic constructions in the country. Before you go in, pause to look at the facade, put up between 1616 and 1621. Although the interior is late Gothic, the exterior is one of the earliest examples of the Classical, or Renaissance, style in France. *Open Tues.–Sun. 6:30–8. The church hosts occasional choral and organ concerts; call 47–26–78–38 for information. Métro: Hôtel de Ville.*

㉕ Don't cross the Seine to Ile St-Louis yet. Take rue de l'Hôtel de Ville to where it meets rue de Figuier. The painstakingly restored **Hôtel de Sens** (1474) on the corner is one of a handful of Parisian homes to have survived since the Middle Ages. With its pointed corner towers, Gothic porch, and richly carved decorative details, it is a strange mixture, half defensive stronghold, half fairytale château. Built at the end of the 15th century for the archbishop of Sens, it was once the home of Henri IV and his queen, Marguerite, philanderers both. While Henri dallied with his mistresses—he is said to have had 56—at a series of royal palaces, Marguerite entertained her almost equally large number of lovers here. Today the building houses a fine-arts library, the **Bibliothèque Forney.** *Admission free. Open Tues.–Fri. 1:30–8:30, Sat. 10–8:30. Métro: Pont Marie.*

㉖ Cross pont Marie to the residential **Ile St-Louis,** the smaller of the two islands in the heart of Paris, linked to the Ile de la Cité by pont St-Louis. There are no standouts here and no great sights, but for idle strolling, window shopping, or simply sitting on one of the little quays and drinking in the views, the Ile St-Louis exudes a quintessentially Parisian air.

Berthillon has become a byword for delicious ice cream. Cafés all over Ile St-Louis sell its glamorous products, but the place to try them is still the little shop on rue St-Louis-en-l'Ile. Expect to wait in line. *31 rue St-Louis-en-l'Ile. Closed Mon. and Tues. Métro: Pont Marie.*

Tour 3: From the Arc de Triomphe to the Opéra

This tour takes in grand, opulent Paris—the Paris of imposing vistas; long, arrow-straight streets; and plush hotels and jewelers. It begins at the Arc de Triomphe, standing sturdily at the top of the most famous street in the city, the Champs-Elysées.

Place Charles-de-Gaulle is known by Parisians as **l'Etoile,** the star—a reference to the streets that fan out from it. It is one of Europe's most chaotic traffic circles, and short of a death-defying dash, your only way of getting to the Arc de Triomphe in the middle is to take an underground passage from the Champs-Elysées or avenue de la Grande-Armée.

★ ㉗ The colossal, 164-foot **Arc de Triomphe** was planned by Napoléon to celebrate his military successes. Unfortunately, the great man's strategic and architectural visions were not entirely on the same plane: When it was required for the triumphal entry of his new empress, Marie Louise, into Paris in 1810, it was still only a few feet high. To save face, he ordered a dummy arch of painted canvas to be put up. (The real thing wasn't finished until 1836.) After recent, extensive cleaning, its elaborate relief sculptures are magnificent. The highlight is the scene by François Rude, illustrated to the right of the arch when viewed from the Champs-Elysées. Called *Departure of the Volunteers in 1792,* it's commonly known as *La Marseillaise* and depicts *La Patrie,* or the Fatherland, with outspread wings exhorting the volunteers to fight for France.

Go up to the viewing platform at the top of the monument, from which you can admire the vista down the Champs-Elysées toward place de la Concorde and the distant Louvre. A small museum halfway up the arch is devoted to its history. France's *Unknown Soldier* is buried beneath the archway; the flame is rekindled every evening at 6:30. *Pl. Charles-de-Gaulle. Admission: 31 frs adults, 20 frs students and senior citizens, 7 frs children. Open daily except public holidays 10–5:30; 10–5 in winter. Métro: Etoile.*

Laid out by landscape gardener André Le Nôtre in the 1660s as a garden sweeping away from the Tuileries, the cosmopolitan **Champs-Elysées** reached its pinnacle at the turn of the century, when the tree- and café-lined avenue was the main drag for Paris's beau monde. The city of Paris has now completed an ambitious reconstruction program that has reestablished this once glorious thoroughfare as one of the world's most beautiful avenues. Improvements include underground parking to alleviate congestion, tree-lined walkways along each side, designer street furniture (coordinated benches, signs, trash cans), Belle Epoque–style newsstands, and stricter regulations to control the garishness of business storefronts. The avenue also occupies a central role in French national celebrations. It witnesses the finish of the Tour de France cycle race on the fourth Sunday of July and is the site of vast ceremonies on Bastille Day, July 14 (France's national holiday), and November 11, Armistice Day. Start by walking down from l'Etoile on the left-hand side, where, 300 yards down, at No. 116-B, is the famous **Lido** nightclub: Foot-stomping melodies in French and English, and champagne-soaked, topless razzmatazz pack in the crowds every night. Avenue George-V leads south to the **Prince de Galles** (Prince of Wales) at No. 33 (with the red awning) and the **George V** (with the blue awning), two of the city's top hotels. Continue down avenue George-V and turn right down Pierre-Ier-de-Serbie to the church of **St-Pierre de Chaillot** on avenue Marceau. The monumental frieze above the entrance, depicting scenes from the life of St. Peter, is the work of Henri Bouchard and dates from 1937. Returning to avenue George-V, continue toward the slender spire of the **American Cathedral of the Holy Trinity**, built by G. S. Street between 1885 and 1888. *Open weekdays 9–12:30 and 2–5, Sat. 9–noon. Services: weekdays 9 AM, Sun. 9 AM and 11 AM; Sun. school and nursery. Guided tours Sun. and Wed. at 12:30. Métro: George V.*

At the bottom of avenue George-V is the place de l'Alma and the Seine. Just across the Alma bridge, on the left, is the entrance to **Les Egouts,** the Paris sewers. Aside from the unpleasant smell, the Egouts are surprisingly interesting. Several underground passages and footbridges carry you along the banks of Paris sewers, marked with signs to mirror the streets above. *Admission: 24 frs. Open Sat.–Wed. 11–4. Métro: Pont de l'Alma.*

Boat rides ★ If you prefer a less malodorous tour of the city, stay on the Right Bank and head down the sloping side road to the left of the bridge, for the embarkation point of the **bâteaux-mouches** motorboat tours of the Seine.

Stylish avenue Montaigne leads from the Seine back toward the Champs-Elysées.

㉘ Two blocks east along the Champs-Elysées on avenue Winston-Churchill sit the **Grand Palais** and the Petit Palais, erected before the Paris World Fair of 1900. As with the Eiffel Tower, there was never any intention that these two buildings would be anything other than temporary additions to the city. Together they recapture the opulence and frivolity of the Belle Epoque. Today the atmospheric iron-and-glass interior of the Grand Palais plays regular host to major exhibitions. *Av. Winston-Churchill. Admission varies according to exhibition. Usually open 10:30–6:30, often until 10 PM on Wed. Métro: Champs-Elysées–Clemenceau.*

㉙ The **Petit Palais** has a beautifully presented permanent collection of lavish 17th-century furniture and French 19th-century paintings, with splendid canvases by Courbet and Bouguereau. Temporary exhibits are often held here, too. The sprawling entrance gallery contains several enormous turn-of-the-century paintings on its walls and ceiling. *Av. Winston-Churchill. Admission: 26 frs adults, 14 frs children. Open Tues.–Sun. 10–5:30. Métro: Champs-Elysées–Clemenceau.*

Cross the Champs-Elysées and head down avenue de Marigny to **rue du Faubourg St-Honoré,** a prestigious address in the world of luxury fashion and art galleries. High security surrounds the French president in the **Palais de l'Elysée.** This "palace," where the head of state works and receives official visitors, was originally constructed as a private mansion in 1718. It has known presidential occupants only since 1873; before then, Madame de Pompadour (Louis XV's influential mistress), Napoléon, Josephine, and Queen Victoria all stayed here. Today the French government, the Conseil des Ministres, meets here each Wednesday. *Not open to the public.*

Turn right on Faubourg St-Honoré and continue down to rue Royale. Lined with jewelry stores, rue Royale links place de la Concorde to the **Eglise de la Madeleine.** With its rows of uncompromising columns, the Madeleine's sturdy neoclassical edifice looks more like a Greek temple than a Christian church. The only natural indoor light comes from three shallow domes. The inside walls are richly and harmoniously decorated, and gold glints through the murk. The church was designed in 1814 but not consecrated until 1842. The portico's majestic Corinthian colonnade—cleaned and renovated in 1991–92—supports a gigantic pediment with a sculptured frieze of *The Last Judgment.* From the top of the steps, stop to admire the view down rue Royale across the Seine.

Alongside the Madeleine, a **ticket kiosk** sells tickets for same-day theater performances at greatly reduced prices. Open Tues.–Fri. 12:30–8; Sat. 12:30 for matinees and 2–8 for evening performances. Métro: Madeleine.

At the far end of the rue Royale, on the right (as you look from La Madeleine), is the legendary **Maxim's** restaurant. Unless you choose to eat here—an expensive and not always rewarding experience—you won't be able to see the interior decor, a riot of crimson velvet and Art Nouveau furniture.

There is a striking contrast between the gloomy, locked-in feel of the high-walled rue Royale and the broad, airy **place de la Concorde.** This huge square is best approached from the Champs-Elysées: The flower beds, chestnut trees, and sandy sidewalks of the avenue's lower section are reminders of its original leafy elegance. Place de la Concorde was built in the 1770s, but there was nothing in the way of peace or concord about its early years. From 1793 to 1795, it was the scene of more than 1,000 deaths by guillotine; victims included Louis XVI, Marie Antoinette, and Danton. The obelisk, a present from the viceroy of Egypt, was erected in 1833. The handsome, symmetrical, 18th-century buildings facing the square include the deluxe **Hôtel Crillon** (far left), though there's nothing so vulgar as a sign to identify it—just an inscribed marble plaque. Facing one side of place de la Concorde are the Tuileries Gardens; two smallish buildings stand here. The one nearer rue de Rivoli is the **Jeu de Paume,** fondly known to many as the former home of the Impressionists (now in the Musée d'Orsay). It underwent extensive renovation in 1990–91 before reopening as a gallery for temporary exhibitions of contemporary art. The building nearer the Seine, identical to the Jeu de Paume, is the recently restored **Orangerie,** containing some early 20th-century paintings by Monet *(Waterlilies)* and Renoir, among others. *Pl. de la Concorde. Admission to Orangerie: 27 frs adults, 18 frs students, senior citizens, and on Sun. Open Wed.–Mon. 9:45–5:45. Admission to Jeu de Paume: 35 frs adults, 25 frs children and on Sun. Open Wed.–Fri. noon–7, Tues. noon–9:30, weekends 10–7. Métro: Concorde.*

㉞ As gardens go, the formal and wonderfully patterned **Jardin des Tuileries** is typically French, a charming place to stroll and survey the surrounding cityscape. Leave the Tuileries by the rue de Rivoli gateway across from rue de Castiglione and the hefty bronze column of place Vendôme.

★ **㉟** The opulent **place Vendôme,** a perfectly proportioned example of 17th-century urban architecture (by Mansart), now holds numerous upscale jewelers and the **Ritz.** Napoléon had the square's central column made from the melted bronze of 1,200 cannons captured at the battle of Austerlitz in 1805. That's him standing at the top.

Cross the square and continue down rue de la Paix to place de
㊱ l'Opéra. The **Opéra,** begun at the behest of Napoléon III and completed in 1875 by Charles Garnier, typifies the pompous Second Empire style of architecture. The monumental foyer and staircase are a stage in their own right, where, on first nights, celebrities perform for their public. If the lavishly upholstered auditorium (ceiling painted by Marc Chagall in 1964) seems small, it is only because the stage is the largest in the world—more than 11,000 square yards. The **Opéra museum,** containing a few paintings and theatrical mementos, is unremarkable. *Tel. 47–42–57–50. Admission: 30 frs adults, 18 frs students and senior citizens. Open daily 10–4:30; closed occasionally. Métro: Opéra.*

Tour 4: From Orsay to Trocadéro

The Left Bank has two faces: the cozy, ramshackle Latin Quarter (*see* Tour 5, *below*) and the spacious, stately 7e, covered in this tour. The latest addition to this area is already the most popular: the
★ **㊲** **Musée d'Orsay,** a stylishly converted train station on the Seine across from the Tuileries. It shows the Impressionist paintings formerly housed in the Jeu de Paume as well as important examples of other 19th- and 20th-century schools. The chief artistic attraction here is the collection of Impressionist works on the top floor, including Whistler's portrait of his mother, *Arrangement in Gray and Black*, and Renoir's *Le Moulin de la Galette*. The Post-Impressionists—Paul Cézanne, Vincent van Gogh, Paul Gauguin, and Henri de Toulouse-Lautrec—are all also represented on this floor.

On the first floor, you'll find the work of Edouard Manet and Edgar Degas. Pride of place, at least in art-history terms, goes to Manet's *Déjeuner sur l'Herbe*, the painting that scandalized Paris in 1863. If you prefer modern developments, head for the exhibit of paintings by the early 20th-century group known as the *Fauves* (fauvists, meaning wild beasts, as they were dubbed by an outraged critic in 1905)—particularly Henri Matisse, André Derain, and Maurice de Vlaminck. Sculpture at the Orsay means, first and foremost, Auguste Rodin. Two further highlights are the faithfully restored Belle Epoque restaurant and the model of the entire Opéra quarter, displayed beneath a glass floor. Prepare for huge crowds: The best times for relatively painless viewing are at lunchtime or on Thursday evening. *1 rue de Bellechasse, tel. 40–49–48–14. Admission: 35 frs adults, 24 frs students, senior citizens, and on Sun. Open Tues.– Wed. and Fri.–Sat. 10–5:45, Thurs. 10–9:30, Sun. 9–5:45. Métro: Solférino.*

㊳ Continue west along the Seine to the 18th-century **Palais Bourbon** (directly across from place de la Concorde), home of the Assemblée Nationale (French Parliament). The colonnaded facade was commissioned by Napoléon. Though it's not open to the public, there is a fine view from the steps across to place de la Concorde and the church of the Madeleine.

Head south on rue de Bougogne to rue de Varenne and turn right to
★ **㊴** the Hôtel Biron, better known as the **Musée Rodin.** The splendid

house, with its spacious vestibule and light, airy rooms, retains much of its 18th-century atmosphere and makes a handsome setting for the sculpture of Rodin (1840–1917), including the famous *Thinker (Le Penseur)* and *Kiss (Le Baiser)*. Don't leave without visiting the garden: It is exceptional, both for its rosebushes (more than 2,000) and its sculptures. *77 rue de Varenne, tel. 47–05–01–34. Admission: 27 frs, 18 frs Sun. Open Tues.–Sun. 10–6, 10–5 in winter. Métro: Varenne.*

40 From the Rodin Museum, you can see the **Hôtel des Invalides** along rue de Varenne, founded by Louis XIV in 1674 to house wounded (or "invalid") veterans. Only a handful of old soldiers lives there today, but the building houses one of the world's foremost military museums, **Musée de l'Armée,** with a vast collection of arms, armor, uniforms, banners, and military pictures. The **Musée des Plans-Reliefs,** housed on the fifth floor of the right-hand wing, contains a fascinating collection of scale models of French towns made to illustrate the fortifications planned by the 17th-century military engineer Sébastien de Vauban. The largest and most impressive is Strasbourg, which takes up an entire room.

The museums are not the only reason for visiting the Invalides, however. The building itself is an outstanding monumental ensemble in late-17th-century Baroque, designed by Libéral Bruant (1635–97) and Jules Hardouin-Mansart (1646–1708). The main, cobbled courtyard is a fitting scene for the parades and ceremonies still occasionally held here. The most impressive dome in Paris towers over the **Eglise du Dôme** (Church of the Dome). The Dôme church was designed by Mansart and built between 1677 and 1735. Napoléon is buried here, in a series of six coffins, one inside the next, within a bombastic tomb of red porphyry. Among others commemorated in the church are French World War I hero Marshal Foch and fortification builder Vauban, whose heart was brought to the Invalides at Napoléon's behest. *Hôtel des Invalides. Admission: 34 frs adults, 24 frs children. Open daily 10–6, 10–4:45 winter. Métro: St-François Xavier.*

★ **41** Turn right out of the Dôme church and follow avenue de Tourville to the Champ de Mars. At the far end looms Paris's best-known landmark, the **Eiffel Tower.** Built by Gustave Eiffel for the World Exhibition of 1889, the centennial of the French Revolution, it was still in good shape to celebrate its own 100th birthday. Such was Eiffel's engineering wizardry that even in the strongest winds, his tower never sways more than a few inches. As you stand beneath its huge legs, you may have trouble believing that it nearly became 7,000 tons of scrap iron when its concession expired in 1909. Only its potential use as a radio antenna saved the day; it now bristles with a forest of radio and television transmitters. You can walk up the stairs as far as the third deck, but if you want to go to the top, 1,000 feet up, you'll have to take the elevator. It's expensive, but on a clear day, the view is definitely worth it. *Pont d'Iéna. Cost by elevator: 2nd floor, 20 frs; 3rd floor, 36 frs; 4th floor, 53 frs. Cost by foot: 12 frs (2nd and 3rd floors only). Open daily 9 AM–11 PM (until midnight July–Aug.). Métro: Bir-Hakeim.*

42 Just across the Pont d'Iéna from the Eiffel Tower, on the heights of Trocadéro, is the massive, sandy-colored **Palais de Chaillot,** a cultural center built in the 1930s. The gardens between the Palais de Chaillot and the Seine contain an aquarium and some dramatic fountains, and the terrace between the two wings of the palace affords a wonderful view of the Eiffel Tower.

The Palais de Chaillot contains four large museums, two in each wing. In the left wing (as you approach from the Seine) are the **Musée de l'Homme,** an anthropological museum, with primitive and prehistoric artifacts from throughout the world (admission: 25 frs adults, 15 frs children; open Wed.–Mon 10–5), and the **Musée de la Marine,** a maritime museum with exhibits on French naval history right up to the age of the nuclear submarine (admission: 31 frs adults, 16 frs senior citizens and children; open Wed.–Mon. 10–6).

The other wing is dominated by the **Musée des Monuments Français,** without question the best introduction to French medieval architecture. Its long, first-floor gallery pays tribute to French buildings, mainly of the Romanesque and Gothic periods (roughly AD 1000–1500), in the form of painstaking copies of statues, columns, archways, and frescoes. Substantial sections of a number of French churches and cathedrals are represented here, notably Chartres and Vézelay. Murals and ceiling paintings—copies of works in churches around the country—dominate the other three floors. *Admission: 21 frs, 14 frs on Sun. Open Wed.–Mon. 9:45–5:15. Métro: Trocadéro.*

The **Musée du Cinéma Henri Langlois,** tracing the history of motion pictures from the 1880s, is located in the basement. *Admission: 25 frs adults, 15 frs senior citizens and children. Open Wed.–Mon., guided tours only, on the hour at 10, 11, 2, 3, 4, and 5. Métro: Trocadéro.*

㊸ The area around the Palais de Chaillot offers a feast for museum lovers. The **Musée Guimet** has three floors of Indo-Chinese and Far Eastern art, including stone Buddhas, Chinese bronzes, ceramics, and painted screens. *6 pl. d'Iéna. Admission: 26 frs, 17 frs students, senior citizens, and on Sun. Open Wed.–Mon. 9:45–5:10. Métro: Iéna.*

㊹ Just across the *place* and up avenue Pierre-Ier-de-Serbie is the **Palais Galliera,** home of the **Musée de la Mode et du Costume** (Museum of Fashion and Costume), a late-19th-century town house that hosts revolving exhibits. *10 av. Pierre-Ier-de-Serbie. Admission: 26 frs. Open Tues.–Sun. 10–5:40. Métro: Iéna.*

㊺ The **Musée de l'Art Moderne de la Ville de Paris** has both temporary exhibits and a permanent collection of modern art. Among the earliest works in the vast galleries are Fauvist paintings by Vlaminck and Derain, followed by Picasso's early experiments in Cubism. Other highlights include works by Robert Delaunay, Georges Braque, and Amedeo Modigliani. There is also a large room devoted to Art Deco furniture and screens; a pleasant, if expensive, museum café; and an excellent bookshop with many books in English. *11 av. du Président-Wilson. Admission: 15 frs, free Sun. for permanent exhibitions only. Open Tues.–Sun. 10–5:40, Wed. 10–8:30. Métro: Iéna.*

Tour 5: The Left Bank

References to the Left Bank have never lost their power to evoke the most piquant images of Paris. Although the bohemian strain the area once nurtured has lost much of its vigor, people who choose to live and work here today are, in effect, turning their backs on the formality and staidness of the Right Bank.

The Left Bank's geographic and cerebral hub is the Latin Quarter, which takes its name from the university tradition of studying and speaking in Latin, a practice that disappeared at the time of the French Revolution. The area is populated mainly by students and academics from the Sorbonne, the headquarters of the University of Paris.

㊻ **Place St-Michel** is a good starting point for exploring the Left Bank. Leave your itineraries at home and wander along the neighboring streets lined with restaurants, cafés, galleries, old bookshops, and all sorts of clothing stores, from tiny boutiques to haute-couture showrooms.

Pick up the pedestrian rue St-André des Arts at the southwest corner of place St-Michel. Just before you reach the carrefour de Buci crossroads at the end of the street, turn onto the cour du Commerce St-André. Jean-Paul Marat printed his revolutionary newspaper, *L'Ami du Peuple*, at No. 8, and it was here that Dr. Guillotin conceived the idea for a new "humane" method of execution that, apparently to his horror, was used during the French Revolution.

47 Continue to the **carrefour de Buci,** once a notorious Left Bank landmark. By the 18th century, it contained a gallows, an execution stake, and an iron collar for punishing troublemakers. Many Royalists and priests lost their heads here during the bloody course of the French Revolution. Nearby rue de Buci has one of the best markets in Paris. The stands close by 1 PM and do not open at all on Monday.

Several interesting, smaller streets of some historical significance radiate from the carrefour de Buci. Rue de l'Ancienne-Comédie is so named because No. 14 was the first home of the now legendary French theater company, the Comédie-Française. Across the street sits the **48** oldest café in Paris, the **Procope** (now a fancy restaurant). Opened in 1686, it has been a watering hole for many of Paris's literati, including Voltaire, Victor Hugo, and Oscar Wilde. Ben Franklin was a patron, as were the fomenters of the French Revolution—Marat, Danton, Desmoulins, and Robespierre. Napoléon's hat, which he forgot here, was encased in a glass dome.

Stretching north from the carrefour de Buci toward the Seine is the rue Dauphine, the street that singer Juliet Greco put on the map when she opened the **Tabou jazz club** here in the '50s. The club attracted a group of young intellectuals who were to become known as the Zazous, a St-Germain movement prompting the jazz culture, complete with all-night parties and "free love."

The next street that shoots out of the carrefour (moving counter-
49 clockwise) is rue Mazarine, housing the **Hôtel des Monnaies,** the national mint. Louis XVI transferred the Royal Mint to this imposing mansion in the late 18th century. Although the mint was moved in 1973, weights and measures, and limited-edition coins are still made here. You can see the vast collection of coins, documents, engravings, and paintings at the **Musée de la Monnaie.** *11 quai Conti. Admission: 20 frs adults, 15 frs students, senior citizens, children, and for all on Sun. Open Tues., Thurs.–Sun. 1–6, Wed. 1–9. Métro: Pont Neuf.*

Next door is the **Institut de France,** a revered cultural institution and one of the Left Bank's most impressive waterside sights, with its distinctive dome and commanding position overlooking the quay. It was built as a college in 1661; in the early 19th century, Napoléon stipulated that the Institut de France be transferred here from the Louvre. The **Académie Française,** the oldest of the five academies that compose the Institut de France, was created by Cardinal Richelieu in 1635. Its first major task was to edit the French dictionary; today, among other functions, it is still charged with safeguarding the purity of the French language. Membership is the highest literary honor in France. Not until 1986 was a woman, author Marguerite Yourcenar, elected to its ranks. *Guided visits are reserved for cultural associations only.*

50 Just west along the waterfront, on quai Malaquais, stands the **Ecole Nationale des Beaux-Arts,** whose students can usually be seen painting and sketching on the nearby quays and bridges. The school, once the site of a convent, was established in 1816 and is still the breeding ground for many of France's foremost painters, sculptors, and architects. Allow yourself time to wander into its courtyard and galleries to see the casts and copies of the statues that were once stored here, or stop in at one of the temporary exhibitions of professors' and students' works. *14 rue Bonaparte. Open daily 1–7. Métro: St-Germain des Prés.*

Tiny **rue Visconti,** running east–west off rue Bonaparte (across from the entrance to the Beaux-Arts), has a lot of history packed into its short length. In the 16th century, it was known as Paris's "Little Geneva"—named after Europe's foremost Protestant city—because of the Protestant ghetto that formed here. Jean Racine, one of France's greatest playwrights and tragic poets, lived at No. 24 until his death in 1699. Honoré Balzac set up a printing shop at No. 17 in 1826, and the fiery Romantic artist Eugène Delacroix (1798–1863) worked here from 1836 to 1844.

Turn right on the gallery-lined rue de Seine, then right again onto the pretty rue Jacob, where both Wagner and Stendhal once lived. Then turn left onto rue de Fürstemberg, which broadens out into one of Paris's most delightful and secluded little squares. Delacroix's studio here has been turned into the charmingly tiny **Musée Eugène Delacroix,** which contains a small collection of sketches and drawings; the garden at the rear is cozy and intimate, like the neighboring square. *6 rue Fürstemberg. Admission: 12 frs adults, 7 frs senior citizens over 60 and youths 18–25. Open Wed.–Mon. 9:15–5:15. Métro: St-Germain des Prés.*

Continue south along rue de Fürstemberg and turn right onto rue de l'Abbaye, which takes you to **St-Germain-des-Prés,** Paris's oldest church. It was built to shelter a relic of the True Cross brought back from Spain in AD 542. Only the church and the adjoining building, the former **Abbey Palace,** remain from the powerful Benedictine monastery that stood here for centuries. Parts of the church date from 990. Interesting interior details include the colorful 19th-century frescoes in the nave by Hippolyte Flandrin, a pupil of the classical painter Ingres. The church stages superb organ concerts and recitals; programs are displayed outside and in the weekly periodicals *Officiel des Spectacles* and *Pariscope.*

Across the cobbled place St-Germain-des-Prés stands the celebrated **Les Deux Magots** café, still thriving on its '50s reputation as one of the Left Bank's prime meeting places for the intelligentsia. These days, you're more likely to rub shoulders with tourists than with philosophers, but a sidewalk table still affords a perfect view of Left Bank life.

In the years after World War II, Jean-Paul Sartre and Simone de Beauvoir would meet "The Family"—their intellectual clique—two doors down at the **Café de Flore,** on the boulevard St-Germain. Today the Flore has become more of a gay hangout, but it is a scenic spot that never lacks for action, often in the form of the street entertainers performing in front of the church.

If you now pick up the long rue de Rennes and follow it south (or travel three stops on the métro to Montparnasse-Bienvenüe), you'll soon arrive in the heart of Montparnasse. The opening of the **Tour Maine-Montparnasse** in 1973 forever changed the face of this former painters' and poets' haunt. The tower, containing offices and a branch of the Galeries Lafayette department store, was part of a vast redevelopment plan that aimed to make the area one of Paris's premier business and shopping districts. As Europe's tallest high rise, it claims to have the fastest elevator in Europe and affords stupendous views of Paris—and you pay dearly to enjoy them. *Admission: 40 frs adults, 30 frs students and senior citizens, 22 frs children 5–14. Open daily 9:30 AM–10:30 PM, weekdays 10–9:30 in winter. Métro: Montparnasse-Bienvenüe.*

Southeast on boulevard du Montparnasse and across from the Vavin métro station are two of the better-known gathering places of Montparnasse's bohemian heyday, the **Dôme** and **La Coupole** brasseries. La Coupole opened in 1927 and soon became a home away from home for some of the area's most famous residents, such as Guillaume Apollinaire, Max Jacob, Jean Cocteau, Erik Satie, Igor Stravinsky, and Ernest Hemingway.

Continue along boulevard du Montparnasse to the intersection with boulevard St-Michel, where the verdant avenue de l'Observatoire sweeps down to the Luxembourg Gardens. Here you'll find perhaps the most famous bastion of the Left Bank café culture, the **Closerie des Lilas.** Now a pricey but pretty bar-restaurant, the Closerie remains a staple on all literary tours of Paris, not least because of the commemorative plaques fastened onto the bar, marking the places where renowned writers used to sit. Charles Baudelaire, Paul Verlaine, Ernest Hemingway, and Guillaume Apollinaire are just a few of the names.

★ Head north on avenue de l'Observatoire (toward the gardens) and then take the first right onto rue du **Val-de-Grâce** to the mighty, domed, Baroque church of the same name, extensively restored in the early 1990s and famous for its cupola frescoes and rhythmic, two-story facade. Retrace your steps to avenue de l'Observatoire and turn right to the **Jardin du Luxembourg,** one of the city's few large parks. Its fountains, ponds, trim hedges, precisely planted rows of trees, and gravel walks are typical of the French fondness for formal gardens. At the far end is the **Palais du Luxembourg,** gray and formal, built, like the park, for Marie de Médicis, widow of Henri IV, at the beginning of the 17th century. The palace remained royal property until the French Revolution, when the state took it over and used it as a prison. Danton, the painter Jacques-Louis David, and American political philosopher and author Tom Paine (1737–1809) were all detained here. Today it is the site of the French Senate and is not open to the public.

If you follow rue Vaugirard two blocks east to boulevard St-Michel, you will come to the place de la Sorbonne, nerve center of the Left Bank's student population. The square is dominated by the **Eglise de la Sorbonne,** whose outstanding exterior features are its 10 Corinthian columns and cupola. Inside is the white marble tomb of Cardinal Richelieu. (The church is open to the public only during exhibitions and cultural events.) The university buildings of La Sorbonne spread out around the church from rue Cujas down to the visitor's entrance on rue des Ecoles.

The **Sorbonne** is the oldest university in France—indeed, one of the oldest in Europe—and has for centuries been one of France's principal institutions of higher learning. It is named after Robert de Sorbon, a medieval canon who founded a theological college here in 1253 for 16 students. By the 17th century, the church and university buildings were becoming dilapidated, so Cardinal Richelieu undertook to have them restored; the present-day Sorbonne campus is largely a result of that restoration. For a glimpse of a more recent relic of Sorbonne history, look for Puvis de Chavannes's painting of the *Sacred Wood* in the main lecture hall, a major meeting point during the tumultuous student upheavals of 1968.

Behind the Sorbonne, bordering its eastern reach, is the rue St-Jacques. The street climbs toward the rue Soufflot, named in honor of the man who built the vast, domed **Panthéon,** set atop place du Panthéon. One of Paris's most physically overwhelming sites—it was commissioned by Louis XV as a mark of gratitude for his recovery from a grave illness in 1744—the Panthéon is now a seldom-used church with monumental frescoes by Puvis de Chavannes and a crypt that holds the remains of such national heroes as Voltaire,

Emile Zola, and Jean-Jacques Rousseau. *Entrance on rue
Clothilde. Admission: 26 frs adults, 19 frs youths 18–24, 6 frs ages
17 and under. Open daily 10–5:30. Métro: Cardinal Lemoine.*

East of the Panthéon is **St-Etienne-du-Mont,** a church with two
claims to fame: its ornate facade and its curly Renaissance rood
screen (1521–35) separating nave and chancel—the only one of its
kind in Paris. Take time to look at the fine 17th-century glass in the
cloister at the back of the church.

★ ⑤⑧ Walk north on rue St-Jacques and turn left on the rue des Ecoles to
reach the square Paul-Painlevé and the distinguished **Musée National du Moyen-Age** (formerly the Musée de Cluny). Built on the site of
the city's enormous Roman baths, the museum is housed in a 15th-
century mansion that originally belonged to the monks of Cluny Abbey in Burgundy. But the real reason anyone comes to the Cluny is
to see its superb tapestry collection. The most famous series is the
graceful *Dame à la Licorne* (*Lady and the Unicorn*), woven in the
15th or 16th century, probably in the southern Netherlands. There
is also an exhibition of decorative arts from the Middle Ages; a
vaulted chapel; and a deep, cloistered courtyard with mullioned
windows, set off by the *Boatmen's Pillar,* Paris's oldest sculpture,
at its center. *Admission: 27 frs adults, 18 frs students, senior citizens, and for all on Sun. Open Wed.–Mon. 9:45–5:15. Métro: Cluny–La Sorbonne.*

⑤⑨ Across boulevard St-Germain, rue St-Jacques reaches toward the
Seine, bringing you past the elegantly proportioned church of
St-Séverin, the parish church of the entire Left Bank during the 11th
century. Rebuilt in the 16th century and noted for its width and its
Flamboyant Gothic architecture, the church dominates a close-knit
neighborhood filled with quiet squares and pedestrian streets. Note
the splendidly deviant spiraling column in the forest of pillars behind the altar. *Open weekdays 11–5:30, Sat. 11–10, Sun. 9–8.
Métro: St-Michel.*

Running riot around the relative quiet of St-Séverin are streets
filled with restaurants of every description and serving everything
from take-out souvlaki to five-course haute cuisine. Rue de la
Huchette is the most heavily trafficked of these and is especially
good for its selection of cheaper Greek food houses and Tunisian pâtisseries.

Cross to the other side of rue St-Jacques. In square René-Viviani,
which surrounds the 12th-century church of **St-Julien-le-Pauvre,**
stands one of two acacias thought to be the oldest tree in Paris (its
rival to this claim is in the Jardin des Plantes). This tree-filled
square also gives you one of the more spectacular views of Notre-
Dame.

Behind the church, to the east, are the tiny, elegant streets of the
recently renovated Maubert district, bordered by quai de Montebello and boulevard St-Germain. Walk south on rue Lagrange to place
Maubert, where public meetings and demonstrations have been
held ever since the Middle Ages. Nowadays, most gatherings are
⑥⓪ held inside or in front of the **Palais de la Mutualité** on the corner of
the square, also a venue for jazz, pop, and rock concerts. On Tuesday, Thursday, and Saturday, it is transformed into a colorful outdoor food market.

Continue east (toward the river) on boulevard St-Germain to the
⑥① **Institut du Monde Arabe,** an Arabic-French cultural center designed
by Jean Nouvel and opened in 1988. The gleaming glass walls combine Muslim decorative motifs with Nouvel's typically sharp, hi-tech
outlines (note the 240 shutterlike apertures on the facade that open
and close to regulate light exposure). Exhibitions with a North African theme are often held here; you may also visit the sound and

image center with its wall of televisions with Arab programming, a museum of Arab-Islamic art, a library, and a documentation center. Glass elevators whisk you to the ninth floor, where you can sip tea on the roof and enjoy a memorable view over the Seine and Notre-Dame. *1 rue des Fossés–St-Bernard, tel. 40–51–38–38. Open Tues.–Sun. 10–6. Métro: Jussieu.*

⑥ Turn left from the institute into rue des Fossés–St-Bernard, then left again along rue Jussieu to the **Jardin des Plantes,** an enormous swath of greenery containing spacious botanical gardens and a number of natural-history museums. It is stocked with plants dating back to the first collections of the 17th century and has since been enhanced by subsequent generations of devoted French botanists. The garden shelters one of at least two brown acacias thought to be Paris's oldest tree, this one planted in 1636. It also contains a small, old-fashioned zoo, an alpine garden, an aquarium, a maze, and a number of hothouses. *Admission to zoo: 25 frs. Open daily 9–5 (until 6 in summer). Métro: Monge.*

The **Grande Galérie de l'Evolution,** at the back of the Jardin des Plantes, reopened to popular acclaim in 1994. This vast, handsome glass-and-iron structure, built, as was the Eiffel Tower, in 1889 but abandoned in the 1960s, contains one of the world's finest collections of stuffed animals, including a section devoted to extinct and endangered species. There are a reconstituted dodo—only a foot actually remains of this heavy, flightless bird from the Indian Ocean island of Mauritius—and a quagga, an extinct relative of the zebra from southern Africa. Stunning lighting effects include push-button spotlighting and a roof that changes color to suggest storms, twilight, or hot savanna sun. *Admission: 40 frs (30 frs before 2 PM). Open Wed. and Fri.–Mon. 10–6, Thurs. 10–10. Métro: Monge.*

Across rue Geoffroy from the Grande Galerie, in place du Puits-de-l'Ermite, you can drink a restorative cup of sweet mint tea in **La Mosquée,** a beautifully kept white mosque, complete with minaret. The sunken garden and tiled patios are open to the public—the prayer rooms are not—as are the restaurant, which serves copious portions of couscous, and the luxurious *hammams,* or Turkish baths (open Fri. and Sun. 11–8 men only; Mon., Wed., Thurs., and Sat. 11–8 women only, 65 frs for baths). *Admission to mosque: 15 frs adults, 10 frs students and senior citizens. Open Sat.–Thurs., guided tours 10–noon and 2–6:30 (5:30 in winter). Métro: Monge.*

Tour 6: Montmartre

Numbers in the margin correspond to points of interest on the Montmartre map.

On a dramatic rise above the city is **Montmartre,** site of the basilica of Sacré-Coeur—Paris's best-known landmark after the Eiffel Tower—and home to a once-thriving artistic community, now reduced to gangs of third-rate painters clustered in the area's most famous square, the place du Tertre. Despite their presence, and the fact that the fabled nightlife of old Montmartre has fizzled down to some glitzy nightclubs and porn shows, the area still exudes a sense of history.

⑥ Begin your tour at **place Blanche** (White Square), which takes its name from the clouds of chalky dust churned up by the windmills that once dotted Montmartre. The windmills were set up here not just because the hill was a good place to catch the wind—at over 300 feet, it's the highest point in the city—but because Montmartre was covered with cornfields and quarries right up to the end of the 19th century. Today only two of the original 20 windmills are intact. The most famous, immortalized on canvas by Toulouse-Lautrec, is the **Moulin Rouge,** or Red Windmill, built in 1885 and turned into a

Montmartre

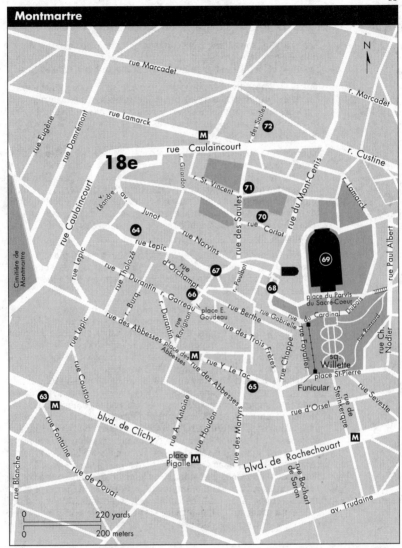

Basilique du Sacré-Coeur, **69**

Bateau-Lavoir, **66**

Chapelle du Martyre, **65**

Lapin Agile, **71**

Moulin de la Galette, **64**

Musée d'Art Juif, **72**

Musée du Vieux Montmartre, **70**

Place Blanche, **63**

Place du Tertre, **68**

Place Jean-Baptiste Clément, **67**

dance hall in 1900; the place is still trading shamelessly on the notion of Paris as a city of sin (*see* Arts and Nightlife, *below*).

For a taste of something more authentically French than the Moulin Rouge's computerized light shows, walk up rue Lepic, site of one of the most colorful and tempting **food markets** in Paris (closed Mon.).

Turn left onto rue Joseph-de-Maistre and walk along to the small **Cimetière de Montmartre.** Among the graves of many prominent French men and women are those of Edgar Degas and Adolphe Sax, inventor of the saxophone. The Russian ballet dancer Vaslav Nijinsky is buried here as well.

64 Retrace your steps and turn left onto rue Tholozé, which leads to the **Moulin de la Galette,** one of the two remaining windmills in Montmartre, now unromantically rebuilt. To reach it you pass **Studio 28:** This seems no more than a generic little movie theater, but when it opened in 1928, it was the first *art et essai*, or experimental theater, in the world, and has shown the works of such directors as Jean Cocteau, François Truffaut, and Orson Welles before their films' official premieres.

Return to rue des Abbesses, turn left, and walk to **place des Abbesses.** Though commercial, the little square has the kind of picturesque and slightly countrified architecture that has made Montmartre famous.

There are two competing attractions just off the square. Theater buffs should head down the tiny rue André-Antoine. At No. 37, you'll see what was originally the **Théâtre Libre,** the Free Theater, which was influential in popularizing the groundbreaking works of naturalist playwrights Henrik Ibsen and August Strindberg. The other attraction is **rue Yvonne Le Tac,** scene of a vital event in Montmartre's early history and linked to the disputed story of how this quarter got its name. Some say the name Montmartre comes from the Roman temple to Mercury that was once here, called the Mound of Mercury, or *Mons Mercurii*. Others contend that it was an adaptation of *Mons Martyrum*, a name inspired by the burial here of Paris's first bishop, St-Denis. (The popular version of his martyrdom is that he was beheaded by the Romans in AD 250 but arose to carry his severed head from rue Yvonne Le Tac to an area 4 miles north, now known as St-Denis.) St-Denis is commemorated by the **65** 19th-century **Chapelle du Martyre** at No. 9. It was in the crypt of the original chapel here that the Italian priest Francis Xavier founded the Jesuit order in 1534, a decisive step in the efforts of the Catholic Church to reassert its authority in the face of the Protestant Reformation.

From rue Yvonne Le Tac, retrace your steps through place des Abbesses. Take rue Ravignon on the right, climbing to the summit via place Emile-Goudeau, an enchanting little cobbled square. Your **66** goal is the **Bateau-Lavoir,** or Boat Wash House, at its northern edge. Montmartre poet Max Jacob coined the name for the old building on this site, which burned down in 1970: Not only did it look like a boat, he said, but the warren of artists' studios within were always paint-spattered and in need of a good hosing down. The drab, present-day concrete building also contains art studios, though none so illustrious as those of Cubist painters Picasso and Braque, which were housed here in years gone by.

67 Continue up the hill to **place Jean-Baptiste Clément.** The Italian painter and sculptor Franco Modigliani (1884–1920) had a studio here at No. 7. Modigliani is thought by some to have been the greatest Italian artist of the 20th century, the man who fused the genius of the Italian Renaissance with the modernity of Cézanne and Picasso. Modigliani claimed he would drink himself to death—he eventually did—and chose the wildest part of town in which to do it.

Rue Norvins runs behind and parallel to the north end of the square. Turn right, walk past the bars and tourist shops, and you'll reach **place du Tertre.** At most times of the year, you'll have to fight your way through the crowds to the southern end of the square and the breathtaking view over the city. The real drawback here, though, is the swarm of artists clamoring to dash off your portrait. Most are licensed, but there is a fair share of con men. If one produces a picture of you without having asked first, you're under no obligation to buy it!

La Mère Catherine, the restaurant at the north end of the square, was a favorite with the Russian cossacks who occupied Paris after Napoléon's 1814 exile to Elba. Little did the cossacks know that when they banged on the tables and shouted "bistro," the Russian word for "quick," they were coining a name for a new breed of French restaurant. Now fairly touristic, La Mère Catherine is surprisingly good, though prices are high.

It was in place du Tertre that one of the most violent episodes in French history began, one that colored French political life for generations. Despite popular images of late-19th-century France—and Paris especially—as a time of freedom and prosperity, the country was desperately divided into two camps for much of this period: a militant underclass, motivated by resentment of what they considered an elitist government, and a reactionary and fearful bourgeoisie and ruling class. In March 1871, the antimonarchist Communards clashed with soldiers of the French government leader, Adolphe Thiers. The Communards formed the Commune, which ruled Paris for three months. Then Thiers ordered his troops to take the city, and upwards of 10,000 Communards were executed after the Commune's collapse.

Looming behind the church of St-Pierre on the east side of the square, the **Basilique du Sacré-Coeur** was erected in 1873 (after Thiers's death) as a kind of guilt offering for the ruthless killing of the Communards. Even so, the building was to some extent a reflection of political divisions within the country, financed by French Catholics fearful of an anticlerical backlash and determined to make a grand statement on behalf of the Church. Stylistically, the Sacré-Coeur borrows elements from Romanesque and Byzantine models, fusing them under its distinctive Oriental dome. The gloomy, cavernous interior is worth visiting for its golden mosaics; climb to the top of the dome for the view over Paris.

More of Montmartre beckons north and west of the Sacré-Coeur. Take rue du Mont Cenis down to rue Cortot and the **Musée du Vieux Montmartre.** Like the Bateau-Lavoir, the building that is now the museum sheltered an illustrious group of painters, writers, and assorted cabaret artists in its heyday toward the end of the 19th century. Foremost among them were Pierre-Auguste Renoir and Maurice Utrillo, who was the Montmartre painter par excellence. Taking the gray, crumbling streets of Montmartre as his subject matter, Utrillo discovered that he worked much more effectively from cheap postcards than from the streets themselves. Look carefully at the pictures in the museum here and you will see the plaster and sand he mixed with his paints to help convey the decaying buildings of the area. The next best thing about the museum is the view over the tiny vineyard on neighboring rue des Saules. *12 rue Cortot. Admission: 25 frs adults, 20 frs senior citizens and children. Open Tues.–Sun. 11–6. Métro: Lamarck Caulaincourt.*

There's an equally famous Montmartre landmark on the corner of rue St-Vincent, just down the road: the **Lapin Agile,** or the Nimble Rabbit. It's a bar-cabaret, originally one of the raunchiest haunts in Montmartre. Today it manages against all odds to preserve at least something of its earlier flavor, unlike the Moulin Rouge.

Behind the Lapin Agile is the **Cimetière St-Vincent** (entrance off little rue Lucien Gaulard), a tiny graveyard sheltering the remains of Maurice Utrillo. Continue north on rue des Saules, across busy rue Caulaincourt, and you'll come to the **Musée d'Art Juif,** the Museum of Jewish Art, containing devotional items, models of synagogues, and works by Camille Pissarro and Marc Chagall. *42 rue des Saules. Admission: 30 frs adults, 20 frs students and children, 15 frs children under 12. Open Sun.–Thurs. 3–6; closed Aug. Métro: Lamarck Caulaincourt.*

Guided Tours

A bus tour of Paris makes a fine introduction to the city but is expensive; we suggest you explore Paris on foot or by the green RATP buses used for public transportation (bus 69 passes a number of major sites on its way from Champ-de-Mars to Père Lachaise, via Invalides, the Louvre, and Bastille). Bateaux-Mouches boat tours provide a pleasant, reasonably priced overview of Paris.

Orientation The two largest bus-tour operators are **Cityrama** (4 pl. des Pyramides, 1er, tel. 44–55–61–00) and **Paris Vision** (214 rue de Rivoli, 1er, tel. 42–60–31–25). Tours are generally in double-decker buses with either a live or a tape-recorded commentary (English is available) and last two hours. Expect to pay about 150 francs.

The **RATP** (Paris Transport Authority) has many guide-accompanied excursions in and around Paris. Inquire at its Tourist Service Board (pl. de la Madeleine, 8e, tel. 40–06–71–45) or at its office (53 quai des Grands-Augustins, 6e, tel. 40–46–44–50).

Special-Interest **Cityrama** and **Paris Vision** offer a variety of theme tours ("Historic Paris," "Modern Paris," "Paris-by-Night") lasting from 2½ hours to all day and costing 150 to 450 francs (more if admission to a cabaret show is included).

Hour-long **boat trips** along the Seine are a must for the first-time visitor. Some boats serve lunch and dinner; make reservations in advance. The following services operate regularly throughout the day and in the evening: **Bateaux-Mouches** has departures from Pont de l'Alma (Right Bank, 8e, tel. 42–25–96–10); **Vedettes du Pont-Neuf** has departures from Square du Vert-Galant (Ile de la Cité, 1er, tel. 46–33–98–38); **Bateaux Parisiens–Tour Eiffel** has departures from Pont d'Iéna (Left Bank, 7e, tel. 47–05–50–00), and **Canauxrama** (tel. 42–39–15–00) organizes half- and full-day barge tours along picturesque canals in eastern Paris (departures from 5 bis quai de la Loire, 19e, or from Bassin de l'Arsenal, 12e, opposite 50 blvd. de la Bastille).

Walking There are plenty of guided tours of specific areas of Paris, often concentrating on a historical or architectural topic—"Restored Mansions of the Marais," for instance, or "Private Walled Gardens in St-Germain." The guides are enthusiastic and dedicated, though not always English-speaking. Charges range from 40 francs to 60 francs, and tours last about two hours. Details are published in the weekly magazines *Pariscope* and *L'Officiel des Spectacles* under the heading "Conférences." You can sometimes make advance reservations for walking tours organized by the **Caisse Nationale des Monuments Historiques,** Bureau des Visites/Conférences (Hôtel de Sully, 62 rue St-Antoine, 4e, tel. 44–61–20–00).

Bicycling **Paris by Cycle** (78 rue de l'Ouest, 14e, tel. 40–47–08–04) organizes daily bike tours around the city and its environs (Versailles, Chantilly, and Fontainebleau) for about 220 francs, 120 francs for bike rental. Bike equipment is also available.

Shopping for Bargains

Paris's reputation as an international capital of such luxury industries as fashion and perfume makes it a great place for window shopping but offers little comfort to the budget traveler; Chanel and Yves Saint-Laurent come no cheaper in Paris than elsewhere. If you are prepared to stray off the tourist path to somewhat uninviting localities such as the Sentier district on the northern edge of the Marais, or the grid of grimy streets at the foot of Montmartre, you can find cheap—and sometimes stylish—clothes without much difficulty. There is a wide choice of affordable souvenirs along the rue de Rivoli, ranging from porcelain boxes, imitation Sèvres china, and miniature Eiffel Towers to printed scarves, tea towels, and busts of Napoléon. Any number of stalls in the métro sell zany jewelry and wool scarves at low prices, while the *bouquinistes* (second-hand bookstores) along the Seine offer browsing and bargaining if you're after old books, posters, photos, or maps.

Shopping Districts   A general rule of thumb is that the Left Bank is geared more to small specialty shops and boutiques, while the Right Bank is home to the high-fashion houses, the most ostentatious shops, and the large department stores.

On the Left Bank, **St-Germain-des-Prés** has long been a center for bookshops, ready-to-wear fashion stores, and specialty shops. Shoe and fabric shops crowd the **rue des Saints-Pères,** while the **rue de Rennes,** running from St-Germain to Montparnasse, is packed with a variety of clothing stores, many quite inexpensive.

On the Right Bank, classic ready-to-wear shops (Chanel, Nina Ricci, Ungaro, Karl Lagerfeld) are found on **avenue Montaigne** and **rue du Faubourg-St-Honoré,** while high-end jewelers are clustered around the **place Vendôme.** The modern, three-tiered **Forum des Halles** is popular with teenage shoppers, as is the **Bastille** area. The **Marais** and the neighborhood around the **place des Victoires** are good sources of avant-garde dress shops; the streets to the north of the Marais, close to the Arts et Métiers métro, are historically linked to the cloth trade, and many shops here offer garments at wholesale prices.

Shopping Arcades   Paris's 19th-century commercial arcades, called *passages,* are the forerunners of the modern mall. Glass roofs, decorative pillars, and mosaic floors give the passages great charm. Shops range from the trendy (**Jean-Paul Gaultier** and **Yukii Tori** fashions in the freshly restored Galerie Vivienne) to the genteel (embroidery supplies and satin ribbons at **Au Bonheur des Dames** in the Passage Jouffroy).

The major arcades are on the Right Bank in central Paris and include **Galerie Vivienne** (4 rue des Petits-Champs, 2e), **Galerie Véro-Dodat** (19 rue J-J Rousseau, 1er) and **Passage des Pavillons** (6 rue de Beaujolais, 1er). Near the Montmartre métro station you'll find the very old (1800) **Passage des Panoramas** (11 blvd. Montmartre, 2e) and the **Jouffroy** (12 blvd. Montmartre, 2e).

Department Stores   Paris has a good selection of department stores, several of which are conveniently grouped on the Right Bank around the Opéra. Both Au Printemps and Galeries Lafayette have multilingual guides, international welcome desks, détaxe offices, and restaurants.

Au Printemps is a three-store complex that includes "La Maison" for housewares and furniture, "La Mode" for women's and children's clothing, and "Brummel" for menswear. Flo Prestige, the celebrated brasserie chain, caters the in-house restaurants. *64 blvd. Haussmann, 9e, tel. 42–82–50–00. Open Mon.–Sat. 9:30–7. Métro: Havre Caumartin, Opéra, Auber.*

Galeries Lafayettes offers stylish, private-label fashions at reasonable prices; the floor-wide gourmet shop includes several snack/wine bars. Be sure to look up while in the main store: The glorious Belle Epoque stained-glass dome is a Paris landmark. *40 blvd. Haussmann, 9e, tel. 42–82–34–56. Open Mon.–Sat. 9:30–6:45. Métro: Chaussée d'Antin, Opéra, Havre Caumartin.*

The budget **Monoprix** and **Prisunic** stores are cheap and cheerful. The largest Prisunic outlets are at 109 Champs-Elysées, on the corner of rue La Boétie, 8e; and 25 avenue des Ternes. Monoprix's handiest outlet for tourists is at 21 avenue de l'Opéra, 1er.

Markets Every *quartier* in Paris has an open-air food market, if only for a few days a week. Sunday morning, until 1 PM, is usually a good time to go; Monday is the most likely closing day. The local markets usually concentrate on food, but they always have a few brightly colored flower stalls. Some markets have stalls that sell antiques, clothing, household goods, and secondhand books. Their lively—sometimes chaotic—atmosphere makes them worth visiting even if you don't intend to buy anything.

Many of the better-known markets are located in areas you'd visit for sightseeing. Our favorites are on **rue de Buci**, 6e (open daily); **rue Mouffetard**, 5e; and **rue Lepic** in Montmartre (the latter two are best on weekends). The **Marché d'Aligre** (open Saturday, Sunday, and Monday mornings) is a bit farther out, beyond the Bastille on rue d'Aligre in the 12th arrondissement, but you won't see many tourists in this less affluent area of town, and Parisians from all over the city know and love it. The prices are slashed as the morning draws to a close.

Paris's main **flower market** is located right in the heart of the city on Ile de la Cité, between Notre-Dame and the Palais de Justice. It's open every day except Monday. On Sunday, it becomes a bird market.

The **Marché aux Puces** on Paris's northern boundary still attracts the crowds, but its once unbeatable prices are now a feature of the past. This century-old labyrinth of alleyways packed with antiques dealers' booths and junk stalls now spreads more than a square mile. Early birds pick up the most worthwhile loot; the pros get out to Clignancourt before breakfast. But be warned—if there's one place in Paris where you need to know how to bargain, this is it! For lunch, stop for mussels and fries in one of the rough-and-ready cafés. *Open Sat.–Mon. Métro: Porte de Clignancourt.*

There are other, less impressive flea markets on the southern and eastern slopes of the city—at **porte de Montreuil** and **porte de Vanves**—but they have a depressing amount of real junk and are best avoided, except by obsessive bargain hunters.

Specialty Those wishing to take home china and crockery should head for the
Stores **rue du Paradis**, 10e; it's lined with china shops selling goods at a wide
Gift Ideas range of prices.

Shoppers looking for bargain fabrics should try **Marché Saint Pierre** (2 rue Charles-Nodier, 18e).

For children, try **Le Monde en Marche** (34 rue Dauphine, 6e), which has a great selection of wooden toys, puppets, and miniatures.

Clothing Bargain hunters like to plan their visits for the January and July sales, although stock shops sell last season's designer clothes at considerable discounts year-round. The rue d'Alésia, on the southern edge of Montparnasse in the 14e, has many of these shops: **Cacharel** (No. 114), **Dorothé bis** (No. 74), and the Sonia Rykiel **SR** shop (No. 64). (There's another SR half-price outlet at 72 rue de Lévis, 17e.) In the Marais, last year's styles from **Azzedine Alaïa** (18 rue de la Verrerie, 4e) and **Lolita Lempicka** (2 rue des Rosiers, 4e) are also sold at half price. **Mendès,** the manufacturer of YSL Rive Gauche fashions, has a discount outlet at 65 rue Montmartre in the second arrondissement, while **Anna Lowe** (35 ave. Matignon) has excellent prices on women's designer fashions from Valentino, Lacroix, Montana, and others in the 8e. **Réciproque** (95, 101, and 123 rue de la Pompe) sells reasonably priced designer resale fashions for men and women in the chic 16e.

For ultra-cheap goods, don't ignore the pink-checked awnings of **Tati,** a downmarket chain of shops that acquired a certain reverse chic when Azzedine Alaïa used its shopping-bag print in one of his collections. Tati has outlets at 140 rue de Rennes, 6e; 4 boulevard Rochouart, 18e; and 13 place de la Republique, 3e.

Perfume Get bargain prices on perfumes at **Michel Swiss,** which has two locations near the Opéra (2e): 16 rue de la Paix and 24 avenue de l'Opéra.

Where to Eat on a Budget

Eating out is one of the perennial delights of this most civilized of cities. Some complain that the French capital is overrated gastronomically and that the Parisian restaurateur is resting complacently on his or her laurels. Of course, not every restaurant offers a gastronomic adventure, and bad meals at unconscionable prices are no more unknown in Paris than at home. The important point to remember is that the city's restaurants exist principally to cater to the demanding needs of the Parisians themselves, and any restaurant that fails to meet their high standards is unlikely to stay in business long.

Dining on a budget in Paris means, first and foremost, the bustling bistros and brasseries where white-aproned waiters scribble your order on paper tablecloths before returning almost immediately with *plats du jour* (plates of the day) and carafes of *vin du patron* (house wine). Steak and *andouillette* (chitterling sausage), served with french fries, are typical main courses. Fast-food chains (McDonald's, Burger King, Quick) are catching on—but more for their novelty impact than for quality or value. Grabbing quick things to eat in Paris on a regular basis is hard on the budget—a sandwich in a bar will set you back $3 and even a street-corner crêpe costs at least $1.50 (usually more)—while a simple, yet wonderfully gratifying, picnic of baguette, ham, and cheese split between a couple of people is a great deal. And if you find the right setting—say the Luxembourg Gardens or the Square Viviani on the Left Bank opposite Notre-Dame—it can be memorable.

Almost all restaurants offer two basic types of menu: à la carte and fixed-price (*prix fixe,* or *un menu*). The fixed-price menu will almost always offer the best value, though choices are limited.

Generally, Paris restaurants are open from noon to about 2, and from 7:30 or 8 to 10 or 10:30. Brasseries have longer hours and often serve all day and late into the evening; some are open 24 hours. The iconoclastic wine bars do as they want, frequently serving hot food only through lunch and cold assortments of charcuterie and cheese until a late afternoon or early evening close.

We have included days closed in all our listings, including yearly vacations when known. Assume a restaurant is open seven days a week, year-round, unless otherwise indicated. Surprisingly, many prestigous restaurants close on Saturday as well as on Sunday. July and August are the most common months for annual closings, but Paris in August is no longer the wasteland it used to be, and many restaurants now close for a few weeks in winter instead. The past couple of years have been hard for many Paris restaurants, and management may hesitate to announce vacation dates too far in advance or suddenly decide not to close after all. We suggest you call ahead.

Because most restaurants are open for only a few set hours for lunch and dinner, and because meals are much longer affairs here than they are in the United States, we strongly advise you to make reservations. Most wine bars do not take reservations; reservations are also unnecessary for brasserie and café meals at odd hours. In the reviews below, we have indicated where reservations are advised or required (and when booking weeks or months in advance is necessary), and where reservations are not accepted. If you want nonsmoking, make this clear when you reserve. Though the law requires all restaurants to provide a nonsmoking area, this is sometimes limited to a very few tables.

What to Wear Perhaps surprisingly, casual dress is acceptable at all but the fanciest restaurants. Use your judgment, of course, and remember that casual to the French does not mean without style. When in doubt, leave the blue jeans behind, and unless you want to be instantly identified as a tourist, pack some comfortable walking shoes instead of sneakers. Use your judgment—the most casual dress will normally be acceptable at less expensive cafés. In the reviews below, we have indicated where a jacket and/or tie are required.

Prices The restaurants reviewed below are grouped in three price ranges: 175 frs–300 frs ($$), 100 frs–175 frs ($), and under 100 frs (¢). Generally these prices are for a first, main, and cheese or dessert course. Sometimes, however, our selections are over budget if you order à la carte; in these cases you must order the fixed-price menu to stay within our price category. This is indicated when appropriate. A few of our selections are affordable only at lunch, and usually with a fixed-price menu only; this is also indicated in the review. All prices include tax and tip (*service compris* or *prix nets*). No additional tip is expected, though pocket change left on the table in simple places, or an additional 5% of the bill in better restaurants, is appreciated.

Highly recommended restaurants are indicated by a star ★.

1st Arrondissement

$$ ★ Pharamond. Pharamond has been a Les Halles landmark since its founding in 1870. No one would dare touch the polychrome tiles and mosaics, mirrors, and handsome woodwork, or the classic bistro menu, with such Norman specialties as scallops in cider, grilled meats, tripe à la mode de Caen (tripe cooked with carrots in a seasoned cider stock), and souffléed potatoes. *24 rue de la Grande-Truanderie, tel. 42–33–06–72. Reservations advised. AE, DC, MC, V. Closed Sun., Mon. lunch, and mid-July–mid-Aug. Métro: Les Halles.*

$ Le Petit Mâchon. This is an authentic version of the uniquely Lyonnais bistro, the *mâchon*. Bring a big appetite, for the long menu offers such robust choices as stuffed pig's foot, duck terrine, braised ham shank, and veal flank with shallots. Wines are overpriced, so stick to a *pichet* (pitcher) of the Coteaux-du-Lyonnais or Beaujolais. Arrive early or book well in advance: The Mâchon gets very busy after 9 PM. *158 rue St-Honoré, tel. 42–60–23–37. Reservations advised. AE, DC, MC, V. Closed Sun. Métro: Louvre.*

¢ A La Cloche des Halles. Get here by 12:30 PM if you want to lunch at this small and popular wine bar. Forgive the tacky decor and enjoy quiches, omelets, and the assortments of high-quality cheeses and charcuterie. Wines, served by the glass or bottle, include some good Beaujolais. The simple menu is served until closing at 10 PM. *28 rue Coquillière, tel. 42–36–93–89. No reservations. No credit cards. Closed Sun. Métro: Les Halles.*

¢ Lescure. Hidden away down short rue de Mondovi next to place de la Concorde, this very old restaurant with a largely foreign clientele offers good bistro cuisine: pâté *en croûte* (in puff pastry), poached haddock, *boeuf bourguignon* (a beef stew cooked in red wine, with onions, mushrooms, and bacon). The tiny, rustic dining room is cozy; a few tables are set on the sidewalk in nice weather. *7 rue de Mondovi, tel. 42-60-18-91. MC, V. Closed Sat. eve., Sun., and Aug. Métro: Concorde.*

¢ **Le Rubis.** One or two hearty *plats du jour,* such as *petit salé* (salted, slow-cooked pork ribs) with lentils and *boudin noir* (sausage made with pig's blood), plus omelets, cheeses, and charcuterie assortments make up the menu at this humble, neighborhood wine bar that enjoys tremendous popularity with everyone from executives to laborers. There's an eclectic selection of adequate wines by the glass or bottle. *10 rue du Marché-St-Honoré, tel. 42-61-03-34. No reservations. No credit cards. Closed Sat. eve., Sun., and mid-Aug. Métro: Tuileries.*

¢ **La Taverne Henri IV.** An excellent choice for a quick lunch or snack, this informal wine bar with rustic charm is near the Pont Neuf, at the tip of the Ile de la Cîté. No full meals are served, but a selection of open-face sandwiches on Poilâne bread (from the celebrated bakery), cheese and charcuterie plates, and varied wines by the glass or bottle make for a satisfying meal. *13 pl. du Pont-Neuf, tel. 43-54-27-90. No reservations. No credit cards. Closed weekends and August. Métro: Pont Neuf.*

2nd Arrondissement

$$ **Le Vaudeville.** Like the other six Parisian brasseries of Jean-Paul Bucher, the Vaudeville has a history and a good-looking clientele (many of them from the stock exchange across the street), and offers excellent value, thanks to its assortment of fixed-price menus. Go for the fixed-price lunch menu or the after-11 PM *Faim de Nuit,* cheaper still. Shellfish, house-smoked salmon, and desserts such as *profiteroles* (small cream puffs with a savory or sweet filling) are particularly fine. You can enjoy the handsome 1930s decor and joyful din until 2 AM daily. *29 rue Vivienne, tel. 40-20-04-62. Reservations advised. AE, DC, MC, V. Métro: Bourse.*

$ **Café Runtz.** Next to the Salle Favart in a neighborhood once full of theaters, this friendly bistro with rich *boiserie* (woodwork) and photos of customers from the entertainment industry serves up an Alsatian feel and cuisine. Tasty, hearty dishes include Gruyère salad, onion tart, choucroute, and fresh fruit tarts. Order a pichet of Riesling or other Alsatian wine. *16 rue Favart, tel. 42-96-69-86. Reservations advised. AE, MC, V. Closed weekends and Aug. Métro: Richelieu Drouot.*

3rd Arrondissement

$ **Au Bascou.** Gregarious proprietor Jean-Guy Lousteau enthusiastically shares his knowledge of the wines of southwestern France at this fashionable little bistro with a simple but imaginative decor, including mosaics of broken mirror. The sturdy, savory cuisine of the Basque country stars on the menu, and the country ham, cod with broccoli puree, and sautéed baby squid are particularly flavorful. *38 rue Réaumur, tel. 42-72-69-25. Reservations advised. MC, V. Closed weekends. Métro: Arts et Métiers.*

¢ **Dame Tartine.** A lively and diverse crowd frequents this restaurant, strategically located between Les Halles and the Marais, just five steps from Beaubourg. You'll look out on the slightly daft but amusing Niki de St-Phalle fountain dotted with knobby modern sculpture while enjoying a classic French light meal—a baguette topped with a variety of fillings, including various cheeses, ham, smoked salmon, vegetables, and pâté. For a more substantial meal, there's a changing selection of hot and cold daily specials. The house wines are fine. *2 rue Brisemiche, tel. 42–77–32–22. No credit cards. Métro: Rambuteau.*

4th Arrondissement

$$ **Le Grizzli.** It's said this turn-of-the-century bistro was one of the
★ last to have dancing bears as entertainment—thus the name.
Today's owner gets many of his ingredients (especially the wonderful ham and cheeses) from his native home of Auvergne. Several dishes are cooked on hot slate, including salmon and lamb. There's an interesting selection of wines from southwestern France. *7 rue St-Martin, tel. 48–87–77–56. Reservations advised. MC, V. Closed Sun., Mon. lunch. Métro: Châtelet.*

¢ **Le Trumilou.** Popular with students, artist types, and others on a budget, the Trumilou serves such unremarkable bistro cuisine as leg of lamb and apple tart. But the homely nondecor is somehow homey, and the staff is friendly despite the crowds. The location facing the Seine and Ile St-Louis is especially pleasant in nice weather, when you can sit on a narrow terrace under the trees. *84 quai de l'Hôtel-de-Ville, tel. 42–77–63–98. MC, V. Closed Mon. Métro: Pont Marie.*

5th Arrondissement

$$ **Chez Toutoune.** Friendly Toutoune, one of the most respected female chefs in Paris, recently redecorated her spacious restaurant in a cheery Provençal theme and introduced a new prix-fixe menu—an excellent value. All meals here begin with complimentary soup (usually vegetable) followed by appetizers such as tabbouleh salad garnished with plump shrimp and fresh herbs. The main course might be roasted salmon with tomato confit, or veal kidneys with bacon and leaf spinach. For dessert, the chocolate tart is superb. Consider splurging on a bottle of the velvety Domaine de la Bernarde 1991 from the admirable wine list. *5 rue de Pontoise, tel. 43–26–56–81. Reservations advised. AE, MC, V. Closed Sun., Mon. lunch, Aug. Métro: Maubert Mutualité.*

$ **Chez René.** This reliable address at the eastern end of boulevard St-Germain has satisfied three generations of Parisians, who count on finding such Burgundian dishes as boeuf bourguignon and coq au vin, and the wines of the Mâconnais and Beaujolais. The dining rooms are cozy, with red leatherette banquettes and white, honeycomb-tile floors. *14 blvd. St-Germain, tel. 43–54–30–23. Reservations advised. MC, V. Closed weekends, Aug., and Dec. 23–Jan. 3. Métro: Cardinal Lemoine.*

¢ **Le Tout Petit Plat.** This charming and conveniently located wine bar, where the food's as good as the wine, occupies the tiny former quarters of the very popular Le Petit Plat (*see below*). All the dishes are paired with a suggested glass of wine, allowing you to discover such mellifluous combinations as a plate of country ham, nutty *Tête-de-Moine* (monk's-head cheese), and a glass of crisp Vouvray. Other light, savory offerings include tomatoes and fennel *à la provençale*, and a delicious stewed chicken with five spices. *3 rue des Grands-Degrés, tel. 40–46–85–34. Reservations advised. MC, V. Closed Thurs. Métro: Maubert Mutualité.*

6th Arrondissement

$$ **La Bastide Odéon.** This little corner of Provence in Paris is just a few
★ steps from the Jardin du Luxembourg. The cooking of southern France continues to increase its popularity in the capital, and this sunny yellow room with old oak tables and chairs is one of the best places to sample the soothing Mediterranean food. Chef Gilles Ajuelos, formerly of Michel Rostang's kitchen at Le Bistrot d'à Côté Flaubert, is a fine fish cook who also prepares wonderful pastas, such as tagliatelle in *pistou* (basil and pine nuts) with wild mush-

rooms, and main courses like peppered tuna steak with ratatouille or roast cod with capers. The best bet on the slightly pricey wine list is the red Côteaux du Tricastin. *7 rue Corneille, tel. 43–26–03–65. Reservations advised. MC, V. Closed Sat., Sun. Métro: Odéon, RER: Luxembourg.*

$$ **Les Bookinistes.** Talented chef Guy Savoy's fifth bistro annex—his
★ first on the Left Bank—is a big success with the locals. The cheery, peach-color, postmodern room, with red, blue, and yellow wall sconces, affords views of the Seine. Savoy's menu of French country cooking changes seasonally, and might include a mussel and pumpkin soup, ravioli stuffed with chicken and celery, or baby chicken roasted in a casserole with root vegetables. The reasonable prices are challenged by a somewhat pricey wine list. The service is friendly and efficient. *53 quai des Grands-Augustins, tel. 43–25–45–94. Reservations advised. AE, DC, MC, V. Closed Sat. lunch, Sun. Métro: St-Michel.*

$ **Le Petit St-Benoît.** This bare-bones bistro has been nurturing poor
★ students and travelers for more than 125 years. Classics of the *cuisine bourgeoise* are served by frequently sassy waitresses in a communal atmosphere. Try veal roast, *blanquette* (a stew, often veal, with a white-sauce base), or *hachis Parmentier* (ground beef-and-mashed-potato pie). *4 rue St-Benoît, tel. 42–60–27–92. Reservations advised. No credit cards. Closed weekends. Métro: St-Germain des Prés.*

$ **Vagenende.** This is a kind of poor man's Maxim's, with an equally gorgeous Belle Epoque interior—but without the pretense. Classic dishes include the house foie gras, sea trout with red-wine sauce, pot-au-feu, and *baba au rhum* (rum-soaked cake). Service can be inept when the large restaurant is full. Prix-fixe menus keep meals in this price range; à la carte is higher. It's open until 1 AM. *142 blvd. St-Germain, tel. 43–26–68–18. Reservations advised. AE, MC, V. Métro: Odéon.*

7th Arrondissement

$$ **L'Oeillade.** Come here for generally good food at good prices. The decor of blond-wood paneling and interesting, 20th-century paintings is without pretense—the same cannot always be said about the clientele. Sample the avocado beignets and move on to the coquilles St-Jacques with endive fondu. Watch out for the wines, which will intoxicate your bill. *10 rue de St-Simon, tel. 42–22–01–60. Reservations advised. MC, V. Closed Sat. lunch, Sun. Métro: Rue du Bac.*

$ **Le Sancerre.** Family-run for several generations, this low-key spot
★ near Les Invalides is a showcase for the wines of Sancerre—white, red, and rosé—available by the glass or bottle. The menu is quite limited but sufficient for a light meal: salads, quiches, omelets, and the tasty Chavignol goat cheese from the Sancerre. The wood-paneled dining room is inviting. *25 av. Rapp, tel. 45–51–75–91. Reservations advised. MC, V. Closed Sat. eve. and Sun. Métro: Ecole Militaire.*

$ **Le Télégraphe.** This cavernous restaurant near the Musée d'Orsay was once a residence for female postal workers. Today's occupants are youngish, fashionable inhabitants of the wealthy neighborhood, who like the reasonable prix-fixe menu (à la carte is more). Although the cuisine is fine—sauté of beef, chocolate surprise—people come here for the atmosphere. *41 rue de Lille, tel. 40–15–06–65. Reservations advised. AE, V. Métro: Bac.*

¢ **Au Sauvignon.** A young, modish, intellectual crowd fills this tiny
★ wine bar, where you'll find the usual limited menu of *tartines*, or open-face sandwiches, on the famous Poilâne loaf, topped with good-quality charcuterie, cheese, or both. The colorful murals will amuse you, but it's even more fun to people-watch from one of the tables set on the narrow sidewalk. *80 rue des Saints-Pères, tel. 45–48–04–69.*

No reservations. No credit cards. Closed Sat. eve., Sun., Aug., Christmas week, Easter. Métro: Sèvres Babylone.

¢ **Thoumieux.** Virtually everything at this third-generation restaurant is made on the premises, including the foie gras, rillettes, *confit de canard* (preserved duck), cassoulet, and the homey desserts. The red velour banquettes, mellow yellow walls, and bustling waiters in long white aprons are delightfully Parisian, but you'll hear a lot of English spoken here. *79 rue St-Dominique, tel. 47–05–49–75. Reservations advised. MC, V. Métro: Invalides.*

8th Arrondissement

$ **Le Petit Yvan.** Personable Yvan, much loved by fashionable Paris, has opened a new annex to his other eponymous restaurant, Yvan. The decor (unremarkable, but comfortable and casual) and menu are both simpler than at his star-studded main outpost, but this place has exceptional food and has become very popular for lunch. The prix-fixe menu, which might include such dishes as lemon-marinated salmon and steak tartare, offers very good value. *1 bis rue Jean Mermoz, tel. 42–89–49–65. Reservations advised. MC, V. Closed Sun., Sat. lunch. Métro: St-Philippe du Roule.*

¢ **La Ferme St. Hubert.** Reserve ahead for lunch, when this unpretentious spot (serving primarily cheese dishes) is mobbed. The owner has one of the city's best cheese shops next door, and from its shelves come the main ingredients for fondue, raclette, and the best *croque St-Hubert* (toasted cheese sandwich) in Paris. The house wines are decent, and the location is convenient to the fancy food shop, Fauchon, on place de la Madeleine. *21 rue Vignon, tel. 47–42–79–20. Reservations essential at lunch, advised at dinner. AE, MC, V. Closed Sun. Métro: Madeleine.*

11th Arrondissement

$$ **Chardenoux.** A bit off the beaten track, this cozy, neighborhood bis-
★ tro with amber walls, etched-glass windows, dark bentwood furniture, tile floors, and a long zinc bar attracts a cross-section of savvy Parisians with its first-rate, traditional cooking. Start with one of the delicious salads, such as the green beans and foie gras, and then try the veal chop with morels, or a game dish. Savory desserts and a nicely chosen wine list with several excellent Côtes-du-Rhônes complete the experience. *1 rue Jules-Vallés, tel. 43–71–49–52. Reservations advised. AE, V. Closed weekends and Aug. Métro: Charonne.*

$ **Astier.** You'll find remarkable value at this pleasant restaurant, where the menu is prix-fixe (there's no à la carte). Among high-quality seasonal dishes, try mussel soup with saffron, fricassee of beef cheeks, and plum *clafoutis* (a hearty, flanlike tart). Service can be rushed, but the enthusiastic crowd doesn't seem to mind. Study the excellent wine list, which has some surprising buys. *44 rue Jean-Pierre Timbaud, tel. 43–57–16–35. Reservations advised. AE, MC, V. Closed weekends, Aug. Métro: Parmentier.*

¢ **L'Ebauchoir.** Trendy, laid-back locals who know a bargain when they see one frequent this old-fashioned bistro with a classic, prewar decor. Don't expect dainty service, but come instead for a hearty feed and good, inexpensive wines. The salad with poached eggs and bacon bits and the confit de canard are delicious, as are the steaks and the homemade dessert tarts. *43–45 rue de Cîteaux, tel. 43–42–49–31. Reservations advised. MC, V. Closed Sun. Métro: Faidherbe Chaligny.*

¢ **Jacques Mélac.** There's robust cuisine to match the noisy camarade-
★ rie at this popular wine bar–restaurant owned by mustachioed Jacques Mélac. Charcuterie, a salad of preserved duck gizzards, braised beef, and cheeses from central France are good choices here. Monsieur Mélac has his own miniature vineyard out the front door and hosts a jolly party at harvest time. *42 rue Léon-Frot, tel.*

43–70–59–27. Reservations advised. MC, V. Closed Mon. dinner, weekends, Aug. Métro: Charonne.

14th Arrondissement

$ **Le Bistrot du Dôme.** Montparnasse is the setting for this fish bistro that belongs to the fancy and expensive Dôme, and that benefits from that elegant brasserie's excellent sources of fish. The many seafood dishes are always very fresh and simply presented; try the poached stingray in a vinaigrette sauce. Colorful tiles and pretty, Italian-glass light fixtures create a cheerful ambience, enhanced by the jovial service. There's a limited but affordable wine list. *1 rue Delambre, tel. 43–35–32–00. Reservations advised. AE, MC, V. Métro: Vavin.*

$ **La Coupole.** La Coupole, the cavernous, world-renowned establishment in Montparnasse, practically defines the term brasserie. Many find it too large, too noisy, and too expensive, and no one likes the long wait at the bar before being seated. Still, everyone from Left Bank intellectuals (Jean-Paul Sartre and Simone de Beauvoir were regulars) to bourgeois grandmothers come here. Owner Jean-Paul Bucher (of the Flo group of brasseries) had the sense to leave well enough alone when he restored it in 1988, simply polishing and cleaning the famous murals. Expect the usual brasserie menu, including perhaps the largest shellfish presentation in Paris, choucroute, and a wide range of desserts. The buffet breakfast from 7:30 to 10:30 daily is an excellent deal. *102 blvd. du Montparnasse, tel. 43–20–14–20. Reservations advised. AE, DC, MC, V. Métro: Vavin.*

15th Arrondissement

$$ **L'Os à Moëlle.** It's unlikely that you'll go away hungry from this small, popular bistro. The very reasonable six-course dinner menu—appetizer, soup, fish, meat, cheese, and dessert—changes daily, and portions are generous (there's no à la carte). A sample menu might include white-bean soup, a country terrine of pork with peppers, rouget, sautéed veal, cheese with a small salad, and a delicious clafoutis of apples and rhubarb. At lunchtime, the à la carte menu is similarly good. The excellent list of wines are fairly priced so your bill should stay comfortably low. *3 rue Vasco-de-Gama, tel. 45–57–27–27. Reservations essential. MC, V. Closed Sun., Mon. Métro: Balard.*

$ **Le Petit Plat.** Originally squeezed into a tiny space in the Latin Quarter (*see* Le Tout Petit Plat, *above*), this bistro was so popular that the owners found a bit more space in a quiet residential area; it's still small, but now the feel is intimate rather than crowded. The kitchen turns out generous portions of the slightly urbanized French country cooking that Parisians are currently mad about: Try the terrine of rabbit in tarragon aspic, sausage with potato salad in shallot vinaigrette, or roast chicken with sautéed mushrooms. The excellent wine list was selected by Henri Gault of Gault-Millau, the famous French food guide (his daughter is one of the three owners). *45 av. Emile-Zola, tel. 45–78–24–20. Reservations advised. V. Closed Mon., Tues. lunch. Métro: Charles Michel.*

16th Arrondissement

$$ **La Butte Chaillot.** A dramatic iron staircase connects two levels decorated in turquoise and earth colors at this, the latest, largest, and most impressive of star-chef Guy Savoy's fashionable bistros. Dining here is part theater, as the à la mode clientele will attest, but it's not all show. The very good food includes tasty ravioli from the town of Royans, roast chicken with mashed potatoes, and stuffed veal breast with rosemary. A wide sidewalk terrace fronts tree-shaded

avenue Kléber. *112 av. Kléber, tel. 47–27–88–88. Reservations advised. AE, MC, V. Métro: Trocadéro.*

$ **Le Petit Rétro.** Two different clienteles—mostly men in expensive suits at noon and well-dressed local couples in the evening—frequent this immaculate little bistro with Art Nouveau tiles and bentwood furniture. You can't go wrong with the daily special, which is written on a chalkboard presented by one of the friendly waitresses. Come in some night when you want a good solid meal, like the perfect *pavé de boeuf* (thick steak) in a ruddy red-wine and stock sauce, accompanied by a baked disk of au gratin potatoes and some deliciously caramelized braised endive. *5 rue Mesnil, tel. 44–05–06–05. Reservations advised. MC, V. Closed Sun., Mon. lunch. Métro: Victor Hugo.*

18th Arrondissement

¢ **Aux Négotiants.** This wine bar in Montmartre has zero decor, but gives a warm welcome to its mix of neighborhood regulars and well-heeled clientele. One or two hot plates are offered daily; otherwise, enjoy the terrines, cheeses, and other simple choices, served with affordable wines by the glass or bottle. *27 rue Lambert, tel. 46–06–15–11. Reservations advised. No credit cards. Closed weekends; dinner served Tues., Thurs., and Fri. only. Closed Aug. Métro: Château Rouge.*

Arts and Nightlife

Arts

Parisians consider their city a bastion of art and culture, and indeed it is. But surprisingly, much of the theater, opera, music, and ballet here is not on a par with what you'll find in London, New York, or Milan. Mime and contemporary dance performances are often better bets, and they pose no language problems.

The music season usually runs from September to June. Theaters stay open during the summer, but many productions are at summer festivals elsewhere in France. The weekly magazines *Pariscope* and *L'Officiel des Spectacles,* published on Wednesday, give detailed entertainment listings, as does *Figaroscope,* a free supplement to the Wednesday edition of the daily newspaper *Le Figaro. Paris Free Voice* gives monthly listings in English—you can find it in bilingual bookstores or at the American Church (65 quai d'Orsay)—and the Paris Tourist Office has set up a **24-hour hot line** (tel. 49–52–53–56) in English with information about weekly events. The best place to buy tickets is at the venue itself; otherwise, try your hotel or a travel agency, such as **Paris-Vision** (214 rue de Rivoli). Tickets for some events can be bought at the **FNAC** stores—especially Alpha-FNAC (1–5 rue Pierre-Lescot, 1e, Forum des halles, 3rd level down, tel. 40–41–40–78, métro Les Halles). **Virgin Megastore** (52 av. des Champs-Elysées, tel. 49–53–50–00, métro Franklin D. Roosevelt) sells theater and concert tickets. Half-price tickets for many same-day theater performances are available at the **Kiosque Théâtre** (across from 15 pl. de la Madeleine; open Tues.–Sat. 12:30–8, Sun. 12:30–6); expect a line. There's another branch at RER station Châtelet (closed Sun.).

Concerts **Salle Pleyel** (252 rue du Fbg. St-Honoré, 8e, tel. 45–61–53–00 or 45–63–07–96, métro Ternes), near the Arc de Triomphe, was Paris's principal home of classical music before the new Opéra Bastille opened. The Paris Symphony Orchestra and other leading international orchestras still play here regularly. Paris may not be as richly endowed as New York or London when it comes to orchestral music, but the city compensates with a never-ending stream of inexpensive lunchtime and evening concerts in churches. **Sainte-Chapelle** (blvd. du Palais, 1er, tel. 43–54–30–09, métro Cité) holds outstanding candlelit concerts—make reservations well in advance. **Notre-Dame** (Ile de la Cité, tel. 42–34–56–10, métro Cité) is another church where you can combine sightseeing with good listening. Other churches with classical concerts ranging from organ recitals to choral music and orchestral works include: **St-Eustache** (rue du Jour, 1er, métro Les Halles), near Les Halles; **St-Germain-des-Prés** (3 pl. St-Germain-des-Prés), 6e, tel. 43–25–41–71, métro St-Germain des Prés, on the Left Bank; **St-Louis-en-l'Ile** (rue St-Louis-en-l'Ile, 4e, tel. 46–34–11–60, métro Pont Marie); **St-Roch** (rue St-Honoré, 1er, tel. 42–44–13–20, métro Tuileries), north of the Louvre; and the lovely **St-Germain l'Auxerrois** (pl. du Louvre, 1er, tel. 42–60–13–96, métro Louvre), at the east end of the Louvre.

Dance The highlights of the Paris dance year usually take place at the **Opéra Garnier** (pl. de l'Opéra, 9e, tel. 47–42–53–71, métro Opéra), which in addition to being the sumptuous home of the well-reputed Paris Ballet also bills dozens of major foreign troupes, ranging from classical to modern. Other major venues include the **Théâtre de la Ville** (2 pl. du Châtelet, 4e, tel. 42–74–22–77, métro Châtelet), the **Palais des Congrès** (pl. de la Porte-Maillot, 17e, tel. 40–68–00–05, métro Porte Maillot), and the **Palais des Sports** (pl. Porte-de-Versailles, 15e, tel. 48–28–40–48, métro Porte de Versailles). The annual **Festival de la Danse** is staged at the **Théâtre des Champs-Elysées** (15 av. Montaigne, 8e, tel. 47–20–36–37, métro Alma Marceau) in October.

Film There are hundreds of movie theaters in the city, and a number of them show English films. Check the *Officiel du Spectacle* or *Pariscope* for a movie of your choice. Look for the initials "v.o.," which means *version original;* that is, not dubbed (but almost always with subtitles). Cinema admission runs from 40 frs to 55 frs; there are reduced rates on Monday, and in some cinemas for morning shows. Old and rare films are often screened at **Beaubourg** and **Musée du Cinema** at Trocadéro.

Opera The "old" Opéra, or Opéra Garnier, has ceded its role as Paris's main opera house to the Opéra Bastille (the old Opéra now devotes itself to classical dance; *see* Dance, *above*). The **Opéra Bastille** (pl. de la Bastille, 12e, tel. 44–43–96–96 or 44–73–13–00, métro Bastille), meanwhile, has had its share of start-up and management problems, and many feel it is not living up to its promise of grand opera at affordable prices. In the lofty old hall of the **Opéra Comique** (5 rue Favart, 2e, tel. 42–60–04–99, métro Richelieu Drouot), you'll hear often excellent comic operas and lightweight musical entertainments. The **Théâtre Musical de Paris**, better known as the Théâtre du Châtelet (2 pl. du Châtelet, 1er, tel. 40–28–28–28, métro Chatelet), offers opera and ballet for a wider audience, at more reasonable prices.

Theater A number of theaters line the grand boulevards between Opéra and République, but there is no Paris equivalent to Broadway or London's West End. Shows are mostly in French. Classical drama is performed at the **Comédie-Française** (Palais-Royal, 1er, tel. 40–15–00–15, métro Palais Royal). You can reserve seats in person about two weeks in advance or turn up an hour beforehand and wait in line for cheap returned tickets.

A completely different sort of pleasure is to be found near place St-Michel at the tiny **Théâtre de la Huchette** (23 rue de la Huchette, 5e, tel. 43–26–38–99, métro St-Michel), where Ionesco's short plays make a deliberate mess of the French language.

A particularly Parisian form of theater is *Café-Théâtre*—a mixture of satirical sketches and variety riddled with slapstick humor, in a café setting. It's fun if you have a good grasp of French. We suggest either the **Café de la Gare** (41 rue du Temple, 4e, tel. 42–78–52–51,

métro Hôtel de Ville) or Montmartre's pricier **Chez Michou** (80 rue
des Martyrs, 18e, tel. 46–06–16–04, métro Abbesses).

Nightlife

The French are definitely nightbirds, though these days that means
smart, elegant *bars de nuit* rather than frenetic discos. The
Champs-Elysées, that ubiquitous cabaret land, is making a comeback, though the clientele remains predominantly foreign. The taw-
dry **Pigalle** and down-at-the-heels **Bastille** areas are trendy these
days, and the **Left Bank** has a bit of everything. During the week,
people usually go home after the closing hour of 2 AM, but weekends
mean late-night partying.

Bars and The more upscale Paris nightclubs tend to be both expensive (1,000
Nightclubs frs for a bottle of gin or whiskey) and private—in other words, you'll
usually need to know someone who's a member to get through the
door. **Club 79** (79 av. des Champs-Elysées, 8e, métro George V) is
probably the handiest bet for dancing the night away.

Other places for a fun evening out include:

Caveau des Oubliettes. Traditional folk singing and ballads are performed in a medieval cellar with Gothic arches and heavy beams. It's
very popular with tourists, but still full of energetic charm. *Admission (with drink): 110 frs. 52 rue Galande, 5e. Open 9 PM–2 AM.
Closed Sun. Métro: St-Michel.*

Le Lapin Agile. This is a touristy but picturesque Montmartre setting: hard wooden benches, brandied cherries, and thumping great
golden French oldies. *22 rue des Saules, 18e. Admission (with
drink): 110 frs. Open 9 PM–2 AM. Métro: Lamarck Caulaincourt.*

La Rôtisserie de l'Abbaye. French, English, and American folk songs
are sung to the accompaniment of a guitar in a medieval setting. The
action starts around 8 PM; come early or you won't get in. You can dine
here, too. *22 rue Jacob, 6e. Admission (including dinner): 200–400
frs. Closed Sun. Métro: St-Germain des Prés.*

Cabaret Paris's nightclubs are household names, at least among foreign tourists. But unless you get standing-only tickets at the Crazy Horse,
Paris cabaret does not come cheap.

The **Crazy Horse** (12 av. George-V, 8e, tel. 47–23–32–32, métro
Alma Marceau) is one of the best known for pretty girls and risqué
dance routines, lots of humor, and scanty clothing. Cheapest ticket:
195 frs (standing), 130 frs under 26.

The **Moulin Rouge** (pl. Blanche, 18e, tel. 46–06–00–19, métro
Blanche) is an old favorite at the foot of Montmartre. Cheapest ticket: 465 frs (seat and champagne).

Nearby is the **Folies-Bergère** (32 rue Richer, 9e, tel. 44–79–98–98,
métro Blanche), which reopened at the end of 1993 after closing
briefly because of financial trouble. The new and improved cabaret
includes ornate costumes, masterful lighting, and a show that returns to its music hall origins. Cheapest seats: 150 frs.

The **Lido** (116 bis av. des Champs-Elysées, 8e, tel. 40–76–56–10,
métro George V), starring the famous Bluebell Girls, underwent a
$10 million face-lift in 1994. Cheapest ticket: 345 frs (standing at the
bar).

Discos **Club Zed** (2 rue des Anglais, 5e, métro Maubert Mutualité) has lively
dancing and some rock-only evenings.

The long-established **Balajo** (9 rue de Lappe, 11e, métro Bastille) is
crowded and lots of fun, with plenty of nostalgic '60s sounds some
nights.

Les Bains (7 rue du Bourg-l'Abbé, 3e, métro Etienne Marcel), once a public bathhouse, now specializes in new-wave music and features live music on Wednesday.

Gay and Lesbian Gay and lesbian bars and clubs are mostly concentrated in the Marais and include some of the most happening addresses in the city. The very trendy **Banana Café** (13 rue de la Ferronnerie, 1er, métro Les Halles) attracts an energetic and scantily clad mixed crowd; dancing on the tables is the norm.

For men, **Le Quetzal** (10 rue de la Verrerie, 4e, métro Hôtel de Ville), which features a chrome-and-blue-light atmosphere, gets very crowded and smoky on weekends; **The Trap** (10 rue Jacob, 6e, métro Mabillon) contains a ground-floor video bar with a staircase leading to a darker, more social area. For a more relaxed atmosphere try **Subway** (35 rue Ste-Croix-de-la-Bretonnerie, 4e, métro Hôtel-de-Ville), a popular hangout that has pinball and pool.

For women, **La Champmeslé** (4 rue Chabanais, 2e, métro Bourse) is the hub of lesbian nightlife with a back room reserved for women only; **Le Memorie's** (2 pl. de la Porte-Maillot, 17e, métro Porte Maillot), though in a staid neighborhood, is Paris's most renowned lesbian dance club.

Jazz Clubs Paris is one of the great jazz cities of the world, with plenty of variety, including some fine, distinctive local coloring. For nightly schedules, consult the magazines *Jazz Hot* or *Jazz Magazine*. Remember that nothing gets going until 10 or 11 PM and that entry prices can vary widely from about 40 frs to more than 100 frs.

The Latin Quarter is a good place to track down Paris jazz. The **Caveau de la Huchette** (5 rue de la Huchette, 5e, métro St-Michel) offers Dixieland in a hectic, smoke-filled atmosphere.

Le Petit Opportun (15 rue des Lavandières-Ste-Opportune, 1er, métro Les Halles) is a converted Latin Quarter bistro with a cramped, atmospheric basement that sometimes features top-flight American soloists with French rhythm sections. At street level, there is a pleasant bar with recorded music and less-expensive drinks.

On the Right Bank is **New Morning** (7 rue des Petites-Ecuries, 10e, métro Château d'Eau), a premier venue for visiting American musicians and top French bands.

Pubs The number of Paris bars that woo English-speaking clients with a pub atmosphere and dark beer are becoming increasingly popular with Parisians, too. The **Académie de la Bière** (88 bis blvd. de Port-Royal, 5e, RER Port Royal) serves more than 100 foreign brews to accompany good french fries and *moules marinières* (mussels cooked in white wine). The **Bar Belge** (75 av. de Saint-Ouen, 17e, métro Guy Môquet) is an authentically noisy Flemish drinking spot, while the **Mayflower** (49 rue Descartes, 5e, métro Cardinal Lemoine) is a classy Left Bank spot, British-style. **Connolly's Corner** (8 rue Mirbel, 5e, métro Censier Daubenton) and **Finnegans Wake** (9 rue des Boulangers, 5e, métro Jussieu) are two of the city's many Irish pubs.

3 Ile-de-France

Including Versailles, Chartres, and Fontainebleau

Far from being a sprawl of faceless gray suburbia, the region surrounding Paris—poetically known as the Ile-de-France—has as much history and beauty as the capital itself. Thanks to a comprehensive rail network, its profusion of cathedrals, châteaus, and picturesque old towns are all within an hour of central Paris. Most visitors are surprised to find such vast forests and swards of lush meadowland so close to the capital.

Ile-de-France never lost favor with the powerful, partly because its many forests—large chunks of which still stand—harbored sufficient game for even bloated, cosseted monarchs to achieve a regular kill. First Fontainebleau, in humane Renaissance proportions, then Versailles, on a minion-crushing, Baroque scale, reflected the royal desire to transform hunting lodges into palatial residences.

The 17th century was a time of prodigious building in the Ile-de-France—a period that bequeathed a vast array of important sights to admire and explore. The château, gardens, and well-preserved town of Versailles should not be overlooked. But do not neglect Versailles's slightly lesser neighbors; Vaux-le-Vicomte, Thoiry, Rambouillet, and Chartres would bask in superstar status anywhere else. And, after the crowds of Versailles in midsummer, you will welcome the relative tranquillity of these smaller châteaus.

By way of contrast, Euro Disney opened in 1992 to an explosion of fanfare and anticipation—which, unfortunately, has faded away. The powers at Disney situated their theme park poorly, 32 kilometers (20 miles) east of Paris, a convenient but rather cold location, and, as the resort's dismal financial returns show, they overestimated the Disney draw. In 1995, after renaming the site Disneyland Paris, they reduced admission prices to halt the slide.

On the whole, however, the architectural impact of the 20th century is discreet in the Ile-de-France, and you may find it disorienting that so many rural backwaters exist within a 30-minute drive of the capital. There is no miracle involved with this, however, just some commonsensical forethought: With the Gallic mania for centralized planning, new developments are assigned to restricted areas. Students of modern architecture may find food for thought in such so-called new towns as St-Quentin-en-Yvelines (near Versailles), and sociologists won't lack material in the concrete ghettos of the "red belt" north of Paris (so-called because its working-class population traditionally votes communist), but the average visitor can comfortably avoid them.

Ile-de-France Basics

Budget Lodging
Remember two things: (1) in summer, hotel rooms are at a premium and reservations are essential, and (2) relative lack of choice means that almost all accommodations in the swankier towns—Versailles, Rambouillet, and Fontainebleau—are on the costly side. Take nothing for granted. Some of the smaller hotels in the region may not accept credit cards, although the Carte Bleue and its international equivalents (MasterCard and Visa) are widely recognized—unlike American Express, which is often refused in all but the plushest establishments.

Budget Dining
With wealthy tourists and weekending Parisians providing the backbone of the region's seasonal clientele, the smarter restaurants of Ile-de-France can be just as pricey as their Parisian counterparts. But in smaller towns, and for those prepared to venture even marginally off the beaten tourist track, it's not difficult to find interesting meals that won't break your budget. The style of cuisine mirrors that of Paris: There is plenty of variety but few things that can be considered specifically regional. In season, sumptuous game and asparagus are found in the south of the region; the soft, creamy cheese of Brie hails from Meaux and Coulommiers to the east.

Bargain Shopping
Most of the Ile-de-France's working population either commutes to Paris or plows farmland. There is little in the way of regional specialties, and, with Paris never more than an hour away, serious shopping—particularly for clothes—means heading back to the capital. However, there are notably fine souvenir shops at Vaux-le-Vicomte, Giverny, and Thoiry (where you can sample cookies and jams made by the American viscountess herself).

Biking
Bicycling is an enjoyable way to explore the area; while occasionally challenging, the terrain is mostly flat or slightly rolling. Wind is negligible, and steep slopes are few. Recommended itineraries include the 90 kilometers (56 miles) of cycling paths that meander through the Rambouillet Forest; the route from Barbizon to the Gorges d'Apremont in the Fontainebleau Forest; or the easy path around the Versailles canal. Bicycles can be rented for a day or weekend in the country from the RATP (contact the Bicyclub de France, 8 rue de la Porte-de-Champerret, Paris, 75017, tel. 47–66–55–92), or from the SNCF (ask for the "Train & Vélo" brochure at any major train station). Local tourist offices can also supply information on bike rentals and itineraries.

Hiking
The Ile-de-France claims 4,200 kilometers (2,600 miles) of marked hiking trails, notably the GR 1, which loops through the forests that surround Paris. Access to the trails is often conveniently near a train station. For maps and detailed itineraries, purchase a copy of the Ile-de-France *Topo Guides*, available at many bookshops. To link up with a group, contact the **Fédération de la Randonnée Pédestre** (64 rue de Gergovie, Paris, 75014, tel. 45–45–31–02).

Festivals
With Paris so close, it seems pointless to detail the comparatively minor offerings of the towns of the Ile-de-France in the domains of theater, music, or cinema. There are, however, a number of arts festivals staged in the Ile-de-France that have earned esteem in their

Ile-de-France

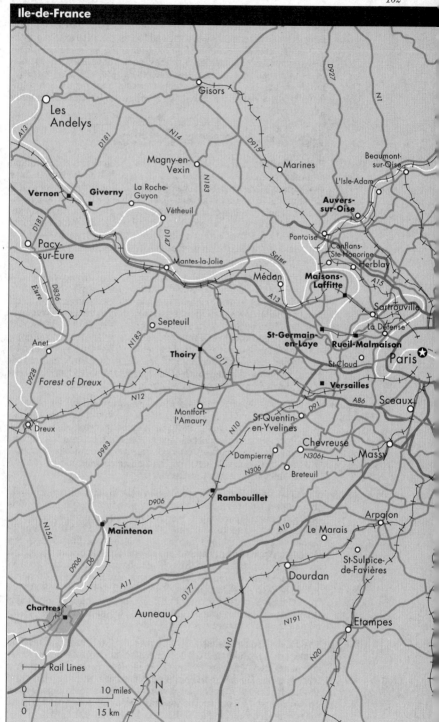

Les Andelys

Gisors

Magny-en-Vexin

Marines

Beaumont-sur-Oise

L'Isle-Adam

Auvers-sur-Oise

Vernon

Giverny

La Roche-Guyon

Vétheuil

Pontoise

Conflans-Ste-Honorine

Herblay

Pacy-sur-Eure

Mantes-la-Jolie

Seine

Maisons-Laffitte

Médan

Sartrouville

Septeuil

St-Germain-en-Laye

La Défense

Anet

Thoiry

Rueil-Malmaison

Paris

St-Cloud

Forest of Dreux

N12

Versailles

Sceaux

Dreux

Montfort-l'Amaury

St-Quentin-en-Yvelines

Chevreuse

Massy

Dampierre

Breteuil

Rambouillet

Arpajon

Maintenon

Le Marais

St-Sulpice-de-Favières

A10

Dourdan

Chartres

Auneau

Etampes

Rail Lines

10 miles

N

0

0

15 km

Émre

D181

A13

D181

N14

D913

D927

N183

D147

D836

D928

D983

N154

D906

D6

A11

D177

A10

N191

N20

N183

D11

N10

N306

N306

D91

A86

A13

A15

D906

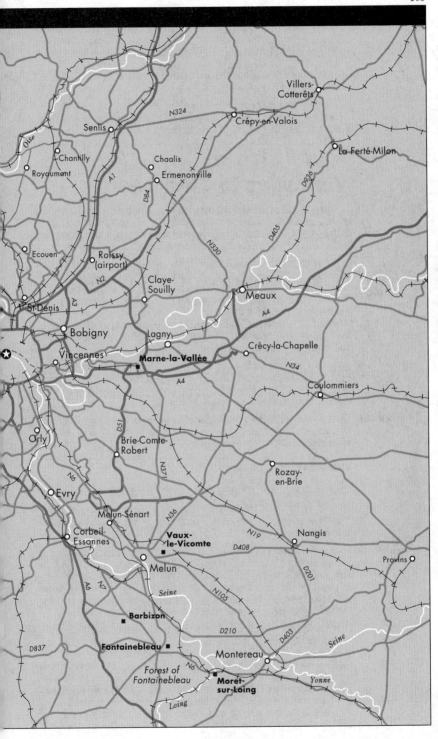

own right. Of these, the largest is the **Festival de l'Ile-de-France** (mid-May–early July), famed for concerts held at châteaus themselves (for details, tel. 42–96–02–32). There are also music festivals in **Provins** (June), **St-Denis** (mid-May–June, with concerts in the basilica, tel. 42–43–30–97), **Versailles** (May–June, concerts and operas, details available at the Tourist Office, or call 30–97–81–03), and at the abbey of **Royaumont** (mid-Aug.–mid-Oct., tel. 34–68–05–50).

An invaluable list of monthly regional events is the *Tourisme Loisirs* brochure produced by the **Comité Régional du Tourisme Ile-de-France** (26 av. de l'Opéra, 75001 Paris, tel. 42–60–28–62).

Tour 1: From Versailles to Chartres

No visit to Paris is complete without an excursion to Versailles, the starting point for this tour, which takes in the châteaus of Thoiry, Rambouillet, and Maintenon, conveniently situated along the Versailles–Chartres rail line, and the cathedral of Chartres itself.

If, after days of museum lines and crowded métros, you feel a sense of escape as you leave Paris, you won't be the first. Back in the 17th century, Louis XIV, the Sun King, no sooner had a firm grip on the throne when he cast his cantankerous royal eye over the Ile-de-France in search of a new power base. Marshy, inhospitable Versailles, 24 kilometers (15 miles) to the west of Paris, was the place of his dreams. Down came its modest royal hunting lodge and up, up, and along went the new château.

From Paris Suburban trains (RER-C) to Versailles's Rive Gauche station leave
By Train central Paris (St-Michel, Musée d'Orsay, Invalides, Eiffel Tower) every ¼ hour. The trip takes 20–25 minutes; the château is 400 yards down avenue de Sceaux from the station.

By Car The drive from Paris (Porte d'Auteuil) to Versailles along A13 takes 20 minutes (longer during the evening rush hour); N185 to N10 is a more scenic route.

Versailles

Tourist office: 7 rue des Réservoirs, to the right of the château close to the park entrance, tel. 39–50–36–22.

Numbers in the margin correspond with points of interest on the Versailles map.

★ ❶ Today the **château of Versailles** seems outrageously big—but it wasn't nearly big enough for the sycophantic army of 20,000 noblemen, servants, and hangers-on who moved in with Louis. A new capital had to be constructed from scratch. Tough-thinking town planners dreamed up vast Baroque mansions and avenues broader than today's Champs-Elysées.

It is hardly surprising that Louis XIV's successors soon felt out of sync with their architectural inheritance. Louis XV, who inherited the throne from the Sun King in 1715, transformed the royal apartments into places to live rather than to pose in. The unfortunate Louis XVI—reigning monarch at the time of the French Revolution—cowered in the Petit Trianon in the leafy depths of Versailles's gardens, well out of the mighty château's shadow. His queen, Marie-Antoinette, lost her head well before her trip to the guillotine in 1793, pretending to be a peasant shepherdess amid the ersatz rusticity of her elaborately landscaped hamlet.

The château was built by French architects Louis Le Vau and Jules Hardouin-Mansart between 1662 and 1690. Enter through the gilt

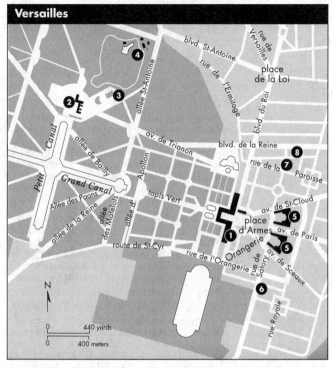

Versailles

iron gates from the huge place d'Armes. On the first floor of the château, right in the middle as you approach across the sprawling cobbled forecourt, is Louis XIV's bedchamber. The two wings were occupied by the royal children and princes of the blood, with courtiers making do in the attics.

The highlight for many on the guided tour of the palace is the **Galerie des Glaces** (Hall of Mirrors), fully restored to sparkling glory. It was here, after France's capitulation, that Prince Otto von Bismarck proclaimed the unified German Empire in 1871, and here, too, that the controversial Treaty of Versailles, asserting Germany's responsibility for World War I, was signed in 1919.

The **Grands Appartements** (State Rooms) that flank the Hall of Mirrors retain much of their original Baroque decoration: gilt stucco, painted ceilings, and marble sculpture. Perhaps the most extravagant of these rooms is the **Salon d'Apollon,** the former throne room, dedicated to the sun god Apollo, Louis XIV's mythical hero. Equally interesting are the **Petits Appartements,** where the royal family and friends lived in (relative) privacy.

In the north wing of the château can be found the solemn white-and-gold **chapel,** designed by J. H.-Mansart and completed in 1710; the intimate **opera house,** built by J.-A. Gabriel for Louis XV in 1770; and, connecting the two, the 17th-century Galleries, with exhibits retracing the château's history. The south wing contains the majestically proportioned **Galerie des Batailles** (Gallery of Battles), lined with gigantic canvases extolling French military glory. *Admission: 40 frs adults, 26 frs students and senior citizens. Open Tues.–Sun. 9–6:30 (9–5:30 in winter). Galerie des Glaces: 9:45–5; Opéra Royal: 9:45–3:30 (tours every 15 min.).*

★ After the awesome feast of interior decor, the **park** outside is an ideal place to catch your breath. The gardens were designed by the French landscape architect André Le Nôtre, whose work here represents classical French landscaping at its most formal and sophisticated. The 250-acre grounds include woods, lawns, flower beds, statues, artificial lakes, and fountains galore. They are at their golden-leafed best in the fall but are also enticing in summer—especially on those Sundays when the fountains are in full flow. They become a spectacle of rare grandeur during the **Fêtes de Nuit** floodlighting and fireworks shows held in July and September. *Grounds open daily, tel. 39–50–36–22 for details of the Fêtes de Nuit. Admission: 20 frs Sun., May–Sept., free other times.*

If you wander too far into the park woods you can easily get lost. Follow signs to skirt the numerous basins (or ponds) until you reach the **Grand Canal.** Move down the right bank, along gravelly paths beneath high-plinthed statues, until you discover that the canal is in the form of a cross—with two smaller arms known as the **Petit Canal.** At the crossing, bear right toward the Grand Trianon (in all, about a mile from the château).

② The **Grand Trianon,** built by Mansart in 1687, is a scaled-down, pink-marble pleasure palace, now used to entertain visiting heads of state. When it is not in use, the palace is opened so that visitors can admire its lavish interior and early 19th-century furniture. *Admission: 21 frs adults, 14 frs students and senior citizens. Open Oct.–Apr., Tues.–Fri. 10–12:30 and 2–5:30, weekends 10–5:30; May–Sept., Tues.–Sun. 10–6:30.*

③ The **Petit Trianon,** close by, was built in the Neoclassical style by architect Jacques-Ange Gabriel in 1768. It is a mansion, not a palace, and is modest by Versailles standards—though still sumptuously furnished. It contains mementos of its most illustrious inhabitant, Marie-Antoinette. Look for her initials wrought into the iron railings of the main staircase. *Admission: 12 frs adults, 8 frs students and senior citizens. Hours same as for Grand Trianon, above.*

Beyond the Petit Trianon and across the Petit Lac, which looks more like a stream as it describes a wriggly semicircle, is the queen's so-**④** called hamlet (**Hameau**). With its watermill, genuine lake (Grand Lac), and pigeon loft, this make-believe village is outrageously pretty; it was here that Marie-Antoinette lived out her romanticized dreams of peasant life.

The town of Versailles is attractive, and its broad, leafy boulevards **⑤** make agreeable places to stroll. Facing the château are the **royal stables,** buildings of regal dimensions and aspect. Take avenue de Sceaux, to the right, and turn right again along rue de Satory, **⑥** which leads to the **Cathédrale St-Louis,** an austere edifice built between 1743 and 1754 by Mansart's grandnephew, with notable paintings and an organ loft.

Turn right out of the cathedral, then left down avenue Thiers, which cuts through the town's three major boulevards—avenues de Sceaux, de Paris, and de St-Cloud—to the ancient market square, **⑦** where rue de la Paroisse heads left to the **Eglise Notre-Dame.** This sturdy Baroque monument was built from 1684 to 1686 (and is therefore older than the cathedral) by Mansart as parish church for the Sun King's new town. Louis XIV himself laid the foundation stone.

Behind the church, in an imposing 18th-century mansion on boule-**⑧** vard de la Reine, is the **Musée Lambinet,** a museum with a wide-ranging collection—a maze of cozy, finely furnished rooms replete with paintings, weapons, fans, and porcelain. *54 blvd. de la Reine. Admission: 19 frs adults, 13 frs students and senior citizens. Open Tues.–Sun. 2–6.*

Lodging **Home St-Louis.** The small, recently modernized Home St-Louis is a
¢ good, cheap, quiet bet—close to the cathedral and not too far from the château. There's no restaurant. *28 rue St-Louis, 78000, tel. 39–50–23–55, fax 39–21–62–45. 27 rooms with bath. MC, V.*

Dining **La Grande Sirène.** An appealing 150-franc lunch menu (wine in-
$ cluded), served every day but Sunday, makes this pretty spot near
the château a popular noontime choice. Try the zesty simmered escargots, or the deftly prepared fish accompanied by fine wines with
service to match. *25 rue du Maréchal-Foch, tel. 39–53–08–08. Reservations advised. AE, MC, V. Closed Mon.*

$ **Quai No 1.** Fish and seafood rule supreme amid the sails, barome-
ters, and model ships of this quaintly decked out restaurant. Home-
smoked salmon and sauerkraut with fish are specialties. Eating à la
carte isn't too expensive, and there are value-priced set menus. *1 av.
de St-Cloud, tel. 39–50–42–26. Reservations advised. MC, V.
Closed Sun. dinner, Mon.*

Shopping Versailles is perhaps the region's most commercial town. After visiting the château, you might want to stop in at **Aux Colonnes,** a highly
rated *confiserie* (confectioner's shop) with an astounding array of
chocolates and candies (14 rue Hoche; closed Mon.). A huge choice of
cheeses—including one of France's widest selection of goat cheeses—can be smelled, admired, and eventually purchased from
Eugène Le Gall (15 rue Ducis; closed Sun. afternoon and Mon.). For
the makings of an impromptu picnic of cold cuts, cheese, salads, and
such, try **Les Délices du Palais** (4 rue du Maréchal-Foch, closed Sun.
PM and Mon.). Anyone in the mood for antiques hunting should visit
Versailles's passage de la Geôle, site of a good, thrice-weekly flea market (10 rue Rameau; open Fri.–Sun. 9–7).

Thoiry

*Hourly trains from Versailles's mainline Chantiers station (less
than a mile from Versailles via avenue de Paris and rue des Etats-
Généraux) take 25 minutes to Montfort-l'Amaury. From here, take
a taxi to reach Thoiry, 10 km (6 mi) away.*

Owner Vicomte de La Panouse and his American wife, Annabelle,
★ have restored the **château of Thoiry** and its park to something of
their former glory, opening both to the public. The result is a splendid combination of history, culture, and adventure. The superbly
furnished 16th-century château has archive and gastronomy museums and overlooks a safari park, where you can picnic near the bears
and lions.

The château was built in 1564. Its handsome Renaissance facade is
set off by gardens landscaped in typically disciplined French fashion
by Le Nôtre. The discipline has unexpected justification: The château is positioned to be directly in line with the sun as it rises in the
east at the summer solstice (June 21) and as it sets in the west at the
winter solstice (December 21). Heightening the effect, the central
part of the château appears to be a transparent arch of light, owing
to its huge glass doors and windows.

The viscountess is a keen gardener and enjoys experimenting in the
less formal **Jardin à l'Anglaise** (English Garden), which also contains
a cricket ground, and in her late-flowering **Autumn Garden.** Visitors
are allowed to wander at leisure, although few dare stray from the
★ official footpath through the **animal reserve.** Note that those parts of
the reserve containing the wilder beasts—deer, zebra, camels, hip-
pos, bears, elephants, and lions—can be visited only by car.

The reserve hit the headlines when the first-ever ligrons—a cross
between a lion and a tiger—were born here several years ago. These
new-look beasts (bigger than either a lion or a tiger) are now into
their second generation and can be seen from the safety of a raised
footbridge in the **Tiger Park.** Nearby, as emus and flamingos stalk in
search of tidbits, there is a **children's play area** that features an
Enchanted Burrow to wriggle through and a huge netted Cobweb to
bounce around in.

Highlights of the château's interior include the **Grand Staircase,** with its 18th-century Gobelins tapestries, and the **Green** and **White salons,** with their antique painted harpsichord, portraits, and tapestries. There is an authentic, homey, faintly faded charm to these rooms, especially when log fires crackle in their enormous hearths on damp afternoons.

The distinguished history of the Panouse family—a Comte César even fought in the American Revolutionary War—is retraced in the **Archive Museum,** where papal bulls, Napoleonic letters, and Chopin manuscripts (discovered in the attic in 1973) mingle with missives from Thomas Jefferson and Benjamin Franklin.

The château pantries house a **Museum of Gastronomy,** whose tempting display of *pièces montées*—virtuoso banquet showpieces—recreate the designs of famed 19th-century chef Antoine Carême. Early recipe books, engravings, and old copper pots are also displayed. *Admission: château 30 frs adults, 25 frs children; animal reserve plus gardens 95 frs adults, 75 frs children. Open Easter–Oct., weekdays 10–6, weekends 10–6:30; Nov.–Easter, weekdays 10–5, weekends 10–5:30.*

Lodging and Dining
¢
Etoile. Handily situated for visitors to Thoiry château and safari park, the Etoile offers a special low-priced tourist menu, as well as a wide choice of à la carte dishes. A garden and a ping-pong table add to the hotel's homey appeal. *38 rue de la Porte St-Martin, 78770, tel. 34–87–40–21, fax 34–87–49–57. 12 rooms with bath. AE, DC, MC, V. Closed Mon. and Jan.*

Rambouillet

Trains leave hourly from Versailles–Chantiers and take 35 minutes to reach Rambouillet. Tourist office: 8 pl. de la Libération, tel. 34–83–21–21.

Surrounded by a huge (34,000 acres) forest, **Rambouillet** is a haughty town once favored by kings and dukes. Today it is home to affluent gentry and, occasionally, the French president. When the president is not entertaining visiting bigwigs, the château and its grounds are open to all.

Make for the **Hôtel de Ville,** an imposing Classical building in red brick, and wander around the corner to the **château.** Most of the buildings you see date from the early 18th century, but the **Tour François I,** a muscular tower named after the king who breathed his last therein in 1547, once belonged to a 14th-century castle. *Admission: grounds free; château (guided tours only), 28 frs adults, 17 frs senior citizens and children. Open Wed.–Mon. 10–11:30 and 2–4:30 (until 5:30 Apr.–Sept.).*

If your appetite for château interiors has already been satisfied, you'll be able to forego Rambouillet's without feeling too guilty. The château's exterior charms are hidden as you arrive, but if you head to the left of the buildings—and if nature is in bloom—you are in for two pleasant surprises. A splendid lake, with several enticing islands, spreads out before you, beckoning you to explore the extensive grounds beyond. Before you do, however, turn around: There, behind you, across trim flower beds awash with color, is the facade of the château—a sight of unanticipated serenity, asymmetry, and, as more flowers spill from its balconies, cheerful informality.

If time allows, veer left around the lake and carry on until you reach two interesting groups of outbuildings: the **Laiterie de la Reine** (built as a dairy for Marie-Antoinette), with its small temple, grotto, and shell-lined **Chaumière des Coquillages** (Shell Pavilion); and the **Bergerie Nationale** (National Sheepfold), site of a more serious agricultural venture; the merino sheep reared here, prized for the quality and yield of their wool, are descendants of beasts imported from Spain by Louis XVI in 1786. *Admission: 15 frs (Laiterie), 22 frs (Bergerie). Laiterie open Wed.–Mon. 10–11:30 and 2–4:30 (until 4 in winter). The Bergerie can be visited Fri.–Sun. 2–6 (Oct.–June, Sun. only 2–5).*

Dining **La Poste.** You can bank on traditional, unpretentious cooking at this
¢ former coaching inn right in the center of town. Service is good, as is the selection of fixed-price menus, weekends included. *101 rue du Général-de-Gaulle, tel. 34–83–03–01. Reservations advised. Jacket and tie. AE, MC, V.*

Maintenon

Trains run from Versailles–Chantiers, via Rambouillet, to Mainte-non every 1¼ hours; journey time is 40 minutes from Versailles and about 15 minutes from Rambouillet. Tourist Office: 2 pl. Aristide-Briand, tel. 37–23–05–04.

The Renaissance **château** of Maintenon once belonged to Louis XIV's mistress (and future morganatic spouse) Madame de Mainte-non, whose private apartments form the hub of the short interior visit. A round brick tower (16th century) and a 12th-century keep are all that remain of the buildings on the site. The formal gardens ease their way back from the château to the unlikely ivy-covered arches of a ruined aqueduct, one of the Sun King's most outrageous projects. His aim: to provide the ornamental lakes in the gardens of Versailles (some 30 miles away) with water from the River Eure. In 1684, 30,000 men were signed up to construct a three-tiered, 3-mile aqueduct as part of the project. Many died of fever in the process, and construction was called off in 1689. *Admission: 28 frs adults, 22 frs students and senior citizens. Open Apr.–Oct., Wed.–Sat. 2–6, Sun. 10–noon and 2–6; Nov.–Mar., Sat. 2:30–6, Sun. 10–noon and 2:30–6.*

Chartres

Trains run from Versailles to Chartres, via Maintenon, every 1½ hours. Journey time is 55 minutes from Versailles and 18 minutes from Maintenon, which is 19 km (12 mi) away. Chartres tourist of-fice: place de la Cathédrale, tel. 37–21–50–00.

★ As you snake along the River Eure from Maintenon, try to spot the noble, soaring spires of **Chartres Cathedral** before you reach the town; they form one of the most famous sights in Western Europe.

Worship on the site of the cathedral goes back to before the Gallo-Roman period; the crypt contains a well that was the focus of Druid ceremonies. In the late 9th century, Charles II (known as the Bald) presented Chartres with what was believed to be the tunic of the Virgin, a precious relic that attracted hordes of pilgrims. Chartres swiftly became a prime destination for the Christian faithful; pil-grims trek here from Paris to this day.

Today's cathedral dates primarily from the 12th and 13th centuries, having been built after the previous, 11th-century edifice burned down in 1194. A well-chronicled outburst of religious fervor followed the discovery that the Virgin's relic had miraculously survived unsinged, and reconstruction moved ahead at a breathtaking pace: Just 25 years were needed for the cathedral to rise from the rubble.

The lower half of the facade is a survivor of the earlier Romanesque church: This can be seen most clearly in the use of round arches rath-er than the pointed Gothic type. The main door (**Portail Royal**) is richly sculpted with scenes from the Life of Christ, and the flanking towers are also Romanesque. The taller of the two spires (380 feet versus 350 feet) dates from the start of the 16th century; its fanciful

Flamboyant intricacy contrasts sharply with the stumpy solemnity of its Romanesque counterpart across the way.

The **rose window** above the main portal dates from the 13th century, and the three windows below it contain some of the finest examples of 12th-century stained glass in France.

The interior is somber, and your eyes will need time to adjust to the dimness. The reward: the gemlike richness of the stained glass, with the famous deep "Chartres blue" predominating. The oldest window is arguably the most beautiful: **Notre-Dame de la Belle Verrière**, in the south choir. The cathedral's windows are gradually being cleaned—a lengthy, painstaking program—and the contrast with those still covered in the grime of centuries is staggering. *Pl. Notre-Dame.*

Just behind the cathedral stands the **Musée des Beaux-Arts,** a handsome 18th-century building that used to be the Bishop's Palace. Its varied collection includes Renaissance enamels; a portrait of the Dutch scholar Erasmus by German painter Hans Holbein; tapestries; armor; and some fine paintings, mainly French, dating from the 17th to the 19th centuries. There is also an entire room devoted to the forceful 20th-century land- and snowscapes of Maurice de Vlaminck, who lived in the region. *29 rue Cloître Notre-Dame. Admission: 10 frs adults (20 frs for special exhibitions), 5 frs students and senior citizens. Open Nov.–Mar., Wed.–Mon. 10–noon and 2–5; Apr.–Oct. 10–6.*

The **museum gardens** overlook the old streets that tumble down to the River Eure. Take rue Chantault down to the river, cross over, and head right along rue de la Tannerie (which, in turn, becomes rue de la Foulerie) as far as rue du Pont St-Hilaire. From here, there is a picturesque view of the roofs of old Chartres nestling beneath the cathedral. Cross over the bridge and head up to the Gothic **Eglise St-Pierre,** whose magnificent windows date to the early 14th century. There is more stained glass (17th century) to admire at the **Eglise St-Aignan** nearby, just off rue St-Pierre. Wander at will among the steep, narrow surrounding streets, using the spires of the cathedral as your guiding landmark.

Lodging **La Poste.** Prices in downtown Chartres tend to reflect the town's appeal to tourists and affluent commuters working in Paris. The Hôtel de la Poste, five minutes' walk from both station and cathedral, is a notable exception. Rooms are comfortable if a little small, and the restaurant offers a choice of set menus. *3 rue du Général-Koenig, 28000, tel. 37–21–04–27, fax 37–36–42–17. 59 rooms, some with shower. Facilities: restaurant, satellite TV. AE, DC, MC, V.*
¢
★

Dining **Le Buisson Ardent.** A wood-beamed, second-floor restaurant, Le Buisson Ardent offers robust, low-priced menus, imaginative food, and a view of Chartres Cathedral (it's just down the street opposite the south portal). Service is gratifyingly attentive. Try the fruity Gamay de Touraine, an ideal wine for lunchtime. *10 rue au Lait, tel. 37–34–04–66. Reservations advised. MC, V. Closed Sun. eve.*
$
★

Shopping Stained glass being the key to Chartres's fame, enthusiasts may want to visit the **Galerie du Vitrail** (17 rue Cloître Notre-Dame), which specializes in the noble art. Pieces range from small plaques to entire windows, and there are books on the subject in English and in French.

Tour 2: Fontainebleau and Environs

Elegant Fontainebleau, home to the finest château in the Ile-de-France after Versailles, is the home base for a short tour that also takes in pretty Moret-sur-Loing (a short train ride away), Barbizon, and Vaux-le-Vicomte.

From Paris
By Train

You can reach Fontainebleau in about 40 minutes by train from Paris's Gare de Lyon (trains leave every 1¼ hours). Disembark in Fontainebleau-Avon, then catch the half-hourly bus at the station for the 1½-mile trip to the château. The bus will let you off near its gardens.

By Car

The 64-kilometer (40-mile) drive from Paris along A6 and N7 takes about an hour.

Fontainebleau

Tourist office: 31 pl. Napoléon-Bonaparte, behind the château, tel. 64–22–25–68.

Numbers in the margin correspond with points of interest on the Fontainebleau map.

★ Like Chambord in the Loire Valley or Compiègne to the north, **Fontainebleau** earned royal esteem as a hunting base. Today's **château** was begun under the flamboyant Renaissance prince François I, the French contemporary of England's Henry VIII. François hired Italian artists Il Rosso (a pupil of Michelangelo) and Francesco Primaticcio, the court architect, to embellish his palace. In fact, they did much more: by introducing the pagan allegories and elegant lines of Mannerism to France, they revolutionized French decorative art. Their extraordinary frescoes and stuccowork can be admired in the **Galerie François I** and the glorious Salle de Bal *(see below)*, completed under Henri II, François's successor.

Although Sun King Louis XIV's architectural energies were concentrated on Versailles, he nonetheless commissioned André Le Nôtre to replant the gardens at Fontainebleau, where he and his court returned faithfully each autumn for the hunting season. But it was Napoléon who spent lavishly to make a Versailles, as it were, out of Fontainebleau. Indeed, the château's collection of Empire furniture is the finest anywhere.

When you get off the bus, walk past the Parterre east of the Etang des Carpes (Carp Pond), and turn left into an alley that leads to the
❶ **Cour Ovale**—a courtyard shaped like a flattened oval with, at the
❷ straight end, the domed **Porte du Baptistère.** The gateway's name commemorates the fact that the Dauphin—the heir to the throne, later to become Louis XIII—was baptized under its arch in 1606.
❸ Opposite is the **Cour des Offices,** a large, severe square built at the same time (1609) as the place des Vosges in Paris.

The hedge-lined alley continues to the Jardin de Diane (Garden of Diana), with its peacocks and statue of the hunting goddess surrounded by mournful hounds. Cross this informal garden and enter
❹ the palace's most majestic courtyard, the **Cour du Cheval-Blanc,** or
❺ Cour des Adieux, dominated by the famous **horseshoe staircase** built by Jean Androuet du Cerceau in the early 17th century, and where Napoléon bade his troops farewell. Climb the steps to the château entrance.

❻ In **Napoléon's apartments** on the second floor is a lock of his hair, his Légion d'Honneur medal, his imperial uniform, the hat he wore on his return from Elba in 1815, and the bed in which he used to sleep.

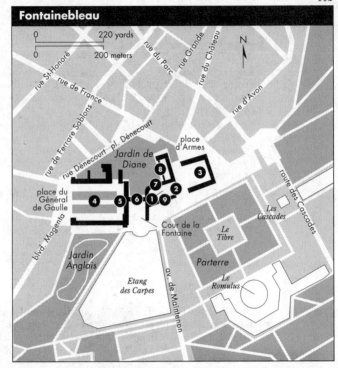

❼ There is also a **throne room**—Napoléon spurned the one at Versailles, a palace he disliked, and established his imperial seat here in the former King's Bedchamber, a room with a suitably majestic decor—and the **Queen's Bedroom,** known as the Room of the Six
❽ Maries. The sweeping **Galerie de Diane,** built during the reign of Henri IV (1589–1610), was converted to a library in the 1860s. Other salons boast 17th-century tapestries, marble reliefs by Jacquet de Grenoble, and paintings and frescoes by Primaticcio, Niccolò dell'Abbate, and other artists of the Fontainebleau School.

The jewel of the interior, though, is the ceremonial ballroom—the
❾ **Salle de Bal**—nearly 100 feet long, with wood paneling, 16th-century frescoes and gilding, and what is reputedly the first coffered ceiling in France. Its intricate pattern is echoed by the splendid 19th-century parquet floor. *Pl. du Général-de-Gaulle, tel. 60–71–50–70. Admission: 31 frs adults, 20 frs students and senior citizens. Open Wed.–Mon. 9:30–12:30 and 2–5; closed holidays.*

If time permits, complete your visit with a stroll around the leafy **Jardin Anglais** (English Garden) west of the Etang des Carpes. Gardens open 9–dusk; admission free.

Lodging **Hôtel de Londres.** The balconies of this tranquil, family-style hotel
$ overlook the château and the Cour des Adieux, where Napoléon bade his troops an emotional farewell; the austere 19th-century facade is a registered landmark. Inside, the decor is dominated by Louis XV gilt furniture. *1 pl. du Général-de-Gaulle, 77300, tel. 64–22–20–21, fax 60–72–39–16. 22 rooms with bath. Facilities: tearoom, bar, parking. AE, DC, MC, V. Closed Dec. 20–Jan. 5.*

Dining **La Route du Beaujolais.** The food is cheap and the atmosphere cheer-
$ ful at this jolly eatery near the château, where Lyonnais-style cold cuts and pots of Beaujolais are the mainstays. For something a little more upscale, try the beef filet with Brie or the braised veal kidney.

Set meals are priced at 88 and 130 frs. *3 rue Montebello, tel. 64–22–27–98. Reservations advised. AE, DC, MC, V.*

Barbizon

Buses travel the 10 km (6 mi) to Barbizon from Fontainebleau 3 times daily. The trip takes 30 minutes. Tourist office: 55 rue Grande, tel. 60–66–41–87.

Barbizon, on the western edge of the 62,000-acre Forest of Fontaine-bleau, retains the atmosphere of a small village, despite the intrusion of expensive art galleries, tacky souvenir shops, and weekending Parisians.

Barbizon owes its renown to the colony of landscape painters—Camille Corot, Jean-François Millet, and Théodore Rousseau, among others—who lived here from the 1830s on. Their innovative commitment to working outdoors paved the way for the Impressionists, as did their willingness to accept nature on its own terms rather than use it as an idealized base for carefully structured compositions.

After working hours, the Barbizon painters repaired to the **Auberge du Père Ganne.** The inn is still standing—now indefinitely closed for restoration—but you can soak up the arty mood at the houses of Millet and Rousseau farther along the single main street (rue Grande), or admire some of their work at the **Ecole de Barbizon** museum. *55 rue Grande. Admission 15 frs. Open Wed.–Mon. 10–12:30 and 2–5.*

Lodging **Auberge des Alouettes.** This delightful, family-run 19th-century inn
¢ is set on two acres of grounds (which the better rooms overlook). The interior has been redecorated in '30s style, but many rooms still have their original oak beams. The popular restaurant (reservations are essential), with its large open terrace, features light cuisine (succinct sauces) and barbecued beef in summer. *4 rue Antoine-Barye, 77630, tel. 60–66–41–98, fax 60–66–20–69. 23 rooms with bath. Jacket and tie required in restaurant. (Restaurant closed Sun. eve. in winter.) Facilities: tennis. AE, DC, MC, V.*

Dining **Le Relais de Barbizon.** Delicious country-French specialties are
$ served here in large portions, and there is a good choice of fixed-price menus. The restaurant is spacious, with a big open fire, and paintings and hunting trophies decorate the walls. The owner is rightly proud of the large terrace, where diners can eat in the shade of lime and chestnut trees. *2 av. Charles-de-Gaulle, tel. 60–66–40–28. Reservations required weekends. MC, V. Closed Tues., Wed., second half Aug., most of Jan.*

Vaux-le-Vicomte

To reach Vaux-le-Vicomte you will need a bike or taxi for the trip from Melun station, 8 km (5 mi) away. Trains make the 13-minute trip from Fontainebleau to Melun every 1½ hours.

★ The **château of Vaux-le-Vicomte,** a masterpiece of 17th-century architecture and design, was built between 1656 and 1661 for finance minister Nicolas Fouquet. The construction process was monstrous even for those days: Entire villages were razed, 18,000 workmen called in, and architect Louis Le Vau, painter Charles Le Brun, and esteemed landscape designer André Le Nôtre hired to prove that Fouquet's supremely refined tastes matched his business acumen. Unfortunately, his house-warming party was too lavish for the likings of star guest Louis XIV. In a fit of jealousy, King Louis hurled the tactless Fouquet in jail (where he died penniless 19 years later), and promptly set Le Vau, Le Brun, and Le Nôtre to work building Versailles.

The high-roofed château, partially surrounded by a moat, is set well back from the roadside behind iron railings topped with sculpted heads. A cobbled avenue stretches up to the entrance. Stone steps lead to the entrance hall, which, given the noble scale of the exterior, seems small. There is no grand staircase, either—the stairs are tucked away in the left wing and lead to the private apartments— rooms designed on an intimate scale for daily living.

Painter Charles Le Brun's lush interior decoration captivates the eye: A major achievement is the ceiling of the **Chambre du Roi** (King's Bedchamber), depicting *Time Bearing Truth Heavenwards*, framed by stucco work by sculptors François Girardon and Legendre. Along the frieze you can make out small squirrels—known as *fouquets* in local dialect. But the masterwork is surely the ceiling of the **Salon des Muses,** a brilliant allegorical composition painted in glowing, sensuous colors, which surpasses anything Le Brun did at Versailles.

Impressive, too, is the **Grand Salon** on the ground floor. With its unusual oval form and 16 caryatid pillars symbolizing the months and seasons, it possesses harmony and style despite its unfinished state. In fact, the lack of decoration only emphasizes Le Vau's architectural genius.

An exhibit, complete with life-size wax figures, explains the rise and fall of Nicolas Fouquet. The version is, not surprisingly, favorable to the château's founder—accused by Louis XIV and subsequent historians of megalomania and shady financial dealings, but apparently condemned on little evidence by a court eager to please the jealous, irascible monarch. The exhibit continues in the basement, whose cool, dim rooms were used to store food and wine and house the château's staff. The **kitchens** are also down here, a more cheerful sight, with their gleaming copperware and old menus.

Although the château's interior is in some respects incomplete, there is no mistaking the grandeur of Le Nôtre's **gardens,** which have been carefully restored. Visit the **Musée des Equipages** (Carriage Museum) in the stables and inspect a host of lovingly restored carriages and coaches. *Tel. 60–66–97–09. Admission: 50 frs adults, 40 frs students and senior citizens (gardens only, 28 frs). Open daily Apr.–Oct. 10–6 (11–5 in winter); closed Dec.–mid-Feb. (except Christmas–New Year's). Candlelight visits May–Oct., Sat. 8:30–11 PM; admission: 68 frs adults, 54 frs students and senior citizens.*

To the right of the château entrance is an imposing barn that has been transformed into a self-serve **cafeteria.** Here, beneath the ancient rafters of a stout wood-beam roof, you can enjoy coffee, cheap pitchers of wine, and good steaks. Insist on *bien cuit* (well done) if you don't want your meat too bloodily rare.

Moret-sur-Loing

Trains make the 8-minute journey from Fontainebleau, 10 km (6 mi) away, every 1¼ hours. Tourist office: place de Samois, tel. 60– 70–41–66.

Close to the confluence of the Rivers Seine and Yonne, the charming village of **Moret-sur-Loing** was immortalized by Impressionist painter Alfred Sisley, who lived here for 20 years at 19 rue Montmartre (not open to the public), around the corner from the church of Notre-Dame. Close by, across the river, is the thatched **house-museum** of another illustrious former inhabitant: truculent World War I leader Georges Clemenceau (1841–1929), known as the Tiger. His taste for Oriental art and his friendship with Impressionist Claude Monet are evoked. *Follow signs to La Grange-Batelière. Tel. 60–70–51–21. Guided tours only: 35 frs. Open Easter–mid-Nov., weekends 3–6.*

The best view of Moret is from the far banks of the Loing. Cross the narrow bridge (one of the oldest in France and invariably clogged with traffic) to gaze back at the walls, rooftops, and church tower. A good time to visit Moret is on a Saturday evening in summer, when locals stage *son-et-lumière* (sound-and-light) pageants illustrating the town's history.

Tour 3: Excursions from Paris

This is not so much a tour as a series of excursions from Paris. A train trip to Vernon brings you within striking distance of Claude Monet's house and garden at Giverny, although a bike or taxi ride is required to complete the trip. Suburban trains whisk you to the painters' village of Auvers-sur-Oise and the superb châteaus of Maisons-Laffitte and St-Germain-en-Laye, and a combination of RER and bus brings you to the Malmaison home of Josephine and Napoléon. The RER also takes you east to the doors of Disneyland Paris.

Vernon and Giverny

Trains leave Paris (Gare St-Lazare) every 2 hours for the 50-minute ride to Vernon. You will need a bike or a taxi, both of which are available for hire at the station, to complete the journey to Giverny. Vernon tourist office: 36 rue Carnot, tel. 32–51–39–60.

The village of **Giverny**, a place of pilgrimage for art lovers, was where Claude Monet lived from 1883 until his death in 1926 at age 86. After decades of neglect, his pretty pink-washed house, with its green shutters, studios, and, above all, the wonderful garden with its famous lily pond, have been lovingly restored.

Monet was brought up in Normandy, in northwestern France, and, like many of the Impressionists, was stimulated by the soft light of the Seine Valley. After several years at Argenteuil, just north of Paris, he moved downriver to Giverny in 1883, along with his two sons, mistress Alice Hoschedé (whom he later married), and her own six children. By 1890, a prospering Monet was able to buy the house outright; three years later, he purchased another plot of land across the road to continue his gardening experiments, diverting the little River Epte to make a pond.

Soon the much-loved and oft-painted waterlilies and Japanese bridges were special features of Monet's garden. They readily conjure up the image of the grizzle-bearded brushman dabbing cheerfully at his canvas—pioneering a breakup of form that was to have a major impact on 20th-century art.

Provided you steer clear of the tourist battalions that tramp through Giverny on weekends and hot summer days, Monet's house—which you enter from the modest country lane that masquerades as Giverny's major thoroughfare—feels refreshingly like a family home after the formal French châteaus. The rooms have been restored to Monet's original designs: the kitchen with its blue tiles, the buttercup-yellow dining room, Monet's bedroom containing his bed and desk. Walls are lined with the Japanese prints Monet avidly collected, as well as with reproductions of his works.

★ The exuberant **garden** breaks totally with French tradition, with flowers spilling over the paths. You can reach the enchanting **water garden,** with its lilies, bridges, mighty willow, and rhododendrons, via an attractively decorated tunnel. *84 rue Claude-Monet, tel. 32–51–28–21. Admission: 35 frs (garden only, 25 frs). Open Apr.–Oct., Tues.–Sun. 10–noon and 2–6 (garden open 10–6).*

Close by is the **Musée Américain,** opened in 1993 and endowed by Chicago art patrons Daniel and Judith Terra. On view are works by American Impressionists who were influenced by Claude Monet. *99 rue Claude-Monet, tel. 32–51–94–65. Admission: 32 frs adults, 21 frs children, students, and senior citizens. Open Apr.–Oct., Tues.– Sun. 10–6.*

Most people visit **Vernon** simply because it's en route to Giverny. However, there are several reasons to stop by when you're in the area, quite apart from its pleasant riverside location on the Seine. There are medieval timber-frame houses; the best of these has been chosen by local authorities to house the Tourist Office, on rue Carnot. Alongside is the arresting rose-windowed facade of **Notre-Dame** church. The facade, like the high nave, dates from the 15th century, but the rounded Romanesque arches in the choir attest to the building's 12th-century origins. The church is a fine sight when viewed from behind—Claude Monet painted it several times from across the Seine.

A few minor Monet canvases, along with other late-19th-century paintings, can be admired in the **Musée Poulain** (Town Museum) at the other end of rue Carnot. This rambling old mansion is seldom crowded, and the helpful curators are happy to explain local history to visitors who are intrigued by the town's English-sounding name. *Rue du Pont, tel. 32–21–28–09. Admission: 15 frs. Open Tues.– Sun. 2–6.*

Maisons-Laffitte

Two trains per hour make the 21-minute trip from Paris (Gare St-Lazare) to Maisons-Laffitte. Tourist office: 48 av. Longueil, tel. 39–62–63–64.

The early Baroque **château of Maisons,** constructed by architect François Mansart from 1642 to 1651, is one of the least-known châteaus in the Ile-de-France. This was not always the case: Sun King Louis XIV came to the housewarming party, and Louis XV (reigned 1715–74), Louis XVI (Marie-Antoinette's husband, reigned 1774–93), Voltaire, and Napoléon all stayed here. The interior clearly met their exacting standards, thanks to the well-proportioned entrance vestibule with its rich sculpture; the winding **Escalier d'Honneur,** a majestic staircase adorned with paintings and statues; and the royal apartments, above, with their parquet floors and elegant wall paneling. *Admission: 27 frs adults, 18 frs students and senior citizens. Open daily 10–6.*

Auvers-sur-Oise

Two trains leave Paris (Gare du Nord) every hour for Auvers; a change in Pontoise is usually necessary, and journey time can vary from 60 to 90 minutes. Tourist office: rue de la Sansonne (opposite the Maison de Van Gogh), tel. 30–36–10–06.

Paul Cézanne, Camille Pissarro, Honoré Daumier, Jean-Baptiste-Camille Corot, Charles-François Daubigny, and Berthe Morisot all painted in **Auvers-sur-Oise** in the 19th century, but it is Vincent van Gogh's memory that haunts every nook and cranny of this pretty riverside **village.** After years of indifference and neglect, his last abode has been turned into a shrine, and the whole village is peppered with plaques enabling you to compare his final works with the scenes as they are today. Little has changed since the summer of 1890, when van Gogh painted no fewer than 70 pictures during the last ten weeks of his life in Auvers before shooting himself behind the village château. He is buried next to his brother Theo in a simple, ivy-covered grave in the village cemetery. You can also visit the medieval village church, subject of one of van Gogh's most famous paintings,

L'Eglise à Auvers, and admire Osip Zadkine's powerful modern statue of him in the village park.

★ Turn left from the train station and walk 600 yards to the Auberge Ravoux, the inn where van Gogh lodged, opened to the public in 1993 after painstaking restoration as the **Maison de Van Gogh.** A dingy staircase leads up to the tiny, spartan, wood-floored attic where van Gogh stored some of modern art's most famous pictures under the bed in which he died. A short film retraces van Gogh's time at Auvers, and there is a well-stocked souvenir shop. *8 rue de la Sansonne. Admission: 25 frs adults, 15 frs students and senior citizens. Open daily 10–6.*

The landscapist Charles-François Daubigny, a precursor of Impressionism, lived in Auvers from 1861 until his death in 1878. The **Musée Daubigny,** upstairs from the Tourist Office and across the lane from the Maison de Van Gogh, contains drawings, lithographs, and oils by Daubigny and other local 19th-century artists. *Manoir des Colombières, rue de la Sansonne, tel. 30–36–80–20. Admission 15 frs adults, 10 frs students and senior citizens. Open Tues.–Wed. and Fri.–Sun. 2:30–6:00 (until 5:30 in winter).*

Daubigny's studio, the **Atelier Daubigny,** has a remarkable array of mural and roof paintings by Daubigny and fellow artists Camille Corot and Honoré Daumier. *61 rue Daubigny. Admission: 20 frs. Open Easter–Oct., Tues.–Sun. 2–6:30.*

The elegant 17th-century village **château,** set above split-level gardens, opened in 1994 as home to a *Voyage au Temps des Impressionistes.* Each visitor receives a set of infrared headphones (English available), with commentary that reacts to your progress through various tableaus of Belle Epoque life. Although there are no Impressionist originals—500 reproductions pop up on screen—this is an imaginative, enjoyable, and innovative museum. Some of the special effects—talking mirrors, computerized cabaret dancers, a train ride past Impressionist landscapes—are worthy of Disney. *Rue de Léry, tel. 34–48–48–48. Admission: 50 frs adults, 40 frs senior citizens, 35 frs students, 100 frs family. Open May–Oct., daily 10–8; Nov.–Apr., Tues.–Sun. 10–5.*

Before it was banned in 1915 because of its effects on the nervous system, absinthe—a forerunner of today's anise-based aperitifs like Ricard and Pernod—was France's national drink. A famous painting by Edgar Degas shows two absinthe drinkers, and van Gogh probably downed a few glasses at the Auberge Ravoux. The small **Musée de l'Absinthe,** near the château, contains publicity posters and other Belle Epoque artifacts, such as the special spoons used to add sugar to absinthe. *44 rue Callé, tel. 30–36–83–26. Admission: 25 frs adults, 20 frs students and senior citizens. Open Apr.–May and Oct., weekends 11–6; June–Sept., Wed.–Sun. 11–6.*

Dining **Auberge Ravoux.** The inn where van Gogh used to take his meals is
$ the obvious choice for lunch here. The 140-franc, three-course menu has a small choice of fish and meat dishes, and changes regularly; there is also a reasonable wine list. But it is the setting, and the history, that make eating here special: The glasswork, lace curtains, and wall decor have been carefully modelled on the designs that van Gogh would have known. *52 rue Général-de-Gaulle, tel. 34–48–05–47. Reservations essential. AE, DC, MC, V. Closed Sat. lunch, Wed., and part of Feb.*

Rueil-Malmaison

Take the RER-A from Paris to La Défense, then switch to bus 158-A.

Rueil-Malmaison is today a faceless, if pleasant, western suburb of Paris, but the memory of star-crossed lovers Napoléon and Josephine still haunts its château on avenue Napoléon-Bonaparte.

Built in 1622, **La Malmaison** was bought by the future Empress Joséphine in 1799 as a love nest for Napoléon and herself (they had married three years earlier). After the childless Josephine was divorced by the heir-hungry emperor in 1809, she retired to La Malmaison and died here on May 29, 1814.

The château has 24 rooms furnished with exquisite tables, chairs, and sofas of the Napoleonic period; of special note are the library, game room, and dining room. The walls are adorned with works by artists of the day, such as Jacques-Louis David, Pierre-Paul Prud'hon, and Baron Gérard. Take time to admire the clothes and hats belonging to Napoléon and Joséphine, particularly the display of the empress's gowns. Their carriage can be seen in one of the garden pavilions, and another pavilion contains a unique collection of snuff-boxes donated by Prince George of Greece. The gardens themselves are delightful, especially the regimented rows of spring tulips. *15 av. du Château. Admission (joint ticket with Bois Préau): 27 frs adults, 18 frs students, senior citizens, and on Sun. Open Wed.- Mon. 10–noon and 1:30–5.*

The **Bois Préau,** which stands close to La Malmaison, is a smaller mansion dating back to the 17th century. It was acquired by Joséphine in 1810, after her divorce, but subsequently reconstructed in the 1850s. Today its 10 rooms, complete with furniture and objects from the Empire period, are devoted mainly to souvenirs of Napoléon's exile on the island of St. Helena. *Entrance from av. de l'Impératrice. Admission (Bois Préau only): 12 frs. Open Wed.- Mon. 10:30–12:30 and 2–5:30.*

St-Germain-en-Laye

The RER-A makes the 30-minute journey from central Paris every 15 minutes. Tourist office: 38 rue au Pain, tel. 34–51–05–12.

The elegant town of **St-Germain-en-Laye,** perched on a hill above the Seine and encircled by forest, has lost little of its original cachet, despite the invasion of wealthy Parisians who commute to work on the RER. Next to the train station, at the heart of St-Germain, is the town's chief attraction—its stone-and-brick **château.**

Most of the impressive château, with its (dry) moat and intimidating circular towers, dates from the 16th and 17th centuries. Yet a royal palace has existed here since the early 12th century, when Louis VI—known as *Le Gros* (The Fat)—exploited St-Germain's defensive potential in his bid to pacify the Ile-de-France. A hundred years later, Louis IX (St. Louis) added the elegant **Sainte-Chapelle,** which is the château's oldest remaining section. The figures on the tympanum (the triangular area inset over the main door) are believed to be the first known representations of French royalty, portraying Louis with his mother, Blanche de Castille, and other members of his family.

Charles V (reigned 1364–80) built a powerful defensive keep in the mid-14th century, but from the 1540s, François I and his successors transformed St-Germain into a palace of more domestic, and less warlike, vocation. Louis XIV was born here, and it was here that his father, Louis XIII, died. Until 1682—when the court moved to Versailles—it remained the country's foremost royal residence outside Paris. Since 1867, the château has housed a major **Musée des Antiquités Nationales** (Museum of Ancient History), holding a trove of artifacts, figurines, brooches, and weapons from the Stone Age through to the 8th century. *Admission: 20 frs (13 frs on Sun.). Open Wed.–Mon. 9–5:15.*

Another place to visit in St-Germain is the quaint **Musée du Prieuré** (Priory Museum), some 600 yards from the château (follow rue au Pain from the church). This museum is devoted to the work of the artist Maurice Denis (1870–1943) and his fellow symbolists and Nabis—painters opposed to the naturalism of their 19th-century Impressionist contemporaries. Denis found the calm of the former Jesuit priory suited to his spiritual themes, which he expressed in stained glass, ceramics, and frescoes, as well as oils. *2 bis rue Maurice-Denis. Admission: 25 frs adults, 15 frs children and senior citizens. Open Wed.–Fri. 10–5:30, weekends 10–6:30.*

Dining **La Petite Auberge.** The specialty here is farmhouse-style cooking
$ from the Aveyron region of southwest France. Aged beef is cooked over an open fire throughout the year, and cheerful red wine (Chinon, from the Loire Valley) is drawn straight from the barrel. Game is served in season. *119-bis rue Léon-Desnoyer, tel. 34–51–03–99. Reservations accepted. Jacket required. MC, V. Closed Sat. lunch, Wed., and second half of Aug.*

¢   **La Feuillantine.** Friendly service and an imaginative, well-priced set menu have made this restaurant a success with locals as well as tourists. Gizzard salad, salmon with endive, and herbed chicken are among the specialties. *10 rue des Louviers, tel. 34–51–04–24. Reservations advised. MC, V. Closed Christmas.*

Disneyland Paris

The RER-A makes the 40-minute journey from central Paris 3 times an hour (more often at peak periods) to Marne-la-Vallée-Chessy; the station is just 100 yards from the theme park entrance. Tourist information: Festival Disney, tel. 64–74–30–00.

Now you can get a dose of American pop culture in between visits to the Louvre and the Left Bank. On April 12, 1992, the Euro Disney (as it was originally called) complex opened in **Marne-la-Vallée,** just 32 kilometers (20 miles) east of Paris. The complex is divided into several areas, including the pay-as-you-enter theme park that is the main reason for coming here. Occupying 136 acres, the theme park is less than half a mile across and ringed by a railroad with whistling steam engines. Smack in the middle of the park is the soaring Sleeping Beauty Castle, which is surrounded by a plaza from which you can enter the four "lands" of Disney: Frontierland, Adventureland, Fantasyland, and Discoveryland. In addition, Main Street U.S.A. connects the castle to Disneyland's entrance, under the pink gabled roofs of the Disneyland Hotel. In June 1995, Disneyland Paris inaugurated its newest attraction, **Space Mountain,** aiming to catapult riders through the Milky Way. *Admission varies by season: 150 frs–195 frs adults, 120 frs–150 frs children under 12. Open Apr.–mid-June, weekdays 9–7, weekends 9–midnight; mid-June–Aug., daily 9–midnight; Sept.–Oct., weekdays 9–7, weekends 9–9; Nov.–Mar., weekdays 10–6, weekends 10–9.*

There are six hotels in the 4,800-acre Disneyland complex, just outside the theme park. The resort also comprises parking lots, a train station, and the Festival Disney entertainment center, with restaurants, a theater, dance clubs, shops, a post office, and a tourist office. Cheaper accommodations—log cabins and campsites—are available at Camp Davy Crockett, but it is located farther away from the theme park.

Future plans at Disneyland call for a second theme park, a convention center, a new golf course, a new campsite, more hotels, and film studios.

Dining Disneyland Paris is peppered with places to eat, ranging from snack
¢–$ carts and fast-food counters to full-service restaurants—all with a distinguishing theme. In addition, all Disney hotels have restau-

rants that are open to the public. But as these are outside the theme park, it is not recommended that you waste time traveling to them for lunch. Be aware that only the hotel, Festival Disney, and the five sit-down theme-park restaurants serve alcoholic beverages; Disney's no-alcohol standard is maintained throughout the rest of the theme park. Eateries serve nonstop as long as the park is open. *Sit-down restaurants: tel. 60–45–65–40; reservations advised. AE, DC, MC, V. Counter-service restaurants: no reservations, no credit cards.*

4 The Loire Valley

Few areas of Europe possess the magic of the Loire Valley, renowned for its constellation of enticing châteaus spanning an architectural range between medieval fortress (Langeais, Angers) and Renaissance pleasure palace (Chenonceau, Cheverny). The whole area exudes a sedate charm barely dispelled by the hordes of midsummer tourists. Woods, vineyards, and venerable towns of white stone line the softly lit valley, once the playground of kings and princes. Although trains speed between the valley's major towns, it takes a chugalong country bus—or a bike—to track down the more secluded sites, such as Ussé, with its fairy-tale turrets, or Chambord, lurking in the heart of a forbidding forest infested with timid deer and ferocious boar.

The Loire Valley was hotly disputed by France and England during the Middle Ages, belonging to England under the Anjou Plantagenet family between 1154 and 1216 and again during the Hundred Years' War (1337–1453). It took the example of Joan of Arc, called the "Maid of Orléans" after the scene of her most rousing military successes, for the French finally to expel the English.

In addition to its abundant châteaus, the Loire Valley offers visitors a host of opportunities for outdoor recreation. Horseback riding, fishing, canoeing, and swimming facilities abound. In the summer, tourists and natives alike flock to concerts, music festivals, fairs, and the celebrated *son-et-lumière* (sound-and-light) extravaganzas held on the grounds of many châteaus. Simply wandering the banks of the placid river and exploring her gentle hills, dotted with woods and castles, provides a welcome break for tired city dwellers.

Loire Valley Basics

Budget
Lodging Even before the age of the train, the Loire Valley drew visitors from far and wide, eager to see the great châteaus and sample the sweet-

ness of rural life. Hundreds of hotels of all kinds have sprung up to accommodate today's travelers. Three smaller groups, the **Château-Accueil, La Castellerie,** and **Bienvenue au Château,** offer pleasant accommodations for a limited number of guests. Illustrated lists of these groups are available from French Government Tourist Offices abroad and in France. At the lower end of the price scale are the **Logis de France** hotels, small, traditional hotels in towns and villages throughout the region that usually offer terrific value for the money. The Logis de France handbook is available free from French Tourist Offices abroad and for 70 francs in French bookshops, or it can be ordered directly from Logis de France Services (83 av. d'Italie, Paris 75013, tel. 45–84–83–84). The Loire Valley is one of the country's most popular vacation destinations, so always make reservations well in advance.

Budget Dining The region known as the "garden of France" produces a cornucopia of farm-fresh products—from beef, poultry, game, and fish to butter, cream, wine, fruit, and vegetables. It sends its early crops to the best Parisian tables, yet keeps more than enough for local use. Loire wines can be extremely good—and varied. Among the best: Savennières and Cheverny (dry white); Coteaux-du-Layon (sweet white); Cabernet d'Anjou (rosé); Bourgueil and Chinon (red); and Vouvray (sparkling white).

Bargain Shopping The region's extraspecial produce is Loire wine. It's not a practical buy for tourists—except for instant consumption—but if wine-tasting tours of vineyards inspire you, enterprising wine makers will arrange shipment to the United States; think in terms of hundreds rather than dozens. Try the **Maison du Vin** in Angers (pl. Président-Kennedy, next to the tourist office), and **Maison des Vins de Touraine** in Tours (19 sq. Prosper Mérimée). Loire food specialties include barley sugar (*sucre d'orge*) and prunes stuffed with marzipan (*pruneaux fourrés*); both are widely available at food shops throughout the valley.

Biking This is excellent country for bicycling—not too hilly, not too flat, and attractions are not too far apart. Bikes can be rented at most train stations and at dozens of other outlets (try **Au Col de Cygne,** 46 bis rue du Dr-Fournier, Tours, tel. 47–46–00–37; and **Leprovost,** 13 rue Carnot, Azay-le-Rideau, tel. 47–45–40–94). **Loisirs Accueil** offices in Blois and Orléans offer organized trips; these often include luggage transportation and camp or youth hostel accommodations (8 rue d'Escures, Orléans, tel. 38–62–04–88; or 11 pl. du Château, Blois, tel. 54–78–55–50).

Hiking Scenic footpaths abound. Long-distance walking paths (*sentiers de grande randonnée*) pass through the Loire Valley and are marked on Michelin maps with broken lines and route numbers with the prefix "GR." Tourist offices will supply sketch maps of interesting paths in their area.

Arts and Nightlife The Loire Valley's most popular form of cultural entertainment is the *son-et-lumière* (sound-and-light show), a dramatic spectacle that takes place after dark on summer evenings on the grounds of major châteaus. Programs sometimes take the form of historical pageants, with huge casts of people in period costume and caparisoned horses, the whole floodlit and backed by music and commentary, a few with earphone translations in English. They may also take the form of spectacular lighting and sound shows, with spoken commentary and dialogue but no visible figures, as at **Chenonceau.** The most magnificent *son-et-lumière* occurs at **Le Lude,** on the River Loir (not the Loire), 48 kilometers (29 miles) northeast of Saumur and 50 kilometers (30 miles) northwest of Tours. (It's an 85-minute bus ride from Le Mans.) Here more than 200 performers present a pageant chronicling the history of the château and region from the

Hundred Years' War on. The spectacle is enhanced by fountains and fireworks.

Festivals   For four weeks, usually beginning in early July, the **Festival d'Anjou** enlivens the area around Angers with music, theater, and dance. In July, the château grounds at **Loches** are the setting for a series of open-air concerts. And in the medieval **Grange du Meslay** near Tours, top-class international musicians gather in late June and July for the **Fêtes Musicales de Touraine.**

Tour 1: The Western Loire Valley—Angers to Tours

Angers, with its sturdy castle and Tapestry of the Apocalypse, is the starting point for this tour. The main rail line from Angers east to Tours goes through Saumur—whence you can take a bus to the medieval abbey at Fontevraud—and through Langeais, a good base for bike excursions to Ussé and Villandry. Several rail excursions are possible from Tours, the largest city on the Loire: to the châteaus of Azay, Chinon, Chenonceau, Loches, or the captivating old towns of Bourges and Vendôme.

From Paris   TGV bullet trains to Angers leave Paris (Gare Montparnasse) 12
By Train   times daily. The trip takes 1½ hours.

By Car   The 295-kilometer (185-mile) drive southwest from Paris along A11 takes 3 hours.

Angers

Tourist office: place Kennedy, opposite the castle, tel. 41–91–96–56.

The former capital of the Anjou region, **Angers** lies on the banks of the River Maine, just north of the Loire, about 105 kilometers (65 miles) west of Tours and 215 kilometers (135 miles) southwest of Orléans. In addition to a towering medieval fortress filled with extraordinary tapestries, the town has a fine Gothic cathedral, a number of art galleries, and a network of pleasant, traffic-free shopping streets. Well served by public transportation, Angers is the starting point for numerous bus, riverboat, hiking, biking, horseback, and ballooning excursions.

The town's principal sights all lie within a compact square formed by the three main boulevards and the River Maine. The castle is a five-minute walk from the station. Take rue de la Gare, turn left onto rue Hoche, then take the next right at place de l'Académie: The castle is across boulevard de Gaulle. Before you go in, stop at the **Maison du Vin** (5 bis pl. Kennedy), the organization that represents Anjou's wine producers. It can provide lots of leaflets about wines, suggestions about which vineyards to visit, and even a free sample or two.

The **château,** a massive, shale-and-limestone castle-fortress dating from the 13th century, glowers over the town from behind its turreted moats. The moats are now laid out as gardens, overrun with deer and blooming flowers. As you explore the grounds, note the startling contrast between the thick, defensive walls and the formal garden, with its delicate, white tufa-stone chapel, erected in the 16th century. For a sweeping view of the city and surrounding countryside, climb one of the castle towers.

A gallery within the castle grounds houses the great **Tapestry of the Apocalypse,** completed in 1390. Measuring 16 feet high and 120 yards long, it shows a series of 70 horrifying and humorous scenes from the Book of Revelation. In one, mountains of fire fall from heaven while boats capsize and men struggle in the water; another shows

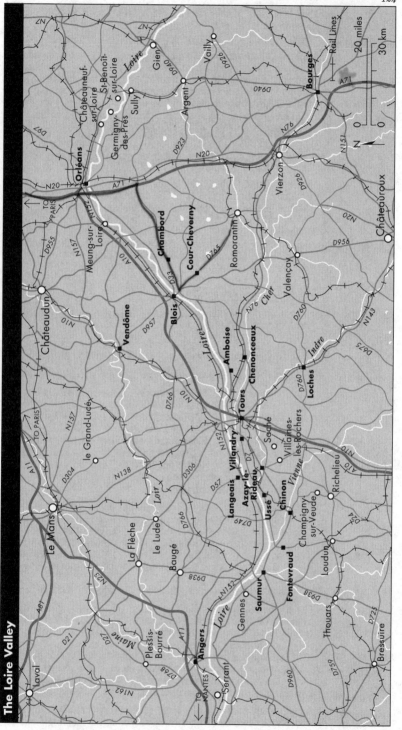

The Loire Valley

an intriguing, seven-headed beast. *Pl. Kennedy. Admission: 31 frs adults, 15 frs students and senior citizens, 6 frs children. Open June–mid-Sept., daily 9–7, mid-Sept.–May, daily 9–12:30 and 2–5:30.*

Just east of the château is the **Cathédrale St-Maurice** (pl. Freppel), a 12th- and 13th-century Gothic cathedral noted for its curious Romanesque facade and original stained-glass windows; you'll need binoculars to appreciate both fully. A few steps north, practically in the cathedral's shadow, lies Angers's large covered food market, **Les Halles** (pl. Mondain; open Tues.–Sat. 9–7; Sun. 9–1). Treat it as a gourmet museum, or stop in for lunch. A modern shopping mall sits right above it.

Just south of the cathedral, in a house that once sheltered Cesare Borgia and Mary, Queen of Scots, is the **Musée des Beaux-Arts** picture gallery. Among the museum's attractions is an impressive collection of Old Masters from the 17th and 18th centuries, including paintings by Raphael, Watteau, Fragonard, and Boucher. *10 rue du Musée. Admission: 12 frs. Open Tues.–Sun. 10–noon and 2–6.*

Around the corner, in the refurbished Eglise Toussaint, is the **Musée David d'Angers,** housing a collection of dramatic sculptures by Jean-Pierre David (1788–1859), the city's favorite son. *33 rue Toussaint. Admission: 10 frs adults. Open Tues.–Sun. 10–noon and 2–6.*

Lodging and Dining
$$

Anjou. In business since 1850, Anjou is currently decorated in a vaguely 18th-century style. Each room is individually furnished, though all are spacious and feature double-glazed windows. The restaurant, Salamandre, offers carefully prepared regional specialties. *1 blvd. du Maréchal-Foch, 49100, tel. 41–88–24–82, fax 41–87–22–21. 53 rooms with bath. Facilities: restaurant. AE, DC, MC, V.*

Lodging
$

Mail. In a 17th-century building on a quiet, central street (near the Hôtel de Ville and place du Ralliement), the Mail is at once modest and refined, and has a loyal clientele. There is no restaurant, however, and the hotel accepts no new guests on Sundays between noon and 6:30. *8 rue des Ursules, 49100, tel. 41–88–41–62, fax 41–20–95–19. 27 rooms, 19 with shower or bath. MC, V.*

Dining
$$
★

Toussaint. Chef Michel Bignon dishes up nouvelle versions of traditional local dishes, plus fine wines and tasty desserts, in a cozy, 400-year-old town house. Loire River fish with *beurre blanc* (white butter sauce) is a specialty. The neoclassical dining room on the second floor provides good views of the castle, and while the first-floor dining room lacks the views, it is less formal. *7 pl. Kennedy, tel. 41–87–46–20. Reservations required. Jacket required. AE, MC, V. Closed Sun. evening, Mon., part of Feb.*

¢

Le Boucherie. If you have an appetite for steak and want value, come here. Various menus offer different cuts of beef, but for 49 frs you can get a sirloin, a small salad, crusty bread, and a ¼ carafe of wine. Service is cheerful and swift. (If you have to wait for a table, don't despair: Dishes are swept away quickly and a new paper tablecloth laid in a matter of moments.) Tables are close together, but the banter of guests only adds to the lively, friendly atmosphere. *27 blvd. du Maréchal-Foch, tel. 41–87–27–85. No reservations. MC, V.*

¢

Jean Foucher. If you're visiting Angers's food market, Les Halles, during the summer, look out for the fish stall of Jean Foucher, who will prepare you a platter of *fruits de mer* (shellfish) to go. The prices are very reasonable. *Les Halles, pl. Mondain, tel. 41–86–06–32. No credit cards. Closed Sun. and Mon.*

¢

Maître Kanter. This chain restaurant, located at the covered market, provides simple food and swift service. It's a convenient refueling spot, and the firm's own beer is available on tap. Try the steak and french fries, or the sauerkraut with sausages and ham. *Les Halles, pl. Mondain, tel. 41–87–93–30. No reservations. V.*

Saumur

Trains make the 25-minute trip from Angers every 2½ hours. Saumur tourist office: Place Bilange, tel. 41–51–03–06.

★ **Saumur,** divided by the Loire, incurred heavy damages during World War II, and so is not, except for its château, visually old and historic. But what it lacks in medievalism it makes up for in wide streets and open spaces. If you arrive by train you'll be on the north-eastern side of the river; walk across the bridge to the other part of town, where most of the attractions are located.

Saumur is known for its wines and a flourishing mushroom industry, which produces 100,000 tons per year. Diagonally across the street from the tourist office, at the **Maison du Vin de Saumur,** local wine producers show off their products and provide information about visits to local vineyards. *25 rue Beaurepaire. Open summer, Mon.–Sat. 9–12:30 and 2–6:30. Closed Mon. in winter.*

★ Towering high above town and river is Saumur's elegant, white, 14th-century **château,** a 10-minute walk from the tourist office. The route takes you through the pretty, old town and place St-Pierre, with its lively Saturday market.

If the château looks familiar, it's probably because you've seen it in countless reproductions from the famous *Très Riches Heures (Book of Hours)* painted for the duc de Berri in 1416, now in the Musée Condé at Château de Chantilly *(see* Tour 3 in Chapter 7). Inside it's bright and cheerful, with a fairy-tale gateway and plentiful potted flowers. The **Musée d'Arts Décoratifs** and the **Musée du Cheval** (Horse Museum) are housed here. The former offers a fine collection of medieval objets d'art and 18th- and 19th-century porcelain, and the latter covers the history of the horse, with exhibits ranging from saddles to skeletons. Both are included in the guided tour. Afterward, climb the **Tour de Guet** (Watchtower) for an impressive view. *Admission: 33 frs adults, 24 frs children, students, and senior citizens. Open July–Sept., daily 9–7; Oct.–June, Mon.–Sat. 9:15–noon and 2–5.*

In the suburb of **St-Hilaire-St-Florent,** 2 kilometers (1 mile) north-west of town via D751, are a series of wine cellars (many open to visitors) that produce the local *vins mousseux* (sparkling wines). These same cool tunnels also harbor mushrooms, about which you can learn all you've ever wanted to know at **La Musée du Champignon,** also in St-Hilaire, on rue de Gennes (tel. 41–50–31–55).

Fontevraud

Three buses daily make the 16-kilometer (10-mile) trip southeast from Saumur to Fontevraud.

Fontevraud is famous for its large **abbey,** which played a key role in the medieval history of France and England. Founded in 1099, the abbey offered separate churches and living quarters for nuns, monks, lepers, "repentant" female sinners, and the sick. Between 1115 and the French Revolution in 1789, 39 different abbesses—among them a granddaughter of William the Conqueror—directed its operations. The abbey church contains the tombs of Henry II Plantagenet, king of England; his wife, Eleanor of Aquitaine; and their son Richard Coeur de Lion—Richard the Lion-hearted. Though their bones were scattered during the Revolution, the effigies remain. Napoléon turned the abbey church into a prison, and so it remained until 1963, when historic restoration—still under way—began.

The great 12th-century abbey church is one of the most eclectic structures in France. The medieval section is built of simple stone and topped with a series of domes; the chapter-house, with its collection of 16th-century religious wall paintings (prominent abbesses served as models), is unmistakably Renaissance; and the paving stones bear the salamander emblems of François I. Next to the long refectory, you will find the unusual octagonal **kitchen**, its tall spire, the **Tour d'Evrault**, serving as one of the abbey's 20 faceted stone chimneys. *Admission: 26 frs adults, 17 frs senior citizens, 5 frs children. Open daily June–mid-Sept. 9–7; mid-Sept.–Oct. 9:30–12:30 and 2–6; Nov.–mid-Apr. 9:30–12:30 and 2–5:30; mid-Apr.–May 9:30–12:30 and 2–6:30.*

Lodging and Dining
$$

Domaine de Mestré. A secluded working farm and home of the charming Dauge family, this ancient, rectangular enclave of creamy stone buildings has cozy guest rooms and a cheerful dining room for breakfast and good, simple, family-style meals. *Fontevraud-l'Abbaye, 49590, tel. 41–51–75–87. 10 rooms. Lunch and dinner (135 frs) by reservation.*

Langeais

Five trains daily make the 25-minute trip northeast from Saumur. Three run daily from Angers (journey time 50–70 minutes). Langeais tourist office: 2 pl. de la Mairie, tel. 47–96–58–22.

Towering over tiny **Langeais** is the uncompromising bulk of **Langeais Castle.** Chunky turrets and a drawbridge guard the entrance at the far end of the main street, but the interior is not so intimidating. A tiered garden sweeps away behind the castle, and the tour of the castle makes it abundantly clear that past inhabitants lived comfortably: This is one of the few Loire châteaus to retain medieval furniture and decoration, perhaps because it was one of the last fortified castles to be built (in the 1460s) prior to the return of peace and the onset of Renaissance prosperity. The upper castle walls are pierced with holes from which boiling oil was never, apparently, poured. *Admission: 30 frs adults, 23 frs senior citizens, 17 frs children. Open mid-Mar.–Oct., daily 9–6:30; Nov.–mid-Mar., Tues.–Sun. 9–noon and 2–5.*

Lodging and Dining
$$

Duchesse Anne. There is something of a dearth of accommodation in tiny Langeais, but this friendly, unpretentious old hotel is fine for a short stay, despite its smallish rooms. The restaurant serves up traditional French cuisine with menus at 90, 120, and 180 francs, and there is a large terrace for outdoor meals. *10 rue de Tours, 37130, tel. 47–96–82–03, fax 47–96–68–60. 23 rooms, 13 with shower. Facilities: restaurant (closed Wed. and Sun. evening). MC, V. Closed Nov. 1–Easter.*

Ussé

Inaccessible by public transportation, Ussé can be reached by bicycle or car from Langeais, 14 km (8½ mi) southeast via D57 and D7. Bike rentals are available at the Langeais train station.

★ **Ussé** is the archetypal fairy-tale **château**, with its astonishing array of delicate towers and turrets. Tourist literature describes it as the original Sleeping Beauty castle—the inspiration for Charles Perrault's beloved 17th-century story. Though parts of the castle date from the 1400s, most of it was completed two centuries later. It is a mix of Gothic and Renaissance styles—stylish and romantic, built for fun, not fighting. Its history supports its playful image: It suffered no bloodbaths—no political conquests or conflicts. And a tablet in the chapel indicates that even the French Revolution passed it by.

After admiring the château's luxurious furnishings and 19th-century French fashion exhibit, climb the spiral stairway to the tower to view the River Indre through the battlements. Here you will also find a waxwork effigy of Sleeping Beauty herself. Before you leave, visit the 16th-century chapel in the garden; its door is decorated with pleasingly sinister skull-and-crossbone carvings. *Admission: 54 frs adults, 27 frs children. Open mid-Mar.–mid-May, daily 9–noon and 2–6.*

Villandry

Inaccessible by public transportation, Villandry can be reached by bike or car from Langeais, 12 km (7½ mi) west via D57 and D7, or from Ussé, 21 km (13 mi) southwest via D7.

★ The **château of Villandry** is renowned for its extravagant, terraced gardens. Both the château and gardens date from the 16th century, but, over the years, they fell into disrepair. In 1906, Spanish doctor Joachim Carvallo and his wife, American heiress Ann Coleman, bought the property and began a long process of restoration. The gardens were replanted according to a rigorous, geometrical design, with zigzagging hedges enclosing flower beds, vegetable plots, and gravel walks. The result is an aristocratic 16th-century *jardin à la française.* Below an avenue of 1,500 precisely pruned lime trees lies an ornamental lake, filled with swans: Not a ripple is out of place. The aromatic and medicinal garden, with plots neatly labeled in three languages, is especially appealing.

The château itself has a remarkable gilded ceiling—imported from Toledo, Spain—and a collection of fine Spanish paintings. However, the garden is unquestionably the main attraction, and as it is usually open during the two-hour French lunch break, you can have it to yourself for a good part of the afternoon. *Admission: château and gardens, 40 frs adults, 37 frs students and senior citizens; gardens only, 24 frs adults, 18 frs students and senior citizens. Château open mid-Feb.–mid-Nov., daily 9–6; garden is open all year, daily 9–sunset (or 8, whichever is earlier).*

Lodging and Dining
$$ **Cheval Rouge.** This is a fine, old-fashioned hotel whose restaurant is popular with the locals. It has an excellent Loire wine list and surprisingly good regional food, considering its touristy location right next to the château. Good bets are the terrine of foie gras, the calf sweetbreads, and the wood-fired grills. The 20 modernized guest rooms are tidy, and all have bath or shower. *37510 Villandry, tel. 47–50–02–07. Reservations advised. Facilities: restaurant (closed Sun. evening and Mon., except in summer). MC, V. Closed Jan.–Feb.*

Tours

Six daily trains make the 20-minute trip east to Tours from Langeais. The Angers–Tours express runs every 2½ hours and takes an hour. Tourist office: rue B. Palissey, opposite the train station, tel. 47–05–58–08.

Numbers in the margin correspond with points of interest on the Tours map.

Tours, the largest town along the Loire Valley, makes a fine base for excursions to numerous châteaus. Though high-rise blocks pepper the city outskirts, the historic center has been lovingly restored and preserved. The town itself is easy to get around by public buses—they run every 10 minutes and cost 6.20 francs in exact fare.

❶ Start your tour at place du Maréchal-Leclerc, usually called the **place de la Gare.** Here you'll find the fine Belle Epoque train station, with its cast-iron curlicues, the bus station, and the tourist office, on the other side of boulevard Heurteloup. Many of the most convenient hotels are situated here or just around the corner.

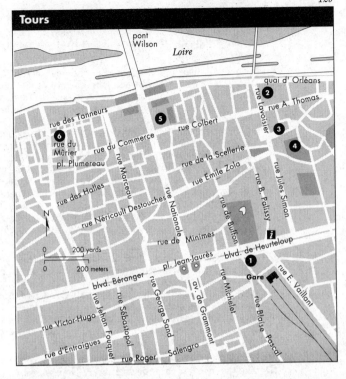

The city plan is fairly simple. Turn left from place du Maréchal-Leclerc, down boulevard Heurteloup, to reach place Jean-Jaurès; then turn right, after the imposing Hôtel de Ville (Town Hall), onto rue Nationale. This street holds many of the city's major shops, and if you continue along it for just more than a half mile, you'll reach the Loire. Turn right a couple of blocks before the river, and you'll soon reach the cathedral, the château, and the Musée des Beaux-Arts. If you turn left, you'll come to the place Plumereau and a quaint pedestrian precinct in the area known as Vieux Tours. Here, small, inexpensive hotels, intimate restaurants, bistros, and antiques and crafts shops line the streets. It has become the scene for many of Tours's evening pleasures as well as a tourist attraction during the day.

② What is left of the château is of minor interest, but, within it, you will find the **Historial de la Touraine**—a group of more than 150 waxwork models representing historic figures, such as St. Martin and Joan of Arc, whose deeds helped shape this region for 15 centuries. There's also a small aquarium. *Quai d'Orléans. Admission: wax museum, 29 frs adults, 25 frs students and children; aquarium, 25 frs adults, 20 frs students, 15 frs children. Open daily 9–11:30 and 2–6:30. Closed mornings Jan.–mid-Mar.*

③ The **Cathédrale St-Gatien**, built between 1239 and 1484, reveals a mixture of architectural styles. Its majestic two-towered facade was cleaned and restored in 1990. The stained glass, in particular, deserves binoculars, and you will want to visit the little children's tomb with its kneeling angels, built in memory of the two children of Charles VIII and Anne of Brittany. *Rue Lavoisier. Open daily 9–noon and 2–6.*

④ Next door, in what was once the archbishop's palace, the **Musée des Beaux-Arts** (Fine Arts Museum) houses an eclectic selection of treasures: works by Rubens, Rembrandt, Boucher, Degas, and Alexander Calder. There's even Fritz the Elephant, stuffed in 1902. *18 pl. François-Sicard. Admission: 30 frs adults, 15 frs students and senior citizens, 12 frs children. Open Wed.–Mon. 9–12:45 and 2–6; closed Tues.*

⑤ Two small museums stand at the river end of rue Nationale: the **Musée des Vins** (Wine Museum) and the **Musée du Compagnonnage** (Guild Museum). You may wish to see the latter, at least. *Compagnonnage* is a sort of apprenticeship-trade-union system, and here you see the masterpieces of the candidates for guild membership: virtuoso craftwork, some of it eccentric (an Eiffel Tower made of slate, for instance, or a varnished-noodle château). These stand as evidence of the devotion to craftsmanship that is still an important feature of French life. Both the guild and the wine museum are set in and around the cloisters of an old church—a pleasant setting, and you are free to visit them at your own pace. *Musée des Vins, 16 rue Nationale. Admission: 20 frs adults, 10 frs students. Open Wed.–Mon. 9–11:30 and 2–4:30. Musée du Compagnonnage, 8 rue Nationale. Admission: 20 frs adults, 10 frs students and children. Open Wed.–Mon. 9–noon and 2–5.*

From rue Nationale, narrow rue du Commerce leads you to the oldest and most attractive part of Tours, the area around **place Plumereau**. It's a great neighborhood for strolling, largely traffic-free, and full of little squares, open-air cafés, and pricey antiques shops. It is also here that the young-at-heart congregate in the evenings; a good place to join the locals is at the **Café du Vieux Marier** (11 pl. Plumereau, tel. 47–61–04–77), whose cluttered decor attracts earnest conversationalists night after night.

⑥ From place Plumereau, head one block along rue Briconnet, and take the first left onto rue du Mûrier. The **Musée du Gemmail,** halfway down on the right in the imposing 19th-century Hôtel Raimbault, houses an unusual collection of three-dimensional colored-glass window panels. Depicting patterns, figures, and even portraits, the panels are both beautiful and intriguing, as most of the gemlike fragments of glass come from broken bottles. *7 rue du Mûrier. Admission: 28 frs adults, 18 frs students and children. Open Mar. 1–Sept. 15, Tues.–Sun. 10–noon and 2:30–6.*

Lodging
$ **Hotel du Cygne.** There's a simple, old-fashioned charm to this quiet, centrally located hotel. Window boxes overflow with flowers, a fire is often crackling in the lounge, and the owners are helpful and kind. These touches and the reasonable price are enough to compensate for a slightly tattered decor. *6 rue du Cygne, 37000, tel. 47–66–66–41. 20 rooms, some with bath. AE, MC, V.*

Lodging and
Dining
$ **Akilène.** In Vieux Tours just off place Plumereau, this two-century-old inn, with exposed blackened beams and creaking timbers, exudes charm. The inn's guest rooms are priced right, even if the furnishings and fixtures do show their age. Rooms range from small with shower only to spacious with a reasonably large bathroom. The small restaurant offers such simple fare as *bifteck*, lamb chops, and *pommes frites* on a fixed menu of 50 frs, and the small bar is where you'll find owner, M. Guilbaud, who speaks excellent English and will happily help you plan your trips. *17, rue de Rôtisserie, 37000 Tours, tel. 47–61–46–04, fax 47–66–15–76. 23 rooms, most with shower. Facilities: restaurant, bar, elevator, direct dial phones, TV. AE, DC, MC, V.*

$ **Moderne.** This old mansion in a quiet street near the Palais des Congrès provides good value in a traditional atmosphere that pleases both tourists and business people. Room sizes vary, with the largest topping 250 frs. The restaurant has a set menu priced at 90 frs. *1 rue Victor-Laloux, 37000, tel. 47–05–32–81, fax 47–05–71–50. 23 rooms, some with bath. Facilities: restaurant (closed lunch, Sun. eve., and Jan.). AE, MC, V.*

Dining
$$

Les Tuffeaux. Facing the château, this restaurant is one of Tours's best, but will not totally break your budget. Chef Gildas Marsollier has been winning customers with his delicious fennel-perfumed salmon, his oysters with an egg-based sauce seasoned with Roquefort, and remarkable desserts. Gentle lighting and a warm, understated decor provide a soothing background. *19 rue Lavoisier, tel. 47–47–19–89. Reservations advised. MC, V. Closed Sun., Mon. lunch, and part of July.*

Shopping

In addition to its wines, **Maison des Vins de Touraine** in Tours (19 sq. Prosper Mérimée; closed Sun. and Mon. mornings) offers a wide selection of local products and crafts, including ceramics.

Azay-le-Rideau

The 6 daily trains west from Tours take 33 minutes to Azay. The château is a short walk from the station.

Nestled in a sylvan setting on the banks of the River Indre, the white, 16th-century **château of Azay-le-Rideau** was—like Ussé—a Renaissance pleasure palace rather than a serious fortress.

A financial scandal forced its builder, royal financier Gilles Berthelot, to flee France shortly after its construction in 1520. For centuries, it passed from one private owner to another and was finally bought by the state in 1905. Though the interior offers an interesting blend of furniture and artwork, you may wish to spend most of your time exploring the enchanting private park. During the summer, visitors can enjoy delightful *son-et-lumière* shows on the castle grounds. *Admission: 26 frs adults, 17 frs students, 6 frs children. Open daily, Apr.–Sept., 9:30–6; Oct.–Mar., 10–12:30 and 2–4:45.*

Lodging and
Dining
$$

Grand Monarque. Just yards from the château, this mildly eccentric, popular hotel draws hundreds of visitors. It has played host to celebrities, royals, and tourists alike. Guest rooms are tastefully and individually decorated. (The firmness of the mattresses varies, so check ahead if this is important to you.) The restaurant has a pleasant, shaded dining garden where good, traditional food is served with an extensive selection of Loire wines. The special 80-franc four-course lunch menu is an especially good value. *3 pl. de la République, 37190, tel. 47–45–40–08, fax 47–45–46–25. 25 rooms with bath. Facilities: restaurant. AE, DC, MC, V. Closed mid-Dec.–Feb. 1.*

Chinon

Five trains a day arrive in Chinon from Tours, 65 minutes northeast, and 7 trains from Azay, 15 minutes northeast. Bicycles can be rented at Chinon station, which is a 10-minute walk from the town center. Tourist office: 12 rue Voltaire, tel. 47–93–17–85.

Located in the fertile countryside between the Loire and the Vienne rivers, **Chinon** is the birthplace of author François Rabelais (1494–1553). Today it is dominated by the towering ruins of its medieval ★ **fortress-castle**, perched high above the River Vienne. Though the main tourist office is in the town below, in summer a special annex operates from the castle grounds. Both the village and the château stand among steep, cobbled slopes, so wear comfortable walking shoes.

The vast fortress dates from the time of Henry II of England, who died here in 1189 and was buried at Fontevraud. Two centuries later, the castle witnessed an important historic moment: Joan of Arc's recognition of the disguised dauphin, later Charles VII. In the early 17th century, the castle was partially dismantled by its then-owner, Cardinal Richelieu (1585–1642), who used many of its stones to build a new palace 21 kilometers (13 miles) away. (That palace no longer exists.)

At Chinon, all but the royal chambers—which house a small museum—is open to the elements. For a fine view of the region, climb the **Coudray Tower,** where, in 1302, leading members of the crusading Knights Templar were imprisoned before being taken to Paris, tried, and burned at the stake. The **Tour de l'Horloge,** whose bell has been sounding the hours since 1399, houses a small **Joan of Arc museum.** *Admission: 26 frs adults, 18 frs students. Open Nov.–mid-Mar., 9–noon and 2–5; mid-Mar.–Jun. and Sept., 9–6; July and Aug., 9–7; Oct. 9–5. Open daily except Wed. in Jan. and Feb.*

Follow the signposted steps down into the old town, or drive your car to the River Vienne pathway. **Place de l'Hôtel-de-Ville**—the main square—is the best place to begin exploring. Stop by the tourist office and pick up a plan of the town's fine medieval streets and alleys. While you are there, visit **Le Musée du Vin** (Wine Museum) in the vaulted, 15th-century cellars. This is a fascinating exhibit, full of information on vine growing and wine- and barrel-making. An English commentary is available, and the admission charge entitles you to a sample of the local product. *Admission: 22 frs. Open May–Oct., Fri.–Wed. 10–noon and 2–6.*

Lodging and Dining | **Hostellerie Gargantua.** In the 15th century, the building housing the Gargantua was a bailiff's palace. Today this small, quiet hotel in the $ | center of the medieval city, close to the St-Maurice church, offers an array of rooms in various sizes and styles. The restaurant, with its charming old dining room and outside tables for summer, serves delicious local specialties. On Friday and Saturday evenings, waitresses dress to give a medieval flare to the dinner, which has mostly traditional fare. The omelets are famous and the filet of barbue fish with a marmalade, thyme, and citron sauce is excellent. *73 rue Haute-St-Maurice, 37500, tel. 47–93–04–71. 9 rooms, most with bath. AE, DC, MC, V. Closed mid-Nov.–Mar.*

Lodging **Hôtel de France.** Just off the main square in one of the oldest (16th $$ | century) buildings in town, the Hôtel de France was given its present name and function during the Revolution. The current owners have been working continuously to restore the building, and so far have refurbished eight of the 30 guest rooms. These are the ones to request, though all rooms are comfortable and have a private shower or bath. There is a restaurant next door where guests dine if they choose the *demi-pension* plan. *47–49 pl. du Général-de-Gaulle, 37500, tel. 47–93–33–91, fax 47–98–37–03. 27 rooms with bath or shower. AE, MC, V. Closed mid-Jan.–Mar.*

Dining **Au Plaisir Gourmand.** Gourmets from all around come here to cele-
$$ | brate, and lucky tourists will get a table only if they make reserva-
★ | tions (the dining room in this charming old house seats 30). Chef Jean-Claude Rigollet makes inventive use of fresh, local produce. For a real treat, try the Vienne River trout. Au Plaisir Gourmand gives top quality without frills and features exceptional local wines, and if you order carefully, you can dine well for less than you'd expect. *Quai Charles VII, tel. 47–93–20–48. Reservations required. Jacket and tie required. MC, V. Closed Sun. dinner, Mon., last 3 weeks in Jan., and 2nd half of Nov.*

¢ | **Jeanne de France.** Local families and swarms of young people patronize this lively little pizzeria in the town's main square. But it's a far cry from an American pizza joint: Here you can also buy jugfuls of local wine, steaks, and french fries. *12 pl. du Général-de-Gaulle, tel. 47–93–20–12. Reservations accepted. Closed Jan., and Wed. Oct.–May.*

Chenonceaux

The 4 daily trains from Tours take 40 minutes east to Chenonceaux.

★ You could happily spend half a day in the village of **Chenonceaux**, visiting its **château** (whose name is for some reason spelled without the final *x*). From long-ago historic figures, such as Diane de Poitiers, Catherine de Médicis, and Mary, Queen of Scots, to a host of modern travel writers, many have called it the "most exciting" and the "most romantic" of all the Loire châteaus. You are free to wander about (there are attendants to answer questions). For most of the year, the château is open—unlike many others—all day. The only drawback is its popularity: If you want to avoid a roomful of English schoolchildren, wander the grounds and come back when they stop for lunch.

More pleasure palace than fortress, Chenonceau was built in 1520 by Thomas Bohier, a wealthy tax collector. When he went bankrupt, it passed to François I. Later, Henri II gave it to his mistress, Diane de Poitiers. After his death, Henri's not-so-understanding widow, Catherine de Médicis, expelled Diane to nearby Chaumont and took back the château. It is to Catherine that we owe the lovely gardens and the handsome three-story extension whose arches span the river.

Before you go inside, pick up a leaflet (English available) at the gate. Then walk around to the right of the main building and admire the peaceful, delicate architecture; the formal garden; and the river gliding under the arches. The romantically inclined may want to rent a rowboat and spend an hour drifting. Inside the château are splendid ceilings, colossal fireplaces, and authentic furnishings. Paintings include works by Rubens, Andrea del Sarto, and Correggio. And as you tour the rooms, be sure to pay your respects to former owner Madame Dupin, whose face is captured in Nattier's charming portrait. Thanks to the great affection Madame Dupin inspired among her proletarian neighbors, the château and its treasures survived the Revolution intact.

A waxworks exhibition (**Musée des Cires**), housed in one of the outbuildings, illustrates four centuries of French history. There are also excellent *son-et-lumière* shows throughout the summer. *Admission: château 45 frs adults, 25 frs children; wax museum 10 frs. Open mid-Feb.–Nov., daily 9–5, 6, or 6:30, depending on the season; mid-Nov.–mid-Feb., daily 9–4:30.*

Lodging and Dining
$$

Bon Laboureur et du Château. In 1882, Bon Laboureur, 250 yards from the château, won Henry James's praise as a simple, rustic inn. It has come up in the world since then, and is now elegantly modern, with a few old oak beams surviving, and a pretty garden where you can eat in summer. Dine on excellent turbot with Hollandaise or braised rabbit with dried fruits. The *poêle de Saint Jacques* (pan-fried scallops) with fresh cèpes from the forest is a must in the autumn. *6 rue du Dr-Bretonneau, 37150, tel. 47–23–90–02, fax 47–23–82–01. 36 rooms with bath. Facilities: restaurant, garden. AE, DC, MC, V. Closed Dec.–mid-Feb.*

Loches

The 5 daily trains from Tours take 80 minutes to get to Loches, which is 18 km (11 mi) due south of Chenonceaux. From the station, take the bridge directly over the Indre; the tourist office (pl. Wermelskirchen; tel. 47–59–07–98) is just on the other side, and the Porte Royale is another 150 yards farther.

Loches, set on a rocky spur just beside the River Indre, is a walled citadel dominating a small, medieval village, like Chinon. But although Chinon's citadel is a ruined shell, much of Loches's is well preserved and stands as a living part of the town.

As you enter the Cité Médiévale through the Porte Royale, the first building you will come across is the church of **St-Ours:** Note its striking roof formed of octagonal pyramids, dating from the 12th century; the doorway sculpted with owls, monkeys, and mythical beasts; and the baptismal font converted from a Roman altar.

The **Logis Royaux** (the château, just north of St-Ours) has a terrace that provides a fine view of the roofs and river below and the towers and swallows' nests above. Inside, keep an eye out for the two-man crossbow that could pierce an oak door at 200 yards. There are some interesting pictures, too, including a copy of the well-known portrait that shows an extremely disgruntled Charles VII and one of his mistresses, Agnès Sorel, posed as a virtuous Virgin Mary (though semitopless). Her alabaster image decorates her tomb, guarded by angels and lambs. Agnès died in 1450, at age 28, probably the result of poisoning by Charles's son, the future Louis XI. The little chapel was built by Charles VIII for his queen, Anne of Brittany, and is lavishly decorated with sculpted ermine tails, the lady's emblem.

After the tour, amble over to the *donjon*, or tower keep. One 11th-century tower, half-ruined and roofless, is open for individual exploration, though the others require guided supervision. These towers contain dungeons and will delight anyone who revels in prison cells and torture chambers. *Admission: château and keep, 26 frs adults, 19 frs students. Open Jan.–mid-Mar. and Sept.–Nov., Thurs.–Tues. 9–noon and 2–5; mid-Mar.–June, daily 9–noon and 2–6; July and Aug., daily 9–6.*

Vendôme

The daily trains from Tours north to Vendôme take 1 hour (26 minutes via TGV). Tourist office: 47–49 rue Poterie, tel. 54–77–05–07.

Charming **Vendôme** is not on most tourists' itineraries, but its picturesque appeal amply merits a visit. To reach the center of town from the station, head south across the Loir and continue past Lycée Ronsard (where Balzac went to high school) and the Ancienne Abbaye de la Trinité, and within 15 to 20 minutes you'll be in place du Château.

Vendôme's château is in ruins, but the **gardens** surrounding it offer knockout views of the town center. From place du Château, head down to admire the Flamboyant Gothic abbey church of **La Trinité,** with its unusual 12th-century clock tower and fine stained glass. Take time to stroll through the narrow streets of this enchanting little town.

Lodging and Dining
$

Auberge de la Madeleine. This venerable hotel lies on a small square by the Madeleine church, just around the corner from the banks of the Loire and a delightful five-minute walk from the town center. The pleasant setting attracts discerning international visitors throughout the summer—as does the splendid 75-franc menu in the hotel restaurant, Le Jardin du Loir. *Rooms start at 150 frs, but expect to pay 220 frs for one with a shower and toilet. 6 pl. de la Madeleine, 41100, tel. 54–77–20–79. 9 rooms with bath or shower. Facilities: restaurant (closed Wed.). MC, V. Closed part of Feb.*

Dining
$

Paris. Don't be put off by the drab postwar exterior of this restaurant close to the train station: It serves generous portions of seasonal produce, with veal and chicken fricassee, as well as grilled boar in autumn, among the specialties. Menus at 90 frs (weekdays) and 128 frs (also at 200 frs and 240 frs) represent excellent value. *1 rue Darreau, tel. 54–77–02–71. Reservations recommended. MC, V. Closed Sun. eve., Mon., last week of Jan., and last 3 weeks in Aug.*

Bourges

Four trains daily make the 95-minute journey to Bourges from Tours. Bourges tourist office: 21 rue Victor-Hugo, tel. 48-24-75-33.

Modern times have largely passed **Bourges** by, and the result is a preserved market town with medieval streets and the 13th-century **Cathédrale-St-Etienne.** You'll see the towers as you approach the town, but once you've arrived, its asymmetrical facade becomes hidden down a narrow street, and it is impossible to photograph. The central portal is a masterpiece: Cherubim, angels, saints, and prophets cluster in the archway above the tympanum, which contains an elaborate representation of the Last Judgment.

The interior is unlike that of any other Gothic cathedral. The forest of tall, slender pillars rising to the vaults is remarkable enough, but the height of the side aisles flanking the nave is unique: 65 feet, high enough to allow windows to be pierced above the level of the second side aisles. The cathedral contains exquisite stained glass, some dating to its construction. *Off rue du Guichet.*

The center of Bourges, downhill from the cathedral, has been restored to its medieval state. Rue Mirabeau and rue Coursalon, pedestrian streets full of timber-frame houses, are charming places for browsing and shopping. At one end of rue Coursalon, across rue Moyenne—Bourges's busy but less distinguished main street—is the **Palais Jacques-Coeur,** one of the most sumptuous Gothic dwellings in France. Note the vaulted chapel, the wooden ceilings covered with original paintings, and the dining room with its tapestries and massive fireplace. *Rue Jacques-Coeur. Admission: 26 frs adults, 17 frs senior citizens and those 18–25; 7 frs children under 18. Open daily Apr.–June and Sept.–Oct., 9–noon and 2–6; Nov.–Mar., 9–noon and 2–5; July–Aug., 9–7. Guided tours only, about 45 min, begin 15 min after the hr.*

Lodging and Dining
$$
Central et Angleterre. This efficient hotel, close to the Palais Jacques-Coeur in the center of town, is popular with business travelers. The interior has been carefully renovated and rooms have been given modern conveniences, from tiled bathrooms to direct-dial telephones and minibars. The restaurant, whose menus start at 120 frs, is quite sedate, done in the style of Louis XVI. The bar off the lobby is a comfortable place to sit before or after dinner. *1 pl. des Quatre-Piliers, 18000 Bourges, tel. 48-24-68-51, fax 48-65-21-41. 31 rooms. Facilities: restaurant. AE, DC, MC, V.*

Tour 2: The Eastern Loire Valley—Blois to Orléans

From homely Blois, our first base, you can visit Amboise (by train) and the châteaus of Cheverny and Chambord (by bus), before heading upriver to Orléans, the nearest Loire city to Paris.

From Paris
By Train
Express trains to Blois leave Paris (Gare d'Austerlitz) about every 2 hours. The trip takes between 1½ and 2 hours depending on the train.

 The 169-kilometer (105-mile) drive from Paris along A10 takes 2 hours.

Blois

Tourist office: 3 av. du Docteur Jean-Laigret, just up from the château, tel. 54-74-06-49.

Perched on a steep hillside overlooking the Loire, about midway between Tours and Orléans, **Blois** is a quaint town, with its white facades, redbrick chimneys, and blue-slate roofs. It is also convenient, thanks to few traffic problems and direct train links not only to Paris but also to all the major towns along the Loire.

★ Avenue Jean-Laigret leads down from the station to the **château**, ¼ mile away. This splendid structure is among the valley's finest. Your ticket entitles you to a guided tour—in English when there are enough visitors who can't understand French—but you are more than welcome to roam around without a guide if you visit between mid-March and August. Before you enter the building, stand in the courtyard and admire four centuries of architecture. On one side stands the 13th-century hall and tower, the latter offering a stunning view of town and countryside. The Renaissance begins to flower in the Louis XII wing (built between 1498 and 1503), through which you enter, and comes to full bloom in the François I wing (1515–24). The masterpiece here is the openwork spiral staircase, painstakingly restored. The fourth side is the classical Gaston d'Orléans wing (1635–38).

At the bottom of the staircase there's a *diaporama*, an audiovisual display tracing the château's history. Upstairs you'll find a series of enormous rooms with tremendous fireplaces decorated with the gilded porcupine, emblem of Louis XII; the ermine of Anne of Brittany; and, of course, François I's salamander, breathing fire and surrounded by flickering flames. There are intricate ceilings, carved and gilded paneling, and a sad little picture of Mary, Queen of Scots. In the great council room, the duc de Guise was murdered on the orders of Henri III in 1588. Don't miss the **Musée des Beaux-Arts,** the art gallery, in the Louis XII wing. The miscellaneous collection of paintings from the 16th to the 19th century is interesting and often amusing. The château also offers a *son-et-lumière* (sound-and-light) display most summer evenings. *Admission: 30 frs adults, 15 frs students and senior citizens. Open May–Aug., daily 9–6; Sept.–Apr., daily 9–noon and 2–5.*

Lodging and Dining
$$
Le Médicis. Located just 1,000 yards from the château, this smart, friendly hotel is your best bet in Blois. The rooms, all with private bath, are roomy, air-conditioned, and sound-proof, and have been newly and individually redecorated. The one suite has a whirlpool. But the restaurant alone would make a stay here worthwhile. Chef-owner Christian Garanger brings an innovative touch to classic dishes. For example, there are *coquille Saint-Jacques* with a pear fondue, and thin slices of roast hare with a black-currant sauce. His presentation, too, is admirable. The maître d' will happily guide you through the menu—indeed, the entire staff here is knowledgeable and helpful. *2 allée François 1er, 41000, tel. 54–43–94–04, fax 54–42–04–05. 12 rooms with bath, 1 suite. Facilities: restaurant (no dinner Sun. in low season). AE, DC, MC, V. Hotel closed Jan. 3–Jan. 24.*

Lodging
$
Anne de Bretagne. Just up from the castle, this small hotel offers street parking, but it's an uphill walk from the city center, and there is no restaurant. The tidy, simple rooms vary in size and shape, though none is especially large. The bar next door is a convenient place for a nightcap. *31 av. du Dr-Jean-Laigret, 41000, tel. 54–78–05–38. 29 rooms, most with bath. AE, DC, MC, V. Closed one week in Feb. and most of Mar.*

Dining
$$
La Péniche. This innovative restaurant is actually a luxurious barge moored along the banks of the Loire. Charming chef Germain Bosque serves up beautifully presented fresh seafood specialties (notably lobsters and oysters). *Promenade du Mail, tel. 57–74–37–23. Reservations advised. AE, DC, MC, V.*

$–$$ **Noë.** It's a good sign that locals crowd the pastel dining room at the

"Noah," half a mile uptown from the château, and you won't be disappointed. They come along to enjoy inexpensive house specialties such as chicken liver, duckling, and carp in a wine sauce—and to enjoy the set menus, priced at 100 frs and 150 frs. *10 bis av. de Vendôme, tel. 54–74–22–26. Reservations recommended. MC, V. Closed Sat. lunch, Tues. and Sun. evening, and Mon.*

Amboise

Trains from Blois southwest to Amboise take 20 minutes and run early morning, lunchtime, and twice in the afternoon. The station is on the north bank of the Loire. To get to the center of town, cross the bridge that leads over Ile-St-Jean to the south bank; the entrance to the château is one street in from the river.

★ **Amboise** is a picturesque little town with bustling markets, plentiful hotels and restaurants, and a historic **château.**

A Stone Age fortress stood here, and an early bridge gave the stronghold strategic importance. In AD 503, Clovis, king of the Franks, met with Alaric, king of the Visigoths, on an island (now the site of an excellent campground). In the years that followed, the Normans attacked the fortress repeatedly. The 15th and 16th centuries were Amboise's golden age, and during this time, the château, enlarged and embellished, became a royal palace. Charles VII stayed here, as did the unfortunate Charles VIII, best remembered for banging his head on a low doorway (you will be shown it) and dying as a result. François I, whose long nose appears in so many château paintings, based his court here. In 1560, his son, young François II, settled here with his wife, Mary Stuart (otherwise known as Mary, Queen of Scots), and his mother, Catherine de Médicis. The castle was also the setting for the Amboise Conspiracy, an ill-fated Protestant plot organized against François II; visitors are shown where the corpses of 1,200 conspirators dangled from the castle walls. In later years, a decline set in, and demolition occurred both before and after the Revolution. Today only about a third of the original building remains standing.

The château's interior is partially furnished, though not with the original objects; these vanished when the building was converted to a barracks and then a button factory. The great round tower is reached by a spiral ramp rather than by a staircase; designed for horsemen, it is wide enough to accommodate a small car. You are free to explore the grounds at your own pace, including the little **Chapelle St-Hubert,** with its carvings of the Virgin and Child, Charles VIII, and Anne of Brittany. There are frequent *son-et-lumière* pageants on summer evenings. *Admission: 30 frs adults, 20 frs students. Open daily, late Sept.–late Mar., 9–noon and 2–5; late Mar.–June, 9–noon and 2–6:30; July–Aug., 9–6:30; Sept. 1–late Sept., 9–noon and 2–6:30.*

In the old powder house at the château is the **Musée de la Figurine-Jouet,** with more than 2,000 pieces of small, humorous, ceramic sculpture on display. *Tel. 41–67–39–23. Admission: 12 frs adults, 7 frs children. Open June and Sept., daily 2–6; July and Aug. 10–6.*

Up rue Victor-Hugo, five minutes from the château, is **Le Clos Lucé,** a handsome Renaissance manor house. François I lent the house to Leonardo da Vinci, who spent the last four years of his life here, dying in 1519. You can wander from room to room at will. The basement houses an extraordinary exhibition: working models of some of Leonardo's inventions. Though impractical in his own time, perhaps, when technology was limited, they were built by engineers from IBM, using the detailed sketches contained in the artist's notebooks. Mechanisms on display include three-speed gearboxes, a military tank, a clockwork car, and even a flying machine. *At the east-*

ern end of rue Victor-Hugo. *Admission: 31 frs adults, 25 frs students. Open daily, Feb.–mid-Mar. and mid-Nov.–Dec. 9–6; mid-Mar.–mid-Nov. 9–7. Closed Jan.*

Lodging and Dining
$$
★

Le Blazon. This delightful small hotel, enlivened by the enthusiasm of the owners, is behind the château, a four-minute walk from the center of town. The old building has been well converted into guest rooms of different shapes and sizes, whose compact, prefabricated bathroom units have showers and toilets. Most rooms have twin beds, though a few have queens. Room 229, with exposed beams and a cathedral ceiling, has special charm; Room 109 is comfortably spacious and has a good view of the square. There's superior fare in the pretty little restaurant, with menus beginning at 95 frs. The menu changes with the seasons, and may include roast lamb with garlic and medallions of pork, and appetizers of salmon carpaccio with mustard dressing and air-dried duck breast scented with herbs and spices. *14 rue Joyeuse, 37400, tel. 47–23–22–41, fax 47–57–56–18. 29 rooms with bath. Facilities: restaurant. MC, V.*

Dining
$

Auberge du Mail. Set in a cozy, rustic, 14-room inn on the banks of the Loire River, this restaurant offers good food at a fair price (there's a 90-franc set menu) and plenty of atmosphere; try the fish stew with baby eels. *32 quai Général de Gaulle, tel. 47–57–60–39. Reservations advised. AE, DC, MC, V. Closed Fri. in winter and 1st 2 wks in Dec.*

Cour-Cheverny

Three daily buses make the 20-minute journey from Blois southeast to Cour-Cheverny (as the château village is officially called). The château is a five-minute walk from the bus station.

The main attraction here is the classical **château of Cheverny,** finished in 1634. The interior, with its painted and gilded rooms, splendid furniture, and rich tapestries depicting the labors of Hercules, is one of the grandest in the Loire region. American visitors will admire the bronze of George Washington in the gallery, alongside a document bearing his signature. Together, Louis XVI and Washington founded the Society of the Cincinnati, reserved for officers who fought in the War of Independence. Three of the present owner's ancestors were members of the group.

One of the chief delights of Cheverny is that you can wander freely at your own pace. Unfortunately, the gardens are off-limits, as is the Orangerie, where the *Mona Lisa* and other masterpieces were hidden during World War II. But you are free to contemplate the antlers of 2,000 stags in the nearby Trophy Room. Hunting, called "venery" in the leaflets, continues vigorously here, red coats, bugles, and all. In the kennels nextdoor, dozens of hounds lounge about dreaming of their next kill. Feeding times—*la soupe aux chiens*—are posted on a noticeboard, and visitors are welcome to watch the dogs gulp down their dinner. *Admission: 29 frs adults, 20 frs students. Open daily, mid-June–mid-Sept., 9:15–6:30; mid-Sept.–mid-June, 9:30–noon and 2:30–5.*

Chambord

Three buses daily travel to Chambord from Blois, 18 km (11 mi) west.

★ The largest of the Loire châteaus, the **château of Chambord** is also one of the valley's two most popular touring destinations (Chenonceau being the other). But although everyone thinks Chenonceau is extravagantly beautiful, reactions are mixed as to the qualities of Chambord. Set in the middle of a royal game forest, Chambord is the kind of place William Randolph Hearst would have built if he had had more money: It's been described as "megalomaniac," "an enormous film-set extravaganza," and, in its favor, "the most outstanding experience of the Loire Valley."

A few facts set the tone: The facade is 420 feet long, there are 440 rooms and 365 chimneys, and a wall 20 miles long encloses the 13,000-acre forest (you can wander in 3,000 of these, the rest being reserved for wild boar and other game). François I started building in 1519; the job took 12 years and required 1,800 workmen. His original grandiose idea was to divert the Loire to form a moat, but someone (probably his adviser, Leonardo da Vinci) persuaded him to make do with the River Cosson. François used the château only for short stays; yet when he first arrived, 12,000 horses were required to transport his luggage, servants, and hangers-on! Later kings also used Chambord as an occasional retreat, and Sun King Louis XIV had Molière perform here. In the 18th century, Louis XV gave the château to Maréchal de Saxe as a reward for his victory over the English and Dutch at Fontenoy in 1745. When not besporting himself with wine, women, and song, the marshal stood on the roof overseeing the exercises of his own regiment of 1,000 cavalry.

Now, after long neglect—all the original furnishings vanished during the French Revolution—Chambord belongs to the state. Vast rooms are open to visitors (you can wander freely), and have been filled with a variety of exhibits—not all concerned with Chambord, but interesting nonetheless. Children will enjoy repeated trips up and down the enormous **double-helix staircase:** It looks like a single staircase, but an entire regiment could march up one spiral while a second came down the other, and they would never meet. Also be sure to visit the roof terrace, whose forest of towers, turrets, cupolas, gables, and chimneys was described by 19th-century novelist Henry James as "more like the spires of a city than the salient points of a single building."

Chambord also offers a short *son-et-lumière* show, in French, English, and German, successively, on many evenings from mid-May to mid-October. *Admission: 31 frs adults, 17 frs students. Open daily, June 15–Sept. 15 9:30–6:45; mid-Sept.–mid-June 9:30–11:45 and 2–4:45 or 5:45, depending on season. Guided tours available Oct.–Apr.*

Lodging and Dining **St-Michel.** Guests enjoy simple and comfortable living in this revamped country house at the edge of the woods across from Chambord château. A few of the more expensive rooms afford spectacular views. There's a pleasant café-terrace for contemplative drinks and a restaurant with reasonably priced à la carte and prix-fixe menus. *103 pl. St-Michel, 41250, tel. 54–20–31–31. 38 rooms, 31 with bath. Facilities: restaurant, tennis, terrace. MC, V. Closed mid-Nov.–Dec. 20.*

$–$$

Orléans

Ten direct trains make the 40-minute run from Blois northeast to Orléans each day. Orleans tourist office: place Albert-Ier, tel. 38–53–05–95.

Numbers in the margin correspond with points of interest on the Orléans map.

The strategic position of **Orléans** as a natural bridgehead over the Loire has long made it the target of hostile confrontations and invasions. Julius Caesar slaughtered its inhabitants and burned it to the ground. Five centuries later, Attila and his Huns did much the same. Next came the Normans; then the Valois kings turned it into a secondary capital. The story of the Hundred Years' War, Joan of Arc, and the siege of Orléans is widely known. During the Wars of

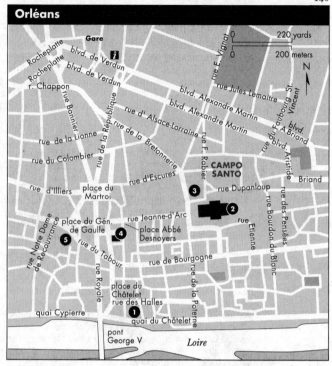

Orléans

Religion (1562–98), much of the cathedral was destroyed, and a century ago, ham-fisted town planners razed many of the city's fine old buildings. During World War II, both German and Allied bombs continued the job. Nevertheless, there is much of interest left, and in recent years dedicated and sensitive planners have done much to bring the city back to life.

The tourist office is on boulevard de Verdun, just in front of the train station. From here, rue de la République takes you 400 yards south to the main square—the **place du Martroi,** with its statue of Joan of Arc. A block farther south, turn left down rue Jeanne-d'Arc for the cathedral, or continue south down **rue Royale;** the latter is lined with excellent shops of all descriptions. Rue Royale brings you to the quai du Châtelet and the banks of the Loire. Make a left turn here to arrive at the **Nouvelle Halle,** the covered market, with its tempting food displays. (Drivers would do best to park at the Campo Santo, by the cathedral, where there's a large underground parking lot.)

2 **Cathédrale Ste-Croix** is a riot of pinnacles and gargoyles, both Gothic and pseudo-Gothic, the whole embellished with 18th-century wedding-cake towers. Novelist Marcel Proust (1871–1922) called it France's ugliest church, but most people find it impressive. Inside you'll see vast quantities of stained glass and 18th-century woodcarving, plus the modern **Chapel of Joan of Arc,** with plaques in memory of the British and American war dead. *Pl. Ste-Croix. Open daily 9–noon and 2–6.*

3 The modern **Musée des Beaux-Arts** is just across the street from the cathedral. Take the elevator to the top and work your way down, viewing works by such artists as Tintoretto, Velázquez, Watteau, Boucher, Rodin, and Gauguin. *1 rue Ferdinand Rabier. Admission: 20 frs adults, 12 frs students. Open Wed.–Mon. 10–noon and 2–6; closed Tues.*

Retrace your steps along the rue Jeanne-d'Arc and turn left onto
④ place Abbé Desnoyers to visit the **Musée Historique.** This Renaissance town house contains both "fine" and "popular" works of art
connected with the town's history and a remarkable collection of pagan bronzes of animals and dancers. These last were hidden from
zealous Christian missionaries in the 4th century and discovered in a
sand pit near St-Benoît in 1861. *Hôtel Cabu, pl. Abbé Desnoyers.
Admission: 12 frs adults, 6 frs students. Open Wed.–Mon. 10–noon
and 2–6.*

Another block west on rue Jeanne-d'Arc, in place du Général-de-
⑤ Gaulle, is **La Maison de Jeanne-d'Arc.** Seventeen-year-old Joan
stayed on the site during the 10-day siege of Orléans in 1429, in a
house that underwent many changes before it was bombed flat in
1940. This reconstruction contains exhibits about her life and costumes of her time. *Pl. du Général-de-Gaulle. Admission: 12 frs
adults, 6 frs students. Open May–Oct., Tues.–Sun. 10–noon and
2–6; Nov.–Apr., Tues.–Sun. 2–6.*

Lodging **Arcade.** This modern, central, chain hotel offers nothing by way of
$ aesthetics, but the rooms are clean and each has its own molded-
plastic bathroom. The restaurant serves light food. *4 rue Maréchal-
Foch, 45000, tel. 38–54–23–11. 125 rooms. Facilities: restaurant.
MC, V.*

$ **Hôtel Central.** Despite its central location, this small hotel has a rus-
tic, provincial charm. The best room is No. 17, which looks out onto a
small courtyard and has a private shower and bathroom. A standard
room has a shower and toilet, though there are some very small
rooms with only a toilet. *6 rue d'Avignon, 45000, tel. 38–53–93–00,
fax 38–77–23–85. 23 rooms. MC, V.*

Dining **L'Assiette.** This is a brisk but comfortable place, right on place du
$–$$ Martroi. Choose your main course (simple grilled meats, mostly),
and while it's cooking, help yourself to a wide variety of hors
d'oeuvres and table wine from the barrel. You're entitled to as much
of both as you want—and desserts are "free," too: The price of your
meal depends on the main dish. *12 pl. du Martroi, tel. 38–53–46–69.
Reservations advised. AE, MC, V.*

Shopping Travelers with a sweet tooth will appreciate the Orléans specialty
known as *cotignac*—an orangey-red molded jelly made from
quinces. It can be bought from most local pâtisseries and is produced
almost exclusively by **Gilbert Jumeau** (1 rue Voisinas, St-Ay), 8 km
(5 mi) west of Orléans.

5 Brittany

Rugged Brittany, occupying the bulbous portion of western France that juts far out into the Atlantic, gazes across the English Channel at Cornwall. The two regions share a Celtic heritage and a wild, untamed feel. Though Brittany became part of France in 1532, Bretons have never felt true kinship with their fellow Frenchmen; many still speak their own language, especially in the remoter parts of the interior, and regional folklore is still very much alive. An annual village *pardon* (a religious festival) will give you a good idea of Breton traditions. At these, banners and statues of saints are borne in colorful parades accompanied by hymns; the whole event is rounded off by food of all kinds. Finistère (from *Finis Terrae*, or Land's End) département, Brittany's westernmost district, is renowned for the costumes worn on such occasions—notably the starched lace bonnets, or *coiffes*, which can tower 15 inches above the wearer's head.

Although Brittany's towns took a mighty hammering from the retreating Nazis in 1944, most have been tastefully restored, the large, concrete-cluttered naval base at Brest being an exception. Rennes, the only Breton city with more than 200,000 inhabitants, retains its traditional charm, as do the towns of Dinan, Quimper, and Vannes. Many ancient man-made delights are found in the region's villages, often in the form of *calvaires* (ornate burial chapels). Other architectural highlights include castles and cathedrals, the most outstanding examples being those of Fougères and Dol, respectively.

Geographically, Brittany is divided in two: maritime Armor ("land of the sea") and hinterland Argoat ("land of the forest"). The north of Brittany tends to be wilder than the south, where the countryside becomes softer as it descends toward Nantes and the Loire. Wherever you go, the coast is close by; the frenzied, cliff-bashing Atlantic surf alternates with sprawling beaches and bustling harbors. Getting around by public transportation is a challenge, and bicycling is the best way to get to remote coastal spots away from towns and villages.

Our tours cover a representative selection of the windswept Brittany that's accessible by train and bus. The first covers the northeastern part of the province, noted for its massive castles and impressive fortifications, and the second takes in highlights of the southern coast.

Brittany Basics

Budget Lodging Although Brittany's economy is somewhat dependent on tourism, the region remains an unspoiled, unhurried spot for visitors on all kinds of budgets. TGV links make the area easily accessible from Paris, bringing larger crowds in the summer, so it is always best to make reservations far in advance. There are an increasing number of luxury hotels (many of which are former châteaus), but the majority of Brittany's lodgings are comfortable and moderately priced. Off-season, many hotels close in coastal areas, but prices drop at those that don't.

Budget Dining Breton cuisine is dominated by fish and seafood. Shrimp, crayfish, crabs, oysters, and scallops are found throughout the region, but the linchpin of Breton menus is often lobster, prepared in sauce or cream or grilled. Popular meats include ham and lamb, frequently served with kidney beans. Fried eel is a traditional dish in the Nantes district. Brittany is particularly famous for its *galettes* and *crêpes*, thin pancakes served with sweet or savory fillings; these are a specialty at the distinctively Breton cafés known as *crêperies*. Accompanied by a glass of local cider, they are ideal for a light, inexpensive meal.

Bargain Shopping Keep an eye out for such typical Breton products as brass and wooden goods, faience pottery, puppets, dolls, locally designed jewelry, and woven or embroidered cloth. Woolens are a specialty, notably thick marine sweaters.

Biking Bikes can be rented at several train stations, including the one in Quimper (tel. 98–98–31–60), and at shops in St-Malo (**Diazo,** 47 quai Duguay-Trouin, tel. 99–40–31–63), Dol (**Cycles Gondange,** 64 rue de Rennes, tel. 99–48–03–20), and Dinard (**Duval Cycles,** 53 rue Gardiner, tel. 99–46–19–63).

Hiking There are three types of long-distance footpaths in Brittany: coastal paths (*sentiers de douanier*), towpaths (*chemins de halage*) along canals between Nantes and Brest, and traditional hiking paths (GR, or *sentiers de grande randonnée*), found throughout France. For more information and detailed guides, contact **L'Association Bretonne des Relais & Itinéraires** (9 rue des Portes-Mordelaises, 35200 Rennes, tel. 99–31–59–44).

Beaches The Brittany coast has any number of clean, sandy beaches; the best are found at Dinard, Perros-Guirec, Trégastel-Plage, Douarnenez, Carnac, and La Baule.

Festivals **Pardons**—traditional religious parades-cum-pilgrimages that invariably showcase age-old local costumes—are the backbone of Breton culture. The pardon held at windswept Ste-Anne-la-Palud, northwest of Locronan, on the last Sunday in August is the most spectacular. There are further manifestations of local folklore, often including dancers and folk singers, at the various Celtic festivals held in summer, of which the **Festival de Cornouaille** in Quimper, in late July, is the biggest.

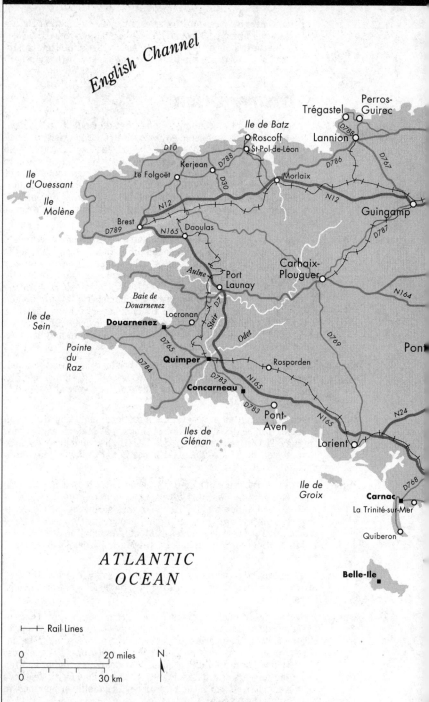

English Channel

Ile de Batz
Roscoff
St-Pol-de-Léon

Trégastel
Perros-Guirec

Lannion

Ile d'Ouessant

Ile Molène

D10
Kerjean
Le Folgoët
D788
D30
Morlaix

D786

D767

N12

N12

Guingamp

Brest
D789
Daoulas
N165
Aulne
Port Launay
D787

Carhaix-Plouguer

N164

Baie de Douarnenez
Locronan
D7
Steir
Odet
D769

Ile de Sein

Douarnenez

D765

Pointe du Raz

D784

Quimper

Rosporden

Pon

Ile de Groix

Concarneau
D783
N165
N165
N24

D783
Pont-Aven

Lorient

Iles de Glénan

D768

Carnac
La Trinité-sur-Mer

Quiberon

ATLANTIC OCEAN

Belle-Ile

⊢—⊢ Rail Lines

0   20 miles
0   30 km

N

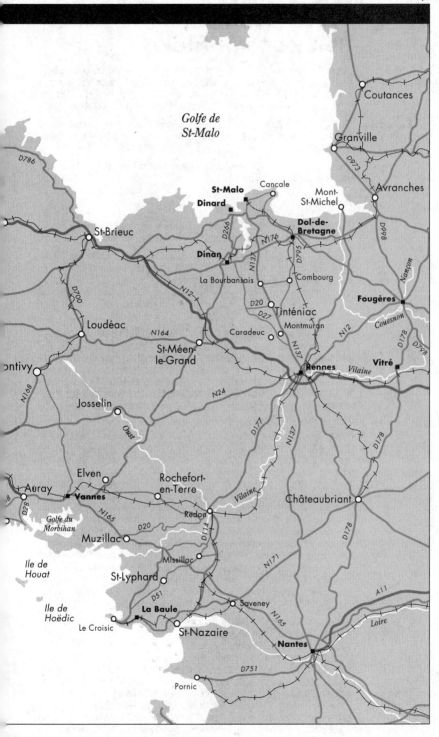

Tour 1: From Rennes to St-Malo

From Rennes and St-Malo, your two base towns on this tour, short train journeys take you to Vitré, Dol, and Dinan. From Vitré, a bus trip brings you to Fougères Castle, and the elegant resort of Dinard lies a short boat ride across the Rance Estuary from St-Malo.

From Paris
By Train TGV bullet trains to Rennes leave Paris (Gare Montparnasse) 12 times daily, several continuing to Quimper. The trip to Rennes takes 2–2½ hours.

By Car The 309-kilometer (193-mile) drive southwest from Paris along A11 and A81 takes 3½ hours.

Rennes

Tourist office: Pont de Nemours, in the middle of the main boulevard south of the cathedral, tel. 99–79–01–98, fax 99–79–31–38.

★ **Rennes,** the traditional capital of Brittany, has a different flavor from other towns in the region, mainly because of a terrible fire in 1720, which lasted a week and destroyed half the city. The remaining cobbled streets and half-timbered, 15th-century houses form an interesting contrast to the classicism of Jacques Gabriel's disciplined granite buildings, broad avenues, and spacious squares.

Head down avenue Janvier from the station and turn left after 600 yards onto quai Emile-Zola. Another 700 yards along, some 200 yards past the tourist office, take the fifth right up into the old town. The **Cathédrale St-Pierre,** a 19th-century building in classical style that took 57 years to construct, looms above rue de la Monnaie. Stop in to admire its richly decorated interior and outstanding 16th-century Flemish altarpiece. *Pl. St-Pierre. Open Mon.–Sat. 8:30–noon and 2–5, Sun. 8:30–noon.*

The pedestrian rue Lafayette and rue Nationale lead to the **Palais de Justice** (Law Courts). This palatial building, originally home to the Breton Parliament, was designed in 1618 by Salomon de Brosse, architect of the Luxembourg Palace in Paris. It was the most important building in Rennes to escape the 1720 fire, but in February 1994, following a massive demonstration by Breton fishermen demanding state subsidies, a disastrous fire broke out at the Parliament building that left it a charred shell. Much of the artwork, though damaged, was saved by firefighters, who arrived at the scene only when the fire was in full flow. It was a case of the fire bell that cried "fire" once too often; a faulty bell, which went off regularly for no reason, led the man on duty to ignore the ringing. As for the cause of the fire itself, rumors abound, but an investigation is still underway. The Parliament has been indefinitely closed for a major restoration.

Head down from the Palais de Justice and left across quai Emile-Zola to the **Palais des Musées,** a huge building containing two museums—the **Musée des Beaux-Arts** and **Musée de Bretagne.** The Fine Arts Museum, on the second floor, houses one of the country's best collections of paintings outside Paris, featuring works by Georges de La Tour, Camille Corot, Paul Gauguin, and Maurice Utrillo, to name only a few. The ground-floor Museum of Brittany retraces the region's history by way of costumes, models, porcelain, furniture, coins, statues, and shiny push-button visual displays. *20 quai Emile-Zola. Admission: joint ticket 18 frs adults, 9 frs children under 14. Open Wed.–Mon. 10–noon and 2–6.*

Northeast of the museum building, a five-minute walk via rue Gambetta and rue Victor-Hugo, is the **Jardin du Thabor,** a large, formal French garden with regimented rows of trees, shrubs, and flowers. Even the lawns are manicured—not often the case in France. There is a notable view of the church of **Notre-Dame-en-St-Mélaine** in one corner.

Lodging **Central.** This stately, late-19th-century hotel, on a narrow back
$$ street close to Rennes Cathedral, lives up to its name. The individually decorated guest rooms look out over the street or courtyard; ask for one of the latter, as they're quieter. The owners have recently renovated the hotel, adding 35 rooms and off-street parking, a big plus in an accommodation so close to the town center. *6 rue Lanjuinais, 35000, tel. 99–79–12–36, fax 99–79–65–76. 78 rooms, most with bath. AE, DC, MC, V.*

$ **Angélina.** This little charmer wins on sheer unpretentiousness: friendly welcome, clean rooms, robust breakfasts, and windows double-glazed to keep out the noise (it is on Rennes's principal boulevard, within a five-minute walk of the old town). Don't be put off by the fact that the hotel begins on the third floor of an ordinary-looking building. *1 quai Lamennais, 35100, tel. 99–79–29–66. 28 rooms, with shower or bath. AE, DC, MC, V.*

Dining **Palais.** The best, though not the most expensive, restaurant in
$$ Rennes must thank its highly inventive young chef, Marc Tizon, for
★ its considerable reputation. Specialties include roast rabbit and, during winter, fried oysters in crab sauce. The lightish cuisine varies according to season and what's freshest in the market. The decor is sharp-edged contemporary, the site conveniently central. *6 pl. du Parlement de Bretagne, tel. 99–79–45–01. Dinner reservations required. Jacket required. AE, DC, MC, V. Closed Sun. dinner, Mon., and Aug.*

$ **Le Grain de Sable.** At the bottom of rue des Dames, which leads to
★ the cathedral, is a thoroughly unusual restaurant. Plants, candelabra, faded photos, and a settee in the middle of the dining room create an ambience that escapes tackiness only by sheer eccentricity. The cuisine is equally offbeat; expect garlic puree or endive with melted cheese to accompany the grilled meats that dominate the menu. Piped music warbles in the background as the playful waitresses receive noisy reprimands from Hervé in the kitchen. *2 rue des Dames, tel. 99–30–78–18. Reservations advised. MC, V. Closed Sun., Mon. dinner.*

Shopping The streets surrounding the cathedral are full of 15th- and 16th-century houses in both medieval and Renaissance styles. Many have been converted for use as shops, boutiques, restaurants, and crêperies; a lively **street market** is held in and around place des Lices on Saturday morning. Places for good textiles are **Tidreiz** (pl. du Palais) and **Au Roy d'Ys** (29 blvd. de Magenta).

Vitré

Seven trains make the 30-minute trip east from Rennes every day. The train station is on the south side of Vitré; if you walk north for less than 200 yards, you'll be in the center of the old town. Tourist office: place St-Yves, tel. 99–75–04–46.

★ Built high above the Vilaine Valley, **Vitré** is one of the age-old gateways to Brittany: There's still a feel of the Middle Ages about its dark, narrow alleys and tightly packed houses. The town's leading attraction is its formidable **castle,** shaped in an imposing triangle with fat, round towers. An 11th-century creation, it was first rebuilt in the 14th and 15th centuries to protect Brittany against invasion and was to prove one of the province's most successful fortresses: During the Hundred Years' War (1337–1453), the English repeatedly failed to take it, even though they occupied the rest of the town.

Time, not foreigners, came closest to ravaging the castle, which was heavily, though tastefully, restored during the past century. The town hall, however, is an unfortunate 1913 addition to the castle courtyard. You can visit the wing to the left of the entrance, beginning with the Tour St-Laurent and continuing along the walls via Tour de l'Argenterie, with its macabre collection of stuffed frogs and reptiles preserved in glass jars, to Tour de l'Oratoire. *Admission: 18 frs. Open Apr.–June, Wed.–Mon. 10–noon and 2:30–5:30; July–Sept., daily 10–12:30 and 2–6:15; Oct.–Mar., Wed.–Fri. 10–noon and 2–5:30, Mon. 2–5:30.*

Vitré's castle makes a splendid sight, especially from a vantage point on rue de Fougères across the river valley below. It faces the narrow, cobbled streets of the remarkably preserved old town. Rue Poterie, rue d'Embas, and rue Beaudrairie, originally the home of tanners (the name comes from *baudoyers*—leather workers), make up a web of medieval streets as picturesque as any in Brittany. Fragments of the town's medieval ramparts remain, including the 15th-century **Tour de la Bridolle** on place de la République, five blocks up from the castle. Built in the 15th and 16th centuries, **Notre-Dame** church has a fine, pinnacled south front and dominates a large square of the same name (you'll have passed it on the left on your way to place de la République).

Lodging **Chêne Vert.** Vitré is badly placed in the hotel stakes, but we suggest
¢ this establishment, which is convenient to D857 (which links Rennes and Laval), just opposite the train station and a 10-minute stroll through cobbled streets from Vitré Castle. It is the epitome of a French provincial hotel: creaky stairs, fraying carpets, oversoft mattresses, and less-than-enthusiastic service—all, including a copious dinner, for next to nothing. Look carefully, however, and you will notice some intriguing touches—an enormous model ship on the second floor, for example, or the zinc-plated walls in the dining room. *Pl. du Général-de-Gaulle, 35500, tel. 99–75–00–58. 22 rooms, a few with bath. Closed mid-Sept.–mid-Oct.; restaurant closed Fri. dinner and Sat., Oct.–May.*

Fougères

Buses run 4 times per day from Vitré north to Fougères. The 32-kilometer (20-mile) trip takes about 40 minutes.

Fougères, a traditional cobbling and cider-making center, was for many centuries a frontier town, valiantly attempting to guard Brittany against attack. Perhaps one of the reasons for its conspicuous lack of success is the site of the **castle:** Instead of sitting high up on the hill, it spreads out down in the valley, though the sinuous River Nançon does make an admirable moat. The 13-towered castle covers more than five acres, making it one of the largest in Europe. Although largely in ruins, the castle is an excellent example of the military architecture of the Middle Ages, and it is impressive both inside and out. The thick walls—up to 20 feet across in places—were intended to resist 15th-century artillery fire, but the castle was to prove vulnerable to surprise attacks and sieges. A visit inside the castle walls reveals three lines of fortification, with the cosseted keep at their heart. There are charming views over Fougères from the Tour Mélusine and, in the Tour Raoul, a small shoe museum. *East end of town on pl. Raoul II. Admission: 13 frs (18 frs with guide). Open Feb.–June and Sept.–Dec., 9:30–noon and 2–5; July–Aug., 9–7.*

The oldest streets of Fougères are alongside the castle, clustered around the elegant slate spire of **St-Sulpice** (rue de Lusignan), a Flamboyant Gothic church with several fine altarpieces. A number of medieval houses line rue de la Pinterie, which leads directly from the castle up to the undistinguished heart of town.

In the 1790s, Fougères was a center of Royalist resistance to the French Revolution. Much of the action in 19th-century novelist Honoré de Balzac's bloodcurdling novel *Les Chouans* takes place hereabouts; the novel's heroine, Marie de Verneuil, had rooms close to the church of **St-Léonard** (follow the river left from the castle), which overlooks the Nançon Valley. Both path and church, with its ornate facade and 17th-century tower, have changed little; the garden through which the path leads is known today as the **Jardin Public.**

Another man who was inspired by the scenery of Fougères was locally born Emmanuel de La Villéon (1858–1944), a little-known Impressionist painter. His works are displayed in the **Musée La Villéon,** in one of the oldest surviving houses (dating from the 16th century) in hilltop Fougères; to reach it from the Jardin Public, head left past St-Léonard, and cross the square onto the adjacent rue Nationale. The more than 100 paintings, pastels, watercolors, and drawings suggest serene, underappreciated talent. *51 rue Nationale. Admission: 8 frs. Open Easter–mid-June, weekends only, 11–12:30 and 2:30–5; mid-June–mid-Sept., weekdays 10:30–12:30 and 2:30–5:30, weekends and holidays 11–12:30 and 2:30–5.*

Dol-de-Bretagne

Trains make the 35-minute trip north to Dol from Rennes 14 times daily. Dol tourist office: 3 Grande-Rue, tel. 99–48–15–37.

The ancient town of **Dol** looks out from its 60-foot cliffs over Le Marais, a marshy plain stretching across to Mont St-Michel, 21 kilometers (13 miles) northeast. The **Promenade des Douves,** laid out along the northern part of the original ramparts, offers extensive views of Le Marais and Mont Dol, a 200-foot granite mound, 3 kilometers (2 miles) north, legendary scene of combat between St. Michael and the devil.

At the end of the promenade, note the **Cathédrale St-Samson** (pl. de la Cathédrale), a damp, soaring, fortresslike bulk of granite dating mainly from the 12th to the 14th century. This mighty building shows just how influential the bishopric of Dol was in days gone by. The richly sculpted Great Porch, carved wooden choir stalls, and stained glass in the chancel all deserve close scrutiny.

Turn down rue des Ecoles to the small **Musée Historique d'Art Populaire** (Museum of Folk Art). During a short, cheerful guided tour, you'll see costumes, weapons, and a series of scale models retracing life in Dol since prehistoric times. The glory of the museum, though, is its assembly of colored wooden religious statues. *Rue des Ecoles. Admission: 23 frs. Open Easter–Oct., Wed.–Mon. 9–noon and 1:30–6:30.*

Rue des Ecoles leads to Dol's picturesque main street, Grande-Rue-des-Stuarts, lined with medieval houses. The oldest, at No. 17, has a chunky row of Romanesque arches.

Lodging and Dining
$

Logis de la Bresche Arthur. With its crisp outlines, white walls, and glassed-in terrace, this hotel may not be quite as historic as it sounds, but it's the coziest lodging place in Dol. Rooms are functional; local character is reserved for the restaurant. Here chef-owner Phillipe Martel serves such classically inspired dishes as roast pigeon with black-currant and ginger sauce, lightly poached scallops with herbs, and ravioli stuffed with *petits gris* (small snails) in a cream sauce. *36 blvd. Deminiac, 35120, tel. 99–48–01–44, fax 99–48–16–32. 24 rooms with bath. Facilities: restaurant. AE, DC, MC, V.*

Dinan

Six trains make the ½-hour journey southwest from Dol each day, and 7 make the 70-minute trip northwest from Rennes (all but 1 require a change in Dol). Dinan tourist office: 6 rue de l'Horloge, tel. 96–39–75–40.

★ **Dinan** has close links with Brittany's 14th-century anti-English warrior-hero Bertrand du Guesclin, whose name is commemorated in countless squares and hostelries across the province. Du Guesclin won a famous victory here in 1359 and promptly married a local girl, Tiphaine Raguenel. When he died in the siege of Auvergne (central France) in 1380, his body was dispatched home to Dinan. Owing to the great man's popularity, however, only his heart completed the journey, the rest of him having been confiscated by devoted followers in towns along the route.

Begin your stroll around the old town at the tourist office, housed in a charming 16th-century building on rue de l'Horloge. For a superb view of the town, climb to the top of the nearby belfry, the **Tour de l'Horloge**. *Admission: 10 frs. Open July–Aug., daily 10:45–1:15 and 3–6.*

Turn left and head half a block along to admire the triangular-gabled wooden houses in **place des Merciers, rue de l'Apport,** and **rue de la Poissonnerie**. With their overhanging balconies and black-and-white half-timbered houses, these cobbled streets are so pretty you may think you've stumbled onto a movie set. Restore your faith with a visit to the nearby church, the **Basilique St-Sauveur** (turn right out of place des Merciers along rue Haute-Voie, then take the second left into the church square). The church is a mixture of styles, ranging from the Romanesque south front to the Flamboyant Gothic facade and Renaissance side chapels. Du Guesclin's heart lies in the north transept.

The **Jardin Anglais** (English Garden) is just behind the church; it's not really much of a garden, but its old trees frame nicely the east end of St-Sauveur. More spectacular views are found at the bottom of the garden, which looks down the plummeting Rance Valley to the river 250 feet below.

Leading down to the harbor, cobblestone rue du Jerzual—a beautifully preserved medieval street—is full of boutiques and crafts shops purveying woodcarvings, jewelry, leather work, glass, painted silk, and other craft items. It is divided halfway down by the town walls and massive Porte du Jerzual gateway. Dinan's harbor seems somewhat forlorn; although there are sailings in summer up the River Rance to Dinard and St-Malo, abandoned warehouses bear witness to vanished commercial activity, with only an occasional restaurant to brighten it up.

Stagger back up the hill (it's steep) and turn right, well after the Porte du Jerzual, onto rue de l'Ecole. This street leads down to another gateway, the Porte St-Malo, from which the leafy Promenade des Grands Fossés heads left on a tour of the best-preserved section of the town walls. Follow these walls around as far as the **castle**. Here you can visit the two-story Coëtquen Tower and 100-foot, 14th-century keep, containing varied displays of medieval effigies and statues, Breton furniture, and local *coiffes* (lace headdresses). *Porte de Guichet. Admission: 15 frs. Open Mar.–Jan., daily 9–noon and 2–6.*

Lodging and Dining
$$
D'Avaugour. This hotel, splendidly situated opposite Dinan Castle's Tour du Connétable, has its own flower garden; most of the cozy guest rooms look out onto either the garden or the castle, and all are being redecorated (completion expected 1997). The hotel restaurant is no more, but owner Mme. Quinton offers a full buffet breakfast

(served in the garden on fine summer days) at the former Continental breakfast rate. Mme. Quinton is fluent in English and enjoys helping guests plan their trips. *1 pl. du Champ-Clos, 22100, tel. 96–39–07–49, fax 96–85–43–04. 27 rooms with bath. Facilities: garden. AE, DC, MC, V.*

Lodging **Arvor.** An English couple, the Bundys, converted an 18th-century
$ convent into this charming, comfortable hotel, which overlooks the quiet cobblestone streets of Dinan's old town. *5 rue A. Pavie, 22100, tel. 96–39–21–22, fax 96–39–83–09. 23 rooms with bath or shower. AE, MC, V.*

Dining **Relais des Corsaires.** The old hilltop town of Dinan is full of restau-
$ rants and cafés specializing in *galettes*, Brittany's distinctive crêpes. But we suggest that you wander down to the old port on the banks of the Rance to dine at this casual spot, named after the pirates who apparently raided the wharves of Dinan. The mid-range prix-fixe menu provides an ample four-course meal, with alternative menus at higher and lower prices. The welcoming propietors, Jacques and Bärbel Pauwels, have also created a more informal grill, Au Petit Corsair, in the 15th-century building next door. *7 rue du Quai, tel. 96–39–40–17. Reservations accepted. AE, DC, MC, V. Closed mid-Jan.–mid-Feb., Sun. dinner, and Mon. in winter.*

Shopping Woolens by the yard and English cakes and scones by the dozen: That's the unlikely combination you'll find at this strange little American-run outfit, **La Toison d'Or** (rue du Jerzual). Long wooden benches add to the atmosphere, if not the comfort, as you settle down for a cup of coffee and a snack.

St-Malo

Five trains make the 1-hour trip north from Dinan each day (with a change at Dol), and 11 trains make the 50-minute journey north from Rennes. St-Malo tourist office: esplanade St-Vincent, tel. 99–56–64–48, fax 99–40–93–13.

★ The ancient walled town of **St-Malo** is a former pirate base whose stone ramparts have stood firm against the Atlantic since the 13th century. The town itself has proved less resistant: A week-long fire in 1944, kindled by retreating Nazis, wiped out nearly all the old buildings. Restoration work was more painstaking than brilliant, but the narrow streets and granite houses of the old town, known as *Intra Muros* ("within the walls"), have been satisfactorily re-created, enabling St-Malo to regain its role as a busy fishing port and seaside resort.

North American visitors can pay homage here to Jacques Cartier, who set sail from St-Malo in 1535 to discover the St. Lawrence River and found Québec. Cartier's tomb is in the church of **St-Vincent** (off Grande-Rue), and his statue looks out over the town ramparts, four blocks away—along with that of swashbuckling corsair Robert Surcouf (he's the one pointing an accusing finger over the waves at *l'Angleterre*). The ramparts themselves date from the 12th century but were considerably enlarged and modified in the 18th. They extend from the castle in St-Malo's northeast corner and ring the old town, with a total length of more than a mile. The views from the ramparts are stupendous, especially at high tide. Five hundred yards offshore is the **Ile du Grand Bé,** a small island housing the somber military tomb of Viscount Chateaubriand, who was born in St-Malo. The islet can be reached by a causeway at low tide, as can the **Fort National,** a massive fortress with a dungeon constructed in 1689 by that military-engineering genius Sébastien de Vauban. *Admission: 10 frs. Open Apr.–Sept., daily 9:30–noon and 2:30–6.*

At the edge of the ramparts, overlooking the Fort National, is **St-Malo Castle,** whose great keep and watchtowers command an impressive view of the harbor and coastline. The castle houses two museums: the **Musée de la Ville,** devoted to local history, and the **Quic-en-Groigne,** a tower where various episodes and celebrities from St-Malo's past are recalled by way of waxworks. *Porte St-Vincent. Admission: 16 frs (Musée de la Ville), 17 frs (Quic-en-Groigne). Musée de la Ville open Mar.–Nov., Wed.–Mon. 9:30–noon and 2–6:30; Quic-en-Groigne open Easter–Oct., daily 9–11:30 and 2–6.*

Lodging
$–$$

Hôtel Elizabeth. In this touristy and slightly honky-tonk town, the Elizabeth is an island of sophistication. It is small, as you would expect of a town house built into the ramparts of the city wall (near Porte Ste-Louis), but each of the compact rooms is tastefully furnished. The hotel is obviously Mme. Raverat's pride and joy, and perhaps for that reason she keeps the rates down. *2 rue des Cordeliers, 35400, tel. 99-56-24-98, fax 99-56-39-24. 17 rooms with bath. AE, DC, MC, V.*

$

Jean-Bart. This clean, quiet hotel next to the ramparts, whose decor makes liberal use of cool blue, bears the stamp of diligent renovation: The beds are comfortable and the bathrooms shiny-modern. Though rooms are on the small side, some have exhilarating sea views. *12 rue de Chartres, 35400, tel. 99-40-33-88. 17 rooms with bath. MC, V. Closed mid-Nov.–mid-Feb.*

Dining
$
★

Café de la Bourse. Wherever you search for a restaurant in the old town of St-Malo, you will feel you are being hemmed into an overcommercialized tourist trap. This restaurant, where prawns and oysters are downed by the shovel, is no exception. However, though its wooden seats and some tacky navigational paraphernalia—ships' wheels and posters of grizzled old sea dogs—are hardly artistic, the large, L-shape dining room makes amends with genuinely friendly service and a bountiful seafood platter for two that includes at least three tanklike crabs, plus an army of cockles, whelks, and periwinkles. *1 rue de Dinan, tel. 99-56-47-17. Reservations accepted. AE, V. Closed Wed. during low season (approximately mid-Sept.–May).*

Shopping

The market held in the streets of old St-Malo on Tuesday and Friday is one of the most colorful in the province.

Dinard

Boats plow frequently across the strait between St-Malo and Dinard. Tourist office: 2 blvd. Féart, tel. 99–46–94–12.

Dinard, a stylish, slightly snobbish vacation resort, may be fraying on the edges these days, but its picture-book setting on the Rance Estuary opposite St-Malo makes up for any shabbiness. Until the middle of the last century, Dinard was a minor fishing village. It became all the rage, thanks to propaganda from a rich American named Coppinger; avenues were baptized Edward VII and George V as English royalty jumped on the bandwagon. Grand hotels and villas are still plentiful.

It's not hard to see why uppercrust Edwardians loved the place, with its dramatic cliffs, lush vegetation, bracing coastal walks, and three sandy beaches. To make the most of Dinard's exhilarating setting, head down to the town's southern tip, the **Pointe de la Vicomte,** where cliffs offer panoramic views across the Baie du Prieuré and Rance Estuary. The **Plage du Prieuré,** named after a priory that once stood here, is a sandy beach ringed by yachts, dinghies, and motorboats. The **Clair de Lune Promenade** hugs the seacoast on its way toward the English Channel, passing in front of the small jetty used by boats crossing to St-Malo. Shortly after, the street reaches the **Musée de la Mer** (Marine Museum and Aquarium). Virtually every known species of Breton bird and sea creature is on display here, in two rooms and 24 pools. Another room is devoted to the polar expeditions of explorer Jean Charcot, one of the first men to chart the Antarctic; there are poignant souvenirs of his last voyage, in 1936, from which he never returned. *Claire de Lune Promenade. Admission: 10 frs. Open Pentecost Sun.–Sept., daily 10–noon and 2–6.*

The Clair de Lune Promenade, lined with luxuriant semitropical vegetation, really hits its stride as it rounds the Pointe du Moulinet to the Prieuré Beach. River meets sea in a foaming mass of rock-pounding surf, and caution is needed as you walk along the slippery path. Your reward: the calm and shelter of the **Plage de l'Ecluse,** an inviting sandy beach, bordered by a casino and numerous stylish hotels. The coastal path picks up again on the far side, ringing the Pointe de la Malouine and Pointe des Etêtés before arriving at Dinard's final beach, the **Plage de St-Enogat.**

Lodging and Dining
$–$$

Altair. In the center of town yet not far from the beach, this traditional family hotel is delightfully unpretentious, though some may consider it old-fashioned. Rooms are clean and comfortable, with well-worn furniture, and there is a small garden for afternoon tea. The restaurant brings in the locals, and though the à la carte dishes can be expensive, the fixed-price menus at 80 francs and 120 francs offer good value. *18 blvd. Féart, 35800, tel. 99–46–13–58, fax 99–88–20–49. 22 rooms. Facilities: restaurant, garden. MC, V. Restaurant closed Sun. dinner. Hotel and restaurant closed mid-Nov.–mid-Dec.*

$

La Vallée. Prices at this traditional, late-19th-century hotel vary according to the room. The best have a sea view: The Clair de Lune Promenade and Prieuré Beach are within shouting distance. The hotel itself is decorated in an elegant, *fin-de-siècle* (turn-of-the-century) style, with an authentic French feel. The restaurant, with moderate and expensive menus, specializes in seafood. *6 av. George-V, 35800, tel. 99–46–94–00, fax 99–88–22–47. 26 rooms with bath. Facilities: restaurant (closed Tues. Oct.–Apr.). V. Closed mid-Nov.–mid-Dec., second half of Jan.*

Tour 2: From Quimper to Nantes

This tour takes in some of Brittany's most distinctive countryside as it follows the main train route down the coast from Quimper, southeast to Nantes. Visiting Douarnenez, Concarneau, and Carnac requires a bus ride from the nearest station, and boats cross to the pretty island of Belle-Ile from sea-swept Quiberon several times daily.

From Paris
By Train

Express trains to Quimper leave Paris (Gare Montparnasse) nine times daily. The trip takes 5–5½ hours.

By Car

The 560-kilometer (350-mile) drive from Paris to Quimper takes about 6 hours. Leave A81 at Rennes, follow N24 southwest to Lorient, then take E60 northwest to Quimper.

Quimper

Tourist office: rue de l'Amiral-de-la-Grandière, across the river from the old town, tel. 98–53–04–05.

Today a lively commercial town, **Quimper** (pronounced cam-*pair*) was the ancient capital of Cornouaille province and was founded, it is said, by King Gradlon 1,500 years ago. It owes its strange-looking name to its site at the confluence *(kemper* in Breton) of the Odet and

Steir rivers. The banks of the Odet are a charming place to stroll. Highlights of the old town include **rue Kéréon**, a lively street for shopping, and the stately **Jardin de l'Evêché** (Bishop's Gardens) behind the cathedral in the center of the old town.

From the station turn right onto avenue de la Gare and continue along the banks of the Odet River (blvd. de Kerguelen) to the **Cathédrale St-Corentin**. This masterpiece of Gothic architecture is the second-largest cathedral in Brittany (after Dol's). Legendary King Gradlon is represented on horseback just below the base of the spires, harmonious, mid-19th-century additions to the medieval ensemble. The luminous 15th-century stained glass is particularly striking. *Pl. St-Corentin.*

Two museums flank the cathedral. Works by major masters, such as Rubens, Corot, and Picasso, mingle with pretty landscapes from the local Gauguin-inspired Pont-Aven school in the **Musée des Beaux-Arts** (admission 25 frs; open July–Aug., daily 9–7, Sept.–June, Wed.–Mon. 10–noon and 2–6), while local furniture, ceramics, and folklore top the bill in the **Musée Départemental** (admission 20 frs; open June–Sept., daily 9–6, Oct.–May, Wed.–Mon. 9:30–noon and 2–6) on adjacent rue du Roi-Gradlon.

Quimper sprang to nationwide attention as an earthenware center in the mid-18th century, when it started producing second-rate imitations of the Rouen ceramics known as faience, featuring blue Asian motifs. Today's more colorful designs, based on floral arrangements and marine fauna, are still often hand-painted. There are tours to the main pottery, the **Faïencerie Henriot,** and its museum on the banks of the Odet south of the old town. *Allée de Locmaria. Admission: 25 frs. Open mid-Apr.–Oct. and school vacations, Mon.–Sat. 10–6.*

Lodging
¢ **Tour d'Auvergne.** Behind the post office and just 350 yards from the cathedral and old Quimper, this small hotel has been entirely renovated to offer pleasant rooms, each with a private bathroom. The restaurant, while serving quite good food, is a tad pricey, with menus beginning at 145 frs. *13 rue des Réguaires, 29000, tel. 98–95–08–70, fax 98–95–17–31. 18 rooms. Facilities: restaurant. MC, V.*

Dining
¢ **Cariatides.** Crêpes are a Brittany specialty, and the best place to sample them in Quimper—with an obligatory bottle of the local cider—is in this bustling crêperie housed in an atmospheric medieval building a stone's throw from the cathedral. The wide choice of traditional sweet crêpes, plus savory versions made from *froment* (white flour) or *blé noir* (buckwheat), pulls in a lively, youthful crowd throughout the year. *4 rue Guéodet, tel. 98–95–15–14. MC, V. Closed Sun.*

Shopping The streets around the cathedral (especially **rue du Parc**) are full of shops, several selling the woolen goods and thick fishermen's sweaters for which Brittany is known. Quimper's hand-painted earthenware can be bought at the **Kéraluc Faïencerie** (14 rue de la Troménie on the Bénodet road) or at **Henriot** (12 pl. St-Corentin).

Douarnenez

Four buses make the 30-minute run daily from Quimper, 22 km (14 mi) to the southeast.

Douarnenez is a charming old fishing town of quayside paths and narrow, zigzagging streets. Boats come in from the Atlantic to offload their catches of mackerel, sardines, and tuna. Sailing enthusiasts will be interested in the town's biennial classic boat rally in mid-August (even years), when traditionally rigged sailing boats of every description ply the waters of the picturesque Bay of Douarnenez.

Concarneau

A dozen trains make the 14-minute run daily from Quimper east to Rosporden, where you connect with a bus that takes another 20 minutes to Concarneau. Tourist office: quai d'Aiguillon, tel. 98–97–01–44.

Located 21 kilometers (13 miles) southeast of Quimper at the mouth of the Baie de la Forêt, **Concarneau** looks south across the Atlantic toward the desolate Iles de Glénan. The third-largest fishing port in France and a busy industrial town, Concarneau has a grain of charm and an abundance of tacky souvenir shops. The town's main attrac-
★ tion, the **Ville Close,** is a fortified islet in the middle of the harbor that you reach by a quaint drawbridge. The islet's narrow streets and huge granite ramparts make for an enjoyable afternoon's roam; the view of the harbor is fantastic.

From early medieval times, Concarneau was regarded as impregnable, and the fortifications were further strengthened by the English under John de Montfort during the War of Succession (1341–64). This enabled the English-controlled Concarneau to withstand two sieges by Breton hero Bertrand du Guesclin; the third siege was successful for the plucky du Guesclin, who drove out the English in 1373. Three hundred years later, Sébastien de Vauban remodeled the ramparts into what you see today: half a mile long and highly scenic, offering views across the two harbors on either side of the Ville Close. *Admission to ramparts: 5 frs. Open Easter–mid-June, daily 10–12:30 and 2–7; mid-June–Sept., 10–7:30.*

At the end of rue Vauban closest to the drawbridge is the **Musée de la Pêche** (Fishing Museum), occupying an enormous hall in the former arsenal. Here you will encounter historical explanations of fishing techniques from around the world, plus such displays as an anti-whale harpoon gun and a giant Japanese crab. Turtles and fish may be seen in the museum's many aquariums. *Admission: 30 frs adults, 20 frs children. Open mid-June–mid-Sept., daily 9:30–7; mid-Sept.–mid-June, 9:30–12:30 and 2–6.*

If you're in Concarneau in the second half of August, you will be able to enjoy the **Fête des Filets Bleus** (Blue Net Festival) in the Ville Close. This festival is a week-long folk celebration during which Bretons in costume swirl and dance to the wail of bagpipes.

Lodging **Sables Blancs.** A great advantage of this old-fashioned hotel is that
$ all guest rooms feature soul-satisfying views of the sea and direct access to the beach: The name is derived from the hotel's location near the Sables Blancs (White Sands) beach. Be sure to request a room in a lower price range, because not all are truly inexpensive. The hotel restaurant is adequate, with set menus at reasonable prices. *Plage des Sables Blancs, 29110, tel. 98–97–01–39, fax 98–50–65–88. 48 rooms, most with bath. Facilities: restaurant. AE, DC, MC, V. Closed mid-Nov.–Mar.*

Dining **Le Galion.** Flowers, wooden beams, silver candlesticks, old stones,
$$ and a roaring hearth form a pleasant backdrop to Henri Gaonach's marine tours de force at this, one of Concarneau's best fish restaurants. The cooking and the decor justify a slight splurge here; several menus start at 150 frs, though the more elaborate menus are tempting. (There are also five guest rooms in the 450-franc range.) *15 rue St-Guénolé, Ville-Close, 29110, tel. 98–97–30–16, fax 98–50–67–88. AE, DC, MC, V. Closed Sun. eve. and Mon. in winter and mid-Jan.–mid-Feb.*

Belle-Ile

Trains from Quimper (via Rosporden) continue southeast to Auray (70 minutes from Quimper), from where 7 buses make the 90-minute trip south to Quiberon each day. Belle-Ile tourist office: quai Bonnelle, tel. 97–31–81–93.

The spa town of Quiberon is famed for its soothing waters and fine beaches. But the best reason to visit is its proximity to 18-kilometer-long (11-mile-long) **Belle-Ile**, Brittany's largest island. Boats leave from the cheerful harbor of Port-Maria and dock at Le Palais, the island's liveliest town, where you can rent bikes (Joël Banet Garage, quai Gambetta, tel. 97–31–50–70).

Despite being a mere 45-minute boat trip from Quiberon, Belle-Ile is much less commercialized, and the scenery is truly exhilarating. Near Sauzon, the island's prettiest settlement, is a staggering view across to the Quiberon peninsula and Golfe du Morbihan from the **Pointe des Poulains,** erstwhile home of the Belle Epoque's femme fatale, actress Sarah Bernhardt. The nearby **Grotte de l'Apothicairerie** is a grotto whose name derives from the local cormorants' nests, said to resemble pharmacy bottles. Farther south, near Port Goulphar, is another dramatic sight—the **Grand Phare** (lighthouse), built in 1835 and rising 275 feet above sea level. Its light is one of the most powerful in Europe, visible from 75 miles across the Atlantic. If the keeper is available, you may be able to climb to the top and admire the view.

Lodging and Dining
¢–$

Bretagne. Staying on Belle-Ile can be pricey, but at this old dockside house by the harbor at Le Palais, the cheapest rooms, the ones without shower or toilet, start at around 130 frs. Better appointed, more spacious accommodations cost 300 frs. Seafood is the specialty of the dining room, which looks out to sea, and you can net a set menu for 70 frs or 130 frs. *Quai Macé, 56360 Le Palais, tel. 97–31–80–14, fax 97–31–51–69. 32 rooms, most with bath or shower. Facilities: bar, restaurant. MC, V.*

Dining
$

La Forge. A sure bet for lunch or dinner, La Forge specializes in traditional cuisine, based on seafood and fish, at affordable prices. Old wooden beams and remnants of the building's original purpose—blacksmithing—contribute to the pleasant, rustic atmosphere. *Rte. de Port-Goulphar, Bangor, tel. 91–31–51–76. Reservations required in summer. AE, DC, MC, V. Closed Wed. and Jan.–Feb.*

Shopping

Henri Le Roux (18 rue du Port-Maria, near the harbor in Quiberon) has taken the art of chocolateiering to dizzying heights.

Carnac

Seven buses daily make the 60-minute run from Quiberon north to Carnac. Tourist office: 74 avenue des Druides, tel. 97–52–13–52.

★ **Carnac** has its beaches, but it's famed for its **megalithic monuments** dating from the Neolithic and Early Bronze ages (3500–1800 BC). The whys and wherefores of their construction remain as obscure as those of their English contemporary, Stonehenge, although religious beliefs and astrology were doubtless an influence. The 2,395 menhirs ("menhir" is a Breton word meaning "standing stone") that make up the three *alignements* (at Kermario, Kerlescan, and Ménec) are positioned with astounding astronomical accuracy in semicircles and parallel lines more than half a mile long. There are also smaller-scale dolmen ensembles and three tumuli (mounds or barrows), including the 130-yard-long, 38-foot-high **Tumulus de St-Michel** (just northeast of Carnac), topped by a small chapel affording fine views of the rock-strewn countryside. *Guided tours of the tumulus daily Apr.–Sept. Cost: 5 frs.*

Lodging and Dining
$–$$

Lann-Roz. This large mansion on avenue de la Poste, the main street connecting the old town to Carnac-Plage, the beach, is a good find in pricey Carnac, although the largest rooms top 300 frs. A veranda overlooks an attractive garden, and bubbly patronne Anne Le

Calvez plays host to a mix of business travelers and international tourists. Unless you opt for the 120-franc menu, the cost of your meal may seem steep. The seafood is a good bet, especially the mussel soup. *12 av. de la Poste, 56340, tel. 97–52–11–01. 14 rooms with bath or shower. Facilities: restaurant. AE, DC, MC, V. Closed Jan. and Wed. out of season.*

Vannes

Eight trains run from Quimper east to Vannes during the day. The trip averages 90 minutes. Trains make the 15-minute trip from Auray to Vannes every 2 hours or so. Vannes tourist office: 1 rue Thiers, tel. 97–47–24–34.

Vannes, scene of the declaration of unity between France and Brittany in 1532, is one of the few towns in Brittany to have been spared damage during World War II, so its authentic regional charm remains intact. Be sure to visit the **Cohue** (medieval market hall—now a temporary exhibition center) and the picturesque **place Henri IV** and browse in the small boutiques and antiques shops in the surrounding pedestrian streets. The ramparts, Promenade de la Garenne, and medieval washhouses are all set against the backdrop of the much-restored **Cathédrale St-Pierre,** with its 1537 Renaissance chapel, Flamboyant Gothic transept portal, and treasury in the old chapterhouse. *Pl. du Cathédrale. Admission: 3 frs. Treasury open mid-June–mid-Sept., Mon.–Sat. 10–noon and 2–6.*

Lodging and Dining **Image Ste-Anne.** This charming hotel is housed in a suitably old, rustic building in the center of historic Vannes. The warm welcome and comfortable guest rooms make the price of a night here seem more than acceptable, as a varied foreign clientele has realized. Mussels, sole in cider, and duck are featured on the restaurant's menus; set menus are all very reasonably priced, beginning at 78 frs. *8 pl. de la Libération, 56000, tel. 97–63–27–36, fax 97–40–97–02. 35 rooms with bath or shower. Facilities: restaurant (closed Sun. dinner Nov.–Mar.). MC, V.*
$

Dining **Lys.** Intricate nouvelle cuisine based on fresh local produce makes this restaurant a pleasant dinner spot close to the agreeable Promenade de la Garenne. Menus are set at 89 frs, 125 frs, and 168 frs. The setting, in a late-18th-century Louis XVI style, is at its best by candlelight, with piano music in the background. *51 rue du Maréchal-Leclerc, tel. 97–47–29–30. Reservations required. Jacket and tie required. AE, DC, MC, V. Closed Mon., mid-Nov.–mid-Dec., and Sun. dinner.*
$–$$

Nantes

There are 3 direct trains daily to Nantes from Quimper (3 hours) and from Vannes (1½ hours away); others require a change at Redon. Nantes tourist office: place du Commerce, tel. 40–47–04–51.

Numbers in the margin correspond with points of interest on the Nantes map.

★ **Nantes** is a tranquil, prosperous city that seems to pursue its existence without too much concern for what's going on elsewhere in France. Although it is not really part of Brittany—it officially belongs to the Pays de la Loire—the dukes of Brittany were in no doubt that Nantes belonged to their domain, and the castle they built is the city's principal tourist attraction.

❶ Turn left out of the station onto cours J.-F. Kennedy, a busy highway that leads to the **Château des Ducs de Bretagne,** 400 yards away. This massive, well-preserved 15th-century fortress with a neatly grassed moat was largely built by François II, who led a hedonistic

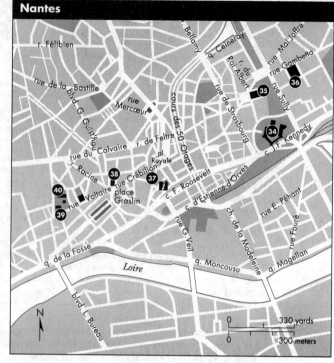

Nantes

existence here, surrounded by ministers, chamberlains, and an army of servants. Numerous monarchs later stayed in the castle, where, in 1598, Henri IV signed the famous Edict of Nantes advocating religious tolerance.

Within the Harnachement—a separate building inside the castle walls—you'll find the **Musée des Salorges** (Naval Museum), devoted principally to the history of seafaring; a separate section outlines the triangular trade that involved transportation of African blacks to America to be sold as slaves. As you cross the courtyard to the Grand Gouvernement wing, home to the **Musée d'Art Populaire Régional** (Regional Folk Art Museum), look for the old well, where the ducal coat of arms is entwined in some magnificent wrought-iron decoration. The Musée d'Art Populaire features an array of armor, furniture, 19th-century Breton costumes, and reconstituted interiors illustrating the former life in the Vendée region to the south. *Just off rue du Château. Admission: 30 frs, free Sun. Castle and museums open Sept.–June, Wed.–Mon. 10–noon and 2–6; July–Aug., daily 10–noon and 2–6.*

❷ Opposite the castle is the **Cathédrale St-Pierre**, one of France's latest Gothic cathedrals; building began only in 1434, well after most other medieval cathedrals had been completed. The facade is ponderous and austere, in contrast to the light, wide, superbly renovated interior, whose vaults rise higher (120 feet) than those of Notre-Dame in Paris. In the transept, notice Michel Colombe's early 16th-century tomb of François II and his wife, Marguerite de Foix, which is one of France's finest examples of funerary sculpture. *Pl. St-Pierre.*

Behind the cathedral, past the 15th-century Porte St-Pierre, is the
❸ **Musée des Beaux-Arts**, with a fine collection of paintings from the Renaissance on, featuring works by Jacopo Tintoretto, Georges de La Tour, Jean-Auguste Ingres, and Gustave Courbet. *10 rue*

Georges-Clemenceau. Admission: 20 frs, free Sun. Open Mon.,
Wed.–Sat. 10–noon and 1–5:15, Sun. 11–5.

The cobbled streets around the castle and cathedral make up the
town's medieval sector. Across cours des 50-Otages, a broad boulevard, is the 19th-century city. From place Royale stroll and window-
shop down busy rue Crébillon. Halfway down on the left is the
④ Passage Pommeraye, an elegant shopping gallery erected in 1843. At
⑤ the far end of rue Crébillon is place Graslin and its 1783 **Grand Théâtre.**

Just along rue Voltaire from place Graslin is the 15th-century
⑥ Manoir de la Touche, once home to the bishops of Nantes. Its medie-
⑦ val silhouette is offset by the mock-Romanesque **Palais Dobrée,** next
door, built by arts connoisseur Thomas Dobrée during the last century. Among the treasures within are miniatures, tapestries, medieval manuscripts, and enamels, and one room is devoted to the
Revolutionary Wars in Vendée. *Pl. Jean V. Admission: 20 frs, free*
Sun. Open Wed.–Mon. 10–noon and 1:30–5:30.

Lodging **Astoria.** An unpretentious hotel in a quiet street near both the train
$$ station and the castle, the Astoria has prices that are as comfortable
as its modern-looking rooms. There's no restaurant. *11 rue*
Richebourg, 44000, tel. 40–74–39–90, fax 40–14–05–49. 45 rooms
with bath or shower. MC, V. Closed Aug. and Dec. 24–Jan. 2.

Dining **L'Embellie.** Chef Claude Scheiber has taken over this small, modern
$$ bistro formerly Le Colvert, serving interesting dishes based on sea-
★ food or game, according to season. The cooking is serious and tradi-
tional, making the most of herbs to bring out a dish's natural flavors.
The lunchtime menu offers a particularly good value. *14 rue*
Armand-Brossard, tel. 40–48–20–02. Reservations advised. MC,
V. Closed Sat. lunch, Sun., and first wk in Sept.

$$ **Mon Rêve.** Fine food and a parkland setting are offered at this cozy
restaurant 8 km (5 mi) east of town. Chef Gérard Ryngel concocts
elegantly inventive regional fare (the duck or rabbit in muscadet are
good choices), while his wife, Cécile, presides over the dining room.
Allow $40 for your round-trip cab fare. *Rte. des bords de Loire,*
Basse-Goulaine, tel. 40–03–55–50. Reservations advised. AE, DC,
MC, V. Closed Tues. eve. and Wed. Oct.–Mar.

$ **La Cigale.** Miniature palm trees, gleaming woodwork, colorful
enamel tiles, and painted ceilings are why this café is officially recog-
nized as a *monument historique.* You can savor its Belle Epoque am-
bience without spending a fortune: The 69-franc and 89-franc menus
are just right for a quick lunch, although the banks of fresh oysters
and the well-stacked dessert cart may tempt you to go for a leisurely
meal à la carte. The wine list is reasonable, and there is also a selec-
tion of wines by the glass. *4 pl. Graslin, tel. 40–69–76–41, fax 40–*
73–75–37. Reservations suggested. MC, V.

Shopping The commercial quarter stretches from place Royale to place
Graslin. For antiques, try **Cibot** (7 rue Voltaire). Don't miss choco-
late specialist **Georges Gautier** (9 rue de la Fosse), with his
Muscadets Nantais—grapes dipped in brandy and covered in choco-
late.

La Baule

Trains make the 1-hour trip west from Nantes every couple of hours.
La Baule tourist office: 9 place de la Victoire, tel. 40–24–34–44, fax
40–11–08–10.

La Baule, one of the most fashionable resorts in France, is a 19th-
century creation that makes the most of the sandy beaches that ex-
tend for some 10 km (6 mi) around the broad, sheltered bay between
Pornichet and Le Pouliguen. A pine forest keeps the shifting sand
dunes firmly at bay.

An air of old-fashioned chic still pervades La Baule's palatial hotels, villas, and gardens, but there's nothing old-fashioned about the prices: Hotels and restaurants should be chosen with care. Night-clubbers will be in their element here, and the resort's summer season buzzes with prestigious events, such as horse shows and classic car contests.

Lodging **Concorde.** This establishment numbers among the least expensive
$$ good hotels in pricey La Baule. It's calm, comfortable, recently modernized, and close to the beach (ask for a room with a sea view). There's no restaurant. *1 bis av. de la Concorde, 44500, tel. 40–60–23–09, fax 40–42–72–14. 47 rooms with bath or shower. Closed Oct.–Easter.*

Dining **La Pergola.** The inventive finesse of its haute cuisine and the warmth
$ of its welcome have given La Pergola a substantial reputation. The restaurant is conveniently situated in the center of La Baule, next to the casino and a stone's throw from the beach. Meat and fish are prepared with aplomb in a variety of subtle sauces. Ordering à la carte is expensive, so stick with the moderately priced set menu. *147 av. des Lilas, tel. 40–24–57–61. Reservations advised. Jacket required. MC, V. Closed for lunch Mon., Wed., and Fri.*

6 Normandy

*Including Rouen and
Le Mont-St-Michel*

Normandy (or Normandie, as the French spell it), the coastal region
northwest of Paris, probably has more associations for English-
speaking visitors than does any other part of France. William the
Conqueror, Joan of Arc, the Bayeux Tapestry, and the D-Day landing beaches have become household names in English, just as they
have in French.

The area has become popular with British vacationers not only because it's right across the Channel but also because of its charming
countryside, from the wild, granite cliffs in the west to the long
sandy beaches along the Channel coast, from the wooded valleys of
the south to the lush green meadows and apple orchards in the center. Normandy is also one of the country's finest gastronomic regions, producing excellent cheeses, such as Camembert, and
Calvados, a powerful apple brandy.

Historic buildings—castles, churches, and monuments—crown the
Norman countryside as reminders of its rich and eventful past. Following the 1066 invasion of England by the Norman duke William
(the Conqueror), Normandy switched between English and French
dominion for several centuries. In Rouen in 1431, Joan of Arc was
burned at the stake, marking a turning point in the Hundred Years'
War, the last major medieval conflict between the French and the
English. The most celebrated building in Normandy is the abbey of
Mont-St-Michel, erected on a 264-foot mound of granite cut off from
the mainland at high tide; it's an architectural marvel and the most
visited site in provincial France.

Normandy features 375 miles of coastline bordering the English
Channel, four major ports—Le Havre, Rouen, Dieppe, and Cherbourg—and coastal towns with seafaring pasts, such as Honfleur,
with its picturesque old harbor, and former fishing villages like
Fécamp. Sandwiched between are the beaches of such fashionable

resorts as Deauville, Cabourg, and Etretat, where visitors can be found reclining in deck chairs, gin-and-tonics in hand.

Normandy Basics

Budget Lodging There are accommodations to suit every taste in Normandy. In the beach resorts, the season is very short, July and August only, but weekends are busy for much of the year; in June and September, accommodations are usually available at short notice. If you're staying on the coast, beware of Deauville and Cabourg, two swanky, outrageously expensive resorts.

Budget Dining Normandy is the land of butter, cream, cheese, and Calvados. Many dishes are cooked with rich sauces; the description *à la normande* usually means "with a cream sauce." The richness of the milk makes for excellent cheese: Pont-l'Evêque (known since the 13th century) is made in the Pays d'Auge (an agricultural region south of Cahors and Deauville) with milk that is still warm and creamy, and Livarot (also produced for centuries) uses milk that has stood for a while; don't be put off by its strong smell. Then there are the excellent Pavé d'Auge and the best known of them all, Camembert, a relative newcomer, invented by a farmer's wife in the late-18th century. There are many local specialties. Rouen is famous for its *canard à la Rouennaise* (duck in blood sauce), Caen for its *tripes à la mode de Caen* (tripe cooked with carrots in a seasoned cider stock), and Mont-St-Michel for *omelette Mère Poulard* (hearty omelet made by a local hotel manager in the late-19th century for travelers to Mont-St-Michel). Then there are *sole dieppoise* (sole poached in a sauce with cream and mussels), excellent chicken from the Vallée d'Auge, and lamb from the salt marshes. Those who like *boudin noir* (blood sausage) have come to the right region, and for seafood lovers, the coast provides oysters, lobster, and shrimp. Normandy is not a wine-growing area but produces excellent cider. The best comes from the Vallée d'Auge and is 100% apple juice; when poured into the glass, it should fizz a bit but not froth.

Bargain Shopping Handmade lace is a great rarity, and admirers will certainly think it's worth spending some time searching it out. Prices are high, but then, this kind of labor-intensive, high-quality creation never comes cheap. In Bayeux, try the **Conservatoire de la Dentelle de Bayeux**, Hôtel de Doyen, on rue Leforestier, near the cathedral.

Normandy is a food lover's region, and some of the best buying is to be done in food markets and charcuteries. Calvados is hard to find outside France, and although it's generally available in wine shops around the country, you'll find a wider choice of good-quality Calvados in Normandy itself.

Biking Roads along the coast and inland along the Seine valley and through the Suisse Normande area around Caen make for pleasant pedaling. You may reserve bicycle rentals (a good idea in high season) at train stations in Bayeux, Caen, Dieppe, Le Tréport, Argentan, Bueil, Granville, Pontorson, and Vernon, and at 30 other stations bicycles may be hired when you arrive. Rental is about 50 frs per day. Or try **Family Home** in Bayeux (39 rue du Gal-de-Dais, tel. 31–92–15–22).

Hiking There are 10 long-distance, signposted itineraries and countless well-indicated footpaths for shorter walks; overnight hostels are found at many points. Contact the **Comité Départemental de la Randonnée Pédestre de Seine-Maritime** (B.P. 680, 76008 Rouen).

Beaches Wherever you go on the Normandy coast, you'll look at the chilly waters of the English Channel: Those used to warmer climes may need all their resolve to take the plunge, even on hot, sunny days. The most fashionable Norman resorts lie along the Floral Coast, the eastern end of the Calvados Coast between Deauville/Trouville and

Cabourg; it's virtually one long, sandy beach, with the different towns overlapping. The rest of the Calvados Coast, which continues west up the Cotentin Peninsula, is also a succession of seaside resorts, though the beaches that saw the Normandy landings have not been so developed as those farther east. While the resort towns of the western Calvados Coast don't lack for charm, they don't have the character of Honfleur or the unspoiled and rugged beauty of the pebbly Alabaster Coast, stretching from Le Havre north and east to beyond Dieppe. The resorts here are more widely spaced, separated by craggy cliffs, and even in the summer months beaches are relatively uncrowded.

Arts and Nightlife Normandy's cultural activities revolve around music, both classical and modern. Many churches host evening concerts, with organ recitals drawing an especially large number of enthusiasts. Jazz aficionados will be interested in the **European Traditional Jazz Festival** held in mid-June at Luneray, 8 km (5 mi) southwest of Dieppe. One of the biggest cultural events on the Norman calendar is the **American Film Festival,** held in Deauville during the first week of September.

Festivals A **Joan of Arc Commemoration** takes place in Rouen at the end of May, featuring a variety of parades, street plays, concerts, and exhibitions that recall the life—and death—of France's patron saint.

Tour 1: Rouen and Upper Normandy

Rouen forms the hub of this tour and is an ideal base for exploring Upper Normandy: by bus toward Le Havre, or by train toward the pretty harbor towns of Dieppe and Fécamp. Traveling along the coast—notably to Etretat—is possible only by bus.

From Paris By Train Express trains to Rouen leave Paris (Gare St-Lazare) hourly. The trip takes 70–90 minutes.

By Car The 135-kilometer (85-mile) drive from Paris along A13 takes 1½ hours.

Rouen

Tourist office: 25 place de la Cathédrale, opposite the cathedral front, tel. 35–71–41–77.

Numbers in the margin correspond with points of interest on the Rouen map.

The city of **Rouen** is a blend of ancient and modern, a large part having been destroyed during World War II. Even before its massive postwar reconstruction, the city had expanded outward during the 20th century with the development of industries spawned by its increasingly busy port, now the fifth largest in France. In its more distant past, Rouen gained celebrity when Joan of Arc was burned at the stake here in 1431. Today it is known as the City of a Hundred Spires, and indeed many of its important edifices are churches.

Head down rue Jeanne d'Arc from the station and turn left after 700 yards onto rue du Gros-Horloge, which leads directly to the magnificent **Cathédrale Notre-Dame.** Dominating the place du Cathédrale, it is one of the masterpieces of French Gothic architecture, immediately recognizable to anyone familiar with the works of Claude Monet, who rendered its west facade in an increasingly misty, yet always beautiful, series, "Cathédrales de Rouen." The original 12th-century construction was replaced after a terrible fire in 1200; only the left-hand spire, the Tour St-Romain, survived the flames.

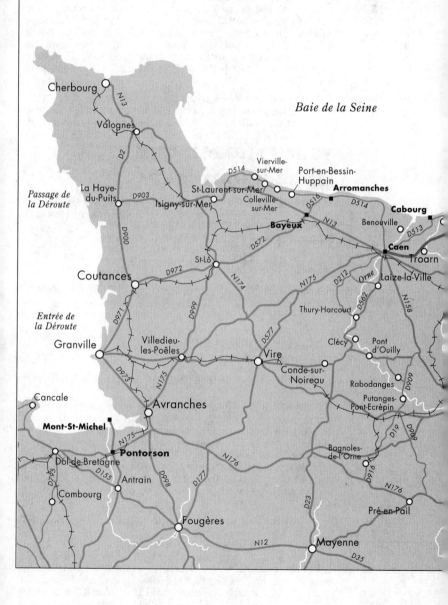

Baie de la Seine

Cherbourg

N13

Valognes

D2

Passage de
la Déroute

La Haye-
du-Puits

D903

Isigny-sur-Mer

D514

Vierville-
sur-Mer

St-Laurent-sur-Mer

Colleville-
sur-Mer

Port-en-Bessin-
Huppain

Arromanches

D514

D514

Cabourg

Bayeux

D572

N13

Benouville

D513

Caen

Troarn

St-Lô

D972

N174

N175

D212

Orne

Laize-la-Ville

N158

Coutances

D999

D971

Thury-Harcourt

D562

Entrée de
la Déroute

Granville

Villedieu-
les-Poêles

D577

Clécy

Pont
d'Ouilly

D909

D973

N175

Vire

Condé-sur-
Noireau

Rabodanges

Putanges-
Pont-Ecrépin

D19

D909

Cancale

Avranches

Mont-St-Michel

N175

Pontorson

N176

Bagnoles-
de-l'Orne

D916

Dol-de-Bretagne

D155

Antrain

D798

D177

D23

N176

D785

Combourg

Fougères

Pré-en-Pail

N12

Mayenne

D35

English Channel

0   20 miles
0   30 km

Rail Lines

Dieppe

St-Valéry-en-Caux

Veules-les-Roses

Varengeville-sur-Mer

D68

Neufchatel-en-Bray

D925

N28

Fécamp

D925

Cany-Barville

Cleres

N27

N29

N15

Forges-les-Eaux

Etretat

D940

D925

N28

Caudebec-en-Caux

St-Wandrille

Villequier

D81

D81

D15

Le Havre

N15

N182

Seine

Jumièges

D982

Rouen

N31

Trouville

Honfleur

St-Martin de Boscherville

A13

Seine

N15

N14

Deauville

D579

D513

Houlgate

Dives-sur-Mer

Pont l'Evêque

Risle

Le Bec-Hellouin

Louviers

Les Andelys

D313

A13

Manerbe

Beuvron-en-Auge

Lisieux

N13

Bernay

Eure

arn

D579

Touques

N138

Conches-en-ouche

Evreux

N13

D316

Vimoutiers

Risle

le

Dives

D840

N183

Argentan

Orne

L'Aigle

N26

Verneuil-sur-Avre

Dreux

Houdan

Eure

N138

N12

Mortagne

N12

Chateauneuf-en-Thymerais

D928

N154

Alençon

Eure

Chartres

Nogent-le-Rotrou

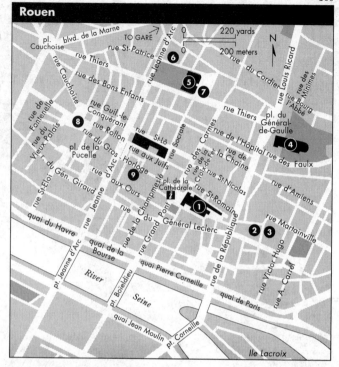

Rouen

The imposing 250-foot tower on the right, known as the Butter Tower, was added in the 15th and 16th centuries and completed in the 17th, when a group of wealthy citizens donated large sums of money—for the privilege of eating butter during Lent.

Interior highlights include the 13th-century choir, with its pointed arcades; vibrant stained glass depicting the crucified Christ (restored after heavy damage during World War II); and massive stone columns topped by some intriguing carved faces. The first flight of the famous Escalier de la Librairie (Booksellers' Staircase) rises up from a tiny balcony just to the left of the transept and is attributed to Guillaume Pontifs, who is also responsible for most of the 15th-century work seen in the cathedral. *Pl. de la Cathédrale. Open daily 7:30–noon and 2:30–6.*

Leaving the cathedral, head east (right) on rue St-Romain and cross rue de la République to place St-Maclou, an attractive square surrounded by picturesque half-timbered houses with steeply pointed roofs. The square's **Eglise St-Maclou** bears testimony to the wild excesses of Flamboyant architecture; take time to examine the central and left-hand portals under the porchway on the main facade, covered with little bronze lion heads and pagan engravings. Inside, note the 16th-century organ, with its Renaissance wood carving, and the fine marble columns. *Open daily 7:30–noon and 2:30–6.*

Continue east to the **Aître St-Maclou** (184–186 rue Martainville), a former ossuary that is one of the last reminders of the plague that devastated Europe during the Middle Ages; these days, it holds Rouen's School of Art and Architecture. The ossuary (a charnel house used for the bodies of plague victims) is said to have inspired the French composer Camille Saint-Saëns (1835–1921) when he was working on his *Danse Macabre*. The building's massive double frieze is especially riveting, carved with some graphic skulls, bones, and grave diggers' tools. *Open daily 8–8.*

Turn north up rue de la République to place du Général-de-Gaulle
❹ and the **Eglise St-Ouen,** a fine example of later Gothic architecture.
The stained-glass windows, dating from the 14th to the 16th centuries, are the most spectacular features of the otherwise spare structure. The church's 19th-century pipe organs have few equals in
France. *Open daily 8–noon and 2–6. Closed Dec. 15–Jan. 15 and
Mon., Tues., and Thurs. Jan. 16–Mar. 14 and Nov. 1–Dec. 14.*

Walk west on rue Thiers to get to a cluster of Rouen's fine museums,
❺ the most important of which is the **Musée des Beaux-Arts** (tel. 35–
71–28–40), on square Vedral. It contains a fine collection of French
paintings from the 17th and 19th centuries, including works by
Claude Monet, Alfred Sisley, and Auguste Renoir. An entire room
is devoted to Rouen-born Théodore Géricault, and there are impressive works by Delacroix and Chassériau. The museum once showcased a superb collection of Norman ceramics, but these are now
❻ housed separately in the **Musée de la Céramique,** a few steps down
the road (rue Faucon, tel. 35–07–31–74; admission 21 frs for both
❼ museums). The **Musée de Ferronerie Le Secq des Tournelles**
(Wrought Ironwork Museum; tel. 35–07–31–74), right behind the
Musée des Beaux-Arts, claims to possess the world's finest collection of wrought iron, with exhibits spanning the 3rd through the
19th centuries. Displays include a range of items used in daily life,
accessories, and professional instruments used by surgeons, bar-
bers, carpenters, clockmakers, and gardeners. *Admission: 13 frs.
All 3 museums open Thurs.–Mon. 10–noon and 2–6, Wed. 2–6.*

Continue down rue Thiers, turn left onto rue Jeanne-d'Arc, then
right onto rue du Gros-Horloge toward place du Vieux-Marché,
❽ dominated by the thoroughly modern **Eglise Jeanne d'Arc.** Dedicated to the saint, the church was built on the spot where she was
burned to death in 1431. Not all is spanking new, however; the
church is graced with some remarkable 16th-century glass windows
taken from the former Eglise St-Vincent, destroyed in 1944. *[Copy
to come]*

The rue du Gros-Horloge is Rouen's most popular attraction. The
★ ❾ name of this little pedestrian street comes from the **Gros-Horloge** itself, a giant Renaissance clock; in 1527, the Rouennais had a splendid arch built especially for it, and today its golden face looks out
over the street (the ticket to the Musée des Beaux-Arts includes admission to the ornate belfry). Though the ancient thoroughfare is
crammed with boutiques and fast-food joints, a few old houses, dating from the 16th century, remain. Wander through the surrounding
old town, a warren of tiny streets lined with more than 700 half-timbered houses. Instead of standing simply as monuments to the past,
these cobbled streets have been successfully transformed into a lively pedestrian shopping precinct, and the old buildings now contain
the most fashionable shops in the city.

Lodging **Hôtel de la Cathédrale.** Housed in a medieval building, and sepa-
$ rated from the back of the cathedral by a narrow, pedestrian-only
★ street, this hotel provides small but neat and comfortable rooms
with either a private bath or shower. (No, the cathedral's bells do
not boom out the hours during the night.) Breakfast only is served,
in the wonderfully beamed *salle à manager.* The owner is very cor-
dial, and will be happy to offer tips on exploring Rouen and to advise
on dining options. *12 rue St-Romain, 76000, tel. 35–71–57–95, fax
35–70–15–54. 25 rooms with bath or shower. Facilities: breakfast
room, public parking nearby. MC, V.*

Dining **Les Maraîchers.** Also called Bistrot d'Adrian, this simple bistro of-
$ fers such dependable classics as fish soup and tête de veau. Daily set
menus at 87 frs and 135 frs are available. *37 pl. du Vieux-Marché,
tel. 35–71–57–73. Reservations advised. AE, DC, MC, V.*

¢ **La Petite Auberge.** This homey inn tucked away on a quiet street serves up typical bistro fare—steamed mussels, chunky pâtés—in generous portions. The crowd is local, the service friendly. There are set menus at 79 frs, 96 frs, 129 francs, and 180 francs. *164 rue Martainville, tel. 35–70–80–18. Reservations advised on weekends. MC, V. Closed Mon. evening.*

¢ **Le Vieux Logis.** This tiny restaurant near the Hôtel de Ville, elegantly fitted out with 18th-century-style furnishings, is the pride and joy of jolly Joseph Guillou. He treats visitors to a 75-franc menu that includes wine and coffee and goes down as the best dining value in Rouen. *5 rue Joyeuse, tel. 35–71–55–30. Reservations essential. No credit cards.*

St-Wandrille

Buses leave Rouen hourly for Le Havre, stopping at St-Martin, St-Wandrille, and Caudebec. The river is just a short walk from the bus stops. The journey time from Rouen northwest to St-Wandrille is about 45 minutes.

The Seine valley between Rouen and Le Havre—called the Val de Seine et des Abbayes—is full of interesting sights, old and new, dotted amid some lovely scenery.

Within 10 minutes of Rouen is the 11th-century abbey church of St-George in **St-Martin de Boscherville.** About 16 km (10 mi) farther along the right bank of the Seine, in **St-Wandrille,** is another Benedictine abbey. The **Abbaye de St-Wandrille** survives as an active monastery to this day; it was founded in the 7th century, sacked (by the Normans), and rebuilt in the 10th century, though what you see today is an ensemble of styles from the 11th century through the early 18th (predominantly the latter). You can still hear the monks sing their Gregorian chants at morning Mass if you're here early in the day (9:25 weekdays and 10 Sunday and holidays). Be sure to visit the abbey shop down the hill. It sells goods made by Benedictine monks, from floor polish to spiritual aids. *Tel. 35–96–23–11. Guided tours at 3 and 4 weekdays and at 11:30 AM Sun. and holidays; cost: 18 frs adults.*

From St-Wandrille, it's only a couple of miles to the charming little village of **Caudebec-en-Caux.** If the day is sunny, be sure to take a stroll along the banks of the Seine. The village's 15th-century Eglise Notre-Dame was described by French monarch Henri IV (1589–1610) as "the most beautiful chapel in the kingdom."

Le Havre

Trains leave Rouen 16 times daily for Le Havre, 55 minutes to the west. The journey takes 3 hours by bus. Le Havre tourist office: 1 pl. de l'Hotel-de-Ville, tel. 35–21–22–88.

Le Havre is a bustling modern town, France's second-largest port (after Marseille). Largely rebuilt after 1945, it was bombarded no fewer than 146 times during World War II, and reinforced concrete and bleak open spaces have not done much for the town's atmosphere. The old seafaring quarter of **Sainte-Adresse** is worth a visit, however. From its fortress, you have panoramic views of the port and the Seine estuary.

★ At the opposite end of the seafront, at the tip of boulevard François-Ier, sits the metal-and-glass **Musée des Beaux-Arts.** On the ground floor there's a remarkable collection of Raoul Dufy's work, including oils, watercolors, and sketches. Dufy (1877–1953) was born in Le Havre and devoted a lot of time to his native region: views of Norman beaches and of Le Havre itself. If you can't spend much time in Normandy, go upstairs to have a look at works by one of the forerunners of Impressionism—Eugène Boudin. Boudin's compelling beach scenes and Norman countrysides will give you a taste of what you're missing. *23 blvd. Clemenceau, tel. 35–42–33–97. Admission free. Open Wed.–Mon. 10–noon and 2–6.*

Lodging **Astoria.** Local charm isn't a characteristic of Le Havre lodging es-
$ tablishments, and this hotel just opposite the train station is no ex-
ception. But if you want a practical, friendly, well-equipped
stopping place, try it. *13 cours de la République, 76600, tel. 35–25–
00–03, fax 35–26–48–34. 37 rooms with bath or shower. Facilities:
restaurant. AE, DC, MC, V.*

Fécamp

*Trains run 9 times daily from Rouen (journey time 65 minutes,
with a change at Bréauté-Beuzeville). Tourist office: place Bellet,
tel. 35–28–20–51.*

Fécamp, an ancient fishing port, was Normandy's primary place of
pilgrimage before Mont-St-Michel stole all the glory. Fécamp no
longer has a commercial fishing fleet, but you will still see lots of
boats in the private yachting marina. The magnificent **Eglise de
La Trinité** (just off boulevard de la République) bears witness to
the town's religious past. The Benedictine abbey was founded by the
Duke of Normandy in the 11th century and became the home of the
monastic order of the Précieux Sang et de la Trinité (referring to
Christ's blood, which supposedly arrived here in the 7th century).
Fécamp is also the home of the liqueur Benedictine. The **Musée de la
Bénédictine,** seven blocks across town on rue Boufart, was rebuilt in
1892 in a florid mixture of neo-Gothic and Renaissance styles and remains one of Normandy's most popular attractions. *110 rue Alex-
andre-le-Grand. Admission: 30 frs adults, 15 frs children 10–17
(including a tasting). Open late Mar.–late May and mid-Sept.–
mid-Nov., daily 10:00–noon and 2–5:30; late May–mid-Sept., daily 10–6; Jan.–late Mar. and mid-Nov.–Dec., 2 guided tours daily at
10:30 and 3:30.*

Dining **L'Escalier.** This delightfully simple little restaurant overlooks the
$ harbor and serves traditional Norman cuisine. The several inexpen-
★ sive fixed-price menus offer mainly seafood. *101 quai Bérigny, tel.
35–28–26–79. Reservations essential in summer. AE, MC, V.
Closed Oct.*

Etretat

*Eight buses run daily from Fécamp southwest to Etretat. Tourist of-
fice: place de la Mairie, tel. 35–27–05–21.*

The most attractive resort along the Alabaster Coast, which
stretches from Le Havre northeast to Dieppe, is **Etretat.** The town's
soaring white cliffs, an inspiration to Monet and many other painters, are almost as famous in France as Dover's are in England. Although the promenade running the length of Etretat's pebble beach
has been spoiled by a proliferation of seedy cafés and french-fry
stands, the town retains its vivacity and charm. Its landmarks are
two arched cliff formations, the **Falaise d'Amont** and the **Falaise
d'Aval,** which jut out over the sea on either side of the bay, and a 300-
foot needle of rock, the **Aiguille,** which thrusts up from the sea near
the Falaise d'Amont. Through the huge archways carved by the sea
into the cliffs, you can walk to neighboring beaches at low tide. For a
breathtaking view of the whole bay, take the path up to the Falaise
d'Aval on the southern side, from which you can hike for miles across
the Manneporte hills.

Dining and **Le Donjon.** This charming little château, set in a park on the hill
Lodging overlooking the village, offers lovely bay views. The individually
Splurge furnished guest rooms are huge, comfortable, and quiet. The per-

sonal and friendly attention paid to guests gives a sense that this is your very own retreat. The pretty, intimate restaurant serves well-prepared provincial French cuisine with flair. *Chemin de St-Clair, 76790, tel. 35–27–08–23, fax 35–29–92–24. 8 rooms, 6 with bath. Facilities: restaurant, pool. AE, DC, MC, V.*

Dining **Les Roches Blanches.** The exterior of this family-owned restaurant,
$ situated back from the beach, is most unattractive: a concrete post–World War II eyesore. But take a table by the window with a view of the sea and the cliffs and order the superbly fresh seafood—and you'll be glad you came. Other dishes, like the veal escalope with mushrooms, flambéed in Calvados, are good, too, but be sure at least to try the mussels. *Rue Abbé-Cochet, tel. 35–27–07–34. Reservations advised, especially for Sun. lunch. MC, V. Closed Tues., Wed., and Thurs. (Wed. only July–early Sept.) and Jan. and Oct.*

Dieppe

Eleven trains make the daily trip north from Rouen, 50–65 minutes away. Tourist office: Pont Jehan Ango, tel. 35–84–11–77.

Dieppe blends the atmosphere of a bustling fishing and commercial port with that of a Norman seaside town. The boulevard du Maréchal-Foch, a seafront promenade, separates an immense lawn from an unspoiled pebble beach where, in 1942, many Canadian soldiers were killed during the so-called Jubilee raid. Overlooking the Channel, at the western end of the bay, stands the 15th-century **Château de Dieppe,** which dominates the town from its clifftop position. It contains the town museum, well known for its collection of ivories. In the 17th century, Dieppe imported vast quantities of elephant tusks from Africa and Asia, and as many as 350 craftsmen settled here to work the ivory; their efforts can be seen in the form of ship models, nautical accessories, and, upstairs, in religious and day-to-day objects. The museum also has a room devoted to sketches by Georges Braque. *Rue de Chaste. Admission: 20 frs adults, 12 frs students and children. Open June–Sept., daily 10–noon and 2–6; Oct.–June, Wed.–Mon. 10–noon and 2–5.*

Lodging **Hotel Epsom.** If you want a hotel fronting the sea, the Epsom is the
$ best choice for the price. Most of the rooms have good views and are comfortably, if uninspiringly, decorated. There's no restaurant, but the bar, styled to resemble a London pub, with easy chairs and a piano, is good for liquid refreshment. *11 blvd. de Verdun, 76200, tel. 35–84–10–18, fax 35–40–03–00. 28 rooms, some with bath. MC, V.*

Tour 2: Caen and Lower Normandy

This tour uses the historic city of Caen as a base, heading east along the coast by bus (there are no trains) to Deauville and Honfleur, and west to Mont-St-Michel via Bayeux, home to the famous tapestry and a launching pad for bus excursions to the D-day landing beaches.

From Paris Express trains to Caen leave Paris (Gare St-Lazare) every 1½
By Train hours. The trip takes 2 to 2½ hours.

By Car The 240-kilometer (150-mile) drive from Paris along A13 takes 2½ hours.

Caen

Tourist office: place St-Pierre, opposite St-Pierre church, tel. 31–27–14–14.

William of Normandy ruled from **Caen,** the capital of lower Normandy, in the 11th century before he conquered England. Nine hundred years later, in 1944, the two-month Battle of Caen devastated the town. Much of the city burned in a fire that raged for 11 days, and the downtown area was almost entirely rebuilt after the war. Caen is now a busy, traffic-congested commercial city, the administrative center for the region. Depending upon the extent of your involvement with William, you may be tempted to bypass the city.

Turn right out of the station and take rue de la Gare across the River Orne. This long, straight street becomes avenue du Maréchal Juin and leads down to the castle. Turn left here and continue half a mile ★ to the town's main tourist attraction, the **Abbaye aux Hommes,** a monastery built by William the Conqueror. "The Men's Abbey" was begun in Romanesque style in 1066 and was added to during the 18th century. Note the magnificent facade of the Eglise St-Etienne, whose spareness is enhanced by two 11th-century towers topped by octagonal spires. Inside, what had been William the Conqueror's tomb was destroyed by 16th-century Huguenots during the Wars of Religion, but the choir still stands; it was the first to be built in Norman Gothic style, and many subsequent choirs were modeled after it. *Pl. Louis-Guillouard, tel. 31–30–41–00. Guided tours of the abbey cost 10 frs and begin daily at 9:30, 11, 2:30, and 4, and last 1–1½ hours.*

Head right up Fosses St-Julien to the Esplanade du Château. The ruins of William the Conqueror's **fortress,** built in 1060 and sensitively restored after the war, glower down on all who approach. The castle gardens are a perfect spot for strolling, and the ramparts afford good views of the city. Within the rampart walls lies the **Musée des Beaux-Arts,** a fine-arts museum whose impressive collection includes Rembrandts and Titians. Also within the castle are the **Musée de Normandie,** displaying regional arts, and the chapel of St-George. *Entrance by the Porte sur la Ville, tel. 31–86–06–24. Admission to each: 10 frs (free Sun.). Open Apr.–Sept., Wed.–Fri. 10–12:30 and 1:30–6, Sat.–Mon. 9:30–12:30 and 2–6; Oct.–Mar., Wed.–Mon. 9:30–12:30 and 2–6.*

Take rue des Chanoines right to the **Abbaye aux Dames,** the "Ladies' Abbey," built by William the Conqueror's wife, Matilda, in 1062. The abbey is now a hospital and is not open to visitors, but you can visit its Eglise de la Trinité. This squat church is a good example of 11th-century Romanesque architecture, though its original spires were replaced by bulky balustrades in the early 18th century. The 11th-century crypt once held Matilda's tomb, which was destroyed during the French Revolution. Note the intricate carvings on columns and arches in the chapel. *Pl. Reine-Mathilde. Admission free. Guided tours daily at 2:30 and 4.*

Head back down rue des Chanoines and continue on rue Montoir-Poissonnerie. Turning left onto place St-Pierre, you'll come face-to-face with the Caen Tourist Office. It merits a visit not only for its excellent information resources but also for its splendid site in the **Hôtel d'Escoville,** a 16th-century mansion built by a wealthy town merchant, Nicolas le Valois d'Escoville. The building was badly damaged during the war but has since been restored; the rather austere facade conceals an elaborate inner courtyard, reflecting the Italian influence on early Renaissance Norman architecture.

A good introduction to the Normandy landings of 1944 can be had at the **Mémorial,** a museum opened in the north of the city in 1988. Videos, photos, arms, paintings, and prints detail the Battle of Normandy and the French Liberation within a historical context from the 1930s to the 1960s. *Esplanade Général-Eisenhower. Admission: 58 frs adults, 32 frs students. Open Wed.–Mon. 9–7.*

Lodging and **Le Dauphin.** Despite its downtown location, Le Dauphin offers
Dining peace and quiet. The building is a former priory dating from the 12th
$$ century, though the smallish guest rooms are briskly modern.
Those overlooking the street are soundproof, and the rooms in back
have views of the serene garden courtyard. The wood-beam break-
fast room is a delightful place to start the day. The service is espe-
cially friendly and efficient, both in the hotel and in the excellent,
though rather expensive, restaurant that specializes in traditional
(though at times inventive) Norman cooking. Fish is featured on the
menu, though the veal sweetbreads in a mushroom sauce is a good
choice as well. The copious 175-franc set menu is an especially good
value. *29 rue Gémare, 14000, tel. 31–86–22–26, fax 31–86–35–14.
21 rooms with bath or shower. Facilities: restaurant (closed Sat. and
several wks in July and Aug.), garden, parking. AE, DC, MC, V.*

Lodging **Hôtel Bernières.** This inexpensive hotel can be recommended for its
$ central location (two blocks from the tourist office) and its enthusi-
astic owners. The rooms are on the small side, though most have a
private toilet and shower. Continental breakfasts are served in a
small room on the second floor. *50 rue de Bernières, 14000, tel. 31–
86–01–26, fax 31–86–51–76. 17 rooms. Facilities: breakfast room.
MC, V.*

Dining **Paquebot.** A young, trendy clientele enjoys the kitschy art deco inte-
$ rior of this establishment near the castle, not to mention its 90-franc
weekday menu. If you spend a little more to eat à la carte, such deli-
cacies as pigeon and foie gras in puff pastry and a tartare of oysters
and scallops await—which is the operative word, as service tends to
be unhurried. There are also menus at 100 frs, 145 frs, and 240 frs. *7
rue des Croisiers, tel. 31–85–10–10. AE, DC, MC, V. Closed Sat.
lunch and Sun.*

Shopping Caen has a morning **market** on Sunday in place Courtonne (where
food and some clothing is sold) and a larger one on Friday in place
St-Sauveur. It also hosts a bric-a-brac and antiques fair in June.

Cabourg

*Buses run from Caen to Cabourg every 2 hours. Cabourg tourist of-
fice: Jardin du Casino, tel. 31–91–01–09.*

Cabourg retains a certain frowsy, 19th-century elegance. Its streets
fan out from a central hub near the seafront where the casino and the
Grand Hôtel are situated. The early 20th-century novelist Marcel
Proust, author of *Remembrance of Things Past*, was a great admirer
of the town's pleasant seaside atmosphere and spent much of his
time here. One of the volumes in his epic paints a perfect picture of
life in the resort, to which the town responded by naming its magnif-
icent seafront promenade after him.

Lodging **Hôtel de Paris.** The Paris is a good, affordable choice in expensive
$ Cabourg. On the main street, a five-minute walk from the beach, it
has modern, comfortable rooms with double-glazed windows. There
is no restaurant, but the owners are happy to advise on suitable
eateries. *39 av. de la Mer, 14390, tel. 31–91–31–34, fax 31–24–54–
61. 24 rooms with bath. MC, V.*

Deauville and Trouville

*The Caen–Le Havre bus runs from Cabourg northeast to Deauville
every 2 hours. Two trains per day make the 25-minute run to
Trouville-Deauville station from Cabourg-Dives (summer only).
Deauville tourist office: place de la Mairie, tel. 31–88–21–43.*

★ The twin but contrasting resorts of **Deauville** and **Trouville** are sepa-
rated only by the estuary of the River Touques. Although Trouville
is now considered an overflow town for its more prestigious neigh-

bor, it became one of France's first seaside resorts when Parisians began flocking here in the mid-19th century.

Deauville is a chic watering hole for the French bourgeoisie and would-be fashionable personalities from farther afield, who are attracted by its racecourse, casino, marina and regattas, palaces and gardens, and, of course, its sandy beach. The **Promenade des Planches**—the boardwalk extending along the seafront and lined with deck chairs, bars, and striped cabanas—is the place for celebrity spotting. Trouville, on the other hand, stands out for authenticity rather than glamour. It, too, has a casino and boardwalk, but also has a bustling fishing port and a native population that makes it a livelier place out of season than Deauville. Both tend to be expensive, but it's possible to get by on a budget if you're careful.

Lodging **Le Continental.** One of Deauville's oldest buildings is home to this $$ provincial hotel, four blocks from the sea; it's within easy walking distance of both the town center and downtown Trouville. The guest rooms are small, but all were refurbished in 1990 to offer simple, pristine accommodations at prices that are reasonable for Deauville. Breakfast is served in your room; there is no restaurant. *1 rue Désiré-le-Hoc, 14800, tel. 31–88–21–06, fax 31–98–93–67. 48 rooms with bath or shower. AE, DC, MC, V. Closed mid-Nov.–mid-Mar.*

$ **Carmen.** This straightforward, unpretentious little hotel is just around the corner from the casino in Trouville and a block from the sea. The rooms range from plain and inexpensive to comfortable and moderate, and the restaurant offers good home cooking at reasonable prices. The owners, the Bude family, are always on hand to advise their guests. *24 rue Carnot, 14360, tel. 31–88–35–43, fax 31–88–08–03. 18 rooms with bath. Facilities: restaurant (closed Mon. dinner and Tues.). AE, DC, MC, V. Closed early Jan.–mid-Feb. and 10 days in Oct.*

Dining **Les Vapeurs.** This friendly, animated brasserie with neon-lit '50s de-$ cor, one of the most popular places in Trouville, serves good, fresh food at any time, day or night, and both the famous and not-so-famous like to meet here after dark. *160 blvd. Fernand-Moureaux, tel. 31–88–51–24. Closed Tues. dinner and Wed. Reservations advised. DC, MC, V.*

$ **La Marine.** Of the many restaurants on the quay, this one offers the best value with its three-course 80-franc menu. Start with a bowl of marinated mussels and then choose from a wide selection of fresh fish from the Channel (avoid the steak). Round out the meal with Camembert or ice cream. The exposed brick walls, a jumble of marine artifacts, and good-humored waiters contribute to a friendly atmosphere. *Sur les Quais, tel. 31–88–12–51. No reservations. AE, DC, MC, V.*

Honfleur

The Caen–Le Havre bus runs from Deauville east to Honfleur every 2 hours. Tourist office: 33 cours des Fossés, tel. 31–89–23–30.

★ **Honfleur**, a colorful port on the Seine estuary, epitomizes Normandy for many people. It was once an important departure point for maritime expeditions, and the first voyages to Canada in the 15th and 16th centuries embarked from here. Its 17th-century harbor is fronted on one side by two-story stone houses with low, sloping roofs and on the other by tall, narrow houses whose wooden facades are topped by slate roofs. The whole town is a museum piece, full of half-timbered houses and cobblestone streets.

Honfleur was colonized by French and foreign painters in the 19th century, and the group later known as the Impressionists used to meet in the **Ferme St-Siméon,** now a luxurious hotel. Honfleur has also inspired artists of other hues: Charles Baudelaire, the 19th-cen-

tury poet and champion of Romanticism, wrote his poem
L'Invitation au Voyage here, and the French composer Erik Satie
was born in Honfleur in 1866.

Today Honfleur is one of the most popular vacation spots in northern
France. During the summer, its hotels rarely have vacancies and its
cafés and restaurants are always packed. Soak up the seafaring atmosphere by strolling around the old harbor, and pay a visit to the
Eglise Ste-Catherine, which dominates the harbor's northern corner
(rue des Logettes). The wooden church was built by townspeople to
show their gratitude for the departure of the English at the end of
the Hundred Years' War (1453), when masons and architects were
occupied with national reconstruction.

Lodging and Dining
$$

Le Cheval Blanc. Occupying a renovated, 15th-century building on
the harborfront, this hotel has a new owner, Alain Petit, who speaks
excellent English. All the guest rooms have recently been redeco-
rated and offer fine views of the fishing boats in the port across the
road. Room 34 is very special (and slightly more expensive than the
others), with a gabled ceiling and a large bathroom with a whirlpool
tub. *2 quai des Passagers, 14600, tel. 31–81–65–00, fax 31–89–52–
80. 35 rooms, 14 with bath. Facilities: breakfast room. MC, V.
Closed Jan.*

$$
Hostellerie Lechat. One of the best-known and -loved establishments
in Honfleur stands in a pretty square just behind the harbor in a typical 18th-century Norman building. The spacious, well-maintained
guest rooms are done in pretty French-provincial decor that makes
good use of cheerful prints and colors. Foreign guests are given a
warm welcome, especially in the American bar. The rustic, beamed
restaurant serves top-notch Norman cuisine; lobster features prominently on the menu. *3 pl. Ste-Catherine, 14600, tel. 31–89–23–85,
fax 31–89–2–61. 23 rooms with bath. Facilities: restaurant (closed
Jan., Wed., and Thurs. lunch mid-Sept.–early June), bar. AE, DC,
MC, V.*

Dining
$

La Terrasse de l'Assiette. One of several restaurants on place Ste-
Catherine with outdoor dining, La Terrasse offers excellent fare at
reasonable prices. Selections from the 120-franc menu might include an appetizer of six oysters taken from local waters or the salmon and haddock marinated in anise, followed by grilled tuna with a
lemon sauce or roast *magret* of duck. Finish with a fondue of apple-
flavored ice cream topped with Calvados or a chocolate mousse cake
with an orange cream sauce. The wine list is limited but extremely
well priced. *8 pl. Ste-Catherine, tel. 31–89–31–33. AE, MC, V.
Closed Wed. in low season.*

Lisieux

*Trains leave Caen for Lisieux, 30 minutes southeast, at least every 2
hours. Lisieux tourist office: 11 rue d'Alençon, tel. 31–62–08–41.*

Lisieux is the main market town of the prosperous Pays d'Auge, an
agricultural region south of Cahors and Deauville famous for
cheeses named after such towns as Camembert, Pont l'Evêque, and
Livarot. It is also a land of apple orchards from which the finest Calvados brandy comes. Characteristic of the countryside are small,
isolated farmhouses surrounded by orchards. Lisieux emerged relatively unscathed from World War II, though it boasts few historical
monuments beyond the **Cathédrale St-Pierre,** built in the 12th and
13th centuries. It is also famous for its patron saint, Ste-Thérèse,
who was born and died in the last quarter of the 19th century, having spent the last 10 of her 25 years as a Carmelite nun. Thérèse was
canonized in 1925, and in 1954 a **basilica**—one of the world's largest
20th-century churches—was dedicated to her; to get there from the
cathedral, walk down avenue Victor-Hugo and branch left onto avenue Ste-Thérèse.

Dining   **France.** Lisieux is better known for providing spiritual sustenance
$–$$ than gastronomic pleasure, but this old-fashioned restaurant with a
stone fireplace, just two minutes' walk from the cathedral, offers a
wide choice of good seafood, salads, and homemade pasta, and there
are set menus at 80 frs, 110 frs, and 155 frs. *5 rue au Char, tel. 31–
62–03–37. Reservations recommended. MC, V. Closed first week in
June, 3 weeks in Jan., and Mon.*

Shopping   The **Distillerie du Père Jules** (rte. des Dives) offers first-rate Calvados.

Bayeux

*Trains make the 15-minute journey from Caen northwest to Bayeux
at least every 2 hours. Tourist office: 1 rue des Cuisiniers, tel. 31–
92–16–26.*

Bayeux, one of the few Normandy towns to have escaped the destruction of World War II (it was the first to be liberated during the
Battle of Normandy), has retained a medieval charm that is only
slightly tarnished by the crowds of tourists who visit each summer.

★ We begin our tour at the **Musée de la Tapisserie,** located in an 18th-
century building on rue de Nesmond and showcasing the world's
most celebrated piece of needlework, the **Bayeux Tapestry.** The
medieval work of art—stitched in 1067—is really a 225-foot-long
embroidered scroll, which depicts, in 58 separate scenes, the epic
story of William of Normandy's conquest of England in 1066, a wa-
tershed in European history. The tapestry's origins remain obscure, though it was probably commissioned from Saxon
embroiderers by the count of Kent—also the bishop of Bayeux—to
be displayed in his newly built cathedral. Despite its age, the tapestry is in remarkably good condition; the extremely detailed scenes
provide an unequaled record of the clothes, weapons, ships, and
lifestyles of the day. *Centre Guillaume Le Conquérant, 13 bis rue de
Nesmond, tel. 31–92–05–48. Admission: 32 frs adults, 15 frs students and children (joint ticket with Musée Baron Gérard). Open
daily June–Sept., 9–7; Oct.–May, 9:30–12:30 and 2–6.*

To reach the **Musée Baron Gérard,** head up rue de Nesmond to rue
Larchet, turning left into lovely place des Tribuneaux. The museum
contains fine collections of Bayeux porcelain and lace, ceramics from
Rouen, and 16th- to 19th-century furniture and paintings. *Pl. des
Tribuneaux, tel. 31–92–14–21. Admission: 18 frs adults, 12 frs stu-
dents and children. Open daily, June–mid-Sept., 9–7; mid-Sept.–
May, 10:00–12:30 and 2–6:00; Closed 2 wks in Jan.*

Behind the museum, with an entrance on rue du Bienvenu, sits
Bayeux's most important historic building, the **Cathédrale Notre-
Dame,** a harmonious mixture of Norman and Gothic architecture.
The portal on the south side of the transept depicts the assassination
of English Archbishop Thomas à Becket in Canterbury Cathedral in
1170, following his opposition to King Henry II's attempts to control
the church. Note the whimsical paintings in the nave. *Closed Sept.–
June 12:30–2:30.*

Return to the 20th century by turning left, walking to place au Blois,
and continuing down rue St-Loup. Turn right on boulevard du Général-Fabian-Ware, site of the **Musée de la Bataille de Normandie,**
whose detailed exhibits trace the story of the Battle of Normandy
from June 7 to August 22, 1944. The ultra-modern museum contains
an impressive array of war paraphernalia, including uniforms,
weapons, and equipment. *Blvd. Général-Fabian-Ware. Admission:
24 frs adults, 12 frs students and children. Open June–Aug., daily
9–7; Sept.–Oct. and Mar.–May, daily 10–12:30 and 2–6:30; Nov.–
Feb., weekends 10:30–12:30 and 2–6:30.*

Lodging
$$

Churchill. This stylish, friendly hotel is popular with foreign visitors. Room sizes and shapes vary according to the irregularities of the several, small town houses occupied by the hotel, and prices reflect this. Bathrooms are functional and clean, though cramped. Solid breakfasts (ham and eggs available on request) are served in the airy veranda. *14 rue St-Jean, 14400, tel. 31–21–32–80, fax 31–21–41–66. 32 rooms with bath or shower. AE, DC, MC, V. Closed mid-Nov.–mid-Mar.*

$$

Hôtel d'Argouges. This lovely 18th-century hotel is an oasis of calm at the northern edge of the city center, and many rooms offer views of the well-tended flower garden. Guest rooms are simply furnished with candlewick bedspreads and rather dowdy carpeting, but you can lie in bed and ponder the sagging wood beams supporting the weight of centuries. Rooms in the main house are quieter than those in the town house, which abuts the street. There's no restaurant. *21 rue St-Patrice, 14400, tel. 31–92–88–86, fax 31–92–69–16. 25 rooms with bath. Facilities: garden. AE, DC, MC, V.*

Dining
$

L'Amaryllis. This restaurant, with fewer than 15 tables, produces good Norman fare at very reasonable prices. A 98-franc three-course dinner with six or so choices for each course will place before you such pleasures as a half dozen oysters, fillet of sole with a cider-based sauce, and pastries for dessert. Decor is simple, with white tablecloths and glistening glasses ready to be filled with reasonably priced wine. *32 rue St-Patrice, tel. 31–22–47–94. AE, DC, MC, V. Closed Mon., and Dec. 20–Jan. 15.*

Lodging and
Dining
Splurge

Le Lion d'Or. The Lion d'Or is a handsome '30s creation, conveniently situated in the center of town. Palm trees arch over the garden courtyard, and flowers cascade from balcony window boxes. Rooms are comfortable and well furnished with pretty fabrics. Fine Norman cuisine is served in the chic, wood-beamed restaurant, decorated in shades of apricot. *71 rue St-Jean, 14400, tel. 31–92–06–90, fax 31–22–15–64. 28 rooms with bath. Facilities: restaurant. AE, DC, MC, V. Closed Christmas–mid-Jan. 380 frs–440 frs.*

$

Notre-Dame. It's difficult to find a better setting for a night in Bayeux than the Notre-Dame, on a charming cobblestone street leading to the west front of the cathedral. You can sit outside on the terrace and drink in the scene with your evening aperitif. Accommodations and cuisine are average, and the place attracts the occasional horde of coach-bound tourists. But with room rates starting at 150 frs, set menus starting at 85 frs, and a cheerful, friendly management, you can't complain. *44 rue des Cuisiniers, tel. 31–92–87–24, fax 31–92–67–11. 24 rooms, some with shower. Facilities: restaurant (closed Sun. eve. and Mon. in winter). MC, V. Closed Mon. mid-Oct.–mid-Apr.*

Arromanches

Three buses daily make the 20-minute run from Bayeux north to Arromanches; the first leaves just after midday.

Operation Overlord, the code name for the Invasion of Normandy, called for five beachheads—dubbed Utah, Omaha, Gold, Juno, and Sword—to be established along the Calvados Coast, to either side of **Arromanches**, a small seaside town that was in the 19th century a popular resort for middle-class Englishmen. Preparations started in mid-1943, and British shipyards worked furiously through the following winter and spring building two artificial harbors (called Mulberries), boats, and landing equipment. The operation was originally scheduled to take place on June 5, but poor weather caused it to be postponed for a day.

The British troops that landed on Sword, Juno, and Gold quickly pushed inland and joined with parachute regiments that had been dropped behind the German lines. U.S. forces met with far tougher opposition on Omaha and Utah beaches, however, and it took them six days to secure their positions and meet the other Allied forces. From there, they pushed south and west, cutting off the Cotentin Peninsula on June 10 and taking Cherbourg on June 26. Meanwhile, British forces were encountering fierce resistance at Caen and did not take it until July 9. By then, U.S. forces had turned their attention southward, but it took two weeks of fighting to dislodge the Germans from the area around St-Lô; the town was finally liberated on July 19.

★ After having boned up on the full story of the Normandy invasion, you'll want to go and see the area where it all took place. The **beaches** are within walking distance of Arromanches and its bus stop. There's little point in visiting all five sites, as not much remains to mark the furious fighting waged hereabouts. In the bay of Arromanches, however, some elements of the floating harbor are still visible. Linger here awhile, contemplating those seemingly insignificant hunks of concrete protruding from the water, and try to imagine the extraordinary technical feat involved in towing the two floating harbors across the Channel from England. (The other was moored at Omaha Beach but was destroyed on June 19, 1944, by an exceptionally violent storm.)

If you're interested in yet more battle documentation, visit the **Musée du Débarquement,** right on the seafront; exhibits include models, mock-ups, and photographs depicting the invasion. *Pl. du 6-Juin, tel. 31-22-34-31. Admission: 30 frs adults, 18 frs senior citizens and students. Open daily June–Aug., 9–7; Sept.–mid. Oct. and Mar.–May, 9:30–12:30 and 2–6:30; mid-Oct.–Mar., 10–12:30 and 2–6. Closed 2 wks in Jan.*

Pontorson and Le Mont-St-Michel

Two trains daily leave for Pontorson from Caen and Bayeux, 1 in the early morning, the other in the late afternoon. The journey lasts around 2 hours. A bus (or taxi) is needed to reach Le Mont-St-Michel from Pontorson station. Tourist office: Corps de Garde des Bourgeois, tel. 33-60-14-30.

★ You can glimpse the spire-topped **Mont-St-Michel,** known as the Merveille de l'Occident (Wonder of the West), long before you reach the causeway that links it with the mainland. Its dramatic silhouette may well be your most lasting image of Normandy. The wonder of the abbey stems not only from its rocky perch a few hundred yards off the coast (it's cut off from the mainland at high tide), but from its legendary origins in the 8th century and the sheer exploit of its construction, which took more than 500 years, from 1017 to 1521. The abbey stands at the top of a 264-foot mound of rock, and the granite used to build it was transported from the Isles of Chausey (just beyond Mont-St-Michel Bay) and Brittany and laboriously hauled up to the site.

Legend has it that the Archangel Michael appeared to Aubert, bishop of Avranches, inspiring him to build an oratory on what was then called Mont Tombe. The original church was completed in 1144, but new buildings were added in the 13th century to accommodate the monks, as well as the hordes of pilgrims who flocked here even during the Hundred Years' War, when the region was in English hands. The Romanesque choir was rebuilt in an ornate Gothic style during the 15th and 16th centuries. The abbey's monastic vocation was undermined during the 17th century, when the monks began to flout the strict rules and discipline of their order, a drift into decadence that culminated in the monks' dispersal and the abbey's conversion into a prison well before the French Revolution. Only within the past 25 years have monks been able to live and work here once more.

A highlight of the abbey is the collection of 13th-century buildings on the north side of the mount. The exterior of the buildings is grimly fortresslike, but inside are some of Normandy's best examples of the evolution of Gothic architecture, ranging from the sober Romanesque style of the lower halls to the masterly refinement of the cloisters and the refectory.

The climb to the abbey is hard going, but worth it. Head first for the Grand Degré, the steep, narrow staircase on the north side. Once past the ramparts, you'll come to the pink-and-gray granite towers of the Châtelet and then to the Salle des Gardes, the central point of the abbey. Guided tours start from the Saut Gautier terrace (named after a prisoner who jumped to his death from it)—you must join one of them if you want to see the beautifully wrought Escalier de Dentelle (Lace Staircase) inside the church. *Admission: 32 frs adults, 18 frs students and senior citizens, 6 frs children under 12. Open mid-May–mid-Sept., daily 9:30–11:30 and 1:30–6; mid-Sept.–mid-May, daily 9:30–11:45 and 1:45–5 or 4:15, depending on month.*

The island village, with its steep, narrow street, is best visited out of season, from September to May. The hordes of souvenir sellers and tourists can be stifling in summer months, but you can always take refuge in the abbey's gardens. The ramparts in general and the North Tower in particular offer dramatic views of the bay.

Be warned: Before you visit this awe-inspiring monument, note that the sea that separates the rock from the mainland is extremely dangerous. It's subject to tidal movements that produce a difference of up to 45 feet between low and high tides, and because of the extremely flat bay bed, the water rushes in at an incredible speed. Also, there are nasty patches of quicksand, so tread with care!

Lodging and Dining
$$

Terrasses Poulard. The hotel is a recent addition to this popular restaurant, a result of the proprietor's buying up and renovating the neighboring houses to create an ensemble of buildings that exude great charm and character, clustered around a small garden in the middle of the mount. The room prices, however, have escalated and only a few remain at 350 frs, most are now in the 500-franc range. The large restaurant attracts hordes of tourists; if you don't mind being surrounded by fellow Americans, Canadians, and Britons, you'll no doubt enjoy the traditional cuisine. *On the main road opposite the parish church, 50116 Le Mont-St-Michel, tel. 33–60–14–09, fax 33–60–37–31. 29 rooms with bath. Facilities: restaurant, library, billiards room. AE, DC, MC, V.*

Lodging
$

La Sirène. Prices for accommodations on this island run high, but several small hotels have converted houses into simple, affordable lodgings, and La Sirène is one. It's actually a crêperie that expanded to a nearby building that overlooks the sands alongside the causeway. The guest rooms are compact, neat, and a very good value. Numbers 1 and 3 have the best views, but cost the most (280 frs), while the others are 230 frs. *50116 Le Mont-St-Michel, tel. 33–60–08–60. 9 rooms. MC, V.*

7 Champagne and the North

Including Reims, Chantilly, and Lille

Too few people visit northern France. The crowd-following French head south each year in search of a suntan. The millions of foreign tourists who flock through the Channel ports of Calais, Boulogne, and Dunkerque make a beeline to Paris. The Channel Tunnel, perhaps the most ambitious engineering project of the late 20th century, could change this. It opened in late 1994, and local tourist authorities have been banking on an influx of British day-trippers and weekenders. The English are already busy buying homes in the region, many with an eye to commuting to London on the TGV. But for now, it's easy to keep a lid on food and lodging costs here, while the dense rail network connecting the region's numerous towns and cities keeps transportation costs low.

It's generally a green and pleasant land where serene, wooded landscapes predominate. To the east, the plains give way to hills. The grapes of Champagne flourish on the steep slopes of the Marne Valley and on the so-called Mountain of Reims. There are no mountains, of course, even though the mighty mound of Laon is known as the Crowned Mountain because of the bristling silhouette of its many-towered cathedral. Reims is the only city in Champagne, and one of France's richest tourist venues. The kings of France were crowned in its cathedral until 1825, and every age since the Roman has left an architectural mark. The small nearby towns of Ay and Epernay play an equally important role in the thriving champagne business, which has conferred wealth and, sometimes, an arrogant reserve on the region's inhabitants. The down-to-earth folk of the North provide a warmer welcome.

This chapter explores the vast region of Champagne and the North in three tours. The first covers the North of France proper, with a look at some windswept Channel beaches, the second stops at towns in the Champagne area, and the third takes in châteaus and a cathedral in the Oise *département* just a short distance from Paris.

Champagne and the North Basics

Budget Lodging   Northern France is loaded with old hotels, often rambling and simple, seldom pretentious. Good value is easy to come by.

Budget Dining   The cuisine of northern France is robust and hearty, like that of neighboring Belgium. Beer predominates and is often used as a base for sauces (notably for chicken). French fries and mussels are featured on most menus, and *friteries* (vans) selling fries and hot dogs are common sights. Great quantities of fish, notably herring, are eaten along the coast, while inland delicacies include *andouillettes* (chitterling sausages), tripe, and pâté made from duck, partridge, or woodcock. Be sure to sample the region's creamy cheeses: Maroilles, Chaource, and the one and only true Brie de Meaux, made with *lait cru* (raw milk). Anyone with a sweet tooth will enjoy the region's ubiquitous macaroons and minty Cambrai *bêtises* (boiled sweets made of sugar, glucose, and mint). Ham, pigs' feet, gingerbread, and a champagne-based mustard are specialties of the Reims area, as is *ratafia*, a sweet aperitif made from grape juice and brandy. To the north, a glass of *genièvre* (a brandy made from juniper berries and sometimes added to black coffee to make a drink called a *bistouille)* is the typical way to conclude a good meal.

Bargain Shopping   Northern France and shopping are intimately associated in the minds of many visitors, especially the English. The cross-Channel ferry trip has become something of an institution, with one rather ignoble aim: to stock up on as much tax-free wine and beer as is physically possible; since 1993, there's no limit to how many liters you can carry across EU borders. Supermarkets along the coast are admirably large and well stocked, though you may want to consider local juniper-based *genièvre* brandy, which is a more original choice. Boulogne, France's premier fishing port, is famous for its kippers (smoked herring). Calais has long been renowned as a lace-making center. Wooden puppets are a specialty at Amiens, and glazed earthenware is part of St-Omer's historical heritage; the nearby Cristallerie at Arques is France's most renowned glass factory. Antiques dealers are legion; some of the best buys can be made at the busy auction houses *(commissaires-priseurs)* at Lille and Calais, among other towns. Note that while Reims owes its prestige to champagne, a number of its central shops duly charge sky-high prices. You'll find the best buys at small producers in the villages along the Montagne de Reims between Reims and Epernay (not at Bouzy, though).

Biking   Bicycles can be rented from the following train stations for around 40 frs a day: Arras, Beauvais, Boulogne, Calais, Compiègne, Etaples, Laon, Rue, St-Amand-les-Eaux, and St-Omer.

Hiking   Favored areas for hiking include the Forêt de Compiègne, the Montagne de Reims, and the Channel coast. For further details contact the regional tourist office (pl. Rihour, 59002 Lille).

Beaches   The northern coast of France, from Calais to Le Touquet, is one long, sandy beach, known as the Côte d'Opale. Apart from swimming in the ocean and in indoor and outdoor pools throughout the region, you may care to try your hand at speed sailing or handling a sand buggy, those windsurf boards on wheels that race along the sands at up to 70 mph. Known as *char à voile*, the sport can be practiced at Le Touquet, Hardelot, Dunkerque, Bray-Dunes, and Berck-sur-Mer; the craft are readily available for rent. For details, contact the **Drakkars** club in Hardelot, south of Boulogne (tel. 21–91–81–96); the cost is 80 frs per hour.

Arts and Nightlife The hub of cultural activity in northern France is **Lille,** a lively museum and concert center where exotic happenings can take place at any time (a recital of traditional music by Tibetan monks, for example).

Festivals The various local carnivals include the **Dunkerque Carnival** at the start of Lent, the **Roses Festival** in Arras in May, and the **Kermesse de la Bêtise** festival in Cambrai in early September.

Tour 1: Lille and the North

Lille is the largest and most interesting city in northern France and, if you're pushed for time, should be your priority. But the new TGV express rail link between Paris and Lille also stops at the attractive old textile town of Arras, so we start our tour there, then continue on to Lille. From Lille we make a quick detour southeast to Le Cateau-Cambrésis (to visit the Musée Matisse) before heading west via the small town of St-Omer to the Channel coast towns of Calais, Boulogne-sur-Mer, Le Touquet, and Montreuil-sur-Mer. Amiens, inland on the Somme, and the capital of Picardy, is our last stop. Except for Le Touquet, which is accesible by bus from nearby Etaples, all towns can be reached by train.

From Paris By Train TGVs to Arras and Lille leave Paris (Gare du Nord) every 1–2 hours. The trip takes 50 minutes to Arras and 1 hour to Lille.

By Car The 225-kilometer (140-mile) drive from Paris along A1 takes 2½ hours to Lille. Allow 1½ hours to Amiens (take the D934 turnoff from Roye) and 2 hours to Arras.

Arras

Tourist office: place des Héros, tel. 21–51–26–95.

The historic core of **Arras,** capital of the historic Artois region between Flanders and Picardy, bears witness to the grandeur of another age, when the town enjoyed medieval importance as a trading and cloth-making center.

Take rue Gambetta from the station and turn right after 500 yards onto rue Delansorne, which winds down to **place des Héros,** separated from **Grand' Place** by a short block. These two main squares are harmonious examples of 17th- and 18th-century Flemish civil architecture, with gabled facades that recall those in Belgium and Holland and testify to the unifying influence of the Spanish colonizers of the "Low Lands" during the 17th century. The smaller, arcaded place des Héros is dominated by the richly worked—and much restored—**Hôtel de Ville,** capped by a 240-foot belfry.

Turn left out of the square, then right onto rue Paul-Doumer. Walking a block along brings you to the imposing 18th-century premises of a former abbey, now the **Musée des Beaux-Arts,** which houses a rich collection of porcelain and paintings, with several major 19th-century French works. *22 rue Paul-Doumer, tel. 21–71–26–43. Admission: 20 frs adults, 12 frs children and senior citizens. Open Apr.–mid-Oct., Wed.–Mon. 10–noon and 2–6; mid-Oct.–Mar., Mon. and Wed.–Fri. 10–noon and 2–5, weekends 10–noon and 2–6.*

The 19th-century **Cathédrale St-Vaast,** a short block farther on, is a white-stone Classical building, almost as vast as its name (pronounced "va") suggests. It replaced the previous Gothic cathedral destroyed in 1799; though it was half-razed during World War I, restoration was so skillfully done you'd never know.

At first glance you might not guess that Arras was badly mauled during World War I. Not far off, though, are parks and memorials recalling the fierce battles. Arras is a convenient base for visiting

Brussels

BELGIUM

Mons

Tournai

Escaut

St-Amand-les-Eaux
Valenciennes
Aulnoye
Avesnes-sur-Helpe
Le Cateau-Cambrésis
La Capelle
Busigny
Cambrai
N43
Iewarde
Douai
A26
Péronne
A1
Lille
Bapaume
Thiepval
Albert
Vimy Ridge
Neuville
Lens
Arras
Béhune
Mont St-Eloi
Doullens
Hazebrouck
Steenvoorde
St-Pol-sur-Ternoise
Amiens
Fruges
Somme
Dunkerque
St-Omer
Arques
Montreuil
Hesdin
Abbeville
Blangy-St-Bresle
Calais
Sangatte
Cap Gris-Nez
Boulogne-sur-Mer
Hardelot
Samer
Le Touquet
Étaples
Rue
St-Valery-sur-Somme

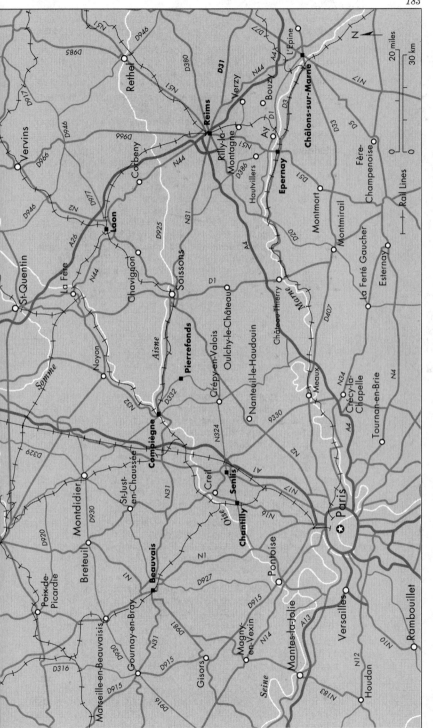

the area's numerous superbly cared-for cemeteries and memorials, which number among the most poignant sights in northern France.

Lodging
$$
★

Univers. This stylish hotel occupies a converted 18th-century monastery and has a pretty garden and a charming restaurant. Its central position and views of the courtyard and garden make it a favorite stopover with vacationers heading south. The interior has recently been modernized, but it retains its rustic provincial furniture. *5 pl. de la Croix-Rouge, 62000, tel. 21–71–34–01, fax 21–71–41–42. 36 rooms, most with bath. Facilities: restaurant (closed Sun. in Aug.), garden. AE, MC, V.*

Dining
$$

La Faisanderie. Housed in a former horse barn, this sumptuous restaurant serves as a landmark nearly as recognized as the arcades that shelter it. Memorable variations on international fare include *pied de veau* (calf's foot), pike baked with frogs' legs, and lobster casserole. A loyal clientele supports its long-standing gastronomic reputation. *45 Grand'Place, tel. 21–48–20–76. Reservations required. Jacket suggested. AE, DC, MC, V. Closed Sun. night, Mon.*

$

La Rapière. This moderate, lively alternative to its posh neighbor offers distinctly local dishes—*andouillettes* (chitterling sausages), *poulet à la bière* (chicken in beer sauce), *tourte au Maroilles* (cheese pie)—as well as a range of specialties like *escalope de veau au Camembert* (veal in Camembert), and foie gras *maison*, all in a casual setting. *44 Grand' Place, tel. 21–55–09–92. AE, MC, V. Closed Sun. evening.*

Lille

Trains run from Arras to Lille every hour or so; the journey takes around 40 minutes. Lille tourist office: Palais Rihour on place Rihour, tel. 20–30–81–00.

For a big city supposedly reeling beneath the problems of its main industry, textiles, **Lille** is a remarkably dynamic, attractive place. The city has had a checkered history, experiencing Flemish, Austrian, and Spanish rule before passing into French hands for good in 1667. Since the arrival of the TGV in 1994, Lille is again a European crossroads—a quick trip by train from Paris, London, and Brussels. Traditionally, the liveliest time to be in Lille is the first weekend of September for its three-day street fair, **La Grande Braderie.** For local ambience at other times, visit the down-to-earth **Wazemmes Market** south of the city center (métro Gambetta).

The shiny glass towers of the new **Euralille** complex, the high-tech commercial center that's Lille's answer to La Défense near Paris, greet travelers arriving at the new TGV station, Lille-Europe. Hotels and shops dominate the complex, and students of modern architecture will find it stimulating.

Avenue Le Corbusier links Euralille to the original rail station, still used for non-TGV services and now renamed Lille-Flandres. The station building, originally the Gare du Nord in Paris, was moved brick by brick to Lille in 1866!

Head down rue Faidherbe from the station, cross place du Théâtre, and turn right onto rue de la Grande-Chaussée. This narrow street rapidly becomes rue des Chats-Bossus, then rue de la Monnaie, and leads to the **Hospice Comtesse** in the heart of the old town. Founded by Jeanne de Constantinople, countess of Flanders, as a hospital in 1237, it was rebuilt in the 15th century after a fire destroyed most of the original building. Local artifacts from the 17th and 18th centuries form the backbone of the museum now housed here, but its star attraction is the Salle des Malades (Sick Room), featuring a majestic wooden ceiling. *32 rue de la Monnaie. Admission: 12 frs adults. Open Wed.–Mon. 10–12:30 and 2–6.*

Follow rue de la Monnaie as it curves right and branch off at rue de la Grande-Chaussée to reach Lille's most famous square, the Grand'Place, officially known as **place du Général-de-Gaulle** (Charles de Gaulle was born in Lille in 1890; his house, at 9 rue Princesse, is a museum). The Déesse (Goddess) atop her giant column, clutching a linstock (used to fire a cannon), has dominated the square since 1845; she commemorates Lille's heroic resistance to an Austrian siege in 1792. Other landmarks include the handsome, gabled 1932 facade of *La Voix du Nord* (the main regional newspaper), topped by three gilded statues symbolizing the three historic regions of Flanders, Artois, and Hainaut; and the Furet du Nord, which immodestly claims to be the world's largest bookshop.

At the far side of the square is the elegant **Vieille Bourse,** the old commercial exchange, one of the most charming buildings in central Lille. The quadrangle of elegant, richly worked buildings was erected by Julien Destrée in the 1650s as a commercial exchange to rival those existing in Belgium and Holland, and was painstakingly restored in 1995. Cross Grand'Place to place Rihour, where the city tourist office is housed in the former chapel of the 15th-century **Palais Rihour,** built for the dukes of Burgundy and now used for exhibitions. Take a look at the staircase, famed for its intricate, swirling-pattern brickwork, then take rue de la Comédie and rue de Béthune to reach the frenzied traffic of boulevard de la Liberté, a vast street that roars through central Lille. Half a block down, on the left, is the **Musée des Beaux-Arts,** the largest fine arts museum in France outside of Paris, which reopened in mid-1995 after extensive renovation. It houses a noteworthy collection of Dutch and Flemish paintings by Anthony Van Dyck, Peter Paul Rubens, Flemish Primitives, and Dutch landscapists as well as some charmingly understated still lifes by Chardin, works by the Impressionists, a few bombastic 19th-century French painters, and dramatic canvases by El Greco, Goya, Tintoretto, and Paolo Veronese. An extensive ceramics section displays some fine examples of Lille faience, which uses opaque glazing techniques to achieve some remarkable effects. *Pl. de la République, tel. 20–57–01–84. Hours and admission details not available at press time.*

Head left out of the art gallery, making for the gigantic **citadel,** which glowers down on the old town from its perch on the west end of the boulevard. Construction started shortly after that of the Vieille Bourse in the mid-17th century; of course that military marvel, Sébastien de Vauban, got the commission. Some 60 million bricks were used, and the result is a fortified town in its own right, with monumental towers and walls. The citadel is now used as a barracks. *Visits on Sun. afternoon Apr.–Oct. Contact tourist office, Palais Rihour, tel. 20–30–81–00.*

Lodging
$$

Paix. Probably the best hotel in central Lille for price and location, the Paix is close to the Vieille Bourse and 200 yards from the train station. Most rooms are large and have modern bathrooms. *46 bis rue de Paris, 59800, tel. 20–54–63–93, fax 20–63–98–97. 35 rooms, most with bath or shower. AE, DC, MC, V.*

Dining
$$
★

Le Hochepot. Just two blocks from place du Général-de-Gaulle, this is a cozy, old-style source of authentic regional specialties, many of them cooked in (and served with) homemade beer. *6 rue Nouveau-Siècle, tel. 20–54–17–59. Reservations advised. Closed Sat. noon, Sun.*

$

La Coquille. The wood beams and pink bricks of this venerable restaurant in a building dating from 1727 set a delightful scene for a quiet, light, fish meal—with delicious chocolate and caramel desserts as a finale. *60 rue St-Etienne, tel. 20–54–29–82. Reservations advised. AE, MC, V. Closed Sat. lunch, Sun., and Aug.*

The Arts The **Orchèstre National de Lille** is a well-respected symphony orchestra (3 pl. Mendès-France, tel. 20–54–67–00), and Lille boasts one of France's few regional opera houses, the **Opéra du Nord** (pl. du Théâtre, tel. 20–55–48–61).

Le Cateau-Cambrésis

Two trains in the morning and 2 in the afternoon leave Lille for Le Cateau; change at Aulnoye and allow at least 1½ hours for the journey.

★ There is one good reason for making the arduous rail excursion from Lille to **Le Cateau**: to visit the **Palais Fénelon**, former home to the archbishops of Cambrai and today the **Musée Matisse**, devoted to the work of artist Henri Matisse (1869–1954), who was born in Le Cateau. Along with a number of early oil paintings and sculptures, there is a superb collection of 50 drawings selected by Matisse himself and arranged in a carefully lighted room on the second floor. *Tel. 27–84–13–15. Admission: 16 frs adults, 4 frs children. Open Wed.–Sat. and Mon. 10–noon and 2–6, Sun. 10–noon and 2:30–6. Free guided tour Sun. at 3.*

St-Omer

Trains run from Lille to St-Omer every hour (except mid-morning and early afternoon). Express trains take 50 minutes, local trains up to 1½ hours. St-Omer tourist office: place du Pain-Levé, tel. 21–98–70–00.

St-Omer is a delightful small town, too often neglected by hasty motorists on their way south. It is not the archetypal northern industrial town; with its yellow-brick buildings, it even looks different from its neighbors, and a distinct air of 18th-century prosperity hovers about the place. Stroll through the narrow streets surrounding the Basilique Notre-Dame and, if time allows, visit the **Hôtel Sandelin** at 14 rue Carnot (open Wed.–Sun. 10–noon and 2–6; Thurs. and Fri. closed at 5; admission: 12 frs). Now the town museum, the 1777 mansion is furnished with 18th-century furniture and paintings and contains an exceptional collection of porcelain and faience.

Dining **Le Cygne.** This simple restaurant, in the old sector of St-Omer near
$ the cathedral, offers four reasonable menus, featuring home-baked ham and duck specialties: breast, liver, even sausage. *8 rue Caventou, tel. 21–98–20–52. MC, V. Closed Mon. eve. and Tues.*

Calais

All trains from Lille to St-Omer continue to Calais, 35 minutes and 40 km (25 mi) to the northeast. Calais tourist office: 12 boulevard Georges-Clemenceau, tel. 21–96–62–40.

Few vestiges remain of old **Calais**, the pretty port town that owed its wealth to the lace industry rather than to day-trippers making the Channel crossing from Dover, 38 km (24 mi) away, by the million every year. You won't want to stay here long, but there are a few sights to see before you dash off.

You don't need to be a lover of sculpture to appreciate Auguste Rodin's bronze **Monument des Bourgeois de Calais,** which lords it over the east end of the Parc St-Pierre next to place du Soldat-Inconnu. The bourgeois in question were townspeople who, in 1347, offered their lives to English king Edward III in a bid to save fellow citizens from merciless reprisals after Calais's abortive attempts to withstand an eight-month siege (Calais was an English possession until 1558 and was the last English toehold in France). Edward's queen, Philippa, intervened on their behalf and the courageous men were spared.

Head up traffic-clogged boulevard Jacquard, turning right onto rue Richelieu. Three blocks along, at No. 25, is the **Musée des Beaux-Arts et de la Dentelle** (Fine Arts and Lace Museum, tel. 21–46–63–17; admission: 10 frs, free Wed.; open Wed.–Mon. 10–noon and 2–5:30), which contains some fine 19th- and 20th-century pictures, local historical displays, some Rodin bronzes, and exhibits documenting the Calais lace industry. Turn left at the next block, making for the much-restored **Eglise Notre-Dame,** where Général de Gaulle was married in 1921. Take time to admire the simple, vertical elegance of the windows and the ornate fan vaulting inside.

Lodging and Dining ¢	**George V.** This clean, pleasant hotel is on rue Royale, the main street through the old town. The restaurant can seem heavy-handed, both for its pseudo-rustic decor and an overambitious cuisine that improbably pairs salmon and beef with endive and wine butter. With its unusually varied, low-priced menus, the Petit George bistro alongside offers a better deal. *36 rue Royale, 62100, tel. 21–97–68–00, fax 21–97–34–73. 45 rooms with bath or shower. Facilities: restaurant (closed Sat. lunch and Sun. evening). AE, DC, MC, V.*
Dining ¢	**Sole Meunière.** As its name suggests, the intimate Sole Meunière is a temple of fish and seafood. Not that anything else could be expected from a restaurant next to Calais harbor! The menus start at a very low price and top out on a moderate level. *1 blvd. de la Résistance, tel. 21–34–43–01. Reservations advised. AE, DC, MC, V. Closed Mon. and mid-Dec.–mid-Jan.*
Shopping	Lace shops still abound in Calais, with its long tradition of lace-making; try **La Dentellière** (30 blvd. de l'Egalité).

Boulogne-sur-Mer

Trains from Calais south to Boulogne run every 1½ hours; journey time varies from 32 to 45 minutes, depending on whether you go via express or local train. Boulogne tourist office: Pont Maquet, by the port, tel. 21–31–68–38.

The contrast between the lower and upper sections of **Boulogne** is startling. The rebuilt concrete streets around the port are gruesome and sinister, but the Ville Haute—the old town on the hill—is a different world, and you can begin to understand why Napoléon chose Boulogne as his base while preparing to cross the Channel. The Ville Haute is dominated by the formidable **Notre-Dame** basilica, its distinctive elongated dome visible from far out at sea. Surrounding the basilica are charming cobblestone streets and tower-flanked ramparts, dating from the 13th century and offering excellent views. The four main streets of the old town intersect at place Bouillon, where you can see the 18th-century brick town hall, and the Hôtel Desandrouins, where Napoléon spent many long nights pondering how to invade England.

Some 2½ km (1½ mi) north of Boulogne just off the main Calais road (N1)—a brisk half-hour walk—is the **Colonne de la Grande Armée.** Work began on this 160-foot marble column in 1804 to commemorate Napoléon's soon-to-be-abandoned plans to invade England, but it was finished 30 years later under Louis-Philippe. The 263 steps take you to the top and a wide-reaching view. If the weather is clear and you're blessed with Napoleonic vision, you may be able to make out the distant cliffs of Dover. *Admission free. Open daily 10–noon and 2–5.*

Lodging $	**Métropole.** This small hotel is handy for ferry passengers but, like most of the Ville Basse (lower town), it is no great architectural

shakes. While no exciting views are to be had from this rather face-less '50s building, the guest rooms are adequately furnished and in-dividually decorated. There is no restaurant. *51 rue Thiers, 62200, tel. 21–31–54–30, fax 21–30–45–72. 27 rooms, some with bath. Fa-cilities: garden. AE, DC, MC, V. Closed Christmas and New Year's.*

Dining
$$
★
Brasserie Liégeoise. Good food spiced with delicious nouvelle touches helps this old, established restaurant remain at the fore-front of the Boulogne eating scene. The decor is modern—an eccen-tric contrast of black and yellow—and so are the prices for both à la carte and set-menu meals. Yet the delicate sauces and interesting combinations, especially the *menu poisson*, are well worth the extra expense. *10 rue Monsigny, tel. 21–31–61–15. Reservations re-quired on weekends. Jacket required. AE, DC, MC, V. Closed Wed., and Sun. dinner.*

Le Touquet

Trains make the 18-minute journey from Boulogne south to Etaples every 2 hours (at least). A shuttle bus completes the trip to Le Touquet, about 5 km (3 mi) distant. Two direct trains a day make the 2-hour trip from Lille to Etaples. Le Touquet tourist office: place de l'Hermitage, tel. 21–05–21–65.

★ **Le Touquet,** though just a short distance down the coast from Bou-logne, is a total contrast. An elegant Victorian seaside resort, it sprang out of nowhere in the 19th century, adopting the name Paris-Plage. Mainly because gambling laws were stricter in Victorian En-gland than in France, Englishmen were the town's mainstay, not Parisians. A cosmopolitan atmosphere remains, although many Frenchmen, attracted by the airy, elegant avenues and invigorating climate, have moved here for good. To one side lies a fine sandy beach; to the other, an artificial forest planted in the 1850s. A casi-no, golf courses, and racetrack cater to fashionable pleasure.

Lodging and
Dining
$$
Red Fox. Le Touquet's determined attachment to its Victorian style and swank often means a lean deal for those with thin wallets. The Red Fox is a good option. Opened in 1993 in a reconstructed building 600 feet from the sea, it offers *style anglais* decor, modern rooms with new baths, and the option of dining at the restaurant next door. *60 rue de Metz, 62520, tel. 21–05–27–58, fax 21–05–27–56. 48 rooms with bath. MC, V.*

Splurge
★
Westminster. With its redbrick facade, this giant—one of the finest hotels in the country—looks as if it were built just a few years ago; in fact, it dates from the 1930s but has been extensively restored by its owners, the personable Flament brothers. The hotel offers a mod-estly priced coffee bar, a swanky French dining room and an "Amer-ican bar" for cocktails. The enormous double rooms represent good value, and the bridal suite is the last word in thick-carpeted extrava-gance. *Av. du Verger, 62520, tel. 21–05–48–48, fax 21–05–45–45. 114 rooms with bath. Facilities: restaurants, bar, squash court, in-door pool, Jacuzzi, sauna, solarium. AE, DC, MC, V. 580 frs–1,080 frs.*

Montreuil-sur-Mer

Six trains daily make the 10-minute run from Etaples to Montreuil, which lies 16 km (10 mi) inland from Le Touquet. Montreuil tourist office: place Darnetal, tel. 21–06–04–27.

Ancient **Montreuil-sur-Mer** features majestic walls and ramparts, as well as faded, nostalgic charm to which various authors, notably Victor Hugo, have succumbed; an important episode of his epic work *Les Misérables* is set here.

Whenever citadels and city walls loom on the French horizon, it's a fair bet that Vauban had a hand in their construction. Montreuil is no exception. In about 1690, he supplemented the existing 16th-century towers of the **citadel** with an imposing wall, whose grassy banks and mossy flagstones can be explored at leisure. There are extensive views on all sides. *Tel. 21–06–10–83. Admission: 8 frs adults, 5 frs children under 18. Open Wed.–Mon. 10–noon and 2–6.*

Lodging and **Bellevue.** This small, old-fashioned hotel is conveniently situated
Dining close to the train station. Room prices start at 210 frs, and the res-
$ taurant offers set menus at 88 frs and 110 frs. *6 av. du 11-novembre, 62170, tel. 21–06–04–19, fax 21–81–01–94. 13 rooms with bath or shower. Facilities: restaurant. MC, V. Closed second half of Dec.*

Amiens

Trains run every 2 hours from Etaples to Amiens, taking 60–80 minutes. Tourist office: 20 pl. Notre-Dame, by the cathedral, tel. 22–91–16–16.

Amiens, the capital of Picardy, is an example of catastrophic post-war reconstruction, with drab gray concrete used in hasty replacement of the region's traditional homely brick. Yet this stolid brick city has a couple of worthwhile attractions, most notably the **Cathédrale Notre-Dame,** the largest church in France. Cross the square in front of the train station, turn right into boulevard d'Alsace-Lorraine, then down rue Gloriette. Go straight for 500 yards until you reach the cathedral.

Although the cathedral lacks the stained glass of Chartres or the sculpture of Reims, for architectural harmony, engineering proficiency, and sheer size, it has no peer. The soaring, asymmetrical facade, with a notable Flamboyant Gothic rose window, dominates the nondescript surrounding brick streets. Inside, the overwhelming sensation of space is enhanced by the absence of pews in the nave, a return to medieval tradition. There is no stylistic disunity to mar the perspective: Construction took place between 1220 and 1264, a remarkably short period in cathedral-building terms. One of the highlights of your visit is hidden from the eye, at least until you lift up the choir stalls and admire the humorous, skillful misericord (seat) carvings executed between 1508 and 1518. *Pl. Notre-Dame, tel. 22–92–77–29. Open all day except noon–2.*

On leaving the cathedral, turn left along rue Cormant and take the second right onto rue Victor-Hugo. Midway down is the **Hôtel de Berny,** an elegant 1634 mansion full of period furniture and devoted to local art and regional history. *36 rue Victor-Hugo. Admission: 16 frs, free on Sun. Open Tues.–Sun. 10–12:30 and 2–6.*

If you have extra time, relax, wander, or spend the evening visiting night spots in the waterfront quarter behind the cathedral called **St-Leu.** It's a lively and novel area to explore, with restored houses painted bright colors, and shops and clubs, mixing nostalgia and contemporary trends. The **hortillonnages,** commercial gardens awash in carefully controlled marshes, are worth some of your time. More than 700 acres have been cultivated since Roman times and can be visited on leisurely trails (54 blvd. Beauvillé, tel. 22–92–12–18. Admission: 25 frs adults. Open Apr.–Oct. daily 9–6) or by small boat (La Capitainerie, quai Bélu, tel. 22–97–88–55). Jules Verne lived in Amiens for 35 years, in the building that's become the **Centre de Documentation Jules Verne** (2 rue Charles Dubois, tel. 22–45–37–84. Admission: 12 frs adults, 6 frs children. Open Tues.–Sat. 9–noon and 2–6). It contains some 15,000 documents as well as original furniture and a reconstruction of the writing studio where Verne created his science fiction. You can visit his dramatically carved tomb in the **cimetière de la Madeleine** (2 rue de la Poudrière, tel. 22–91–90–15).

Lodging **Hôtel de la Paix.** Near the Picardy Museum, the hotel is housed in a
$ building reconstructed after World War II. Private parking and the
view of a nearby church from some of the rooms offset a certain lack
of personality, although the breakfast room tries valiantly to suggest an 18th-century Louis XV salon. Foreign visitors are frequent,
and English is spoken. *8 rue de la République, 80000, tel. 22–91–39–
21, fax 22–92–02–65. 26 rooms, 11 with bath. Facilities: breakfast
room. AE, MC, V. Closed Sun. and mid-Dec.–mid-Jan.*

Dining **Les Marissons.** This restaurant, in the prettiest and oldest section of
$$ Amiens, near the cathedral, features the laudable cuisine of chef
Antoine Benoît: burbot (a local river fish) in apricot, rabbit with
goat cheese and mint, pigeon in *cassis* (black-currant liqueur).
Weekday menus offer modest alternatives to pricey à la carte. *68 rue
des Marissons, tel. 22–92–96–66. Reservations advised. Jacket and
tie required for dinner. MC, V. Closed Mon., Sat. lunch, Sun. eve-
ning, and part of Jan.*

$ **Joséphine.** This unpretentious restaurant in central Amiens is a reli-
able choice for good value. Solid regional fare, decent wines, and
rustic decor (a bit on the stodgy side, like the sauces) pull in many
foreign customers, notably the British. *20 rue Sire-Firmin-Leroux,
tel. 22–91–47–38. Reservations advised in summer. MC, V. Closed
Sun.*

Tour 2: Reims and Champagne Country

Using venerable Reims as a hub, this tour makes rail excursions
north to Laon and south through the champagne vineyards to
Epernay and Châlons-sur-Marne.

From Paris Express trains to Reims leave Paris (Gare de l'Est) 8 times daily.
By Train The trip takes 1½ hours.

By Car The 150-kilometer (95-mile) drive from Paris along the A4 express-
way also takes about 1½ hours.

Reims

*Tourist office: 2 rue Guillaume-de-Machault, off to the left as you
view the cathedral facade, tel. 26–77–45–25.*

*Numbers in the margin correspond with points of interest on the
Reims map.*

Several major producers are headquartered in **Reims**, the spiritual
capital of the champagne industry, and you won't want to miss the
chance to visit the chalky maze of cellars that tunnel under the city
center.

Cross the garden opposite the train station, take rue Thiers, and
turn right after 150 yards onto cours Langlet, which cuts through
★ ❶ the city's shopping district to the **Cathédrale Notre-Dame,** one of the
most famous in France and the age-old setting for the coronations of
the French kings (Clovis, 6th-century king of the Franks, was bap-
tized in an early structure; Joan of Arc led her recalcitrant Dauphin
here to be crowned King Charles VII; Charles X's coronation was
the last, in 1825). Its glory is its facade, which is so skillfully propor-
tioned that initially you have little idea of the building's monumental
size. Above the north (left) door hovers the *Laughing Angel*, a de-
lightful statue whose famous smile threatens to melt into an acid-
rain scowl. Pollution has succeeded war as the ravager of the build-

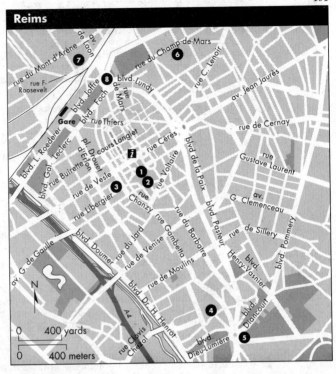

Basique St-
Rémi, **4**

Cathédrale
Notre-Dame, **1**

Mumm, **6**

Musée des
Beaux-Arts, **3**

Palais du Tau, **2**

Porte Mars, **8**

Salle de
Reddition, **7**

Taittinger, **5**

ing's fabric. Restoration is an ongoing process; take a look in the postcard shops opposite to get an idea of the pounding the cathedral took between 1914 and 1918.

The high, solemn nave is at its best in summer, when the plain lower walls are adorned by 16th-century tapestries relating the life of the Virgin. The east-end windows include stained glass by Marc Chagall. Admire the vista toward the west end, with an interplay of narrow pointed arches of different sizes.

With the exception of the 15th-century towers, most of the original building went up in the 100 years after 1211. A stroll around the outside will reinforce the impression of harmony and decorative richness. The east end presents an idyllic sight across well-tended lawns. There are spectacular light shows both inside (45 frs) and outside the cathedral (free) in July and August. *Pl. du Cardinal-Luçon. Open daily 7:30–7:30.*

② Next door, the **Palais du Tau** (former archbishop's palace) houses an impressive display of tapestries and coronation robes, as well as several statues "rescued" from the cathedral facade. The second-floor views of Notre-Dame are terrific. *2 pl. du Cardinal-Luçon, tel. 26-47–74–39. Admission: 26 frs adults, 15 frs senior citizens, 6 frs children. Open July–Aug., daily 9:30–6:30; mid-Mar.–June and Sept.–mid-Nov., daily 9:30–12:30 and 2–6; mid-Nov.–mid-Mar., weekdays 10–noon and 2–5, weekends 10–noon and 2–6.*

③ Two blocks from the cathedral, on the right, is the **Musée des Beaux-Arts,** with an outstanding collection of paintings spearheaded by no fewer than 27 Corots and Jacques-Louis David's celebrated portrait of Revolutionary leader Jean-Paul Marat, stabbed to death in his bath by a disillusioned female supporter. *8 rue Chanzy. Admission: 11 frs alone, 16 frs for joint ticket including the Salle de Reddition (Surrender Room; see below). Open Wed.–Mon. 10–noon and 2–6.*

4 As you leave the museum, turn right and continue along rue Chanzy and rue Gambetta to the 11th-century **Basilique St-Rémi,** honoring the 5th-century saint who gave his name to the city. St-Rémi is nearly as long as the cathedral, and its interior seems to stretch into the endless distance, an impression created by the nave's relative murk and lowness. The airy, four-story Gothic choir contains some fine original 12th-century stained glass.

5 Several champagne producers organize visits to their cellars, combining video presentations with guided tours of their cavernous, chalk-hewn underground warehouses. **Taittinger** has the most spectacular cellars. *9 pl. St-Nicaise, tel. 26–85–45–35. Open weekdays 9:30–1 and 2–5:30, weekends 9–noon and 2–6; closed weekends Dec.–Feb.*

6 Few show much generosity when it comes to pouring samples, though, so we recommend you double back across town to **Mumm,** which does.(If the 2½ km/1½ mi from Taittinger is too much, either take a taxi from the station or skip St-Rémi and Taittinger and concentrate on the cathedral and Mumm.) *34 rue du Champ-de-Mars. Open Mar.–Oct., daily 9–11 and 2–5.*

7 From Mumm, head down rue du Champ-de-Mars toward the train station, turn right onto avenue de Laon, then left onto rue Franklin-Roosevelt. A short way along is the **Salle de Reddition,** where General Eisenhower established Allied headquarters at the end of World War II. It was here, in a well-preserved, map-covered room, that the German surrender was signed in May 1945. *12 rue Franklin-Roosevelt, tel. 26–47–84–19. Admission: 11 frs adults. Open Wed.–Mon. 10–noon and 2–6.*

8 The **Porte Mars,** an unlikely but impressive 3rd-century AD Roman arch ornately adorned by faded bas-reliefs depicting Jupiter, Romulus, and Remus, looms up just across from the train station.

Lodging   **Hôtel de la Paix.** A modern, eight-story hotel, 10 minutes' walk from
$$ the cathedral, La Paix has admirably equipped, stylish rooms, plus a pretty garden, a swimming pool, and a rather incongruous chapel. Its brasserie-style restaurant, Drouet, serves generous breakfasts and good, though not inexpensive, cuisine (mainly grilled meats and seafood). *9 rue de Buirette, 51000, tel. 26–40–04–08, fax 26–47–75–04. 105 rooms with bath. Facilities: restaurant (closed Sun.), pool, patio bar. AE, DC, MC, V.*

$ **Gambetta.** Its location close by the Cathédrale Notre-Dame is the Gambetta's main claim to fame. Guest rooms are small and somewhat featureless but clean and acceptable for the price. *9 rue Gambetta, 51000, tel. 26–47–41–64, fax 26–47–22–43. 14 rooms with bath. Facilities: restaurant (closed Sun. dinner and Mon.). AE, V.*

Dining   **Le Vigneron.** This friendly little brasserie in a 17th-century mansion
$$ is cozy and cheerful, with two tiny dining rooms that display a jum-
★ ble of champagne-related paraphernalia—from old advertising posters to barrels and other tools of the trade. The food is delightful as well: distinctly hearty, prepared with finesse—and relatively cheap. Try the pigs' feet or *andouillettes* (chitterling sausages) slathered with Reims's delicious champagne-spiked mustard. *Pl. Paul-Jamot, tel. 26– 47–00–71. Reservations strongly advised. MC, V. Closed Sat. lunch, Sun., Christmas–New Year's, and most of Aug.*

Dining and   **Boyer–Les Crayères.** Gérard Boyer, justifiably one of the country's
Lodging most highly rated chefs, continues to draw kudos for the highly per-
Splurge sonal simplicity of his preparations, from wild mushrooms in cream
★ or scallops with endive confit to grilled St-Pierre (John Dory) or oysters with turbot. The setting, not far from the Basilique St-Rémi, is magnificent, too: a 19th-century château surrounded by an extensive, well-tended park. The decor is opulent, typified by ornate

chandeliers, towering ceilings, gilt mirrors, intricate cornices, and glossy paneling. There are 19 luxurious suites as well. *64 blvd. Henry-Vasnier, tel. 26–82–80–80, fax 26–82–65–52. Reservations required. Jacket and tie required. 19 rooms. Facilities: restaurant (closed Mon., Tues. lunch), indoor pool, tennis. AE, DC, MC, V. Closed Christmas–New Year's. 500–750 frs.*

Laon

Six trains daily make the 50-minute journey from Reims northwest to Laon. Tourist office: place du Parvis, to the right of the cathedral, tel. 23–20–28–62.

With its splendid hilltop site, **Laon** is sometimes called the "crowned mountain"—a reference to the forest of towers sprouting from its ancient cathedral. The site, cathedral, and enchanting old town are worth seeing. Strangely, not many people do; few Parisians, for instance, have ever heard of the place.

★ Dominating the old town, the **Cathédrale Notre-Dame,** constructed between 1160 and 1235, is a superb example of early Gothic. The light, creamy-stone interior gives the impression of order and immense length (120 yards in total). The flat east end, an English-inspired feature, is unusual in France. The upper galleries that extend around the building are typical of early Gothic; what isn't typical is that you can actually visit them (and the towers) with a guide from the tourist office on the cathedral square. (Tours last about 2 hours and take place weekend afternoons.) The filigreed elegance of the five remaining towers is audacious by any standards, and rare: Medieval architects generally preferred to concentrate on soaring interiors, with just two towers at the west end. Even those not usually affected by architecture will appreciate the sense of movement about Laon's majestic west front; compare it with the more placid, two-dimensional feel of Notre-Dame in Paris. Look, too, for the stone bulls protruding from the towers, a tribute to the stalwart, 12th-century beasts that carted up blocks of stone from quarries far below.

★ The medieval **ramparts,** virtually undisturbed by passing traffic, provide a ready-made itinerary for a tour of old Laon. Panoramic views, sturdy gateways, and intriguing glimpses of the cathedral lurk around every bend. Another notable survivor from medieval times is the **Chapelle des Templiers,** a small, well-preserved octagonal 12th-century chapel on the grounds of the town museum. *Porte d'Ardon. Admission: 11 frs. Open Apr.–Oct., Wed.–Mon. 10–noon and 2–6; Nov.–Mar. until 5.*

Lodging and Dining
$
Bannière de France. In business since 1685, the old-fashioned, uneven-floored Bannière de France is just five minutes' walk from Laon's picturesque cathedral and the medieval Ville Haute (upper town). Madame Lefèvre, the *patronne*, speaks fluent German and English. Guest rooms are cozy and quaintly decorated with ubiquitous flowered wallpaper, and new showers were installed in 1993. The restaurant's venerable dining room features sturdy cuisine (trout, guinea fowl) and well-priced set menus. *11 rue Franklin-Roosevelt, 02000, tel. 23–23–21–44, fax 23–23–31–56. 18 rooms, 15 with bath or shower. Facilities: restaurant. AE, DC, MC, V. Closed Christmas and New Year's.*

Dining
$$
La Petite Auberge. Young chef Willy-Marc Zorn dishes up modern, imaginative cuisine at this 18th-century-style restaurant close to the train station in Laon's Ville Basse. The 165-franc menu is a good bet, as prices continue to climb. Those in search of more modest fare can have a satisfying meal in the adjoining wine bar, **Le Saint-Amour,** with its good steaks, local andouillettes, inexpensive menus, and a staggering variety of wines to sample. *45 blvd. Pierre-*

Brossolette, tel. 23–23–02–38. Reservations advised. AE, DC, MC, V.

Epernay

There are no trains between Reims and Epernay between 8:15 AM and noon; they make the 20-minute journey south every hour or so at other times. Tourist office: 7 av. de Champagne, tel. 26–55–33–00.

Unlike Reims with its abundant treasures, **Epernay**, on the banks of the River Marne, appears to live only for champagne; there seems to be little relation between the fabulous wealth of Epernay's illustrious inhabitants and the drab, dreary appearance of the town as a whole. Most of the champagne houses are spaced out along the long, straight avenue de Champagne, and although their names may provoke sighs of wonder, their functional or overdressy facades are a disappointment.

The attractions are underground, in the cellars. Of the various houses open to the public, **Mercier** offers the best deal; its sculpted, labyrinthine caves contain one of the world's largest wooden barrels (with a capacity of more than 200,000 bottles) and can be visited in the speed and comfort of a small train. A generous glass of champagne is your posttrip reward. *75 av. de Champagne, tel. 26–54–71–11. Admission free. Open Mar.–Oct., daily 10–noon and 2–5; Nov.–Feb., Mon.–Sat. 10–noon and 2–5.*

Dining **Terrasse.** Local champagne executives jostle with discerning tour-
 ¢ ists for tables at this friendly spot on the banks of the Marne. There are four set menus—those at 75 and 130 francs are particularly good bets. *7 quai de la Marne, tel. 26–55–26–05. Reservations recommended. AE, MC, V. Closed Sun. evening, Mon., and Feb.*

Shopping Champagne is not the only Epernay specialty. At **La Chocolaterie,** Monsieur Thibaut performs confectionary miracles before your eyes—and you can take a seat in the adjoining Salon de Thé if you feel the urge to indulge on the spot. *9 rue Gallice, tel. 26–51–58–04. Closed Sun. and Mon.*

Châlons-sur-Marne

Two trains in the early morning and 1 in the afternoon make the trip from Epernay, which is 16 minutes and 35 km (22 mi) to the west. Three trains daily cover the 38-minute run southeast from Reims. Tourist office: 3 quai des Arts, tel. 26–65–17–89.

Strangely enough, the official administrative center of the champagne industry is not Reims or Epernay but **Châlons-sur-Marne.** Yet the principal interest of this large town is to fans of medieval architecture. The **Cathédrale St-Etienne** is a pure, harmonious 13th-century construction with large nave windows and tidy flying buttresses; the overall effect is marred only by the bulky 17th-century Baroque west front. Of equal merit is the church of **Notre-Dame des Vaux,** with its twin spires, Romanesque nave, and early Gothic choir and vaults. The small **museum** beside the excavated cloister contains outstanding medieval statuary. *Rue Nicolas-Durand. Admission: 20 frs adults, 6 frs children 7–18. Open Apr.–Sept., Wed.–Mon. 10–noon and 2–6; Oct.–Mar., Wed.–Mon. 10–noon and 2–5.*

Tour 3: The Oise Département

Haughty Chantilly, worth visiting to see its château and forest, forms the base for two excursions. Antique Senlis is accessible by bus, and Beauvais, home to France's tallest cathedral, is a short journey by rail. The tour then continues by train to Compiègne, site of another château and base for bus trips to splendidly restored Pierrefonds Castle.

From Paris
By Train
Express trains to Chantilly leave Paris (Gare du Nord) every 30 minutes during the early morning and evening, and 3 times during the rest of the day. The trip takes 30 minutes.

By Car
The 51-kilometer (32-mile) drive from Paris to Senlis along A1 takes about ½ hour. Chantilly is another 10 km (6 mi) west via D924.

Chantilly

Tourist office: 23 av. du Maréchal-Joffre, down a short street opposite the station, tel. 44–57–08–58.

★ To reach the **château of Chantilly,** about a mile from the station, head down to avenue du Maréchal-Joffre, turn left, then go right onto rue du Connétable, Chantilly's main street. This leads past the stables, then veers right, affording the first glimpse of the imposing, golden-hued château, sitting snugly behind an artificial, carp-filled lake.

Despite appearances, much of the current building is not old but a 19th-century Renaissance pastiche, rebuilt in the 1870s. The lavish interior contains the outstanding **Condé Collection** of illuminated medieval manuscripts, tapestries, furniture, and paintings. The most famous room, the **Santuario,** contains two celebrated works by Raphael (1483–1520)—the *Three Ages of Woman* and *The Orleans Virgin*—plus an exquisite ensemble of 15th-century miniatures by the most illustrious French painter of his time, Jean Fouquet (1420–81). Farther on, in the Cabinet des Livres, is the *Book of Hours* of the Duc de Berri, one of the finest medieval manuscripts.

Other highlights of this unusual museum are the **Galérie de Psyché,** with 16th-century stained glass and portrait drawings by Flemish artist Jean Clouet II; the **chapel,** with sculptures by Jean Goujon and Jacques Sarrazin; and the extensive **collection of paintings** by 19th-century French artists, headed by Jean-Auguste Ingres. *Tel. 44–57–08–00. Admission: 35 frs adults, 27 frs students, 10 frs children. Park only: 15 frs. Open Easter–Oct., Wed.–Mon. 10–6; Nov.–Easter, 10:30–12:45 and 2–5.*

Behind the château is a large **park,** based on that familiar combination of formal bombast and romantic eccentricity. The neatly planned parterres and mighty straight-banked canal contrast pleasantly with the Jardin Anglais, with its waterfall, and the make-believe village that inspired Marie-Antoinette's version at Versailles.

Across the lake from the château is the Chantilly racecourse, inaugurated in 1834 by the prestigious French Jockey Club. In one corner (to the right as you leave the château) are the majestic 18th-century stables (**Grandes Ecuries**), where up to 240 horses and 400 hounds for stag and boar hunts could be accommodated in straw-lined comfort. Today the stables host the **Musée Vivant du Cheval** (Living Horse Museum), so dubbed because 35 different breeds of horse live here and are featured in classes and demonstrations for the public. *Tel. 44–57–40–40. Admission: 45 frs adults, 35 frs students and senior citizens. Open Apr.–Oct., Mon., Wed.–Fri. 10:30–*

5:30; weekends 10:30–6. Nov.–Mar., Mon., Wed.–Fri. 2–4:30; weekends 10:30–5:30.

Lodging **La Calèche.** This small, underwhelming hotel and restaurant is con-
$$ veniently placed on the avenue leading from the train station to the château. It's cheap and acceptable for a night's stopover, though your reception may be somewhat lacking in warmth. *3 ave. du Maréchal-Joffre, 60500, tel. 44–57–02–55. 10 rooms, 6 with shower, 4 with bath. MC, V.*

Dining **Relais Condé.** What is probably the most sophisticated restaurant in
$$ Chantilly is pleasantly situated opposite the racecourse, in a build-
★ ing that originally served as an Anglican chapel. A reasonably priced menu makes it a suitable lunch spot. An extensive wine list and the specialties of chef Jacques Legrand warrant a lengthier (if more expensive) visit in the evening: Try the duck wings in honey. *42 av. du Maréchal-Joffre, tel. 44–57–05–75. Reservations required. Jacket and tie required for dinner. AE, MC, V. Closed Mon. eve. and Tues.*

$–$$ **Relais du Coq Chantant.** The discreet, upmarket style of this well-established restaurant attracts a clientele of golfers and horse fanciers. They may be willing to splash out à la carte, but we suggest that you opt for a set menu to sample a traditional meal based on fowl or rabbit. *21 rte. de Creil, tel. 44–57–01–28. Reservations advised. Jacket required. AE, DC, MC, V.*

¢ **Capitainerie.** As the château of Chantilly is a fair walk from the town's main street, it makes sense to have a quick lunch on the spot at this self-service restaurant. Situated in the château's medieval basement and adorned with old kitchen utensils, it offers a buffet of salads, cheeses, and desserts, complemented by the occasional hot dish—and service is nonstop from about 10:30 to 6:30. *Château, tel. 44–57–15–89. No reservations or credit cards. Closed Tues.*

Senlis

Buses meet most trains at Chantilly for the drive east to Senlis, which is 25 minutes and about 10 km (6 mi) away. Tourist office: place du Parvis, tel. 44–53–06–40.

The crooked, mazelike streets of **Senlis** are dominated by the svelte, soaring spire of the Gothic cathedral of **Notre-Dame,** recently cleaned and looking glorious. This is prime hunting country. On the grounds of the ruined royal castle opposite the west front of the cathedral is the **Musée de la Véneric,** one of Europe's few full-fledged hunting museums. Suitable artifacts, prints, and paintings rekindle the atmosphere of the kingly pursuit. *Château Royal. Admission: 14 frs adults, 7 frs students and senior citizens. Open for guided visits on the hr, Wed. 2–6, Thurs.–Mon. 10:30–noon and 2–6. Closed mid-Dec.–Jan.*

No one with even a glimmer of interest in antiquities should miss the town's **Musée d'Art et d'Archéologie,** built atop an ancient Gallo-d'Roman residence. The excavated foundations are on display in the museum's basement. Fascinating too are Gallo-Roman votive objects, unearthed in the neighboring Halatte Forest. Upstairs, the museum presents paintings by—among others—Thomas Couture, Manet's teacher, who lived in Senlis. *Pl. du Parvis-Notre-Dame. Admission: 15 frs. Open Mar.–Oct., weekdays except Tues. 9–noon and 2–6, weekends 10–noon and 2–7; Nov.–Apr., Wed.–Mon. 1:30–6:30; closed 3 wks in winter.*

Down the lane behind the cathedral is the former church of **St-Pierre,** with its Flamboyant facade; across place Notre-Dame, the large square beside the cathedral, is the **Fondation Cziffra,** the former church of St-Frambourg, converted into an exhibition center by Hungarian-born pianist Gyorgy Cziffra in 1977, with a small adjoining museum devoted to regional architectural finds. *1 pl. St-Frambourg, tel. 44–53–39–99. Admission: 20 frs adults, 10 frs students. Open May–Oct., weekends 3–6.*

Lodging **Hostellerie Porte-Bellon.** This is the closest you'll get to spending a
$ night in the historic center of Senlis. A modest yet efficient hotel, the Porte-Bellon is just a five-minute walk from the cathedral and is close to the bus station. *51 rue Bellon, 60300, tel. 44–53–03–05, fax 44–53–29–94. 20 rooms, most with bath. Facilities: restaurant. MC, V. Closed Fri. (except in summer) and mid-Dec.–mid-Jan.*

Dining **Les Gourmandins.** This cozy, two-floor restaurant in old Senlis
$–$$ serves some interesting dishes—try the marjoram-scented rabbit
★ with tiny vegetable ravioli—and offers a fine wine list. The fixed-price menu is a bargain for a weekday lunch; dining à la carte can nudge the expensive range. *3 pl. de la Halle, tel. 44–60–94–01. Reservations advised. MC, V. Closed Tues.*

Beauvais

Five trains daily make the 8-minute trip from Chantilly to nearby Creil, where you can change for Beauvais, 35 minutes northwest. Beauvais tourist office: 1 rue Beauregard, tel. 44–45–08–18.

Like Reims, **Beauvais** still bears the painful scars of two world wars. It was savagely bombed in June 1940, and the ramshackle streets of the old town have resurfaced as characterless modern blocks. One survivor is the beautiful old Bishop's Palace, now the **Musée Départemental de l'Oise,** where you'll find a varied collection of paintings, ceramics, and regional furniture. Highlights include an epic canvas of the French Revolution by 19th-century master Thomas Couture, complete with preparatory sketches, and the charming attic under the sloping roofs, one of the loveliest rooms in all France. *1 rue du Musée, tel. 44–48–48–48. Admission: 16 frs adults, 8 frs students. Open Wed.–Mon. 10–noon and 2–6.*

★ The town's showpiece is unquestionably the **Cathédrale St-Pierre,** adjacent to the art museum (pl. St-Pierre). You may have an attack of vertigo just gazing up at its vaults, which, at 153 feet, are the highest in France. Such daring engineering was not without risk: The choir collapsed in 1284, shortly after completion. The transept, an outstanding example of Flamboyant Gothic, was not attempted until the 16th century. It was crowned by an improbable 450-foot spire that promptly came crashing down. With funds rapidly dwindling, the nave was never begun, delivering the final coup de grâce to Beauvais's ambition of becoming the largest church in Christendom. Experts now say the cathedral is starting to lean and they worry about cracks that have appeared in the choir vaults. The 10th-century church, known as the **Basse Oeuvre** (closed to the public), juts out impertinently where the nave should have been.

From 1664 to 1939, Beauvais was one of France's leading tapestry centers; it reached its zenith in the mid-18th century under the direction of renowned artist Jean-Baptiste Oudry. The **Galerie Nationale de la Tapisserie,** a modern museum next to the cathedral, has examples from all periods. *1 rue St-Pierre, tel. 44–05–14–28. Admission: 20 frs. Open Mar.–Oct., Tues.–Sun. 9:30–11:30 and 2:30–6; Nov.–Feb., Tues.–Sun. 10–11:30 and 2:30–4:30.*

Lodging **Palais.** This small, family-run hotel is no palace, but it's quiet,
¢ cheap, and central—just three minutes' walk from the cathedral. *9 rue St-Nicolas, 60000, tel. 44–45–12–58. 15 rooms, some with shower or bath. AE.*

Dining **Marignan.** Sturdy bourgeois dishes such as duck with orange and
$ trout with almonds are the mainstay at the Marignan, located near St-Etienne church just off place Hachette. Go for the filling, low-

priced menu, as eating à la carte will cost more than 200 frs. If you're
in a hurry or want a cheaper meal, try the bustling ground-floor
brasserie, where sauerkraut and andouillette stand out. *1 rue Mal-
herbe, tel. 44–48–15–15. Reservations suggested. AE, MC, V.
Closed Sun. eve., Mon.*

Compiègne

*From Beauvais, change at Creil for Compiègne. From Chantilly
there are 6 trains to Compiègne during the day. The trip takes 45
minutes. Compiègne tourist office: place de l'Hôtel-de-Ville, tel. 44–
40–01–00.*

Compiègne, a bustling town of some 40,000 people, stands at the
northern limit of the Ile-de-France forest, on the edge of the misty
plains of Picardy: prime hunting country, a sure sign that there's a
former royal palace in the vicinity. The one here enjoyed its heyday
in the mid-19th century under Napoléon III. But the town's place in
history looks both further back—Joan of Arc was held prisoner
here—and further forward: The World War I armistice was signed
in Compiègne Forest on November 11, 1918.

The 18th-century **Palais de Compiègne** was restored by Napoléon I
and favored for wild weekends by his nephew Napoléon III. The
first Napoléon's legacy can be more clearly felt, however. His state
apartments have been refurnished, using the original designs for
wall hangings and upholstery; brightly colored silk and damask
adorn every room. Much of the elegant mahogany Empire furniture
gleams with ormolu, and the chairs sparkle with gold leaf. (In contrast, Napoléon III's furniture looks ponderous and ostentatious.)

In the gardens, a gently rising, 4-kilometer (2½-mile) vista leads
back from the palace, inspired by the park at Schönbrunn in Vienna,
where Napoléon I's second wife, empress Marie-Louise, was
brought up. You should also visit the **Musée de la Voiture** to admire
its large collection of carriages, coaches and old cars, including the
Jamais Contente ("Never Satisfied"), the first car to reach 100 kph
(62 mph). *Pl. du Palais, tel. 44–40–04–37. Admission: 30 frs (19 frs
Sun.). Open Wed.–Mon. 9:30–5.*

One of the central highlights of Compiègne is the late-15th-century
town hall, or **Hôtel de Ville,** which possesses an exceptional Flamboyant Gothic facade with fine statuary. Make time to visit the
Musée de la Figurine for its amazing collection of 85,000 lead soldiers
depicting military uniforms through the ages. *28 pl. de l'Hôtel-de-
Ville, tel. 44–40–72–55. Admission: 12 frs. Open Mar.–Oct., Wed.–
Sun. 9–noon and 2–6; Nov.–Feb. to 5.*

**Lodging and
Dining
$**
France. This 17th-century house, on a narrow street in the old town
near the ornate Hôtel de Ville, is calm, comfortable, and inexpensive; rates start at 175 frs for its rooms, many of which have period
furniture. Though service in the restaurant sometimes lacks enthusiasm, it does have style—lace tablecloths, wooden beams, and Louis XVI furniture—and its wide selection of half bottles is welcome.
*17 rue Eugène-Floquet, 60200, tel. 44–40–02–74, fax 44–40–48–37.
21 rooms, some with bath or shower. Facilities: bar, restaurant.
MC, V.*

**Dining
$**
Picotin. Its three inexpensive menus make the old-fashioned Picotin
a good choice for lunch or dinner after you've visited the nearby château. The traditional cuisine (salads, steaks, and chocolate desserts)
offers few surprises—or disappointments. *22 pl. de l'Hôtel-de-Ville,
tel. 44–40–04–06. Reservations strongly advised. MC, V. Closed
Tues.*

Pierrefonds

There are 3 daily buses from Compiègne to Pierrefonds, 14 km (9 mi) to the southeast.

★ Attractive, lakeside **Pierrefonds** is dominated by its huge 12th-century **château,** comprehensively restored to imagined former glory by the noted architect Viollet-le-Duc at the behest of upstart emperor Napoléon III in the 1860s. What he left is a crenellated fortress with a fairy-tale silhouette. (Like the fortified town of Carcassonne, which Viollet-le-duc also restored, Pierrefonds is considered more a construct of what Viollet-le-Duc thought it should have looked like than what it really was.) A visit takes in the chapel, barracks, and the majestic keep holding the lord's bedchamber and reception hall. *Tel. 44–42–80–77. Admission: 30 frs adults, 10 frs children 7–17. Guided tours only, May–Aug., daily 10–5:15; Apr. and Sept., daily 10–noon and 2–6; Oct.–Mar., Thurs.–Mon. 10–noon and 2–4:30.*

Lodging **Etrangers.** A lakeside terrace, château views, bike and horse rental,
$ and a comfortable restaurant make this an ideal halting place beneath the mighty castle of Pierrefonds. The three-story hotel was modernized in 1994, although it still lacks an elevator; American and English visitors are frequent. *10 rue Beaudon, 60350, tel. 44–42–80–18, fax 44–42–86–74. 18 rooms, most with bathroom. Facilities: restaurant (closed Sun. dinner and Mon. mid-Nov.–mid-Mar.), terrace, bike and horse rental. AE, DC, MC, V.*

8 Alsace-Lorraine

Including Strasbourg, Nancy, and Franche-Comté

Who put the hyphen in Alsace-Lorraine? Though the names to this day are often linked, the two regions, long distinct geologically and politically, have always had strong individual cultures, cuisines, and architectural styles. Only their recent past ties them together: In 1871, after France's defeat in the Franco-Prussian War, Alsace and Lorraine, sutured together by Kaiser Wilhelm I, were ceded to Germany as part of the spoils of war. The region was systematically (but unsuccessfully) Teutonized, and two generations grew up culturally torn—until 1919, when, after World War I, France took its revenge and reclaimed the territory.

But no matter how forcefully the French tout its Frenchness, Alsace's German roots go deeper than the late 19th century, as one look at its storybook medieval architecture will prove. In fact, this strip of flatland and vine-covered hills squeezed between the Rhine and the Vosges mountains was called Prima Germania by the Romans and belonged to the fiercely German Holy Roman Empire for more than 700 years. A heavy German influence is still evident. Regional dialect is widespread; conversations between locals are incomprehensible even to most French; town names look German; and the main daily paper, *Les Dernières Nouvelles d'Alsace*, is published in both languages.

The prettiest parts of Alsace are the vineyards that nestle amid the Vosges foothills. The Route du Vin (Wine Road) weaves its way through flower-strewn villages with medieval towers, walls, and houses built in the unmistakable red Vosges sandstone. The pointed, half-timber houses, ornate wells and fountains, oriels, and carved-wood balustrades would serve well on a film set for William Tell. Storks flutter overhead; their large, distinctive nests crown the spires of church towers. Strasbourg, the capital and unofficial "capital" of Europe—and the symbol of Franco–German reconciliation—is a city of great cultural, historic, and architectural interest, perhaps France's most fascinating outside Paris. And throughout Alsace, hotels are well scrubbed, with tiled bathrooms, good mattresses, and geraniums spilling from every windowsill. Sauerkraut, foie gras, and tobacco are among the region's specialties, and though France's major breweries are here, Alsace is more famous for its white wine, named not by locality but by grape variety.

Lorraine, west of the Vosges, creased by the cheerful Moselle Valley, evolved as decidedly less German than its neighbor. It served French and Burgundian lords as well as the Holy Roman Empire, coming into its own under the powerful Dukes of Lorraine in the Middle Ages and the Renaissance. Its historic glories are long past, though, and the present-day decline of the steel and coal industries and the miseries of its small farmers have left much of it tarnished and neglected—or, some might say, unspoiled. At its heart is majestic Nancy, a city of great appeal imbued with medieval, classical, and Art Nouveau elegance. And the rich, rolling countryside is dotted with orchards of the yellow, plumlike mirabelle and with crumbling stucco villages, abbeys, fortresses, and historic towns. It is the home of Baccarat and St-Louis crystal, the birthplace of Joan of Arc, Gregorian chant, and Art Nouveau. Yes, it lacks the Teutonic comforts of Alsace, subscribing to the more Latin laissez-faire school of innkeeping (concave mattresses, dusty bolsters, creaky floors), but it serves its regional delicacies with flair: *tourte Lorraine* (a pork and beef pie), madeleines, mirabelles, and the famous quiche Lorraine.

To the south of Alsace-Lorraine is the Jura–Franche-Comté region. Better known to Europeans than Americans, the Jura Mountains form a natural border some 150 miles long that curves between France and Switzerland. The birthplace of Louis Pasteur and Victor Hugo, and home to the celebrated aperitif Pernod, the Jura is dotted with picturesque little towns where local craftsmen still make wooden toys, clocks, and pipes. The area is renowned for its wines and cheese, and a cuisine that draws on the plentiful local lake and river fish—especially trout.

Alsace-Lorraine Basics

Budget Lodging Hotel accommodations are easier to find in Lorraine than in Alsace, where advance reservations are essential during summer months (especially in Strasbourg and Colmar). Glamorous Strasbourg, a leading tourist venue and home to a multitude of Eurocrats, is one of France's most expensive cities.

Budget Dining Alsatian cooking is distinctive in its marriage of German and French tastes. It tends to be heavy: *Choucroute* (sauerkraut), served with ham and sausages, or *Baeckoffe* (a hearty meat and potato casserole), washed down with a mug of local beer or a pitcher of wine, are filling means of combating the cold of winter or fueling up during long walks through the Vosges. But there is some sophistication, too. The local foie gras is admirably accompanied by a glass of sweet, spicy Gewürztraminer, preferably late-harvested *(vendanges tardives)* for extra sweetness. Round, fruity Riesling, the classic wine of Alsace, is often used to make a sauce that goes exceptionally well with trout or chicken. Red pinot noir, served chilled, offers a light, flexible compromise for fish-and-meat menus. Snails and seasonal game (pheasant, partridge, hare, venison, and boar) are other favorites, as are Munster cheese, salty *Bretzel* loaves, and flaky, briochelike *Kouglof* bread.

Salmon, pike, eel, and trout can be found in rivers throughout Alsace and Lorraine. Carp fried in breadcrumbs is a specialty of southern Alsace. Lorraine, renowned for its famous quiches, is also known for its Madeleines, almond candies *(dragées)*, and macaroons. Lorraine shares the Alsatian love of pastry and fruit tarts, often made with mirabelles, a yellow, cherrylike plum that flourishes in the region, but only in German-influenced Alsace will you find *winstubs*, down-to-earth café-wine bars serving wine by the jug and snacks and meals heavy on local specialties such as sauerkraut, sausage, and snails. Restaurant prices tend to be lower in Lorraine than in Alsace.

Bargain Shopping Among the specialties of Alsace are the handwoven checkered napkins and tablecloths known as **kelches** and the hand-painted **earthenware molds** for *Kouglof* bread. These goods can be found throughout this tourist-oriented province, where every pretty village has a souvenir shop of greater or lesser standing. You'll find the traditionally dressed **Hansi** characters, named for their Colmar-born creator, on everything from china to dish towels. Green-stemmed, Germanic **wine glasses** are typical of Alsace; more universal glass, and crystal are produced by skilled artisans at **Baccarat,** 60 km (37 mi) east of Nancy; its town center is dominated by attractive crystal shops, including the factory's opulent showroom. And the lively city centers of Strasbourg and Colmar are crammed with specialty shops and boutiques.

Biking A guide for biking in Lorraine is available from the **Comité Regional de Cyclotourisme VTT de Franche-Comté** (12 rue Charles Dornuer, 25000 Besançon, tel. 81–52–18–13). Bikes can be rented at many local train stations—including those in Verdun and Gérardmer in Lorraine, and Strasbourg, Saverne, Sélestat, and Colmar.

Hiking Hiking in the Vosges foothills is a rewarding pastime; for a list of signposted trails, contact the **Sélestat** tourist office (10 blvd. Leclerc, tel. 88–92–02–66). The Vosges Mountains, which often act as a cloud buffer, ensure that rain is less frequent in Alsace than in Lorraine.

Arts and Nightlife Strasbourg is a lively cultural center. Not only does it have its own orchestra, the **Strasbourg Philharmonic Orchestra** (Palais des Congrès, tel. 88–52–18–45), but it also hosts a variety of seasonal arts events. The annual **Festival de Musique** is held in Strasbourg from June to early July at the modern Palais des Congrès and at the cathedral (tel. 88–32–43–10 for details). A monthly handbook, *Strasbourg Actualités*, is a mine of information on local cultural events.

Festivals Many regional towns and villages, especially the wine villages of Alsace, stage festivals in summer. Note the spectacular, pagan-inspired burning of the three pine trees at **Thann** (late June) and the Flower Carnival at **Sélestat** (mid-August). There are impressive *son-et-lumière* (sound-and-light) performances at the château of **Saverne,** the cathedral of **Strasbourg,** and occasionally on place Stanislas in Nancy (check dates and times locally).

Tour 1: Alsace

Elegant Strasbourg, sitting proudly by the German frontier, is the star of Alsace. Trains head south through this narrow province to the towns of Obernai, Sélestat, and Colmar, whose churches, museums, and old streets deserve scrutiny. Use Colmar as a base for an excursion to Mulhouse, home to outstanding rail and automobile museums.

From Paris By Train Express trains to Strasbourg leave Paris (Gare de l'Est) 10 times daily. The trip takes about 4 hours.

By Car The 490-kilometer (305-mile) drive along A4 from Paris to Strasbourg takes 5 hours.

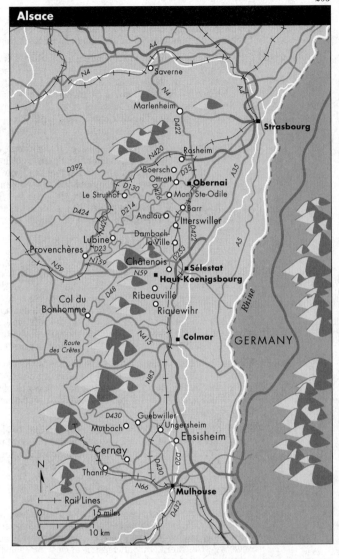

Alsace

Saverne
N4
Marlenheim
D422
N4
Strasbourg
A4
N420
Rosheim
A35
D392
Boersch
D35
Ottrott
D130
Obernai
D426
Le Struthof
Mont Ste-Odile
D424
D214
Barr
D420
Andlau
Itterswiller
D422
Lubine
Dambach-
la-Ville
D253
Provenchères
D23
Châtenois
A5
N159
N59
Sélestat
N59
Haut-Koenigsbourg
Rhine
D48
Ribeauvillé
Riquewihr
Col du
Bonhomme
Colmar
GERMANY
N415
Route
des Crêtes
N83
D430
Guebwiller
Mutbach
Ungersheim
Cernay
Ensisheim
D20
N
Thann
D430
N66
Mulhouse
Rail Lines
D432
0   15 miles
0   10 km

Strasbourg

Tourist office: 17 place de la Cathédrale, tel. 88–52–28–28.

Numbers in the margin correspond with points of interest on the Strasbourg map.

Perhaps the most interesting and attractive French city after Paris, **Strasbourg** is an irresistible mixture of old houses, waterways, and museums; looming above them all is the colossal single spire of the cathedral.

The Romans knew Strasbourg as Argentoratum before it came to be called Strateburgum, or city of (cross)roads. After centuries as part of the Germanic Holy Roman Empire, the city was united with France in 1681 but retained independence regarding legislation, education, and religion under the honorific title Free Royal City. Since World War II, Strasbourg has become a symbol of Franco-German reconciliation and the wider idea of a united Europe. It plays host to

the European Parliament and Council of Europe and acts as a neu-
tral stomping ground for such controversial political figures as
Yasser Arafat, leader of the Palestinian Liberation Organization.

★ ❶ The **Cathédrale Notre-Dame** is a tortuous ¾-mile walk from the station. To get there, take rue du Maire-Küss, which becomes rue du
22-novembre after the canal and arrives at the bottom corner of
place Kléber; skirt the square and turn right at the far end onto rue
des Grandes-Arcades, then turn left after 250 yards up pedestrian
rue des Hallebardes. The cathedral itself, with its splendid openwork spire, is at the hub of Strasbourg, on place de la Cathédrale.

Local pink sandstone covers the facade. Not content with the outlines of the walls themselves, medieval builders stuck huge, slender,
rodlike shafts of stone everywhere: You feel as if you can reach up
and snap one off. The ornately sculpted facade—a triumph of Gothic
art—was completed in 1284. The spire, finished in 1439, looks ab-
surdly fragile as it tapers skyward like some elongated, 466-foot
wedding cake; only the 528-foot spire of Ulm, in Germany, climbs
higher.

The interior presents a stark contrast to the facade. For a start, it is
older, virtually finished by 1275. Then, at 105 feet, the nave does not
create the same impression of soaring height: Its broad windows
emphasize the horizontal rather than the vertical. In the nave, note
Hans Hammer's elaborately worked pulpit (1484–86), with its 50
statuettes, and the richly painted 14th- to 15th-century organ loft
that rises from pillar to ceiling. Along the left wall, magnificent
stained-glass windows commemorate the early Holy Roman Emperors—Karls and Ottos clearly labeled in order of their reign.

Another contrast—that between the choir and the nave—is apparent within. The stolid choir is not ablaze with stained glass but is
framed by chunky masonry. The original brickwork of the cupola is
visible, as if no one had ever gotten around to decorating it. The Byz-
antine-style mosaic is modern.

The elaborate 16th-century **Chapelle St-Laurent,** to the left of the
choir, merits a visit, but most visitors turn to the right to admire the
Angels' Column, an intricate pillar dating from 1230, formed by clus-
tering, tubelike colonnettes harboring three tiers of delicate statues. Nearby, the daring Renaissance machinery of the 16th-century
Astronomical Clock whirs into action at 12:30 PM daily: Macabre
clockwork figures—including a skeletal Father Time and the screeching rooster that reminds the Apostle Peter of his broken promise—enact the story of Christ's Passion. The cathedral is closed from 11:30 to 1
so that only paying visitors can view the clock in full action. In this
Spielberg-spoiled era, only aficionados of early mechanical clocks will
find the special effects are worth the wait. And in fact, a few of the figures perform on the hour all day, enough to give the visitor a good idea
of the clock's marvelous actions. *Admission to view clock performance: 5 frs. Line forms around 11:30, doors open at noon, and
clock starts at 12:30.*

There is a *son-et-lumière* (sound-and-light) performance in the cathedral every evening from April through the end of October. The
text is in French or German, but virtuoso lighting effects translate
into any language. *Admission: 29 frs adults, 16 frs children under
18. Performances in German at 8:15 and in French at 9:15 PM.*

❷ A worthy complement to the cathedral is the **Musée de l'Oeuvre
Notre-Dame,** opposite the south front. There is more to this museum
than the usual assembly of dilapidated statues rescued from the local cathedral before they fell off. A conscious effort has been made to
create a church atmosphere and provide an appropriate setting for
the works of art. Part of one room evokes a narrow, low-roofed cloister. A dimly lighted, high-walled chamber, reached through a

creaky wooden door, is ringed by stone screens with pinnacles and pointed gables. Soon you'll find yourself in the stonemasons' workshop. A polished wooden staircase leads to a suite of small passages and large rooms, with drawings, stained glass, and gold objects. All the architectural elements of the Renaissance—pediments, spiral pillars, and cornices—can be found on the bulky wardrobes and cupboards produced by local cabinetmakers. There are some fine Old Master paintings as well. *Pl. du Château, tel. 88–52–50–00. Admission: 15 frs adults, 8 frs students and children. Open Tues.–Sun. 10–noon and 1:30–6, Sun. 10–5.*

★ ❸ Alongside the Musée de l'Oeuvre Notre-Dame, between the cathedral and the river, is the **Château des Rohan,** onetime palace of the powerful Rohans, a dynasty of prince-bishops who held both political and spiritual sway over the city and region. The exterior of Robert de Cotte's Neoclassical building (1732–42) is starkly austere. The glamour is inside, in Robert le Lorrain's magnificent groundfloor rooms, led by the great **Salon d'Assemblée** (Assembly Room) and the book- and tapestry-lined **Bibliothèque des Cardinaux** (Cardinals' Library).

The library leads to a series of less august rooms that house the **Musée des Arts Décoratifs** and its elaborate display of ceramics. Works by Hannong, a porcelain manufacturer active in Strasbourg from 1721 to 1782, are comprehensively represented; dinner services by other local kilns reveal the influence of Chinese porcelain in their delicate patterns. Equally interesting are the dishes and terrines in animal form (turkeys' and hogs' heads), or table decorations imitating plums and cauliflowers—of doubtful taste but technical tours de force. Furniture, tapestries, and silver-gilt complete the collection. The **Musée des Beaux Arts,** also in the château, features masterworks of European paintings from Giotto and Memling through El Greco, Rubens, and Goya. Downstairs, the **Musée Archéologique** displays regional findings from the prehistoric era through Roman and Merovingian times. *Pl. du Château, tel. 88–52–50–00. Admission: 30 frs adults, 16 frs students and children for all museums; each museum: 15 frs adults, 8 frs students. Open Mon. and Wed.–Sat. 10–noon and 1:30–6, Sun. 10–5 (free entry to 2 PM).*

About 50 yards north of the cathedral, and running parallel to it, is rue des Hallebardes, Strasbourg's most stylish pedestrian-only shopping street. It leads to **place Gutenberg,** dominated by an elegant three-story building with large windows, constructed between 1582 and 1585, now used as the Chamber of Commerce. Johannes Gutenberg (1400–68), after whom the square is named, invented the printing press in Strasbourg in 1434. On one side of his statue, executed in 1840 by sculptor David d'Angers, is a plaque bearing the U.S. Declaration of Independence, in acknowledgment of its influence on French revolutionary soldiers from Alsace.

❹ The **Musée Historique** (Local History Museum) stands between place Gutenberg and the river. Closed for renovation until the end of 1996, it will on reopening continue to display its broad collection of maps, armor, arms, bells, uniforms, printing paraphernalia, cardboard toy soldiers, and two huge relief models of Strasbourg, one made in 1727, the other in 1836. *3 rue de la Grande-Boucherie. Post-renovation prices and hours not set at press time.*

❺ The **Ancienne Douane,** opposite, was constructed in 1358 to serve as a customs house. It now serves as a small gallery housing temporary exhibitions. *Admission and hours vary with exhibitions.*

❻ Across the River Ill is the **cour du Courbeau,** a ramshackle 14th-century courtyard whose hostelry once welcomed kings and emperors.

❼ Facing the Ancienne Douane is the **Musée Alsacien.** If you want a glimpse of how Alsace families used to live, this is the place to visit. Local interiors—kitchens, bedrooms, and sitting rooms (the last

Strasbourg

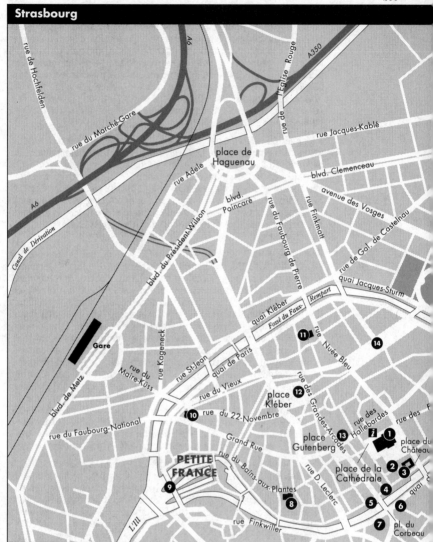

Ancienne Douane, **5**
Cathédrale
Notre-Dame, **1**
Château des Rohan, **3**
Cour du Courbeau, **6**
Musée Alsacien, **7**
Musée de l'Oeuvre
Notre-Dame, **2**
Musée Historique, **4**
Orangerie, **19**
Palais de l'Europe, **18**
Palais de
l'Université, **17**
Place Broglie, **14**

Place de la
République, **15**
Place du
Marché-Neuf, **13**
Place Kléber, **12**
Ponts Couverts, **9**
St-Paul, **16**
St-Pierre-le-Jeune, **11**
St-Pierre-le-Vieux, **10**
St-Thomas, **8**

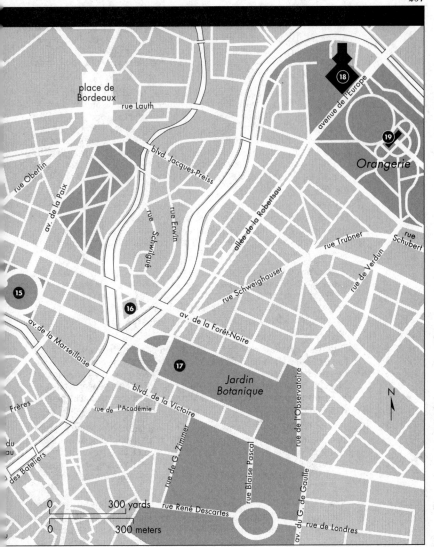

two often combined)—have been faithfully reconstituted. The diverse activities of blacksmiths, clog makers, saddlers, and makers of artificial flowers are explained with the help of old-time artisans' tools and equipment. *23 quai St-Nicolas, tel. 88–35–55–36. Admission: 15 frs adults, 8 frs students and children. Open Mon. and Wed.–Sat. 10–noon and 1:30–6, Sun. 10–5.*

⑧ Cross the river two bridges farther west to admire the church of **St-Thomas** (quai Finkwiller), particularly the mausoleum of Marshal Maurice of Saxony (1696–1750), a key figure in the 1740–48 War of Austrian Succession. Follow the banks of the river toward the picturesque quarter of **La Petite France,** whose cobblestone streets are lined with richly carved, half-timbered Renaissance houses. The Ill, **⑨** which branches into several canals here, is spanned by the **Ponts Couverts,** three connected 14th-century covered bridges, each with its tall, stern, stone tower.

⑩ Follow the waterfront north to the church of **St-Pierre-le-Vieux,** whose choir is decorated with scenes from the Passion (circa 1500) by local painter Henri Lutzelmann. Continue along the quay around **⑪** to **St-Pierre-le-Jeune,** consecrated in 1320, to admire its painted rood screen, immense choir, and 14th-century frescoes.

Alsace provided the French Revolution with 64 generals and marshals. One of the most famous was Jean-Baptiste Kléber (1753–1800), assassinated in Cairo after being left in charge of Egypt by Napoléon in 1799. Kléber's statue lords it over Strasbourg's busiest **⑫** square, **place Kléber,** up rue des Grandes-Arcades from St-Pierre-le-Jeune.

Rue des Orfèvres, one of the lively pedestrian streets leading off from rue des Hallebardes, is connected to the noisy, commercial rue **⑬** des Grandes-Arcades by a leafy, cobblestone square—the **place du Marché-Neuf**—seldom discovered by visitors. This peaceful oasis is a fine place to stop for a drink, and its two open-air cafés are open till late at night.

⑭ Rue de l'Outre leads off place Kléber to another large square, **place Broglie,** home of the city hall, the 18th-century Municipal Theater, and the Banque de France. The bank occupies the site of the house where the *Marseillaise* (composed by Rouget de Lisle, and originally entitled *Battlesong of the Rhine Army)* was sung for the first time in 1792.

⑮ Across the river, the spacious layout and ponderous architecture of **place de la République** have nothing in common with the old town except the local red sandstone. A different hand was at work here—that of occupying Germans, who erected the former Ministry (1902); the Academy of Music (1882–92), former Regional Parliament; and the Palais du Rhin (1883–88), destined to be the German imperial palace.

Much of northern Strasbourg bears the stamp of German rule. Head east out of place de la République, past the neo-Gothic church of **⑯ ⑰** St-Paul, to the pseudo-Renaissance **Palais de l'Université**—constructed between 1875 and 1885 (though Strasbourg University itself dates from 1621). Heavy, turn-of-the-century houses, some betraying the whimsical curves of the Art Nouveau style, frame allée de la Robertsau, a tree-lined boulevard that would not look out **⑱** of place in Berlin; follow its length to reach the modern **Palais de l'Europe,** designed by Paris architect Henri Bernard in 1977. The Palais houses the European Court of Human Rights and the Council of Europe, founded in 1949 and independent of the European Union (founded as the European Community in 1957), whose 12 members are joined here by representatives from the traditionally nonallied countries—Austria, Norway, Sweden, and Switzerland—plus Cyprus, Iceland, Liechtenstein, Malta, and Turkey. The European flag that flutters in front of the Palais—a circle of 12 gold stars on a blue background—was created for the Council of Europe in 1955 and adopted by the European Community in 1986. *Av. de l'Europe. Guided tours by appointment only; tel. 88–41–20–29.*

★ ⑲ Just across the street from the Palais de l'Europe, the **Orangerie** is a delightful park filled with flowers and punctuated by copper beeches. It contains a lake and, close by, a small reserve of rare birds, including flamingos and noisy local storks.

Lodging **Gutenberg.** A 200-year-old mansion is the setting of this charming hotel, just off place Gutenberg and only a few hundred yards from the cathedral. Several rooms and the reception and breakfast area have been modernized with a sleek, scrubbed decor, though enough antique oak details remain to remind you of the building's history. There's no restaurant. Be sure to ask for one of the lower-priced rooms, as some are more expensive than others. *31 rue des Serruriers, 67000, tel. 88–32–17–15, fax 88–75–76–67. 50 rooms, 17 with bath, 27 with shower and bath, 6 with bidet only. MC, V. Closed first wk in Jan.*

¢ **Michelet.** First impressions of the Michelet may be a shade gloomy, but students and foreign tourists flock here. Rooms are clean, if small, and offer unbeatable value given the location near the cathedral, off place Gutenberg. *48 rue du Vieux-Marché-aux-Poissons, 67000, tel. 88–32–47–38. 16 rooms, some with shower. V.*

Dining **Au Gourmet Sans Chiqué.** This intimate little restaurant, sophisti-
$$ cated but *sans chiqué* (without pretense), offers a selection of exqui-
★ site, if nouvelle-proportioned, experiments from the kitchen of chef Daniel Klein: foie gras in Szechuan pepper with caramelized choucroute, roast turbot in salsify, tenderloin of rabbit in hazelnut oil, and airy chocolate soufflé. Aim for the weekday lunch menu, and delve into the deep selection of local wines. Sans Chiqué is two crooked blocks south of place Kléber. *15 rue Ste-Barbe, tel. 88–32–04–07. Reservations advised. AE, DC, MC, V. Closed Sun., Mon. lunch, 1 wk in Feb., and 2 wks in Aug.*

$–$$ **Au Sanglier.** Step off the busy rue des Hallebardes and settle by the
★ fireplace in this dark-timbered, lace-clothed old dining room, where you can tuck into a flavorful choucroute, crisp *jambonneau* (ham shank), trout in white-wine cream sauce, or cheese-crusted onion soup. Choose a wine from a list that's local and reasonable. *11 rue du Sanglier, tel. 88–32–64–58. Jacket suggested. MC, V.*

¢ **Au Tire Bouchon.** Just beyond the cathedral on a small backstreet, this comfortable winstub offers a simple *plat du jour*, as well as lighter options: *salade de Gruyère* (nutty cheese and onion bits in a rich vinaigrette), omelets, and sausages—and, of course, local wines by the carafe. *5 rue des Tailleurs de Pierre, tel. 88–32–47–86. MC, V.*

Obernai

Local trains make the 30-minute journey southwest from Strasbourg in the early morning, at lunchtime, and in the late afternoon. Obernai tourist office: Chapelle du Beffroi, place du Marché, tel. 88–95–64–13.

At the heart of **Obernai**, a colorful, thriving market town well developed for tourism, is the medieval place du Marché, dominated by the stout, square, 13th-century **Kappellturm Beffroi** (Belfry), topped by a pointed steeple flanked at each corner by frilly openwork turrets added in 1597. The nearby **Puits à Six-Seaux,** constructed in the 1570s, is an elaborate Renaissance well whose name recalls the six buckets suspended from its metal chains. Just behind the belfry is Obernai's **Hôtel de Ville,** rebuilt in 1848 but incorporating much of the original Renaissance building, notably its richly carved balcony.

North of the town hall, the twin spires of the parish church of **St-Pierre-et-St-Paul** compete with the belfry for skyline preeminence. They date, as does the rest of the church, from the 1860s, although the 1504 Holy Sepulcher altarpiece in the north transept is a survivor from the previous church, along with some 15th-century stained glass.

Sélestat

Seven trains a day make the 30-minute trip from Obernai south to Sélestat. Hourly trains from Strasbourg make the 20- to 40-minute trip. Sélestat tourist office: 10 blvd. Leclerc, tel. 88–92–02–66.

Sélestat is a busy town with two impressive churches. On place du Marché Vert, **St-Foy** dates from between 1155 and 1190; its Romanesque facade remains largely intact (the spires were added in the 19th century), as does the 140-foot octagonal tower over the crossing. Sadly, the interior was mangled during the centuries, chiefly by the Jesuits; their most inspired legacy is the Baroque pulpit of 1733 illustrating the life of the founder of their movement, St. Francis Xavier. Note the Romanesque bas-relief next to the baptistery, originally the lid of a sarcophagus.

Take rue de Babil one block south to the later, Gothic church of **St-Georges.** It, too, has a fine tower, built in 1490 and some 200 feet tall. There is medieval stained glass in the rose window above the south door and in the windows of the choir, telling the tales of saints Catherine, Helen, and Agnes.

Head left down rue du Sel to the **Bibliothèque Humaniste,** a major library founded in 1452 and installed in the former Halle aux Blés. Among the precious manuscripts on display are a 7th-century lectionary and a 12th-century Book of Miracles. Altarpieces, jewelry, sculpture, and earthenware are also exhibited. *1 rue de la Bibliothèque. Admission: 10.50 frs adults, 5.50 frs students. Open weekdays 9–noon and 2–6, Sat. 9–noon; July–Aug., also weekends 2–5.*

Dining **Vieille Tour.** Rustic decor and waiters decked out in local costume
$ entice diners to the far side of place d'Armes from St-Foy church to enjoy the healthy contrast of traditional dishes (choucroute, beef in pinot noir) and more unexpected fare such as leek and mushroom salad. The best value is the 90-franc menu, as à la carte dining can push your check up to 200 frs or more. *8 rue Jauge, tel. 88–92–15–02. Reservations recommended. MC, V. Closed Mon. and 2 wks in July.*

Haut-Koenigsbourg

Haut-Koenigsbourg is inaccessible by public transportation, so you'll need to take a pricey taxi ride from Sélestat, 8 km (5 mi) away, or rent a bike at the train station for an ambitious switchback climb.

★ The romantic, crag-top castle of **Haut-Koenigsbourg** looks just as a kaiser thought it should: In 1901, German emperor Wilhelm II was presented with the 13th-century ruins by the town of Sélestat (or Schelestadt, the German name used then); he restored them with some diligence and no lack of imagination—squaring the main tower's original circle, for instance. Today Haut-Koenigsbourg is besieged by tourists and should be avoided on sunny summer days. At other times, the site, panorama, drawbridge, and amply furnished imperial chambers merit a visit. *Admission: 35 frs adults, 10 frs children 7–17. Open daily June–Sept. 9–6; Apr.–May 9–noon and 1–6; Oct. and Mar. 9–noon and 1–5; Nov.–Feb. 9–noon and 1–4.*

Colmar

Trains make the 15-minute run south from Sélestat every 1½ hours or so. There are hourly trains from Strasbourg, 35 minutes away. Colmar tourist office: 4 rue Unterlinden, tel. 89–20–68–92.

The heart of the proud merchant town of **Colmar** remains intact: A web of pedestrian streets fans out from the beefy-towered church of **St-Martin.** To the east lies Grand'Rue, with its 15th-century **Ancienne Douane** (Customs House) and twin-turreted **Maison aux Arcades** (1609). To the south is the pretty, water-crossed district known as **Petite Venise.**

Alongside St-Martin's, at 11 rue Mercière, is the **Maison Pfister** (1537), which, with its decorative frescoes and medallions, counts as one of the most impressive dwellings in town. On the other side of rue des Marchands is the **Musée Bartholdi,** former home of Frédéric Auguste Bartholdi (1834–1904), the local sculptor who designed the Statue of Liberty. *30 rue des Marchands, tel. 89–41–90–60. Admission: 20 frs adults, 10 frs students. Open Apr.–Dec., Wed.–Mon. 10–noon and 2–6.*

In the nearby **Eglise des Dominicains** (Dominican Church) can be seen the Flemish-influenced *Madonna of the Rosebush* (1473) by Martin Schongauer (1445–91), a talented engraver as well as a painter. This work, stolen from St-Martin's in 1972 and later recovered and hung here, has almost certainly been reduced in size from its original state. Realistic birds, buds, thorns, and flowers add life to the gold-background solemnity. *Place des Dominicains, tel. 89–24–46–57. Admission: 8 frs adults, 5 frs students. Open mid-Mar.–Dec., daily 10–6.*

★ Take rue des Têtes past the Maison des Têtes (1608)—so called because of the carved heads proliferating on its facade—to the **Musée d'Unterlinden,** France's best-attended provincial museum. The star attraction of this former medieval convent is the **Isenheim Altarpiece** (1512–16) by Matthias Grünewald, majestically displayed in the convent's Gothic chapel. The altarpiece was originally painted for the Antoine convent at Isenheim, 32 kilometers (20 miles) south of Colmar, and was believed to have miraculous healing powers over ergot, a widespread disease in the Middle Ages caused by poisonous fungus found in moldy grain. The altarpiece's emotional drama moves away from the stilted restraint of earlier paintings toward the humanistic realism of the Renaissance: The blanched despair of the Virgin, clutched by a weeping St. John, is balanced, on the other side of the cross, by the grave expression of John the Baptist. The blood of the crucified Christ gushes forth, and his face is racked with pain. A dark, simple background heightens the composition's stark grandeur.

The altarpiece was closed and folded according to the religious calendar and contains several other scenes apart from the *Crucifixion:* The *Incarnation* features angelic musicians playing celestial melodies as a white-bearded God, the Father, patrols the heavens; to the left, an incredulous Mary receives the Angel Gabriel; to the right, Christ rises from his tomb amid a bold halo of orange and blue. The third arrangement portrays, to the left, St. Anthony in conversation with St. Paul in a wild, overgrown landscape, while to the right, nightmarish beasts, reminiscent of Hieronymous Bosch, make up the torturous *Temptation of St. Anthony.* Modern art, stone sculpture, and local crafts cluster around the 13th-century cloisters to complete Unterlinden's folksy charm. *1 rue Unterlinden, tel. 89–20–15–50. Admission: 28 frs adults, 18 frs students. Open Apr.–Oct., daily 9–noon and 2–6; Nov.–Mar., Wed.–Mon. 9–noon and 2–5.*

Lodging
$
★

Colbert. The plus here is a convenient location, halfway between the train station and the ancient town center. Ask for one of the quieter rooms along rue des Taillandiers. Guest rooms are well equipped and air-conditioned, though the decor is a little loud. *2 rue des Trois-Epis, 68000, tel. 89–41–31–05, fax 89–23–66–75. 50 rooms with bath or shower. Facilities: bar. MC, V.*

Dining
$
★

Buffet de la Gare. Not all train-station buffets can claim gastronomic fame, but hungry travelers will enjoy this one. With its stained-glass windows, Buffet de la Gare looks more like a church than a station, and the waiters exude pastoral concern rather than ticket-collecting officiousness: They will happily advise you how best to connect between choucroute, *tête de veau* (calf's head), and pike in Riesling. Order carefully and the low tab will surprise you. *9 pl. de la Gare, tel. 89–41–21–26. Reservations accepted. MC, V.*

$

Koïfhus. Here on a beautiful old-town summer terrace, you can dive into a massive, classic choucroute, *baeckoffe* (meat and potato stew), or tender-crisp tarte flambée without dealing with stuffy service or heavy *additions* (bills). Have another pitcher of Riesling and spend the evening. Reserve in summer for a seat outdoors. *2 pl. de l'Ancienne-Douane, tel. 89–23–04–90. DC, MC, V. Closed Thurs. and Jan.*

$

La Cave Gourmande. This restaurant, in an atmospheric vaulted crypt, tries a little harder than most to break away from local standards, serving such dishes as snails with pasta, Muenster pastry, and cod in mustard sauce. The weekday lunch is a bargain. *22 rue des Marchands, tel. 89–24–37–94. MC, V. Closed Jan.*

Splurge

Schillinger. Displaying not a trace of Alsatian influence in either menu or decor, genial Jean Schillinger lords it over one of the smoothest-run restaurants in Alsace. Impeccable service, velvet upholstery, and gleaming silver cutlery complement an exhaustive wine list and adventurous cooking: monkfish with garlic and bacon, squid salad with herb pasta, and rouget with marrow, to name just a few dishes. *16 rue Stanislas, tel. 89–41–43–17. Reservations required. Jacket and tie required. AE, DC, MC, V. Closed Sun. dinner, Mon. 280–600 frs.*

Mulhouse

Trains south from Colmar run every ½ hour and take 25 minutes. Trains run from Strasbourg every 1½ hours and take an hour. Mulhouse tourist office: 9 av. Foch, tel. 89–45–68–31.

Mulhouse, a pleasant if unremarkable industrial town, is worth visiting for its museums. Dutch and Flemish masters of the 17th to 18th centuries top the bill at the **Musée des Beaux-Arts.** *14 pl. Guillaume Tell, tel. 89–32–58–58. Admission: 29 frs adults, 15 frs children 6–16. Open Oct.–mid-June, Fri.–Mon., and Wed. 10–noon and 2–5, Thurs. 10–5; mid-June–Sept., Fri.–Mon., and Wed. 10–noon and 2–6, Thurs. 10–5.* But it is cars and trains that attract most visitors. Some 500 vintage and modern cars, dating from the steam-powered Jacquot of 1878 and spanning 100 different makes, are featured in the **Musée National de l'Automobile.** The highlights are the two Bugatti Royales. Only a handful of these stately cars were ever made; one was auctioned in 1987 for $8 million. *192 av. de Colmar. Admission: 56 frs adults, 26 frs students. Open June–Sept., daily 10–6; Oct.–May, Wed.–Mon. 10–6.*

A reconstructed Stephenson locomotive of 1846 sets the wheels rolling at the **Musée Français du Chemin de Fer** (National Train Museum), a 10-minute walk west down rue J.-Hofer. Rolling stock is spread over 12 tracks, including a vast array of steam trains and the BB 9004 electric train that held the rail speed record of 207 mph from 1955 to 1981. A section of the museum also houses a display of firefighters' equipment. *2 rue de Glehn. Admission: 43 frs adults, 20 frs students. Open daily 9–5.*

Tour 2: Lorraine

If you visit just one place in Lorraine, it should be Nancy, a city of ducal splendor with a mix of medieval and Neoclassical architecture. Historic Toul and Metz—each with venerable cathedrals and many old buildings—make rewarding excursions by train.

From Paris By Train Express trains to Nancy leave Paris (Gare de l'Est) 10 times a day. The trip takes about 2 hours 40 minutes.

By Car The 335-kilometer (210-mile) drive to Nancy from Paris via A4 (branching off onto A31 at Metz) takes 3½ hours.

Nancy

Tourist office: 14 place Stanislas, opposite the Hôtel de Ville, tel. 83–35–22–41.

Numbers in the margin correspond with points of interest on the Nancy map.

★ **Nancy** is one of France's richest cities architecturally. Medieval ornament, 18th-century grandeur, and Belle Epoque fluidity rub shoulders in a town center that combines commercial bustle with stately elegance.

Turn left out of the station, then right down rue Stanislas, which leads down to **place Stanislas,** the symbolic heart of Nancy. The severe, gleaming-white classical facades of this stylish square are given a touch of rococo jollity by fancifully wrought gilt-iron railings. Stanislas Leszczyński, twice dethroned as King of Poland, was offered the throne of Lorraine by Louis XV (his son-in-law) in 1736. Knowing that after his death the independent duchy of Lorraine would fall under French rule, Stanislas sweetened the transition with a legacy of spectacular buildings, undertaken between 1751 and 1760 under the artistry of architect Emmanuel Héré and ironwork-genius Jean Lamour. A sculpture of Stanislas dominates the square's center, though he didn't commission the work himself; his grand statue of Louis XV, which ornamented what was then called the place Royale, was destroyed in the Revolution. In the 1830s, the statue of the beloved Polish king was erected when the place was named after him.

❶ One side of place Stanislas is occupied by the **Hôtel de Ville** (Town
❷ Hall), another by the **Musée des Beaux-Arts.** On the ground floor of the latter, 19th- and 20th-century pictures by Claude Monet, Edouard Manet, Maurice Utrillo, and Amedeo Modigliani mingle with 150 works in glass and crystal by local Art Nouveau master Antonin Daum. A hefty *Transfiguration* by Rubens adorns the staircase that leads to the second floor and its wealth of Old Masters from the Italian, Dutch, Flemish, and French schools. *Pl. Stanislas. Admission: 20 frs adults, 30 frs for joint admission with the Musée de l'Ecole de Nancy, below. Open Wed.–Sun. 10:15–12:30 and 1:30–5:45, Mon. 1:30–5:45.*

Before leaving place Stanislas, take a look down rue Maurice-Barrès
❸ at the twin towers of the **cathedral.** This vast, frigid edifice was built in the 1740s in a chunky Baroque style that has none of the ease and grace of the 18th-century place Stanislas. Its most notable interior feature is a murky 19th-century fresco in the dome; restoration is promised and sorely needed.

From place Stanislas, place de la Carrière, lined with pollards and handsome 18th-century mansions, leads to the colonnaded facade of

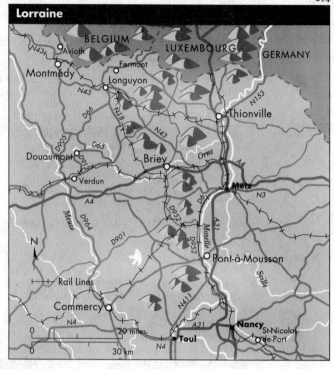

the **Palais du Gouvernement,** former home to the governors of Lorraine. To the east are the spacious formal gardens known as **La Pépinière;** to the west is the 275-foot spire of **St-Epvre,** a splendid neo-Gothic church rebuilt in the 1860s. Thanks to the efforts of Monsignor Trouillet, an entrepreneurial builder-priest, St-Epvre embodies craftsmanship of a cosmopolitan kind. Most of the 2,800 square yards of stained glass were created by the Geyling workshop in Vienna; the chandeliers were made in Liège, Belgium; many carvings are the work of Margraff of Munich; the heaviest of the eight bells was cast in Budapest; and the organ, though manufactured by Merklin of Paris, was inaugurated in 1869 by Austrian composer Anton Bruckner.

Running north–south near St-Epvre is the old town's principal medieval thoroughfare, the **Grande-Rue,** lined with bookshops, antiques dealers, restaurants, and bakeries, and dominated by the majestic **Palais Ducal,** built in the 13th century and completely restored at the end of the 15th century by René II, the hero who defeated Charles the Bold in 1476. Duke Antoine, his heir, contributed the elaborate front entry (that's his statue, on a rearing horse, above the door) and the Galerie des Cerfs (*see below*). The main entrance to the palace, and to the **Musée Historique Lorrain,** which it now houses, is 80 yards farther down the street. The museum has a delightfully far-flung assembly of exhibits. Your visit begins in a low, terracelike building across the palace lawn, with several showcases of archaeological finds ranging from Stone Age implements and ancient pottery to Roman coins and sculpture. Across the courtyard is the poorly indicated entrance to the main building, which welcomes visitors into a long, narrow room lined with medieval statues.

A spiral stone staircase leads up to the palace's most impressive room, the **Galerie des Cerfs;** exhibits here (including pictures, armor, and books) recapture the Renaissance mood of the 16th and 17th centuries—one of elegance and jollity, though not devoid of

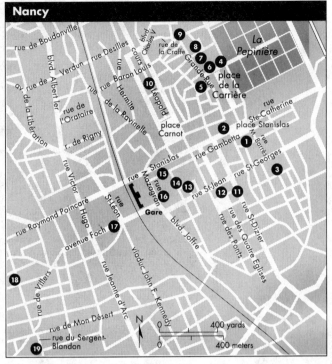

stern morality, as shown by an elaborate series of huge tapestries, *La Condamnation du Banquet*, that expounds on the evils of drink and gluttony with their allegorical sermon.

The rest of the museum is taken up mainly with paintings (including several by Lorrainer Georges de La Tour), furniture, and an extensive display of porcelain and earthenware. In a series of attic rooms, posters, proclamations, and the inevitable *tricolor* banners retrace local history from Napoléon up to World War I. *64 Grande-Rue, tel. 83–32–18–74. Joint admission to Musée des Arts et Traditions Populaires and Eglise des Cordeliers (see below): 20 frs adults, 15 frs children. Open May–Sept., Wed.–Mon. 10–6; Jan.–Apr. and Oct.–Dec., Wed.–Mon. 10–noon and 2–5, Sun. to 6.*

7 Continue along Grande-Rue to the Couvent des Cordeliers, a former convent that contains the **Musée des Arts et Traditions Populaires,** a branch of the history museum that's a minutely researched combination of scholarship and theatrical realism. It shows how local people lived in a series of rural interiors equipped with craftmen's tools, colorful crockery, and regional furniture stained a rich black-brown with pigs' blood. There are butter molds, cheese presses, choucroute graters, rush-woven beehives, and massive stone fireplaces with iron firebacks that, through open cupboard doors in the adjoining room, warmed the children in their carved-box beds.

8 The dukes of Lorraine are buried in the crypt of the adjoining **Eglise des Cordeliers,** a Flamboyant Gothic church; the intricately sculpted limestone tombs of René II and his wife Philippa de Gueldra are impressive. The octagonal Ducal Chapel was begun in 1607 in the classical style, modeled on the Chapel of the Médicis in Florence. *66 Grande-Rue, tel. 83–32–18–74. Joint admission: see above. Open May–Sept., Wed.–Mon. 10–6; Oct.–Apr., Wed.–Mon. 10–noon and 2–5, Sun. to 6.*

⑨ Wander to the end of the Grande-Rue to the **Porte de la Craffe,** the last vestige of Nancy's medieval fortifications. Built in the 14th and 15th centuries, this striking group of towers served as a prison through the Revolution.

Nancy has yet another face: It was a principal source of the revolution in decorative arts that produced Art Nouveau and Jugendstil. Inspired and coordinated by the glass master Emile Gallé, the local movement, formalized in 1901 as l'Ecole de Nancy, nurtured the floral *pâte de verre* (literally, glass dough) and stained-glass works of Daum and Gruber as well as Gallé; the fluid furniture of Louis Majorelle; and the sinuous architecture of Lucien Weissenburger, Emile André, and Eugène Vallin. With a good pair of walking shoes, you can head from the Porte de la Craffe along a route that takes in many of Nancy's best Art Nouveau buildings and end up at the Musée de l'Ecole de Nancy (*see below*). Allow a good 1½ hours for the stroll; in poor weather, you may opt for bus No. 5 from the gare, which heads directly to the museum.

Around the corner from rue de la Craffe, at 1 **boulevard Charles-V,** is a house by Lucien Weissenburger (1904) with windows by Jacques Gruber, including one in the form of the double-armed cross of Lor-
⑩ raine. The adjacent **cours Léopold** has another Weissenburger creation (1905) at No. 52, and you'll see more Gruber windows at No. 40.

Continue to the end of cours Léopold, cross place Carnot, turn left onto rue Stanislas, then take the second right into the busy shop-
⑪ ping district along **rue St-Dizier.** At No. 42 is a bank designed in 1903 by French architects Biet and Vallin; its interior can be inspected during working hours (9–5 weekdays). Turn west onto rue St-Jean,
⑫ then left onto **rue Raugraff.** At No. 86 is a house by Vallin (1906).
⑬ Return to rue St-Jean and continue to **rue Bénit.** At No. 2 is the first building in Nancy with a metallic structure: not just iron girders, either, but intricately wrought metal pillars, the work of Schertzer to the design of Gutton. There is more stained glass by Gruber, while the exterior decoration tells us that the building began life as a
⑭ seed shop. The next street along, parallel to rue Bénit, is **rue Chanzy;** at No. 9 is another bank, designed by Emile André, with interior furnishings by Majorelle and yet more Gruber windows.

⑮ At 40 **rue Henri-Poincaré,** a street running parallel to rue Stanislas, is a commercial building of 1908 by Toussaint and Marchal, with metal structure by Schertzer, glass by Gruber, and wrought iron by Majorelle. The facade is adorned with the Lorraine thistle, and
⑯ hops—used to make beer—symbolize local breweries. **Rue Mazagran** greets you at the far end of the street with, at No. 5, the Excelsior Brasserie; its rhythmic facade, severe by Art Nouveau standards, is illuminated at night.

⑰ Intersecting the south end of rue Mazagran is **avenue Foch,** a busy boulevard that heads past the train station into a district lined with solid, serious mansions clearly built for Nancy's affluent 19th-century middle class. At No. 41, more ironwork by Majorelle can be admired; yet another architect, Paul Charbonnier, was responsible for the overall design, in 1905. At No. 69, the occasional pinnacle suggests Gothic influence on a house built in 1902 by Emile André, who designed the neighboring house at No. 71 two years later.

⑱ On the right, past rue de Villers, is **rue Louis-Majorelle.** At No. 1 stands a villa built in 1902 by Paris architect Henri Sauvage for Majorelle himself. Sinuous metal supports seem to sneak up on the unsuspecting balcony like swaying cobras, scrutinizing the spacious windows and reckoning them to be yet further productions of that in-demand glazier Jacques Gruber.

⑲ End your Art Nouveau survey at the **Musée de l'Ecole de Nancy,** at 36 rue du Sergent-Blandan. This airy, turn-of-the-century town house was built by Eugène Corbin, an early patron of the School of Nancy. His personal collection forms the basis of this, the only museum in France devoted to Art Nouveau. Lamps, chairs, beds, stained glass, paintings, tables, and silverware are arrayed over two creaky stories. *36 rue Sergent-Blandon, tel. 83–40–14–86. Admission: 20 frs adults, 15 frs children; 30 frs for joint ticket with Musée des Beaux-Arts, above. Open Apr.–Oct., Wed.–Mon. 10–noon and 2–6; Nov.–Mar., Wed.–Mon. 10–noon and 2–5.*

Lodging   **Carnot.** A rather generic downtown hotel with 1950s-style comforts
$ and mostly tiny rooms, the Carnot is handy to cours Léopold parking and backs the old town. Corner rooms are sizable, back rooms quiet. *2 cours Léopold, tel. 83–36–59–58, fax 83–37–00–19. 33 rooms, most with bath. MC, V.*

$ **Central.** Located next to the train station, the Central makes a less expensive but equally convenient alternative to the Grand Hôtel de la Reine. It is fully modernized, with double glazing to keep out the noise, and has a charming courtyard garden. There's no restaurant. *6 rue Raymond-Poincaré, 54000, tel. 83–32–21–24, fax 83–37–84–66. 68 rooms with bath or shower. AE, MC, V.*

$ **Deguise.** Deep in the shuttered old town, this formerly grand mansion features a magnificent stone-floor entry and a dramatic sweeping staircase, which unfortunately winds up to rooms that have been given a standard, creaky, pasteboard renovation job. Breakfast on the noble main floor and an excellent location make this a good choice for bargain-hunting romantics. *18 rue Guise, tel. 83–32–24–68, fax 83–35–75–63. 45 rooms. AE, MC, V.*

Splurge   **Grand Hôtel de la Reine.** Definitely worth a splurge, this hotel is ev-
★   ery bit as swanky as the place Stanislas on which it stands; the magnificent 18th-century building it occupies is officially classified as a historic monument. The guest rooms are decorated in a suitably grand Louis XV style, and the most luxurious look out onto the square. The classic-nouvelle restaurant, Le Stanislas, is costly, although the set menu at weekday lunch is a good value. *2 pl. Stanislas, 54000, tel. 83–35–03–01, fax 83–32–86–04. 51 rooms with bath. Facilities: restaurant, bar, TV. Restaurant reservations required. Jacket and tie required. AE, DC, MC, V. 700 frs and up.*

Dining   **Petit Gastrolâtre.** Admirers of sophisticated regional cooking
$ shouldn't pass up a visit to Nancy's most famous purveyor of the art, under the direction of chef Patrick Tanesy. Recommended dishes include baeckoffe with foie gras, salmon—try it any way it's offered—and a delectable fricassee of snails. *7 rue des Maréchaux, tel. 83–35–51–94. Reservations required. Jacket and tie required. V. Closed Sun., Mon. lunch.*

¢   **La Gourmandière.** In this tiny storefront opposite St-Epvre, a friendly young couple serves up an inexpensive daily lunch menu with a surprising variety of choices, from quiche and crudités to turkey in tarragon, pork chops in mustard sauce, and a delicate fish *feuilleté* in lemon sauce with saffron rice. With paper mats over pink linens, a mustard pot on every table, good pitcher wines, and attentive service, it's a far cry from the touristy lunch scene off place Stanislas. *13, pl. du Colonel-Fabien, tel. 83–32–80–95. MC, V.*

Shopping   Nancy has less regional cachet for shoppers than Strasbourg, though the streets next to the cathedral are full of life, and the old town's Grand-Rue is lined with antiques shops, secondhand bookstalls, and bakeries. At 9 place Stanislas is the Dickensian **La Cave du Roy,** where old wines, champagne, and spirits are arranged in endearing confusion as mustachioed Monsieur Henné chuckles his way around with Gallic courtesy. His rare red Côtes de Toul is highly recommended.

Toul

Frequent trains throughout the day make the 20-minute trip from Nancy west to Toul. Tourist office: Parvis de la Cathédrale, tel. 83–64–11–69.

★ The charming old town of **Toul** nestles behind mossy, star-shaped ramparts. The ramshackle streets of the central part of the town can't have changed much for centuries—not since the embroidered, twin-towered facade, a Flamboyant Gothic masterpiece, was woven onto the **Cathédrale St-Etienne** in the second half of the 15th century. The cathedral's interior, begun in 1204, is long (321 feet), airy (105 feet high), and more restrained than the exuberant facade. The tall, slender windows of the unusually shallow choir sparkle in the morning sunshine. *pl. Charles-de-Gaulle. Open daily, summer 9–6; winter until dark.*

The cathedral is flanked on one side by 14th-century **cloisters** and on the other by a pleasant garden behind the **Hôtel de Ville,** built in 1740 as the Bishop's Palace. Continue down rue de Rigny, turn right onto rue Michâtel, and then take a second right onto rue de Ménin, which winds its way down to the Porte de Metz. Veer left at the gateway, then left again onto rue Gouvion St-Cyr; at No. 25 is the **Musée Municipal,** housed in a former medieval hospital. The museum's well-preserved Salle des Malades (Patients' Ward) dates from the 13th century and displays archaeological finds, ceramics, tapestries, and medieval sculpture. *25 rue Gouvion St-Cyr, tel. 83–64–13–38. Admission: 16 frs. Open Apr.–Oct., Wed.–Mon. 10–noon and 2–6; Nov.–Mar., 2–6 only.*

Fork right onto rue de la Boucherie, which, over a 300-yard stretch lined with old houses, becomes successively rue du Collège, rue Pont-de-Vaux, and rue Gengoult. Eventually rue Sonaire leads off (right) to the attractive church of **St-Gengoult,** whose choir boasts some of the finest 13th-century stained glass in eastern France. The Flamboyant Gothic **cloisters** are later than those of the cathedral but equally picturesque. Because of vandalism, St-Gengoult is closed to viewing, but you can see them from inside by attending Sunday mass at 10:30 AM. The lovely cloister remains open at all hours.

Dining   **Belle Epoque.** Except for the odd, seedy bar selling steak and french
  $ fries at lunchtime, historic downtown Toul is woefully short on places to eat. The homey, intimate Belle Epoque, situated on the road leading from the train station to the old town, is an exception. Its French cuisine is reliable, and there's a set menu for 98 frs. *31 av. Victor-Hugo, tel. 83–43–23–71. Reservations essential. MC, V. Closed Sat. lunch, Sun., and the first 3 wks in July.*

Metz

Two or three trains an hour make the 40-minute trip from Nancy north to Metz. Tourist office: place d'Armes, tel. 87–75–65–21.

Despite its industrial background, **Metz** is officially classed as one of France's greenest cities: Parks, gardens, and leafy squares crop up everywhere. At its heart, towering above the Hôtel de Ville and the
★ 18th-century place d'Armes, is the **Cathédrale St-Etienne,** one of the finest Gothic cathedrals in France.

At 137 feet from floor to roof, Metz Cathedral is also one of the highest in France, and, thanks to nearly 1½ acres of window space, one of the lightest. The narrow 13th- to 14th-century nave channels the eye toward the dramatically raised 16th-century choir, whose walls have given way to huge sheets of gemlike glass by masters old and modern, including Russian-born artist Marc Chagall (1887–1985). The oldest windows actually date from the 12th century and, in their dark, mosaiclike simplicity, offer stark contrast to the ethereal new stained glass. You'll find them on the right rear wall of the transepts, over the modern organ. Binoculars magnify moving details and reveal, flanking the full length of the clerestory above the nave, marvelously quirky gargoyles.

A pair of symmetrical 290-foot towers flank the nave, marking the medieval division between two churches that were merged to form the cathedral. The tower with a fussy 15th-century pinnacle houses **Dame Mutte,** an enormous bell cast in 1605 and tolled on momentous occasions. The Grand Portal beneath the large rose window was reconstructed by the Germans at the turn of the century. The statues of the prophets include, on the right, Daniel, sycophantically sculpted to resemble Kaiser Wilhelm II (his unmistakable upturned mustachios were shaved off in 1940). *Pl. d'Armes.*

Up the street, in a 17th-century former convent, is the **Musée d'Art et d'Histoire;** turn left out of the cathedral and take rue des Jardins. The museum's wide-ranging collections encompass French and German paintings from the 18th century on, military arms and uniforms, and archaeology; local finds evoke the city's Gallo-Roman, Carolingian, and medieval past. Religious works of art are stored in the **Grenier de Chèvremont,** a granary built in 1457, with a many-windowed facade and stone-arcade decoration. *2 rue du Haut-Poirier, tel. 87–75–10–18. Admission: 20 frs adults, 10 frs students. Open daily 10–noon and 2–5.*

Now walk back past the cathedral, continuing for another two blocks. At one end of the **Esplanade,** an agreeable terraced park overlooking the Moselle, is the 18th-century **Palais de Justice,** noted for the sculpted bas-reliefs in the courtyard (the one on the right portrays the 1783 Peace Treaty between France, England, Holland, and the United States) and its ceremonial staircase with wrought-iron banisters. Farther down the Esplanade is the small, heavily restored church of **St-Pierre-aux-Nonnains** (rue Poncelet). Parts are thought to date from the 4th century, making it the oldest church in France. The neighboring 13th-century **Chapelle des Templiers** (blvd. Poincaré) is also rare: It's the only octagonal church in Lorraine.

Lodging **Métropole.** This large, tastefully modernized station hotel is clean, ¢ comfortable, and well run. Rooms vary considerably in size and price. The brasserie alongside, under the same ownership, provides quick, straightforward meals. *5 pl. du Gal-de-Gaulle, 57000, tel. 87–66–26–22, fax 87–66–29–91. 80 rooms, most with bath or shower. AE, MC, V.*

Dining **A La Ville de Lyon.** Just behind the cathedral is this charming $$ eaterie in a venerable vaulted structure. It's well worth checking out for its fabulous wine list (30,000 bottles in stock) and no-nonsense menu. Dishes range from grilled veal kidneys to frozen mirabelle soufflé. *7 rue des Piques, tel. 87–36–07–01. Reservations advised. AE, DC, MC, V. Closed Sun. dinner, Mon., end of July and Aug.*

$ **La Baraka.** Below the cathedral, this classic French-Moroccan couscous spot with a lively, unstuffy ambience offers a fiery but digestible break from heavy *cuisine bourgeoise.* If you burned out on couscous in Paris, venture toward *méchoui* (lamb shish kebab) or *tajine,* a meat stew simmered in terra-cotta. *24 pl. de Chambre, tel. 87–36–33–92. MC, V. Closed Wed.*

¢ **Le Dauphiné.** En route from the cathedral to the museum, stop at this charming bistro/tearoom where, under a low barrel vault, you can sample *tourte lorraine* (meat pie), an inexpensive *plat du jour* with creamy potato gratin, or a slice of fruit tart. *8 rue du Chanoine-Collin, tel. 87–36–03–04. MC, V. Closed Tues.*

Tour 3: Jura–Franche-Comté Region

This tour takes in the hilly Jura region south of Alsace—France's "Switzerland," known for its leafy valleys and towering rock formations. Picturesque Besançon, the wine town of Arbois (boyhood home of Pasteur), and the royal salt works at Arc-et-Senans number among the highlights.

From Paris
By Train Fourteen TGVs daily make the 2½-hour trip from Paris (Gare de Lyon) to Besançon; several require a change at Dijon. A change at Besançon is usually necessary for the 70-minute ride to Belfort.

By Car The 400-kilometer (250-mile) drive from Paris to Besançon along the A6/A36 takes 3½–4 hours. Belfort is 75 km (47 mi) farther along the A36.

Belfort

Tourist office: rue Jules-Vallès, tel. 84–28–12–23.

Leave the station via rue Thiers and turn left after crossing the Savoureuse River. On place des Bourgeois, the celebrated 36-foot-high **Lion of Belfort,** sculpted in red sandstone by Félix-Auguste Bartholdi (best known as the sculptor of the Statue of Liberty in New York) towers over the heart of Belfort. The lion was commissioned to celebrate Belfort's heroic resistance during the Franco-Prussian war of 1870–71.

As the Prussians slashed through French defenses at Sedan (in the Ardennes), forcing Emperor Napoléon III to abdicate and making short shrift of French efforts to stop their advance on Paris, the town of Belfort, under the leadership of General Denfert-Rochereau, withstood a 103-day siege and only surrendered after the rest of France had capitulated. The Prussian leader Otto van Bismarck was so impressed by Belfort's plucky resistance that he declined to incorporate it into the German Empire along with neighboring Alsace, granting Belfort independent status. Although Alsace was returned to France in 1918, Belfort maintained its special status—making the *Territoire de Belfort* by far the smallest *département* in France. (A smaller replica of the Lion of Belfort can be found on place Denfert-Rochereau in Paris.) It costs 3 frs to visit the lion close-up.

Belfort's lion sits proudly at the foot of Vauban's impregnable hilltop château, now home to the **Musée d'Art et d'Histoire,** which contains Vauban's 1687 scale model of the town, plus a detailed section on military history. From the castle you can look out over the old town toward the Vosges Mountains to the north and the Jura to the south. *Tel. 84–28–52–96. Admission to château free. Admission to museum: 11 frs. Open May–Sept., daily 10–7; Oct. and Apr., Wed.–Mon. 10–noon and 2–5.*

Lodging and Dining
$$ **Château Servin.** No surprises at this quiet, traditional hotel, set amid expansive grounds; Louis XV rooms are comfortable and fully modernized; although some are small, many overlook the garden. In the plush dining room, chef Dominique Mathy serves such dishes as smoked salmon with cabbage and steaming cherry soufflé. *9 rue du Général-Négrier, 90000, tel. 84–21–41–85, fax 84–57–05–57. 10 rooms with bath or shower. Facilities: restaurant (closed Sun. eve., Fri.). AE, DC, MC, V. Closed Aug.*

Dining
$ **Pot au Feu.** This rustic, red-sandstone bistro at the foot of the citadel offers tasty salads, smoked fish, and pot-au-feu. Two well-priced

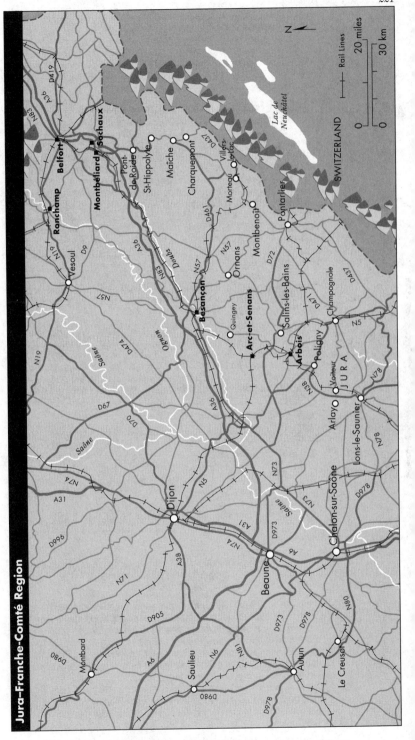

Jura–Franche-Comté Region

lunch menus include wine. *27 bis Grande Rue, tel. 84–28–57–84. Reservations advised. MC, V. Closed Sun., Mon., and 1 wk in Aug.*

Ronchamp

Three trains daily (1 in the early morning, 2 more in the early evening) make the 25-minute run west from Belfort.

The little town of **Ronchamp** constitutes our sole excursion into the windswept *département* of Haute-Saône. Small it may be—containing a population of around 3,000—but Ronchamp has one of Europe's most famous postwar buildings, the hilltop chapel of ★ **Notre-Dame-du-Haut,** designed by Swiss-born French architect Le Corbusier to replace the church destroyed here during World War II. The chapel's curved, sloping white walls, small, irregularly placed windows, and unadorned, slug-shaped gray concrete roof have no architectural equivalent. Many consider it Le Corbusier's masterpiece—utterly individual, yet imbued with peace and calm. *Tel. 84–20–65–13. Admission: 10 frs. Open daily mid-Mar.–Oct. 9–7; Nov.–mid-Mar. 9–4.*

Montbéliard

Trains run every 1 or 2 hours from Belfort south to Montbéliard; the trip takes 13 minutes. Montbéliard tourist office: 1 rue Henri-Mouhot, tel. 81–94–45–60.

Industrial **Montbéliard,** base for the giant Peugeot automobile company, is redeemed by a stately, round-towered **château** a stone's throw from the train station. Its museum is devoted to zoology (with a special section on insects), geology, archaeology, and traditional local industries (clocks and music boxes). Etienne Oehmichen studied in Montbéliard before inventing the helicopter back in 1924. *Tel. 81–99–22–61. Admission free except during special exhibitions. Open Wed.–Mon. 10–noon and 2–6.*

Across the rail line in the neighboring suburb of Sochaux, Peugeot's production methods and colorful history can be explored at the **Musée de l'Aventure Peugeot,** and you can tour the factory. The company originally concentrated on steel before producing its first bicycles, in 1886, and its first automobiles, in 1891. *Carrefour de l'Europe, Sochaux, tel. 81–94–48–21. Admission: 30 frs adults, 15 frs children. Open daily 10–6. Free guided tours of automobile factory leave museum weekdays at 8:30 AM.*

Besançon

Trains run most hours from Montbéliard southwest to Besançon; the trip takes 50–65 minutes. Besançon tourist office: 2 pl. de la Première-Armée-Française, tel. 81–80–92–55.

The capital of Franche-Comté, **Besançon** nestles in a vast bend of the River Doubs. Its defensive potential was quickly spotted by Vauban, whose imposing citadel remains the town's architectural highlight. Besançon has long been a clock-making center and is the birthplace of the synthetic silk (rayon) industry. The town's famous offspring includes Auguste and Louis Lumière, the inventors of a motion-picture camera, and writer Victor Hugo, born while his father was garrisoned here in 1802. Hugo is no local hero, though, having dismissed Besançon as an "old Spanish town," a disparaging reference to its medieval lip service to the Austro-Spanish Habsburgs.

From the station, follow signs for Centre Ville. Ignore the first bridge across the River Doubs and continue another 200 yards to the Pont de la République, where you can get a good introduction to the town by taking a 75-minute trip on a 110-seater *vedette* motorboat. The trip takes in a lock and a 400-yard tunnel underneath the citadel. *Tel. 81–68–13–25. Ticket: 43 frs adults, 33 frs children 3–10. Boats depart July–early Sept., weekdays 10:30, 2:30, 4:30; weekends also at 6:15; May–June, weekends at 2:30 and 4:30.*

Wander around the quayside to the **Musée des Beaux-Arts** to see its collection of tapestries, ceramics, and paintings by Bonnard, Renoir, and Courbet. There's also a section devoted to clocks and watches through the ages. *1 pl. de la Révolution, tel. 81–81–44–47. Admission: 20 frs adults, free Sun. Open Wed.–Mon. 9:30–noon and 2–6.*

Continue to the nearby Pont Battant and the start of **Grande-Rue**, Besançon's oldest street. This leads to the citadel, past fountains, wrought-iron railings, and stately 16th- to 18th-century mansions, the most stunning of which is the Renaissance Palais Granvelle (1540). Hugo was born at No. 140, the Lumière brothers just opposite. At the foot of the citadel, notice the **Horloge Astronomique**, a stupendous 19th-century astronomical clock with 62 dials, 30,000 working parts, and an array of automatons that spurt into action just before the hour. *2 rue du Chapitre, tel. 81–81–12–76. Admission: 20 frs. Open Wed.–Mon. 9:45–11:45 and 2:45–5:45; closed Wed. in winter.*

The **Citadelle** is perched on a rocky spur 350 feet above the town. (In summer, a small independent tourist train carries you, with commentary, on a round-trip to the Citadelle, but the fare does not include admission.) Its triple ring of ramparts, now laid out as promenades and peppered with Vauban's original watch towers, offers extensive views of the city and countryside. The buildings contain a series of museums devoted to natural history, regional folklore, agricultural tools, and the French Resistance during World War II. *Rue des Fusillés, tel. 81–65–07–44. Admission to citadel and museums: 30 frs adults, 20 frs students and senior citizens. Open late Mar.–Sept., Wed.–Mon. 9–6:30; Oct.–Mar., Wed.–Mon. 9:45–4:45.*

Lodging **Paris.** With few decent hotels in the attractive heart of Besançon,
$ this is the best; it's well run, unpretentious, old-fashioned, and brightened by a tree-lined garden courtyard. *33 rue des Granges, 25000, tel. 81–81–36–56, fax 81–61–94–90. 60 rooms, most with bath or shower. Facilities: breakfast room. AE, DC, MC, V.*

$ **Poker d'As.** Wood carvings and gleaming brasswork lend an alpine chalet feel to this popular restaurant, but judging from such adventurous cuisine as mussels in kirsch, salmon and herring tartare, and rhubarb soup, we suspect that Benoît Ferreux is something of a city slicker. Menus offer excellent value for brave forays into *cuisine du terroir* (regional cooking). Jura wines are showcased. *14 rue du Clos St-Amour, tel. 81–81–42–49. Reservations advised. AE, DC, MC, V. Closed Sun. dinner, Mon., and most of July.*

Arc-et-Senans

Four trains daily (none in the morning) make the 35-minute journey southwest from Besançon.

The **royal saltworks** at Arc-et-Senans, built 1774–79 by Claude-Nicolas Ledoux, are an extraordinary example of Neoclassical industrial architecture. With their Palladian porticoes, rustication, and towering columns, the buildings—arranged in a gracious semicircle around sweeping lawns—have an almost palatial grandeur. Originally they were meant to form part of a rationally planned, circular *ville idéale* (ideal town), visions of which are conjured up by the Musée Ledoux's exhibition of scale models. Wander around the various buildings, admire their intricate wood-beam roofs, and learn about the long-gone salt industry. The caucuses of chatting foreign students that pour in to attend the conferences and training courses held here lend an international atmosphere to the tiny town. *Saline Royale, tel. 81–54–45–45. Admission: 29 frs. Open daily July–Aug. 9–7; Mar.–June, Sept.–Oct. 9–noon and 2–6; Nov.– Feb. 10–noon and 2–5.*

Arbois

Two trains each afternoon make the 20-minute trip from Arc-et-Senans south to Arbois; the early-morning train from Besançon, which does not stop at Arc, reaches Arbois in 45 minutes. Arbois tourist office: rue de l'Hôtel-de-Ville, tel. 84–37–47–37.

Arbois is a pretty wine village, worth an overnight stop at its fine hotel-restaurant, Jean-Paul Jeunet (*see* Lodging and Dining, *below*). The famous bacteriologist Louis Pasteur (1822–95) grew up here and returned each year on vacation. His family home, still housing many of his possessions—his inkstand, school prizes, science books, and laboratory—is being renovated to honor the centennial of his death. *83 rue de Courcelles, tel. 84–66–11–72. New admission hours unavailable at press time.*

The vines owned by Pasteur (he used grapes for his experiments on fermentation) have also been preserved and can be viewed just north of the town at the intersection of the main highway and the road to Montigny-lès-Arsures. The Arbois vineyard is one of the finest in eastern France; to learn more about it, visit the newly remounted **Musée de la Vigne et du Vin de Franche-Comté and peruse its collection of tools and documents.** *Château Pecauld, tel. 84–66–26–14. Admission: 17 frs. Open Feb.–Nov., Wed.–Mon. 10–noon and 2–6.*

Lodging and Dining
$$

Jean-Paul Jeunet. This ancient stone convent, its massive beams enhanced with subtle lighting and contemporary art, has surged to the fore as the most popular and recognized eatery in the Jura. Chef Jean-Paul Jeunet's devotion to the flora and fauna of the local wilderness has allowed him to evolve a bold, earthy, high-flavored cuisine: smoked carp pancakes, snails in anise sauce, prawns with heather flowers, crisp beet chips, even sheeps' milk sorbet—though occasionally his classic *coq au vin jaune* (chicken made with cream and a flavorful regional wine) reappears. The chef's father, once an award-winning sommelier himself, has laid down a worthy *cave* (cellar) that focuses, naturally, on regional treasures. The hotel rooms have pleasant modern fittings and pretty pine furniture. *9 rue de l'Hôtel-de-Ville, 39600, tel. 84–66–05–67, fax 84–66–24–20. 17 rooms with bath or shower. Facilities: restaurant (closed Tues., Wed. lunch). DC, MC, V. Closed Dec.–Jan.*

9 Burgundy

Including Vézelay, Beaune, and Cluny

It's no coincidence that the emblem of Burgundy is a snail. The people of Burgundy eat snails regularly and often seem to move at a snail's pace. So do the area's sluggish, cross-country trains—and so will you. Not that you'd want to do otherwise: This is a region for relaxing, for lingering over rich food and extraordinary wines, ambling around ancient towns, strolling through verdant meadows, and taking in antique pilgrimage sites. Tiny Vézelay is topped by the most important church in medieval Christendom, whence pilgrims set out on the 900-mile journey to Spain's Santiago de Compostela; the now ruined Abbey of Cluny was once equally important.

There is just one city in Burgundy: Dijon, the former capital of the all-powerful dukes of Burgundy. Today, their elegant palace houses one of France's finest provincial museums, and the city challenges Lyon as France's capital of gastronomy. Its principle industries are wine, mustard, and cassis (black currant liqueur).

The famous vineyards south of Dijon—the Côte de Nuits and Côte de Beaune—are among the world's most distinguished and picturesque. You need a car to visit the growers, and in any case you can't expect to unearth many bargains here. But there is plenty of wine to be had in Dijon and in Beaune, a charming old town clustered around the elaborately tile-roofed Hôtel-Dieu, the town's medieval hospital; its Marché aux Vins is a particularly good place for sampling.

Burgundy Basics

Budget Lodging For all its charms, Burgundy is seldom deluged by tourists, and finding accommodations is not hard. But there are few towns with so many hotels that you can be sure to find something, so always make advance reservations, especially in the wine country (from Dijon to Beaune). If you intend to visit Beaune for the Trois Glorieuses wine festival in November, make your hotel reservation several months in advance. Note that nearly all country hotels have restaurants, and you are usually expected to eat in them.

Budget Dining The Burgundians are hearty eaters; whatever the class of restaurant, you are unlikely to go hungry—and even wealthy towns such as Dijon and Beaune offer an abundance of restaurants where you get plenty of value for your restaurant dollar.

Game, freshwater trout, garlicky ham in a pailey aspic, goat cheese, coq au vin, snails, mustard, and mushrooms number among the region's specialties. Meat is often served in rich, wine-based sauces. There is wine of all types and prices: Whites range from cheapish Aligoté and classy Chablis to legendary Meursault; and reds, from unpretentious Mâcon to indescribable Gevrey-Chambertin and Romanée-Conti.

Bargain Shopping Shopping is not one of life's major activities in sleepy Burgundy, where eating and drinking are most important. Mustard, snails, and all manner of candies (including chocolate snails—*escargots de Bourgogne)* may be found without difficulty, especially in the commercial heart of Dijon, with its numerous pedestrian streets. You can get the famous Burgundy wine at a relatively good price if you buy it from an individual producer. Note: Cassis, the local black currant liqueur, can be found easily enough anywhere else in France for much the same price.

Biking Rolling green vineyards, pastures lined with hedgerows, dense forest, light traffic, and terrain that is seldom more than gently rolling make this a good area for bicycling; most tourist offices can give details about recommended routes. Bikes are available for rent at train stations in Autun, Auxerre, Avallon, Beaune, Chalon-sur-Sâone, Clamecy, Dijon, Mâcon, Saulieu, and Tonnerre. Cycle tours are organized by **Service Quatre Chemins** (33 Grande Rue Chauchien, 71400 Autun, tel. 85–52–07–91).

Hiking Enthusiastic hikers should consult **La Peurtantaine** (Accueil Morvan Environnement, Ecole du Bourg, 71550 Anost, tel. 85–82–77–74) for information on paths and circuits. The Morvan Forest and vineyards between Dijon and Beaune make fine itineraries.

Arts and Nightlife Cultural activity is best represented by music. The august ruined abbey of Cluny is one of the backdrops for the **Festival des Grands Crus,** held in August and September (tel. 85–59–05–34 for details). Autun Cathedral provides a stunning setting for the **Musique en Morvan** festival in the second half of July, and Nevers the base for **Musique en Nivernais** during September and October. Dijon stages its own **Eté Musical** in June and July. Check local tourist offices for details of the programs.

Festivals Wine lovers from all over world pour into Burgundy in the third week of November to celebrate the **Trois Glorieuses,** three days of bucolic festivities culminating in a monster charity wine auction at (and benefitting) the Hospices de Beaune.

Tour 1: Troyes and Northern Burgundy

This tour makes extensive use of slow-moving regional train lines. It heads south by train from Troyes to Auxerre, then travels through the wooded Morvan region of nothern Burgundy to the old Roman town of Autun. A bus excursion from Avallon is required to reach secluded Vézelay.

From Paris **By Train** Express trains to Troyes leave Paris (Gare de l'Est) 9 times daily. The trip takes 1½ hours.

Burgundy

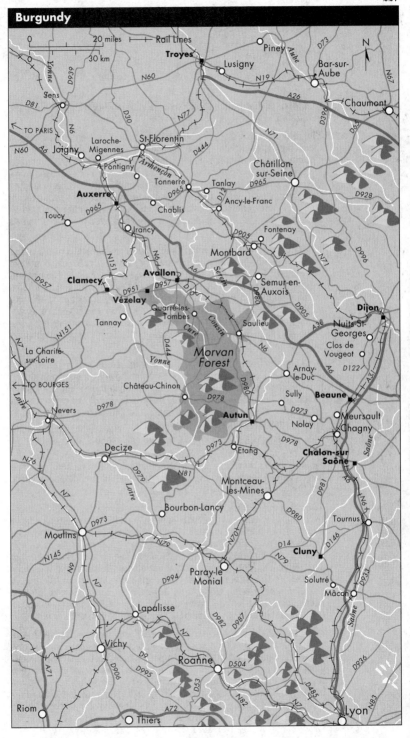

0   20 miles   ┤─┤─ Rail Lines

0   30 km

N

TO PARIS

Sens

Joigny

Laroche-Migennes

Pontigny

St-Florentin

Troyes

Piney

Lusigny

Bar-sur-Aube

Chaumont

Châtillon-sur-Seine

Tonnerre

Tanlay

Ancy-le-Franc

Auxerre

Chablis

Toucy

Irancy

Fontenay

Montbard

Clamecy

Avallon

Vézelay

Quarré-les-Tombes

Semur-en-Auxois

Dijon

Nuits-St-Georges

Clos de Vougeot

Tannay

Saulieu

La Charité-sur-Loire

TO BOURGES

Château-Chinon

Morvan Forest

Arnay-le-Duc

Sully

Beaune

Meursault

Chagny

Nevers

Autun

Nolay

Decize

Etang

Chalon-sur-Saône

Montceau-les-Mines

Bourbon-Lancy

Tournus

Moulins

Cluny

Solutré

Paray-le-Monial

Mâcon

Lapalisse

Vichy

Roanne

Riom

Thiers

Lyon

By Car The 160-kilometer (100-mile) drive from Paris southeast to Troyes takes 2¼ hours via N19.

Troyes

Tourist office: 16 boulevard Carnot, opposite the station, tel. 25–73–00–36.

Numbers in the margin correspond with points of interest on the Troyes map.

★ The inhabitants of **Troyes** would be seriously insulted if you mistook them for Burgundians. This old town is the capital of southern Champagne; as if to prove the point, its historic town center is shaped like a champagne cork. Visitors will be struck by the town's phenomenal number of old buildings, magnificent churches, and fine museums: Few, if any, French town centers contain so much to see and do. A wide choice of restaurants and a web of enchanting pedestrian streets with timber-framed houses add even more to Troyes's appeal.

Follow broad, leafy boulevard Gambetta from the station and swing right at the far end into quai Dampierre, which divides the center of Troyes. A good place to begin exploring is **place de la Libération,** where quai Dampierre meets the rectangular artificial lake known as the Bassin de la Préfecture. Although Troyes stands on the Seine, it is the capital of the département named after the River Aube, administered from the elegant **Préfecture** that gazes across both the lake and place de la Libération from behind its gleaming gilt-iron railings.

But the most charming view from place de la Libération is undoubtedly that of the cathedral, whose 200-foot tower peeps through the trees above the statue and old lamps of the square's central flower garden. The **Cathédrale St-Pierre St-Paul** is just a five-minute walk away, in a tumbledown square that, like the narrow surrounding streets, has not changed for centuries.

The cathedral is most striking for its incomplete one-towered facade; the small Renaissance campaniles on top of the tower; and the artistry of Martin Chambiges, who worked on the facade (note the large rose window). Try to see it at night, when its floodlit features are thrown into dramatic relief.

The cathedral's vast, five-aisled interior, refreshingly light thanks to large windows and the near-whiteness of the local stone, dates mainly from the 13th century. Its renowned stained glass includes the fine examples of primitive 13th-century glass in the choir as well as the richly colored 16th-century glass of the nave and rose window on the facade. The arcaded triforium above the pillars of the choir was one of the first in France to be glazed rather than filled with stone. *Pl. St-Pierre. Open daily 10–noon and 2–6. Son et lumière shows are held in the cathedral at variable hours in summer months: contact the tourist office for details. Admission free.*

❸ Just south of the cathedral is the **Musée d'Art Moderne,** housed in the 16th- to 17th-century former Bishop's Palace. Its magnificent interior, with huge fireplaces, carved wood-beamed ceilings, and a Renaissance staircase, plays host to the Levy Collection of modern art, featuring drawings, sculpture, and nearly 400 paintings. The assembly of Fauve works—a short-lived style that succeeded Impressionism at the start of the 20th century—is exceptional, notably the frenzied, hotly colored canvases by Maurice de Vlaminck, Georges Braque, and André Derain. *Pl. St-Pierre, tel. 25–80–57–30. Admission: 15 frs adults; free Wed. Guided tours: 20 frs adults, 10 frs those 18 and under. Admission ticket is good for length of stay in town.*

Abbaye
St-Loup, **4**

Basilique
St-Urbain, **6**

Cathédrale
St-Pierre
St-Paul, **2**

Hôtel-Dieu, **5**

Hôtel de
Ville, **7**

Maison
de l'Outil, **10**

Musée d'Art
Moderne, **3**

Musée
Historique/
Musée de la
Bonneterie, **12**

Préfecture, **1**

Ste-Madeleine, **9**

St-Jean, **8**

St-Nicolas, **13**

St-Pantaléon, **11**

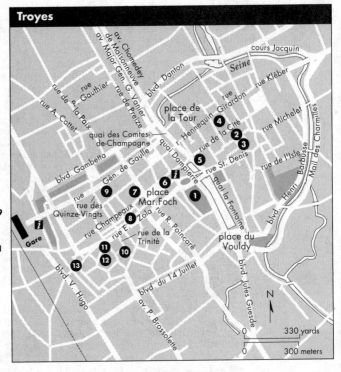

Joint ticket covering all town museums: 20 frs. Open Wed.–Mon. 11–6.

④ On the other side of the cathedral square are the former abbey buildings of the **Abbaye St-Loup,** containing two museums. The ground-floor display is devoted to natural history, with impressive collections of birds and meteorites; the Musée des Beaux- Arts et d'Archéologie is confusingly spread over two floors. In the former abbey cellars are local archaeological finds, especially gold-mounted 5th-century jewelry and a Gallo-Roman bronze statue of Apollo. There is also a section devoted to medieval statuary and gargoyles. Paintings from the 15th to the 19th centuries are exhibited on the second floor and include works by Rubens, Anthony Van Dyck, Antoine Watteau, François Boucher, and Jacques-Louis David. *21 rue Chrétien-de-Troyes, tel. 25–42–33–33. Admission: 15 frs adults, 5 frs children under 18. Joint ticket: 20 frs. Open Wed.–Mon. 10–noon and 2–6.*

⑤ From the Abbaye St-Loup, rue de la Cité, packed with restaurants, leads back to quai Dampierre, passing in front of the superb wrought-iron gates of the 18th-century **Hôtel-Dieu** (hospital), topped with the blue-and-gold fleurs-de-lis emblems of the French monarchy. Around the corner is the entrance to the **Pharmacie,** the only part of the Hôtel-Dieu open to visitors. Take time to inspect the former medical laboratory, with its quaint assortment of pewter dishes and jugs, earthenware jars, and painted wooden boxes designed to contain herbs and medicines. *Quai des Comtes-de-Champagne, tel. 25–42–33–33, ext. 3592. Joint ticket: 20 frs. Open Wed.–Mon. 10–noon and 2–6.*

⑥ The cathedral quarter north of quai Dampierre seems quiet and drowsy compared with the more upbeat, commercial southern part of Troyes. Cross over from the Hôtel-Dieu and continue down rue Clemenceau to the **Basilique St-Urbain,** built between 1262 and 1286 by Pope Urban IV, who was born in Troyes. St-Urbain is one of the most remarkable churches in France, a perfect culmination of Gothic's quest to replace stone walls with stained glass. Huge windows, containing much of their original glass, ring the church, while the exterior bristles with the thrust-bearing flying buttresses that made this daring structure possible. Inquire at the tourist office (*see above*) about summer hours of this and other area churches.

Follow rue Urbain-IV down to **place du Maréchal-Foch,** the main square of central Troyes, flanked by cafés, shops, and the delightful early 17th-century facade of the **Hôtel de Ville.** In summer, the square throbs from morning to night as residents and tourists swarm in to drink coffee or eat crêpes in the various cheap restaurants that spill into the rue Champeaux, Troyes's liveliest pedestrian street. Rue Champeaux runs parallel to **St-Jean,** a lengthy church where England's warrior king, Henry V, married Catherine of France in 1420. The church's tall 16th-century choir contrasts with the low, earlier nave; the clock tower is an unmistakable landmark of downtown Troyes.

A little farther along rue Champeaux, the **ruelle des Chats** wanders off toward the church of Ste-Madeleine. The *ruelle*, or alley, is the town's narrowest thoroughfare: Its overhanging dwellings practically bump attics. Halfway down is the tastefully restored cour du Mortier d'Or, a tiny medieval courtyard.

The church of **Ste-Madeleine** (rue du Général-de-Gaulle), the oldest in Troyes, is best known for its elaborate triple-arched stone rood screen separating the nave and the choir. Only six other such screens still remain in France—most were dismantled during the French Revolution—and this one was carved with panache by Jean Gailde between 1508 and 1517. The church's west tower and main door also date from the early 16th century.

Take rue des Quinze-Vingts, which runs parallel to the ruelle des Chats, as far as rue Emile-Zola. Turn right, then second left, onto rue de la Trinité. The museum known as **Maison de l'Outil** stands at No. 7 in the 16th-century Hôtel de Mauroy. Upstairs is a collection of pictures, models, and tools relevant to such traditional wood-related trades as carpentry, clog making, and barrel making. *7 rue de la Trinité, tel. 25–73–28–26. Admission: 30 frs adults, 20 frs children. Open daily 9–noon and 2–6.*

Close to the Maison de l'Outil, via rue Bordet, is another 16th-century building: the church of **St-Pantaléon.** A number of fine stone statues, surmounted by canopies, cluster around its pillars. The tall, narrow walls are topped not by stone vaults but by a wooden roof, unusual for such a late church. Just as unexpected are the red-and-white streamers and *Solidarnosc* (Solidarity) banners sometimes found next to the altar: St-Pantaléon is used for services by the Polish community. *Rue de Turenne. Open 10–noon and 2–6 in summer months only; at other times apply to the tourist office.*

The Renaissance Hôtel de Vauluisant, opposite, houses two museums. The **Musée Historique** traces the development of Troyes and southern Champagne, with a section devoted to religious art. The **Musée de la Bonneterie** (Textile Museum) outlines the history and manufacturing process of the town's traditional bonnet-making industry; some of the bonnets on display are more than 200 years old. *4 rue Vauluisant, tel. 25–42–33–33, ext. 3592. Joint ticket: 20 frs. Open Wed.–Mon. 10–noon and 2–6.*

Close by, beyond place Jean-Jaurès, is yet another church: that of **St-Nicolas.** You may not be tempted by its grimy exterior, but undaunted souls will be rewarded by the chance to scale a wide stone staircase up to an exuberantly decorated chapel and an unexpected view over the nave. Notice the funny little spiral staircase on the left of the nave that appears to vanish into mid-wall. Open daily 3–6.

Lodging **Le Marigny.** Churches, crêperies, and pizza parlors dominate the
$ cobbled, half-timbered core of Troyes. Le Marigny sits in their midst, on a quiet street adjacent to the narrow ruelle des Chats. With its tottering, 500-year-old gables, the hotel looks pretty shaky from the outside; creaking floorboards confirm that it's shaky inside, too. The guest rooms are few, small, and faintly run-down—but prices are suitably old-fashioned. Rooms 3 and 5 face the inner courtyard and so are the quietest. There is no restaurant. *3 rue Charbonnet, 10000, tel. 25–73–10–67. 15 rooms, 6 with bath or shower. V.*

Dining **Bouchon Champenois.** Large mirrors in this wood-beamed dining
$$ room reflect the striped, timbered patterns of the cour du Mortier d'Or, a tiny restored courtyard just outside, and make the restaurant an ideal place to savor Troyes's medieval ambience. Lunches are savory and light, and evening meals are plentiful, despite the moderate cost. Try salmon in Bouzy (from Champagne) or a *cassolette d'escargots* with almonds. *1 cour du Mortier d'Or, tel. 25–73–69–24. MC, V. Closed Sun. eve., Mon., and 2 wks in Dec.*

$$ **Le Chanoine Gourmand.** Tucked away on a charming old street behind the cathedral and not far from some of the town's best museums, this tiny restaurant offers creative cuisine at reasonable prices; there's a 165-franc set menu with an astonishing range of adventuresome choices. In summer, choose a table in the back garden from which to enjoy an appetizer of homemade duck liver in porto with pastry; St-Pierre in langoustine butter; very local andouillettes sausages in champagne sauce; and good regional cheeses. *32 rue de la Cité, tel. 25–80–42–06. Reservations advised on weekends. AE, DC, MC, V. Closed Sun. dinner and Mon.*

Shopping Numerous clothing manufacturers are established just outside the town, with the result that clothes prices in stores can be up to 50% cheaper than elsewhere in France. Rue des Bas-Trévois, rue Bégand (leather goods also), and rue Cartalon are good places to look; the best buys on jeans can be had at the **Jeans Shop** (64 rue Emile-Zola).

Auxerre

There are 2 trains daily from Troyes southwest to Auxerre, 1 in late morning, 1 in late afternoon. Both take 2½–3 hours and require changes at St-Florentin and Laroche-Migennes. Auxerre tourist office: 1 quai de la République, tel. 86–52–06–19.

Auxerre is a small, peaceful town dominated by its cathedral. If you have arrived by train, prepare yourself for a good 15-minute walk to the center of town. Head west from the station and cross the River Yonne via Pont Paul-Bert. To the right on quai de la République is the tourist office, behind which is the **Cathédrale St-Etienne,** perched on a steep hill overlooking the river. The 13th-century choir, the oldest part of the edifice, contains its original stained glass, dominated by dazzling reds and blues. Beneath the choir is the frescoed 11th-century Romanesque crypt; alongside is the Treasury, which features medieval enamels, manuscripts, and miniatures. *Pl. St-Etienne, tel. 86–52–31–68. Admission to crypt and treasury: 5 frs each. The Passport Ticket (20 frs) gives entry to the crypt and treasury plus St-Germain (below). Open daily 9–noon and 2–6, 2–5 on Sun.*

Fanning out from Auxerre's main square, place des Cordeliers (just up from the cathedral), are a number of venerable streets lined by 16th-century houses. Explore these before heading north toward the town's most interesting church, the former abbey of **St-Germain,** which stands parallel to the cathedral some 300 yards away.

The church's earliest section aboveground is the 11th-century Romanesque bell tower, but the extensive underground crypt dates from the 9th century and preserves its original frescoes, some of the oldest in France. *Pl. St-Germain, tel. 86–51–09–74. Admission: 20 frs. Guided tours of the crypt every half hour Wed.–Mon. 9–11:30 and 2–5:30.*

Lodging
$
Le Normandie. The picturesque, vine-covered Normandie occupies a grand-looking building in the center of Auxerre, a short walk from the cathedral. The guest rooms are unpretentious but reasonably priced and spanking clean, with such amenities as hair dryers in the bathrooms. You can relax in the charming garden, but there is no restaurant on the premises. *41 blvd. Vauban, 89000, tel. 86–52–57–80, fax 86–51–54–33. 48 rooms with bath or shower. Facilities: garden, garage, sauna, gym, bar. AE, DC, MC, V.*

Dining
$$
Jardin Gourmand. As its name implies, this restaurant features a pretty garden where you can eat *en terrasse* during summer months; the interior, dominated by light-colored oak, is equally congenial. The cuisine is innovative—try the ravioli and foie gras or the duck with black currants—and the service is discreet. *56 blvd. Vauban, tel. 86–51–53–52. Reservations advised. MC, V. Closed Mon., Tues. lunch.*

Clamecy

Six daily trains travel from Auxerre south to Clamecy. The trip takes 65 minutes, and the station is a stiff 15-minute walk north of the town center. Clamecy tourist office: rue du Grand-Marché, tel. 86–27–02–51.

Slow-moving **Clamecy** is not on many tourist itineraries, but its tumbling alleyways and untouched, ancient houses epitomize *La France Profonde* (the sleepy heartland of France). Clamecy's multishaped roofs, dominated by the majestic square tower of St-Martin's collegiate church, are best viewed from the banks of the Yonne. The river played a crucial role in Clamecy's development; trees from the nearby Morvan Forest were chopped down and floated in huge convoys to Paris. The history of this form of transport (*flottage*), which lasted until 1923, is detailed in the town museum housed in two mansions. The **Musée d'Art et d'Histoire Romain Rolland** is named for a native son, a Nobel laureate for literature in 1915. *Av. de la République, tel. 86–27–17–99. Admission: 15 frs adults. Open Wed.–Mon. 10–noon and 2–6; closed Sun. Nov.–Easter.*

Lodging and Dining
¢
Boule d'Or. This down-to-earth country hotel (not particularly comfortable but oh-so-cheap) boasts a delightful setting by the River Yonne. Ask for a room facing the river—there are lovely views of Old Clamecy. The restaurant is housed in a former medieval chapel, which, together with absurdly inexpensive set menus, more than compensates for the often apathetic service. *5 pl. Bethléem, 58500, tel. 86–27–11–55, fax 86–24–47–02. 12 rooms, most with bath. Facilities: restaurant (closed Sun. evening and Mon. off-season). AE, MC, V.*

Dining
$$
L'Angélus. The cuisine in this restaurant is as charming as the setting—opposite the collegiate church, in a wood-beamed medieval landmark. The chef, Thierry Lambelin, turns out a fine, lighter version of the region's traditional cuisine. Set menus start at 90 frs. *11 pl. St-Jean, tel. 86–27–23–25. Reservations advised. AE, DC, MC, V. Closed Wed. evening and Thurs.*

Shopping
In homage to the logs that used to be floated downriver from Clamecy to Paris, a log-shaped, sugared-almond candy has long been chewed by *Clamecyçois*, as the local inhabitants are known. You can find your *bûchettes* at **Avignon** (22 rue de la Monnaie), a pas-

try shop–cum–tearoom close to the steps leading up to the church square.

Avallon

Six trains daily make the 60- to 70-minute trip from Auxerre southeast to Avallon. Tourist office: 6 rue Bocquillot, tel. 86–34–14–19.

Avallon is spectacularly situated on a promontory jutting over the Cousin Valley. Its old streets and ramparts are pleasant places for strolling, before or after viewing the works of medieval stone carvers whose imaginations ran riot on the portals of the venerable church of **St-Lazarus.**

Lodging and Dining
$-$$
★

Les Capucins. On a peaceful square 10 minutes from the town center, this intimate hotel offers rooms in a wide range of prices. It is better known for its restaurant, however, which features four set menus dominated by regional cooking. Dishes of especially good value are the duck, the trout in flaky pastry, and the very local *oeufs en meurette* (eggs poached in broth and red wine). The desserts are excellent. There's a pleasant garden for breakfast and aperitifs, and small, cozy rooms for postprandial *digestits*. *6 av. Paul-Doumer (also known as av. de la Gare), 89200, tel. 86–34–06–52, fax 86–34–58–47. 8 rooms with bath. AE, MC, V. Facilities: restaurant (closed Wed., Tues. dinner Nov.–Mar.). Closed mid-Nov.–mid-Jan.*

Dining
$$

Morvan. Solid, filling dishes are offered at this folksy eatery just outside town; fish terrine, rabbit, and chocolate cake number among the menu's best. There is an adjoining rock garden. *7 rte. de Paris, tel. 86–34–18–20. Reservations accepted. AE, DC, MC, V. Closed Sun. evening, Mon., most of Jan. and Feb., and second half of Nov.*

Vézelay

A bus for Vézelay leaves daily at 8 AM from place Vauban in Avallon, which is about 6 km (10 mi) northeast. The return bus departs at 5 PM. Tourist office: rue St-Pierre, tel. 86–33–23–69.

★ In the 11th and 12th centuries, the crag-top basilica in picturesque old **Vézelay** was one of the focal points of Christendom. Pilgrims poured in to gasp at the relics of St. Mary Magdalene before setting off on the great medieval trek to the shrine of St. James at Santiago de Compostela in northwest Spain.

By the mid-13th century, the authenticity of St. Mary's relics was in doubt; others had been discovered in Provence. The decline continued until the French Revolution, when the basilica and adjoining monastery buildings were sold by the state. Only the basilica escaped demolition and was itself falling into ruin when architect Viollet-le-Duc rode to the rescue in 1840 (he also restored the cathedrals of Laon and Amiens, and Paris's Notre-Dame).

Today the **basilica** at Vézelay has recaptured its onetime glory and is considered France's most prestigious Romanesque showcase. Nowhere is this more evident than in the nave, whose carved column capitals are imaginatively designed and superbly executed, representing miniature medieval men in all manner of situations—working in the fields, wielding battle swords, or undergoing the tortures of hell.

The basilica's exterior is best seen from the leafy terrace to the right of the facade. Opposite is a vast, verdant panorama encompassing lush valleys and rolling hills. In the forefront is the Flamboyant Gothic spire of St-Père-sous-Vézelay, a tiny village a couple of miles away.

A somewhat isolated hill town, Vézelay rarely becomes as crowded as it deserves. You can climb the cobblestone streets and ramparts, admire restored private homes and eclectic (but not kitschy) shops, or relax in cloistered rose gardens with a feeling of unfettered calm.

Lodging **Relais du Morvan.** With its delightful setting, Vézelay makes a great
$ place to stay. But it is, after all, a mere village (500 inhabitants) and contains just a handful of hotels. Don't opt for the large, unfriendly, and astronomically expensive Lion d'Or; try instead to reserve a room at the cozy, budgetwise Relais du Morvan. The welcome is cheerful, the rooms functional and unpretentious (ask for one on the second floor). There is a choice of three very affordable set menus in the restaurant. *89450 Vézelay, tel. 86–33–25–33. 13 rooms, most with bath. Facilities: restaurant (closed Tues. evening and Wed.). MC, V. Closed early Jan.–mid-Feb.*

Autun

The rail trip takes 1¾–2¼ hours from Avallon south to Autun (2¾–3½ hours from Auxerre). There are 3 trains daily. Autun tourist office: 3 av. Charles-de-Gaulle, tel. 85–52–20–34.

Autun's importance since Roman times is immediately apparent at the well-preserved archways, **Porte St-André** and **Porte d'Arroux,** and at the **Théâtre Romain,** once the largest arena in Gaul. Julius Caesar even referred to Autun as the "sister and rival of Rome itself." Another famous warrior, Napoléon, studied here in 1779 at the military academy (now the Lycée Bonaparte).

Autun's principal monument, however, is its **cathedral,** built from 1120 to 1146 to house the relics of St. Lazarus; the main tower, spire, and upper reaches of the chancel were added in the late-15th century. The influx of medieval pilgrims accounts for the building's size (35 yards wide and nearly 80 yards long). Lazarus's tomb was dismantled in 1766 by canons who were believers in the rationalist credo of the Enlightenment. These clergy did their best to transform the Romanesque-Gothic cathedral into a Classical temple at the same time, adding pilasters and classical ornament willy-nilly. Fortunately, some of the best Romanesque stonework, including the inspired nave capitals and the tympanum above the main door—a gracefully elongated *Last Judgment* sculpted by Gislebertus in the 1130s—emerged unscathed. Jean Auguste Ingres's painting depicting the *Martyrdom of St-Symphorien* has been relegated to a dingy chapel in the north aisle of the nave. *Pl. St-Louis.*

Across from the cathedral, the **Musée Rolin** houses several fine paintings from the Middle Ages and good examples of Burgundian sculpture, including another Gislebertus masterpiece, the *Temptation of Eve*, which originally topped one of the side doors of the cathedral. *Pl. St-Louis, tel. 85–52–09–76. Admission: 14 frs. Open Apr.–Sept., Wed.–Mon. 9:30–noon and 1:30–6; Oct.–Mar., Mon. and Wed.–Sat. 10–noon and 2–5 or 6, Sun. 10–noon and 2–5.*

On the outskirts of town, off the Nevers road, are the ruins of the so-called **temple of Janus,** an ancient Roman temple dedicated to an unknown god. And on the opposite side of town, in the direction of Chalon-sur-Saône, is a 2,000-year-old Roman **amphitheater,** an ideal picnic spot.

Lodging **St-Louis.** This quiet comfortable hotel dates from the 17th century;
$$ legend has it that Napoléon once slept here. Guest rooms are cozily decorated and have a slightly faded charm. The hotel has a pleasant patio-garden and its own restaurant, La Rotonde. *6 rue de l'Arbalète, 71400, tel. 85–52–21–03, fax 85–86–32–54. 52 rooms, some with bath. Facilities: restaurant, garden. AE, DC, MC, V.*

Dining **Chalet Bleu.** In the center of Autun, this restaurant serves solid tra-
$ ditional French cuisine at prices that can be refreshingly low if you order carefully. The fresh, green setting, complemented by spruce

white furniture, resembles a converted conservatory. Foie gras and beef with shallots are trustworthy choices. *3 rue Jeannin, tel. 85-86-27-30. Reservations advised. AE, DC, MC, V. Closed Mon. dinner, Tues.*

Tour 2: From Dijon to Cluny

Dijon, the capital of Burgundy and a major cultural and gastronomic venue, is the base of this tour, which heads south through the wine town of Beaune to Chalon-sur-Saône, where buses leave for the delightful old town of Cluny, whose ruined abbey was once the most powerful religious center of western Europe.

From Paris   TGV bullet trains to Dijon leave Paris (Gare de Lyon) 8 times daily.
By Train   The trip takes 1 hour 40 minutes.

By Car   The 312-kilometer (193-mile) drive to Dijon from Paris southeast along A6/A38 takes 3 hours.

Dijon

Tourist office: 29 place Darcy, down avenue Foch from the station, tel. 80–44–11–44.

Numbers in the margin correspond with points of interest on the Dijon map.

Dijon is the age-old capital of Burgundy. Throughout the Middle Ages, Burgundy was a duchy that led a separate existence from the rest of France, culminating in the rule of the four "Grand Dukes of the West" between 1364 and 1477. A number of monuments date from this period, such as the Palais des Ducs (Ducal Palace), now largely converted into an art museum.

Dijon's fame and fortune outlasted its dukes, and the city continued to flourish under French rule from the 17th century on. It has remained the major city of Burgundy—the only one, in fact, with more than 100,000 inhabitants. Its site, on the major European north–south trade route and within striking distance of the Swiss and German borders, has helped maintain its economic importance. The same can be said of its numerous gastronomic specialties: snails, mustard, and cassis, which is often mixed with white wine—preferably Burgundy Aligoté—to make Kir, one of France's most popular aperitifs. Dijon is a cultural center as well, with no fewer than 10 museums.

From the station take avenue Foch down to place Darcy and head off right along pedestrian rue de la Liberté to the Palais des Ducs.

★ ❶   The **Palais des Ducs** is Dijon's leading testimony to bygone splendor. These days, it's home to one of France's major arts museums, the **Musée des Beaux-Arts,** where tombs of two of the aforementioned dukes—Philip the Bold and John the Fearless—spearhead a rich collection of medieval objects and Renaissance furniture. Among the paintings are works by Italian Old Masters, and French 19th-century artists, such as Théodore Géricault and Gustave Courbet, and their Impressionist successors, notably Edouard Manet and Claude Monet. The **ducal kitchens** (circa 1435), with their six huge fireplaces, and the 14th-century chapter house catch the eye, as does the 15th-century **Salle des Gardes** (Guard Room), with its richly carved and colored tombs and late-14th-century altarpieces. The elegant, classical exterior of the former palace can best be admired from place de la Libération and cour d'Honneur. *Pl. de la Ste-Chapelle, tel. 80–74–52–70. Admission: 12 frs adults, 5 frs stu-*

236

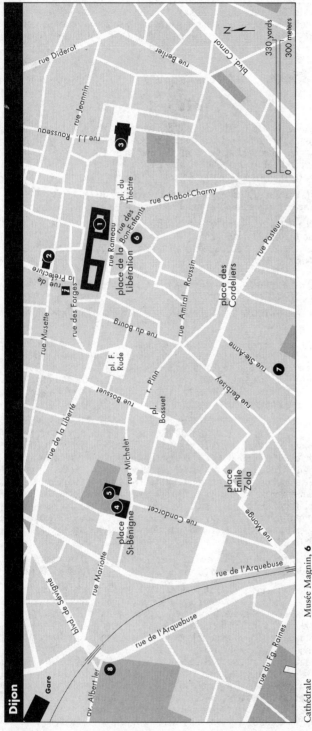

Dijon

rue Diderot

rue Berlier

blvd Carnot

N

330 yards

300 meters

rue Jeannin

rue J.J. Rousseau

pl. du Théâtre

rue des Bon-Enfants

rue Chabot-Charny

1

3

2

rue Rameau

rue de la Préfecture

rue de la Libération

place de la Libération

6

rue des Forges

rue Musette

rue du Bourg

rue Amiral Roussin

rue Pasteur

place des Cordeliers

pl. F. Rude

r. Piron

rue Berbisey

rue Ste-Anne

7

rue Bossuet

pl. Bossuet

rue de la Liberté

rue Michelet

place Émile Zola

rue Monge

rue Condorcet

blvd de Sévigné

rue Mariotte

place St-Bénigne

5

4

rue de l'Arquebuse

rue de l'Arquebuse

av. Albert ler

rue du Fg. Raines

Gare

8

Cathédrale
Ste-Bénigne, **4**
Musée
Archéologique, **5**
Musée d'Art Sacré, **7**
Musée d'Histoire
Naturelle/Jardin
Botanique, **8**

Musée Magnin, **6**
Notre-Dame, **2**
Palais des Ducs, **1**
St-Michel, **3**

dents; ticket valid for all town museums. Open Wed.–Mon. 10–6 (contemporary section closed noon–2:30).

Further links with Dijon's medieval past are found west of the town center, just off the avenue Albert Ier beyond the train station. Keep an eye out for the exuberant 15th-century gateway to the Chartreuse de Champmol—all that remains of a former charterhouse—and the adjoining **Puits de Moïse,** the so-called Well of Moses, with six large, compellingly realistic medieval statues on a hexagonal base (1395–1405).

② Among the city's outstanding old churches is **Notre-Dame** (rue de la Préfécture), with its elegant towers, delicate nave stonework, 13th-
③ century stained glass, and soaring chancel. The church of **St-Michel** (rue Rameau) takes us forward 300 years with its chunky Renais-
④ sance facade. **Cathédrale Ste-Bénigne** (off rue Mariotte) is comparatively austere; its chief glory is the 10th-century crypt—a forest of pillars surmounted by a rotunda.

Dijon is rich in museums, which all can be visited on a single 12-franc
⑤ ticket. The **Musée Archéologique,** housed in the former abbey buildings of Ste-Bénigne, traces the history of the region through archaeological discoveries. *5 rue du Docteur-Maret, tel. 80–30–88–54. Open Sept.–May, Wed.–Mon. 9–noon and 2–6; June–Aug., Wed.–Mon. 9:30–6.*

⑥ The **Musée Magnin** is a 17th-century mansion showcasing original furnishings and a variety of paintings from the 16th to the 19th centuries. *4 rue des Bons-Enfants, tel. 80–67–11–10. Open June–Sept., Tues.–Sun. 10–6; Oct.–May, Tues.–Sun. 10–noon and 2–6.*

⑦ The **Musée d'Art Sacré,** devoted to religious art, has a collection of sculpture and altarpieces in the appropriate setting of a former church. *17 rue Ste-Anne, tel. 80–30–65–91. Open Wed.–Mon. 9–noon and 2–6.*

⑧ The **Musée d'Histoire Naturelle** (tel. 80–76–82–76) and the **Jardin Botanique** (tel. 80–76–82–84), behind the train station, encompass a natural-history museum and impressive botanical gardens, with a wide variety of trees and tropical flowers. *1 av. Albert Ier. Museum open Wed.–Mon. 9–noon and 2–6; garden open daily 7:30–6 (8 PM in summer).*

Lodging and Dining
$$
Central Ibis. This central, long-established hotel has benefited from recent modernization: Its sound-proof, air-conditioned rooms offer a degree of comfort in excess of their price. The adjoining grill room, the Central Grill Rôtisserie, offers a good alternative to the gastronomic sophistication that is difficult to avoid elsewhere in Dijon; there's carpaccio and smoked salmon in addition to heavier *abats* (organ meats). *3 pl. Grangier, 21000, tel. 80–30–44–00, fax 80–30–77–12. 90 rooms, most with bath. Facilities: restaurant (closed Sun.). AE, DC, MC, V.*

Dining
$$
★
Dame Aquitaine. A happy marriage between two of France's greatest gastronomic regions—the chef comes from Aquitaine in the deep southwest, her husband from Burgundy—has produced a wonderful blend of regional cuisines in this atmospheric medieval crypt. The foie gras and duck, either in confit or with cèpes, come from her native Pau; the coq au vin, boeuf bourguignon, snails, and *lapin à la moutarde* (rabbit in a mustard sauce) from her husband's region. The moderate menus—especially the *menu terroir* (regional menu)—are good value. *23 pl. Boussuet, tel. 80–30–36–23. Reservations and jacket suggested. AE, DC, MC, V. Closed Mon. lunch, Sun.*

$$
★
Thibert. Chef Jean-Paul Thibert has no need to give his restaurant a fancy name. The art-deco setting is perhaps a trifle severe, but the cuisine is refined and imaginative. The menu changes regularly. Cabbage stuffed with snails and prawns with peas and truffles fig-

ure among the *tours de force;* sorbets encased in black-and-white mixed chocolate will tempt you to indulge in dessert. Thibert continues to represent remarkable value for the money—for the moment at least—though it's possible to run up quite a tab if you feel like a splurge. *10 pl. Wilson, tel. 80–67–74–64. Reservations required. Jacket and tie required. AE, MC, V. Closed Sun., Mon. lunch, early Jan. and Aug.*

$$ **Toison d'Or.** A collection of superbly restored 16th-century build-
★ ings belonging to the Burgundian Company of Winetasters forms the backdrop to this fine restaurant, which features a small wine museum in the cellar. Toison d'Or is lavishly furnished and quaint (candlelight de rigueur in the evening), and the food is increasingly sophisticated. Try the langoustines with ginger and the nougat and honey dessert. *18 rue Ste-Anne, tel. 80–30–73–52. Reservations accepted. Jacket required. AE, DC, MC, V. Closed Sun. evening.*

Beaune

Trains from Dijon south to Beaune leave every two hours and take 20 minutes. Tourist office: rue de l'Hôtel-Dieu, tel. 80–22–24–51.

Wine has been made in nearby **Nuits-St-Georges** since Roman times; its "dry, tonic, and generous qualities" were recommended to Louis XIV for medicinal use. It is appropriate, then, that some of the region's finest vineyards should be owned by the **Hospices de Beaune,** founded in 1443 as a hospital, which carried on its medical activities until 1971, its nurses still sporting their strange medieval uniforms.

★ A visit to the Hospices is one of the highlights of a stay in **Beaune,** one of the most charming and attractive French provincial towns despite the hordes of tourists. The hospital's medical history is retraced in a museum whose wide-ranging collections feature some of the weird and wonderful instruments used by doctors back in the 15th century. You can also see a collection of tapestries and Rogier Van der Weyden's medieval Flemish masterpiece, *The Last Judgment.* A suspended magnifying glass allows you to scan the extraordinary details of the work. (Another good series of tapestries, relating the life of the Virgin, can be admired in Beaune's main church, the 12th-century **Collégiale Notre-Dame,** just off avenue de la République.) Each year, as part of the Trois Glorieuses, an auction of wines is held at the Hospices on the third Sunday of November; it's attended by connoisseurs and dealers from around the world. *Rue de l'Hôtel-Dieu. Museum admission: 27 frs. Open Apr.–Nov., daily 9–6; Dec.–Mar., daily 9–11:30 and 2–5:30.*

There are few more delightful experiences than a visit to the
★ candlelit cellars of the **Marché aux Vins** (rue Nicolas Rolin). Here you can taste as many of the regional wines as you wish—beginning with whites and fruity Beaujolais and ending with such big reds as Gevrey-Chambertin—for the price of admission. *7 rue Nicolas Rolin, tel. 80–22–27–69. Admission and tasting: 40 frs. Open daily 9:30–11:30 and 2–6; closed mid-Dec.–Jan.*

Lodging **Hostellerie de Bretonnière.** This small, unpretentious hotel, a 10-
$$ minute walk from the center of town, has very comfortable rooms; some (at 340 frs) look out onto the garden, where breakfast is served in fine weather. There is no restaurant. *43 rue du faubourg Bretonnière, 21200, tel. 80–22–15–77, fax 80–22–72–54. 25 rooms. MC, V. Closed 1st 2 wks in Feb. and in Dec.*

$$ **Hôtel de la Cloche.** Though some of the rooms here are on the small side, all are neat and clean, all have private bath, and all are reasonably priced, ranging from about 290 frs to 360 frs (affordable lodging is increasingly hard to find in the center of town). The hotel's restaurant has good prices as well, and there are a couple of even less expensive places to eat nearby. The staff is helpful, and there's a parking lot across the street. *40–42 rue du faubourg Madeleine,*

21200, tel. 80–24–66–33, fax 80–24–04–24. 21 rooms, all with bath. Facilities: restaurant (closed Tues.). MC, V. Closed Dec. 20–Jan. 20.

Dining **Auberge des Vignes.** This friendly, traditional auberge, just 4 km (6
$$ mi) outside Beaune in the Volnay vineyards, offers excellent values for simple, dependable regional specialties and standards of cuisine bourgeois: richly sauced steaks, hearty stews, and very local wines. *On N 74, southwest of town. Tel. 80–22–24–48. Reservations advised. Closed Sun. dinner and Mon.*

$$ **L'Ecusson.** Don't be put off by its unprepossessing exterior. This is a comfortable, friendly, thick-carpeted restaurant whose four variously priced set menus offer outstanding value and a showcase to chef Jean-Pierre Senelet's sure-footed culinary mastery: duck sweetbreads with ham and spinach, rabbit terrine with tarragon, and leg of duck in oxtail sauce, to name just a few dishes. *Pl. Malmédy, tel. 80–24–03–82, fax 80–24–74–02. Reservations advised. AE, DC, MC, V. Closed Sun. (open for Sun. lunch Easter–mid-Nov.) and most of Feb.*

$ **Le Gourmandin.** This is just what the center of Beaune needed: a nononsense restaurant that serves regional fare—boeuf bourguignon, *quenelles de brochet* (light dumplings of pike), and *tourte de canard* (duck pie), for example—at reasonable prices. Prepared under the guidance of Jean Crotet, the food is excellent. The wine list, too, has a superb selection from small vineyards at affordable prices. Decor is simple, in the style of a 1930s café, and the small dining area is on two levels. *8 pl. Carnot, tel. 80–24–07–88. Closed Sun. dinner and Tues.*

$ **La Grilladine.** This small restaurant can be recommended on three
★ counts: The cooking, while not elaborate, produces good, hearty, Burgundian dishes (boeuf bourguignon; eggs poached in a red wine and bacon sauce); the prices are reasonable, with a three-course meal starting at 78 frs; and the ambience is warm, intimate, and cheerful. Of the two rooms here, the one on the right as you enter is the cozier, with exposed stone walls, an ancient beam supporting the ceiling, and tables set with rose-pink tablecloths. *17 rue Maufoux, tel. 80–22–22–36. Reservations advised. MC, V. Closed Mon.*

Chalon-sur-Saône

Trains south from Beaune take 20–25 minutes to Chalon-sur-Saône; note that there is none in the early afternoon. Tourist office: boulevard de la République, tel. 85–48–37–97.

Chalon-sur-Saône has its medieval heart near the **Eglise St-Vincent**—a former cathedral displaying a jumble of styles—close to the banks of the River Saône. This area has been reconstructed to have an Old World charm, but the rest of Chalon is modern and cosmopolitan, the cultural and commercial center of southern Burgundy. Chalon is the birthplace of Nicéphore Niepce (1765–1833), whose early experiments, developed further by Jacques Daguerre, qualify him as the father of photography. The **Musée Nicéphore Niepce**, a fine museum occupying an 18th-century house overlooking the Saône, retraces the early history of photography and motion pictures with the help of some pioneering equipment. It also includes a selection of contemporary photographic work and a lunar camera used during the U.S. Apollo program. But the star of the museum must be the primitive camera used to take the first photographs, in 1816. *Hôtel des Messageries, 20 quai des Messageries, tel. 85–48–41–98. Admission: 10 frs adults, 5 frs children; free Wed. Open Sept.–June, Wed.–Mon. 9:30–11:30 and 2:30–5:30, July–Aug. 10–6.*

Lodging and Dining **St-Georges.** Close to the train station and the town center, the
friendly, white-walled St-Georges hotel has been tastefully moder-
$$ nized and possesses many spacious rooms. Its cozy restaurant is
known locally for its efficient service and set menus of outstanding
value. You can't go wrong with the duck in white pepper, foie gras
with truffles, or roast pigeon. *32 av. Jean-Jaurès, 71100, tel. 85–48–
27–05, fax 85–93–23–88. 48 rooms, most with bath. Facilities: res-
taurant (closed Sat. lunch). AE, DC, MC, V.*

Cluny

*Six buses daily make the pretty, 90-minute run south to Cluny from
Chalon-sur-Saône. Cluny tourist office: 6 rue Mercière, tel. 85–59–
05–34.*

★ Though the old town of **Cluny** is charming in its own right, most visi-
tors come to admire the magnificent ruins of the Benedectine **Abbey
of Cluny.** Founded in the 10th century, it was the biggest church in
Europe until the 16th century, when Michelangelo built St. Peter's
in Rome. Cluny's medieval abbots were as powerful as popes. In
1098, Pope Urban II (himself a Cluniac) assured the head of his old
abbey that Cluny was the "light of the world." That assertion, of du-
bious religious validity, has not stood the test of time, and Cluny's
remains today stand as a reminder of the limits of human grandeur.

The ruins nonetheless suggest the size and glory of Cluny Abbey at
its zenith. Only the Clocher de l'Eau-Bénite (a majestic bell tower)
and the right arms of the two transepts, climbing 100 feet above
ground, remain. The 13th-century *farinier* (flour mill), with its fine
chestnut roof and collection of statues, can also be seen. The gardens
contain an ancient lime tree, several hundred years old, named Abé-
lard after the controversial philosopher who sought shelter at the
abbey in 1142. No one is sure the tree is quite that old, though! A
small museum, with separate entry price, displays religious paint-
ings, sculptures from demolished portions of the abbey, and the re-
mains of the *bibliothèque des moines*, or monks' library. *Admission:
29 frs adults, 15 frs senior citizens, 9 frs children 7–17. Museum
only: 13 frs. Open daily Nov.–Mar. 10:30–11:30 and 2–4; Apr.–
June 9:30–noon and 2–6; July–Sept. 9–7; Oct. 10–noon and 2–5.
Museum closed Tues.*

Lodging and Dining **Hôtel de l'Abbaye.** The parents of the owner-chef, M. Lassagne, used
$ to have a small hotel next to the abbey, but the Germans blew it up
during World War II. They then opened this modest, simple hotel on
the outskirts of the village (a 5-minute walk from the center) and
kept the name of the original establishment. The three rooms to the
right of the dining room have been more recently decorated than the
others, and at 250 frs are an especially good value. The restaurant
offers regional cooking that's less elaborate than at the Bourgogne,
but better (according to the chef, who did his training there). Prices
are reasonable, too, with a three-course menu starting at 98 frs. *Av.
Charles-de-Gaulle, 71250, tel. 85–59–11–14, fax 85–59–09–76. 16
rooms, 9 with bath. Facilities: restaurant (closed Mon., Tues.
lunch). MC, V. Hotel and restaurant closed Jan.–mid-Feb.*

Dining **Potin Gourmand.** Original dishes prepared with super-fresh, sea-
$–$$ sonal ingredients make this simple spot a favorite with townspeople
as well as visitors. The reasonable prices make it even more appeal-
ing. *Pl. Champ de Foire, tel. 85–59–02–06, fax 85–59–22–58. AE,
MC, V. Closed early Jan.–early Feb. and Mon.*

Reality check. Call home.

—— *AT&T USADirect® and World Connect®. The fast, easy way to call most anywhere.* ——

Take out AT&T Calling Card or your local calling card.** Lift phone. Dial AT&T Access Number for country you're calling from. Connect to English-speaking operator or voice prompt. Reach the States or over 200 countries. Talk. Say goodbye. Hang up. Resume vacation.

Austria*†††..............**022-903-011**	Luxembourg............................0-800-0111	**Turkey***.........................**00-800-12277**
Belgium*.........................**0-800-100-10**	**Netherlands***...................**06-022-9111**	**United Kingdom**................**0500-89-0011**
Czech Republic*..............**00-420-00101**	**Norway**..............................**800-190-11**	
Denmark **8001-0010**	**Poland**†◆¹..................0◊**010-480-0111**	
Finland **9800-100-10**	**Portugal**†.......................**05017-1-288**	
France..................................**19-0011**	**Romania***.......................**01-800-4288**	
Germany.............................**0130-0010**	**Russia***†(Moscow)................**155-5042**	
Greece*............................**00-800-1311**	**Slovak Rep.***..................**00-420-00101**	
Hungary*.......................**00◊-800-01111**	**Spain**●............................**900-99-00-11**	
Ireland **1-800-550-000**	**Sweden** **020-795-611**	
Italy*....................................**172-1011**	**Switzerland***.......................**155-00-11**	

AT&T
Your True Choice

For a free wallet sized card of all AT&T Access Numbers, call: 1-800-241-5555.

What to do when your *money* is done traveling before you are.

Don't worry. With **MoneyGram**,^{SM} your parents can send you money in usually 10 minutes or less to more than 19,000 locations in 80 countries. So if the money you need to see history becomes history, call us and we'll direct you to a **MoneyGram**^{SM} agent closest to you.

USA: **1-800-MONEYGRAM**   Canada: **1-800-933-3278**   France: **05-905311**
Germany: **0130-8-16629**   England: **0800-89-7198**   Spain: **900-96-1218**

or call collect **303-980-3340**

10 Lyon and the Alps

Including the Rhône and Grenoble

In the heavily industrialized countries of northern Europe, big cities mean grimy factories, snarling traffic, and blocks of post-war concrete. Most French cities are different, and none more so than Lyon, where the silk weavers who made the city's fame beavered away in house attics before scuttling along narrow passages to transport their precious cloth. Much of central Lyon remains curiously intimate, especially the medieval streets around the cathedral. Museums, restaurants, Roman remains, lively pedestrian shopping streets, and not one, but two rivers—the Saône and the Rhône—complete the scene.

The TGV bullet train has put Lyon within just two hours of Paris and made it the obvious gateway to the French Alps. The boom in winter sports has hurtled the once-backward Alpine region into the 20th century, and rail and bus lines were further extended for the 1992 Winter Olympics in Albertville. Nonetheless, reaching many high-up villages remains an arduous proposition, but in both winter and summer, these journeys are definitely worthwhile. Though expensive for skiing, compared to the Pyrenees or the Vosges, the Alps usually offer better snow. In summer, they're unparalleled for hiking.

The character of the countryside away from Lyon and the mountains is determined by the Saône and Rhône rivers. Before reaching Lyon, the Saône flows between the lush hillside of the Beaujolais vineyards and the flat marshland of the Dombes. The Rhône, the great river of southern France, actually trickles to life high up in the Swiss mountains, then comes to life at Lyon, where it merges with the Saône and plummets due south in search of the Mediterranean. Its progress south from Lyon is often spectacular, as steep-climbing vineyards conjure up vistas that are more readily associated with the river's Germanic cousin, the Rhine.

Lyon and the Alps Basics

Budget Lodging The entire region is filled with hotels and country inns; at many, you'll be expected to take your evening meal there (especially in summer), but this tends to be more a pleasure than an obligation. The Alps' extensive hotel infrastructure is geared primarily to winter visitors, who are invariably expected to take *demi-pension* or *pension complète* (with two or three meals a day in the hotel).

Budget Dining Lyon is a renowned capital of good cuisine. Both gourmets and gourmands will enjoy the robust local specialties, such as *saveloy* (sausage) and *quenelles* (fish dumplings). The *marrons glacés* (chestnuts poached in syrup and glazed) of Privas and the nougats of Montélimar delight a sweet tooth. The rivers and lakes of the Alps teem with pike and trout, and the hills are a riot of wild raspberries and black currants during summer months. *Raclette* is a warming Alpine winter specialty: melted cheese served with boiled potatoes, inch-long sour pickles called *cornichons*, and salami or ham. Mountain herbs form the basis of traditional drinks—try a tangy, dark **Suédois** or a bittersweet **Suze** (made from gentian), and round off your meal with a green **Chartreuse.**

Hiking Spectacular scenery and an invigorating mountain climate make the Alps a perfect base for a summer hiking holiday—and chair lifts can frequently help you negotiate the more daunting slopes. The Beaujolais hills north of Lyon are a gentler proposition.

Skiing In this region, whose ski season begins in December and lasts through April, the most famous ski resort is **Chamonix** (6,063 feet), beloved of experts. **Val d'Isère** (6,068 feet) ranks as one of Europe's swankiest resorts, with lots of cross-country runs as well as downhill slopes. Nearby **Tignes,** the highest of the Savoie resorts (6,930 feet), offers slopes to suit skiers of all abilities. Family groups favor **Morzine** (3,280 feet), a popular small resort with gentle slopes geared to the inexperienced. Chic, expensive **Megève** (3,650 feet) offers a lively nightlife and a particularly impressive network of *téléfériques* (cable cars) and helicopter services. **Courchevel** (6,068 feet) is renowned for its après-ski, while across the mountain, fashionable **Méribel** (5,428 feet) boasts lots of difficult runs.

Arts and Nightlife Lyon is the region's liveliest arts center, with dozens of discos, piano bars, and nightclubs, and a full calender of concerts, theater, and arts events.

Festivals September in Lyon sees the internationally renowned **Biennale de la Danse** (even years). October brings the **Festival Bach** (tel. 78–72–75–31) and the Contemporary Art Festival, **Octobre des Arts** (odd years; tel. 78–30–50–66). Jazz enthusiasts will want to catch Grenoble's popular **Cinq Jours de Jazz** (Five Days of Jazz) in February or March.

Tour 1: Lyon and the Northern Rhône

There is enough to see and visit in Lyon to warrant a stay of several days. Frequent trains whistle down the Rhône Valley to the towns of Vienne, Tournon, and Valence, which make for pleasant day trips.

From Paris By Train TGVs to Lyon leave Paris (Gare de Lyon) every hour. The trip takes 2–2¼ hours.

By Car Allow 4½ hours for the 465-kilometer (290-mile) drive to Lyon southeast from Paris along the A6 expressway.

Lyon

Tourist offices: in a freestanding building in place Bellecour, tel. 78–42–25–75; and in the Perrache train station. The easiest way to get around Lyon is by métro, which runs from 5 AM to midnight: a daily ticket costs 20 frs and a set of 10 tickets costs 65 frs. There are no ticket booths, so make sure to have plenty of change to buy your tickets from the automatic vending machines on station platforms.

Numbers in the margin correspond with points of interest on the Lyon map.

★ **Lyon** and Marseille both like to claim they are France's "second city." In terms of size and commercial importance, Marseille probably grabs that title. But when it comes to tourist appeal, Lyon's a clear winner. It's first of all a human-size town. You can encompass it in a glance from high on the bank of the Saône, and you can walk all its pedestrian streets and see all its sights in a few days. But it would take a lifetime to discover all of its food.

Lyon's development owes much to its position halfway between Paris and the Mediterranean and within striking distance of Switzerland, Italy, and the Alps. The city's exceptional site is physically impressive, with steep cliffs dominating the River Saône, which parallels the Rhône before the two converge south of the city center.

Because Lyon has never really had to endure hard times, a mood of untroubled content prevails. The Lyonnais bask in the knowledge that their city has been important for more than 2,000 years: The Romans made it the capital of Gaul around 43 BC. Its name derives from the Roman Lugdunum, or "Hill of the Crow."

❶ Few, if any, crows, rooks, or ravens are found these days on **place Bellecour**, midway between the Saône and the Rhône. (To get here from La Part Dieu or Perrache stations, take the métro to Bellecour.) This imposing, tree-shaded square, the largest in the city and one of the largest in France, derives its architectural distinction from the classical facades erected along its narrower sides in 1800. The large bronze statue of Louis XIV on horseback is the work of local sculptor Jean Lemot, installed in 1828.

Stop in at the tourist office in place Bellecour for a city map and information leaflets. (A 30-franc day pass for admission to all municipal museums, once available here, can now be bought at the museums themselves.) Then cross the square and head 500 yards north along lively rue du Président-Herriot before turning left onto rue Grenette. Take the Pont du Maréchal-Juin over the Saône to the old town at the foot of Fourvière Hill, crowned by the imposing silhouette of **Notre-Dame** basilica.

❷ On the right bank of the Saône lies **Vieux Lyon** (Old Lyon), an atmospheric warren of streets and alleys. Turn right after the bridge, then take the first left down a little alley to **place de la Baleine,** a small square lined with 17th-century houses. At the far end of place de la Baleine lies **rue St-Jean,** one of the many streets that weave their way around the banks of the Saône. Many of the area's elegant houses were built for the town's most illustrious denizens—bankers and silk merchants—during the French Renaissance under the 16th-century king François I. Originally, they had four stories; the upper floors were added in the last century. Look for the intricate old iron signs hanging over the shop doorways—many gave the streets their names.

A peculiarity of the streets of old Lyon are the *traboules*, quaint little passageways that cut under the houses from one street to another. Don't hesitate to venture in; they aren't private. There's a fine example at 24 rue St-Jean, just off place de la Baleine (to the left), which leads through to rue du Boeuf via an airy, restored courtyard.

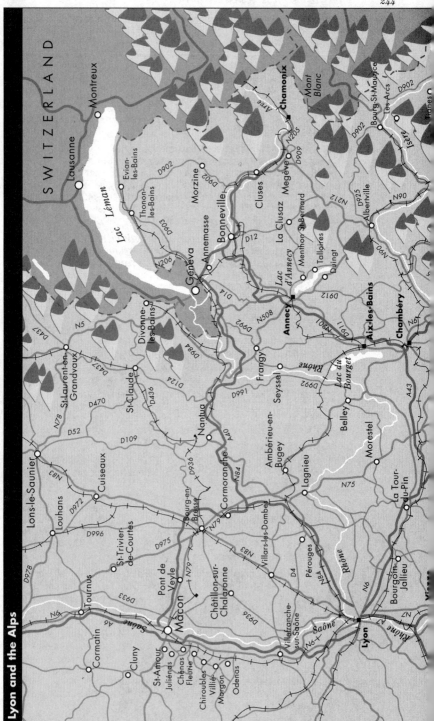

Lyon and the Alps

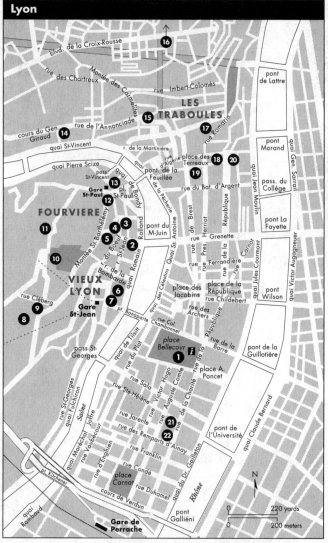

Rue St-Jean was old Lyon's major thoroughfare. Stop in the elegant courtyard of No. 27 on your way north from place de la Baleine to place du Change, where money changers would operate during Lyon's medieval trade fairs. The **Loge du Change** church, on one side of the square, was built by Germain Soufflot (best known as architect of the Panthéon in Paris) in 1747.

Take rue Soufflot to one side of the church and turn left onto rue de Gadagne, where the largest Renaissance ensemble in Lyon is located: the Hôtel de Gadagne, built between the 14th and the 16th centuries and now home to the **Musée Historique de Lyon.** The first floor of this history museum contains medieval sculpture from long-gone local churches and abbeys, while other floors showcase local furniture, pottery, paintings, engravings, and antique playing cards. On the second floor is the **Musée de la Marionnette,** which traces the history of marionnettes from Guignol and Madelon (Lyon's local equivalent of Punch and Judy, created by Laurent Mourguet in 1795) through to contemporary hand and string puppets from across the globe. *1 pl. du Petit-Collège, tel. 78–42–03–61. Admission: 20 frs. Open Wed.–Mon. 10:45–6 (Fri. to 8).*

Continue through tiny place du Petit-Collège to rue du Boeuf. One of old Lyon's finest mansions lies farther down rue du Boeuf, at No. 16: ❺ the 17th-century **Maison du Crible** (now a pricey restaurant called La Tour Rose). Venture into its courtyard to glimpse the original Tour Rose—an elegant, pink-washed tower—and the charming terraced garden. Close by, in a niche high up at the corner of place Neuve St-Jean, is one of the most famous sculptures in old Lyon, the work of Giambologna (1529–1608), a renowned French sculptor who honed his skills in Renaissance Italy; the white marble sculpture portrays the bull for which rue du Boeuf is named. Head down place Neuve and turn right onto rue St-Jean. A hundred yards farther, turn right onto rue de la Bombarde, which leads to the peaceful ❻ **Jardin Archéologique,** with its excavated remains of the four churches that succeeded one another on the spot.

Alongside is one church that has withstood the onslaught of time: ❼ the **Primatiale St-Jean,** Lyon's somewhat disappointing cathedral. You won't find any soaring roof or lofty spires here. Instead, a stumpy facade is stuck almost bashfully onto the nave, and while the interior mishmash has its moments—the 13th-century stained-glass windows in the choir or the variety of window tracery and vaulting in the side chapels—it lacks drama and a sense of harmony. The cathedral dates from the 12th century, and the chancel is Romanesque, but construction continued over three centuries and most of the building is Gothic (note the high pointed windows). Pope John XXII was consecrated here in 1316, and Henri IV married Marie de Médicis here in 1600. The 14th-century astronomical clock, in the north transept, chimes a hymn to St-Jean on the hour from noon to 3 PM as a screeching rooster and other automatons enact the Annunciation.

To the right of the cathedral facade—at its best at night when subtle lighting accents the relief of the stonework—stands the venerable 12th-century **Manécanterie** (choir school); upstairs you'll find a small Treasury museum housing medieval Limoges enamels, fine ivories, and embroidered robes. *70 rue St-Jean, tel. 78–92–82–29. Admission: 18 frs adults, 10 frs students and senior citizens. Open weekdays 10–noon and 2–6:30; weekends 9–5.*

To continue your tour, take the *ficelle* (funicular) at the left of the cathedral up to the top of Fourvière Hill. Head along the Montée de ❽ Fourvière to the ruins of the **Théâtres Romains** nearby. There are two semicircular theaters here: the **Grand Théâtre,** the oldest Roman theater in France, built in 15 BC to seat 10,000 spectators, and the smaller **Odéon,** with its geometric-patterned tiled flooring. The best time to appreciate the theaters is September, when they are used to stage events during the Lyon International Arts Festival. *Fourvière Hill. Admission free. Open daily 9–dusk.*

Since 1933, systematic excavations have unearthed many vestiges of the opulent Roman city of Lugdunum. These remains can be viewed ❾ in the **Musée de la Civilisation Gallo-Romaine,** which overlooks the theaters. The museum's semisubterranean open-plan design is an unusual showcase for the collection of statues, mosaics, vases, coins, and tombstones. One of the museum's highlights is a large bronze plaque, the **Table Claudienne,** upon which is inscribed part of Emperor Claudius's speech to the Roman Senate in AD 48, conferring senatorial rights on the Roman citizens of Gaul. *17 rue Clébert, tel. 78–25–94–68. Admission: 20 frs adults, 10 frs students. Open Wed.–Sun. 9:30–noon and 2–6.*

Head back to the spot where the ficelle dropped you off. You won't be ❿ able to miss the pompous, late-19th-century basilica of **Notre-Dame-de-Fourvière,** which has unfortunately become one of the symbols of Lyon. In terms of its mock-Byzantine architecture and hilltop site, it's a close cousin of Paris's Sacré-Coeur. Both were built for a similar reason: to underline the might of the Roman Catholic Church when the Prussian defeat of France in 1870 gave rise to the birth of the anticlerical Third Republic. The riot of interior decoration—an overkill of gilt, marble, and colorful mosaics—reveals that the Church had mind-boggling wealth to compensate for its waning political clout. *pl. de Fourvière. Open daily 8–noon and 2–6.*

One of the few places in Lyon from which you can't see the Fourvière basilica is the terrace alongside it. The plummeting panorama reveals the city laid out on either side of the Saône and Rhône rivers, with the St-Jean cathedral facade in the foreground and the huge glass towers of the reconstructed Part-Dieu business complex glistening behind. For an even more sweeping view—encompassing the surrounding hills—climb the 287 steps of the basilica's **observatory.** *Admission: 6 frs. Open Easter–Oct., daily 10–noon and 2–6; Nov.–Easter, weekends 10–noon and 2–5.*

⑪ Looming beyond the basilica is a skeletal metal tower, **Tour Métallique,** built in 1893 and now used as a television transmitter. Take the stone staircase, **Montée Nicolas-de-Lange,** at the foot of the tower; this sneaks back down to old Lyon, emerging alongside the St-Paul train station at place St-Paul. Turn right onto rue Juiverie, resplendent with new wrought-iron signs displaying colorful medie-
⑫ val coats-of-arms; the **Hôtel Paterin** at No. 4 is a splendid Renaissance mansion, and the Hôtel Bullioud (No. 8) has a courtyard with an ingenious gallery constructed in 1536 by Philibert Delorme, one of France's earliest and most accomplished exponents of Classical architecture (he worked at the châteaus of Fontainebleau and Chenonceau in the Loire Valley). Alongside at No. 2 is the **Palais de la Miniature,** a folksy two-story museum with an extensive array of scale models, dollhouses, and miniature figures, including a minute Garden of Eden made up of tiny origami animals. Children will be enthralled. *Admission: 22 frs adults, 6 frs children. Open Tues.–Sun. 10–noon and 2–7.*

⑬ North of place St-Paul is the 12th-century church of **St-Paul;** the octagonal lantern, the frieze of animal heads in the chancel, and the Flamboyant Gothic chapel are all worth a look. Head around the church, take the St-Vincent footbridge over the Saône, and turn left along quai St-Vincent. Two hundred yards along, to the right, is the
⑭ **Jardin des Chartreux,** a small, leafy park. Cut through the park up to cours du Général Giraud, then turn right onto place Rouville, pausing to admire the splendid view of the river and Fourvière Hill.

⑮ Rue de l'Annonciade leads from place Rouville to the **Jardin des Plantes,** 250 yards away, a haven of peace in this otherwise busy quarter. These luxurious botanical gardens contain remnants of the **Amphithéâtre des Trois Gauls,** a once-huge circular amphitheater built in AD 19. From the gardens, you'll be able to survey the hilly, surrounding **Croix Rousse** district, which once resounded to the clanking of weaving looms that churned out yards of the silk and cloth for which Lyon became famous. By the 19th century, more than 30,000 *canuts* (weavers) were working in Lyon; they set up their looms on the upper floors—the brightest—of the tightly packed houses. The houses were so tightly packed, in fact, that the only way to transport the finished fabrics was through the *traboules* (long narrow corridors leading through buildings and providing public access to other streets), which had the additional advantage of protecting the fabrics from bad weather.

Armed with a detailed map, you could spend hours "trabouling" your way across the Croix Rousse, still a hive of activity despite the industrialization of silk and textile production and the ensuing demise of most of the original workshops. Old-time "Jacquard" looms

🔟 can still be seen in action at the **Maison des Canuts;** the weavers—many surprisingly young—are happy to show children how to operate a miniature loom. (Take the métro from Hôtel de Ville to Croix-Rousse, head up Grande-Rue Croix-Rousse, and turn right into rue d'Ivry.) *12 rue d'Ivry, tel. 78–28–62–04. Admission: 10 frs adults, 5 frs students and senior citizens. Open weekdays 8:30–noon and 2–6:30, Sat. 9–noon and 2–6.*

For an impromptu tour of the Croix Rousse, leave the gardens and head along rue Imbert-Colomès as far as No. 20. Here, turn right through the *traboule* that leads to rue des Tables-Claudiennes, then veer right across place Chardonnet. Take the Mermet stairway
🔟 down past **St-Polycarpe** church, then turn left into rue Leynaud. A *traboule* at No. 32 leads to Montée St-Sébastien. Keep right, cross place Croix-Paquet, and take rue Romarin down to place des Terreaux. The north side of the sizable place des Terreaux is lined
🔟 with cafés, from which you can survey the facade of the **Hôtel de Ville,** redesigned by architects Jules Hardouin-Mansart and Robert de Cotte after a serious fire in 1674 (the rest of the building dates to the early 17th century). In the middle of the square, four majestic horses rear up from a monumental 19th-century fountain by Frédéric Auguste Bartholdi, whose most famous creation is New York's Statue of Liberty. On the south side of the square is the elegant 17th-century front of the former Benedictine abbey **Palais St-Pierre,** now the city's art museum.

★ 🔟 The **Musée des Beaux-Arts** showcases the country's largest collection of art after the Louvre. The cloister gardens are studded with a number of worthy statues, including three works by Rodin: *The Walker, The Shadow,* and *The Bronze Age.* Inside, the wide-ranging collections include enamels, Byzantine ivories, Etruscan statuettes, 4,000-year-old Cypriot ceramics, and a plethora of Egyptian archaeological finds. Amid the usual wealth of Old Master, Impressionist, and modern paintings is a unique collection of works by the tight-knit Lyon School, whose twin characteristics are exquisitely painted flowers and an overbearing religious sentimentality. Note Louis Janmot's *The Poem of the Soul,* a series of immaculately painted visions that seesaw among the heavenly, the hellish, and the downright spooky. *Pl. des Terreaux, tel. 78–28–07–66. Admission: 20 frs adults, 10 frs students. Open Wed.–Sun. 10:30–6.*

Leave the museum and walk west across place des Terreaux and through the ground floor of the Hôtel de Ville (go around if it's
🔟 closed) to the **Opéra de Lyon.** This wonderful, barrel-vaulted reincarnation of a moribund building from 1831 was built in the early 1990s at a cost of 478 million frs. The columned exterior and neoclassic public spaces blend beautifully with the latest in backstage high-tech magic and the soaring double glass vaulting. And above it all, looking out between heroic-size statues of the muses lined up along the parapet, sits Philippe Chavent's small restaurant, Les Muses (*see* Dining, *below*). *Pl. de la Comédie, tel. 72–00–45–00 (information) or 72–00–45–45 (reservations), fax 72–00–45–01.*

If you're in the mood for browsing, head south by way of shop-lined rue de la République, which becomes rue de la Charité after skirting place Bellecour. Some 300 yards down are two major museums. Alternatively, you can take the métro from Hôtel de Ville, alight at Ampère, and take rue des Remparts to the museums.

★ 🔟 The **Musée des Arts Décoratifs** occupies an 18th-century mansion, with fine displays of silverware, furniture, objets d'art, ceramics, and tapestries. Take time to admire the outstanding array of Italian Renaissance porcelain. *34 rue de la Charité. Admission: 25 frs (joint ticket with Fabrics Museum). Open Tues.–Sun. 10–noon and 2–5:30.*

❷ The **Musée Historique des Tissus** (Fabrics Museum) contains a stream of intricate carpets, tapestries, and silks. You'll see Oriental tapestries dating as far back as the 4th century and a fabulous assembly of Turkish and Persian carpets from the 16th to the 18th centuries. European highlights include Italian Renaissance fabrics, Hispano-Moorish cloth from Spain, and 18th-century Lyon silks. *20 rue de la Charité. Admission: 25 frs (joint ticket with Arts Musuem). Open Tues.–Sun. 10–noon and 2–5:30.*

Lodging **Bellecordière.** This clean and pleasant no-frills hotel is right in the
$ heart of the city. Rooms are small, with simple, modern furniture
★ and gray, industrial carpeting, but all have televisions, direct-dial telephones, and modern bathrooms. The management is friendly and serves a good and copious breakfast, and the neighborhood is quiet. *18 rue Bellecordière, 69001, tel. 78–42–27–28. 25 rooms with bath. AE, MC, V.*

$ **Bristol.** This large, well-kept hotel, midway between the city-center and Perrache station, has been modernized and soundproofed. It counts as one of the best-priced and most convenient bases for exploring Lyon. *28 cours de Verdun, 69002, tel. 78–37–56–55. 134 rooms, most with bath or shower. Facilities: sauna, gym. Closed Christmas through New Year's. AE, DC, MC, V.*

$ **Morand.** This quiet and delightfully idiosyncratic hotel is in a residential area of the city, a 10-minute taxi ride from the station. Flowers abound in the pretty inner courtyard that doubles as a breakfast veranda, and the smiles at the front desk foster a mood of good cheer and friendliness. Guest rooms are on the small side but feature lots of homey knickknacks. There's no restaurant. *99 rue de Créqui, 69006, tel. 78–52–29–96. 33 rooms, 27 with bath. AE.*

Dining **Le Bar du Passage.** Despite a wonderful burl veneer Art Deco bar,
$$ where you can savor a preprandial cocktail atop a brass stool by Philippe Starck, the enfant terrible of modern French design, this is not just a bar but a stylish eatery adjoining the top-ranking **Passage** restaurant. Both belong to chef Daniel Ancel, but here you can sample his creations for half the price you'd pay next door: Try the duck and gizzard salad, guinea-fowl with cabbage, or warm *tricolor terrine* (carrots, broccoli, and celery) washed down with a *pot* (the local word for a carafe or small bottle) of Côtes du Rhône. The scarlet wallpaper, imitating stage curtains, and sturdy velvet-lined seats revived from a defunct local cinema create a cheerful, whimsical mood at odds with the gloomy passageway that provides access from rue du Plâtre near place des Terreaux. *8 rue du Plâtre, tel. 78–28–12–61. AE, DC, MC, V. Closed Sat. lunch and Sun.*

$$ **Les Muses.** High up under the glass vault of the Opéra de Lyon is a small restaurant run by Philippe Chavent. The restaurant's glass front looks out between the buxom statues of the muses to the splendid Hôtel de Ville across the street; but if you can drag your attention back to your plate and Chavent's classic-inspired nouvelle cuisine, you'll be hard put to choose between the salmon in butter sauce with a watercress mousse and the 59-franc *plat du jour*—perhaps chicken in tarragon cream with sautéed zucchini. *Opéra de Lyon, tel. 72–00–45–58. Reservations advised. AE, MC, V.*

$$ **Le Vivarais.** This simple, tidy restaurant, run by Roger Duffaud, a
★ pupil and former colleague of the superstar chef Alain Chapel, is one of the city's outstanding gourmet good buys. Don't expect napkins folded into flower shapes here—all the excitement happens on your plate. The menu offers a perfect contemporary take on the lyonnaise classics. Try the *lièvre royale* (hare cooked with onions, red wine, and cinnamon and then rolled and stuffed with truffles and pâté), the superb cheese tray, and the daily dessert, maybe a pear tart. *1 pl. du Dr-Gailleton, tel. 78–37–85–15. Reservations advised. MC, V. Closed Sun.*

$ **Brasserie Georges.** One of the city's oldest and largest brasseries,
★ this inexpensive spot boasts high-backed red benches and thirties

decor. At any hour of the day or evening, you can relax over hearty dishes such as veal stew or sauerkraut, or go for more refined fare. The 85-franc local "Gone" menu includes lentil salad, beef *joue* (cheek), and a cream-cheese and olive oil delicacy known as a *cervelle des canuts*. Wash it all down with a fruity Coteaux du Lyonnais, and enjoy musical accompaniment from an old-time hurdy-gurdy. *30 cours de Verdun, tel. 78–37–15–78. AE, DC, MC, V.*

$ **Café des Fédérations.** For more than 80 years, this sawdust-strewn café has reigned as one of the city's friendliest eating spots, and even newcomers are treated as one of the gang. Jocular Raymond Fulchiron not only serves up deftly prepared lyonnais classics such as hearty *boudin blanc* (white-meat sausage), but he also comes out to chat and make sure everyone feels at home. The decor is a homey mix of red-checked tablecloths, wood paneling, and old-fashioned bench seating. *8 rue du Major-Martin, tel. 78–28–26–00. Reservations advised. AE, DC, MC, V. Closed weekends and Aug.*

$ **Chez Sylvain.** The old-fashioned decor of Chez Sylvain is a delightful reminder of its days as a favorite neighborhood beanery. Little has changed since, and the huge wooden counter, turn-of-the-century wall decorations, and original spiral staircase are the ideal backdrop for Sylvain's robust lyonnaise cuisine; the tripe and andouillettes are especially good. *4 rue Tupin, tel. 78–42–11–98. Reservations accepted. V. Closed Sun., Mon., and Aug.*

Splurge **Paul Bocuse.** One of the country's most celebrated gourmet temples,
★ this restaurant is no budget standby, and it's easy to get to only with a car, as it is 12 km (7 mi) north of town in Collonges-au-Mont-d'Or. But if you want to splurge, this is the place. The grandiose decor is perfectly matched by the excellence of the cuisine from the kitchen of the larger-than-life chef Paul Bocuse. Bocuse is often away on the lecture-tour trail, but his restaurant continues to please its elegantly dressed diners, who feast on such house specialties as truffle soup and succulent sea bass. *50 quai de la Plage, 69660 Collonges-au-Mont-d'Or, tel. 72–27–85–85, fax 72–27–85–87. Reservations required. Jacket and tie required. AE, DC, MC, V.*

Shopping **Lyon** makes for the region's best shopping for chic clothing; try the stores on **rue du Président Edouard-Herriot** and **rue de la République** in the center of town. Lyon has maintained its reputation as the French silks-and-textile capital, and all the big-name French and international designers have shops here; Lyonnais designer **Clémentine** (18 rue Emile-Zola) is a good bet for well-cut clothes, or, for trendy outfits for youngsters, try **Etincelle** (34 rue St-Jean) in the old town. If it's antiques you're after, wander down **rue Auguste-Comte** (from place Bellecour to Perrache); you'll find superb engravings at **Image en Cours** (26 rue du Boeuf) and authentic Lyonnais puppets on **place du Change,** both in the old town. Two excellent Lyon charcuteries are **Reynon** (13 rue des Archers) and **Vital Pignol** (17 rue Emile-Zola). For chocolates, try **Bernachon** (42 cours Franklin-Roosevelt), which many people consider to be the best chocolaterie in France.

The Arts *Lyon-Poche,* a weekly guide published on Wednesday and sold at any newsstand, will give details. The café-theater, a Lyonnais specialty, fuses art with café society: **Espace Gerson** (1 pl. Gerson, tel. 78–27–96–99) or **Café-Théâtre de l'Accessoire** (26 rue de L'Annonciande, tel. 78–27–84–84). Lyon's Société de Musique de Chambre performs at **Salle Molière** (18 quai Bondy, tel. 78–28–03–11).

Nightlife As for nightlife, laser beams and video screens make **L'Aquarius** (47 quai Pierre-Scize) a frenetic place for dancing the night away in Lyon. **Comoëdia** (30 rue Neuve) is more low-key, with a downstairs disco and an old-fashioned piano bar upstairs. Expect anything from the tango to rock-and-roll at **Palace Mobile** (2 rue René-Leynaud). The **Hot Club** (26 rue Lanterne) has been going strong for more than

40 years in a vaulted stone basement that features live jazz. **Le Melhor** (20 quai Dr-Gailleton) is a more restrained cocktail bar catering to the city's intellectual set. If you'd like a casual game of darts and a pint of bitter, head to the **Albion Public House** (12 rue Ste-Catherine). The **Bouchon à Vins** wine bar (62 rue Mercière) has more than 30 vintages for you to choose from; for a more romantic evening, make it a champagne toast in the intimate, wood-paneled **Metroclub** (2 rue Stella). For a sampling of local slapstick *café-théâtre*—jolly, though hard to follow for non-French speakers—head up to the **Nombril du Monde** above place des Terreaux (1 pl. Chardonnet).

Vienne

Trains make the ½-hour journey from Lyon south to Vienne every hour or so. Tourist office: cours Briller, tel. 74–85–12–62.

★ **Vienne** was one of the most important towns of Roman Gaul and a religious and cultural center under its count-archbishops in the Middle Ages, and despite its role today as a major road and train junction, it retains abundant historic charm.

The tourist office stands at the river end of cours Brillier in the leafy shadow of the **Jardin Public** (the train station is at the opposite end of cours Brillier). Begin your tour here, turning right along quai Jean-Jaurès, beside the Rhône, to the nearby church of **St-Pierre.** Note the rectangular 12th-century Romanesque bell tower with its arcaded tiers. The lower parts of the church walls date from the 6th century.

Head down the left-hand side of the church and turn left again onto rue Boson, which leads to the cathedral of **St-Maurice.** Although the religious wars deprived this cathedral of many statues, much of the original decoration is intact; the arches of the portals on the 15th-century facade are carved with Old Testament scenes. The cathedral was built between the 12th and 16th centuries, with later interior additions, such as the splendid 18th-century mausoleum to the right of the altar, which contains the tombs of two of Vienne's archbishops. The entrance to the vaulted passage that once led to the cloisters, but now opens onto place St-Paul, is adorned with a frieze of the zodiac.

Place St-Paul and rue Clémentine bring you to place du Palais and the remains of the **Temple d'Auguste et de Livie,** thought to date, in part, to the earliest Roman settlements in Vienne (1st century BC). The slender Corinthian columns that ring the temple were filled in with a wall during the 11th century, when the temple was used as a church; today, however, the temple has been restored to its original appearance.

Take rue Brenier to rue Chantelouve, site of a **Roman gateway** decorated with delicate friezes (the last vestige of the city's sizable Roman baths), then continue to rue de la Charité and the **Théâtre Romain.** This was one of the largest Roman theaters in Gaul (143 yards in diameter) and is only slightly smaller than Rome's famed Theater of Marcellus. Vienne's theater was buried under tons of rubble until 1922, but since then, the 46 rows of seating and parts of the marble flooring and frieze on the original stage have been excavated and renovated. Shows and concerts are staged here on summer evenings. *7 rue du Cirque, tel. 74–85–39–23. Admission: 9 frs. Open Apr.–mid-Oct., Wed.–Mon. 9:30–1 and 2–6; mid-Oct.–Mar., Wed.–Sat. 10–noon and 2–5, Sun. 1:30–5:30.*

Take rue de la Charité back down to rue des Orfèvres, lined with Renaissance facades, and continue on to the church of **St-André-le-Bas,** once part of a powerful abbey. Venture inside to see the finely sculpted 12th-century capitals and the 17th-century wooden statue of St. Andrew. The adjacent cloisters are at their best during the summer music festival held here (and at the cathedral) from June to August. *Cour St-André, tel. 74–85–18–49. Admission: 9 frs. Open Apr.–mid-Oct., Wed.–Mon. 9:30–1 and 2–6; mid-Oct.–Mar., Wed.– Sat. 10–noon and 2–5, Sun. 2–6.*

Take the nearby bridge across the Rhône to inspect the excavated Cité Gallo-Romaine, where the Romans built most of their sumptuous private villas. *Admission free. Open daily.*

Lodging **Central.** Of Vienne's few good, inexpensive hotels, this house in the
$–$$ old town, close to the cathedral, is the most convenient. Medium-size rooms start at 280 frs. *3 rue de l'Archevêché, 38200, tel. 74–85–18–38. 27 rooms with bath or shower. AE, MC, V. Closed Christmas through New Year's.*

Dining **Le Bec Fin.** An inexpensive weekday menu makes the Bec Fin a good
$ lunch spot, and a serious dinner venue as well. The well-run, unpretentious eatery is just opposite the cathedral; its main dishes—steak and freshwater fish—seldom disappoint and occasionally display a deft touch (as with the burbot cooked with saffron). The gray-and-white dining room has an understated elegance. *7 pl. St-Maurice, tel. 74–85–76–72. Reservations accepted. Jacket required. MC, V. Closed Sun. dinner and Mon.*

Tournon

Trains run from Vienne south to Tournon every 2 hours or so (journey time 35–50 minutes).

A hefty 15th- to 16th-century **château** is the chief attraction in **Tournon**, which stands on the banks of the Rhône at the foot of some impressive granite hills. From the château's two terraces there are sumptuous views of the old town, river, and—towering above the village of Tain-l'Hermitage across the Rhône—the steep-climbing vineyards that produce Hermitage wine, one of the Rhône Valley's most refined (and costly) reds. The château houses a museum of local history, the **Musée Rhodanien**, which features an account of the life of locally born Marc Seguin (1786–1875), the engineer who built the first suspension bridge over the Rhône at Tournon in 1825 (the bridge was demolished in 1965). *Pl. Auguste-Faure, tel. 75–07–15–96. Admission: 14 frs adults, 7 frs children. Open June–Aug., Wed.–Mon. 10–noon and 2–6; Apr.–May and Sept.–Oct., Wed.–Mon. 2–6; closed Tues.*

Lodging and **Château.** This fine old hotel stands just across the Rhône from the
Dining wine village of Tain-l'Hermitage, and the restaurant, where set
$$ menus start at 110 francs, looks out on the famous, steeply terraced Hermitage vineyard. Most accommodations have been modernized and fitted with double-glazed windows; ask for a room that overlooks the river, although the best nudge past 400 francs. *12 quai Marc-Séguin, 07300, tel. 75–08–60–22. 14 rooms with bath or shower. Facilities: restaurant (closed Sat. lunch). AE, DC, MC, V. Closed Nov. and weekends out of season.*

Valence

Trains make the 15-minute run from Tournon south to Valence every 1½ hours. Tourist office: boulevard Maurice-Clerc, tel. 75–43–04–88.

Valence, capital of the Drôme *département*, is the principal fruit-and-vegetable market for the surrounding region. Steep-curbed alleyways—known as *côtes*—extend from the banks of the Rhône to the heart of the old town around the cathedral of **St-Apollinaire**. Although the cathedral was begun in the 12th century in the Romanesque style, it's not altogether as old as it looks: Parts were rebuilt in the 17th century, and the belfry in the 19th. Alongside the cathedral, in the former 18th-century Bishops' Palace, is the **Musée des Beaux-Arts,** featuring local sculpture and furniture and a collection of 96 red-chalk drawings by deft landscapist Hubert Robert (1733–1808). *Pl. des Ormeaux, tel. 75–79–20–80. Admission: 14 frs adults. Open Wed. and weekends 9–noon and 2–6; Mon.–Tues. and Thurs.–Fri. 2–6.*

Turn left out of the museum and cross hectic avenue Gambetta to the Champ-de-Mars, a broad terraced garden overlooking the Rhône, where there are fine views across to Crussol Castle. Just below the Champ-de-Mars is the **Parc Jouvet,** with 14 acres of pools and gardens.

Lodging and Dining

¢

Chaumont. A warm, friendly welcome and reliable home cooking make this small hotel-restaurant, a 10-minute walk up avenue Carnot from the tourist office, a hit with travelers. Service in the restaurant is speedy, and there is an extensive choice of set menus (four for less than 130 frs); you can choose among pâtés, coq au vin, and andouillette in white wine sauce. *79 av. Sadi-Carnot, 26000, tel. 75–43–10–12. 11 rooms, some with shower. Facilities: restaurant (closed Fri. evening and Sat.). MC, V. Closed 1st 3 wks in Aug. and part of Dec.*

Tour 2: Grenoble and the Alps

The Alps are captivating whatever the season. In winter, the dramatic, snow-carpeted slopes offer some of the best skiing in the world; in summer, chic spas, shimmering lakes, and breathtaking hilltop trails come into their own.

Grenoble, within sight of the peaks, forms a natural gateway to this mountain range, Europe's mightiest. Trains wind their way through the valleys to such attractive towns as Briançon, Chambéry, Aix-les-Bains, Chamonix, and Annecy. Reaching many of the high mountain ski resorts, among them pricey Val d'Isère, requires a bus ride from the valley villages along narrow, twisting alpine highways—an experience that's exhilarating or terrifying, depending on how distracting you find the stupendous vistas en route.

From Paris By Train

TGV trains to Grenoble leave Paris (Gare de Lyon) 6 times daily. The trip takes 3 hours 20 minutes.

By Car

Allow up to 6 hours for the 560-kilometer (350-mile) drive from Paris to Grenoble via A6, A43, and A48.

Grenoble

Tourist office: 14 rue de la République, opposite the covered market and close to the art museum, tel. 76–42–41–41.

★ Located 104 km (65 mi) southeast of Lyon, **Grenoble** is a large, cosmopolitan city. Its skyscrapers and forbidding gray buildings—intimidating by homey French standards—bear witness to Grenoble's fierce desire to move with the times, as does the city's nuclear research plant. The city is also home to a large university and is the birthplace of Stendhal, one of the most famous French novelists of the 19th century.

Head down avenue Viallet from the station and cross the Jardin de la Ville at the far end to reach the banks of the Isère River. A cable car (30 frs round-trip; operates Apr.–Oct., 9–midnight, Nov.–Dec. and Feb.–Mar., 10–6) starting at quai St-Stéphane-Jay whisks you up to the hilltop and its **Fort de la Bastille,** offering splendid views of the city and the River Isère. Walk down rue Maurice-Gignoux, past gardens, cafés, and stone mansions, to the **Musée Dauphinois,** a lively regional museum in a 17th-century convent, featuring displays of local folk arts and crafts. *30 rue Maurice-Gignoux, tel. 76–85–19–01. Admission: 15 frs adults, 10 frs children, free Wed. Open Wed.– Mon. 9–noon and 2–6.*

Heading left from the museum, make for the church of **St-Laurent,** which contains an atmospherically murky 6th-century crypt (one of the country's oldest Christian monuments) supported by a row of formidable marble pillars. *2 pl. St-Laurent, tel. 76–44–78–68. Admission: 15 frs adults, 10 frs children. Open June–Sept., Wed.– Mon. 10–noon and 2–6.*

★ Art buffs will want to cross the river to place de Lavalette, the new home to the **Musée de Peinture et de Sculpture,** one of France's oldest museums (founded in 1796) and the first to concentrate on modern art (Picasso donated his *Femme Lisant* in 1921). The collection now runs to 4,000 pictures and 5,500 drawings, and a new museum to house them opened in January 1994. It incorporates the medieval Tour de l'Isle, a noted Grenoble landmark, into the long and low modern section, designed to harmonize with the backcloth of the old town. The collection predating 1900 highlights the Italian Renaissance, Rubens, Flemish still lifes, Zurburan, a Canaletto view of Venice, and culminates in the Impressionists (Renoir, Monet). The 20th-century art includes works by Matisse (*Intérieur aux Aubergines* of 1911), Signac, Derain, Vlaminck, Magritte, Ernst, Miró, Dubuffet, and Hans Hoffmann. An array of modern sculpture adorns the gardens. *5 pl. de Lavalette, tel. 76–63–44–44. Admission: 25 frs adults, 15 frs senior citizens and children. Open Wed. 11–10, Thurs.–Mon. 11–7.*

Leave place Verdun by rue Blanchard and follow it five blocks to **place Grenette,** a lively pedestrian mall abloom with flowers and lined with sidewalk cafés.

Lodging **Alpes.** This modest hotel escapes being average by its reasonably
$ comfortable rooms with Skai armchairs and attractive wallpaper), calm (windows overlooking the street are double-glazed), and above all handy location midway between the station and downtown. *45 av. Félix-Viallet, 38000, tel. 76–87–00–71. 67 rooms with bath or shower. MC, V.*

Dining **Berlioz.** This restaurant near place de Verdun is a favorite with Gre-
$ noble food-lovers thanks to its light, airy decor, and its imaginative ways with French cuisine—exemplified by dishes such as marinated halibut with ginger. Best bets are set menus at 120 frs and 154 frs. *4 rue de Strasbourg, tel. 76–56–22–39. Reservations recommended. AE, MC, V. Closed Sat. lunch, Sun., and mid-July–mid-Aug.*

Briançon

Three trains daily make the picturesque 4-hour trip from Grenoble southeast to Briançon. Tourist office: 1 place du Temple, tel. 92–21–08–50.

Reputedly the highest town in Europe, at 4,350 feet above sea level, **Briançon** combines historic appeal with an Alpine backdrop and di-
★ rect access to the Serre-Chevalier ski complex (take the Prorel cable car from the Lower Town). The **old town,** referred to as the Ville Haute (Upper Town) or Briançon-Vauban, was remodeled by military engineer Vauban from 1692 onward. His three-tiered fortifications proved their worth in 1815 when, in the aftermath of Waterloo, marauding Austro-Sardinian troops were kept at bay for several months.

From the station, turn left and walk for about 10 minutes on avenue du Général-de-Gaulle. Turn right at the roundabout and go up the hill until you come to avenue de la République. A steep, straight climb up avenue de la République leads to the old town, which you'll enter through the beefy **Porte d'Embrun,** one of four gateways. Head left along Petite Gargouille—past **place d'Armes,** once a parade square, with two sundials high on the walls of the district law court (the Briançon region enjoys 300 days of sunshine a year)—and continue up to the triangular place du Temple, crushed beneath the early 18th-century church of **Notre-Dame** (completed by Vauban). The tourist office is housed on the *place* in the elegant, pilastered Maison des Templiers. Continue up rue du Temple and turn right into **Grande Gargouille** (also called Grande-Rue), the old town's liveliest street, with shops, restaurants, a gutter down the middle, and crumbling facades on either side.

Halfway down is the **Fontaine François I,** a fountain with whimsical spouts in the form of elephants' heads. Turn left here into narrow rue du Pont-Asfeld, which leads past the Chapelle des Pénitents and above the **Eglise des Cordeliers,** renowned for its 15th-century frescoes (access via a stone staircase), and continue as far as the Porte de la Durance. Venture through this stone gateway and cross what looks like a humdrum parking lot for a glimpse of the daring **Pont d'Asfeld** (built 1731), which straddles the Durance River 180 feet below. Then head up the Chemin de Rond, beneath the hilltop citadel (built over several periods and of little interest) for a panoramic view of the town and mountains.

Dining and Lodging
$$
★

Vauban. The polyglot Sémiond family has run this spacious, four-square hotel—halfway between the train station and cable car, and a 10-minute walk from the Upper Town—since it opened in 1956. While Odile—and a bust of the ubiquitous Vauban—survey the reception area, dignified *patron* André Sémiond, Odile's husband, patrols the restaurant in blazer and tie, offering advice about the wine (try the Chinon), local cuisine (try the river trout in a delicate butter sauce), and, of course, how to appreciate the great Vauban himself (prints of meatily fortified towns adorn the dining room walls). The five-course, 125-franc set menu changes twice daily, and by the time you've done justice to the local cheeseboard, André will be waiting for you behind the bar after a quick change into a rather less dignified checkered shirt and sheriff's vest. The best rooms are on the fourth floor, with small balconies and south-facing mountain views. *13 av. du Général-de-Gaulle, 05100, tel. 92–21–12–11, fax 92–50–58–20. 44 rooms, 26 with bath, 12 with shower. Facilities: restaurant, bar, parking. MC, V. Closed early Nov.–Christmas.*

Chambéry

Trains make the 40-minute trip from Grenoble north to Chambéry every 2 hours or so. Chambéry tourist office: 24 boulevard de la Colonne, tel. 79–33–42–47.

Tasteful restorations have helped lively **Chambéry** recapture some of its past glory as capital of Savoy. Stop for coffee on the pedestrian **place St-Léger** before heading two blocks to visit the 14th-century **Château des Ducs de Savoie.** The château's Gothic Sainte-Chapelle contains some good stained glass and houses a replica of the notorious Turin Shroud, once thought to have been used to wrap up the crucified Christ (but probably, according to recent scientific analysis, a medieval hoax). *Rue Basse du Château. Admission: 20 frs. Guided tours July and Aug., daily at 10:30, 2:30, 3:30, 4:30, and 5:30; June and Sept., daily at 10:30 and 2:30; Mar.–May and Oct.–Nov., Sat. at 2:15, Sun. at 3:30.*

Dining
$

Trois Voûtes. A sense of spaciousness and the view of the street outside create an informal mood at this large, lively restaurant near the cathedral. Fondue is one of the local specialties on the long, varied menu, and there are several set menus (two for under 100 frs). *110 rue de la Croix-d'Or, tel. 79–33–38–56. Reservations not required. MC, V.*

Aix-les-Bains

Hourly trains take 10–15 minutes for the trip from Chambéry north to Aix-les-Bains. Tourist office: place Mollard, tel. 79–35–05–92.

The gracious spa town of **Aix-les-Bains** lies on the eastern shore of Lac du Bourget. Although swimming in the lake is not advised (it's freezing cold), you can sail, fish, play golf and tennis, or picnic on the 25 acres of parkland that stretches along the lakefront. Visit the ruins of the original Roman baths, under the present **Thermes Nationaux** (Thermal Baths), built in 1934 and renovated in 1972 (guided tours only; Apr.–Oct., Mon.–Sat. at 3 PM; Nov.–Mar., Wed. at 3 PM). The Roman Temple of Diana (2nd–3rd centuries AD) now houses an **archaeology museum** (entrance via the tourist office on place Mollard).

There are half-hour boat trips from Aix-les-Bains across Lac du Bourget to the **Abbaye de Hautecombe,** where mass is celebrated with Gregorian chant. *Tel. 79–54–26–12. Cost: 60 frs. Departures from the Grand Pont, Mar.–June and Sept.–Oct., daily at 2:30; July–Aug. at 9:30, 2, 2:30, 3, 3:30, and 4:30.*

Dining **Dauphinois.** The long dining room of this large, cheerful hotel-res-
$ taurant, 300 yards south of the train station, has an adjacent garden where you can enjoy alfresco meals in summer. Local ham and fresh-water fish usually figure on the 125- and 150-franc set menus. *14 av. de Tresserve, tel. 79–61–22–56. Reservations recommended. AE, DC, MC, V. Closed mid-Dec.–mid-Feb.*

Annecy

Trains run every 1½ hours from Aix-les-Bains north to Annecy. The trip takes 35 minutes. Tourist office: Clos Bonlieu, 1 rue Jean-Jaurès, tel. 50–45–00–33.

Annecy stands on the shores of crystal-clear Lac d'Annecy and is surrounded by rugged, snow-tipped peaks. The canals, flower-covered bridges, and cobblestone pedestrian streets of old Annecy are at their liveliest on market days, Tuesday and Friday, though the town park and the tree-lined boulevard have tranquil, invigorating appeal any day of the week.

Start a meander through the old town on a small island in the River Thiou at the 12th-century Palais de l'Isle, once home to courts of law and a prison, and now containing a small museum of local history. You may notice that the Thiou seems to be flowing the "wrong way," that is, out of the lake. It does in fact drain the lake, feeding the net-work of Annecy's canals. There are views over the lake from the towers of the 12th-century **castle,** set high on a hill opposite the Palais.

Dining **Le Petit Zinc.** This reasonably priced bistro is the perfect place for a
$ delicious lunch after you've finished wandering around the old quar-ter of Annecy. The cozy, beamed dining room is very popular with locals, who come for the cheese croquettes and salad, roast pork, and good carafe wines. There are also a wonderful cheese tray and home-baked desserts. *11 rue du Pont-Morens, tel. 50–51–12–93. MC, V. Closed Sun.*

Chamonix

Trains make the 2½-hour run from Annecy east to Chamonix every 3 hours. You'll make a change at St-Gervais. Chamonix tourist office: 85 place Triangle-de-l'Amitié, tel. 50–53–00–24.

Chamonix, the oldest and perhaps most prestigious French winter sports resort, is a charmer of an Alpine mountain town, despite its size, so it's not surprising that it was a favorite of European vacationers long before it hosted the first Winter Olympics in 1924. Here, you don't have to be a skier or mountain climber to penetrate the lonely mountain fastnesses. In an incredible, spine-tingling trip, ★ the world's highest **cable car** soars 12,000 feet from Chamonix up the Aiguille du Midi, from which there are staggering views of Europe's loftiest peak, the 15,700-foot **Mont-Blanc.** Be prepared for a lengthy wait, though, to go up and come down—and take warm clothing. *Cost: 170 frs. round-trip. Open May–Sept., daily 8–4:45; Oct.–Apr., daily 8–3:45.*

Apart from its history and the spectacular backdrop of the Alps' highest peaks, Chamonix owes its popularity to excellent snow (especially the slopes facing northwest), which lasts from November through mid-May. You can enjoy 62 slopes from altitudes of 10,500 feet down to 3,900 feet with the Ski Pass Mont-Blanc.

Lodging and Dining
Splurge

Albert I & Milan. Though the prices can be high at this welcoming chalet-style hotel (some rooms go for as much as 800 frs), it does offer the best value among Chamonix's quality lodging establishments. Many guest rooms were renovated in 1992; most have balconies, and all are furnished with elegant period reproductions. The dining room offers stupendous views of Mont Blanc, and the cuisine scales heights of invention and enthusiasm; try the oysters fried with asparagus. *119 impasse du Montenvers, 74400, tel. 50–53–05–09, fax 50–55–95–48. 17 rooms and 12 suites, all with bath. Facilities: restaurant (closed Wed. lunch), pool, tennis, sauna, hot tub. AE, DC, MC, V. Closed last wk of Oct., Nov., and first wk of Dec.*

11 Corsica

Including Bastia, Calvi, Ajaccio, and Corte

A combination of ancient Mediterranean ports, crystalline waters, archaeological treasures, and high mountains makes Corsica one of the most scenic and unspoiled regions of France. And while prices can be high during July and August, off-season visits in spring and fall offer hotel and restaurant deals that make this an economical alternative to the Riviera.

The island is roughly the shape of an inverted triangle, with the cities of Calvi and Bastia in the top corners and Bonifacio in the southern tip. The capital, Ajaccio (a-*jack*-sio), lies on the western side of the island halfway between Calvi and Bonifacio, and the lonely peninsula of Cap Corse juts north of Bastia toward France. Ferry service links Marseille, Nice, and Toulon with Bastia, Calvi, and Ajaccio, Corsica's main cities, which are connected by a single train line that traverses some of the most spectacular mountain scenery on the island. A two-car train follows the northern coast between L'Ile Rousse and Calvi, stopping on request at any of the beach coves, and bus routes fan out from these towns to all other points of interest.

For thousands of years, its natural resources and strategic location, 168 km (105 mi) south of the French coast and just 81 km (50 mi) west of Italy, have made Corsica a prize hotly contested by many Mediterranean civilizations. You can still see vestiges of those invaders, from primitive stone statues of prehistoric warriors to exquisite Grecian urns and crumbling Roman ruins. The city-state of Genoa ruled Corsica for hundreds of years, leaving behind impressive citadels and bridges and a network of nearly 100 medieval watchtowers that still encircle the island. The Italian influence is also apparent in village architecture and in the Corsican language, a combination of Italian and Latin. Corsican is still spoken among island residents, but everyone except the oldest villagers also speaks French.

Corsica

TO MARSEILLE

TO NICE

TO MARSEILLE, TOULON

TO MARSEILLE, TOULON

TO NICE

TO GENOA, LIVORNO

Centuri

Pino

Rogliano

Cap Corse Peninsula

D80

D180

Canari

Cannelle

Nonza

Monte Stello

D80

Erbalunga

Patrimonio

St-Florent

Oletta

Bastia

D81

D82

N193

L'Ile Rousse

Algajola

Pigna

Sant'Antonio

Cateri

Cassano

Calvi

N197

D151

Calenzana

N197

D84

Casamozza

Mariana

N193

Golo

D506

Haut-Asco

Asco

Piedicroce

Scala di

Santa Regina

Calacuccia

D84

N193

D71

Castagniccia

Partinello

Corte

Golfe de Porto

Porto

Evisa

Ota

D84

Riventosa

Piana

Monte d'Oro

N200

N28

TO SARDINIA

Cargèse

Vico

Sagone

Tiuccia

Vizzavona

Vivario

Aléria

D81

N193

Ghisoni

Golfe de Sagone

Gravona

D69

Ghisonaccia

D344

N198

Ajaccio

N196

Cauro

Tavaro

D69

Solenzara

TO MARSEILLE

Iles Sanguinaires

Golfe d'Ajaccio

Porticcio

Petreto-Bicchisano

D268

Col de Bavella

TO NICE, TOULON, MARSEILLE

Filitosa

Zonza

Capo di Muro

Olmeto

TO MARSEILLE

Propriano

D368

Golfe de Porto-Vecchio

TO PORTO SAN STEFANO

Cauria

Sartène

TO POZZUOLI

Mediterranean Sea

N196

Porto-Vecchio

Figari

D859

Tyrrhenian Sea

N

N198

N196

0

40 miles

0

60 km

Bonifacio

Iles Lavezzi

TO SARDINIA

TO PALAU

While Corsica is only 215 km (133 mi) long and 81 km (50 mi) wide, it seems much larger—partly because rugged, mountainous terrain makes for slow traveling and partly because the landscape varies so much from region to region. Bastia and Ajaccio are big cities with urban sprawl but colorful old quarters. The area surrounding the capital is rural and hilly, while the Calvi region has sand-colored villages and crescent beaches. The eastern part of the island is a marshy plain with long sandy beaches, the southern region around Bonifacio contains austere granite hill towns, and the entire interior is a chain of dramatic mountaintops. Unlike many other Mediterranean islands, Corsica is green year-round and has plentiful supplies of fresh water; 14 rivers tumble down from the mountains through wooded valleys, full of cork-oak trees and ancient laricio pines, Europe's tallest conifer. All of Corsica that is not wooded or cultivated is covered with a dense thicket of undergrowth called the *maquis*. The maquis is made up of a variety of such sweet-smelling plants as lavender, myrtle, and heather that turn the hillsides white with tiny flowers in the spring, and gave Corsica its nickname "the perfumed isle."

There's always been a kind of black legend associated with the island that stems mainly from a tradition of clannishness; but while Corsican clans often fought each other in endless cycles of revenge, they also took care of each other. Corsica is also famous as the birthplace of Napoléon Bonaparte. Although he never returned to the island after beginning his military career, Napoléon is honored with statues in Ajaccio, where you can visit his family's home. Perhaps a better representative of the individualistic character of the island is Corsica's other hero, Pasquale Paoli, who framed the world's first constitution for the island in 1755. Paoli's ideas greatly influenced the French Revolution as well as the founding fathers of the United States, who drew upon Corsica's constitution in writing their own version some 30 years later.

Corsica Basics

Budget Lodging When tourism began in Corsica in the 1960s, the majority of hotels were built in a modern, boxy style. But as a second generation of hoteliers begins to take over the family businesses, more attention is being paid to decor and service. Restored country inns are beginning to appear, and tastefully designed new hotels are being built at the rate of three or four a year. Prices at the best seaside hotels are only slightly lower than on the Riviera, but villages in the interior remain substantially cheaper. Good prices can be found everywhere on the island during the off-season, although many hotels close for half the year from November 1 to Easter. During the peak season (July 1–Sept. 15) prices shoot up, and some hotels will insist that you take your meals there. There are more than 700 *gîtes* of one kind or another all over the island. These farmhouses, inns, and hikers' way stations offer good value and good company as well. *Gîtes de France, 6 ave. Pasquale Paoli, 20000 Ajaccio, tel. 95–20–51–34, fax 95–20–28–96.*

Budget Dining Many things about Corsica may strike you as Italian, but the islanders are thoroughly French their regional cooking. There are a number of excellent regional restaurants, most with moderate prices. Attractive harborside cafés offer classic French and nouvelle cuisine: Their best dishes use fresh Mediterranean seafood—lobster, oysters, mussels, and a variety of fish such as sea bream, red mullet, sole, and sardines—many of which go into a rich bouillabaisse called *aziminu*.

Corsica also offers a variety of delicious local cheeses and *charcuterie*. The best-known cheese, *brocciu* (pronounced BRO-choo), similar to ricotta, serves as a filling in a variety of sweet and savory dishes such as omelets with mint, cannelloni, and *fritelli* (doughnuts made with chestnut flour). Other cheeses to look for are the mild *basteliccacis* and the *bleu de Corse*. Cold meats, including *figatelli* (pork sausages), *lonzu* (pork tenderloin), *coppa* (pork shoulder), and *prisuttu* (ham) are all made from free-range chestnut-fed pigs and wild boar and smoked with a combination of herbs from the maquis. Traditional stews of wild boar, lamb, and *merle* (blackbird) feature prominently on menus, often accompanied by slices of polenta made from chestnut flour. Fresh mountain trout is also popular in the interior. For those with a sweet tooth, *fiadoni* (brocciu cheesecake) and *canistrelli* (anise cookies) make a good ending to a meal.

Corsica, with no fewer than eight separate wine-growing regions, produces many fine wines to accompany any meal. Worth looking for are an excellent berry-flavored red wine from Ajaccio made with the local sciacarello grapes and warm, full-bodied reds produced in Patrimonio. Sartène's Fumicicoli is one of the smoothest reds, while the Domaine San Quilico is a top rosé from Patrimonio. A highly prized muscatel is made on Cap Corse, and local liqueurs include a curiously refreshing myrtle-flavored brandy.

Bargain Shopping
Artisans use the wood from Corsica's rich chestnut and juniper forests to craft beautifully carved letter openers, pipes, and other objects. Island potters craft colorful modern ceramics, while antique-style ceramic reproductions are produced near the Roman ruins in **Aléria.** Small packages of herbs from the sweet-smelling maquis, chestnut cakes and cookies, local wines, or myrtle liqueur make good presents and are easy to carry home. A fun place to buy them is at the **outdoor markets** in Bastia, Ile Rousse, or Ajaccio.

Biking
Only expert cyclists will want to attempt the rugged terrain of interior Corsica, although bicycles can be useful for coastal rides to find secluded beaches. Rental shops include **Moto Corse Evasion** (3 Montée St-Jean, Ajaccio, tel. 95–20–52–05), **Locacycles** (40 rue César-Campinchi, Bastia, tel. 95–31–02–43), and **Location Ambrosini** (pl. Bel Ombra, Calvi, tel. 95–65–02–13).

Hiking
Next to sunbathing, hiking ranks as one of Corsica's main outdoor attractions. The opportunities for scenic strolls range from simple one-hour walks in the pine forests of **Col de Bavella** to technical climbing and arduous trails like the **GR** (Grand Randonée) **20,** which travels 160 km (100 mi) across the island from north to south and takes two weeks to complete. One of the island's most beautiful and popular day hikes can be found in an area called the **Restonica,** outside of Corte. Leaflets covering most walking paths are available from local tourist offices. The **Associaciu di i muntagnoli corsi** (quartier Pentaniedda, 20122 Quenza, tel. 95–78–64–05) offers two- and three-day guided hikes through the mountains and lake regions.

Beaches
Corsica's beaches range from the wide sandy strands of Porto-Vecchio on the east coast to the rocky cliffs off Piana in the west to the tiny beaches along the lovely private *criques* (creeks) of the Cap Corse peninsula in the north. Calvi is deservedly famous for its lovely fine sand beach and for the *petit train côtier* (little coastal train) that makes several runs daily to the beaches between Calvi and L'Ile Rousse. The windswept dunes of the Saleccia beach, once used to film Robert Mitchum in *The Longest Day,* are now frequented by nudists, while the beach at Nonza is known for its carpet of black pebbles.

Arts and Nightlife
Singing plays an important role in both traditional and daily island life. You'll doubtless come across impromptu café gatherings where amateur vocalists give impressive renderings of a traditional *paghiella* (a three-voice harmony), a *voceru* (funeral chant), or a *chjama e rispondi* duel in which two singers rival each other in a lyrical ping-pong match, throwing questions and answers in an at-

tempt to outdo one another by the wit, beauty, or rhyme of their invention.

Festivals The island has three major **carnivals**—one in Bastia at the end of August, another in Ajaccio celebrating Napoléon's birthday in mid-August, and a third the second half of September in Calvi—when the towns come alive with song, costumed processions, and outdoor theater. Other island festivals include a **Mediterranean Film Festival** in Bastia in October and November; a **Jazz Festival** in Calvi in mid-June; a classical **International Music Meeting** in Ajaccio in July; Calvi's late-October **Festiventu** wind festival (hang-gliding, kite-flying, and the like); and an **International Music Festival** in Bastia in early December.

Tour 1:
From Bastia to Calvi

This tour focuses on the northern towns of Bastia and Calvi, connected by train, and includes excursions to the rugged Cap Corse peninsula and the historic farming region of the Balagne, which can be made by car or local bus.

From Mainland France
By Plane **Air France** has daily flights from Paris to Bastia (tel. 45–35–61–61, Paris; 95–32–10–29, Bastia), while **Air Inter** flies daily from Marseille or Nice to Bastia and Calvi (tel. 95–65–20–09, Calvi; 95–54–54–95, Bastia). Shuttle buses meet flights and run to the center of each town (except Calvi) and cost about 25 frs. (A taxi ride from the airport to Calvi costs about 100 frs.)

By Ferry **SNCM** (Société Nationale Maritime Corse Méditerranée, tel. 49–24–24–24, Paris; 91–56–30–10, Marseille; 93–89–89–89, Nice; 94–41–25–76, Toulon; 95–54–66–66, Bastia; 95–65–01–38, Calvi) operates ferries to Calvi and Bastia from Marseille, Toulon, and Nice. **Corsica Ferries** (tel. 95–31–18–09) also connects Calvi and Bastia with Genoa and Livorno in Italy. Crossings take from five to eight hours. Ferries dock near the center of town in all cases.

From Ajaccio
By Train **SNCF** (tel. 95–23–11–03, Ajaccio; 95–32–60–06, Bastia; 95–65–00–61, Calvi) operates a slow train along the scenic route between Ajaccio and Bastia or Calvi, making stops at all the towns in between. Travel time is three to four hours.

By Bus **Les Rapides bleus** (1 rue Maréchal-Sebastiani, Bastia, tel. 95–31–03–79; quai l'Herminier, Ajaccio, tel. 95–21–28–01) and **Société des autocars cortenais** (route de St-Pancrace, Corte, tel. 95–46–02–12) connect Ajaccio by bus with Calvi and Bastia.

Bastia

Tourist office: place St-Nicolas, tel. 95–31–00–89.

We begin our tour in **Bastia,** whose name comes from *bastaglia* (fortress). The Genoese built a prodigious one here in the 14th century as a stronghold against rebellious islanders and potential invaders from across the Tuscan Straits. Today the city is Corsica's business center and largest town, and despite sprawling suburbs filled with supermarkets, apartment towers, and giant hardware stores, the center of town retains the timeless salty flavor of an ancient Mediterranean port.

The **Terra Vecchia** (Old Town) is small enough to be explored on foot. Start at the wide, palm-filled **place St-Nicolas,** bordered on one side by the sea and on the other by two blocks of cafés that stretch along boulevard Général-de-Gaulle. These cafés, with their tables spilling into the square, are the hub of Bastia's social life. (A good one to try is the wood-paneled Les Palmiers.)

Head south on boulevard Général-de-Gaulle, which becomes rue Napoléon, and in two blocks on the left you will see the **Eglise de la Conception,** occupying a pebble-studded square. Step inside to admire the church's ornate, dimly lit, 18th-century interior. The walls are covered with gold, maroon Genoan velvet, and marble, and the ceiling is painted with vibrant frescoes.

Walk around the back of the church and you will come out on the **place du Marché**—the market square—where every morning except Monday black-swathed grandmothers haggle over the price of fish and fruit. This is a good place to stroll around and familiarize yourself with Corsican varieties of fish and cheese before faced with dinnertime decisions. Continue across the market, opposite the town hall, to a warren of tiny streets that make up the old **fishermen's quarter.** Here the sky disappears above the tall buildings, plaster crumbles, laundry drips from overhead, children scoot by on bikes, and sounds of family life drift out the windows into the pungent air trapped between the houses.

Continue south through to the picturesque **old port,** dominated by the hilltop citadel. The harbor, now lined with excellent seafood restaurants, is home to million-dollar yachts, but you can still find many bright red and blue fishing boats and tangles of old nets and lines. A walk around the port brings you to **Terra Nova** (New Town), a maze of 16th- to 18th-century streets and houses at the base of the 16th-century fortress. Climb to the top of the stairs for a sweeping view of the Italian islands of Capraia, Elba, and Montecristo. On a clear day you'll be able to make out the hills of Tuscany.

At the place de la Citadelle, stop in at the **Genoese Governor's Palace,** whose vaulted, colonnaded galleries now house the **Musée d'Ethnographie Corse,** with collections detailing peasant life and the island's history. There are exhibits of archaeology, botany, and anthropology, including a life-size reproduction of a shepherd's hut. Be sure to look for the 18th-century rebel flag with the black head and white headband. This symbol of Corsican nationalism frequently appears throughout the island on everything from bags of cookies to political posters. The palace's courtyard is the setting for local fairs and historical pageants. Behind the ancient defense tower, a tiny stairway leads to the governor's private gardens, an intimate oasis offering a superb view over the port to the towers of the Church of St. John the Baptist. *Pl. du Donjon, tel. 95–31–09–12. Admission: 15 frs. Open weekdays 9–noon and 2–6, weekends 10–noon and 2–5.*

Opposite the museum, a network of cobbled alleyways rambles across the citadel to the 15th-century **Cathédrale Ste-Marie** on rue Notre-Dame. Inside, classic Baroque abounds in an explosion of gilt decoration. The church's 18th-century silver statue of the Assumption is paraded at the head of a solemn religious procession through the streets of the Old Town each August 15. Just behind the church stands the **Chapelle Ste-Croix,** with a sumptuous Baroque style that makes it look more like a theater than a church. The chapel owes its name to a blackened oak crucifix, "Christ of the Miracles," discovered at sea by fishermen in 1428 and venerated to this day by Bastia's fishing community.

Lodging
$$
★

Castel Brando. One of Bastia's most congenial hotels, Castel Brando is about 15 minutes north of the city in the picturesque coastal village of Erbalunga, easily reached by local buses that run every half hour. Owners Joëlle and Jean Paul Pieri have refurbished the 19th-century mansion with extremely good taste, using a cool buff color, dark green shutters, and terra-cotta tile. The large guest rooms are furnished with country-style antiques, dried flowers, and decorative tile in the baths, and each comes equipped with a kitchenette. The hotel's garden has a large swimming pool and a terrace where guests enjoy breakfast, which is included in the room rate. *B.P. 20 Erbalunga 20222, tel. 95–30–10–30, fax 95–33–98–18. 16 rooms with bath. Facilities: pool, tennis. AE, MC, V. Closed late Oct.– Apr.*

$ **Posta Vecchia.** An old building overlooking the port was renovated and transformed into the Posta Vecchia hotel in 1978. The unpretentious guest rooms, decorated with floral wallpaper and print bedspreads, have wood-beamed ceilings that add a rustic touch. Some rooms are small; the best are in the main house facing the port. *Quai des Martyrs, 20200, tel. 95–32–32–38, fax 95–32–14–05. 49 rooms with bath. AE, DC, MC, V.*

Dining **La Voûte.** Kids come here for the pizza cooked in a wood-fired oven,
$$ while their parents dip into excellent fish and steaks, making La Voûte one of Bastia's most popular restaurants. Vaulted brick ceilings, exposed stone, and indirect lighting add an authentic Corsican atmosphere. The smoked salmon and rockfish soup are superb. *6 bis rue Luce de Casabianca, tel. 95–32–47–11. Reservations advised. AE, MC, V. Closed Sun. lunch.*

¢–$ **La Cave Gaetan.** This stone-and-brick-lined hideaway 50 yards behind the Posta Vecchia hotel serves Corsican specialties and fresh seafood—try the fish soup or the *cabrit* (baby goat)—at alarmingly low prices. The owners are friendly and fun, and the place is well known among locals looking for good value and a relaxed venue. *1 rue de St-Erasme, tel. 95–31–55–13. No reservations. No credit cards. Closed Sun.*

Cap Corse

Every half hour, Bastia city buses (information: tel. 95–31–06–65) head up Cap Corse as far as Erbalunga. **Cars Micheli** *(1 rue de Nouveau Port, Bastia, tel. 95–35–61–08) offers a daily excursion around the cape throughout the year and connects Cap Corse towns with Bastia during the summer on Tuesday, Thursday, and Saturday afternoons.*

The rugged **Cap Corse peninsula** juts out toward France's south coast, and its wild scenery and atmospheric villages make for rewarding adventures. A scenic coastal road (D80) runs around the peninsula, skirting either side of a mountain range that culminates at Monte Stello, soaring skyward near the tiny port of **Erbalunga** on the east coast. Erbalunga is one of the cape's prettiest villages, its tiny stone houses tumbling to the water's edge. To the north the scenery grows wilder as maquis covers the slopes. The road cuts across the tip of the peninsula from the fishing port of **Macinaggio** through the hinterlands of Rogliano and on to **Centuri,** a picturesque 18th-century port on the west coast of the peninsula famous for its underwater scenery.

From all the coastal villages it is possible to make challenging hikes into the interior hills of the cape. At the top of Col de Sainte Lucie stands the **Tour de Sénèque,** a tower to which the luckless Seneca was exiled for having seduced the Roman emperor Claudius's niece. Along the west coast are more pretty villages, notably **Pino, Canari,** and **Cannelle. Nonza,** the largest of the west coast villages, enjoys a particularly appealing location—overlooking the sea and a stretch of blue-gray beaches on one side and an expanse of terraced vineyards on the other.

Lodging and **Le Vieux Moulin.** If you're after Old World charm and an authentic
Dining Corsican flavor, Le Vieux Moulin is the place to try. The main house
$$ was built in 1870 as a private residence; the eight-room annex is
★ more recent, but no less inviting, with bougainvillea cascading from

its balconies. The friendly staff will arrange boat rides and fishing trips around the coast of the Cap Corse peninsula, and there's a tennis court and golf course nearby. The restaurant specializes in seafood; try the bouillabaisse. *Centuri Port, 20238, tel. 95–35–60–15, fax 95–35–60–24. 14 rooms with bath. Facilities: restaurant. AE, DC, MC, V. Closed Nov.–Mar.*

Calvi

*Three trains a day make the trip southwest from Bastia and another three link Calvi and Ajaccio. **Agence Les Beaux Voyages** (tel. 95–65–11–35) offers daily bus service between Bastia and Calvi. Tourist office: port de Plaisance, tel. 95–65–16–67.*

Calvi is one of Corsica's most sophisticated resort towns and the port closest to mainland France. As headquarters of the Balagne, known as the garden of Corsica, Calvi grew rich by supplying its products to Genoa. Citizens always considered themselves somewhat superior to other Corsicans and remained loyal supporters of Genoa long after the rest of the island had declared independence. Calvi also claims to be the birthplace of Christopher Columbus, the most famous Genoese of them all. The evidence is slight, but the crew lists from Columbus's voyages to the New World do contain the names of many Calvi residents.

Like Bastia, Calvi's location has made it a strategic spot for warriors and tourists alike. During the 18th century the town endured assaults from Corsican nationalists, the most prominent being the celebrated patriot Pasquale Paoli. Today's Calvi sees a summertime invasion of mainly French and Italian visitors, drawn by the resort's four-mile-long white sand beach flanked by graceful umbrella pines, a perfectly carved bay, and a busy marina.

The **Genoese Citadel,** perched on a rocky promontory at the tip of the bay, competes with the beach as a major attraction. The ramparts are the natural place to begin your tour of the city. As you cross the drawbridge, notice the plaque above. The inscription *Civitas Calvi semper fidelis,* "The citizens of Calvi always faithful," reflects the town's unswerving allegiance to Genoa. At the welcome center, just inside the gates, you can see a video on the city's history; a guided tour is available in English three times a day at 10, 4:30, and 6:30 from Easter to October 1. You may also conduct a self-guided walking tour. *Tel. 95–65–36–74. Guided tour and video show: 45 frs adults, 15 frs children 10–15.*

The historic circuit takes you around the rampart walls for great views and a peek inside the gardens of the luxurious villas that look out on the sea. It continues up into the center of the Old Town to the **place du Donjon.** The old governor's palace is now a barracks for the French foreign legion, but you can visit the **Oratoire de la Confrérie St-Antoine,** a 15th-century chapel showcasing Calvi's religious art.

From the citadel, descend to the elegant **quai Landry,** lined with attractive restaurants and cafés. Rue Clemenceau and boulevard Wilson, behind the harbor, are major shopping streets. Stop in at the 13th-century church of **St-Jean-Baptiste** on the place d'Armes, which contains an interesting baptismal font dating from the Renaissance. Look up at the dome to see the rows of pews screened by grillwork. The chaste young women of Calvi's upper classes would sit here to say their prayers, protected from the hot glances of any lusty peasant who might happen to look up.

Before leaving the Calvi region make an excursion on the coastal train, which runs as far as L'Ile Rousse, picking up and depositing sun worshippers at beach coves not accessible by road. Named for the mass of reddish rock now connected to the town by a causeway, **L'Ile Rousse** is a favorite with French vacationers. More charming is the village of **Algajola,** the last and smallest of the seven citadel towns built by the Genoese on Corsica's shores. Its perfect crescent beach draws a big holiday crowd, but the tiny old town retains its medieval history.

Another excursion possible by bus is to **Calenzana,** the largest of the rose-colored hill towns of the **Balagne.** This was the so-called land of lords and remained a feudal society until the French Revolution. Calenzana, once a hideout for Corsica's notorious bandits, lies among olive groves and boasts the 11th-century **church of Ste-Restitute,** a short walk beyond the town. The church's marble and granite altar is backed by medieval frescoes depicting the life of Sainte Restitute. Legend has it that the saint was martyred here in the third century, and when the people of the town began building a church on another site, the stone blocks were moved here each night by two huge white bulls. Apparently, this happened several times before the townsfolk finally got the divine message and changed building sites.

Lodging and Dining
$ **Casa Musicale.** Don't miss this unusual place, with traditional local cuisine, music of all kinds—authentic Corsican polyphonic singing more often than not—and a lovely view over the Balagne down to Calvi. The rooms are simple but elegant, with whitewashed walls and rustic furniture. *20220 Pigna, tel. 95–61–77–31, fax 95–61–77–81. 7 rooms that sleep 2, 3, or 4. MC, V.*

Lodging
$$ **La Balanea.** This friendly place overlooking the port is filled with good cheer, good taste, and interestingly designed furniture shaped like whales and dolphins. The rooms are as impeccable as the location, across the street from Calvi's best-value restaurant, U San Carlu, and literally on top of all the movement, day and night, along quai Landry. *6 rue Clemenceau, 20260, tel. 95–65–00–45, fax 95–65–29–71. 38 rooms with bath. AE, DC, MC, V.*

$$ **L'Ondine.** Nestled into the rocks at the edge of a sandy cove, L'Ondine is a village of beige, single-story, stucco buildings pleasantly landscaped with trees and flowering shrubs. The southern-style rooms are simple but have everything you'll need for a comfortable stay, including TVs. Rooms on the second floor overlook the garden. The swimming pool commands a stunning view of the beach and the 16th-century citadel town of Algajola. *7 rue à Marina, Algajola 20220, tel. 95–60–70–02, fax 95–60–60–43. 55 rooms with bath. Facilities: restaurant, bar, pool. MC, V. Closed Oct. 15–Easter.*

Dining
$$
★   **Chez Tao.** At Chez Tao, a mandatory stop on almost everyone's itinerary, you can rub elbows with French film stars and the rest of the island's glitterati, and dine in ocher-colored 16th-century vaults that afford views of the bay through arched picture windows. Seafood is what everyone eats here, but food and wine play second fiddle to the atmosphere, which includes Corsican folk singing and dancing until the wee hours. Carefully selecting your dinner will bring the price down somewhat, or you can stop in for a drink only. *Pl. de la Citadelle, tel. 95–65–00–73. Reservations advised. AE, MC, V. Closed Nov.–Easter.*

$ **U San Carlu.** Good, classic Corsican and French cooking at reasonable prices makes U San Carlu a favorite with tourists and locals alike. The restaurant, with its brick-vaulted dining room, is in a restored 16th-century building that once housed the town hospital. In summer you can eat outdoors on a palm-shaded patio. Specialties include Corsican soup (a thick soup of vegetables, beans, and pork), steak in Roquefort sauce, and prawns flamed in brandy. The warm goat cheese salad is great and the daily menu is an excellent value. *10 pl. St-Charles, tel. 95–65–21–93. Reservations advised weekends. AE, DC, MC, V. Closed Tues. eve. and Wed. in winter.*

Tour 2: Ajaccio and Southern Corsica

Ajaccio, the capital of Corsica and the birthplace of Napoléon, is the start of this tour, which fans out along bus routes past the archaeological site of Filitosa to the granite hill town of Sartène, the cliff-top fortress and port of Bonifacio, the east coast beaches of Porto-Vecchio, and the west coast rock formations—Les Calanches—near Piana. The interior nationalist stronghold of Corte is reached by a railroad that passes along Corsica's backbone of mountains.

From Mainland France By Plane Air France and Air Inter connect Ajaccio's Campo-Dell'Oro airport (tel. 95–20–52–29) to mainland France with daily flights to Paris, Nice, and Marseille. Delta Airlines flies to Ajaccio via Paris between May 1 and October 30. Buses meet flights and run into town and cost about 25 frs.

By Ferry SNCM (quai l'Hermanier, tel. 95–29–66–99) plies between Ajaccio and Nice, Marseille, or Toulon.

From Bastia and Calvi By Train Three trains a day from Bastia and another three from Calvi pull into the SNCF station in Ajaccio (tel. 95–23–11–03). The trip takes three to four hours.

By Bus All buses in Ajaccio arrive and depart from a central terminal at the port (quai l'Hermanier; information: tel. 95–21–28–01). Several buses a day link Bastia and Ajaccio; the trip takes 3½ hours. Other towns on the island generally have two connections a day, one in the early morning and another in the afternoon.

Ajaccio

Tourist offices: Corsica regional office, 17 blvd. Roi-Jérôme, tel. 95–21–56–56; Ajaccio, Hôtel de Ville, pl. Maréchal-Foch, tel. 95–21–40–87.

Numbers in the margin correspond with points of interest on the Ajaccio map.

★ **Ajaccio** is a busy commercial city with high-rise buildings and urban sprawl, but the center remains historic and all the important sights are close to one another.

❶ Begin your tour at **place Maréchal-Foch,** the city's main square, right on the waterfront. Rows of stately palm trees create a tropical atmosphere and lead to a marble statue of Napoléon dressed in a Ro-
❷ man toga and surrounded by four lions. Stop in at the **Hôtel de Ville** (100 yards toward the port), whose Empire-style Grand Salon is hung with portraits of a long line of Bonapartes. There is a fine bust of Letizia, Napoléon's formidable mother, and a bronze death mask of the emperor. The frescoed ceiling portrays Napoléon's meteoric rise to fame. *Pl. Maréchal-Foch. Admission: 2 frs. Open Apr.–Oct., weekdays 9–noon and 2:30–5:30; Nov.–Mar., weekdays 9–noon and 2–5.*

❸ Behind the town hall look for the **city market,** a lovely square where every morning except Monday you can ogle the enticing array of sausages, cheeses, and vegetables fresh from the city's surrounding farms. Be sure to try the unusual beignets that village women still make in the traditional way, with chestnut flour and brocciu cheese.

Walk back to place Maréchal-Foch and head down rue Bonaparte for two blocks. Just up rue St-Charles stands the large middle-class
❹ 18th-century **Maison Bonaparte,** where Napoléon was born on August 15, 1769. His father, Carlo, was a lawyer, and the status-conscious family, interested in the prominent address, rented out only

Cathedral, **6**
Chapelle Impériale, **7**
City market, **3**
Hôtel de Ville, **2**
Maison Bonaparte, **4**
Musée Fesch, **8**
Oldest houses, **5**
Place Maréchal-Foch, **1**

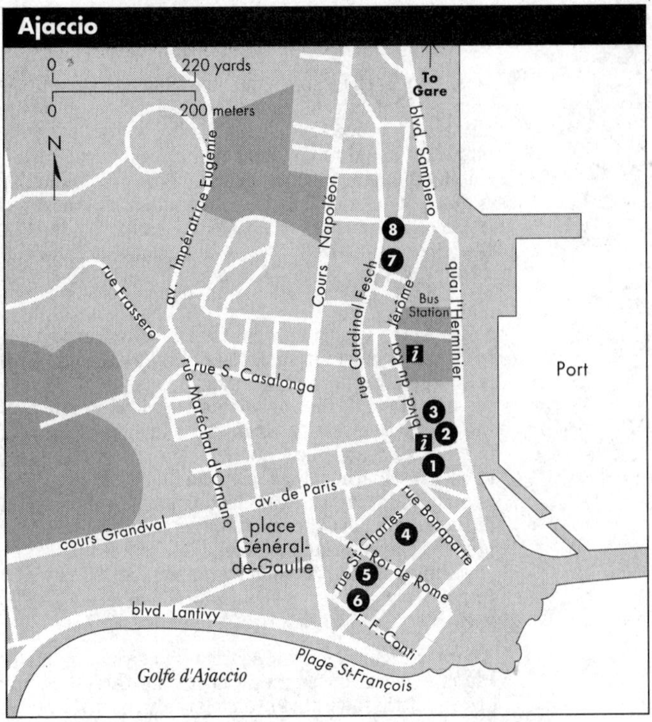

the first floor of this attractive residence. The building houses a museum featuring the original Louis XV and XVI interiors designed by Napoléon's mother. Glass cases display mementos, and another room contains portraits and cameos of the entire Bonaparte clan. Search out the two family trees, one spanning nearly 200 years (1769–1959) and the other dating from the 19th century and, remarkably, woven out of human hair. *Rue St-Charles. Admission: 17 frs. Open Apr.–Oct., Tues.–Sat. 9–noon and 2–6, Sun. 9–noon and Mon. 2–6; Nov.–Mar., Tues.–Sun. 10–noon and Mon. 2–5.*

Turn left outside the Maison Bonaparte down rue St-Charles and
5 you'll come to the city's **oldest houses** on the corner of rue Roi de Rome, opposite the tiny church of St. John the Baptist. These simple homes were built shortly after the town was founded in 1492. They suffer the fate of most buildings in Corsica: No effort has been made to repair the crumbling plaster. It's not a case of poverty, because the island enjoys a relatively high standard of living, nor is it squalor, as you'll notice the streets and parks are kept clean and tidy—Corsica is just now beginning to appreciate its historic buildings.

At the end of rue St-Charles stands the 16th-century Baroque
6 **cathedral** where Napoléon was baptized. The interior is covered with newly restored trompe-l'oeil frescoes, and the high altar, from an old church in Lucca, Italy, was donated by Napoléon's sister Eliza after he made her princess of Tuscany. Look for Eugène Delacroix's famous painting *Virgin of Sacré Coeur* just over the Chapelle de la Madonna del Pianto.

Before leaving Ajaccio, walk back to the Napoléon statue on place Maréchal-Foch and head four blocks up rue Cardinal Fesch to the
7 Renaissance-style **Chapelle Impériale,** built in 1857 by Napoléon's nephew, Napoléon III, to accommodate the tombs of the Bonaparte family. (The great man himself is buried in the Hôtel des Invalides in Paris, however.) A Coptic crucifix taken from Egypt during the

general's 1798 campaign hangs over the main altar. *50 rue Fesch. Admission: 10 frs. Open Tues.–Sat. 10–12:30 and 3–7.*

❽ Next door is the island's finest art museum, the **Musée Fesch,** which houses what is considered the best collection of Italian paintings outside Florence and Paris. This is just part of a collection of 30,000 paintings bought up at bargain prices following the French Revolution by Napoléon's uncle, Cardinal Fesch, the archbishop of Lyon. Among the works are canvases by Bellini, Andrea de Firenza, and Botticelli. *50 rue Cardinal Fesch, tel. 95–21–48–17. Admission: 25 frs. Open Apr.–Oct., Wed.–Mon. 9:30–noon and 3–6:30 (also in July and Aug., Tues.–Sat. 9–midnight); Nov.–Mar., Wed.–Mon. 9:30–noon and 2:30–6.*

★ From Ajaccio you may want to take an organized one-day excursion to Corsica's most interesting archaeological site, **Filitosa,** which has the largest grouping of megalithic menhirs on the island. Bizarre, life-size stone figures of ancient warriors rise up mysteriously from the undulating terrain, many with images of human faces that have been eroded and flattened by time. A small museum on the site houses fascinating archaeological finds, including the menhir known as Scalsa Murta, whose delicately carved spine and rib cage make it difficult to believe the statue dates from some 3,000 years before the birth of Christ. During June, July, and August there are English-speaking guides to show you around. *Tel. 95–74–00–91. Admission: 25 frs. Open daily 8–7. Bus tour information from Ollandini Voyages, 3 pl. Général-de-Gaulle, tel. 95–21–10–12.*

Another excursion from Ajaccio takes you north along the coast to **Piana** (several buses a day make the three-hour trip). Piana is a drowsy little town that seems largely unexcited by its proximity to **Les Calanches,** the extraordinary pink and orange rock formations that are among Corsica's most memorable sights. Self-guided walking tours, which take about 50 minutes to complete, have been laid out among the rocks; look for signs for Château Fort (Stronghold) or Tête de Chien (Dog's Head) on the road between Piana and Porto to the northeast. Boat tours can also be arranged in Porto, whose tourist office will provide you with further information on Piana (tel. 95–26–10–55).

Lodging **Stella di Mare.** A low-slung, motel-style hotel built in the '60s, the
$ Stella di Mare is easygoing and friendly, fine for families and for those who want to spend most of their time outdoors on the white-sand beach. Frequent buses will take you into the center of town, about 10 minutes away. *Rte. des Iles Sanguinaires km 7, 20000, tel. 95–52–01–07, fax 95–52–08–69. 60 rooms with bath. Facilities: restaurant, bar, pool, nursery. AE, DC, MC, V. Closed Nov.–Easter.*

Dining **Le Point U.** Named for the spot it occupies at the point of merging
$$ streets, this attractive restaurant remains fiercely Corsican. Spe-
★ cialties include fish soup, roast lamb, duck with chestnuts, and cannelloni stuffed with brocciu cheese. Stone walls, red hardwood floors, and dramatic spot lighting create a modern ambience. *59 bis rue Cardinal Fesch, tel. 95–21–59–92. V. Closed Sun.*

$ **Restaurant de France.** A few blocks away from the old quarter, the France is popular with locals. The old-fashioned dining room, with starched white linens, serves up three-course menus featuring such fare as smoked salmon, steak with Roquefort sauce, and walnut torte at very good prices. Also available are Corsican specialties like wild boar stew and chestnut ice cream. *59 rue Cardinal Fesch, tel. 95–21–11–00. AE, DC, MC, V. Closed Sun. and Christmas week.*

Sartène

Two buses a day depart from the station in Ajaccio, stopping in Sartène and continuing on to Bonifacio and Porto-Vecchio. Tourist office: rue Borgo, tel. 95–77–15–40.

Often called the "most Corsican of all Corsican towns," **Sartène** dates from the 16th century and has survived pirate raids as well as bloody feuding among the town's families. The word *vendetta* comes from Sartène as a result of a notorious family feud, and centuries of fighting have left the town with a slightly spooky atmosphere.

As you draw near, a line of fortresslike granite houses rise in surly greeting. The most interesting part of town is **Vieux Sartène** (Old Sartène), surrounded by ancient ramparts. Cross the bridge from the bus station and walk up Sartène's only street to start your walking tour at the place de la Libération, the main square and town meeting place. To one side of the square is the **Hôtel de Ville,** the former Genoese governor's palace, which retains a decorative coat of arms. For a taste of the Middle Ages, slip through the tunnel in the building to place du Maggiu and the **old quarter of Santa Anna,** an eerie warren of narrow cobblestone streets lined with granite houses. Scarcely 100 yards from the Town Hall, down a steep and winding street, a **12th-century watchtower** stands out in sharp contrast to the modern apartment buildings behind.

Sartène is the center for research into Corsica's prehistory, due to its proximity to a region rich in dolmens and megalithic statues just to the south. For a look at some of the island's best prehistoric relics, stop by the **Musée Départemental de la Préhistoire Corse** in the town's former prison just outside the walls. *Rue Croce, tel. 95–77–01–09. Admission: 10 frs. Open Apr.–Oct., Mon.–Sat. 10–noon and 2–6; Nov.–Mar., weekdays 10–noon and 2–5.*

Bonifacio

Several buses a day connect Ajaccio and Bonifacio. Tourist office: place de l'Europe, tel. 95–73–11–88.

★ The ancient walled city of **Bonifacio** occupies a spectacular clifftop setting, with a handsome fjordlike harbor carved into the limestone cliffs at its feet. The southernmost town in France, it's just 13 km (8 mi) from Sardinia, and local speech is heavily influenced by the accent and idiom of the neighboring Italian island. Don't be surprised if you find the inhabitants difficult to understand—many Corsicans do too!

Established in the 12th century as Genoa's first Corsican stronghold against the Moors, Bonifacio remained Genoese through centuries of battles and sieges. (Throughout the village are circular silos that were used to hoard food and supplies needed to survive lengthy sieges.) As you wander the narrow streets of the **Haute-Ville** (Upper Village), inside the walls of the citadel, think of Homer's *Odyssey*. It was here, in the bottleneck harbor at Bonifacio, that Ulysses' fleet, according to classics scholars, was bombarded by the vicious Laestrygonians.

From the place d'Armes at the city gate, enter the **Bastion of the Standard,** where you can still see the system of weights and pulleys used to pull up the drawbridge. The chambers of the former garrison now house life-size dioramas from Bonifacio's history. One depicts the visit in 1541 of Emperor Charles V. A local nobleman lent the emperor his best horse to ride from the Gulf of Santa Manza into the center of town. After Charles arrived and dismounted, the man took out a pistol and shot the horse dead, reasoning that the horse could never have another rider that would equal the emperor in greatness. *Admission: 15 frs. Open June 15–Sept. 15, daily 9–7.*

In the center of the maze of cobblestone streets that makes up the citadel you'll find the 12th- to 13th-century church of **Ste-Marie-Majeure,** with buttresses attaching it to surrounding houses. Inside the church, look for the Renaissance baptismal font, carved in bas relief, and a white marble Roman sarcophagus that dates from the 3rd century. Walk around the back to see the loggia, built above a huge water cistern, where town elders once held court and dispensed justice.

Lodging and Dining
$$

La Caravelle. This quayside restaurant opening onto Bonifacio's mast-filled port specializes in seafood (particularly shellfish), as well as dishes with a decidedly Italian accent. The food is prepared by Madame Filippeddu and served by her son. The hotel next door is operated under different management, but it offers comfortable rooms, most with unbeatable harbor views. *37 quai Comparetti, tel. 95–73–00–03. 30 rooms with bath. Facilities: restaurant. MC, V. Closed Oct.–Easter.*

Dining
$
★

Les 4 Vents. An informal, family-style place with kids and dogs running underfoot and bright flowers tumbling from a wooden balcony in the dining room, this friendly restaurant is popular with the yachting crowd. In winter the kitchen serves up such Alsatian specialties as sauerkraut and sausages, but it concentrates on barbecued fish and meats in summer. Typical Corsican dishes change daily, but they are always cheap, delicious, and filling. *29 quai Banda del Ferro, tel. 95–73–07–50. Reservations advised weekends. No credit cards. Closed Tues.*

$

Restaurant du Pêcheur. This tiny place has only six tables, and people often line up on the sidewalk for a chance to dine at the most authentic seafood spot in town. True to its name, the restaurant is run by fishermen who serve the catch of the day straight from the sea. There's no written menu, but you can ask to see what's available. *14 rue Doria, tel. 95–73–12–56. No reservations. No credit cards. Closed Oct.–Easter.*

Porto-Vecchio

Two buses a day depart from Ajaccio, stopping in Sartène and continuing on to Bonifacio and Porto-Vecchio. Tourist office: place de l'Hôtel-de-Ville, tel. 95–70–03–72.

Third largest of Corsica's cities, **Porto-Vecchio** triples its population in summer, when bathers, sun worshipers, and windsurfers arrive, predominantly from Italy. Founded in 1539 as a Genoan stronghold, Porto-Vecchio has its historic stone corners but is primarily popular as a jumping-off point for spectacular nearby beaches. South of town are the strands of **Palombaggia** and **Golfe de Santa Giulia,** while to the north the bays of San Ciprianu and Pinarello lead up to the **Côte des Nacres,** a series of long, sandy beaches that settle into Corsica's eastern flats.

Corte

The hub of Corsica's rail system, Corte is just 90 minutes by train from Bastia, Ajaccio, and Calvi. (Hikers may want to stop at villages with direct access to trails, such as Vizzavona, Vivario, or Riventosa.) Bonifacio can be reached from Corte by a high-speed bus (2½ hours) that travels down the flat, straight highway of Corsica's eastern coast, a much more comfortable ride than the Ajaccio–Bonifacio route. Tourist office: La Citadelle, tel. 95–46–24–20.

Corte, spectacularly sited among cliffs and gorges at the confluence of the Tavignano, Restonica, and Orta rivers, is the spiritual heart and soul of Corsica (if there is one). It was the capital of Pasquale Paoli's government from 1755 to 1769 and where he established the

Corsican University in 1765. Closed by the French in 1769, the university, always a symbol of Corsican identity, was reopened in 1981 and now has more than 2,000 students.

To reach the upper town, from where the 15th-century château looks out over the rivers, walk up the cobblestone ramp from place Pasquale-Paoli (a five-minute walk from the bus and train stations) to the lovely **place Gaffori.** Here are several cafés and restaurants, and the bullet-pocked house where the Corsican hero Gian Pietro Gaffori and his wife, Faustina, held off the Genoans in 1750. Continue up, passing under a beautiful stone archway, to the Palais National (open weekdays 2–6) and the **Citadelle.** This Vauban-style fortress (1769–1778) is built around the château—the "Eagle's Nest"—the original, 15th-century fortification, at the highest point of the cliff; it also houses the **Musée de la Corse,** with exhibits on the island's history and ethnography. *Tel. 95–61–00–61. Admission: 20 frs adults, 10 frs children. Open weekdays 9–6.*

Walk left along the Citadelle wall to the belvedere for an unforgettable view of the river junction and the Genoan bridge below, the tiny watch tower of the Citadelle above, and the mountains behind. Now follow the cobblestones down, bearing right at the St-Théophile chapel through the Quartier de Chiostra. To the left is a minuscule patio with an excellent pottery shop. Over the door to the left is a small stone carving said to be a prehistoric goddess of fertility. Don't miss the flying stone staircase sticking out of the opposite wall; it looks precarious, but the treads are seated about 31 inches into the stone wall. Continue down to the ramp back to place Pasquale-Paoli.

Corte is an ideal starting point for exploring interior Corsica's soaring mountains, plentiful streams, and quiet alpine pastures. Hiking is popular all along the spine of the island; a favorite excursion is to the Restonica Gorge and lakes above Corte.

Lodging and Dining

$ **Auberge de la Restonica–Hôtel Dominique Colonna.** This fine auberge and restaurant, known for its cuisine, has inaugurated a sister establishment across the parking lot. The seven rooms in the original building, rather like a hunting lodge, are now joined by 28 modern double rooms in the functional but pleasant new hotel. The Normandy-born chef, David Verger, has a light nouvelle touch with powerful Corsican ingredients, and owner Dominique "Dumé" Colonna, one of France's all-time soccer stars, is a gracious host. You'll fall asleep at night to the soothing sound of the Restonica torrent rushing by. Ask for one of the more rustic rooms in the auberge. *Vallée de la Restonica, 20250, tel. (auberge) 95–46–20–13; (hotel) 95–61–03–91; fax 95–61–03–91; (restaurant) 95–46–09–58. 35 rooms with bath. Facilities: restaurant. AE, DC, MC, V.*

¢–$ **Le Refuge.** Two kilometers (3 miles) west of Corte up the Restonica River gorge, this simple, casual inn offers rooms and *table d'hôte* (home cooking served at a communal table) at more than reasonable rates. The views over the cascading Restonica are superb; and the nights are cool in summer. *Vallée de la Restonica, 20250, tel. 95–46–09–13. MC, V. Closed Oct.–May.*

12 Provence

*Including
Avignon and Marseille*

Away from the Riviera, the coastal part of the province described in Chapter 13, Provence offers ideal possibilities for memorable travel on a tight budget. Quite apart from the vineyards, olive groves, Roman remains, and near-permanent sunshine that form a backcloth accessible to all, it is a very practical region to visit: Excellent rail service (supplemented by regular buses) links major towns to country villages, and the distances involved are relatively minor. Marseille provides big-city bustle in a breathtaking setting between rocky hills and the Mediterranean, and Avignon, Arles, and Aix, along with Nîmes nearby in Languedoc, all have plenty to see yet are small enough to visit on foot.

Located in the south of France, bordered by Italy to the east and the blue waters of the Mediterranean, the area was known by the Romans as Provincia—the Province—for it was the first part of Gaul they occupied. Roman remains litter the ground in well-preserved profusion. The theater and triumphal arch at Orange, the amphitheater at Nîmes, the aqueduct at Pont-du-Gard, and the mausoleum at St-Rémy-de-Provence are considered the best of their kind in existence.

Provençal life continues at an old-fashioned pace. Hot afternoons tend to mean siestas, with signs of life discernible only as the shadows under the *platanes* (plane trees) start to lengthen and lethargic locals saunter out to play *boules* (the French version of bocce) and drink long, cooling *pastis*, an anise-based aperitif.

Provence means dazzling light and rugged, rocky countryside, interspersed with vineyards, fields of lavender, and olive groves. Any Provençal market provides a glimpse of the bewildering variety of olives and herbs cultivated, and the local cuisine is pungently spiced with thyme, rosemary, basil, and garlic.

The famous mistral—a fierce, cold wind that races through the Rhône Valley—is another feature of Provence. It's claimed that the extensive network of expressways has lessened the mistral's effect, but you may have trouble believing this as the wind whistles around your ears. Thankfully, clear blue skies usually follow in its wake.

Provence Basics

Budget Lodging
Accommodations are varied in this much-visited part of France, ranging from luxurious *mas* (converted farmhouses) to modest downtown hotels convenient for sightseeing. Service is often less than prompt, a casualty of the sweltering summer heat. Reservations are essential for much of the year, and many hotels are closed during winter.

Budget Dining
There's a lot to be said for simple Provençal food on a vine-shaded terrace. Have a pale green *pastis* as an aperitif with savory local black olives, or try the *tapenade*, a delicious paste of capers, anchovies, olives, oil, and lemon juice, best smeared on chunks of garlic-rubbed bread. Follow it up with crudités served with aïoli and a simple dish of grilled lamb or beef, accompanied by a bottle of chilled rosé. Locals like to end their meal with a round of goat cheese and fruit.

A trip to the fish market at Marseille will reveal the astronomical price of the fresh local catch; in the Mediterranean there are too few fish chased by too many boats. Steer clear of the multitude of cheap Marseille fish restaurants; any inexpensive fish menu must use frozen imports. The Marseille specialty of bouillabaisse is a case in point: Once a fisherman's cheap stew of spanking-fresh specimens too small or bony to put on sale, it has now become a celebration dish, with such heretical additions as lobster. The high-priced versions can be delicious, but avoid the cheaper ones, undoubtedly concocted with canned, frozen, and even powdered ingredients.

Bargain Shopping
Santons, painted clay figures traditionally placed around a Christmas crèche, make excellent gifts or souvenirs and can be found throughout the region. The hundreds of characters range from Mary, Joseph, and the Wise Men to fictional characters and notable personalities, both historic and contemporary. Two specialties of Aix-en-Provence are deliciously fragrant soaps with natural floral scents, and *calissons d'Aix*, ingeniously sculpted marzipan. Beautiful, delicately patterned Provençal fabrics made by Souleïado can be bought in lengths or already fashioned into dresses, scarves, and other items. You can find the prints in better-quality shops throughout the region, though Arles and Aix-en-Provence seem to have cornered most of the market.

Biking
Bikes can be rented from train stations at Aix-en-Provence, Arles, Avignon, Marseille, Montpellier, Nîmes, and Orange; the cost is about 55 frs per day. Contact the **Comité Départemental de la Fédération Française de Cyclo** (2 rue Lavoisier, Avignon) for a list of the area's more scenic bike paths.

Hiking
Contact the **Comité Départemental de Tourisme** (pl. Campagna, B.P. 147, 84008 Avignon) for a detailed list of blazed trails (marked by discreet paint splashes) and outfitters.

Beaches
Marseille has a large artificial beach (the sand was imported from elsewhere) with good facilities, and there are narrow sandy beaches on either side of Toulon (west at Bandol and Sanary, east at Hyères). Cliffs dominate the coastline east of Marseille, and access to the sea is often difficult.

Festivals
The summer music and drama festivals at Aix-en-Provence, Arles, Avignon, and Orange attract top performers. At Aix, the **International Arts and Music Festival,** with first-class opera, symphonic concerts, and chamber music, flourishes from mid-July to mid-August; its principal venue is the Théâtre de l'Archevêché in the court-

yard of the Archbishop's Palace (pl. des Martyrs de la Résistance). At Arles, the **Music and Drama Festival** takes place in July in the Théâtre Antique (rue de la Calade/rue du Cloître). Avignon's prestigious **International Music and Drama Festival,** held during the last three weeks of July, is centered on the Grand Courtyard of the Palais des Papes (pl. du Palais, tel. 90–82–67–08). The **International Opera Festival** in Orange, during the last two weeks of July, takes place in the best-preserved Roman theater in existence, the Théâtre Antique (pl. des Frères-Mounet).

Tour 1: Roman Provence

This tour takes the form of a triangle, with three base towns. From Avignon, you'll take a short rail trip north to Orange; from Nîmes, ride the bus northeast to the Pont du Gard aqueduct and east to Tarascon; and from Arles, travel by bus northeast to Les Baux and St-Rémy.

From Paris TGVs to Avignon leave Paris (Gare de Lyon) 6 times daily. The trip
By Train takes a bit less than 4 hours.

By Car The 690-kilometer (430-mile) drive to Avignon from Paris via A6 and A7 takes about 6½ hours.

Avignon

Tourist office: 41 cours Jean-Jaurès, 400 yards down from the station, tel. 90–82–65–11.

Numbers in the margin correspond with points of interest on the Avignon map.

A warren of medieval alleys nestling behind a protective ring of chunky towers, **Avignon** is possibly best known for the Pont St-Bénezet, immortalized in a nursery rhyme. No one dances across the bridge these days, however—it was amputated in midstream in the 17th century, when a cataclysmic storm washed half of it away. Still, Avignon has lots to offer, starting with the Palais des Papes (Papal Palace), where seven exiled popes camped between 1309 and 1377 after fleeing from the corruption of Rome. Avignon remained papal property until 1791, and elegant mansions and a late-18th-century population of 80,000 bear witness to the town's former prosperity.

★ ❶ Avignon's main street, rue de la République, leads from the station and tourist office past shops and cafés to place de l'Horloge and place du Palais, site of the colossal **Palais des Papes.** This "palace" creates a disconcertingly fortresslike impression, underlined by the austerity of its interior decor; most of the furnishings were dispersed during the French Revolution. Some imagination is required to picture it in medieval splendor, awash with color and with worldly clerics enjoying what the 14th-century Italian poet Petrarch called "licentious banquets."

On close inspection, two different styles of building emerge: the severe **Palais Vieux** (Old Palace), built between 1334 and 1342 by Pope Benedict XII, a member of the Cistercian order, which frowned on frivolity, and the more decorative **Palais Nouveau** (New Palace), built in the following decade by the arty, extravagant Pope Clement VI. The Great Court, where visitors arrive, links the two.

The main rooms of the Palais Vieux are the consistory (council hall), decorated with some excellent 14th-century frescoes by Simone Martini; the Chapelle St-Jean, with original frescoes by Matteo Giovanetti; the Grand Tinel, or Salle des Festins, with a majestic vaulted roof and a series of 18th-century Gobelin tapestries; the Chapelle St-Martial, which has more Matteo frescoes; the Chambre du Cerf, with a richly decorated ceiling, murals featuring a stag

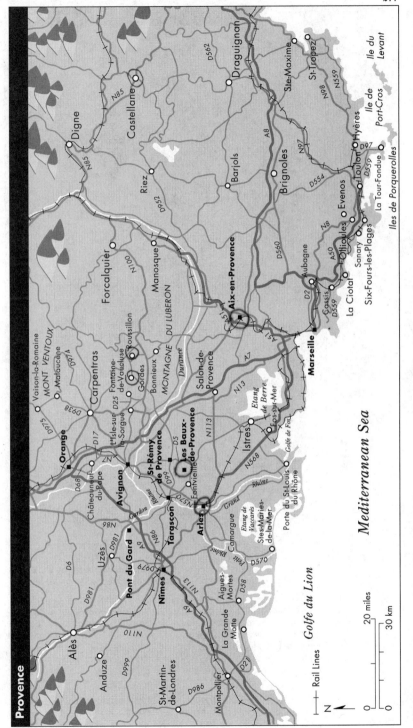

Provence

Mont Ventoux · Malaucène · Vaison-la-Romaine · D975 · Orange · Châteauneuf-du-Pape · D68 · Avignon · D17 · L'Isle-sur-la-Sorgue · D938 · Carpentras · Fontaine-de-Vaucluse · D25 · Gordes · Roussillon · Bonnieux · MONTAGNE DU LUBERON · Forcalquier · N100 · Manosque · Digne · N85 · Riez · D952 · Castellane · N85 · Draguignan · D562

Alès · N110 · Anduze · D907 · D6 · Uzès · D981 · St-Martin-de-Londres · D986 · Montpellier · D21 · La Grande Motte · Aigues-Mortes · D58 · Nîmes · N113 · A9 · D979 · Pont du Gard · 98N · N86 · Tarascon · St-Rémy-de-Provence · Les Baux-de-Provence · D5 · Fontvieille · D99 · Arles · N570 · Camargue · Grand Rhône · Petit Rhône · Stes-Maries-de-la-Mer · D570 · Etang de Vaccarès · Porte du St-Louis du Rhône

Salon-de-Provence · N113 · Istres · N568 · Etang de Berre · Fos-sur-Mer · Golfe de Fos · Aix-en-Provence · A51 · A7 · N13 · Marseille · A50 · Aubagne · D2 · Cassis · La Ciotat · D559 · Bandol · Sanary · Six-Fours-les-Plages · Ollioules · N8 · Evenos · Toulon · N97 · La Tour-Fondue · Hyères · D97 · D559 · N559 · St-Tropez · Ste-Maxime · N98 · A8 · Brignoles · D554 · Barjols · D560

Mediterranean Sea

Golfe du Lion

Ile du Levant · Ile de Port-Cros · Iles de Porquerolles

N

├── Rail Lines

20 miles

30 km

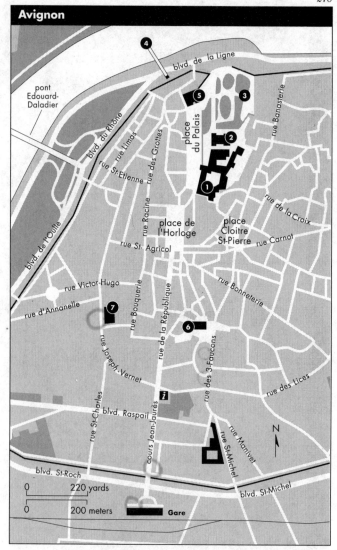

hunt, and a delightful view of Avignon; the Chambre de Parement
(papal antechamber); and the Chambre à Coucher (papal bedchamber).

The principal attractions of the Palais Nouveau are the Grande Audience, a magnificent two-naved hall on the ground floor, and, upstairs, the Chapelle Clémentine, where the college of cardinals
gathered to elect the new pope. *Pl. du Palais-des-Papes. Admission: 45 frs adults, 34 frs students. Guided tours only Mar.–Oct.
Open Easter–Sept., daily 9–7; Oct.–Easter, daily 9–12:30 and 2–6.*

2 The 12th-century **cathedral** nearby contains the Gothic tomb of Pope
3 John XII. Beyond is the **Rocher des Doms**, a large, attractive garden
4 offering fine views of Avignon, the Rhône, and the celebrated **Pont
St-Bénezet**—built, according to legend, by a local shepherd named
Bénezet in the 12th century. The first bridge to span the Rhône at
Avignon, it was originally 900 yards long. Though only half of the
bridge remains, it's worth strolling along for the views and a visit to

the tiny Chapelle St-Nicolas, which juts out over the river. *Tel. 90–85–60–16. Admission: 10 frs adults, 5 frs children. Open Apr.–Sept., daily 9–6:30; Oct.–Mar., Tues.–Sun. 9–1 and 2–5.*

❺ The medieval **Petit Palais,** between the bridge and the Rocher des Doms, was once home to cardinals and archbishops. Nowadays it contains an outstanding collection of Old Masters, led by the Italian schools of Venice, Siena, and Florence (note Sandro Botticelli's *Virgin and Child). 21 pl. du Palais, tel. 90–86–44–58. Admission: 20 frs adults, 10 frs children; free Sun. in winter. Open Wed.–Mon. 9:30–noon and 2–6.*

Double back past the Papal Palace and venture into the narrow, winding, shop-lined streets of old Avignon. Halfway down rue de la
❻ République is the **Musée Lapidaire,** which displays a variety of archaeological finds—including the remains of Avignon's Arc de Triomphe—in a sturdy 17th-century Baroque chapel fronted by an imposing facade. *27 rue de la République, tel. 90–85–75–38. Admission: 5 frs adults. Open Wed.–Mon. 10–noon and 2–6.*

Cross rue de la République and turn right onto rue Joseph-Vernet.
❼ A few minutes' walk will lead you to the **Musée Calvet,** an 18th-century town house featuring an extensive collection of mainly French paintings from the 16th century on; highlights include works by Théodore Géricault, Camille Corot, Edouard Manet, Raoul Dufy, Maurice de Vlaminck, and the Italian artist Amedeo Modigliani. Greek, Roman, and Etruscan statuettes are also displayed. *65 rue Joseph-Vernet, tel. 90–86–33–84. Admission free. Open Wed.–Mon. 10–6.*

Lodging **Médiéval.** As the building dates from the 17th century, the name of
$ this hotel is almost appropriate; its antique decor seems right at home among the narrow streets behind St-Pierre church. Rooms overlooking the street are predictably on the dark side; try for one overlooking the pretty patio-garden. *15 rue de la Petite-Saunerie, 84000, tel. 90–86–11–06, fax 90–82–08–64. 20 rooms, some with shower. MC, V. Closed Jan.–Feb.*

$ **Mignon.** Near the top of rue Joseph-Vernet, close to St-Agricol church, the small, cheerful Mignon provides excellent value in a hotel so central—rates start at just 175 frs. *12 rue Joseph-Vernet, 84000, tel. 90–82–17–30. 15 rooms, some with shower. Facilities: boutique. MC, V.*

Dining **Hiély-Lucullus.** According to most authorities, this establishment
$$ numbers among the top 50 restaurants in France. The upstairs din-
★ ing room, run with aplomb by Madame Hiély, has a quiet, dignified charm. Chef André Chaussy's delights include crayfish tails in scrambled eggs hidden inside a puff-pastry case. Save room for the extensive cheese board. The prices, often moderate enough for a budgeting traveler, are an additional plus (have the 220-franc set menu). *5 rue de la République, tel. 90–86–17–07. Reservations required. AE, MC, V. Closed Mon., Tues., most of Jan., and last 2 wks in June.*

$–$$ **Le Petit Bedon.** Locals flock to this cheerful restaurant 300 yards from the station to sample Jean Férigoule's hearty cuisine: Try the liver and veal sweetbreads or the burbot fricassee in red wine sauce. The 105-franc lunch menu is a particularly good value (the evening menu costs 160 frs). *70 rue Joseph-Vernet, tel. 90–82–33–98. MC, V. Closed Mon. eve. Sun., and second half of Aug.*

Orange

Trains to Orange make the 15-minute trip north from Avignon at least every 2 hours. Tourist office: cours Aristide-Briand, tel. 90–34–70–88.

Orange is a small, pleasant town that sinks into total siesta somnolence during hot afternoons but, at other times, buzzes with visitors who are keen on admiring its Roman remains. Allow for a 10-minute walk from the station to the town center. Take avenue Frédéric-Mistral to avenue Fabre (which becomes rue de la République); turn left and you'll soon come to place de la République in the heart of town.

★ The magnificent, semicircular **Théâtre Antique,** just south of place de la République, is the best-preserved ancient theater. It was built just before the birth of Christ, to the same dimensions as that of Arles. Orange's theater, however, has a mighty screen wall, more than 100 yards long and 120 feet high, and steeply climbing terraces carved into the hillside. Seven thousand spectators can crowd in, and regularly do, for open-air concerts and operatic performances; the acoustics are superb. This is the only Roman theater that still possesses its original Imperial statue, of Caesar Augustus, which stands in the middle of the screen. At nearly 12 feet, it's one of the tallest Roman statues in existence. *Pl. des Frères-Mounet, tel. 90–34–70–88. Admission: 25 frs adults, 20 frs students and senior citizens; joint ticket with Musée Municipal. Open Apr.–Oct., daily 9–6:30; Nov.–Mar., daily 9–noon and 1:30–5.*

The **Parc de la Colline St-Eutrope,** the banked garden behind the theater, yields a fine view of the theater and of the 6,000-foot Mont Ventoux to the east. Walk up cours Aristide-Briand, turn right at the top, then left immediately after to the venerable **Arc de Triomphe**—composed of a large central arch flanked by two smaller ones, the whole topped by a massive entablature. The 70-foot arch, the third-highest Roman arch still standing, towered over the old Via Agrippa between Arles and Lyon and was probably built around AD 25 in honor of the Gallic Wars. The carvings on the north side depict the legionnaires' battles with the Gauls and Caesar's naval showdown with the ships of Marseille. Today the arch presides over a busy traffic circle.

Dining
$
★
Le Pigraillet. One of Orange's best lunch spots is Le Pigraillet, on the Chemin Colline St-Eutrope at the far end of the gardens. You may want to eat in the garden, but most diners seek shelter from the mistral in the glassed-in terrace. The modern cuisine includes crab ravioli, foie gras in port, and duck breast in the muscat wine of nearby Beaumes-de-Venise. Prices, which start in the moderate range, go high enough to raise your check if you don't watch it. *Chemin de la Colline St-Eutrope, tel. 90–34–44–25. Reservations advised. MC, V.*

$ **Le Yaka.** Wood beams, old stonework, and fresh flowers on the tables give Le Yaka more character than most of the restaurants in touristy Orange. There is plenty of choice, ranging from liver pâté with onion jam to leg of lamb au gratin with olive purée or pork fillet with lemon. An appetizing dessert trolley rounds off the meal—try the chocolate cake. *24 pl. Sylvain, tel. 90–34–70–03. MC, V. Closed Tues. eve., Wed., and Nov.*

Nîmes

Trains run from Avignon southwest to Nîmes most hours and take around 25 minutes. Tourist office: 6 rue Auguste, tel. 66–67–29–11.

Numbers in the margins correspond with points of interest on the Nîmes map.

★ Few towns have preserved such visible links with their Roman past as **Nîmes.** Nemausus, as the town was then known, grew to prominence during the reign of Caesar Augustus (27 BC–AD 14) and still boasts a Roman amphitheater (Arènes), temple (Maison Carrée), and watchtower (Tour Magne). Luckily, these monuments emerged relatively unscathed from the cataclysmic flash flood that devastated Nîmes in 1988, leaving thousands homeless.

Head straight down avenue de Feuchère from the station, then spin left around the esplanade de Gaulle to reach place des Arènes, site of ❶ the **Arènes,** more than 140 yards long and 110 yards wide, with a seating capacity of 21,000. A smaller version of the Colosseum in Rome, the arena is considered the world's best-preserved Roman amphitheater. Despite its checkered history—it was transformed into a fortress by the Visigoths and used for housing in medieval times—the amphitheater has been restored to most of its original splendor. A roof has even been installed to facilitate its current use for theatrical performances, tennis matches, and bullfights. *Blvd. Victor-Hugo, tel. 66–67–45–76. Admission: 22 frs adults, 16 frs students; joint ticket to Tour Magne: 30 frs adults, 21 frs students. Open mid-June–mid-Sept., daily 8–8; mid-Sept.–Oct. and Apr.–mid-June, daily 9–noon and 2–6; Nov.–Mar., daily 9–noon and 2–5.*

❷ Take rue de la Cité-Foulc behind the Arènes to the **Musée des Beaux-Arts,** where you can admire a vast Roman mosaic discovered in Nîmes during the last century; the marriage ceremony depicted in the center of the mosaic provides intriguing insights into the Roman aristocratic lifestyle. Old Masters (Nicolas Poussin, Pieter Brueghel, Peter Paul Rubens) and sculpture (Auguste Rodin and his pupil Emile Bourdelle) form the mainstay of the collection. *Rue de la Cité-Foulc, tel. 66–67–38–21. Admission: 22 frs adults, 16 frs students. Open Tues.–Sat. 9:30–12:30 and 2–6, Sun. and Mon. 2–6.*

Return to the Arènes and turn right along boulevard de la Libération, which soon becomes boulevard de l'Amiral-Courbet. A hun-❸ dred and fifty yards down on the left is the **Musée Archéologique et d'Histoire Naturelle,** rich in local archaeological finds, mainly statues, busts, friezes, tools, glass, and pottery. It also houses an extensive collection of Greek, Roman, and medieval coins. *Blvd. de l'Amiral-Courbet, tel. 66–67–25–57. Admission: 22 frs adults, 16 frs students. Open Tues.–Sun. 11–6.*

Turn right onto Grand' Rue behind the museum, then take the sec-❹ ond left up toward the **cathedral.** This uninspired 19th-century reconstruction is of less interest than either the surrounding ❺ pedestrian streets or the **Musée du Vieux Nîmes** (Museum of Old Nîmes), opposite the cathedral in the 17th-century Bishop's Palace. Embroidered garments and woolen shawls fill the rooms in an exotic and vibrant display. Nîmes used to be a cloth-manufacturing center and lent its name to what has become one of the world's most popular fabrics, denim (*de Nîmes*—from Nîmes). Two rooms contain colorful, sometimes grisly, exhibits on the regional sport of bullfighting. *Pl. aux Herbes, tel. 66–36–00–64. Admission: 22 frs adults, 16 frs students. Open Tues.–Sun. 11–6.*

Head right from the cathedral along rue des Halles, then left down ❻ rue du Général-Perrier, to reach the **Maison Carrée.** Despite its name ("square house"), this Roman temple dating from the 1st century AD is oblong. Transformed down the ages into a stable, a private dwelling, a town hall, and a church, the building is now a museum that contains an imposing statue of Apollo and other antiquities. The exquisite carvings along the cornice and on the Corinthian capitals rank as some of the finest in Roman architecture. Thomas Jefferson admired the Maison Carrée's chaste lines of columns so much that he had them copied for the Virginia state capitol at Richmond. *Blvd. Victor-Hugo. Admission free. Open mid-June–mid-Sept., daily 9–7; mid-Sept.–Oct. and Apr.–mid-June, daily 9–noon and 2–6; Nov.–Mar., daily 9–noon and 2–5.*

❼ Opposite the Maison Carrée is the **Carrée d'Art,** a swanky contemporary art museum that opened in 1993, showcasing international pictures and sculpture from 1960 onward. *Pl. de la Maison Carrée, tel.*

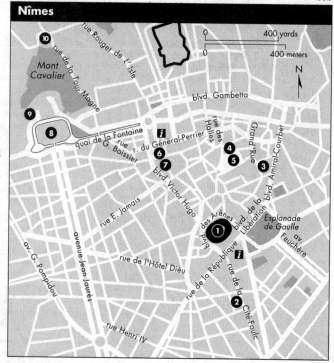

Nîmes

66–76–35–35. Admission: 22 frs adults, 16 frs students. Open Tues.–Sun. 10–6.

⑧ Rue Molière and rue Gaston-Boissier lead from the Maison Carrée to the **Jardin de la Fontaine.** This elaborate formal garden was land-scaped on the site of the Roman baths in the 18th century, when the Source de Nemausus, a once-sacred spring, was channeled into **⑨** pools and a canal. Close by is a Roman ruin known as the **Temple of ⑩ Diana,** and at the far end of the garden is the **Tour Magne**—a stumpy tower probably used as a lookout post, which, despite having lost 30 feet in the course of time, still provides fine views of Nîmes for any-one who is energetic enough to climb the 140 steps to the top. *Quai de la Fontaine, tel. 66–67–65–56. Admission to Tour Magne: 12 frs adults, 10 frs students; joint ticket as described above at Les Arènes. Open mid-June–mid-Sept., daily 9–7; mid-Sept.–Oct. and Apr.– mid-June, daily 9–noon and 2–6; Nov.–Mar., daily 9–noon and 2–5.*

Lodging and Dining
$$
★
Louvre. In a 17th-century house on a leafy square near the Roman arena, the Louvre is the best sort of carefully run provincial hotel. The guest rooms are spacious and have high ceilings, and they man-age to retain the feel of a private house; ask for one that faces the courtyard. The restaurant, which caters only to guests of the hotel and to groups, serves well-prepared traditional cuisine. Seafood ad-dicts will enjoy the lobster or the mussels in a flaky pastry crust. *2 sq. de la Couronne, 30000, tel. 66–67–22–75. 33 rooms with bath. Facilities: restaurant. AE, DC, MC, V.*

Dining
¢
★
Nicolas. Locals have long known about this homey place, which is al-ways packed; you'll hear the noise before you open the door. A friendly, frazzled staff serves up delicious *bourride* (a garlicky fish soup) and other local specialties—all at unbelievably low prices. *1 rue Poise, tel. 66–67–50–47. Reservations advised. MC, V. Closed Mon., 1st 2 wks July, and mid-Dec.–1st wk Jan.*

Pont du Gard

Eight buses make the ½-hour trip daily northeast from Nîmes.

★ The **Pont du Gard** is a huge, three-tiered aqueduct erected 2,000 years ago as part of a 48-kilometer (30-mile) system for supplying water to Roman Nîmes. It is astonishingly well preserved. Its setting, spanning a rocky gorge 150 feet above the River Gardon, is nothing less than spectacular. There is no entry fee or guide, and at certain times you can have it all to yourself: Early morning is best, when the honey-colored stone gleams in the sunlight. The best way to gauge the full majesty of the Pont du Gard is to walk right along the top.

Tarascon

Trains make the 15-minute run east from Nîmes at least every 1½ hours.

Tarascon was once home of the mythical Tarasque, a monster that would emerge from the Rhône to gobble children and cattle. Luckily St. Martha, washed up with the three Maries at Stes-Maries-de-la-Mer, allegedly tamed the beast with a sprinkle of holy water, after which the inhabitants clobbered it senseless and slashed it to pieces. This dramatic event is celebrated on the last Sunday in June with a colorful parade.

Ever since the 12th century, Tarascon has possessed a formidable **castle** to protect it from any beast or man that might be tempted to emulate the Tarasque's fiendish deeds. The castle's massive stone walls, towering 150 feet above the rocky banks of the Rhône, are among the most daunting in France, so it's not surprising that the castle was used as a prison for centuries. Since 1926, however, the chapels, vaulted royal apartments, and stone carvings of the interior have been restored to less-intimidating glory. *Admission: 26 frs adults, 18 frs senior citizens, 10 frs students. Open July and Aug., daily 9–7; Sept.–June, daily 9–noon and 2–5.*

Arles

Trains run every 2 hours to Arles from Tarascon, 20 minutes north, and from Nîmes, 25 minutes northwest. Tourist office: esplanade Charles-de-Gaulle, tel. 98–18–41–20.

The first inhabitants of **Arles** were probably the Greeks, who arrived from Marseille in the 6th century BC. The Romans, however, left a stronger mark, constructing the theater and amphitheater that remain Arles's biggest tourist attractions. Arles used to be a thriving port before the Mediterranean receded over what is now the Camargue, a marshy realm of birds and beasts, pink flamingos and wild horses. It was also the site of the southernmost bridge over the Rhône, and became a commercial crossroads; merchants from as far afield as Arabia, Assyria, and Africa would linger here to do business on their way from Rome to Spain or northern Europe.

Vincent van Gogh produced much of his best work—and chopped off his ear—in Arles during a frenzied 15-month spell (1888–90) just before his suicide at age 37. Unfortunately, the houses he lived in are no longer standing—they were destroyed during World War II—but part of one of his most famous subjects remains: the **Pont de Trinquetaille** across the Rhône. Van Gogh's rendering of the bridge, painted in 1888, was auctioned a century later for $20 million.

Local art museums such as the **Musée Réattu**, 300 yards from the bridge along quai Marx-Dormoy, can't compete with that type of bidding—which is one reason none of Van Gogh's works are displayed here. Another is that Arles failed to appreciate Van Gogh; he was jeered at and eventually packed off to the nearest lunatic asylum. To add insult to injury, Jacques Réattu, after whom the museum is named, was a local painter of dazzling mediocrity. His works fill three rooms, but of much greater interest is the collection of modern drawings and paintings by Pablo Picasso, Fernand Léger, and Maurice de Vlaminck, as well as the photography section containing images by some of the field's leading names. *Rue du Grand-Prieuré, tel. 90–49–37–58. Admission: 15 frs; passport to all monuments and museums: 55 frs adults, 35 frs students. Open June–Sept., daily 9:30–7; Nov.–Mar., daily 10–12:30 and 2–5; Apr.–May and Oct., daily 9:30–12:30 and 2–6.*

The museum facade, facing the Rhône, dates from the Middle Ages and formed part of a 15th-century priory. Beside it are the ruins of the **Palais Constantin,** site of Provence's largest Roman baths, the **Thèrmes de la Trouille.** *Entrance on rue Dominique-Maisto. Admission: 12 frs adults, 7 frs students; joint ticket as above. Same opening times as above.*

Most of the significant sights and museums in Arles are set well away from the Rhône. The most notable is the 26,000-capacity ★ **Arènes,** built in the 1st century AD to showcase circuses and to-the-death gladiator combats. The amphitheater is 150 yards long and as wide as a football field, with each of its two stories composed of 60 arches; the original top tier has long since crumbled, and the three square towers were added in the Middle Ages. Climb to the upper story for some satisfying views across the town and countryside. Despite its venerable age, the amphitheater still sees a lot of action, mainly Sunday-afternoon bullfights. *Rond-Point des Arènes. Admission: 15 frs adults, 9 frs students; joint ticket as above. Open June–Sept., daily 8:30–7; Nov.–Mar., daily 9–noon and 2–4:30; Apr.–May and Oct., daily 9–12:30 and 2–6:30.*

Just 100 yards from the Arènes are the scanty remains of Arles's **Théâtre Antique;** the bits of marble column scattered around the grassy enclosure hint poignantly at the theater's onetime grandeur. The capacity may have shrunk from 7,000 to a few hundred, but the orchestra pit and a few tiers of seats are still used for the city's Music and Drama festival each July. *Rue du Cloître, tel. 90–96–93–30 for ticket information. Admission: 15 frs adults, 9 frs students; joint ticket as above. Open June–Sept., daily 8:30–7; Nov.–Mar., daily 9–noon and 2–4:30; Apr.–May and Oct., daily 9–12:30 and 2–6:30.*

Follow rue de la Calade to place de la République. To the left is the church of **St-Trophime,** dating mainly from the 11th and 12th centuries; subsequent additions have not spoiled its architectural harmony. Take time to admire the accomplished 12th-century sculptures flanking the main portal, featuring the Last Judgment, the apostles, the Nativity, and various saints. There are other well-crafted sculptures in the cloisters. *Rue de l'Hôtel-de-Ville, tel. 90–49–36–36. Admission to cloisters: 15 frs adults, 9 frs students; joint ticket as above. Open June–Sept., daily 8:30–7; Nov.–Mar., daily 9–noon and 2–4:30; Apr.–May and Oct., daily 9–12:30 and 2–6:30.*

Opposite St-Trophime is the **Musée d'Art Païen** (Museum of Pagan Art), housed in a former church next to the 17th-century Hôtel de Ville. The "pagan art" displays encompass Roman statues, busts, mosaics, and a white marble sarcophagus. You'll also see a copy of the famous statue the *Venus of Arles*; Sun King Louis XIV waltzed off to the Louvre with the original. *Pl. de la République. Admission: 12 frs adults, 7 frs students; joint ticket as above. Open June–Sept., daily 8:30–7; Nov.–Mar., daily 9–noon and 2–4:30; Apr.–May and Oct., 9–12:30 and 2–6:30.*

Turn left alongside the Hôtel de Ville onto plan de la Cour. A hundred yards down, in a former 17th-century Jesuit chapel, is the **Musée d'Art Chrétien** (Museum of Christian Art). One of the highlights is a magnificent collection of sculpted marble sarcophagi, second only to the Vatican's, that date from the 4th century on. Downstairs, you can explore a vast double gallery built in the 1st century BC as a grain store and see part of the great Roman sewer built two centuries later. *Rue Balze. Admission: 12 frs adults, 7 frs students; joint ticket as above. Open June–Sept., daily 8:30–7; Nov.–Mar., daily 9–noon and 2–4:30; Apr.–May and Oct., daily 9–12:30 and 2–6:30.*

The **Museon Arlaten,** an old-fashioned folklore museum, is housed next door in a 16th-century mansion. The charming displays include costumes and headdresses, puppets, and waxworks, lovingly assembled by the great 19th-century Provençal poet, Frédéric Mistral. *29 rue de la République, tel. 90–96–08–23. Admission: 15 frs adults, 10 frs students; joint ticket as above. Open June–Sept., daily 8:30–7; Nov.–Mar., Tues.–Sun. 9–noon and 2–4:30; Apr.–May and Oct., Tues.–Sun. 9–12:30 and 2–6:30.*

Head down rue du Président-Wilson opposite the museum to the **boulevard des Luces,** a broad, leafy avenue flanked by trendy shops and sidewalk cafés. Locals favor it for leisurely strolls and aperitifs.

At the east end of the boulevard is the **Jardin d'Hiver,** a public garden whose fountains figure in several of Van Gogh's paintings. Cross the gardens to rue Fassin and head left to place de la Croisière and the start of the allée des Sarcophages, which leads to the **Alyscamps,** a Provençal term meaning "mythical burial ground." This was a prestigious burial site from Roman times through the Middle Ages. A host of important finds have been excavated here, many of which are exhibited in the town's museums. Empty tombs and sarcophagi line the allée des Sarcophages, creating a powerfully gloomy atmosphere in dull weather. *Tel. 90–49–36–87. Admission: 12 frs adults, 7 frs students. Open daily 9–5.*

Lodging **St-Trophime.** This impressive town house, close to the Arènes and
$ the eponymous church, has old-fashioned rooms and a nice courtyard. It can be a little noisy in the height of summer, but with prices as low as 200 francs for the smallest rooms, you can't complain. *16 rue Calade, 13200, tel. 90–96–88–38, fax 90–96–92–19. 22 rooms, some with bath or shower. AE, DC, MC, V. Closed mid-Nov.–mid-Dec. and most of Jan.*

Dining **Le Vaccarès.** In an upstairs restaurant overlooking place du Forum,
$$ chef Bernard Dumas serves classic Provençal dishes with a touch of invention and some particularly good fish creations. Try his mussels dressed in herbs and garlic. The dining-room decor is as elegant as the cuisine, and many of the prices, though not all, will keep your tab to a moderate level. *11 rue Favorin, tel. 90–96–06–17, fax 90–96–24–52. Reservations advised. MC, V. Closed end of Dec.–end of Jan., Sun. dinner, and Mon.*

$ **Côte d'Adam.** This country-style restaurant near place du Forum offers the best dining value in the historic town center: three different set menus for under 100 frs, showcasing such tasty, unpretentious fare as chicken salad and mussel soup. *12 rue de la Liberté, tel. 90–49–62–29. Reservations advised. AE, DC, MC, V. Closed Mon. and the second half of Nov.*

Les Baux-de-Provence

Four buses leave Arles daily on the ½-hour trip northeast to Les Baux.

★ **Les Baux-de-Provence** is an amazing place perched on a mighty spur of rock high above the surrounding countryside of vines, olive trees, and quarries, (the mineral bauxite was discovered here in 1821). Half of Les Baux is composed of tiny climbing streets and ancient stone houses inhabited, for the most part, by local craftsmen selling pottery, carvings, and assorted knickknacks. The other half, the **Ville Morte** (Dead Town), is a mass of medieval ruins, vestiges of Les Baux's glorious past, when the town boasted 6,000 inhabitants and the defensive impregnability of its rocky site far outweighed its isolation and poor access.

Close to the 12th-century church of St-Vincent (where local shepherds continue an age-old tradition by herding their lambs to midnight mass at Christmas) is the 16th-century **Hôtel des Porcelets,** featuring some 18th-century frescoes and a small but choice collection of contemporary art. *Pl. Hervain, tel. 90–54–36–99. Admission: 32 frs adults, 22 frs children under 18 (joint ticket with Musée Lapidaire and Ville Morte). Open Easter–Oct., daily 9–noon and 2–6.*

Rue Neuve leads around to the **Ville Morte.** Enter through the 14th-century Tour-de-Brau, which houses the **Musée Lapidaire,** displaying locally excavated sculptures and ceramics. You can wander at will amid the rocks and ruins of the Dead Town. A 13th-century castle stands at one end of the clifftop, and at the other, the Tour Paravelle and the Monument Charloun Rieu. From here, you can enjoy a magnificent view of Arles and the Camargue as far as Stes-Maries-de-la-Mer. *La Citadelle, tel. 90–54–37–37. Admission: 32 frs (joint ticket with above museums). Open daily 9:15–6:15.*

St-Rémy-de-Provence

Two buses daily run between Les Baux and St-Rémy (15 minutes), and 3 between St-Rémy and Tarascon (30 minutes). Tourist office: place Jean-Jaurès, tel. 90–92–05–22.

St-Rémy-de-Provence, founded in the 6th century BC and known as Glanum to the Romans, is renowned for its outstanding Roman remains: Temples, baths, forum, and houses have been excavated, and the Roman mausoleum and Arc Municipal (Triumphal Arch) welcome visitors as they enter the town.

The **Roman mausoleum** was erected around AD 100 to the memory of Caius and Lucius Caesar, grandsons of the emperor Augustus; the four bas-reliefs around its base, depicting ancient battle scenes, are stunningly preserved. The mausoleum is composed of four archways topped by a circular colonnade. The nearby **Arc Municipal** is a few decades older and has suffered heavily; the upper half has crumbled away, although you can still make out some of the stone carvings.

Excavations of **Glanum** begun in 1921 have uncovered about a tenth of the original Roman town. The remains, spread over 300 yards along what was once the Aurelian Way between Arles and Milan, are less spectacular than the arch and mausoleum, but students of archaeology won't mind paying for the privilege of admiring what were once temples, fountains, gateways, baths, houses, and a forum. *Tel. 90–92–23–79. Admission: 32 frs adults, 10 frs children under 10. Open Apr.–Sept., daily 9–noon and 2–6; Oct.–Mar., daily 9–noon and 2–5.*

Many of the finds—statues, pottery, and jewelry—can also be examined at the town museum, the **Musée Archéologique,** in the center of St-Rémy. *Hôtel de Sade, rue Parage, tel. 90–92–13–07. Admission: 14 frs adults, 7 frs children under 10. Open June–Oct., daily 9–noon and 2–6; Apr.–May and Oct., weekends 10–noon, weekdays 3–6.*

Opposite the Hôtel de Sade, in a grand 16th-century mansion, is the **Musée des Alpilles,** with a fine collection of minerals found in the nearby hills (the Alpilles), plus items of regional folklore: costumes, furniture, and figurines. Exhibits also touch on the 16th-century astrologer Nostradamus, who was born in St-Rémy (his house can be seen on the other side of the church, on rue Hoche, but it's not open to the public). *Pl. Favier. Admission: 14 frs. Open Apr.–Oct., Wed.–Mon. 10–noon and 2–6; Mar. and Nov., weekends 10–noon and 2–4.*

Tour 2: Marseille and Aix

The two towns in this tour, though just a short train ride apart, couldn't be more different. Marseille is big, brash, and busy, while Aix-en-Provence is elegant, proud, and almost haughty.

From Paris By Train TGV trains to Marseille leave Paris (Gare de Lyon) every 2 hours. The trip takes 4 hours 40 minutes.

By Car The 785-kilometer (490-mile) drive from Paris to Marseille via A6 and A7 takes around 7 hours.

Marseille

Tourist office: 4 La Canebière, close to the Vieux-Port, tel. 91–13–89–00.

Numbers in the margin correspond with points of interest on the Marseille map.

Marseille is not crowded with tourist goodies, nor is its reputation as a big, dirty city entirely unjustified, but it still has more going for it than many realize: a craggy mountain hinterland that provides a spectacular backdrop, superb coastal views of nearby islands, and the sights and smells of a Mediterranean melting pot where different peoples have mingled for centuries—ever since the Phocaean Greeks invaded around 600 BC. The most recent immigrants come from North Africa.

★ ❶ Marseille is the Mediterranean's largest port. The sizable, ugly, industrial docks virtually rub shoulders with the intimate, picturesque old harbor, the **Vieux-Port,** packed with fishing boats and pleasure craft. This is the heart of Marseille, with La Canebière, the city's main street, leading down to the water's edge.

Take the métro from Gare St-Charles to the Vieux-Port, or descend the majestic stone staircase outside the station and follow boulevard d'Athènes before turning right onto La Canebière. Pick up your leaflets and town map at the tourist office and peruse them on a café terrace overlooking the Vieux-Port, where a forest of yacht and fishing-boat masts creates a colorful scene. Restaurants line the quays, and fishwives spout incomprehensible Provençal insults as they serve gleaming fresh sardines each morning. The Marseillais can be an irascible lot: Louis XIV built the Fort St-Nicolas, at the entry of the Vieux-Port, with the guns facing inland to keep the citizens in order.

❷ A short way down the quai du Port is the elegant 17th-century Hôtel de Ville. Just behind, on rue de la Prison, is the Maison Diamantée, a 16th-century mansion with an elaborate interior staircase. The mansion, renovated in 1995, houses the **Musée du Vieux Marseille,** with displays of costumes, pictures, and figurines that depict old Marseille. *2 rue de la Prison, tel. 91–55–10–19. Admission: 10 frs adults, 5 frs students and senior citizens. Open Tues.–Sun. 10–5.*

❸ Marseille's pompous, striped, neo-Byzantine **cathedral** stands around the corner, its various domes looking utterly incongruous against the backdrop of industrial docks. If, however, you skirt around the colossal edifice and climb up rue du Panier behind the city police station, or *"archevêché"* ("archbishop's seat"), as it is irreverently known, the cathedral's Oriental silhouette, facing out

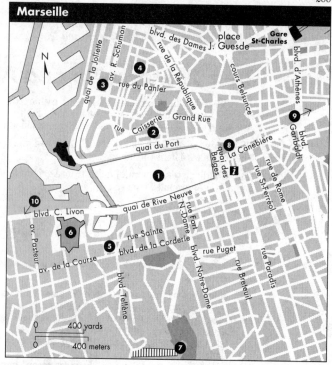

Marseille

over the Mediterranean, acquires fresh significance as a symbol of Marseille's role as gateway to the Levant.

The grid of narrow, tumbledown streets leading off rue du Panier is called simply *Le Panier* (The Basket). There is a claustrophobic feel here, heightened by the lines of washing strung from window to window, sometimes blotting out the sky. Apart from the colorful, sleazy ambience, the Panier is worth visiting for the elegantly restored 17th-century hospice now known as the **Musée de la Vieille-Charité.** Excellent art exhibits are held here, and the architecture—an arcaded, three-story courtyard built around a shallow-domed chapel—displays a subtlety and restraint lacking in the cathedral. *2 rue de la Charité, tel. 91–56–28–38. Admission: 10 frs adults (25 frs for exhibitions). Open Tues.–Sun. 10–5.*

Now return to the Hôtel de Ville and take the barge that plows across the Vieux Port every few minutes (6 frs). Head right along the quay toward the **Basilique St-Victor** (rue Sainte), in the shadow of the **Fort St-Nicolas** (which can't be visited). With its powerful tower and thick-set walls, the basilica resembles a fortress and boasts one of southern France's oldest doorways (circa 1140), a 13th-century nave, and a 14th-century chancel and transept. Downstairs, you'll find the murky 5th-century underground crypt, with its collection of ancient sarcophagi.

Just up the street from the basilica at 136 rue Sainte is the **Four des Navettes,** a bakery that has been producing slender, orange-spiced, shuttle-shape *navette* loaves for more than 200 years. Because the navettes can last for up to a year, they make good take-home presents as well as on-the-spot snacks.

A brisk half-mile walk up boulevard Tellène, followed by a trudge up a steep flight of steps, will bring you to the foot of **Notre-Dame de la Garde** (blvd. A. Aune). This church, a flashy 19th-century cousin of the Sacré-Coeur in Paris and Fourvière in Lyon, features a similar hilltop location. The expansive view, clearest in early morning (especially if the mistral is blowing), stretches from the hinterland mountains to the sea via the Cité Radieuse, a controversial '50s housing project by Swiss-born architect Le Corbusier. The church's interior is generously endowed with bombastic murals, mosaics, and marble, and at the top of the tower, the great gilded statue of the Virgin stands sentinel over the old port, 500 feet below.

Return to the Vieux-Port and venture onto the legendary **La Canebière**—the "Can O' Beer" to prewar sailors—where stately mansions recall faded glory. La Canebière has been on the decline in recent years, but cafés and restaurants continue to provide an upbeat pulse. A hundred yards down on the left is the big white Palais ⑧ de la Bourse (stock exchange) and, inside, the **Musée de la Marine,** with a rundown on the history of the port and an interesting display of model ships. *Tel. 91–39–33–33. Admission: 10 frs. Open Wed.– Mon. 9–noon and 2–6.*

Behind the bourse is the **Jardin des Vestiges,** a public park that holds the remains of Roman foundations. Here you will find the little **Musée de l'Histoire de Marseille,** featuring exhibits related to the town's history. One of the highlights is the 60-foot Roman boat. *Cours Belsunce. Admission: 10 frs. adults, 5 frs. senior citizens and children. Open Tues.–Sat. 10–4:45.*

Continue past such busy shopping streets as rue Paradis, rue St-Ferréol, and rue de Rome, and turn right onto boulevard Garibaldi to reach **cours Julien,** a traffic-free street lined with sidewalk cafés, restaurants, bookshops, and boutiques. The atmosphere is that of a scaled-down St-Germain-des-Prés wafted from Paris to the Mediterranean.

Return to La Canebière and, at the undistinguished church of St-Vincent de Paul, fork left along cours Jeanne-Thierry (which becomes boulevard Longchamp) to the imposing **Palais Longchamp,** built in 1860 by the same architect who built Notre-Dame de la Garde, Henri Espérandieu (1829–74). The palais is home to the ⑨ **Musée des Beaux-Arts;** its collection of paintings and sculptures includes works by 18th-century Italian artist Giovanni Battista Tiepolo, Rubens, and French caricaturist and painter Honoré Daumier. *Tel. 91–62–21–17. Admission: 10 frs adults, 5 frs students and senior citizens. Open Tues.–Sun. 10–5.*

Marseille is no seaside resort, but a scenic 5-kilometer (3-mile) coast road known as the **Corniche du Président J. F. Kennedy** links the Vieux-Port to the newly created Prado beaches in the swanky parts of southern Marseille. To get there, take any 19, 83, or 72 bus. There are breathtaking views across the sea toward the rocky Frioul Islands, which can be visited by boat. Boats leave the Vieux-Port hourly in summer and frequently in winter for the 90-minute trip (40 ⑩ frs) to the **Château d'If,** a castle in which various political prisoners were held captive down the ages. Alexandre Dumas condemned his fictional hero, the count of Monte Cristo, to be shut up in a cell here, before the wily count made his celebrated escape through a hole in the wall. *Admission: 21 frs. Open June–Sept., daily 8:30–noon and 1:30–6:30; Oct.–May, daily 8:30–noon and 1:30–4.*

Lodging **Lutétia.** There's nothing remarkable about this small hotel, but its
$ rooms are quiet, airy, modern, and a good value for the money, given the handy setting between La Canebière and St-Charles rail station. *38 allée Léon-Gambetta, 13001, tel. 91–50–81–78, fax 91–50–23–52. 29 rooms with bath or shower. DC, MC, V.*

Splurge **Pullman Beauvau.** Right on the Vieux Port, a few steps from the end
★ of La Canebière, the Beauvau is the ideal town hotel. The 200-year-old former coaching inn was totally modernized in 1986 and its facade cleaned in 1992. Its charming, Old World opulence is enhanced

by wood paneling, designer fabrics, fine paintings, genuine antique
furniture—and exceptional service. The best rooms look out onto
the Vieux Port. There's no restaurant, but you can start your day in
the cozy breakfast room. *4 rue Beauvau, 13001, tel. 91–54–91–00
(U.S. reservations, 800/223–9868; in the U.K., 0171/621–1962), fax
91–54–15–76. 71 rooms with bath. Facilities: bar, breakfast room.
AE, DC, MC, V. 600 frs–750 frs.*

Dining **Chez Madie.** Every morning *patronne* Madie Minassian bustles
$ along the quayside to trade insults with the fishwives at the far end
of the Vieux Port—and to scour their catch for the freshest ingredients, which swiftly end up in her bouillabaisse, fish soup, *favouilles*
sauce (made from tiny local crabs), and other dishes you'll savor at
her restaurant. *138 quai du Port, tel. 91–90–40–87. Reservations
advised. AE, DC, MC, V. Closed Mon., Sun. dinner, and most of
Aug.*

$ **Dar Djerba.** This is perhaps the best of the North African restau-
★ rants that are scattered throughout Marseille. The cozy, white-
walled Dar Djerba on bustling cours Julien specializes in couscous of
all kinds (with lamb, chicken, or even quail) as well as in Arab coffees
and pastries. The Moorish tile patterns and exotic aromas will waft
you away on a Saharan breeze. *15 cours Julien, tel. 91–48–55–36.
Reservations advised in summer. DC, MC, V. Closed Tues. and second half of Aug.*

Aix-en-Provence

*Trains make the 30-minute run from Marseille north to Aix every
1½ hours or so. Tourist office: 2 place du Général-de-Gaulle, tel. 42–
26–02–93.*

Many villages, but few towns, are as well preserved as the tradition-
★ al capital of Provence: elegant **Aix-en-Provence**. The Romans were
drawn here by the presence of thermal springs; the name Aix origi-
nates from *Aquae Sextiae* (the waters of Sextius) in honor of the consul who reputedly founded the town in 122 BC. Twenty years later, a
vast army of Germanic barbarians invaded the region but was defeated by General Marius at a neighboring mountain, known ever
since as the Montagne Sainte-Victoire. Marius remains a popular local first name to this day.

Aix-en-Provence counts two of France's creative geniuses among its
sons: Paul Cézanne (1839–1906), many of whose paintings feature
the nearby countryside, especially Montagne Sainte-Victoire
(though Cézanne would not recognize it now, after the forest fire
that ravaged its slopes in 1990), and novelist Emile Zola (1840–
1902), who, in several of his works, described Aix (as "Plassans")
and his boyhood friendship with Cézanne.

The celebrated **cours Mirabeau**, flanked by intertwining plane
trees, is the town's nerve center, a gracious, lively avenue with the
feel of a toned-down, intimate Champs-Elysées. It divides Old Aix
into two, with narrow medieval streets to the north and sophisticated 18th-century mansions to the south. Begin your visit at the
west end of cours Mirabeau (the tourist office is close by). Halfway
down is the **Fontaine des Neuf Canons** (Fountain of the Nine Cannons), dating from 1691, and farther along is the **Fontaine d'Eau
Thermale** (Fountain of Thermal Water), built in 1734.

Turn left down rue Clemenceau to place St-Honoré, with another
small fountain, then make a left again onto rue Espariat. The sumptuous Hôtel Boyer d'Eguilles at No. 6, erected in 1675, is worth a
visit for its fine woodwork, sculpture, and murals but is best known
as the **Muséum d'Histoire Naturelle**. The highlight is its rare collection of dinosaur eggs, accompanied by lifesize models of the dino-
saurs that roamed locally 65 million years ago. *6 rue Espariat, tel.*

*42–26–23–67. Admission: 15 frs adults, 9 frs students. Open Mon.–
Sat. 10–noon and 2–6, Sun. 2–6.*

Continue on rue Espariat past the sculpted facade of the Hôtel
d'Albertas (built in 1707) at No. 10, then turn right onto rue Aude,
lined with ancient town houses. Wend your way down to the **Hôtel de
Ville,** pausing to admire its 17th-century iron gates and balcony, and
the 16th-century **Tour de l'Horloge** (former town belfry) alongside.
Toward the far end of the street (now known as rue Gaston-de-
Saporta), just past the intimate square of place des Martyrs, stands
the **Cathédrale St-Sauveur.** Its mishmash of styles lacks harmony,
and the interior feels gloomy and dilapidated, but there's a remarkable 15th-century triptych by Nicolas Froment, entitled *Tryptique
du Buisson Ardent (Burning Bush),* depicting King René (duke of
Anjou, Count of Provence, and titular king of Sicily) and Queen Joan
kneeling beside the Virgin. Ask the sacristan to spotlight it for you
(he'll expect a tip) and to remove the protective shutters from the
ornate 16th-century carvings on the cathedral portals. Afterward,
wander into the tranquil Romanesque cloisters next door to admire
the carved pillars and slender colonnades.

The adjacent Archbishop's Palace is home to the **Musée des
Tapisseries.** Topping the bill are 17 magnificent tapestries made in
Beauvais that date, like the palace itself, from the 17th and 18th cen-
turies. Nine woven panels illustrate the adventures of the bumbling
Don Quixote. *28 pl. des Martyrs de la Résistance. Admission: 14 frs
adults, 8 frs students. Open Wed.–Mon. 10–noon and 2–5:45.*

Return past the cathedral and take rue de la Roque up to the broad,
leafy boulevard that encircles Old Aix. Head up avenue Pasteur, opposite, then turn right onto avenue Paul-Cézanne, which leads to
the **Musée-Atelier de Paul Cézanne** (Cézanne's studio). Cézanne's pioneering work, with its interest in angular forms, paved the way for
the Cubist style of the early 20th century. No major pictures are on
display here, but his studio remains as he left it at the time of his
death in 1906, scattered with the great man's pipe, clothing, and
other personal possessions, many of which he painted in his still
lifes. *9 av. Paul-Cézanne, tel. 42–21–06–53. Admission: 15 frs
adults, 9 frs students. Open Wed.–Mon. 10–noon and 2–5.*

Make your way back to cours Mirabeau and cross into the southern
half of Aix. The streets here are straight and rationally planned,
flanked by symmetrical mansions imbued with classical elegance.
Rue du Quatre-Septembre, three-quarters of the way down cours
Mirabeau, leads to the splendid **Fontaine des Quatre Dauphins,**
where sculpted dolphins play in a fountain erected in 1667. Turn left
along rue Cardinale to the **Musée Granet,** named after another of
Aix's artistic sons: François Granet (1775–1849), whose works are
good examples of the formal, at times sentimental, style of art popular during the first half of the 19th century. Cézanne is also represented here with several oils and watercolors. An impressive
collection of European paintings from the 16th to the 19th century,
plus archaeological finds from Egypt, Greece, and the Roman Empire, complete the museum's collections. *13 rue Cardinale, tel. 42–
38–14–70. Admission: 18 frs adults, 10 frs students. Open Wed.–
Mon. 10–noon and 2–6.*

Lodging **Caravelle.** There is nothing remarkable about the Caravelle—except
$–$$ that it is just five minutes' walk from cours Mirabeau and one of the
few affordable options in central Aix. Streetside rooms are small and
sometimes noisy, but you'll have to pay more than 350 frs for the quieter back rooms that look out over a flower garden. *29 blvd. du Roi-
René, 13100, tel. 42–21–53–05. 32 rooms with bath or shower. AE,
DC, MC, V.*

Dining **Brasserie Royale.** This noisy, bustling eatery on cours Mirabeau
$ serves up hearty Provençal dishes amid a background din of banging

pots, vociferous waiters, and tumultuous cries for more wine. The best place to eat is in the glassed-in patio out front, so you can soak up the Champs-Elysées–style atmosphere of the leafy boulevard while enjoying your meal. *17 cours Mirabeau, tel. 42–26–01–63. Reservations advised. MC, V.*

Shopping Two Aix specialties are fragrant soaps with natural floral scents, and *calissons d'Aix*, ingeniously sculpted marzipan. Delicately patterned Provençal fabrics can be found at **Souleïado** (8 pl. des Chapeliers). **Fouque** (65 cours Gambetta) is a good source of *santons*, clay crêche figures. In addition, several **markets** are a delight to explore: the flower market on Tuesday, Thursday, and Saturday mornings at place de l'Hôtel-de-Ville; the fruit and vegetable market every morning at place Richelme; and the fruit, vegetable, and herb market on Tuesday, Thursday, and Saturday mornings at place des Prêcheurs. There is also an antiques market on Tuesday, Thursday, and Saturday mornings at place de Verdun.

13 The Riviera

The Riviera is not the cheapest area of France. So before you make the journey, it's important to know what you'll really find when you get here. If you're expecting fabulous yachts and villas, movie stars and palaces, and budding starlets sunning themselves on ribbons of golden sand, think again. The truth is that most beaches, at least east of Cannes, are small and pebbly. And in summer, hordes of visitors are stuffed unglamorously into concrete high rises or roadside campsites. Yes, the film stars are here—but in their private villas. The merely wealthy wisely favor off-seasons—spring and fall.

That said, we can still recommend the Riviera, even in summer, as long as you're selective about the places you choose to visit. Cannes and Monaco are basically jet-set haunts; you visit quickly to soak up the atmosphere, then move on. But other resorts have something for every purse; Nice has downtown color and swing, and a wide choice of affordable hotels and restaurants. A few miles inland, fortified medieval towns perch on mountaintops high above the sea amid headily scented fields of roses and lavender. Craftspeople here still make and sell their wares, as their predecessors did in the Middle Ages. Only minutes from the beaches are some of the world's most famous museums of modern art, featuring the works of painters who were captivated by the colors here: Fernand Léger, Marc Chagall, Henri Matisse, Pablo Picasso, Auguste Renoir, Jean Cocteau. And the light is as magical as ever.

The only problem is accessibility—the spectacular rail line sticks stubbornly to the coast. Nonetheless, buses and trains serve most of the area's high points, so you don't need your own wheels to absorb the essence of this world-famous resort area.

Riviera Basics

Budget Lodging The Riviera is unquestionably the most expensive region of France, so brace youself. Affordable hotels do exist—Nice is your best bet—but they fill up days, if not weeks, in advance. Unless you're prepared to splurge, Cannes and Monaco are not places to spend a night.

Budget Dining Though prices often scale Parisian heights, the Riviera shares its cuisine with Provence, enjoying the same vegetable and fish dishes prepared with the same vivid seasonings. The most famous is bouillabaisse, a fish stew from around Marseille. Genuine bouillabaisse combines *rascasse* (scorpion fish), eel, and half a dozen other types of seafood; crab and lobster are optional. Local fish is scarce, however, so dishes like *loup flambé* (sea bass with fennel and anisette), braised tuna, and even fresh sardines are priced accordingly.

With Italy so close, it's no surprise that many menus feature such specialties as ravioli and potato gnocchi. Try vegetable *soupe au pistou*, an aromatic brew seasoned with basil, garlic, olive oil, and Parmesan cheese; or *pissaladière*, a pastry-based version of pizza, topped with tomato, olives, anchovy, and plenty of onion. Nice claims its own specialties: *pan bagna* (salad in a bun) and *poulpe à la niçoise* (octopus in a tomato sauce). Of the various vegetable dishes, the best is ratatouille, a stew of tomatoes, onions, eggplant, and zucchini.

Anise-flavored *pastis* is the Riviera's most popular drink.

Bargain Shopping Spending money is easy on the Riviera, where you'll find Paris fashions at Paris prices (the sales are in January). Some better buys may be found in food—crystallized fruits or olive oil in Nice, for example, make good gifts. In Cannes, visit the Saturday market at allées de la Liberté, where secondhand cookware is sold alongside strings of garlic. St-Paul and Vence will tempt you with paintings and artifacts that may seem exorbitantly priced until you realize that the frame usually comes with the painting. Grasse's perfume is famous worldwide; a few ounces taken home will win hearts. In general, though, the Riviera is not a place to find bargains.

Biking Bikes can be rented from train stations at Antibes, Cannes, Juan-les-Pins, and Nice. Two especially scenic trips on fairly level ground are from Nice to Cap Ferrat via Villefranche, and to the area around Cap d'Antibes, including Juan-les-Pins, from Cannes. Both trips are around 25 kilometers (16 miles).

Hiking The hilly hinterland, spangled with old villages, makes good rambling country; write to the **Comité Départemental de la Randonnée Pédestre** (La Chenaie, Chemin Martourette, 06530 Le Tignet) for maps and recommended routes.

Beaches If you like your beaches sandy, stick to those between St-Tropez and Antibes; most of the others are pebbly, though Menton and Monaco have imported vast tons of sand to spread around their shores. Private beaches are everywhere. Though you'll have to pay between 60 frs and 140 frs a day to use them, you get much in return: a café or restaurant, cabanas and showers, mattresses and umbrellas, and the pleasure of watching the perpetual parade of stylish swimwear and languid egos.

La Napoule has no fewer than eight beaches, offering facilities for waterskiing, windsurfing, diving, and snorkeling, or you can just swim or stretch out on a lounge chair. In **Nice**, beaches extend along the Baie des Anges; **Ruhl Plage** is one of the most popular, with a good restaurant and facilities for waterskiing, windsurfing, and children's swimming lessons. Not to be outdone, **Neptune Plage** has all that plus a sauna.

Arts and
Nightlife The Riviera's cultural calendar is splashy and star-studded, and never more so than during the region's world-famous festivals. The biggest and most celebrated is the **Cannes Film Festival** in May, rivaled by Monte Carlo's arts festival, **Printemps des Arts** (late March through late April). Antibes and Nice both host **jazz festivals** during July, drawing international performers.

Casinos are very much part of the nightlife of Cannes and Monaco, but a spell at the games table will be beyond the budget of all but the best-heeled travelers. And although Riviera resorts buzz after dark, discos require snappy dressing and ready funds.

Festivals The celebrated **Carnival** in Nice mixes parades and other revelry during the weeks preceding Lent. The two weekends preceding Mardi Gras are a swirl of parades, fireworks, and masked balls.

Exploring the Riviera

Nice is a logical base for exploring the Riviera. By rail, you can then head west to Antibes, Cannes (from where you can take a ferry to the Iles de Lérins), La Napoule, and Fréjus; travel east to Villefranche-sur-Mer, Beaulieu, Eze, Monaco, and Menton; and make excursions to such ancient hinterland villages as St-Paul-de-Vence (by bus, and then by another bus to Vence) and Peillon (by train).

From Paris Six TGVs to Nice leave Paris (Gare de Lyon) each day. A change of
By Train trains at Marseille is often necessary, and the trip takes 7–7½ hours.

By Car Allow at least 8 hours—in fact, a full day—for the 930-kilometer (580-mile) journey from Paris via A6, A7, and A8.

Nice

Tourist office: avenue Thiers, by the train station, tel. 93–87–07–07.

Numbers in the margin correspond with points of interest on the Nice map.

Nice is less glamorous, less sophisticated, and less expensive than Cannes. It is also older—weathered-old and faded-old—like a wealthy dowager who has seen better days but who still maintains a demeanor of dignity and poise. Nice is a big, sprawling city of 350,000 people—five times as populous as Cannes—and has a life and vitality that survive when tourists pack their bags and go home.

Turn left out of the station, then right onto bustling avenue Jean-Medécin, Nice's main shopping street, where all needs and most tastes are catered to in its big department stores (Nouvelles Galeries, Prisunic, and the split-level Etoile mall). Continue on
❶ down to arcaded **place Masséna**, the city's main square and the logical starting point for the three Nice minitours we've mapped out.
❷ First, head west through the fountains and gardens of the **Jardin Al-**
❸ **bert I** to the **Promenade des Anglais,** built, as the name indicates, by the English community in 1824. Traffic on this multilane highway can be heavy, but once you have crossed to the seafront, there are fine views, across private beaches, of the Baie des Anges.

Walk as far as the Neptune Plage (beach) and cross over to the **Hôtel Négresco** (37 promenade des Anglais); spend a few dollars on a cup of coffee here and think of it as an admission charge to this palatial hotel.

❹ Just up rue de Rivoli from the Hôtel Négresco is the **Musée Masséna,** concerned principally with the Napoleonic era and, in particular, with the life of local-born general André Masséna (1756–1817). Bonaparte rewarded the general for his heroic exploits during the Ital-

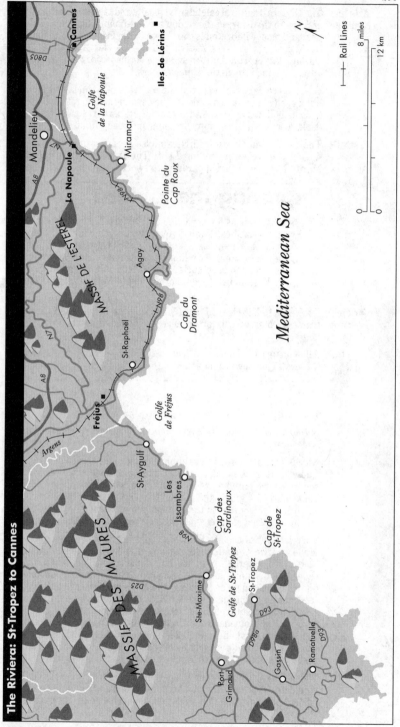

296

The Riviera: St-Tropez to Cannes

Cannes

Iles de Lérins

Mandelieu

D805

A8

N7

Golfe
de la Napoule

MASSIF DE L'ESTEREL

La Napoule

Miramar

N98

Pointe du
Cap Roux

Agay

N98

St-Raphaël

Cap du
Dramont

Fréjus

Argens

Golfe de Fréjus

St-Aygulf

Mediterranean Sea

MASSIF DES MAURES

Les
Issambres

N98

Cap des
Sardinaux

D25

Ste-Maxime

Golfe de St-Tropez

St-Tropez

Cap de
St-Tropez

Port-
Grimaud

D98a

D98a

Gassin

Ramatuelle

D93

D93

Rail Lines

N

0   8 miles
0   12 km

297

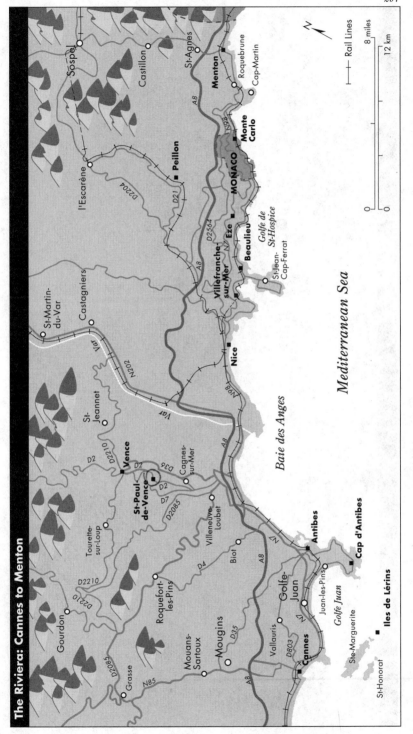

The Riviera: Cannes to Menton

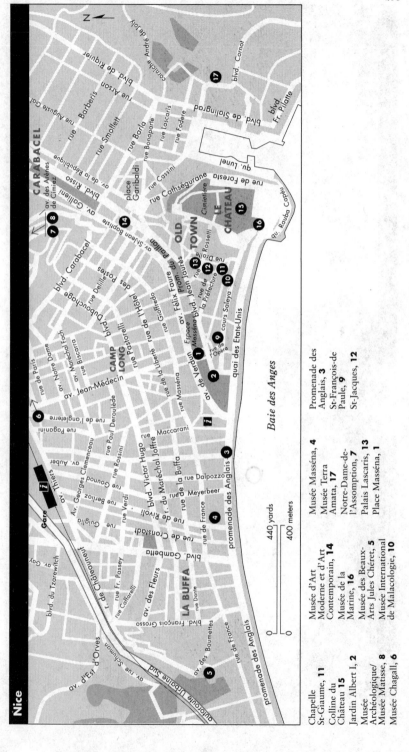

Nice

N

CARABACEL

OLD TOWN

LE CHÂTEAU

CAMP LONG

LA BUFFA

Baie des Anges

Gare

corniche André de Joly

blvd. de Riquier
blvd. Carnot
blvd. Fr. Pilatte
blvd. de Stalingrad
rue Arson
rue Barberis
rue de la République
av. de la République
blvd. Risso
rue Smollett
rue Barla
rue Bonaparte
rue Lascaris
rue Fodéré
qu. Lunel
rue de Foresta
Cimetière
av. Rauba Capeu
rue Cathségurane
rue Cassini
place Garibaldi
rue Droite
rue Rossetti
rue de la Préfecture
cours Saleya
quai des États-Unis
promenade des Anglais
rue de l'Opéra
Espace Masséna
blvd. Jean Jaurès
av. Félix Faure
rue de Gioffredo
rue de l'Hôtel des Postes
blvd. Dubouchage
blvd. Carabacel
rue Delille
av. des Arènes de Cimiez
blvd. Risso
av. Gallieni
av. Sévan Baptiste
Pavillon
av. de Verdun
rue Masséna
rue de la Liberté
rue Pastorelli
rue Biscarra
av. Maréchal Foch
rue Notre-Dame
rue de Paris
av. Jean-Médecin
rue Paganini
rue de l'Angleterre
rue Paul Déroulède
av. Georges Clemenceau
av. Auber
av. Thiers
av. Guiglia
rue Gounod
rue Rossini
av. Gay
blvd. du Tzarewitch
rue de Châteauneuf
r. Fr. Passey
rue Caffarelli
blvd. François Grosso
rue Berlioz
rue Verdi
blvd. Victor Hugo
rue du Maréchal Joffre
rue Maccarani
rue de la Buffa
rue Meyerbeer
rue Dalpozzo
rue de France
av. des Fleurs
rue Dante
autoroute Urbaine Sud
av. d'Est d'Orves
av. rue de Schnnon
rue de Cronstadt
rue de Rivoli
blvd. Gambetta
av. des Baumettes
rue de France
promenade des Anglais
440 yards
400 meters

Chapelle
St-Giaume, **11**
Colline du
Château **15**
Jardin Albert I, **2**
Musée
Archéologique/
Musée Matisse, **8**
Musée Chagall, **6**

Musée d'Art
Moderne et d'Art
Contemporain, **14**
Musée de la
Marine, **16**
Musée des Beaux-
Arts Jules Chéret, **5**
Musée International
de Malacologie, **10**

Musée Masséna, **4**
Musée Terra
Amata, **17**
Notre-Dame-de-
l'Assomption, **7**
Palais Lascaris, **13**
Place Masséna, **1**

Promenade des
Anglais, **3**
St-François-de-
Paule, **9**
St-Jacques, **12**

ian campaign with the sonorous sobriquet *l'enfant chéri de la
victoire* (the cherished child of victory). Sections of the museum
evoke the history of Nice and its carnival; there are also some fine
Renaissance paintings and objects. *67 rue de France. Admission
free. Open Dec.–Oct., Tues.–Sun. 10–noon and 2–5 (3–6 May–
Sept.).*

Head left along rue de France, then turn right up avenue des
⑤ Baumettes to the **Musée des Beaux-Arts Jules Chéret,** Nice's fine-
arts museum, built in 1878 as a palatial mansion for a Russian princess. The rich collection of paintings includes works by Auguste Renoir, Edgar Degas, Claude Monet, Raoul Dufy, Oriental prints,
sculptures by Auguste Rodin, and ceramics by Picasso. Jules Chéret
(1836–1932) is best known for his Belle Epoque posters; several of
his oils, pastels, and tapestries can be admired here. *33 av. des
Baumettes, tel. 93–62–18–12. Admission free. Open May–Sept.,
Tues.–Sun. 10–noon and 3–6; Oct. and Dec.–Apr., Tues.–Sun. 10–
noon and 2–5.*

Our second minitour brings you back up avenue Jean-Médecin from
place Masséna and then right on avenue Thiers. Pass the train station, turn left on avenue Malausséna, and across from the railway
⑥ take the first right down to the **Musée Chagall**—built to show off the
paintings of Marc Chagall (1887–1985) in natural light. The Old Testament is the primary subject of the works, which include 17 huge
canvases covering a period of 13 years, together with 195 prelimi-
nary sketches, several sculptures, and nearly 40 gouaches. In summertime, you can buy snacks and drinks in the garden. *Av. du Dr-
Ménard, tel. 93–81–75–75. Admission: 27 frs adults, 18 frs children
and senior citizens. Open July–Sept., Wed.–Mon. 10–7; Oct.–July,
Wed.–Mon. 10–12:30 and 2–5:30.*

Boulevard de Cimiez, just east of the museum, runs northeast to the
residential quarter of Nice—the hilltop site of **Cimiez,** occupied by
the Romans 2,000 years ago. The foundations of the Roman town can
be seen, along with vestiges of the arena; these are less spectacular
than those at Arles or Nîmes but are still in use (notably for a summer jazz festival). Close by is the Franciscan monastery of
⑦ **Notre-Dame-de-l'Assomption,** with some outstanding late-medieval
religious pictures; guided tours include the small museum and an
audiovisual show on the life and work of the Franciscans. *Pl. du
Monastère, tel. 93–81–00–04. Admission free. Open Mon.–Sat. 10–
noon and 3–6.*

A 17th-century Italian villa amid the Roman remains contains two
⑧ museums: the **Musée Archéologique,** with a plethora of ancient objects, and the **Musée Matisse,** with paintings and bronzes by Henri
Matisse (1869–1954), illustrating the different stages of his career.
The Matisse Museum reopened in mid-1993 after a five-year renovation program. *164 av. des Arènes-de-Cimiez, tel. 93–81–08–08.
Musée Matisse, admission: 25 frs. Open Apr.–Sept., Wed.–Mon.
11–7; Oct.–Mar., Wed.–Mon. 10–5. Musée Archéologique, admission free. Open Tues.–Sat. 10–noon and 2–5, Sun. 2–5.*

★ Our third tour takes in the **old town** of Nice, one of the delights of the
Riviera. Cars are forbidden on streets that are so narrow that their
buildings crowd out the sky. The winding alleyways are lined with
faded 17th- and 18th-century buildings, where families sell their
wares. Flowers cascade from window boxes on soft pastel-colored
walls. You wander down cobblestone streets, proceeding with the
logic of dreams, or sit in an outdoor café on a Venetian-looking
square, basking in the purest, most transparent light.

To explore the old town, head south from place Masséna along rue de
l'Opéra, and turn left onto rue St-François-de-Paule. You'll soon
⑨ come to the 18th-century church of **St-François-dePaule,** renowned
for its ornate Baroque interior and sculpted decoration.

Rue St-François-de-Paule becomes the pedestrian-only cours
Saleya, with its colorful morning market selling seafood, flowers,
and orange trees in tubs. Toward the far end of cours Saleya is the
⑩ **Musée International de Malacologie,** with a collection of seashells
from all over the world (some for sale) and a small aquarium of Mediterranean sea life. *3 cours Saleya, tel. 93–85–18–44. Admission
free. Open Dec.–Oct., Tues.–Sat. 10:30–1 and 2–6 (until 6:30 June–
Sept.).*

⑪ Next, stroll left up rue la Poissonnerie and pop into the **Chapelle St-
Giaume** to admire its gleaming Baroque interior and grand altarpieces. Continue to rue de Jésus; at one end is the church of
⑫ **St-Jacques,** featuring an explosion of painted angels on the ceiling.
⑬ Walk along rue Droite to the elegant **Palais Lascaris,** built in the
mid-17th century and decorated with paintings and tapestries. The
palace boasts a particularly grand staircase and a reconstructed
18th-century pharmacy. *15 rue Droite. Admission free. Open Dec.–
Oct., Tues.–Sun. 9:30–noon and 2:30–6.*

Continue up rue Droite, turn left across place St-François, then
⑭ right along boulevard Jean-Jaurès to reach the **Musée d'Art Moderne
et d'Art Contemporain.** This state-of-the-art museum with four mar-
ble-fronted towers overlooking a sculpture-laden concourse, has an
outstanding collection of French and international abstract and figurative art from the late 1950s onward: "New Realists" like local-
based Arman, Martial Raysse, and Yves Klein, American moderns
like LeWitt and Stella, plus pop-art popes such as Warhol,
Rauschenberg, Lichtenstein, and Wesselmann. Temporary exhibits
are held on the ground floor. *Promenade des Arts, tel. 93–62–61–
62. Admission free. Open Wed.–Mon. 11–6 (Fri. 11–10).*

⑮ Old Nice is dominated by the **Colline du Château** (Castle Hill), a romantic cliff fortified many centuries before Christ. The ruins of a
6th-century castle can be explored and the views from the sur-
⑯ rounding garden admired. A small naval museum, the **Musée de la
Marine,** is situated in the 16th-century tower known as the **Tour
Bellanda** here, with models, instruments, and documents charting
the history of the port of Nice. *Rue du Château, tel. 93–80–47–61.
Admission free. Open June–Sept., Wed.–Mon. 10–noon and 2–7;
Oct.–mid-Nov. and Jan.–May, Wed.–Mon. 10–noon and 2–5. Elevator between Tour Bellanda and the quayside in operation daily
9–7 in summer, 2–7 in winter.*

The back of Castle Hill overlooks the harbor. On the other side,
⑰ along boulevard Carnot, is the **Musée Terra Amata,** containing relics
of a local settlement that was active 400,000 years ago. There are recorded commentaries in English and films explaining the lifestyle of
prehistoric dwellers. *25 blvd. Carnot, tel. 93–55–59–93. Admission
free. Open Oct.–mid-Sept., Tues.–Sun. 9–noon and 2–6.*

Lodging **Little Palace.** M. and Mme. Loridan run the closest thing to a coun-
$ try-house hotel in Nice. The old-fashioned decor, the jumble of bric-
★ a-brac, and the heavy wooden furniture lend an Old World air; some
may say it's like stepping onto a film set. *9 av. Baquis, 06000, tel.
93–88–70–49, fax 93–88–78–89. 36 rooms, 31 with bath. MC, V.
Closed Nov.*

¢–$ **La Mer.** This small hotel is handily situated on place Masséna, close
to the old town and seafront. Rooms are spartan (and carpets sometimes frayed), but all have a minibar and represent good value. Ask
for a room away from the square to be sure of a quiet night. *4 pl.
Masséna, 06000, tel. 93–92–09–10, fax 93–85–00–64. 12 rooms with
bath or shower.*

Dining **La Diva.** This simply decorated restaurant in the old town, halfway
$ between place Masséna and the seafront, provides cheerful service,
good value, and a three-course lunch menu at around 85 frs that features ravioli, mussels, and fillet of sea bream with basil. Dinner is

more expensive (first menu 105 frs); the fish and pasta specialties—seafood stew, duck ravioli, fettucini with mushrooms, among others—are quite good. *4 rue de l'Opéra, tel. 93–85–96–15. MC, V. Closed Mon.*

¢ **Le Tire Bouchon.** This small restaurant in the heart of old Nice only has 10 tables, but the narrow room is made to seem wider by mirrors on the wall. Currently very popular, it serves good simple fare at very reasonable prices: three-course menus cost 69 frs and 94 frs. The salade niçoise is an obvious choice; less obvious is the salad with smoked duck. Other dishes include curries, entrecôte, and grilled fish. If you cannot obtain a table here, wander up to the parallel street, rue de l'Abbaye, which is packed with mostly Italian restaurants (try the Casa di Pompeii). *19 rue de la Préfecture, tel. 63–92–63–64. Reservations advised. Closed Sun. MC, V.*

Shopping Crystallized fruit is a Nice specialty; there's a terrific selection at **Henri Auer** (7 rue St-François-de-Paule). Locals and visitors alike buy olive oil by the gallon from tiny **Alziari,** just down the street at No. 14; the cans have colorful, old-fashioned labels, and you can also pick up lots of Provençal herbs and spices. In addition to plants, Nice's famous flower market at **cours Saleya** also features mounds of fish, shellfish, and other food items; on Monday, there's a flea market at the same spot.

Antibes

There are trains from Nice every 30 minutes. Expresses take 14 minutes, locals 40 minutes. Tourist office: 11 place du Général-de-Gaulle, tel. 93–33–95–64.

Founded as a Greek trading port in the 4th century BC, **Antibes** is now a center for fishing and rose growing. Avenue de l'Amiral-de-Grasse runs along the seafront from the harbor to the **marketplace,** a colorful sight most mornings, and to the church of the **Immaculate Conception,** with intricately carved portals (dating from 1710) and a 1515 altarpiece by Nice artist Louis Bréa (c. 1455–1523).

★ The **Château Grimaldi,** built in the 12th century by the ruling family of Monaco and extensively rebuilt in the 16th century, is reached by nearby steps. Tear yourself away from the sun-baked terrace overlooking the sea to go inside to the **Musée Picasso.** There are stone Roman remains on show, but the works of Picasso—who occupied the château during his most cheerful and energetic period—hold center stage; they include an array of paintings, pottery, and lithographs inspired by the sea and Greek mythology. *Pl. du Château, tel. 93–34–91–91. Admission: 20 frs adults, 10 frs students and senior citizens. Open Dec.–Oct., Wed.–Mon. 10–noon and 2–6 (3–7 in summer).*

Continue down avenue de l'Amiral-de-Grasse to the St-André Bastion, constructed by Sébastien de Vauban in the late 17th century and home to the **Musée Archéologique.** Here 4,000 years of local history are illustrated by continually expanding displays. *Bastion St-André, tel. 93–34–48–01. Admission: 10 frs adults, 5 frs children and senior citizens. Open Dec.–Oct., weekdays 9–noon and 2–6.*

Antibes officially forms one town (dubbed "Juantibes") with the more recent resort of **Juan-les-Pins** to the south, where beach and nightlife attract a younger and less affluent crowd than in Cannes. In the summer, the mood is especially frenetic.

The **Cap d'Antibes** peninsula, jutting out into the sea beyond Juan-les-Pins, is rich and residential, with beaches, views, and large villas hidden in luxurious vegetation. Barely 2 miles long by 1 mile wide, it offers a perfect day's outing. An ideal walk is along the
★ **Sentier des Douaniers,** the customs officers' path.

From Pointe Bacon there is a striking view over the Baie des Anges toward Nice; climb up to the nearby Plateau de la Garoupe, the highest point of the headland, for a sweeping view inland over the Estérel massif and the Alps. The **Sanctuaire de la Garoupe** (sailors' chapel) up here has a 14th-century icon, a statue of Our Lady of Safe Homecoming, and numerous frescoes and votive offerings. The lighthouse alongside, which can be visited, has a powerful beam that carries more than 40 miles out to sea. *Admission free. Open Nov.– Mar., daily 10:30–12:30 and 2–5.*

Nearby, along the boulevard du Cap, which runs along the middle of the peninsula, is the **Jardin Thuret**, established by botanist Gustave Thuret (1817–75) in 1856 as France's first garden for subtropical plants and trees. The garden, now run by the Ministry of Agriculture, remains a haven for rare, exotic plants. *41 blvd. du Cap. Admission free. Open weekdays 8–12:30 and 2–5:30.*

At the southwest tip of the peninsula, opposite the luxurious and ultra-expensive Grand Hôtel du Cap d'Antibes, is the **Musée Naval & Napoléonien,** a former battery, where you can spend an interesting hour scanning Napoleonic proclamations and viewing scale models of oceangoing ships. *Batterie du Grillon, av. Kennedy, tel. 93–61– 45–32. Admission: 15 frs adults, 7 frs children and senior citizens. Open Apr.–Oct., weekdays 10–noon and 3–7, Sat. 10–noon; Dec.– Mar., weekdays 10–noon and 2–5, Sat. 10–noon.*

Lodging **Manoir Castel Garoupe Axa.** This old inn, known locally as Motel
$ Axa after owner Mme. Axa, is not a deluxe resort by any means, but the atmosphere is friendly and the beach is a 2-minute walk away. Each room has a kitchenette and balcony with views of the countryside. There is no restaurant; just breakfast is served. *959 blvd. de la Garoupe, 06600 Cap d'Antibes, tel. 93–61–36–51, fax 93–67–74–88. 22 rooms with bath. Facilities: pool, tennis court. Closed Jan. MC, V.*

Lodging and **Auberge de l'Estérel.** The affable Denis Latouche runs the best mod-
Dining erately priced (average price for dinner per person is 100 frs) restau-
$ rant in Juan-les-Pins, lending a nouvelle twist to local dishes; try the monkfish and, for dessert, the lemon tart. The secluded garden is a romantic setting for dining under the stars. There are 15 bedrooms (six with bath) in the attached hotel. The hotel-restaurant, in a quiet residential area, is just 1,000 yards from both the town center and the train station. *21 rue des Iles, 86160 Juan-les-Pins, tel. 93–61– 74–11. Reservations advised. MC, V. Closed mid-Nov.–mid-Dec., part of Feb., Sun. dinner, and Mon.*

Cannes

Trains run every ½ hour from Antibes to Cannes and take 10 minutes. Trains run frequently from Nice and take 23 minutes via express service or 50 minutes via local. Tourist office: Palais des Festivals, 1 La Croisette, tel. 93–39–24–53.

Unlike Nice, which is a city, **Cannes** is a resort town, existing only for the pleasure of its guests. Cosmopolitan, sophisticated, and smart, it's a tasteful and expensive breeding ground for the upscale (and those who are already "up"), and a sybaritic heaven for those who believe that life is short and that sin has something to do with the absence of a tan.

Alongside the long, narrow beach is a broad promenade called La Croisette, bordered by palm trees and flowers. At one end of the promenade is the modern Festival Hall, a summer casino, and an old harbor where pleasure boats are moored. At the other end is a winter casino and a modern harbor for some of the most luxurious yachts in the world. All along the promenade are cafés, boutiques, and luxury hotels like the Carlton and the Majestic. Speedboats and

waterskiers glide by; little waves lick the beach, lined with pros-
trate bodies. Behind the promenade lies the town, filled with shops,
restaurants, and hotels, and behind the town are the hills with the
villas of the very rich.

★ The first thing to do is to stroll along **La Croisette,** stopping at cafés
and boutiques along the way. Near the eastern end (turning left as
you face the water), before you reach the new port, is the **Parc de la
Roserie,** where some 14,000 roses nod their heads in the wind. Walking west takes you past the **Palais des Festivals** (Festival Hall), where
the famous film festival is held each May. Just past the hall is **place
du Général-de-Gaulle,** and on your left is the **old port.** If you continue
straight beyond the port on **allées de la Liberté,** you'll reach a tree-
shaded area, where flowers are sold in the morning, *boules* is played
in the afternoon, and a flea market is held on Saturday. If instead of
continuing straight from the square you turn inland, you'll quickly
come to rue Meynadier. Turn left. This is the old main street, which
has many 18th-century houses—now boutiques and specialty food
shops.

Lodging **Mondial.** A three-minute walk from the beach takes you to this six-
$$ story hotel, a haven for the traveler seeking solid, unpretentious
lodging in a town that leans more to tinsel. Many guest rooms offer
sea views and most have small terraces, though the hotel is in the
heart of the commercial center and only 250 yards from the train sta-
tion. There's no restaurant. *77 rue d'Antibes, 06400, tel. 93–68–70–
00, fax 93–99–39–11. 58 rooms, all with bath. AE, DC, MC, V.*

$ **Hôtel Select.** Just 70 yards from the main street, rue d'Antibes, and
200 yards from La Croisette, the Select offers a convenient location
and reasonable prices. Rooms are typically small but clean and func-
tional: they are both soundproof and air-conditioned. There is no
restaurant. *16 rue Hélène-Vagliano, 06400, tel. 93–99–51–00, fax
92–98–03–12. 26 rooms, most with bath. MC, V.*

Dining **Au Bec Fin.** A devoted band of regulars will attest to the quality of
¢ this family-run restaurant near the train station. Don't look for a
carefully staged decor: It's the spirited local clientele and the homey
food that distinguish this cheerful bistro. The fixed-price menus,
which often have choucroute and fish as the main course, are a fan-
tastic value at 80 frs or 100 frs. *12 rue du 24-Août, tel. 93–38–35–86.
Reservations advised. AE, DC, MC, V. Closed Sat. dinner, Sun.,
Christmas–late Jan., and last wk of June.*

¢ **Chez Astoux.** There are dozens of restaurants along this popular
people-watching street, one block from the sea in a small park dot-
ted with flower sellers. But Chez Astou, which ranks highly for its
seafood, stands out. (Indeed, it has a seafood stall next door, where
locals come to buy for their own kitchens.) The ambience at Chez
Astou is plain and simple, and you have the choice of sitting on the
terrace (heated when necessary) or inside. The local mussels, known
as *bouchots*, are strongly recommended. They're small and meaty,
ideal served either marinière or à la crème. At lunch there's a three-
course menu for 98 frs—very reasonable compared to prices at the
other restaurants nearby. *43 rue Felix-Faure, tel. 93–39–06–22.
Reservations accepted. AE, DC, MC, V.*

Shopping Cannes is one of the Riviera's top spots for chic—and expensive—
clothing. More fun is the local market, which sells everything from
strings of garlic to secondhand gravy boats every Saturday on allées
de la Liberté.

Iles de Lérins

*Ferries leave hourly from Cannes harbor (near the Palais des Festi-
vals); it's 15 minutes and 40 frs to Ste-Marguerite and 30 minutes
and 45 frs to St-Honorat. (A combined ticket for both islands costs 60
frs). Call 93–39–11–89 for information.*

Ste-Marguerite, the larger of the two **Iles de Lérins** (Lerin Islands), is all wooded hills, with a tiny main street lined with fishermen's houses. Visitors enjoy peaceful walks through a forest of enormous eucalyptus trees and parasol pines. Paths wind through a dense undergrowth of tree heathers, rosemary, and thyme. The main attraction is the dank cell in **Fort Royal,** where the Man in the Iron Mask was imprisoned (1687–98) before going to the Bastille, where he died in 1703. The mask, which he always wore, was in fact made of velvet. Was he the illegitimate brother of Louis XIV or Louis XIII's son-in-law? No one knows. The fort also contains a marine museum. *Tel. 93–43–18–17. Admission: 10 frs adults; free Wed. Open Wed.– Mon., 10:30–noon and 2–4:30 (6:30 in summer.) Closed Jan.*

St-Honorat is less tamed but more tranquil than its sister island. It was named for a hermit-monk who came here to escape his followers; but when the hermit founded a monastery here in AD 410, his disciples followed and the monastery became one of the most powerful in all Christendom. It's worth taking the two-hour walk around the island to the **old fortified monastery,** where noble Gothic arcades are arranged around a central courtyard. Next door to the "new" 19th-century monastery (open on request) is a shop where the monks sell handicrafts, lavender scent, and a home-brewed liqueur called Lérina. *Monastère de Lérins, tel. 93–48–68–68. Admission: 10 frs. Open daily 10–noon and 2–4:45. High mass at the abbey 9:45 Sun.*

La Napoule

Four trains run daily to La Napoule from Cannes, 8 minutes away, and from Nice, 50 minutes distant. Tourist office: 274 av. Henri-Clews, tel. 93–49–95–31.

La Napoule, forming a unit with the older, inland village of **Mandelieu,** is known for its extensive modern sports facilities: swimming, boating, waterskiing, deep-sea diving, fishing, golf, tennis, horseback riding, and parachuting. It explodes with color during the Fête du Mimosa (Mimosa Festival) in February. Stop in at the **Château de La Napoule Art Foundation** to see the eccentric work of the American sculptor Henry Clews. A cynic and sadist, Clews had, as one critic remarked, a knowledge of anatomy worthy of Michelangelo and the bizarre imagination of Edgar Allan Poe. *Av. Henry-Clews. Admission: 25 frs. Guided tours only, Sept.–Oct. and Dec.– June, Wed.–Mon. at 3 and 4; July and Aug., Wed.–Mon. at 3, 4, and 5. Closed Tues. and Nov.*

Fréjus

Three trains run daily to Fréjus from Cannes, 30 minutes away, and from Nice, 70 minutes away. Tourist office: 325 rue Jean-Jaurès, tel. 91–51–54–14.

Fréjus, a family resort, was founded by Julius Caesar as Forum Julii in 49 BC, and it is thought that the Roman city grew to 40,000 people—10,000 more than the population today. The Roman remains are unspectacular, if varied, and consist of part of a theater, an arena, an aqueduct, and city walls.

Fréjus Cathedral dates to the 10th century, although the richly worked choir stalls belong to the 15th century. The baptistery alongside it, square on the outside and octagonal inside, is thought to date from AD 400, making it one of France's oldest buildings. The adjacent cloisters feature an unusual contrast between round and pointed arches.

St-Raphaël, next door to Fréjus, is another family resort with holiday camps, best known to tourists as the railway stop to the teeming

resort of St-Tropez, where Brigitte Bardot and her director Roger
Vadim filmed *And God Created Woman* in 1956 (and changed the resort forever). It was in St-Raphaël that the Allied forces landed in
their offensive against the Germans in August 1944.

Lodging and **L'Aréna.** This former bank in the heart of the old town has been
Dining tastefully transformed: The cozy rooms—some a little small—have
$ brightly patterned wallpaper, curtains, and tiled bathrooms. Chef
Bruno Bluntzer serves up king-size prawns in cream, turbot, and
iced nougat, with set-price menus starting at 115 frs. *139 rue du
Général-de-Gaulle, 83600, Fréjus, tel. 94-17-09-40, fax 94-52-01-
52. 19 rooms with bath or shower. Facilities: restaurant. MC, V.
Closed mid-Nov.–mid-Dec.*

St-Paul-de-Vence

*Buses leave Nice's Gare Routière every ½ hour for St-Paul-de-
Vence, 50 minutes away, continuing to Vence.*

Not even hordes of tourists can destroy the ancient charm of
★ **St-Paul-de-Vence**, a gem of a town whose medieval atmosphere has
been perfectly preserved. You can walk the narrow, cobblestone
streets in perhaps 15 minutes, but you'll need another hour to explore the shops—mostly galleries selling second-rate landscape
paintings, but also a few serious studios and gift shops offering
everything from candles to dolls, dresses, and hand-dipped chocolate strawberries. Your best bet is to visit in the late afternoon,
when the tour buses are gone, and enjoy a drink among the Klees
and Picassos in the Colombe d'Or, a charming inn (*see* Lodging and
Dining, *below*). Be sure to visit the remarkable 12th-century Gothic
church; you'll want to light a candle to relieve its wonderful gloom.
The treasury is rich in 12th- to 15th-century pieces, including pro-
cessional crosses, reliquaries, and an enamel Virgin and Child.

At La Gardette, within walking distance just northwest of the vil-
★ lage, is the **Fondation Maeght,** one of the world's most famous small
museums of modern art. Monumental sculptures are scattered
around its pine-tree park, and a courtyard full of Alberto
Giacometti's elongated creations separates the two museum buildings. The rooms inside showcase the works of Joan Miró, Georges
Braque, Wassily Kandinsky, Bonnard, Matisse, and others. Few
museums blend form and content so tastefully and imaginatively.
There are also a library, cinema, and auditorium. *Tel. 93-32-81-63.
Admission: 40 frs adults, 30 frs children. Open July–Sept., daily
10-7; Oct.–June, daily 10-12:30 and 2:30-6.*

Lodging and **Colombe d'Or.** Anyone who likes the ambience of a country inn will
Dining feel right at home here. You'll be paying for your meal with cash or
Splurge credit cards; Picasso, Klee, Dufy, Utrillo—all friends of the former
★ owner—paid with the paintings that now decorate the walls. The
restaurant is competent in its cooking, but the prices—count on
spending at least 400 frs—reflect the fame of the hotel rather than
the creativity of the kitchen. The Colombe d'Or is certainly on the
tourist trail, but many of the tourists who stay here are rich and famous—if that's any consolation. *Pl. du Général-de-Gaulle, 06570
St-Paul-de-Vence, tel. 93-32-80-02, fax 93-32-77-78. 24 rooms
with bath. Facilities: restaurant, pool. AE, DC, MC, V. Closed mid-
Nov.–late Dec. 1,150 frs and up.*

Vence

*Buses depart every ½ hour from St-Paul-de-Vence and take 5 min-
utes.*

A few miles farther up into the hills from St-Paul is **Vence.** Unlike
St-Paul, which is confined to a promontory, Vence has had room to

breathe and grow, and is home to merchants and farmers coming to town to sell their produce as well as to its share of artists. Stay here if you prefer mountain air to the humidity of the Mediterranean; you'll find lower prices in the shops up here as well.

The Romans were the first to settle on the 1,000-foot hill; the **cathedral** (built between the 11th and 18th century), rising above the medieval ramparts and traffic-free streets, was erected on the site of a temple to Mars. Of special note are a mosaic by Marc Chagall of Moses in the bullrushes and the ornate 15th-century wooden choir stalls.

★ At the foot of the hill, on the outskirts of Vence, is the **Chapelle du Rosaire,** a small chapel decorated with beguiling simplicity and clarity by Matisse between 1947 and 1951. The walls, floor, and ceiling are gleaming white and are pierced by small stained-glass windows in cool greens and blues. "Despite its imperfections I think it is my masterpiece . . . the result of a lifetime devoted to the search for truth," wrote Matisse, who designed and dedicated the chapel when he was in his eighties and nearly blind. *Av. Henri-Matisse, tel. 93–58–03–26. Admission free. Open Tues. and Thurs. 10–11:30 and 2:30–5.*

Lodging and Dining
$

Le Roseraie. Although there's no rose garden here, a giant magnolia spreads its venerable branches over the terrace of this turn-of-the-century hotel, which offers a fine view of Vence and the surrounding hillside. All the rooms have a sunny southern exposure overlooking the garden and, like the entire hotel, are furnished with antiques that the owners have gathered over the years from auctions and fairs. The warm welcome here, plus the owners' determination to keep three-quarters of their rooms under 500 frs (including breakfast), make La Roseraie one of the best values in the region. *51 av. Henri-Giraud, 06140, tel. 93–58–02–20, fax 93–58–99–31. 12 rooms with bath. Facilities: restaurant (closed Tues. lunch and Wed.), pool. AE, MC, V. Closed Jan.*

Peillon

Two trains run from Nice to Peillon daily. The trip, about 10 km (6 mi) northeast, takes 25 minutes.

★ Situated on a craggy mountaintop more than 1,000 feet above the sea, the fortified medieval town of **Peillon** is the most spectacular and the least spoiled of all the Riviera's cliffside villages. Unchanged since the Middle Ages, it has only a few narrow streets and many steps and covered alleys. And because there's really nothing to do here but look, tour buses stay away, leaving Peillon uncommercialized for its 50 resident families—including professionals summering from Paris and artists who want to escape the insanity of the world below. Stop at the charming **Auberge de la Madame** to pick up the key to the **Chapel of the White Penitents,** a short walk away; spend a half hour exploring the ancient streets; then head back down the mountain to Nice.

Villefranche-sur-Mer

Hourly trains to Villefranche take 6 minutes from Nice, 4 km (2½ mi) to the west.

The harbor town of **Villefranche-sur-Mer** is a miniature version of old Marseille. The sort of place where *Fanny* could have been filmed, it's a stage set of brightly colored houses—orange buildings with lime-green shutters, yellow buildings with ice-blue shutters—with steep narrow streets winding down to the sea. (One, **rue Obscure,** is an actual tunnel.)

The 17th-century **St-Michel** church has a strikingly realistic Christ, carved of boxwood by an unknown convict. The chapel of St-Pierre-des-Pêcheurs, known as the **Cocteau Chapel,** is a small Romanesque chapel once used for storing fishing nets, which the French writer and painter Jean Cocteau decorated in 1957. Visitors walk through the flames of the Apocalypse (represented by staring eyes on either side of the door) and enter a room filled with frescoes of St. Peter, Gypsies, and the women of Villefranche. *Admission: 15 frs. Open May–Oct., Tues.–Sun. 9–noon and 2:30–7; Dec.–Apr., Tues.–Sun. 9:30–noon and 2:30–5.*

To see the chapel, arrive by 4 PM. If you skip the chapel, your best bet is to come at sundown (for dinner, perhaps) and enjoy an hour's walk around the harbor, when the sun turns the soft pastels to gold.

Beaulieu

There are hourly trains to Beaulieu from Villefranche, 3 minutes away, and from Nice, 9 minutes away.

Beaulieu, just next door to Villefranche, was a playground for high society at the turn of the century. Stop and walk along the promenade, sometimes called Petite Afrique (Little Africa) because of its magnificent palm trees, to get a flavor of how things used to be.

The one thing to do in Beaulieu is visit the **Villa Kérylos.** In the early part of the century, a rich amateur archaeologist named Theodore Reinach asked an Italian architect to build an authentic Greek house for him. The villa, now open to the public, is a faithful reproduction, made from cool Carrara marble, alabaster, and rare fruitwoods. The furniture, made of wood inlaid with ivory, bronze, and leather, is copied from drawings of Greek interiors found on ancient vases and mosaics. *Rue Gustave-Eiffel, tel. 93–01–01–44. Admission: 35 frs adults, 15 frs children and senior citizens. Open July–Aug., weekdays 3–7, weekends 10:30–12:30 and 3–7; Sept.–June, Tues.–Fri. 2–5:30, weekends 10:30–12:30 and 2–5:30.*

Eze

There are hourly trains to Eze, which is 5 minutes from Beaulieu and 14 minutes from Nice.

Almost every tour from Nice to Monaco includes a visit to the medieval hill town of **Eze,** perched on a rocky spur some 1,300 feet above the sea. (Don't confuse Eze with the beach town of **Eze-sur-Mer,** which is down by the water.) Be warned that because of its accessibility the town is also crowded and commercial: Eze has its share of serious craftspeople, but most of its vendors make their living selling perfumed soaps and postcards to the package-tour trade.

Enter through a fortified 14th-century gate and wander down narrow, cobblestone streets with vaulted passageways and stairs. The church is 18th century, but the small Chapel of the White Penitents dates to 1306 and contains a 13th-century gilded wooden Spanish Christ and some notable 16th-century paintings. Tourist and crafts shops line the streets leading to the ruins of a castle, which has a scenic belvedere. Some of the most tasteful crafts shops are in the hotel-restaurant **Chèvre d'Or.**

Near the top of the village is a garden with exotic flowers and cacti. (It's worth the admission price, but if you have time for only one exotic garden, visit the one in Monte Carlo.) Also stop in at **La Parfumerie Fragonard,** a branch of a Grasse perfumerie located in front of the public gardens.

Monaco

There are hourly trains to Monaco. The trip takes 8 minutes from Eze, 22 from Nice. Tourist office: 2a boulevard. des Moulins, tel. 93–30–87–01.

Numbers in the margin correspond with points of interest on the Monaco map.

Covering just 473 acres, the **Principality of Monaco** would fit comfortably inside New York's Central Park or a family farm in Iowa. Its 5,000 citizens would fill only a small fraction of the seats in Yankee Stadium. The country is so tiny that residents have to go to another country to play golf.

The present ruler, Prince Rainier III, traces his ancestry to Otto Canella, who was born in 1070. The Grimaldi dynasty began with Otto's great-great-great-grandson, Francesco Grimaldi, also known as Frank the Rogue. Expelled from Genoa, Frank and his cronies disguised themselves as monks and seized the fortified medieval town known today as the Rock in 1297. Except for a short interlude under Napoléon, the Grimaldis have been here ever since, which makes them the oldest reigning family in Europe. On the Grimaldi coat of arms are two monks holding swords (look up and you'll see them above the main door as you enter the palace).

In the 1850s, a Grimaldi named Charles III made a decision that turned the Rock into a figurative giant blue chip. Needing revenues but not wanting to impose additional taxes on his subjects, he contracted with a company to open a gambling facility. The first spin of the roulette wheel was on December 14, 1856. There was no easy way to reach Monaco then—no carriage roads or railroads—so no one came. Between March 15 and March 20, 1857, one person entered the casino—and won 2 frs. In 1868 the railroad came to Monaco, filled with wheezing Englishmen looking to escape the London fog. The effects were immediate. Profits were so great that Charles eventually abolished all direct taxes.

Almost overnight, a threadbare principality became an elegant watering hole for European society. Dukes and duchesses (and their mistresses and gigolos) danced and dined their way through a world of spinning roulette wheels and bubbling champagne—preening themselves for nights at the opera house, where such artists as Vaslav Nijinsky, Sarah Bernhardt, and Enrico Caruso came to perform.

Monte Carlo—the modern gambling town with elegant shops, man-made beaches, high-rise hotels, and a few Belle Epoque hotels—is actually only one of four parts of Monaco. The second is the medieval town on the Rock (**Old Monaco**), 200 feet above the sea, which is where Prince Rainier lives. The third area is **La Condamine,** the commercial harbor area with apartments and businesses, and the fourth is **Fontvieille,** the industrial district situated on 20 acres of reclaimed land.

Start at the Monte Carlo tourist office just north of the casino gardens (ask for the useful English-language booklet *Getting Around in the Principality*), a 10-minute walk downhill from the train station. The **Casino** is a must-see, even if you don't bet a cent. You may find it fun to count the Jaguars and Rolls-Royces parked outside and breathe on the windows of shops selling Saint-Laurent dresses and fabulous jewels. Within the gold-leaf splendor of the casino, where fortunes have been won and shirts have been lost, the hopeful traipse in from tour buses to tempt fate at the slot machines beneath the gilt-edged ceiling.

The main gambling hall, once called the European Room, has been renamed the American Room and fitted with 150 one-armed bandits

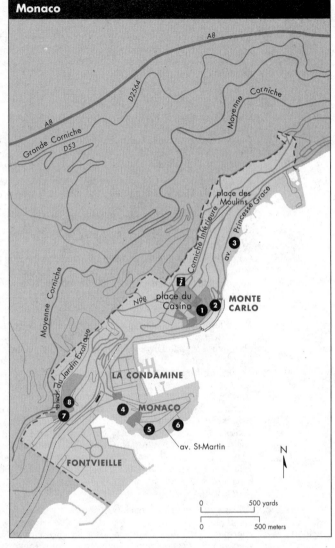

from Chicago. Adjoining it is the Pink Salon, now a bar where unclad nymphs float about on the ceiling smoking cigarillos. The Salles Privées (private rooms) are for high rollers. The stakes are higher here, so the mood is more sober, and well-wishers are herded farther back from the tables.

On July 17, 1924, black came up 17 times in a row on Table 5. This was the longest run ever. A dollar left on black would have grown to $131,072. On August 7, 1913, the number 36 came up three times in a row. In those days, if a gambler went broke, the casino bought him a ticket home.

The casino opens at 10 AM and continues until the last die is thrown. Ties and jackets are required in the back rooms, which open at 3 PM. Bring your passport.

Place du Casino is the center of Monte Carlo, and, in the true spirit of this place, it seems that the **Opera House,** with its 18-ton gilt bronze chandelier, is part of the casino complex. The designer, Charles Garnier, also built the Paris Opéra.

② The serious gamblers, some say, play at **Loews Casino,** nearby. It opens weekdays at 4 PM and weekends at 1 PM. You may want to try parking here, as parking near the old casino is next to impossible in season.

From place des Moulins there is an escalator down to the Larvotto **③** beach complex, artfully created with imported sand, and the **Musée National,** housed in a Garnier villa within a rose garden. This museum has a beguiling collection of 18th- and 19th-century dolls and mechanical automatons, most in working order. *17 av. Princesse-Grace, tel. 93–30–91–26. Admission: 26 frs adults, 15 frs students. Open daily 10–12:15 and 2:30–6:30. Closed holidays.*

Prince Rainier spends much of the year in his grand Italianate **④ palace** on the Rock. The changing of the guard takes place here each morning at 11:55, and the State Apartments can be visited in summer. *Tel. 93–25–18–31. Admission: 26 frs adults, 15 frs children. Joint ticket with Musée Napoléon: 40 frs adults, 20 frs children. Open June–Oct., daily 9:30–6:30.*

One wing of the palace, open throughout the year, is taken up by a museum full of Napoleonic souvenirs and documents related to Monaco's history. *Admission: 20 frs adults, 10 frs children. Joint ticket with palace apartments as above. Open Tues.–Sun. 9:30–6:30.*

From here, a stroll through the medieval alleyways takes you past **⑤** the **cathedral,** a neo-Romanesque monstrosity (1875–84) with several important paintings of the Nice school. Continue to one of **⑥** Monaco's most outstanding showpieces, the **Musée Océanographique,** an important research institute headed by celebrated underwater explorer and filmmaker Jacques Cousteau. Prince Rainier's great-grandfather Albert I (1848–1922), an accomplished marine biologist, founded the institute, which now boasts two exploration ships, laboratories, and a staff of 60 scientists. Nonscientific visitors may wish to make straight for the well-arranged and generously stocked aquarium in the basement. Other floors are devoted to Prince Albert's collection of seashells and whale skeletons, and to Cousteau's diving equipment. *Av. St-Martin, tel. 93–15–36–00. Admission: 60 frs adults, 30 frs students and children. Open July–Aug., daily 9–8, Sept.–June, daily 9:30–7 (6 in winter).*

⑦ A brisk half-hour walk back past the palace brings you to the **Jardin Exotique** (Tropical Garden), where 600 varieties of cacti and **⑧** succulents cling to a sheer rock face. The **Museum of Prehistoric Anthropology,** on the grounds, contains bones, tools, and other artifacts. Shapes of the stalactites and stalagmites in the cavernous grotto resemble the cacti outside. *Blvd. du Jardin-Exotique. Admission: 39 frs adults, 26 frs senior citizens, 16 frs children. Open daily 9–7 (dusk in winter).*

Lodging **Alexandra.** Shades of the Belle Epoque linger in this comfortable ho-
$$ tel's spacious lobby and airy guest rooms. Tan and rose colors dominate the newer rooms, and the friendly proprietress, Madame Larouquie, makes foreign visitors feel right at home. *35 blvd. Princesse-Charlotte, 98000, tel. 93–50–63–13, fax 92–16–08–48. 55 rooms, 46 with bath. AE, DC, MC, V.*

Dining **Polpetta.** This popular little trattoria is close enough to the Italian
$ border to pass for the real McCoy and is an excellent value for the
★ money. If it's on the menu, go for the vegetable *soupe au pistou. 2 rue Paradis, tel. 93–50–67–84. Reservations required in summer. V. Closed Tues., Sat. lunch, and most of Feb.*

Menton

Hourly trains operate from Monaco, 18 minutes away, and from Nice, 40 minutes away. Tourist office: Palais de l'Europe, avenue Boyer, tel. 93–57–57–00.

Menton, a comparatively quiet all-year resort that likes to call itself the Pearl of the Riviera, boasts the area's warmest climate. Lemon trees flourish here, as do senior citizens, enticed by a long strand of beaches. It's beautiful, respectable, and not grossly expensive.

Walk eastward from the casino along promenade du Soleil to the harbor, where there is a small 17th-century fort in which writer, artist, and filmmaker Jean Cocteau (1889–1963) once worked. The fort now houses the **Cocteau Museum**'s collection of fantastical paintings, drawings, stage sets, and a large mosaic. *Bastion du Port, 111 quai Napoléon III, tel. 93–57–72–30. Admission free. Open Apr.–Oct., Wed.–Sun. 10–noon and 2–6; Nov.–Mar., Wed.–Sun. 10–noon and 3–6.*

The quaint old town above the jetty has an Italian feel to it. Visit the church of **St-Michel** for its Baroque interior and altarpiece of St. Michael slaying a dragon. Concerts of chamber music are held on the square on summer nights.

Higher still is the **Vieux Cimetière** (old cemetery), affording a magnificent view of the old town and coast. Here lie Victorian foreigners—Russians, Germans, English—who hoped (in vain, as the dates on the tombstones reveal) that Menton's balmy climate would reverse the ravages of tuberculosis.

Return to the center and the pedestrian rue St-Michel. On avenue de la République, which runs parallel, is the **Hôtel de Ville.** The room where civil marriage ceremonies are conducted has vibrant allegorical frescoes by Cocteau; a tape in English helps to interpret them. *17 rue de la République. Admission 5 frs. Open weekdays 8:30–12:30 and 1:30–5.*

Two other places of interest lie at opposite ends of Menton. To the west is the **Palais Carnolès,** an 18th-century villa once used as a summer retreat by the princes of Monaco. The gardens are beautiful, and the collection of European paintings spanning the 13th to 18th centuries is extensive. *3 av. de la Madone. Admission free. Open Wed.–Sun. 10–noon and 2–6. Closed holidays.*

At the other end of Menton, above the Garavan harbor, lie the **Jardins des Colombières,** where follies and statues lurk among 15 acres of hedges, yew trees, and Mediterranean flowers. *Chemin de Valleya. Admission: 20 frs. Open Feb.–Sept., daily 9–noon and 3–8 (or sunset if earlier).*

Lodging and Dining
$

Londres. The restaurant of this small hotel, close to the beach and casino, serves solid, traditional French fare, and there's a small garden for outdoor dining in summer. *15 av. Carnot, BP 73, 06502 Cedex, tel. 93–35–74–62, fax 93–41–77–78. 26 rooms with shower or bath. Facilities: restaurant (closed Wed.), bar. AE, MC, V. Closed mid-Nov.–mid-Jan.*

14 Toulouse, the Midi-Pyrénées, and Roussillon

Toulouse is a long way from Paris, and the Pyrénées are poorly equipped with public transportation. But with 28,500 square miles stretching from the Massif Central in the north to the Spanish border in the south, the surrounding Midi-Pyrénées—the largest region in France—offers an abundance of historic towns and spectacular mountain scenery. In addition, skiing is less expensive in the Pyrénées than in the Alps, though ski stations are fewer and may have insufficient snow in mild winters.

The Pyrénées, western Europe's highest mountain range after the Alps, are the source of the Garonne, the great river of Toulouse and Bordeaux. The Garonne is joined by the Aveyron, Lot, and Tarn rivers, which cross the region from east to west, carving out steep gorges and wide green valleys. The Pyrenean foothills are riddled with streams, lakes, and spas established in Roman times. Armagnac brandy has its home among the gently undulating hills of the Gers, while farther north, hearty red wine has been produced in the rugged country around Cahors for more than 2,000 years.

Toulouse, known as the Ville Rose because of its soft pink brick, is an upbeat university center whose energetic nightlife smacks more of Spain (less than 2 hours' drive away) than of the drowsy French provinces. The Canal du Midi, built in the 17th century, passes through Toulouse and continues east near the medieval walls of Carcassonne on its way from the Atlantic to the Mediterranean. Smaller towns offer equal charms. Don't miss the fortified medieval bridge at Cahors or the extensive town walls at Carcassonne. Pilgrims flock to Lourdes as they once flocked to the dramatic cliffside village of Rocamadour, the architectural embodiment of vertical takeoff. At Montauban is the Musée Ingres, devoted to one of France's most accomplished pre-Impressionist painters. Albi stands out for the Musée Toulouse-Lautrec, with its racy testimony to the acuity of the leading observer of Belle Epoque cabaret, and the redbrick cathedral of Ste-Cécile, the most impressive monument in the Midi-Pyrénées, with slits for windows and walls like cliffs.

The attractive Mediterranean coast between Narbonne and the Spanish border can easily be reached from Toulouse and is covered on our tour of Roussillon. Perpignan, its capital, has a bustling, Spanish feel: Roussillon has strong linguistic and historic ties with Catalonia, across the Pyrénées, and was ceded by Spain to France as recently as 1659. The streets of even the smallest towns are awash with the proud Catalan colors of *sang et or* (blood and gold).

Midi-Pyrénées Basics

Budget Lodging Hotels in this vast region range from Mediterranean-style modern to Middle Ages baronial; most are small and cozy rather than luxurious. Toulouse, the area's only major town, has the usual range of big-city hotels; make reservations well ahead if you plan to visit in spring or fall. As with most of France, many of the hotels we list offer excellent eating opportunities.

Budget Dining The cuisine in Toulouse and the southwest is rich and strongly seasoned, making generous use of garlic and goose fat. This is the land of foie gras, especially delicious when sautéed with grapes. The most famous regional dish is *cassoulet*, a succulent white-bean stew with *confit* (preserved goose), spicy sausage, pork, and sometimes lamb; there are a number of local versions around Toulouse and Carcassonne. Goose and duck dishes are legion: Try a *magret de canard* (a steak of duck breast). Cheaper specialties include *garbure*, mixed vegetables served as a broth or puree; *farci du lauragais*, a kind of pork pancake; and *gigot de sept heures*, a leg of lamb. Béarn, west of Toulouse around Pau, is great eating country, famous for richly marinated stews made with wood pigeon (*civet de palombes*) or wild goat (*civet d'isnard*). The local *poule au pot* of stuffed chicken poached with vegetables is memorable.

Bargain Shopping Don't leave the Midi-Pyrénées without buying some of the region's renowned foie gras and preserved duck (*confit de canard*). Two manufacturers in particular, **Aux Ducs de Gascogne** and **Comtesse de Barry**, offer beautifully packaged tins that make ideal gifts. You'll find their products in most good grocery stores and general food shops throughout the region.

Biking The attractive, varied terrain north of Toulouse and the desperately flat Garonne Valley make for enjoyable cycling; you can rent bikes at the Cahors, Rocamadour, Albi, and Rodez rail stations. The banks and tow paths of the Canal du Midi offer less strenuous terrain (you can rent a bike from the Carcassonne station). Sturdier cyclists may opt to attack the Pyrenean foothills; contact **Cycles Fun** (3 pl. Comminges) in Bagnères-de-Luchon, or **Marc de Baudoine** (28 rue Polinaires) in Toulouse, which specialize in mountain bikes. You can also rent bikes at the Luchon, Foix, and Lourdes stations.

Hiking The Midi-Pyrénées offers more than 2,000 miles of marked paths for walkers and hikers, all designed to pass natural and historical sights. Local tourist offices have detailed maps, or, for advance information, contact **Comité Régional du Tourisme Midi-Pyrénées** (54 blvd. de l'Embouchure, B.P. 2166, 31022 Toulouse cedex, tel. 61–13–55–55, fax 51–47–17–16).

Beaches The long beaches of coarse sand along the Mediterranean coast attract French families who do not want the glitz or expense of the Riviera. Few foreign tourists, however, make these beaches their base for a vacation.

Arts and Nightlife Toulouse, the region's cultural high spot, is also recognized as one of France's most art-rich cities. Its classical, lyrical, and chamber music orchestras, dramatic-arts center, and ballet are all listed as national companies—no mean feat in this arts-oriented country. So many opera singers have come to sing here at the Théâtre du Capitole or the Halle aux Grains that the city is known as the *capitale du bel canto.*

Festivals The medieval city of Carcassonne has a major arts festival in July, featuring dance, theater, classical music, and jazz; for details, contact the Théâtre Municipal (B.P. 236, rue Courtejaire, 11005 Carcassonne cedex, tel. 68–25–33–13).

Tour 1:
The Toulouse Region

Swinging Toulouse, rosy with its pink-brick buildings, is the base for a counterclockwise tour through Rodez, Cahors, and Montauban, with visits to other points of interest en route.

From Paris Express trains to Toulouse leave Paris (Gare d'Austerlitz) six times
By Train daily. The trip takes 6–6½ hours.

By Car Allow 8–9 hours for the arduous 705-kilometer (440-mile) drive from Paris to Toulouse via A10 and A71, then N20 from Vierzon.

Toulouse

Tourist office: Donjon du Capitole, behind the Capitole itself, tel. 61–23–32–00.

Numbers in the margin correspond with points of interest on the Toulouse map.

Ebullient **Toulouse** lies just 96-odd km (60 mi) from the Spanish border, and its flavor is more Spanish than French. The city's downtown sidewalks and restaurants are thronged way past midnight as foreign tourists mingle with immigrant workers, college students, and technicians from the giant Airbus aviation complex headquartered outside the city. Toulouse is a hectic place, its streets jammed with cars and its pavements with people. However, most sights are within easy walking distance, and a new métro system that runs east–west and costs 7 frs for one zone (most of central Toulouse is within a zone) eases congested bus routes.

Head over the canal in front of Gare Matabiau and take rue de Bayard. Cross boulevard de Strasbourg and continue down rue de Rémusat to the town center. **Place du Capitole**, a vast, open square lined with shops and cafés, is the best spot for getting your bearings. One side of the square is occupied by the 18th-century facade of the
❶ **Capitole** itself, home of the Hôtel de Ville and the city's highly regarded opera company. The coats of arms of the Capitouls, the former rulers of Toulouse, can be seen on the balconies in the Capitole's courtyard, and the building's vast reception rooms are open to visitors when not in use for official functions. Halfway up the Grand Escalier (Grand Staircase) hangs a large painting of the *Jeux Floraux*, the Floral Games organized by the Compagnie du Gai-Savoir—a literary society created in 1324 to promote the local language, Langue d'Oc. The festival continues to this day: Poets give public readings here each May, the best receiving silver- and gold-plated flowers as prizes.

Four more giant paintings in the Salle Henri-Martin, named after the artist (1860–1943), show how important the River Garonne has always been to the region. Look out for Jean Jaurès, one of France's greatest Socialists (1859–1914), in *Les Rêveurs* (*The Dreamers*); he's wearing a boater and a beige-colored coat. *Pl. du Capitole, tel.*

61–22–29–22 (ext. 3412) to check opening times. Admission free. Closed Tues. and weekends.

② Head north from place du Capitole along rue du Taur, lined with tiny shops. Half a block up is the 14th-century church of **Notre-Dame du Taur,** built on the spot where St-Saturnin (or Sernin), the martyred bishop of Toulouse, was dragged to his death in AD 257 by a rampaging bull. The church is famous for its *cloche-mur,* or wall tower; the wall looks more like an extension of the facade than a tower or steeple and has inspired many similar versions throughout the Toulouse region.

★ ③ The basilica of **St-Sernin,** Toulouse's most famous landmark, lies at the far end of rue du Taur. The basilica once belonged to a Benedictine abbey built in the 11th century to house pilgrims on their way to Santiago de Compostela in Spain. When illuminated at night, St-Sernin's five-tiered octagonal tower glows red against the sky, dominating the city. Not all the tiers are the same: The first three, with their rounded windows, are Romanesque; the upper two, with their pointed Gothic windows, were added around 1300.

The size of the basilica—particularly the width of the transept, more than 68 feet—is striking. It's worth paying the token entry fee to the crypt and ambulatory to admire the tomb of St-Sernin and seven exquisitely preserved marble bas-reliefs of Christ and his apostles, dating from the end of the 11th century. *Rue du Taur, tel. 61–21–70–18. Admission to crypt: 10 frs. Open daily 10–11:30 and 2:30–5:30.*

④ Opposite the basilica is the **Musée St-Raymond,** the city's archaeological museum. The ground floor has an extensive collection of imperial Roman busts, and the second floor is devoted to the applied arts, featuring ancient and medieval coins, lamps, vases, and jewelry. *Pl. St-Sernin, tel. 61–22–21–85. Admission: 10 frs adults, 5 frs children. Open Wed.–Mon. 8–noon and 2–6 (closed Sun. morning).*

⑤ Retrace your steps down rue du Taur, turn right at place du Capitole and then left onto rue Lakanal to arrive at the **Jacobins church,** built in the 1230s for the Dominicans; the name Jacobins was given to the Dominicans in 1217 when they set up their Paris base at the Porte St-Jacques. The church was harmoniously restored in the 1970s, its interior retaining the original orange-ocher tones. The two rows of columns running the length of the nave—to separate the monks from their congregation—is a feature of Dominican churches, though this one is special, as the column standing the farthest from the entrance is said to support the world's finest example of palm-tree vaulting. The original refectory is used for temporary art exhibitions, and the cloisters provide an atmospheric setting for the city's summer music festival.

⑥ Around the corner, on rue Gambetta, stands the **Hôtel de Bernuy,** built during the 16th century, when Toulouse was at its most prosperous. Merchant Jean de Bernuy made his fortune exporting pastel, a blue dye made from the leaves of a plant cultivated around Toulouse and Albi and used to color cloth, especially bed linen. Merchant wealth is reflected in the mansion's use of stone, a costly material in this region of brick, and by the octagonal stair tower, the highest in the city. Building such towers was a rarely bestowed privilege, and this one makes its opulent point by rising above the ceiling of the top floor. The Hôtel de Bernuy is now part of a school, but you may wander freely around its courtyard.

⑦ Walk down rue Jean-Suau to place de la Daurade and the 18th-century church of **Notre-Dame de la Daurade,** overlooking the River Garonne. The name "Daurade" comes from *doré* (gilt), referring to the golden reflection given off by the mosaics decorating the 5th-centu-

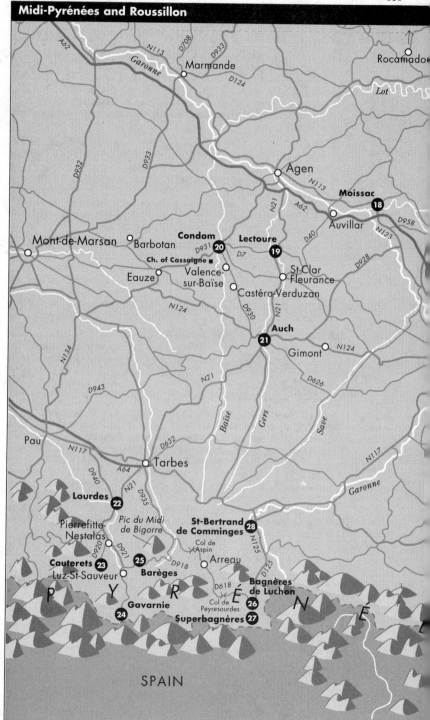

A62
Garonne
N113
D708
D933
Marmande
D124
Rocamado[...]
Lot

D832
D633
Agen
N113
Moissac **18**
A62
N21
Auvillar
D40
D958
D133

Mont-de-Marsan
Barbotan
Condom
20
Lectoure
D931
D7
19
D928
Ch. of Cassaigne ■
Valence-sur-Baïse
St-Clar
Fleurance

Eauze
Castéra-Verduzan
N124
D920
N21
Auch **21**
Gimont
N124

N134
N21
D626
Baïse
Gers
Save
D943

Pau
N117
D632
N117
Garonne
D940
A64
N21
Tarbes

Lourdes
22
D935
St-Bertrand de Comminges **28**
Pierrefitte-Nestalas
Pic du Midi de Bigorre
Col de Aspin
D125
D220
D22
25
D918
Arreau
Cauterets **23**
Luz-St-Sauveur
Barèges
D618
Bagnères de Luchon
P   Y   R
Col de Peyresourdes **26**
Gavarnie
24
Superbagnères **27**
N   É

SPAIN

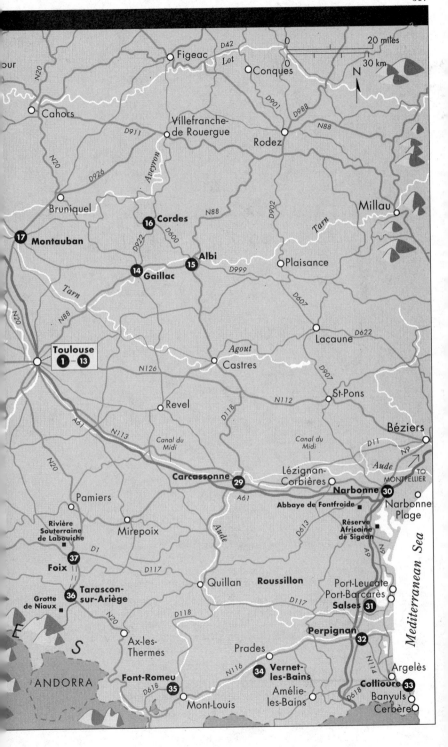

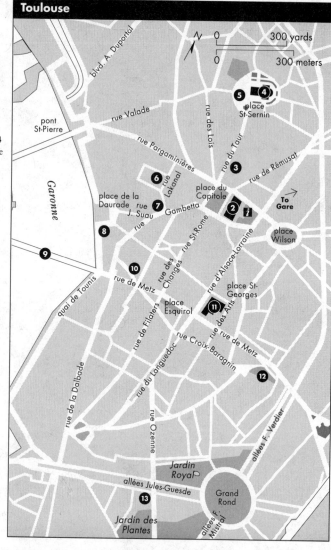

ry temple to the Virgin that once stood on this site. The flowers presented to the winners of the Floral Games are blessed here.

Take time to saunter along quai de la Daurade, beside the church,
and admire the view from **Pont Neuf** across to the left bank. Then
head east along rue de Metz. A hundred yards down, on the left, is
the **Hôtel d'Assézat,** built in 1555 by Toulouse's top Renaissance architect, Nicolas Bachelier. The facade is particularly striking: Su-
perimposed classical orders frame alternating arcades and
rectangular windows, with ornately carved doorways below. Climb
to the top of the tower for splendid views over the city rooftops. *Rue
de Metz. Admission free. Open daily 10–noon and 2–6.*

Continue along rue de Metz. The second road on the left (rue des
Changes, which becomes rue St-Rome) was once part of the Roman
road that sliced through Toulouse from north to south; today it's a
chic pedestrian shopping area. Running parallel is the swinging rue
d'Alsace-Lorraine, a center of nightlife, luxury boutiques, and de-

partment stores. On the corner of rue d'Alsace-Lorraine and rue de Metz, just beyond busy place Esquirol, is the largest museum in Toulouse: the **Musée des Augustins,** housed in a medieval Augustinian convent whose sacristy, chapter house, and cloisters provide an attractive setting for an outstanding array of Romanesque sculpture and religious paintings by such renowned artists as Spain's Bartolomé Esteban Murillo (1618–82) and Flemish maestro Peter Paul Rubens (1577–1640). *21 rue de Metz, tel. 61–23–55–07. Admission: 10 frs (free Sun.). Open Wed. 10–9, Thurs.–Mon. 10–5.*

From the Musée des Augustins, cross rue de Metz and head down rue des Arts, then turn left along rue Croix-Baragnin to place St-Etienne, site of both the city's oldest fountain, in marble (16th century), and of the cathedral of **St-Etienne,** erected in stages between the 13th and the 17th centuries. The nave and choir look awkward because they are not properly aligned. A fine collection of 16th- and 17th-century tapestries traces the life of St. Stephen (Etienne, in French).

The broad allées François-Verdier leads to the leafy, circular Grand Rond, flanked by the **Jardin Royal** (royal gardens) and **Jardin des Plantes** (botanical gardens)—home of the **Musée d'Histoire Naturelle** and its varied collection of stuffed birds and prehistoric exhibits. *35 allées Jules-Guesde, tel. 61–52–00–14. Gardens admission free; open daily dawn to dusk. Museum admission: 8 frs; open Wed.–Mon. 10–5.*

Lodging **Hotel Albert 1er.** The new building appears rather ordinary and the
$
★ reception area is merely pleasant and functional, but the newly furnished guest rooms are cheerful and as spacious as you can expect for a hotel in the heart of Toulouse. The extremely personable owner, Mme. Hilaire, is usually on hand for a chat and to give suggestions on where to dine and to shop. There is a small lounge and breakfast room, but no restaurant. *8 rue Rivals, 31000, tel. 61–21–17–91, fax 61–21–09–64. 46 rooms with bath. MC, V.*

$ **Taur.** If you want to be in the hub of things without paying grand-hotel prices, the Taur, just a stone's throw from the Capitole, is a workmanlike option. Its labyrinthine corridors have a faded, creaky charm, and the welcome is courteous. But be prepared for soft mattresses, viewless rooms, and gaudily florid wallpaper. *2 rue du Taur, 31000, tel. 62–21–17–54. 41 rooms, most with shower. AE, MC, V.*

Dining **La Belle Epoque.** Owner Pierre Roudgé's approach to cooking is
$$ novel: Tell him what you don't like and he'll invent your menu on the spot. The ginger-spiced lobster in a flaky pastry is as good as it sounds, especially in the handsomely renovated 1920s setting. However, be prepared for prices that nudge toward the expensive range. *3 rue Pargaminières, tel. 61–23–22–12. Reservations advised. AE, DC, MC, V. Closed Sat. and Mon. lunch, Sun., and July.*

$ **Chez Emile.** There are two dining rooms at this restaurant overlooking place St-Georges. The ground floor is modern and elegant, specializing in light, contemporary fish dishes that change daily; if it's on the menu, try the turbot in ginger. Upstairs is a cozy hideaway for those who appreciate a more traditional taste of Toulouse: cassoulet, *magret de canard* (duck), and other filling fare. *13 pl. St-Georges, tel. 61–21–05–56. Reservations required. AE, DC, MC, V. Closed last wk in Aug., Sun., and Mon.*

$ **La Cave Bistro.** Just a few minutes' walk away from the Capitole, this tiny hideaway with stucco walls and a heavy beamed ceiling offers good provincial fare with very reasonable fixed-price menus. A three-course lunch that may include salad with locally cured ham, a grilled entrecôte, and fruit flan for dessert is only about 55 frs—add another 30 frs for a carafe of wine. *18 rue du Taur, tel. 61–22–47–94. AE, DC, V. Closed Sun.*

Shopping The **Centre Commercial St-Georges**, a frenetic, modern shopping mall downtown (rue du Rempart St-Etienne), offers a vast array of clothing, jewelry, books—and just about anything else you'd possibly want to buy or admire. For upscale clothes, try the chic shops on **rue St-Rome** and **rue d'Alsace-Lorraine,** home to Toulouse's main department store, **Nouvelles Galeries,** which, like its sister store in Paris, Galeries Lafayette, provides a good range of services for foreign visitors (including overseas shipment and payment with any major credit card).

The Arts The performing arts season here lasts from October until late May, though there are occasional summer presentations. Toulouse's **Ballet du Capitole** stages classical ballets, and the **Ballet-Théâtre Joseph Russilo** and **Compagnie Jean-Marc Matos** put on modern-dance performances. The **Centre National Chorégraphique de Toulouse** welcomes international companies each year in the St-Cyprien quarter. For performing arts schedules, get in touch with the city tourist office.

Nightlife For a complete list of clubs and discos, buy a copy of *Toulouse Pratique* at any bookshop or newspaper stand. One of the best spots is **L'Art Club** (1 rue de l'Echarpe), a trendy club in a vaulted brick cellar in the Esquirol quarter. If you like a more intimate setting, try **La Cendrée** (15 rue des Tourneurs), which has lots of cozy nooks and crannies. **L'Ubu** (16 rue St-Rome), the city's top night spot for more than 20 years, is where the local glitterati and concert and theater stars come to relax. Liberated couples love **Victory-Clippers Club** (Canal de Brienne, 90 allée de Barcelone), though it may be a bit daring for some. **Le Café des Allées** (64 allées Charles-de-Fitte) is a hot spot among local jazz musicians. **Le Père Bacchus** (20 pl. St.-Georges) is the trendiest jazz club on the city's trendiest square.

Albi

Trains make the 65-minute run from Toulouse every 2 hours. Tourist office: place Ste-Cécile, tel. 63–54–22–30.

Albi, a tastefully preserved old town full of narrow streets and redbrick buildings, was once a major center for Cathars, members of an ascetic religious sect that rejected earthly life as evil and criticized the worldly ways of the Catholic Church; the town's huge ca-
★ thedral of **Ste-Cécile** was meant to symbolize the Catholic Church's return to power after the crusade against the Cathars (or Albigensians, as they came to be known) at the start of the 13th century. With its intimidating clifflike walls, the cathedral appears as a cross between a castle, a power station, and an ocean liner.

Its interior is an ornate reply to the massive austerity of the ocher outer walls. Every possible surface has been painted; the leading contributors were a 16th-century team of painters from Bologna, Italy, who splattered the main vault with saints and Old Testament *venerati*, then lined the bays with religious scenes and brightly colored patterns. The most striking fresco, however, is a 15th-century depiction of the Last Judgment, which extends across the west wall beneath the 18th-century organ loft. Unfortunately, its central section was demolished in 1693, to make the St-Clair chapel.

Between the cathedral and the Pont Vieux (Old Bridge) spanning
★ the River Tarn stands the **Palais de la Berbie.** Built in 1265 originally as a fortress, then converted into the Bishop's Palace, it has now been transformed into a museum honoring Albi's most famous son: Belle Epoque painter Henri de Toulouse-Lautrec (1864–1901).

Toulouse-Lautrec left Albi for Paris in 1882 and soon made his name with racy evocations of the bohemian glamour of the cabarets, music halls, bars, and cafés in and around Montmartre. Despite his aristocratic origins (Lautrec is a town not far from Toulouse), Henri cut a far-from-noble figure. He was less than 5 feet tall (his growth was stunted by slipping on the floor in his bedroom and not, as a popular movie on his life suggests, by a childhood riding accident) and he pursued a decadent life that led to an early grave. The Albi exhibit is the country's largest collection of Toulouse-Lautrecs, with 600 works beautifully presented, notably in the lengthy Galérie Ambrie (holding his earliest efforts) and in the rooms leading from the Salon Rose (portraits and lithographs). *Just off pl. Ste-Cécile, tel. 63–54–14–09. Admission: 22 frs adults, 12 frs children. Open Easter–Oct., daily 10–noon and 2–6; Nov.–Easter, Wed.–Mon. 10–noon and 2–5.*

Before leaving Albi, stroll around the old town to admire its pedestrian-only streets and elegant shops. You may also be able to visit Lautrec's birthplace, **Maison Natale de Toulouse-Lautrec** (14 rue Henri de Toulouse-Lautrec, along blvd. Sibille from the cathedral), to see more of his early works, as well as his personal possessions and memorabilia. The house is privately owned, and occasionally during the summer it is opened to the public. Check with the tourist office for schedules.

Lodging
$$
Orléans. Despite its ritzy modern facade, the Orléans is a large, traditional station hotel. Room rates are reasonable, the welcome is cheerful, and the set menus start at 85 frs. *Pl. de Stalingrad, 81000, tel. 63–54–16–56, fax 63–54–43–41. 55 rooms with bath or shower. Facilities: restaurant (closed Sat. lunch and Sun.), exercise room. AE, DC, MC, V. Closed Christmas through New Year's.*

Dining
$$
Le Jardin des Quatre Saisons. There are two reasons for this restaurant's excellent reputation: value for the money and very good seafood. Ask the sommelier to help you choose a bottle from the extensive wine list to accompany one of the chef's fish dishes. House specialties include mussels baked with leeks and *suprême de sandre* (a type of perch) in wine. Desserts are surprisingly light. Try for a table in the garden. *19 blvd. de Strasbourg, tel. 63–60–77–76. Reservations advised. Jacket and tie required. AE, MC, V. Closed Mon.*

Lodging and Dining
$$
Mercure Albi Bastides. Ask for a room with a view in this converted 18th-century mill, which overlooks the River Tarn. The ones on the second and fourth floor are best (those on the third and top floors have tiny windows), but all are functional, modern, and fairly cramped, with utilitarian bathrooms. The hotel's restaurant is a stylish place to try Eric Sanchez's regional specialties, such as *fritons*—peanut-size chunks of duck lard in flaky pastry with capers; they're a great deal more appetizing than they sound. Dine on the terrace in summer. *41 rue Porta, 81000, tel. 63–47–66–66, fax 63–46–18–40. 56 rooms with bath. Facilities: restaurant, terrace. AE, DC, MC, V.*

$
Hôtel du Vieil-Alby. On a pedestrian-only street in the center of the old town, the Vieil-Alby is a small, simple hotel in a very old building. Rooms are small and oddly shaped but clean, and each has a shower or bath. The restaurant offers a good three-course menu for 75 frs during weekdays (110 frs on weekends for a different menu). Half-pension is required in September. *25 rue Henri-de-Toulouse-Lautrec, 81000, tel. 63–54–14–69, fax 63–54–96–75. 19 rooms. Facilities: restaurant (closed Sun. dinner and Mon., except in July and Aug.). MC, V.*

Rodez

Five trains daily make the 85-minute run from Albi, 78 km (48 mi) southwest. The center of town is a stiff 15-minute walk uphill. Tourist office: place du Maréchal-Foch, tel. 65–68–02–27.

Rodez, capital of the Aveyron *département,* sits on a windswept hill between the arid, Causses plateau and the verdant Ségala hills.

Towering over the town is the pink sandstone cathedral of **Notre-Dame** (13th to 15th centuries). Its awesome bulk is lightened by the decorative upper stories, completed in the 17th century, and by the magnificent 285-foot bell tower. The interior contains ornamental altarpieces, an elaborate 15th-century choir screen, and a 17th-century organ within an intricate wooden casing.

The renovated **Cité quarter,** once ruled by medieval bishops, lies behind the cathedral; attractive pedestrian zones surround place du Bourg. On tiny place de l'Olmet, just off place du Bourg, stands the 16th-century **House of Armagnac,** a fine Renaissance mansion with a courtyard and an ornate facade covered with medallion emblems of the counts of Rodez.

Farther on, at place de la Madeleine, is the 18th-century church of **St-Amans,** featuring finely preserved Romanesque capitals and, inside, some colorful 16th-century tapestries. The extensively modernized **Musée Denys Puech,** an art gallery noted for works by local painters and sculptors, lies just east of the wide boulevard that encircles the old town. *Pl. Clemenceau, tel. 65–42–70–64. Admission: 17 frs adults, 12 frs children under 18 (free Wed.). Open Mon. 2–8, Wed.–Sat. 10–noon and 3–7, Sun. 3–7.*

Lodging and Dining
¢
Midi. Pierre and Martine de Schepper are the enthusiastic hosts at this pleasant hotel near the cathedral in the old part of town. To savor the filling regional cuisine, you can't do better than to sample the 70- and 105-franc menus offered in the spacious dining room. *1 rue de Béteille, 12000, tel. 65–68–02–07, fax 65–68–66–93. 34 rooms, most with shower. Facilities: restaurant (closed Sun. and Mon.). MC, V. Closed mid-Dec.–mid-Jan. and Sat. in winter.*

Figeac

Five trains daily make the 85-minute run northwest from Rodez. The 3 daily trains north from Toulouse take 2¼ hours. The train station is a 10-minute walk south of the town center. Tourist office: place Vival, tel. 65–34–06–25.

Figeac, a charming old town with a lively Saturday-morning market, grew up around an abbey in the 9th century, becoming, in turn, a stopping point for pilgrims plodding from Conques to Compostela. Many houses in the old part of town, from the 13th, 14th, and 15th centuries, have been carefully restored to preserve their octagonal chimneys, rounded archways and arcades, and *soleilhos,* open attics used for drying flowers and stocking wood.

The 13th-century **Hôtel de la Monnaie,** a block from the River Célé, is a characteristic example, an elegant building probably used as a medieval money-changing office. These days it houses the tourist office and a museum displaying fragments of sculpture and religious relics found in the town. *Pl. Vival, tel. 65–34–06–25. Admission free. Open July–Aug., daily 10–noon and 2:30–6:30; Sept.–June, Mon.–Sat. 3–5.*

Figeac was the birthplace of Jean-François Champollion (1790–1832), one of the first men who deciphered Egyptian hieroglyphic script. The **Musée Champollion** (leave place Vival on rue 11-novembre, take the first left, and follow it as it bends right) contains a casting of the Rosetta stone, discovered in the Nile delta; the stone's three renderings of the same inscription—in hieroglyphic and demotic Egyptian and in ancient Greek—enabled the mysteries of the Pharaonic dialect to be penetrated for the first time. On the ground floor of the museum, a film traces Champollion's life. *5 impasse Champollion, tel. 65–34–66–18. Admission: 22 frs adults, 14 frs children. Open May–Sept., Tues.–Sat. 10–noon and 2:30–6:30.*

Rocamadour

There are five daily trains northwest from Figeac; the trip takes 40 minutes. The station is 5 km (3 mi) from the village—walk or take a taxi. Tourist office: Hôtel de Ville, tel. 65–33–62–59.

★ The medieval village of **Rocamadour** seems to defy the laws of gravity as it surges out of a cliff 1,500 feet above the Alzou River gorge.

Rocamadour got its name after the miraculous discovery in 1166 of the body of St-Amadour "quite whole" under a sanctuary. (This was a major event: Amadour had died a thousand years earlier and was allegedly none other than Zaccheus, the tax collector of Jericho, who had come to live in Gaul as a hermit after Christ persuaded him to give up his money-grubbing ways.) Amadour's body was displayed in the church and began to work miracles. Its fame soon spread to Portugal, Spain, and Sicily, and pilgrims flocked to the site, climbing the 216 steps to the church on their knees. Making the climb on foot is sufficient reminder of the medieval penchant for agonizing penance, and today an elevator assists weary souls.

The staircase and elevator start from place de la Carreta; those on foot can pause at a landing after the first 141 steps to admire the **Fort,** as the 14th-century Bishop's Palace is invitingly called. The remaining steps lead to tiny place St-Amadour and its seven sanctuaries: the basilica of **St-Sauveur** opposite the staircase; the **St-Amadour crypt** under the basilica; the chapel of **Notre-Dame** to the left; the chapels of **John the Baptist, St-Blaise,** and **Ste-Anne** to the right; and the Romanesque chapel of **St-Michel,** built into the overhanging cliff. St. Michel's two 12th-century frescoes—depicting the Annunciation and the Visitation—are in superb condition. *Centre d'Accueil Notre-Dame. English-speaking guide available. Guided tours Mon.–Sat. 9–5; tips at visitors' discretion.*

The village itself is full of beautifully restored medieval houses. One of the finest is the 15th-century **Hôtel de Ville,** near the Porte Salmon, which also houses the tourist office and a fine collection of tapestries. *Admission free. Open Mon.–Sat. 10–noon and 3–8.*

At the **Rocher des Aigles**, about 3 km (2 mi) outside of town, a hundred different species of birds of prey, including condors and vultures as well as eagles, swoop high and low at the command of their expert handlers. *Rte. du Château, tel. 65–33–65–45. Admission: 30 frs adults, 15 frs children. Open Apr.–mid-Nov. for demonstrations daily at 11, 3, 4, 5, and 6.*

Lodging and Dining
$$
Le Beau Site. How often can you spend the night in a medieval village in a building clinging to a rock face? This is the best hotel of the few in the old town, which is where you really want to stay. It has ordinary but comfortable rooms (the antique charm of the ancient beams, exposed stone, and open hearth in the foyer ends as you climb the stairs), many with wonderful views (but not the three new rooms at the back), and a staff that's helpful and friendly. The dining room is across the street on the edge of a ravine, affording dramatic views. The fare is straightforward French. *rue Roland-le-Preux, Cité Médiévale, 46500, tel. 65–33–63–08, fax 65–33–65–23. 55 rooms with bath or shower. Facilities: restaurant. MC, V. Closed mid-Dec.–mid-Jan.*

$ **Panoramic.** Most restaurants and hotels in Rocamadour have terrific views. But this cheerful family hotel perched on the clifftop near the castle, a short stroll from the elevator, has a better view than most—and a leafy dining terrace from which to enjoy it. There are 95- and 120-franc menus in the restaurant, and the management organizes excursions for guests along the Dordogne and Lot valleys. *L'Hospitalet, 46500, tel. 65–33–63–06, fax 65–33–69–26. 21 rooms with bath or shower. Facilities: bar, restaurant, pool. AE, DC, MC, V. Closed Nov.–mid-Feb.*

Cahors

The eight direct trains per day from Toulouse north to Cahors take about 70 minutes. The train station is on the western edge of town, a 10-minute walk from the cathedral. Tourist office: place Aristide-Briand, tel. 65–35–09–56.

Once an opulent Gallo-Roman settlement, **Cahors** sits snugly within a loop of the River Lot. The town is perhaps best known for its tannic red wine—often, in fact, a deep purple, and known to the Romans as "black wine"—which you can taste at many of the small estates nearby. The finest sight in Cahors is the **Pont Valentré,** a spellbinding feat of medieval engineering whose tall, elegant towers have loomed over the river since 1360.

Rue du Président-Wilson cuts across town from the bridge to the old quarter of Cahors around the kathedral of **St-Etienne,** easily recognized by its cupolas and fortresslike appearance. The tympanum over the north door was sculpted around 1135, with figures portraying the Ascension and the life of St-Etienne. The cloisters, to the right of the choir, contain a corner pillar embellished with a charmingly sculpted Annunciation Virgin with long, flowing hair. The cloisters connect with the courtyard of the archdeaconry, awash with Renaissance decoration and thronged with visitors viewing its temporary art exhibits.

Lodging and Dining $–$$ **Terminus.** This small, ivy-covered hotel is deep in the heart of truffle country yet just two minutes' walk from Cahors train station; its restaurant, La Balandre, is the city's best. The decor is mainly Roaring Twenties and the atmosphere is comfortably traditional, emphasized by the filtered light from the stained-glass windows in the lobby. Gilles Marre and his wife, Jacqueline, specialize in truffles but also serve an exceptional fresh cod *brandade* (mousse) and foie gras in flaky pastry. There's a good range of local wines, and the service is sophisticated yet friendly. The guest rooms are cozily traditional in feel. *5 av. Charles-de-Freycinet, 46000, tel. 65–35–24–50, fax 65–37–95–93. 31 rooms with bath. Facilities: restaurant (reservations advised; closed 2 wks in Feb., 1 wk in June, Sun. dinner and Mon. Jan.–Mar., and Sat. lunch July–Aug.) AE, MC, V.*

Dining ¢ **Le Coq & La Pendule.** This small café-restaurant on a pedestrian street near the cathedral offers homey French cooking in a down-home setting. Space is tight and it's all hustle-bustle, but service is friendly and portions generous. And a five-course meal with wine and coffee won't cost much more than 80 frs. *10 rue St-James, tel. 65–35–28–84. No credit cards.*

Montauban

There are seven daily trains from Cahors; the trip takes 45 minutes. Hourly trains make the 30-minute journey north from Toulouse. Tourist office: 2 rue du Collège, tel. 63–63–60–60.

Perched above the rich alluvial plains of the Tarn and Garonne rivers, **Montauban** was, in the 13th century, a *bastide*, a fortified town particular to the southwest. Today it is known for the deep rose color of its brickwork, especially beautiful at sunset.

Montauban was the birthplace of the great painter Jean Auguste Dominique Ingres (1780–1867). Ingres was the last of the great French Classicists, who took their cue from Raphaël, favoring line over color and taking much of their subject matter from the antique world. Ingres's personal dislike of Eugène Delacroix (the earliest and most important French Romantic painter), his sour personality, and (for some) his arid painting style, with its worship of line and technical draftsmanship, led many contemporaries to ridicule his work. These days, Ingres is undergoing a considerable revival in popularity.

★ The **Musée Ingres** is housed in the sturdy, brick 17th-century Bishop's Palace overlooking the River Tarn. Ingres has the second floor to himself; note the contrast between his love of myth *(Ossian's Dream)* and his deadpan, uncompromising portraiture *(Madame Gonse)*, underscored by a closet eroticism (silky-skinned nudes) that belies the staid reputation of academic art. The exhibit also includes hundreds of Ingres's drawings, plus some of his personal possessions—including his beloved violin. Most of the paintings are from Ingres's excellent private collection, ranging from his followers (Théodore Chassériau) and precursors (Jacques-Louis David) to Old Masters. *Pl. Bourdelle, tel. 63–63–18–04. Admission: 15 frs adults, 10 frs students. Open July–Aug., Mon.–Sat. 9:30–noon and 1:30–6, Sun. 1:30–6; Sept.–June, Tues.–Sat. 10–noon and 2–6.*

Take some time to explore the old streets of Montauban, especially the pedestrian zone around the restored place Nationale (home to a lively morning market). Check out the classical cathedral of **Notre-Dame** on place Roosevelt: Its white stone is an eye-catching contrast to the pink brick of other buildings; inside there is a major Ingres painting, the *Vow of Louis XIII.*

Lodging and Dining   **Midi.** This friendly, rambling old hotel near the cathedral offers spacious rooms with bath priced at all of 290 frs as well as smaller, spartan ones that go for as little as 210 francs a night. The restaurant's 85-franc menu is a good bet. *12 rue Notre-Dame, 82000, tel. 63–63–17–23, fax 63–66–43–66. 64 rooms, some with bath or shower. Facilities: bar, restaurant (closed mid-Dec.–mid-Jan.). AE, DC, MC, V.*

$

Moissac

The six daily trains covering the 29 km (18 mi) northwest from Montauban take 20 minutes. There are five trains daily from Toulouse, taking between 45 minutes and 1 hour.

★ **Moissac,** on the right bank of the River Tarn, was once a stop for pilgrims on their way to Santiago de Compostela. Today it is a sleepy market town serving the surrounding agricultural region that happens to hold one of the most remarkable abbey churches, **St-Pierre.** Little is left of the original 7th-century abbey, while religious wars laid waste its 11th-century replacement. Today's abbey, dating mostly from the 15th century, narrowly escaped demolition earlier in this century when the Bordeaux–Sète railroad was rerouted within feet of the cloisters, sparing the precious columns around the arcades, carved in different shades of marble. Each of the 76 capitals has its own unique pattern of animals, geometric motifs, and religious or historical scenes. Conserved in the corner chapels of the cloisters are local religious sculpture and photographs of similar sculpture from throughout the Quercy region. The highlight of the abbey church is the 12th-century south portal, topped with carvings illustrating the Apocalypse. The sides and vaults of the porch are adorned with historical scenes sculpted in intricate detail. *6 bis rue de l'Abbaye, tel. 63–04–03–08. Admission: 24 frs. Open daily 9–noon and 2–5 (2–6 in June and Sept., 2–7 in July and Aug.).*

Tour 2: The Pyrénées

This tour, which follows the main Paris–Spain train route after it forks at Dax (northeast of Biarritz) and turns east, hits the central Pyrénées and the towns of Pau and nearby Lourdes. Cauterets, known for its thermal springs, and Gavarnie, a great base for hiking, can be reached by bus from Lourdes.

From Paris Eight TGVs daily make the 5½-hour run southwest to Pau from Par-
By Train is (Gare Montparnasse).

By Car Pau is 785 km (490 mi) from Paris: Take the A10 to Bordeaux, switch
to the A63/N10 (in the direction of Spain), and then branch off along
D947 via Dax to catch the A64 expressway at Orthez. Allow 8 hours
for the trip.

Pau

*The train station is across the boulevard des Pyrénées from the tour-
ist office. Tourist office: place Royale, tel. 59–27–27–08.*

Elegant **Pau,** 192 km (120 mi) southwest of Toulouse, is the historic
capital of Béarn, a state annexed to France in 1620. Pau rose to
prominence after being "discovered" in 1815 by British officers returning from the Peninsular War in Spain and was soon launched as a
winter resort. Fifty years later, English-speaking inhabitants
made up one-third of Pau's population. They launched the Pont-
Long steeplechase, still one of the most challenging in Europe, in
1841; created France's first golf course here in 1856; and introduced
fox hunting to the region. In 1970 a university was established in
Pau, somewhat offsetting this administrative center's tendency to
stuffiness.

★ Pau's regal past is commemorated at the **château,** begun in the 14th
century by Gaston Phoebus, the flamboyant count of Béarn. The
building was transformed into a Renaissance palace in the 16th century by Marguerite d'Angoulême, sister of François I. Marguerite's
grandson, the future King Henri IV, was born in the château in
1553. Temporary exhibits connected to Henri's life are mounted regularly here. His cradle—a giant turtle shell—is on show in his bedroom, one of the sumptuous, tapestry-lined royal apartments. Other
highlights are the 16th-century kitchens and the imposing dining
hall, which could seat up to 100 guests. *Rue du Château, tel. 59–82–
38–00. Admission: 26 frs (14 frs Sun.). Open Apr.–Oct., daily 9:30–
11:30 and 2–5:45; Nov.–Mar., daily 9:30–11:30 and 2–4:30.*

On the fourth floor of the château, the **Musée Béarnais** offers an
overview of the region, encompassing everything from fauna to furniture to festival costumes. There is a reconstructed Béarn house
and displays of such local crafts as cheese- and béret-making. *Admission: 8 frs adults. Open Apr.–Oct., daily 9:30–12:30 and 2:30–
6:30; Nov.–Mar., daily 9:30–12:30 and 2:30–5:30.*

Lodging **Montpensier.** This sturdy, old, pink-brick mansion with well-kept
$ rooms and a colorful garden has an air of calm despite its location in
the bustling center of Pau, 600 yards from place Clemenceau via rue
Serviez. *36 rue Montpensier, 64000, tel. 59–27–42–72, fax 59–27–
70–95. 22 rooms, most with bath or shower. AE, DC, MC, V.*

Dining **Au Fin Gourmet.** This airy, elegant rotunda surrounded by its own
$–$$ garden strikes an incongruous note in its rather unbeautiful location
near the station. Service is bashfully discreet, but the cuisine can be
bold and inventive—take the veal with raspberry vinegar, for instance—or authentically regional. There is a set menu at 160 frs
(and another at 85 frs on weekdays); eating à la carte tends to be
much more expensive. *24 av. Gaston-Lacoste, tel. 59–27–47–71.
Reservations advised. AE, DC, MC, V. Closed Mon.*

Lourdes

*Trains run from Pau southeast to Lourdes, 25 minutes away, every
2 hours or so. Tourist office: place du Champ-Commun, tel. 62–94–
15–64.*

More than 5 million pilgrims flock to **Lourdes** each year, many in quest of a miracle cure for their sickness or disability. In February 1858, Bernadette Soubirous, a 14-year-old miller's daughter, claimed the Virgin Mary had appeared to her in the **Massabielle grotto** near the Gave de Pau river. The visions were repeated. During the night, Bernadette dug at the ground in the grotto, releasing a gush of water from a spot where no spring existed. From then on, pilgrims thronged the Massabielle rock in response to the water's supposed healing powers.

Church authorities reacted skeptically. It took four years of inquiry for the miracle to be authenticated by Rome and a sanctuary erected over the grotto. In 1864, the first organized procession was held. Today there are six official annual pilgrimages, the most important on August 15. In 1958, Lourdes celebrated the centenary of the apparitions by constructing the world's largest underground church, the basilica of **St-Pie X**. The basilica looks more like a parking lot, but it can accommodate 20,000 people—more than the permanent population of the whole town. Above the basilica stand the neo-Byzantine basilica of **Rosaire** (1889) and the tall, white basilica of **Supérieure** (1871). Both are open throughout the day, but their spiritual function far outweighs their aesthetic appeal.

The area surrounding the churches and grotto (between the basilicas and the river) is woefully lacking in beauty. Out of season, the acres of parking space beneath the basilicas echo like mournful parade grounds to the steps of solitary visitors. Shops are shuttered and restaurants are closed. In season, a milling throng jostles for postcards, tacky souvenirs, and a glimpse of the famous grotto, lurking behind a forest of votive candles struggling to remain aflicker in the Pyrenean breeze.

The Pavillon Notre-Dame, across from the underground basilica, houses the **Musée Bernadette,** with mementoes of her life (she died at a convent in Nevers, Burgundy, in 1879) and illustrated history of the pilgrimages. In the basement is the **Musée d'Art Sacré du Gemmail,** *gemmail* being a modern approach to the stained-glass technique involving the assembly of broken glass, lit from behind, often by electric light. *72 rue de la Grotte, tel. 62–94–13–15. Admission free. Open July–Nov., daily 9:30–11:45 and 2:30–6:15; Dec.–June, Wed.–Mon. 9:30–11:45 and 2:30–5:45.*

Just across the river are the **Moulin des Boly,** where Bernadette was born on January 7, 1844 (12 rue Bernadette-Soubirous; open Easter–mid-Oct., daily 9:30–11:45 and 2:30–5:45), and, close to the parish church where she was baptized, the **Cachot,** a shabby little room where Bernadette and her family lived. *15 rue des Petits-Fossés, tel. 62–94–51–30. Admission free. Open Easter–mid-Oct., daily 9:30–11:45 and 2:30–5:30; mid-Oct.–Easter, daily 2:30–5:30.*

Despite the town's fame and Bernadette's compelling story, in the opinion of many Lourdes is a tourist center to be missed. It is lucky to have an authentic historic attraction to complement the commercialized aura of its pilgrim sites. **Lourdes Castle** stands on a hill above the town and can be reached on foot or by escalator. In the 17th and 18th centuries, the castle was used as a prison; now it contains the **Musée Pyrénéen,** one of France's best provincial museums, devoted to customs and arts throughout the Pyrénées region, from Bayonne on the Atlantic to Perpignan by the Mediterranean. *25 rue du Fort, tel. 62–94–02–04. Admission: 28 frs adults, 14 frs students. Open Easter–mid-Oct., daily 9–noon and 2–7 (last admission at 6); mid-Oct.–Easter, Wed.–Mon. 9–noon and 2–7.*

Lodging and Dining
$

Albret. The Albret's modern rooms are cheap and comfortable, if characterless, and from this town-center location you are only half a mile from the pilgrimage site. At the hotel's restaurant, La Taverne de Bigorie, chef Claude Moreau's cabbage-and-bacon stew is excellent fuel for your own Lourdes pilgrimage. Lighter fish dishes are on the menu as well, and prices start at 70 frs for a three-course meal. *21 pl. du Champ Commun, 65100, tel. 62–94–75–00, fax 62–94–78–45. 27 rooms, some with shower. Facilities: restaurant (closed Sun.). AE, MC, V. Closed Nov.–Feb.*

¢ **Notre-Dame de Lorette.** In Lourdes's mix of small, seedy hotels and glitzy modern establishments, this featureless structure with small rooms is no great shakes. But the welcome is friendly, the housekeeping just fine, and the setting—across the river from the grotto—very pleasant. The restaurant serves honest French cuisine and prices its three-course menu at 75 frs. *12 route de Pau, 65100, tel. 62–94–12–16. 20 rooms, some with shower. Facilities: restaurant. No credit cards. Closed mid-Oct.–Easter.*

Cauterets

Five coaches make the 30-kilometer (19 mile) run daily from Lourdes south to Cauterets, 55 minutes away. Tourist office: 2 place Georges-Clemenceau, tel. 62–92–50–27.

Snug in a valley embraced by the Pyrénées, **Cauterets** makes an excellent base for hiking and skiing. And the thermal springs here have been revered since Roman times as a miracle cure for female sterility. Victor Hugo (1802–85) womanized here, and Lady Aurore Dudevant—better known as the writer George Sand (1804–76)—discovered the thrill of adultery. Poetic viscount François René Chateaubriand (1768–1848) stayed determinedly chaste, however, pining for his "inaccessible Occitan girl." It is still a spa-resort, but today's visitors often ski until May.

Gavarnie

Two coaches run daily from Cauterets southeast to Gavarnie, via Pierrefitte.

Pretty **Gavarnie,** a great base for hiking, stands at the foot of the **Cirque de Gavarnie,** one of the world's most remarkable examples of glacial erosion. When the upper snows melt, numerous streams whoosh down from the cliffs to form spectacular waterfalls; the greatest of them—the **Grande Cascade**—drops nearly 427 meters (1,400 feet). The Cirque presents a daunting challenge to mountaineers; if you've forgotten your climbing boots, a horse or donkey can take you partway into the mountains from the village.

Lodging and Dining **Marboré.** This family hotel is Gavarnie's most appealing. Its veranda offers splendid views of the magnificent Cirque, and the old-fashioned main restaurant serves filling meals from 80- and 160-franc set menus while an adjoining brasserie offers quicker, less expensive alternatives. The Marboré comes into its own in winter, when skiers warm up around the open hearth in the Swan Bar after their days on the nearby slopes. *Le Village, 65120, tel. 62–92–40–40, fax 62–92–40–30. 24 rooms with shower. Facilities: restaurant, bar, exercise room. MC, V. Closed first half of Nov.*

Tour 3: Roussillon

We now head east from Toulouse to the historic region of Roussillon. Once part of Spain, Roussillon's culture and dialect retain close ties with neighboring Catalonia. We start at the hilltop town of Carcassonne and then visit Narbonne, Perpignan, and the pretty Mediterranean coastal town of Collioure.

From Paris By Train Two trains during the day (one requiring a change at Toulouse) and two more overnight make the 8-hour trip from Paris (Gare d'Austerlitz) to Carcassonne.

By Car The Paris–Carcassonne drive is a very long one. You can travel either via Bordeaux/Toulouse (A10/A62), a journey of 870 km (540 mi), or via Lyon/Montpellier (A6/A7/A9/A61), a 910-kilometer (570-mile) drive. Both routes take at least 8 hours.

Carcassonne

Tourist office: 15 boulevard Camille-Pelletan, tel. 68–25–07–04.

There are two **Carcassonnes**, the new and the medieval. The new is uninteresting—commercial, traffic-clogged, and location of the train station. It's a stiff uphill walk from here to the medieval town, ★ whose surrounding **walls** are the longest in Europe. The mighty circle of towers and battlements stands high on a hilltop above the River Aude and is said to be the setting for Charles Perrault's *Puss in Boots*. The earliest sections of wall were built by the Romans in the 1st century AD, and the Visigoths later enlarged the settlement into a true fortress in the 5th century. In the 13th century, Louis IX (Saint Louis) and his son, Philip the Bold, strengthened the fortifications and gave Carcassonne much of its present-day appearance. Much, but not all: In 1835, the Historic Monument Inspector (and poet) Prosper Mérimée was appalled by the dilapidated state of the walls, and by 1844 Viollet-le-Duc was at work restoring them.

Plan on spending at least a couple of hours exploring the walls and peering over the battlements across sun-drenched plains toward the distant Pyrénées. The old streets inside the walls are lined with souvenir shops, crafts boutiques, and restaurants; be sure to visit the **Château Comtal,** with its drawbridge and Musée Lapidaire, home to stone sculptures found in the area. *Tel. 68–25–01–66. Admission: 26 frs adults, 17 frs students. Open daily 9–noon and 2–5 (9–6 June–Sept.).*

The *ville basse* (lower town), a good mile below the ramparts between the River Aude and the Canal du Midi, is the commercial part of Carcassonne (the train station is here). It is less captivating than the upper town, but it does have the **Musée des Beaux-Arts,** housing a fine collection of porcelain, 17th- and 18th-century Flemish paintings, and works by local artists—including some stirring battle scenes by Jacques Gamelin (1738–1803). *Rue Verdun, tel. 68–72–47–22. Admission free. Open Mon.–Sat. 10–noon and 2–5.*

Dining **Auberge du Pont-Levis Pontard.** At the foot of the medieval city gate-
$$ way, the Porte Narbonnaise, the Pont-Levis provides a welcome shelter from tourist crowds. Chefs Olivier and Thierry Pautard serve traditional cassoulet and foie gras alongside a more inventive terrine marbled with artichokes and leeks, accompanied by a truffle vinaigrette. Otherwise, try the *méli-mélo du pêcheur,* a refreshing mix of mussels, cockles, and other seafood of the season. In summer you can eat on the terrace or in the garden. *Chemin des Anglais, tel. 68–25–55–23. Reservations advised. Jacket required. AE, DC, MC, V. Closed Nov., Feb., Sun. dinner, and Mon.*

Lodging and **Hôtel Montségur** and **Le Languedoc.** The mother runs the hotel and
Dining the sister and brother-in-law manage the restaurant two blocks
$$ away, both in new Carcassonne. The compact hotel fits into a large town house. Rooms on the first two floors feature Louis XV and Louis XVI furniture, some of it genuine, while those above are more romantic, with gilt-iron bedsteads set under the sloping oak beams. The restaurant (32 allée d'Iéna, tel. 68–25–22–17), under chef Didier Faugeras, offers a light version of the region's specialties, from confit to game. The setting is quite romantic and the enthusiasm is there, but the food lacks a certain robustness. *27 allée d'Iéna, 11000, tel. 68–25–31–41, fax 68–47–13–22. 21 rooms with bath. Facilities: restaurant. DC, MC, V. Restaurant and hotel closed mid-Dec.–mid-Jan.; restaurant closed Sun. and Mon. Sept.–June.*

Narbonne

*Trains make the 32-minute run east from Carcassonne every 1½
hours. The train station is a 30-minute walk north of the town center. Tourist office: place Roger-Salengro, tel. 68–65–15–60.*

A bustling industrial town, **Narbonne** was in Roman times the second-largest town in Gaul (after Lyon) and an important port, though
little remains of its Roman past. Until the sea receded in the Middle
Ages, Narbonne prospered. You will appreciate its one-time wealth
when you enter the 14th-century cathedral; its vaults rise 133 feet
from the floor, making it the tallest cathedral in southern France.
Only Beauvais and Amiens, in Picardy, are taller, and as at Beauvais, the nave at Narbonne was never built. Richly sculpted cloisters
link the cathedral to the former **Archbishop's Palace,** now home to
the Museum of Archaeology and the Museum of Art and History.
Note the enormous palace kitchen, with its ornate central pillar, and
check out the late-13th-century keep, Donjon Gilles-Aycelin; climb
the 180 steps to the top for a view of the region as well as the town.
*Palais des Archevêques, tel. 68–90–30–30. Admission: 25 frs (joint
ticket for all town museums). Open May–Sept., daily 9–noon and
2–6; Oct.–Apr., Tues.–Sun. 10–noon and 2–5:30.*

Cross the nearby canal to visit the **Musée Lapidaire** (sculpture museum), housed in the handsome, 13th-century former church of Notre-
Dame de la Mourguié. Classical busts, ancient sarcophagi, lintels,
and Gallo-Roman inscriptions await you. *Pl. Lamourguier, tel. 68–
65–53–58. Joint admission with and same hours as Palais des
Archevêques, above.*

Lodging and   **Languedoc.** This old-fashioned, turn-of-the-century hotel is a 10-
Dining   minute walk from the train station. The smallish rooms have been
$$ renovated, but they vary in style and comfort—ask to check yours
out before you book a room—and you pay an extra 100 frs for a full
bath. La Coupole restaurant serves inexpensive regional dishes, Sir
John's Piano Bar stays open until 2 AM, and there is also a billiards-
snooker parlor. *22 blvd. Gambetta, 11100, tel. 68–65–14–74, fax 68–
65–81–48. 38 rooms (34 with bath or shower), 2 suites. Facilities:
restaurant (closed Sun. dinner, Mon.), piano bar. AE, DC, MC, V.*

Perpignan

*Trains make the 40-minute run south from Narbonne every 1½
hours. Tourist office: place Armand-Lanoux, tel. 68–66–30–30.*

With a population of 120,000, **Perpignan**—Roussillon's historic capi-
tal—is the largest French town south of Toulouse. In medieval
times, Perpignan was the Second City of Catalonia (after Barcelo-
na), before falling to Louis XIII's army in 1642.

Take avenue du Général-de-Gaulle from the station, turn right onto
cours Escarguel, and follow this broad boulevard for 458 meters (500
yards). A left onto avenue Brutus will take you to Perpignan's lead-
ing monument, the fortified **Palais des Rois de Majorque** (Palace of
the Majorcan Kings), begun in the 14th century by James II of Ma-
jorca. Highlights here are the majestic Cour d'Honneur, the two-
tiered Flamboyant Gothic Chapel of Sainte-Croix, and the Grande
Salle, with its monumental fireplaces. *Rue des Archers, tel. 68–34–
48–29. Admission: 10 frs. Open daily 9–5.*

Head back across town toward the River Têt and the medieval monu-
ment of **Le Castillet,** with its tall, crenellated twin towers. The Casa
Pairal, a museum devoted to Catalan art and traditions, is housed
here. *Pl. de Verdun, tel. 68–35–42–05. Admission free. Open Wed.–
Mon. 9–noon and 2–6.*

Across boulevard Wilson from Le Castillet is the **Promenade des Platanes,** a cheerful stretch of flowers, trees, and fountains. Perpignan may not be rich in outstanding tourist sites, but the streets near Le Castillet and the adjacent place de la Loge, the town's nerve center, contain interesting medieval buildings. Among them are the **Cathédrale St-Jean** (distinguished by a frilly, wrought-iron campanile and a dramatic medieval crucifix), the **Loge de Mer** (formerly a maritime exchange), and the **Palais de la Députation** (once home to the Spanish law courts). The **Petite Rue des Fabriques d'En Nabot,** opposite the Palais, is Perpignan's best-preserved medieval street.

Lodging and Dining $$
Park. This family-run hotel with its own garden is unquestionably the smartest in Perpignan; although some rooms are small, most are positively luxurious, and all are soundproof and air-conditioned. Ask for one that has been refurbished; these have a Catalonian feel. The local bourgeouisie pours in to the excellent **Chapon Fin** restaurant to sample the subtle cuisine of chef Eric Cerf, who spent seven years working with Joël Robuchon in Paris before coming to Perpignan in 1993. Now he is a star in his own right. Three set menus showcase authentic Mediterranean food. A second, newer restaurant, **Le Bistro du Park,** specializes in seafood. Choose from the array laid out on the ice-bar at the entrance and discuss with the maître d' how you want it prepared. Not only is the cooking excellent, but the prices are very reasonable. *18 blvd. Jean-Bourrat, 66000, tel. 68–35–14–14, fax 68–35–48–18. 67 rooms with bath or shower. Facilities: 2 restaurants (Chapon Fin closed Sat. dinner, Sun., and mid-Aug.–early Sept.). MC, V.*

Dining $
La Serre. Regional dishes such as artichoke in pastry with garlic or duck with honey and grapefruit are showcased in this friendly restaurant in the old heart of town. We recommend the 90-franc menu. *2 bis rue Dagobert, tel. 68–34–33–02. Reservations advised. AE, DC, MC, V. Closed Sat. lunch.*

Collioure

Nine trains daily make the 25-minute run south from Perpignan. Tourist office: place du 18-juin, tel. 68–82–15–47.

Collioure, with its sheltered natural harbor, was originally a fishing town; anchovies are still caught here at night using the *lamparo* technique (powerful lamps to which anchovies are irresistibly attracted). The town's picture-postcard setting makes it a mecca for tourists, the first of whom were such turn-of-the-century painters as Henri Matisse, André Derain, Henri Martin, Georges Braque, and Emile-Othon "Everyone" Friesz.

The view they admired remains largely unchanged. To the north, the rocky Ilot St-Vincent juts out into the sea, a modern lighthouse at its tip. The first building on the mainland is the 17th-century church of Notre-Dame-des-Anges—observe the exuberantly carved altarpieces—whose pink-domed bell tower doubled as the original lighthouse. Behind the church lie the tumbling streets of the old Quartier du Mouré. A slender jetty divides the Boramar beach, beneath the church, from the small landing area at the foot of the **Château Royal.** This 15th-century castle, remodeled by Vauban 200 years later, can be visited and has fine views of the bay. *Tel. 68–82–06–43. Admission: 20 frs. Open Mar.–Oct., daily 10–noon and 2–5.*

Lodging and Dining *Splurge*
Relais des Trois Mas. Snuggled in the cliff that curves around the bay and looks over the harbor to the old fort, this hotel has charm enough to warrant staying here even if Collioure itself were not so picturesque. The rooms have spectacular views, and each is named for a particular painter. A group of glazed tiles behind the whirlpool tub in each bathroom reproduces a work of that painter, and a print reproduction of another hangs in the bedroom. Rooms are small but

interestingly furnished, with antique Spanish doors for headboards. The more expensive rooms have separate sitting areas with huge armchairs; four rooms have private patios that lead out to a little garden. Though there is a pebble beach below the hotel, most guests linger around the small pool (hewn from rock) and, before dressing for dinner, visit the solarium to take a dip in the huge Jacuzzi. Dinner is at **La Balette** restaurant, where you may dine either on the terrace or indoors in one of the two small dining rooms where there are views of the harbor. The food, cooked by chef Christian Peyre, from Avignon, is varied, using local produce but with recipes from throughout France. Try the rabbit terrine or the duck in a red-berry sauce. *Rte. de Port-Vendres, 66190, tel. 68–82–05–07, fax 68–82–38–08. 19 rooms, 4 suites, all with bath. Facilities: restaurant, bar, pool, whirlpool. AE, DC, MC, V. Closed mid-Nov.–mid-Dec. Rates begin at 550 frs (50% less between Oct.–Apr.).*

Lodging **Les Caranques.** There are no frills at this small seaside hotel, but
  $ service is efficient and friendly, and you'll enjoy the view from one of the rooms overlooking the picturesque bay. *Rte. de Port-Vendres, 66190, tel. 68–82–06–68. 16 rooms, 14 with bath or shower. Facilities: restaurant. MC, V. Closed Oct.–May.*

15 The Atlantic Coast

Including Bordeaux, the Dordogne, and Basque Country

It would be hard to visit the area of western France described in this chapter without finding something that captures your imagination. Poitou-Charentes, the rural, gently rolling region described in our first tour, contains France's finest Romanesque architecture, as the cathedrals of Poitiers, Saintes, and Angoulême testify. And La Rochelle, also in this tour, is one of France's prettiest harbor towns. Dramatic scenery and castles are featured in our second tour, which heads east from Bordeaux along the Dordogne Valley—the best example is cliff-top Beynac. City lovers have just one choice, urbane, sophisticated Bordeaux: It's the only town with more than 80,000 inhabitants between Nantes and the Spain border. It is also the wine capital of the world, and trips to the famous vineyards of St-Emilion and the Médoc are relatively easy by public transportation. Brandy drinkers can tour one of the world's most famous producers in Cognac. The third tour is to a different France, the Basque country. Here the architecture, language, and culture are neither French nor Spanish but unique to themselves; the geography, too, is a dramatic contrast to the mountains of the Pyrénées and the shores of the Atlantic.

It's not hard to eat well while visiting the Atlantic coast. Truffles, plums, trout, eel, and myriad succulent species of mushrooms vie for the diner's attention. And wherever you are, you'll sense the influence of the Atlantic on restaurant menus: Shellfish predominates, especially oysters. If you enjoy rich, hearty food such as goose and duck, the Dordogne Valley will spoil you.

Note that the region is well served by trains and that Dax, Poitiers, and Bordeaux can be reached from Paris by the superfast TGV.

Atlantic Coast Basics

Budget Lodging In summer, France's western coast provides extreme contrasts of crowds and calm. Vacationers flock to La Rochelle, Royan, and the islands of Ré and Oléron, and for miles around, hotels are booked solid months in advance. Farther inland the situation is easier, but there is a dearth of hotel accommodations in Bordeaux. Advance booking is recommended here and in the Dordogne, whose few towns fill up quickly in summer.

Budget Dining The cuisine of this ocean-facing region centers on fish and seafood. Oysters and mussels are major industries, while carp, eel, sardines, sole, and even sturgeon form the basis of menus in fish restaurants.

Futher inland in Périgord, along the Dordogne Valley, the cooking becomes richer. Truffles lead the way, followed by many types of game, fowl, and mushrooms. The goose market in the quaint old town of Sarlat is proof of the local addiction to foie gras. The River Dordogne is home to that rarest of western European fish, sturgeon, whose eggs—better known as caviar—surpass even foie gras as a sought-after delicacy.

The versatile wines of Bordeaux make fine accompaniments to most regional dishes, but don't overlook their less prestigious cousins (Bergerac, Pécharmant, Fiefs Vendéens, Monbazillac, Charentes). Cognac is de rigueur at the end of a meal.

Bargain Shopping The Périgord region owes much of its fame to such gastronomic specialties as truffles, *fruits confits* (fruit preserved in brandy), and foie gras (ask for a sealed can rather than a glass jar, and it will last for months). Regional gifts include embroidery, wooden models, and, more exceptionally, the small green animals made from the stems of the wild angelica found around Poitiers and Niort. Poitiers is also known for its delicious nougat.

Biking You can rent bikes from a number of train stations, notably La Rochelle, Bordeaux, Bergerac, Libourne, Le Verdon, and Sarlat. Ile de Ré makes an excellent place for bike vacations (accessible from La Rochelle), as do the rolling vineyards around St-Emilion/ Libourne or in the Médoc peninsula.

Hiking Enthusiastic walkers can choose a varied landscape of coast, vineyards, forest, and river valleys. For details of the best routes, contact the **Grande Randonnée en Aquitaine** (Maison du Tourisme, Rond-Point du Figuier, 33115 Pila-sur-Mer, tel. 56–54–02–22).

Beaches The Atlantic coast presents an outstanding, uninterrupted vista of sandy beaches from Rochefort south to Royan and from the Pointe de Grave south to Biarritz, a stretch known as the **Côte d'Argent** (Silver Coast). Biarritz is an expensive resort—try St-Jean-de-Luz or Hendaye, as they're more affordable.

Arts and Nightlife A wide range of music is available during **Bordeaux's International Musical May,** a leading event on France's cultural calendar (tel. 56–44–28–41). A smaller summer festival, the **Festival de la Musique Ancienne,** is held at **Saintes** in early July (tel. 46–92–51–35). Modern music gets a week-long airing at **La Rochelle's Franco-Folies** festival, also in July (tel. 46–50–56–39). Drama and music combine to make up the **Festival International de l'Entre-Deux-Mers** in August (tel. 56–71–51–35).

Festivals Other major festival activities in this ocean-bordered region are inspired by the sea. **"Fêtes de la Mer"** (Sea Festivals)—sometimes including carnival parades—are frequent, with one of the biggest at **La Rochelle** at Pentecost. A **Bande Dessinée** (comic book) festival takes place in **Angoulême** in January, and there's a **Crime Film** festival in **Cognac** each September.

Tour 1: Poitou-Charentes

The region of Poitou-Charentes occupies the middle band of France's Atlantic coast, extending east to include the inland swampy area known for its mussels and south to the rolling countryside where the cows produce the best sweet butter in all of France. Excellent rail links mean easy access to the region's principal towns. Follow the main line from Poitiers southwest to La Rochelle, with a brief stop along the way in Niort; take a boat ride to charming Ile de Ré before veering south to stately Saintes; then return east along the Charente Valley branch line to the brandy towns of Cognac and Jarnac.

From Paris TGVs to Poitiers leave Paris (Gare Montparnasse) every 2 hours.
By Train The trip takes 1 hour 40 minutes.

By Car The 335-kilometer (210-mile) drive southwest to Poitiers from Paris via A10 takes 3¼ hours.

Poitiers

Tourist office: 15 rue Carnot, tel. 49–41–58–22.

★ Thanks to its majestic hilltop setting above the River Clain, and its position halfway along the Bordeaux–Paris trade route, **Poitiers** became an important commercial, religious, and university town in the Middle Ages. Since the 17th century nothing much has happened, but visitors will find that this is not such a bad thing; stagnation equals preservation, and Poitiers's architectural heritage is correspondingly rich.

Boulevard Solférino climbs up from the station to the old town on the hilltop, continuing as rue Boncenne directly to the church of **Notre-Dame-la-Grande,** one of the most impressive examples of the Romanesque architecture so common in western France (rue des Cordeliers). Its 12th-century facade is framed by rounded arches of various sizes and decorated with a multitude of bas-reliefs and sculptures. The interior is dark. Its painted walls and pillars are not original; such decoration was a frequent ploy of mid-19th-century clerics keen to brighten up their otherwise austere churches.

Just off Grand'Rue, a few hundred yards beyond Notre-Dame-la-Grande, is the cathedral of **St-Pierre,** built during the 13th and 14th centuries (pl. de la Cathedrale). The largest church in Poitiers, it has a distinctive facade featuring two asymmetrical towers, as well as the usual rose window and carved portals. The imposing interior is noted for its 12th-century stained glass, especially the Crucifixion in the chancel, and 13th-century wooden choir stalls, thought to be the oldest in France.

Head down Grand'Rue, taking the second left and first right onto rue Jean-Jaurès. The town museum, **Musée Ste-Croix,** is a modern building housing archaeological discoveries and European paintings from the 15th to the 19th centuries; these are of good, though not outstanding, quality. *61 rue St-Simplicien, tel. 49–41–07–53. Admission: 15 frs (joint ticket with the museums of Chièvre-Croix and Hypogée). Open Tues.–Sun. 10–noon and 1–5 (2–6 on weekends).*

Next to the museum is the 4th-century **Baptistère St-Jean,** the oldest Christian building in France. Its heavy stone bulk, some 12 feet beneath ground level, consists of a rectangular baptismal chamber and an eastern end added during the 6th and 7th centuries. The porch, or narthex (restored in the 10th century), is linked to the main building by three archways. Go inside to see the octagonal basin, a larger version of a font for baptism by total immersion, and a collection of sarcophagi and sculpture. *Rue Jean-Jaurès. Admission: 4 frs. Open summer, daily 10–12:30 and 2–4:30; winter, Thurs.–Tues. 2–4:30.*

The Atlantic Coast

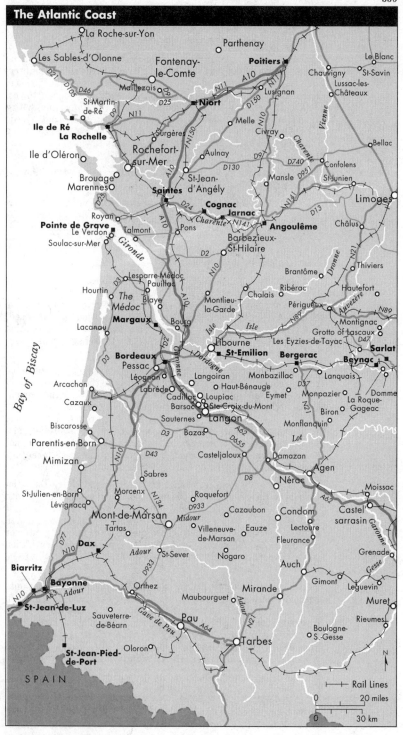

La Roche-sur-Yon
Parthenay
Les Sables-d'Olonne
Le Blanc
Fontenay-le-Comte
Poitiers
St-Savin
Chauvigny
Maillezais
Lussac-les-Châteaux
St-Martin-de-Ré
Lusignan
Niort
Ile de Ré
La Rochelle
Melle
Civray
Ile d'Oléron
Surgères
Rochefort-sur-Mer
Aulnay
Vienne
Charente
Bellac
Confolens
Mansle
Brouage
Marennes
Saintes
St-Jean-d'Angély
St-Junien
Limoges
Royan
Cognac
Jarnac
Angoulême
Châlus
Pointe de Grave
Le Verdon
Pons
Charente
Talmont
Soulac-sur-Mer
Barbezieux-St-Hilaire
Thiviers
Brantôme
Dronne
Hautefort
Lesparre-Médoc
Pauillac
Ribérac
Hourtin
The Médoc
Blaye
Chalais
Périgueux
Montignac
Margaux
Bourg
Montlieu-la-Garde
Grotto of Lascaux
Sarlat
Lacanau
Isle
Isle
Libourne
Les Eyzies-de-Tayac
Beynac
Bordeaux
St-Emilion
Bergerac
Pessac
Léognan
Langoiran
Haut-Bénauge
Monbazillac
Lanquais
Arcachon
Labrède
Cadillac
Loupiac
Eymet
Monpazier
La Roque-Gageac
Cazaux
Barsac
Ste-Croix-du-Mont
Domme
Biscarosse
Sauternes
Langon
Biron
Parentis-en-Born
Bazas
Monflanquin
Lot
Mimizan
Casteljaloux
Damazan
Agen
St-Julien-en-Born
Sabres
Roquefort
Nérac
Moissac
Lévignacq
Morcenx
Cazaubon
Condom
Castel-sarrasin
Mont-de-Marsan
Midour
Villeneuve-de-Marsan
Eauze
Lectoure
Garonne
Tartas
Fleurance
Grenade
Dax
Adour
St-Sever
Nogaro
Auch
Biarritz
Bayonne
Orthez
Mirande
Gimont
Leguevin
Muret
St-Jean-de-Luz
Maubourguet
Rieumes
Sauveterre-de-Béarn
Pau
Tarbes
St-Jean-Pied-de-Port
Oloron
Boulogne-S.-Gesse

Bay of Biscay

Gironde

SPAIN

Rail Lines

N

0   20 miles

0   30 km

Make your way back into the town center, pausing to admire the beautifully preserved houses lining the way. Perhaps stop to pick up some nougat. The best is sold at La Boutique du Patisserie on the north side of place M. Leclerc. Then walk across the square to rue Carnot. Shortly after this street has become rue de la Tranchée, the oldest of Poitiers's churches, **St-Hilaire-le-Grand,** appears on the right (rue St. Hilaire). Parts of St-Hilaire date from the early 11th century, but unfortunately, the original church had to be reduced in width in the 12th century when its roof was destroyed by fire; local masons lacked the expertise to cover large expanses with the fireproof stone vaulting used in its replacement. The semicircular, mosaic-floor choir rises high above the level of the nave. Cupolas, mighty columns, frescoes, and finely carved capitals add to the church's interest.

Lodging **Europe.** In an early 19th-century building in the middle of town, the
$ Europe is a comfortable, traditional hotel, though some rooms occupy a modern extension. Foreign visitors often stay here, attracted by the private garden used for summer breakfasts and afternoon tea, and competitive prices. There is no restaurant. *39 rue Carnot, 86000, tel. 49–88–12–00, fax 49–88–97–30. 88 rooms with bath or shower. Facilities: garden. MC, V.*

Dining **Maxime.** This crowd-pleaser lives up to its famous name, thanks to a
$ wide choice of set menus, the personal recipes of chef Christian Rougier (foie gras and duck salad, for instance), and a pastel-toned decor featuring frescoes from the '20s and '30s. *4 rue St-Nicolas, tel. 49–41–09–55. Reservations required. AE, MC, V. Closed Sat., Sun., and much of July and Aug.*

Niort

Six trains daily make the 50-minute run from Poitiers, 72 km (45 mi) northeast. The train station is a 15-minute walk southeast of the town center. Niort tourist office: place de la Poste, tel. 49–24–18–79.

Niort, a complacent, middle-class town, is best known as the capital of the French insurance business. The massive keep (Le Donjon), with its two square towers dominating the River Sèvre, is all that remains of the **Plantagenet castle** built at the end of the 12th century by English kings Henry II and Richard the Lion-Hearted. Inside there is a museum with an extensive collection of arms and local costumes. *Rue Duguesclin, tel. 49–28–14–28. Admission: 14 frs. Open Apr.–Oct., Wed.–Mon 9–noon and 2–6; Nov.–Mar., Wed.–Mon. 9–noon and 2–5.*

Just off the nearby rue Victor-Hugo is the old town hall, a triangular building completed in 1535. It now houses the **Musée du Pilori,** with a collection of local archaeological finds and Renaissance artifacts. The highlight is an ebony chest encrusted with gold and silver. *Just off rue Victor-Hugo, tel. 49–28–51–73. Admission: 13 frs. Open Apr.–Oct., Wed.–Mon. 9–noon and 2–6; Nov.–Mar., Wed.–Mon. 9–noon and 2–5.*

Do an about-face and amble down rue St-Jean, the oldest street in Niort, to the **Musée des Beaux-Arts,** where tapestries, gold and enamelware, wooden statues and effigies, and 17th- to 18th-century paintings are on display. At press time the museum was closed for renovations; call for details about hours and admission fees. *Rue St-Jean, tel. 49–24–97–84.*

La Rochelle

Six trains daily link Niort to La Rochelle, 55 minutes southwest. Avenue de Gaulle leads north from the station to the Old Port, less than 1 km (½ mi) away. Tourist office: place de la Petite-Sirène, tel. 46–41–14–68.

★ **La Rochelle** is an appealing old town; its ancient streets are centered on its harbor, the remarkably picturesque Vieux-Port. Standing on either side of the harbor are the fortresslike 14th-century towers known as **Tour St-Nicolas** (to the east) and the **Tour de la Chaîne** (to the west). From the top of Tour St-Nicolas, visitors can admire the view over the surrounding bay toward the Ile d'Aix. *Admission: 13 frs to each tower. Open Wed.–Mon. 9:30–12:30 and 2:30–6 (until 5 in winter).*

Take cours des Dames, a spacious avenue lined with sturdy trees and 18th-century houses, back to the Porte de la Grosse-Horloge, a massive stone gate marking the entrance to the straight, narrow, bustling streets of the old town. Head down rue du Palais and onto rue Gargoulleau. Halfway down on the left is the 18th-century Bishop's Palace, now home to a museum of paintings. Opposite is the **Musée d'Histoire Naturelle,** housed in an elegant mansion and containing extensive collections of rocks, coral, and shellwork. Other items range from a tribal idol from Easter Island in the South Pacific to a giraffe (now stuffed) given as a gift to King Charles X (reigned 1824–30). *28 rue Albert-Ier, tel. 46–41–18–25. Admission: 16 frs. Open Apr.–Oct., Tues.–Sun. 10–noon and 2–6; Nov.–Mar., Tues.–Sat. 10–noon and 2–5, Sun. 2–5.*

Farther down rue du Palais (which becomes rue Albert-Ier) is another 18th-century building containing the **Musée du Nouveau-Monde** (New World Museum). Old maps, engravings, watercolors, and even wallpaper evoke the commercial links between La Rochelle and the New World. *10 rue Fleuriau, tel. 46–41–46–50. Admission: 16 frs. Open Wed.–Mon. 10:30–12:30 and 1:30–6, Sun. 3–6.*

La Rochelle will impress you as more than a port if you are here on a Wednesday or Saturday, when a market takes place all around the covered market in the old town. A good way to get around is on a bicycle. There are several *location de vélos;* try **Centre de Location Agrée** (48 rue St-Jean, tel. 46–41–84–32).

Lodging **Hôtel St-Nicolas.** This restored mansion in the heart of the old town
$$ and a block and a half from the quay offers clean, functional rooms. The cheerful lobby and public area are flooded with light that streams through the indoor garden to a sunken sitting area, warmed in the winter by an open fire. There is no restaurant, but the bar serves as a gathering spot in the evenings. *13 rue Sardinerie, 17000, tel. 46–41–71–55, fax 46–41–70–46. 76 rooms with bath or shower. Facilities: bar, outdoor garden, parking. AE, DC, MC, V.*

$ **Tour de Nesle.** This modernized hotel may be a bit cramped, but it is clean, cheerful, and ideally placed for exploring the harbor and the old town. Ask for a room with a view across the canal toward St-Sauveur church—these are the least expensive. There is no restaurant, but *petit déjeuner* (Continental) is served in the breakfast room. *2 quai Louis-Durand, 17000, tel. 46–41–30–72, fax 46–41–95–17. 28 rooms with shower or bath. Facilities: breakfast room. MC, V.*

Dining **André.** The salty decor is somewhat excessive—fishing nets flutter
$ overhead, and posters of ocean liners billow from the walls—but the food and service have such gusto that you'll be caught up in the mood, especially if you order the monumental seafood platter (washed down with white Charentes wine). *5 rue St-Jean, tel. 46–41–28–24. Reservations advised. AE, DC, MC, V.*

¢ **Pré Vert.** Decorated throughout in shades of green, this restaurant is hidden down a discreet pedestrian street close to the harbor. It offers three inexpensive set menus and a good selection of regional specialties, such as foie gras, eel, and duck. *43 rue St-Nicolas, tel.*

46–41–24–43. Reservations advised in summer. AE, DC, MC, V. Closed Sun., Nov.–Feb.

Dining and
Lodging
$$
★
33 Thiers. It would be tempting to stay here just for the welcome and charm of this inn. Actually, it's not an inn but a private town house owned by the amiable Mme. Iribe, who in addition speaks fluent English and is a gourmet cook and an enthusiast of the region. With advance notice she will prepare a splendid dinner made from products bought at the lively market that's held twice weekly a few blocks away. You'll likely eat in the country kitchen and, if you want, pick up some cooking tips while she works (Mme. Iribe teaches cooking classes). She also knows the best restaurants in town. The guest rooms are large and wonderfully furnished, expressing the owner's idiosyncracies. The Mexican Room is gaily decorated with cheerful colors. The Blue Room is also a delight, in its cool, refreshing tones. Both are at the back of the house, removed from any street noise. *33 rue Thiers, 17000, tel. 46–41–62–23, fax 46–41–10–76. 8 rooms with bath. Facilities: dining room (by reservation). MC, V.*

Ile de Ré

Boats leave La Rochelle harbor daily in summer for the nearby islands of Ré (72 frs adults, 40 frs children, round-trip), d'Aix (82 frs), and Fort Boyard (62 frs).

Cheerful **Ile de Ré** is just 26 km (16 mi) long and 6 km (4 mi) at its widest. Vineyards sweep over the eastern part of the island while oyster beds straddle the shallow waters to the west. Many visitors are content to hang around in **St-Martin-de-Ré,** where the ferry docks, while others rent bicycles to explore the island and its 10 villages. The largest village, St-Martin-de-Ré (population 3,000) has a lively harbor and a citadel built by ace military architect Sébastien de Vauban in 1681. Many of its streets also date from the 17th century, and the villagers' low, white houses, often embellished with window boxes full of flowers, are typical of the island as a whole. Head down to the far end of the island to climb up the **Phare des Baleines** (lighthouse) for sweeping views, and check out the village of **Ars,** with its black-and-white church spire and cute harbor.

Ile d'Aix is the smallest of these three offshore islands, with a tiny village and quiet beaches (and no cars). It is also the island from which Napoléon departed for his exile to St-Helena on July 15, 1815. **Fort Boyard,** on its own little rock of an island, was built during Napoléon's tenure and is now an armory museum.

Dining
¢
Café du Phare. This spot at the foot of Ile de Ré's lighthouse serves excellent meals and snacks in a Art Deco setting full of arty '30s lamps. Try the *poutargue,* a local specialty made from smoked cod roe and served with shallots and sour cream. *Route du Phare, St-Clément-des-Baleines, tel. 46–29–46–66. No reservations or credit cards. Closed Oct.–Easter.*

Saintes

Eight trains daily run down the coast from La Rochelle to Saintes, 50 minutes southeast. The station is about 1 km (½ mi) from the center of town via avenue Gambetta. Tourist office: 62 cours National, tel. 46–74–23–82.

★ **Saintes** is a city of stately serenity. Its **cathedral** seems to stagger beneath the weight of its chunky tower, which climbs above the red roofs of the old town. Engineering caution foiled plans for the traditional pointed spire, so the tower was given a shallow dome—incongruous, perhaps, but distinctive. Angels, prophets, and saints decorate the Flamboyant Gothic main door of the cathedral, and the austere 16th-century interior is lined with circular pillars of formidable circumference.

The narrow pedestrian streets clustered around the cathedral contrast with the broad boulevard that slices through the town and over the River Charente, but both are full of life and color. Just across the bridge, to the right, is the impressive Roman **Arc de Germanicus,** built in AD 19. Ahead, reached by rue de l'Arc-de-Triomphe, is the sturdy octagonal tower of the **Abbaye aux Dames.** Consecrated in 1047, this abbey church is fronted by an exquisite, arcaded facade, whose portals and capitals, carved with fantastic beasts, deserve more than a quick look. Although the Romanesque choir remains largely in its original form, the rest of the interior is less harmonious, having been periodically restored. The abbey fell on hard times after the death of the last abbess—the 30th—in 1792. First it became a prison and then a barracks. It was recently converted into a cultural center for expositions. *Tel. 46–97–48–48. Open June–Sept., daily 10–12:30 and 2–7; Oct.–May, Thurs. and Sat. 10–12:30 and 2–7, Mon., Tues., Fri., and Sun. 2–7.*

Saintes owes its development to the salt marshes that first attracted the Romans to the area some 2,000 years ago. The Romans left their mark with an arch, which we've already seen, and with an impressively restored **amphitheater:** There are several better-preserved examples in France, but few as old. To reach the amphitheater, take the boulevard back across the river and veer left onto cours Reverseaux. Access is via rue St-Eutrope.

Dining **L'Abbatial.** When the abbey complex was reopened in 1989 after a
¢ thorough overhaul, this brasserie opened opposite the abbey portals. The design is state-of-the-art, and the set menus at lunchtime, starting at 75 frs, no less than astounding. Try the broccoli flan. *7 pl. de l'Abbaye, tel. 46–92–05–25. Reservations advised. V. Closed Sun.*

Cognac

Six trains daily make the 30-minute journey east from Saintes. The station is a 10-minute walk north of the city center. Tourist office: 16 rue du XIV-Juillet, tel. 45–82–10–71.

Compared with Saintes, dull, black-walled **Cognac** seems an unlikely hometown for one of the world's most successful drink trades. You may be disappointed initially by its unpretentious appearance but, like the drink, it tends to grow on you. Cognac owed its early development to the transport of salt and wine along the River Charente. When 16th-century Dutch merchants discovered that the local wine was both tastier and easier to transport if distilled, the town became the heart of the brandy industry and remains so to this day.

The leading monument in Cognac is its former **castle,** now part of the premises of Otard Cognac, a leading merchant. Volatile Renaissance monarch François I was born here in 1494. The castle has changed quite a bit since then. The remaining buildings are something of a hodgepodge, though the stocky towers that survey the Charente recall the site's fortified origins. The tour of Otard Cognac combines its own propaganda with historical comment on the drink itself. The slick audiovisuals are tastefully done, and you will visit some interesting rooms and receive a free taste of the firm's product, which is available for sale at vastly reduced prices. *127 blvd. Denfert-Rochereau, tel. 45–82–40–00. Admission free. Guided tours daily on the hour 10–noon and 2–5 (except Sun. during Oct.–May).*

Most cognac houses organize visits of their premises and *chais* (warehouses). **Hennessy,** a little farther along the banks of the Charente (note the company's mercenary emblem: an ax-wielding arm carved in stone), and **Martell** both give polished guided tours, an ideal introduction to the mysteries of cognac. Martell's *chais* are perhaps more picturesque, but the Hennessy tour includes a cheerful jaunt across the Charente in old-fashioned boats. Wherever you decide to go, you will literally soak up the atmosphere of cognac; 3% of the precious cask-bound liquid evaporates every year! This has two consequences: Each *chais* smells delicious, and a small, black, funguslike mushroom, which feeds on cognac's alcoholic fumes, forms on walls throughout the town. *Hennessy, rue Richonne, tel. 45-82-52-22. Open Oct.-May, Mon.-Thurs. 8:30-11 and 2-5, Fri. 8:30-noon; June and Sept., weekdays 8:30-11 and 2-5; July and Aug., Mon.-Sat. 8:30-11 and 1:30-5. Martell, pl. Martell, tel. 45-82-44-44. Open mid-June-mid-Sept., weekdays 9-5:30; mid-Sept.-mid-June, weekdays 8:30-11.*

Rue Saulnier, alongside the Hennessy premises, is the most atmospheric of the somber, sloping, cobblestone streets that compose the core of Cognac, dominated by the tower of **St-Léger,** a church with a notably large Flamboyant Gothic rose window. Busy boulevard Denfert-Rochereau twines around the old town, passing in front of the manicured lawns of the town hall and the gravelly drive of the neighboring **Musée du Cognac,** which contains good ceramics and Art Nouveau glass but is worth visiting mainly for its section on cognac itself. The history and production of cognac are clearly explained, and one room is devoted to amusing early advertising posters. *48 blvd. Denfert-Rochereau, tel. 45-32-07-25. Admission 15 frs. Open Wed.-Mon. 10-noon (summer only) and 2-5:30.*

Lodging and Dining
$$
★

Pigeons Blancs. "White Pigeons," a converted and modernized coaching inn in spacious grounds, has been owned by the same family since the 17th century. The welcome is warm, the hotel comfortable and intimate, and worth the 2-kilometer (1¼-mile) trek from the train station. Each room has its own charm. Number 32, a particular favorite, has a gabled ceiling supported by an ancient beam, an extremely comfortable bed, a skylight, and a small bathroom en suite. Though the rooms are charming and reasonable (380 frs), the major draw is chef Jacques Tachet's cuisine, which includes milk-fed lamb with *jus d'ail doux* (sweet garlic) and lightly grilled escargots with locally cured ham. He also has a three-course menu of the day (155 frs). *110 rue Jules-Brisson, tel. 45-82-16-36, fax 45-82-29-29. 6 rooms with bath. Facilities: restaurant (closed Sun. dinner). AE, DC, MC, V. Closed first half of Jan.*

¢-$

Hôtel d'Orléans. In the center of town not far from the train station, this 17th-century building has been turned into a most agreeable small hotel with reasonable rates (120 frs with only a toilet, 250 frs for toilet and bath). The lobby is quite splendid, with a marvelous stairway and wall mosaics. The restaurant, **La Brasserie,** is popular with locals as a place to hang out and drink as well as to eat. *25 rue d'Angoulême, 16100, tel. 54-82-01-26, fax 45-82-20-33. 23 rooms, some with shower or bath. Facilities: restaurant, live music. MC, V.*

Shopping

An old bottle of cognac makes a fine souvenir; try **La Cognathèque** (10 pl. Jean-Monnet). Though you'll find the same stuff, but infinitely cheaper, at any local producer, this is perhaps the most convenient source.

Jarnac

Trains continue from Cognac to Jarnac, 10 minutes and 16 km (10 mi) upriver.

Several cognac firms are found in the charming village of **Jarnac,** also famous as the birthplace of former French president François Mitterrand. **Hine** (quai de l'Orangerie, tel. 45-81-11-38) and **Courvoisier** (pl. du Château, tel. 45-35-55-55) organize visits of their riverside premises, though Hine's cozy buildings in local chalky stone have more appeal than does Courvoisier's bombastic redbrick factory by the bridge.

Angoulême

Six trains daily link Saintes to Angoulême via Cognac-Jarnac; the journey from Jarnac, 26 km (16 mi) east, lasts 20 minutes. Tourist offices: place St-Pierre, tel. 45–95–16–84, place de la Gare, tel. 45–92–27–57.

Angoulême is divided, as are many other French towns, between an old, picturesque sector perched around a hilltop cathedral and a modern, industrial part sprawling along the valley and railroad below. Don't let the outskirts deter you—the initial depression soon wears off.

Angoulême Cathedral, in place St-Pierre, bears little resemblance to the majority of its French counterparts because of the cupolas topping each of its three bays. This style was popular in the southwest, and Angoulême's cathedral was influenced by the one in Périqueux. Though it dates from the 12th century (the fourth construction), the cathedral was partly destroyed by Calvinists in 1562, then restored in a heavy-handed manner in 1634 and 1866. Its principal attraction is the magnificent Romanesque facade, whose layers of rounded arches boast 70 stone statues and bas-reliefs illustrating the Last Judgment. The interior is austere and massive with a few odd points of interest. Collect the free pamphlet from the tourist office, across the street, which gives a detailed description.

The cathedral dominates the *ville haute* (upper town), known as the "plateau." There are stunning views from the ramparts alongside, and a warren of quaint old streets to explore in the shadow of the Hôtel de Ville, with its colorful garden. The 19th-century novelist Honoré de Balzac is one of the town's adopted sons; Balzac described Angoulême in his novel *Lost Illusions*.

Dining
$

La Tour des Valois. Of the many small restaurants in the old quarter, this one diagonally across from the market offers a good selection of local produce. Try one of the veal dishes—the one using the local mustard from Jarnac for the sauce is particularly good. Start with the locally made pâté de foie gras and finish with the *duchesses d'Angoulême* (petits fours). *7 rue Massillon, tel. 45–95–91–76. No reservations. Closed Sat. lunch and Sun. MC, V.*

Dining and Lodging
$

Terminus. Stay at this convenient, if run-of-the-mill, station hotel to avoid lugging your bags up Angoulême's steep hill to the old town. The ground-floor restaurant is actually under different management but makes an excellent venue for regional specialties like burbot with leeks or veal kidneys in a mustard sauce, showcased in a plethora of fixed-price menus. *1 pl. de la Gare, 16000, tel. 45–95–27–13, fax 45–94–09–04. 33 rooms, some with bath or shower. Facilities: adjoining restaurant. AE, MC, V.*

Tour 2: Bordeaux and the Dordogne

Dignified Bordeaux is the base for this tour, which features rail excursions through the vineyards of the Médoc peninsula and east along the picturesque castle-lined Dordogne Valley to St-Emilion, one of France's prettiest wine towns, and historic Sarlat, famed for its goose fair and foie gras.

From Paris
By Train

TGVs to Bordeaux leave Paris (Gare Montparnasse) just about every hour. The trip takes 3–3¼ hours.

By Car The 575-kilometer (360-mile) drive from Paris southwest to Bordeaux along A10 takes 5½ hours.

Bordeaux

Tourist office: 12 cours du 30-Juillet, opposite the CIVB wine center, tel. 56–44–28–41.

Numbers in the margin correspond with points of interest on the Bordeaux map.

★ The capital of southwest France, **Bordeaux** is renowned worldwide for its wines. Vineyards extend on all sides: Graves and pretty Sauternes to the south; flat, dusty Médoc to the west; and Pomerol and St-Emilion to the east. Stylish châteaus loom above the most famous vines, but much of the wine-making area is unimpressive, with little sign of the extraordinary regional affluence it promotes.

There are signs enough in the city itself, however, where wine shippers have long based their headquarters along the banks of the Garonne. An aura of 18th-century elegance permeates the downtown area, whose fine shops and pedestrian precincts invite leisurely exploration.

❶ If you turn right upon exiting Gare St-Jean and head left down rue de Tauzia you'll reach the heart of the **old dockland** to the south of the city's center. For the time being, however, you may want to pass by this area. The town planners promise to resurrect the dockland by attracting artisans and shopkeepers to the warehouses connected by narrow streets, but enthusiasm for the project is still lukewarm, and nothing has happened yet. Currently the area has a forbidding feel; indeed, Bordeaux as a whole is a less exuberant city than most in France, with an almost British reserve.

❷ For a better view of the picturesque quayside, stroll across the **Pont de Pierre,** which spans the Garonne; built by Napoléon at the start of the 19th century, the bridge makes spectacular viewing itself, thanks to a multitude of gracefully curving arches.

From the bridge, head north along the river until you come to cours Chapeau-Rouge. Turn left and after two blocks you'll come to the ❸ city's leading 18th-century monument: the **Grand Théâtre,** built between 1773 and 1780 to the plans of architect Victor Louis. Its exterior is ringed by graceful Corinthian columns and pilasters. The majestic foyer, with its two-winged staircase and cupola, inspired Charles Garnier's design for the Paris Opéra. The theater hall itself has a frescoed ceiling and a shimmering chandelier composed of 14,000 Bohemian crystals; the acoustics are said to be perfect. *Pl. de la Comédie, tel. 57–81–90–81. Contact the tourist office for guided tours. Cost: 25 frs adults, 20 frs children.*

The allées de Tourny and cours du 30-Juillet, tree-lined boulevards, reel off north from the Grand Théâtre. At the start of the cours du ❹ 30-Juillet is the **CIVB,** headquarters of the Bordeaux wine trade, where information can be had and samples tasted. The **Vinothèque,** opposite, sells Bordeaux by the bottle to suit every purse. At the far end of the cours is the **esplanade des Quinconces,** a vast square overlooking the Garonne.

Dedicated oenophiles only should turn left from the esplanade and ❺ head half a mile along the quay to the **Cité Mondiale du Vin** (enter at 25 quai des Chartrons). This ambitious complex is part office block, part shopping mall, and part culture center; a museum, bars, and exhibition hall all have a common theme: the world of wine.

❻ Head back along the river, past the esplanade, as far as **place de la Bourse,** the city's second most important 18th-century landmark after the Grand Théâtre. A provincial reply to Paris's celebrated place

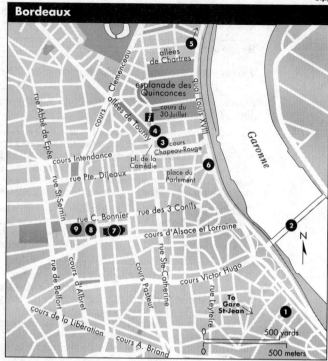

Cathedral
St-André, **7**

Cité Mondiale
du Vin, **5**

CIVB, **4**

Grand
Théâtre, **3**

Hôtel de
Ville, **8**

Musée des
Beaux-Arts, **9**

Old dockland, **1**

Place de la
Bourse, **6**

Pont de
Pierre, **2**

Bordeaux

Vendôme, the square (built 1730–55) features airy, large-windowed buildings designed by the country's most esteemed architect of the era, Jacques-Ange Gabriel.

Head two blocks down rue F-Philippart to the 18th-century **place du Parlement,** and you'll have no problem finding a promising lunch spot. No fewer than six bistros and restaurants, some with outdoor tables, line the square.

7 A maze of narrow streets wends its way from the river to the **Cathédrale St-André,** located in place Pey-Berland. This hefty edifice, 135 yards long, isn't one of France's better Gothic cathedrals, and the outside has a dirty, neglected look. The interior, though, rewards your scrutiny, as the soaring 14th-century chancel makes an interesting contrast with the earlier, more severe nave. Excellent—albeit grimy—stone carvings adorn the facade (notably that of the Porte Royale, to the right), as well as the 15th-century Pey-Berland Tower, which stands nearby.

8
9 Across the tidy gardens behind the opulent **Hôtel de Ville** (opposite the cathedral) is the busy cours d'Albret and the **Musée des Beaux-Arts.** This fine-arts museum has a notable collection of works spanning the 15th to the 20th centuries, with important paintings by Paolo Veronese (*Apostle's Head*), Camille Corot (*Bath of Diana*), and Odilon Redon (*Chariot of Apollo*), and sculptures by Auguste Rodin. *20 cours d'Albret, tel. 56–10–17–49. Admission: 15 frs. Open Wed.–Mon. 10–6.*

Lodging **Hôtel des Quatre Soeurs.** This inexpensive find, between the Grand
$ Théâtre and the city tourist office, offers well-kept rooms of varying sizes and prices. The adjoining café, excellent for coffee and light meals, treats guests to classical music on many afternoons. The charming owner, Mme. Defalque, will help direct you to the best of Bordeaux. *6 cours du 30-Juillet, 33000, tel. 57–81–19–20, fax 56–*

01–04–28. 35 rooms with bath or shower. Facilities: bar, café. MC, V.

$ **Pyrénées.** In a turn-of-the-century building close to the theater and the older part of town, the Pyrénées provides typically earnest provincial comfort (deep, slightly worn armchairs and effusive decor). American and British guests are common. There is no restaurant. *12 rue St-Rémi, 33000, tel. 56–81–66–58. 18 rooms with bath. AE, V. Closed second half Aug. and Christmas–New Year's.*

$ **Royal Médoc.** This Bordeaux hotel is admirably situated near the esplanade des Quinconces in the city center, in a building that dates from 1720. English-speaking guests form the backbone of the foreign clientele attracted by the Neoclassical architecture and cheerful, efficient service. There is no restaurant. *5 rue de Sèze, 33000, tel. 56–81–72–42, fax 56–51–74–98. 45 rooms, many with bath. AE, MC, V.*

Dining **Vieux Bordeaux.** This much-acclaimed haunt of nouvelle cuisine lies
$$ on the fringe of the old town. Chef Michel Bordage concentrates on
★ fresh produce. His menu is therefore limited but of high quality, complemented by three set-price menus. His fish dishes are particularly good; try the steamed turbot. The wine is well priced, the decor modern, and the ambience lively. *27 rue Buhan, tel. 56–52–94– 36. Reservations advised. AE, MC, V. Closed Sat. lunch, Sun., Aug., and 1 wk in Feb.*

$ **Clavel.** The sister restaurant to a center-city establishment of the
★ same name, Clavel adds a note of gastronomic good value to the undistinguished St-Jean quarter near the train station. It is one of the few places in town where you can sample claret by the glass, though any number of fruity young Bordeaux are available by the bottle for under 120 frs. The squeaky-clean, modern-rustic decor, varied cuisine (including salmon, ravioli stuffed with lobster, duck with orange and chocolate sauces), and true bistro prices make this an excellent choice. *44 rue Charles-Domercq, tel. 56–92–63–07. Reservations advised. MC, V. Closed Sun., Mon. lunch, and 2nd half of July.*

¢ **Ombrière.** The friendly Ombrière looks out over one of the finest squares in old Bordeaux, and on fine days you can eat outside. The food is pleasant in an unexciting, brasserie sort of way (steak and fries), but for central Bordeaux its set menu is fairly priced, and even a choice à la carte dinner won't seem extravagant. *14 pl. du Parlement, tel. 56–44–82–69. MC, V. Closed Sun., Mon., and Aug.*

Shopping Stylish shops abound in the commercial heart of Bordeaux, on the numerous pleasant pedestrian streets between the cathedral and Grand Théâtre. A top-ranking Bordeaux is not likely to represent top value, though at the **Vinothèque** (8 cours du 30-Juillet) you'll have a wide choice.

Médoc

Trains from Bordeaux head up the Médoc peninsula six times daily to Margaux (45 minutes away) and Pauillac (70 minutes away). One midday train stops at St-Estèphe (80 minutes away), and three trains stop at Le Verdon, near Pointe de Grave (2 hours from Bordeaux).

Médoc is strange, dusty territory. Even the vines look dusty, as does the ugly town of **Margaux**, the area's unofficial capital. Yet the soil hereabouts is sown with the seeds of grandeur. The small, arid communes and châteaus of Haut-Médoc feature such venerable names as Margaux, St-Julien, Pauillac, and St-Estèphe. Château Margaux, an elegant, coolly restrained classical building of 1802, and three wineries at Pauillac—Lafite-Rothschild, Latour, and Mouton-Rothschild—are recognized as producers of *premiers crus*, their wines qualifying with Graves's Haut-Brion as Bordeaux's top five reds. But unless you propose to buy wine from a vineyard or get a thrill out of seeing billboards announce the names of famous vineyards, you may not wish to make the effort of touring the Médoc.

Trains chug through the less prestigious wine fields of northern, or Bas, Médoc, toward **Pointe de Grave,** at the tip of the Médoc peninsula, the site of an American memorial commemorating the landing of U.S. troops in 1917. From the surrounding sand dunes, there are views over the Gironde estuary to Royan and back across the Atlantic. A car-ferry plows across to Royan four times daily (cost: 125 frs per car, 35 frs per passenger). Another ferry, closer to Bordeaux, crosses the Gironde from Lamarque to Blaye four times a day (cost: 78 frs per car, 20 frs per passenger).

St-Emilion

Two trains each day, one in the early morning and one in early afternoon, make the ½-hour run east from Bordeaux. It's a 10-minute walk uphill from the station to the center of town. Tourist office: place des Créneaux, tel. 57–24–72–03.

★ **St-Emilion** is a jewel of a town, with old buildings of golden stone, ruined town walls, well-kept ramparts offering charming views, and a church hewn into a cliff. Sloping vines invade from all sides—and lots and lots of tourists invade down the middle.

The medieval streets are filled with wine stores and crafts shops. Macaroons are a specialty. The local wines offer the twin advantages of reaching maturity earlier than other Bordeaux reds and representing better value for the money. Tours of the pretty **St-Emilion vineyard,** including wine tastings, are organized by the Syndicat d'Initiative (tourist office) on place des Créneaux, a bulky square with a terrace overlooking the lower part of St-Emilion. A stroll along the 13th-century ramparts helps you appreciate St-Emilion's ancient, unspoiled, stone-walled houses, and soon brings you to the Royal Castle, or **Château du Roi,** built by occupying sovereign Henry III of England (1216–72). *Admission: 26 frs. Open daily 9:30–12:30 and 2–6:30.*

Steps lead down from the ramparts to place du Marché, a wooded square where cafés remain open late into the night. Lining one side are the east windows of the **Eglise Monolithe,** one of France's largest underground churches, hewn out of the rock face between the 9th and 12th centuries. *Tel. 57–24–72–03. Visits organized by the Syndicat d'Initiative start from the Office du Tourisme and cover the Citadel, the Eglise Monolithe, the Catacombes, and the Grotte de l'Ermitage. Cost: 34 frs adults, 17 frs children. Tours every 45 min, 10–5.*

You may also wish to take the tourist train for a 30-minute ride with commentary through a St-Emilion vineyard. *Admission: 25 frs. Book through the tourist office.*

Just south of the town walls is **Château Ausone** (not open to the public), an estate that is ranked with Cheval Blanc as producing the finest wine of St-Emilion.

Lodging and Dining
$
★
Auberge de la Commanderie. For such a pretty town, St-Emilion is a bit short on accommodations. Luckily, this two-story, 19th-century hotel is admirable in every sense. It is close to the ramparts and has its own garden and views of the vineyards; rooms are small but clean and individually decorated; and the attractive restaurant is often frequented by nonresidents and has a good selection of local wines. *Rue des Cordeliers, 33300, tel. 57–24–70–19, fax 57–74–44–53. 15 rooms, most with bath. Facilities: restaurant (closed Tues., Sept.– June), garden. MC, V. Closed late Dec.–Feb.*

Dining **Chez Germaine.** Family cooking and regional dishes are featured at
$ this central St-Emilion eatery. The stylish upstairs dining room,
candlelit and adorned with flowers, is a pleasant place to enjoy the
reasonably priced set menus. Grilled meats and fish are house specialties; for dessert, try the almond macaroons. There's also a terrace for outdoor eating. *Pl. du Clocher, tel. 57–24–70–88.
Reservations advised. DC, MC, V. Closed Sun., Mon., and mid-
Dec.–mid-Jan.*

Bergerac

*Seven trains operate daily from Bordeaux and take 75 minutes to
reach Bergerac. There are three trains daily from St-Emilion, an
hour away. The station is a fairly long walk north of the town center; you may want to take a taxi or a bus along avenue Président
Wilson. Tourist office: 97 rue Neuve d'Argenson, tel. 53–57–03–11.*

You expect vines to be cultivated around **Bergerac**—but not tobacco. Learn about this local industry at the **Musée du Tabac,** a museum
housed in the 17th-century Maison Peyrarède near the quayside.
The manufacture, uses, and history of tobacco, from its American
origins to its spread worldwide, are explained with the help of maps,
pictures, documents, and other exhibits, including a collection of
pipes and snuff bottles. *10 rue de l'Ancien-Pont, tel. 53–63–04–13.
Admission: 15 frs. Open Tues.–Fri. 10–noon and 2–6, Sat. 10–
noon and 2–5, Sun. 2:30–6:30.*

Head left from the tobacco museum, past place de la Myrpe, to the
Couvent des Récollets. This former convent's stone-and-brick buildings range in date from the 12th to the 17th century and include galleries, a large, vaulted cellar, and a cloister, where the Maison du
Vin dishes out information on—and samples of—local wines. From
the first floor of the convent, treat yourself to a view of the sloping
vineyards of Monbazillac across the Dordogne. *Just off pl. de la
Myrpe. Admission: 12 frs. Open July–Aug., tours every hr from
10:30–11:30 and 1:30–5:30; mid-May–June and Sept.–mid-Oct., at
3:30 and 4:30. Closed Sun. and Mon.*

The regional wines of Bergerac range from red (popular and inexpensive table wines) and rosé to dry and sweet whites. While you're
in town, you might like to purchase a bottle or two of the town's most
famous vintage: Monbazillac, a sweet wine made from overripe
grapes that enjoyed an international reputation long before its Bordeaux rival, Sauternes.

Guided, 90-minute walking tours of the old town of Bergerac leave
from the tourist office (tel. 53–57–03–11; cost: 22 frs). You can also
take an hour-long cruise on the Dordogne for 35 frs. Check the
schedules with the tourist office or the cruise company (tel. 53–24–
58–06).

Lodging and **Bordeaux.** The Bordeaux, one of Bergerac's better hotels, has been
Dining refurbished recently and given contemporary furnishings. Rooms
$$ are neat, with tiled bathrooms en suite; those facing the garden-
courtyard are preferred (No. 22 is slightly roomier than the others).
The restaurant is better than average; its moderately priced (145
frs) traditional menu of the Périgord offers three courses, including
confit of duck and foie gras. Though guests are not obliged to eat
here, who can refuse the marinated salmon in anisette and lime or
the pan-fried escalope de foie gras? The owner, M. Maury, speaks
fluent English and is usually on hand to give advice on the area. *38
pl. Gambetta, 24100, tel. 53–57–12–83, fax 53–57–72–14. 40 rooms
with bath. Facilities: restaurant (closed Mon. and Sat., Nov.–
Mar.), pool, garden. AE, DC, MC, V. Closed mid-Dec.–Jan.*

Sarlat-la-Canéda

The three daily trains east from Bergerac take 80 minutes. The station is on the southern edge of town, about a 10-minute walk up avenue A. Briand, which becomes avenue Thiers, to the medieval town center. Tourist office: place de la Liberté, tel. 53–59–27–67.

★ To do justice to the golden-stone splendor of **Sarlat**, you may want to take advantage of the guided tour offered by the tourist office on place de la Liberté, or at least pick up their informative walking map, which dates and briefly describes virtually every significant building. Rue de la Liberté leads to place du Payrou, occupied on one corner by the pointed-gable Renaissance house where writer-orator Etienne de la Boétie (1530–63) was born. Diagonally opposite is the entrance to **Sarlat Cathedral**. An elaborate turret-topped tower, begun in the 12th century, is the oldest part of the building and, along with the choir, all that remains of the original Romanesque church. A sloping garden behind the cathedral, the Cour de l'Evêché, affords good views of the choir and contains a strange, conical tower known as the **Lanterne des Morts** (Lantern of the Dead), which was occasionally used as a funeral chapel.

Rue d'Albusse, adjoining the garden, and rue de la Salamandre are narrow, twisty streets that head back to place de la Liberté and the 17th-century town hall. Opposite the town hall is the rickety former church of St-Marie, overlooking place des Oies and pointing the way to Sarlat's most interesting street, **rue des Consuls.** Among its medieval buildings are the Hôtel Plamon, with broad windows that resemble those of a Gothic church, and, opposite, the 15th-century Hôtel de Vassal.

Across the undistinguished rue de la République, which slices Sarlat in two, is the Quartier Ouest (Western Quarter), many of whose streets are too narrow to be used by cars. Rue Rousseau leads past the Chapelle des Récollets and Abbaye St-Claire to the 16th-century Tour du Bourreau and a remnant of the former town walls.

Lodging and Dining $ ★ **Hôtels St-Albert et Montaigne.** The Garrigou family has two hotels on a delightful square in the center of Sarlat. The entirely renovated Montaigne reincarnated a former manor house. Freshly decorated guest rooms have neatly tiled bathrooms and double-glazed windows to silence street noise. Room 33, with exposed beams, is especially charming. The St-Albert offers another 31 rooms of varying sizes, all simply furnished with basic comforts. Bathrooms either have a shower or bath. The dining room for both hotels is in the St-Albert, where wholesome and hearty regional fare is on hand at very reasonable prices. Enjoy the three complimentary pâtés and a local aperitif as you look over the menu. After that, the choices are yours, but the traditional confit is worth trying. *10 pl. Pasteur, 24200, tel. 53–31–55–55, fax 53–59–19–99. 56 rooms and 6 suites, all with bath or shower. Facilities: restaurant (closed Sun. dinner and Mon. from Nov.–mid-Apr.). AE, MC, V.*

Dining $ **Jardin des Consuls.** If you feel like lunch or a snack, make your way to this establishment in the heart of old Sarlat. Part restaurant, part tearoom, it has a pleasant stone-walled dining room and a courtyard in back that's idyllic in sunny weather. Soups and *cassoulet* stews head the filling 100-franc menu, best accompanied by a young, *gouleyant* (fruity) Cahors. Or just enjoy the sorbets and crêpes. *4 rue des Consuls, tel. 53–59–18–77. V. Closed Mon.*

Beynac

Three buses run daily from Sarlat west to Le Buisson, stopping at La Roque-Gageac and Beynac.

★ The 13th-century **castle of Beynac** is daringly perched atop a sheer cliff face beside an abrupt bend in the Dordogne. Restoration of this privately owned castle is an ongoing process, but its muscular architecture and the staggering views from its battlements make a visit imperative. *Tel. 53–29–50–40. Admission: 25 frs. Open Mar.–mid-Nov., daily 10–noon and 2:30–5 or 6 (7 in July and Aug.).*

A short distance upriver, huddled beneath a towering gray cliff, is **La Roque-Gageac,** one of the prettiest and best-restored villages in the Dordogne Valley. Crafts shops line its low, narrow streets, dominated by the outlines of the 19th-century mock-medieval Château de Malartrie and the round-turreted Manoir de Tarde.

Lodging and **La Plume d'Oie.** This small inn overlooking the Dordogne and its
Dining limestone cliffs has neat guest rooms furnished in light fabrics and
$ wicker furniture. Rooms vary in size and are priced accordingly (275 frs–380 frs), but all have a bath or shower, hair dryer, minibar, and telephone. La Plume d'Oie's major raison d'être, however, is the pretty beamed and stone-walled restaurant at which all hotel guests are expected to have at least one meal during their stay. Chef Marc-Pierre Walker, owner of the inn and husband of Hiddy, who will greet you on your arrival, prepares a fairly classical cuisine of the region: fillet of beef cooked in red wine and ragout of foie gras. *24250 La Roque Gageac, tel. 53–29–57–05, fax 53–29–15–28. 4 rooms with bath or shower. Facilities: restaurant (closed Mon.). AE, DC, MC, V. Closed late Nov.–mid-Dec. and Feb.*

¢ **La Belle Etoile.** This cozy old stone hotel fits snugly into La Roque-Gageac's spectacular cliffside setting on the banks of the Dordogne. Several rooms overlook the river, as does the restaurant, where you'll prefer the set menus (starting at 100 francs) to the pricey à la carte choices, both prepared by the father and son team, Guy and Regis Ongaro. *24250 La Roque-Gageac, tel. 53–29–51–44, fax 53–29–45–63. 17 rooms, 15 with bath or shower. Facilities: restaurant. MC, V. Closed mid-Oct.–Easter.*

Tour 3: Basque Country

This tour, which follows the main Paris–Spain train route as it forks at Dax and heads west, leads you into Basque country and the attractive towns of Bayonne, St-Jean-Pied-de Port, Biarritz, and St-Jean-de-Luz.

From Paris Six TGVs to Dax leave Paris (Gare Montparnasse) each day. The
By Train trip takes 4 hours 7 minutes.

By Car The 735-kilometer (460-mile) drive from Paris takes about 7½ hours. Follow A10 and N10 from Bordeaux, then D947 from Castets.

Dax

Tourist office: place Thiers, by Pont St-Esprit, tel. 58–90–20–00.

Dax, known in Roman times as Aquae Tarbellicae, has been famous for 2,000 years for its thermal springs. The daughter of Caesar Augustus came here to soothe her aches and pains, and she was the first in a long line of seasonal guests whose numbers have swollen to 50,000 each year, making Dax the country's premier warm-water spa. Steaming water gushes out of the lion-headed Néhé fountain in the center of town. The local mud (containing radioactive algae) is also reputed to have healing qualities.

Dax, though short on outstanding sites, is an open, airy town ideal for peaceful walks through its parks and gardens or along the banks of the River Adour. Follow signs from the train station to the Centre Ville, half-mile distant on the other side of the river. To the left as you cross Pont St-Esprit is the Parc Denis, with its bullring and traces of the old city walls. To the right along cours de Verdun is the ornate casino. Rue des Carmes, midway between the bridge and the casino, cuts through the old town toward the classical, 17th-century cathedral, which contains a variety of fine sculpture, some inherited from the previous Gothic structure. (Architecture enthusiasts should make a trip back across the river to the church of St-Paul-lès-Dax, which has 11th-century bas-reliefs adorning its east end.)

Lodding
¢ **Nord.** This clean but unremarkable hotel is not only very inexpensive but also the most convenient for rail travelers, as it's close to the station near Pont St-Esprit. Rooms are smallish. *68 av. St-Vincent-de-Paul, 40100, tel. 58–74–19–87. 19 rooms, some with bath or shower. MC, V. Closed Christmas through New Year's.*

Lodging and Dining
$$ **Régina.** A heated corridor runs between the thermal baths and this large, calm, modern hotel. Rooms are individually decorated, and the best have balconies. In the restaurant, set menus start at 90 frs. *Blvd. des Sports, 40100, tel. 58–74–84–58, fax 58–74–88–31. 88 rooms with bath or shower. Facilities: bar, restaurant. DC, MC, V. Closed Dec.–Feb.*

$ **Richelieu.** The smattering of elderly guests who come to Dax to take the waters across town seem right at home in the spacious, slightly old-fashioned rooms of this hotel, which is centrally located south of the cathedral. The solid, filling local specialties available in the restaurant—mainly variations on poultry and foie gras—have eternal appeal, and there are set menus at 85, 100, and 180 francs. *13 av. Victor-Hugo, 40100, tel. 58–74–81–81, fax 58–74–87–84. 17 rooms with bath or shower. Facilities: restaurant (closed Sun. out of season). AE, DC, MC, V.*

Bayonne

Eight trains daily make the ½-hour run from Dax, 48 km (30 mi) northeast. Most continue to Biarritz and St-Jean-de-Luz. Tourist office: place de la Liberté, tel. 59–59–31–31.

Bayonne is the gateway to Basque country, a territory stretching across the Pyrénées to Bilbao in Spain. Bayonne stands at the confluence of the Rivers Adour and Nive; the port of Bayonne extends along the valley to the sea about 5 kilometers (3 miles) away. You could easily spend an enjoyable few hours here, admiring the town's 13th-century cathedral, cloisters, old houses, and 17th-century ramparts. The airy, modernized **Musée Bonnat** houses a notable collection of 19th-century paintings. *5 rue Jacques-Lafitte, tel. 59–59–08–52. Admission: 15 frs. Open Wed.–Mon. 10–noon and 2:30–6:30.*

Lodging and Dining
$$ **Loustau.** This comfortable hotel with modern amenities stands near the old town ramparts, just 100 yards from the station by Pont St-Esprit. Priced at 330 frs to 420 frs, its well-appointed rooms attract tourists and business travelers alike; the hotel's Clos St-Esprit restaurant offers a buffet at lunchtime, together with 85- to 180-franc menus. *1 pl. de la République, 64100, tel. 59–55–16–74, fax 59–55–69–36. 44 rooms with bath or shower. Facilities: bar, restaurant (closed mid-Dec.–mid-Jan.). AE, DC, MC, V.*

St-Jean-Pied-de-Port

Three trains daily make the 55-minute run southeast from Bayonne. Tourist office: 14 place Charles-de-Gaulle, tel. 59–37–03–57.

The journey itself is one good reason for making an excursion from Bayonne to **St-Jean-Pied-de-Port**, 8 km (5 mi) from the Spanish border. The train hugs the banks of the sinuous River Nive as the valley grows ever steeper and the Pyrénées loom in the distance. Pilgrims

once used St-Jean as a launching pad for their assault on the Pyrénées, preferring to tarry a while in the tumbling street of the old
town. In fact, the winding main street is lined with century-old
houses that are beautifully tended; its cobblestones are worn
smooth, and no cars are allowed to squeeze across the ancient bridge
that once clattered with departures to Santiago de Compostela.
Parts of the original town wall stand, too, but this didn't prevent
Vauban from erecting a fort on a hill above the town, just in case.
Scramble up for sweeping views across the valley and local vineyards, which produce Irouleguy wine.

Dining **Relais de la Nive.** Full of babbling French families eating lunch, this
$ family-run restaurant by the river offers plain, honest Basque fare.
A three-course meal may consist of *jambon de Bayonne* (locally
cured ham), *poulet Basquaise* (chicken cooked in white wine and
served with a heavy piperade sauce), and Pyrénées cheese. Try for a
table looking out at the bridge and river, even if it means waiting a
while and having a drink at the bar. *2 pl. Charles-de-Gaulle, tel. 59-
37-04-22. Closed Mon. MC, V.*

Biarritz

*Trains run from Bayonne to Biarritz every 1½ hours and take 10
minutes to travel the 8 km (5 mi) west. Tourist office: 1 sq. d'Ixelles,
tel. 59-24-20-24.*

The celebrated resort of **Biarritz**, set on a particularly sheltered
part of the Atlantic coast, rose to prominence in the 19th century
when upstart emperor Napoléon III took to spending his holidays
here on the prompting of his Spanish wife, Eugénie. You'll soon understand why: The crowded Grande Plage and neighboring Plage
Miramar provide fine sand and friendly breakers amid a setting of
craggy natural beauty. Biarritz would like to remain a high-brow resort, but the fashionable crowd has dispersed and many of the hotels
have discounted their rooms. Once so stylish, the resort struggles to
keep its head above water, although there are still some smart hotels, in particular Hôtel Le Palais. And with a new casino facing the
sea and a convention center under construction, Biarritz may be on
the road to a comeback, enabling it to challenge its rival to the south,
St-Jean-de-Luz, and San Sebastian, across the border in Spain. Certainly the down-to-earth charm of the former fishing village remains
to counterbalance the uppercrust ambience. The narrow streets
around the 16th-century church of St-Martin are delightful to stroll
and, together with the harbor of Port des Pêcheurs, offer a tantaliz-
ing glimpse of the Biarritz of old.

Lodging **Windsor.** Built in the 1920s, this hotel is handy for the casino and the
$$ beach, and has its own restaurant as well (fish predominates; the
cheapest menu is around 100 francs). The guest rooms—some mod-
erately priced and some more expensive—are modern yet cozy, and
some offer sea views. The least expensive rooms face the inner
courtyard. Guests, including many foreigners, tend to come here
because they can't afford the majestic Palais or the slick Miramar. *19
blvd. du Général-de-Gaulle, 64200, tel. 59-24-08-52, fax 59-24-
98-90. 49 rooms with bath. Facilities: restaurant. AE, MC, V.
Closed mid-Nov.-mid Mar.*

St-Jean-de-Luz

*Trains link Biarritz to St-Jean-de-Luz, 10 minutes southwest, ev-
ery 2 hours. Six trains daily make the 80-minute journey between
St-Jean-de-Luz and Dax. Tourist office: place Foch, tel. 59-26-
03-16.*

★ **St-Jean-de-Luz** deserves a visit for its old streets, curious church,
colorful harbor, and elegant beach. The tree-lined place Louis-XIV,

alongside the Hôtel de Ville with its narrow courtyard and dainty statue of Louis XIV on horseback, is the quaint hub of the town. Nearby are the **Eglise St-Jean-Baptiste**, where unusual wooden galleries line one wall to create a theaterlike effect, and the **Maison de l'Infante,** where Maria Teresa of Spain stayed prior to her wedding to the Sun King. The foursquare mansion contains worthy 17th-century furnishings. *Quai de l'Infante, tel. 59–26–01–56. Admission: 25 frs. Open June–Sept. 10:30–noon and 3–6:30; closed Sun. AM.*

Lodging and Dining $$

Bel Air. There's a family holiday mood at this large villa with an unbeatable location near the beach and next to the casino. The hotel has its own garden and a terrace overlooking the bay; rooms, many of which also overlook the bay, are spacious. In the restaurant there is a set menu at 125 frs. Only MAP and AP reservations are accepted during the high season. *Promenade Jacques-Thibaud, 64500, tel. 59–26–04–86, fax 59–26–62–34. 23 rooms with bath or shower. Facilities: restaurant (June–Sept. only). AE, DC, MC, V. Closed mid-Nov.–Apr.*

Conversion Tables

Clothing Sizes

Men
Suits

To change American suit sizes to French suit sizes, add 10 to the American suit size.
To change French suit sizes to American suit sizes, subtract 10 from the French suit size.

U.S.	36	38	40	42	44	46	48
French	46	48	50	52	54	56	58

Shirts

To change American shirt sizes to French shirt sizes, multiply the American shirt size by 2 and add 8.
To change French shirt sizes to American shirt sizes, subtract 8 from the French shirt size and divide by 2.

U.S.	14	14½	15	15½	16	16½	17	17½
French	36	37	38	39	40	41	42	43

Shoes

French shoe sizes vary in their relation to American shoe sizes.

U.S.	6½	7	8	9	10	10½	11
French	39	40	41	42	43	44	45

Women
Dresses and Coats

To change U.S. dress/coat sizes to French dress/coat sizes, add 28 to the U.S. dress/coat size.
To change French dress/coat sizes to U.S. dress/coat sizes, subtract 28 from the French dress/coat size.

U.S.	4	6	8	10	12	14	16
French	32	34	36	38	40	42	44

Blouses and Sweaters

To change U.S. blouse/sweater sizes to French blouse/sweater sizes, add 8 to the U.S. blouse/sweater size.
To change French blouse/sweater sizes to U.S. blouse/sweater sizes, subtract 8 from the French blouse/sweater size.

U.S.	30	32	34	36	38	40	42
French	38	40	42	44	46	48	50

Shoes

To change U.S. shoe sizes to French shoe sizes, add 32 to the U.S. shoe size.
To change French shoe sizes to U.S. shoe sizes, subtract 32 from the French shoe size.

U.S.	4	5	6	7	8	9	10
French	36	37	38	39	40	41	42

French Vocabulary

Words and Phrases

	English	*French*	*Pronunciation*
Basics	Yes/no	Oui/non	wee/no
	Please	S'il vous plaît	seel voo play
	Thank you	Merci	mare-**see**
	You're welcome	De rien	deh ree-**en**
	Excuse me, sorry	Pardon	pahr-**doan**
	Sorry!	Désolé(e)	day-zoh-**lay**
	Good morning/ afternoon	Bonjour	bone-**joor**
	Good evening	Bonsoir	bone-**swar**
	Goodbye	Au revoir	o ruh-**vwar**
	Mr. (Sir)	Monsieur	mih-see-**oor**
	Mrs. (Ma'am)	Madame	ma-dam
	Miss	Mademoiselle	mad-mwa-**zel**
	Pleased to meet you	Enchanté(e)	on-shahn-**tay**
	How are you?	Comment allez-vous?	ko-men-tahl-ay-**voo**
Numbers	one	un	un
	two	deux	dew
	three	trois	twa
	four	quatre	**cat**-ruh
	five	cinq	sank
	six	six	seess
	seven	sept	set
	eight	huit	wheat
	nine	neuf	nuf
	ten	dix	deess
	eleven	onze	owns
	twelve	douze	dooz
	thirteen	treize	trays
	fourteen	quatorze	ka-torz
	fifteen	quinze	cans
	sixteen	seize	sez
	seventeen	dix-sept	deess-**set**
	eighteen	dix-huit	deess-**wheat**
	nineteen	dix-neuf	deess-**nuf**
	twenty	vingt	vant
	twenty-one	vingt-et-un	vant-ay-**un**
	thirty	trente	trahnt
	forty	quarante	ka-**rahnt**
	fifty	cinquante	sang-**kahnt**
	sixty	soixante	swa-**sahnt**
	seventy	soixante-dix	swa-sahnt-**deess**
	eighty	quatre-vingts	cat-ruh-**vant**
	ninety	quatre-vingt-dix	cat-ruh-vant-**deess**
	one-hundred	cent	sahnt
	one-thousand	mille	meel
Colors	black	noir	nwar
	blue	bleu	blu
	brown	brun/marron	brun
	green	vert	vair
	orange	orange	o-**ranj**

	red	rouge	rouge
	white	blanc	blahn
	yellow	jaune	jone

Days of the Week	Sunday	dimanche	dee-**mahnsh**
	Monday	lundi	lewn-**dee**
	Tuesday	mardi	mar-**dee**
	Wednesday	mercredi	mare-kruh-**dee**
	Thursday	jeudi	juh-**dee**
	Friday	vendredi	van-dra-**dee**
	Saturday	samedi	sam-**dee**

Months	January	janvier	jan-**vyay**
	February	février	feh-vree-**ay**
	March	mars	marce
	April	avril	a-**vreel**
	May	mai	meh
	June	juin	jwan
	July	juillet	jwee-**ay**
	August	août	oot
	September	septembre	sep-**tahm**-bruh
	October	octobre	oak-**toe**-bruh
	November	novembre	no-**vahm**-bruh
	December	décembre	day-**sahm**-bruh

Useful Phrases	Do you speak English?	Parlez-vous anglais?	par-lay vooz ahng-**glay**
	I don't speak French	Je ne parle pas français	jeh nuh parl pah fraun-**say**
	I don't understand	Je ne comprends pas	jeh nuh kohm-prahn **pah**
	I understand	Je comprends	jeh kohm-**prahn**
	I don't know	Je ne sais pas	jeh nuh say **pah**
	I'm American/British	Je suis américain/anglais	jeh sweez a-may-ree-**can**/ahng-**glay**
	What's your name?	Comment vous appelez-vous?	ko-mahn voo za-pel-ay-**voo**
	My name is . . .	Je m'appelle . . .	jeh muh-**pel** . . .
	What time is it?	Quelle heure est-il?	kel ur et-**il**
	How?	Comment?	ko-**mahn**
	When?	Quand?	kahnd
	Yesterday	Hier	yair
	Today	Aujourd'hui	o-zhoor-**dwee**
	Tomorrow	Demain	deh-**man**
	This morning/afternoon	Ce matin/cet après-midi	seh ma-**tanh**/set ah-pray-mee-**dee**
	Tonight	Ce soir	seh **swar**
	What?	Quoi?	kwah
	What is it?	Qu'est-ce que c'est?	kess-kuh-**say**
	Why?	Pourquoi?	poor-**kwa**
	Who?	Qui?	kee

Where is . . .	Où est . . .	oo ay
the train station?	la gare?	la gar
the subway station?	la station de métro?	la sta-syon deh may-**tro**
the bus stop?	l'arrêt de bus?	la-ray deh **booss**
the terminal (airport)?	l'aérogare?	lay-ro-**gar**
the post office?	la poste?	la post
the bank?	la banque?	la bahnk
the . . . hotel?	l'hôtel . . . ?	low-**tel**
the . . . museum?	le musée . . . ?	leh mew-**zay**
the hospital?	l'hôpital?	low-pee-**tahl**
the elevator?	l'ascenseur?	la-sahn-**seur**
the telephone?	le téléphone?	leh te-le-**phone**
Where are the restrooms?	Où sont les toilettes?	oo son lay twah-**let**
Here/there	Ici/lá	ee-**see**/la
Left/right	A gauche/à droite	a goash/a drwat
Is it near/far?	C'est près/loin?	say pray/lwan
I'd like . . .	Je voudrais . . .	jeh voo-**dray**
a room	une chambre	ewn **shahm**-bra
the key	la clé	la clay
a newspaper	un journal	un joor-**nahl**
a stamp	un timbre	un **tam**-bruh
I'd like to buy . . .	Je voudrais acheter . . .	jeh voo-**dray** ahsh-**tay**
cigarettes	des cigarettes	day see-ga-**ret**
matches	des allumettes	days a-loo-**met**
city plan	un plan de ville	un plahn de la **veel**
road map	une carte routière	ewn cart roo-tee-**air**
magazine	une revue	ewn reh-**view**
envelopes	des enveloppes	dayz ahn-veh-**lope**
writing paper	du papier à lettres	deh-pa-pee-ay a **let**-ruh
airmail writing paper	du papier avion	deh pa-pee-ay a-vee-**own**
postcard	une carte postale	ewn cart post-**al**
How much is it?	C'est combien?	say comb-bee-**en**
It's expensive/cheap	C'est cher/pas cher	say sher/pa sher
A little/a lot	Un peu/beaucoup	un puh/bo-**koo**
More/less	Plus/moins	ploo/mwa
Enough/too (much)	Assez/trop	a-**say**/tro
I am ill/sick	Je suis malade	jeh swee ma-**lahd**
Call a doctor	Appelez un docteur	a-pe-lay un dohk-**tore**
Help!	Au secours!	o say-**koor**
Stop!	Arrêtez!	a-ruh-**tay**
Dining Out A bottle of . . .	une bouteille de . . .	ewn boo-**tay** deh
A cup of . . .	une tasse de . . .	ewn tass deh

A glass of . . .	un verre de . . .	un vair deh
Ashtray	un cendrier	un sahn-dree-**ay**
Bill/check	l'addition	la-dee-see-**own**
Bread	du pain	due pan
Breakfast	le petit déjeuner	leh pet-**ee** day-zhu-**nay**
Cocktail/aperitif	un apéritif	un ah-pay-ree-**teef**
Dinner	le dîner	leh dee-**nay**
Fixed-price menu	le menu	leh may-**new**
Fork	une fourchette	ewn four-**shet**
I am vegetarian	Je suis végétarien(ne)	jeh swee vay-jay-ta-ree-**en**
I cannot eat . . .	Je ne peux pas manger de . . .	jeh nuh puh pah mahn-**jay** deh
I'd like to order	Je voudrais commander	jeh voo-**dray** ko-mahn-**day**
I'd like . . .	Je voudrais . . .	jeh voo-**dray**
I'm hungry/thirsty	J'ai faim/soif	jay fam/swahf
Is service/the tip included?	Est-ce que le service est compris?	ess keh leh sair-veess ay comb-**pree**
It's good/bad	C'est bon/mauvais	say bon/mo-**vay**
It's hot/cold	C'est chaud/froid	say sho/frwah
Knife	un couteau	un koo-**toe**
Lunch	le déjeuner	leh day-juh-**nay**
Menu	la carte	la cart
Napkin	une serviette	ewn sair-vee-**et**
Pepper	du poivre	due **pwah**-vruh
Plate	une assiette	ewn a-see-**et**
Please give me . . .	Donnez-moi . . .	doe-nay-**mwah**
Salt	du sel	dew sell
Wine list	la carte des vins	la cart day **van**

Menu Guide

English	French
Set menu	Menu à prix fixe
Dish of the day	Plat du jour
Drink included	Boisson comprise
Local specialties	Spécialités locales
Choice of vegetable accompaniment	Garniture au choix
Made to order	Sur commande
Extra charge	Supplément/En sus
When available	Selon arrivage

Breakfast

Jam	Confiture
Croissants	Croissants
Honey	Miel
Boiled egg	Oeuf à la coque
Bacon and eggs	Oeufs au bacon
Ham and eggs	Oeufs au jambon
Fried eggs	Oeufs sur le plat
Scrambled eggs	Oeufs brouillés
(Plain) omelet	Omelette (nature)
Rolls	Petits pains

Starters

Anchovies	Anchois
Chitterling sausage	Andouille(tte)
Assorted cold cuts	Assiette anglaise
Assorted pork products	Assiette de charcuterie
Small, highly seasoned sausage	Crépinette
Mixed raw vegetable salad	Crudités
Snails	Escargots
Ham (Bayonne)	Jambon (de Bayonne)
Bologna sausage	Mortadelle
Devilled eggs	Oeufs à la diable
Liver purée blended with other meat	Pâté
Tart with a rich, creamy filling of cheese, vegetables, meat or seafood	Quiche (lorraine)
Cold sausage	Saucisson
Pâté sliced and served from an earthenware pot	Terrine
Cured dried beef	Viande séchée

Salads

Diced vegetable salad	Salade russe
Endive salad	Salade d'endives
Green salad	Salade verte
Mixed salad	Salade panachée
Tuna salad	Salade de thon

Soups

Clear soup	Consommé, bouillon
Cold leek and potato cream soup	Vichyssoise
Cream of . . .	Crème de . . .

Cream of . . .	Velouté de . . .
Hearty soup	Soupe
Day's soup	Soupe du jour
French onion soup	Soupe à l'oignon
Provençal vegetable soup	Soupe au pistou
Light soup	Potage
Fish and seafood stew	Bouillabaisse
Seafood stew (chowder)	Bisque
Stew of meat and vegetables	Pot-au-feu

Fish and Seafood

Bass	Bar
Carp	Carpe
Clams	Palourdes
Cod	Morue
Creamed salt cod	Brandade de morue
Crab	Crabe
Crayfish	Ecrevisses
Eel	Anguille
Fish stew from Marseille	Bourride
Fish stew in wine	Matelote
Frog's legs	Cuisses de grenouilles
Herring	Harengs
Lobster	Homard
Mackerel	Maquereau
Mussels	Moules
Octopus	Poulpe
Oysters	Huîtres
Perch	Perche
Pike	Brochet
Dublin bay prawns (scampi)	Langoustines
Red mullet	Rouget
Salmon	Saumon
Scallops in creamy sauce	Coquilles St-Jacques
Sea bream	Daurade
Shrimps	Crevettes
Sole	Sole
Squid	Calmar
Trout	Truite
Tuna	Thon
Whiting	Merlan

Methods of Preparation

Baked	Au four
Fried	Frit
Grilled	Grillé
Marinated	Mariné
Poached	Poché
Sautéed	Sauté
Smoked	Fumé
Steamed	Cuit à la vapeur

Meat

Beef	Boeuf
Beef stew with vegetables, braised in red Burgundy wine	Boeuf bourguignon
Brains	Cervelle
Chops	Côtelettes

Cutlet	Escalope
Double fillet steak	Chateaubriand
Kabob	Brochette
Kidneys	Rognons
Lamb	Agneau
Leg	Gigot
Liver	Foie
Meatballs	Boulettes de viande
Pig's feet (trotters)	Pieds de cochon
Pork	Porc
Rib	Côte
Rib or rib-eye steak	Entrecôte
Sausages	Saucisses
Sausages and cured pork served with sauerkraut	Choucroute garnie
Steak (always beef)	Steak/steack
Stew	Ragoût
T-bone steak	Côte de boeuf
Tenderloin steak	Médaillon
Tenderloin of T-bone steak	Tournedos
Tongue	Langue
Veal	Veau
Veal sweetbreads	Ris de veau

Methods of Preparation

Very rare	Bleu
Rare	Saignant
Medium	A point
Well-done	Bien cuit
Baked	Au four
Boiled	Bouilli
Braised	Braisé
Fried	Frit
Grilled	Grillé
Roast	Rôti
Sautéed	Sauté
Stewed	A l'étouffée

Game and Poultry

Chicken	Poulet
Chicken breast	Suprême de volaille
Chicken stewed in red wine	Coq au vin
Chicken stewed with vegetables	Poule au pot
Spring chicken	Poussin
Duck/duckling	Canard/caneton
Duck braised with oranges and orange liqueur	Canard à l'orange
Fattened pullet	Poularde
Fowl	Volaille
Guinea fowl/young guinea fowl	Pintade/pintadeau
Goose	Oie
Partridge/young partridge	Perdrix/perdreau
Pheasant	Faisan
Pigeon/squab	Pigeon/pigeonneau
Quail	Caille
Rabbit	Lapin
Turkey/young turkey	Dinde/dindonneau
Venison (red/roe)	Cerf/chevreuil

Vegetables

Artichoke	Artichaut
Asparagus	Asperge
Brussels sprouts	Choux de Bruxelles
Cabbage (red)	Chou (rouge)
Carrots	Carottes
Cauliflower	Chou-fleur
Eggplant	Aubergines
Endive	Endives
Leeks	Poireaux
Lettuce	Laitue
Mushrooms	Champignons
Onions	Oignons
Peas	Petits pois
Peppers	Poivrons
Radishes	Radis
Spinach	Epinards
Tomatoes	Tomates
Watercress	Cresson
Zucchini	Courgette
White kidney/French beans	Haricots blancs/verts
Casserole of stewed eggplant, onions, green peppers, and zucchini	Ratatouille

Spices and Herbs

Bay leaf	Laurier
Chervil	Cerfeuil
Garlic	Ail
Marjoram	Marjolaine
Mustard	Moutarde
Parsley	Persil
Pepper	Poivre
Rosemary	Romarin
Tarragon	Estragon
Mixture of herbs	Fines herbes

Potatoes, Rice, and Noodles

Noodles	Nouilles
Pasta	Pâtes
Potatoes	Pommes (de terre)
matchsticks	*allumettes*
mashed and deep-fried	*dauphine*
mashed with butter and egg yolks	*duchesse*
in their jackets	*en robe des champs*
french fries	*frites*
mashed	*mousseline*
boiled/steamed	*nature/vapeur*
Rice	Riz
boiled in bouillon with onions	*pilaf*

Sauces and Preparations

Brown butter, parsley, lemon juice	Meunière
Curry	Indienne
Egg yolks, butter, vinegar	Hollandaise
Hot pepper	Diable
Mayonnaise flavored with mustard and herbs	Tartare

Mushrooms, red wine, shallots, beef marrow	Bordelaise
Onions, tomatoes, garlic	Provençale
Pepper sauce	Poivrade
Red wine, herbs	Bourguignon
Vinegar, egg yolks, white wine, shallots, tarragon	Béarnaise
Vinegar dressing	Vinaigrette
White sauce	Béchamel
White wine, mussel broth, egg yolks	Marinière
Wine, mushrooms, onions, shallots	Chasseur
With goose or duck liver purée and truffles	Périgueux
With Madeira wine	Madère

Cheeses

Mild:	Beaufort
	Beaumont
	Belle étoile
	Boursin
	Brie
	Cantal
	Comté
	Reblochon
	St-Paulin
	Tomme de Savoie
Sharp:	Bleu de Bresse
	Camembert
	Livarot
	Fromage au marc
	Munster
	Pont-l'Évêque
	Roquefort
Swiss:	Emmenthal
	Gruyère
	Vacherin
Goat's milk:	St-Marcellin
	Crottin de Chavignol Valençay
Cheese tart	Tarte au fromage
Small cheese tart	Ramequin
Toasted ham and cheese sandwich	Croque-monsieur

Fruits and Nuts

Almonds	Amandes
Apple	Pomme
Apricot	Abricot
Banana	Banane
Blackberries	Mûres
Blackcurrants	Cassis
Blueberries	Myrtilles
Cherries	Cerises
Chestnuts	Marrons
Coconut	Noix de coco
Dates	Dattes
Dried fruit	Fruits secs
Figs	Figues
Grapefruit	Pamplemousse
Grapes green/blue	Raisin blanc/noir

Hazelnuts	Noisettes
Lemon	Citron
Melon	Melon
Orange	Orange
Peach	Pêche
Peanuts	Cacahouètes
Pear	Poire
Pineapple	Ananas
Plums	Prunes
Prunes	Pruneaux
Raisins	Raisins secs
Raspberries	Framboises
Strawberries	Fraises
Tangerine	Mandarine
Walnuts	Noix
Watermelon	Pastèque

Desserts

Apple pie	Tarte aux pommes
Baked Alaska	Omelette norvégienne
Caramel pudding	Crème caramel
Chocolate cake	Gâteau au chocolat
Chocolate pudding	Mousse au chocolat
Custard tart	Flan
Custard	Crème anglaise
Ice cream	Glace
Layer cake	Tourte
Pear with vanilla ice cream and chocolate sauce	Poire Belle Hélène
Soufflé made with orange liqueur	Soufflé au Grand-Marnier
Sundae	Coupe (glacée)
Water ice	Sorbet
Whipped cream	Crème Chantilly
Creamy dessert of egg yolks, wine, sugar, and flavoring	Sabayon
Puff pastry filled with whipped cream or custard	Profiterole

Index

Maison des Canuts (Lyon), *312–315, 318–325. See also* Toulouse

Maison du Crible (Lyon), *247*

Maison du Vin (Angers), *123*

Maison du Vin de Saumur, *126*

Maison Natale de Toulouse-Lautrec (Albi), *321*

Maison Pfister (Colmar), *211*

Maisons-Laffitte, *116*

Malmaison, *118*

Mandelieu (La Napoule), *304*

Manécanterie (Lyon), *247*

Manoir de la touche (Nantes), *159*

Marais (Paris), *59, 69–72, 87*

Marché aux Fleurs (Paris), *68*

Marché aux Vins (Beaune), *238*

Margaux (Médoc), *345–346*

Marie Antoinette, *67, 74, 104, 106, 108*

Marine Museum and Aquarium (Dinard), *153*

Maritime Museum (Paris), *77*

Marquis de Sade, *71*

Marseille, *40, 287–290*

Martell (Cognac), *340–341*

Massabielle grotto (Lourdes), *327*

Matisse, Henri, *186*

Mediterranean Film Festival (Bastia), *263*

Médoc, *345–346*

Megalithic monuments, Ajaccio, Carnac, *156*

Megère, *242*

Mémorial (Caen), *171*

Menton, *311*

Mercier (champagne cellar; Epernay), *194*

Méribel, *242*

Merveille de l'Occident (Mont-St-Michel), *177–178*

Métro (Paris), *47, 50*

Metz, *218–219*

Midi-Pyrénées,

Modern Art Museum (Troyes), *228–229*

Modigliani, *84*

Moissac, *325*

Mona Lisa, *66*

Monaco, *35, 308–310*

Monet, Claude, *115*

Money, *9–10, 27–29*

Mont-Blanc (Chamonix), *258*

Mont-St-Michel, *39, 177–178*

Montauban, *324–325*

Montbéliard, *222*

Monte Carlo (Monaco), *35, 308–310*

Monte Carlo Open Tennis Championships, *35*

Montée Nicolas-de-Lange (Lyon), *248*

Montmartre (Paris), *59, 82, 84–86*

Montmartre Cemetery (Paris), *84*

Montparnasse (Paris), *60*

Montreuil-sur-Mer, *188–189*

Monument des Bourgeois de Calais, *186–187*

Moret-sur-Loing, *114–115*

Morzine, *242*

Mosque (Paris), *82*

Moulin de la Galette (Paris), *84*

Moulin des Boly (Lourdes), *327*

Moulin Rouge (Paris), *82, 84*

Mulhouse, *212–213*

Mumm (champagne cellar; Reims), *192*

Musée Alsacien (Strasbourg), *205, 208*

Musée Américain (Giverny), *116*

Musée Archéologique (Antibes), *301*

Musée Archéologique (Dijon), *237*

Musée Archéologique (Nice), *299*

Musée Archéoligique (St-Rémy-de-Provence), *286*

Musée Archéologique (Strasbourg), *205*

Musée Archéologique et d'Histoire Naturelle (Nîmes), *281*

Musée Baron Gérard (Bayeux), *173*

Musée Bartholdi (Colmar), *211*

Musée Béarnais (Pau), *326*

Musée Bernadette (Lourdes), *327*

Musée Bonnat (Bayonne), *350*

Musée Bricard de la Serrure (Paris), *70*

Musée Calvet (Avignon), *279*

Musée Chagall (Nice), *299*

Musée Champollion (Figeac), *322*

Musée Cognacq-Jay (Paris), *71*

Musée Daubigny (Auvers-sur-Orse), *117*

Musée Dauphinois (Grenoble), *255*

Musée David d'Angers, *125*

Musée d'Art Chrétien (Arles), *284–285*

Musée d'Art et d'Archéologie (Senlis), *196*

Musée d'Art et d'Histoire (Belfort), *220*

Musée d'Art et d'Histoire (Metz), *219*

Musée d'Art et d'Histoire Romain Rolland (Clamecy), *232*

Musée d'Art Juif (Paris), *86*

Musée d'Art Moderne (Troyes), *228–229*

Musée d'Art Moderne et d'Art Contemporain (Nice), *300*

Musée d'Art Païen (Arles), *284*

Musée d'Art Populaire Régional (Nantes), *158*

Musée d'Art Sacré (Dijon), *237*

Musée d'Art Sacré du Gemmail (Lourdes), *327*

Musée d'Arts Decoratifs (Saumur), *126*

Musée d'Ethnographie Corse (Bastia), *264*

Musée d'Histoire Naturelle (Aix-en-Provence), *290–291*

Musée d'Histoire Naturelle (Dijon), *237*

Musée d'Histoire Naturelle (La Rochelle), *338*

Musée d'Histoire Naturelle (Toulouse), *319*

Musée d'Orsay (Paris), *75*

Musée d'Unterlinden (Colmar), *211*

Musée de Bretagne (Rennes), *146*

Musée de Ferronerie Le Secq des Tournelles (Rouen), *167*

Musée de l'Absinthe (Auvers-sur-Oise), *117*

Musée de l'Armée (Paris), *76*

Musée de l'Art Moderne de la Ville de Paris, *77*

Musée de l'Aventure Peugeot (Montbéliard), *222*

Musée de l'Ecole de Nancy, *217*

Musée de l'Histoire de France (Paris), *70*

Musée de l'Histoire de Marseille, *289*

Musée de l'Histoire de Paris, *71*

Musée de l'Homme (Paris), *76–77*

Musée de l'Oeuvre Notre Dame (Strasbourg), *204–205*

Musée de la Bataille de Normandie (Bayeux), *175*

Musée de la Bénédictine (Fécamp), *169*

Musée de la Bonneterie (Troyes), *230*

NOTES

NOTES

NOTES

NOTES

Fodor's Travel Publications

Available at bookstores everywhere, or call 1–800–533–6478, 24 hours a day.

Gold Guides

U.S.

Alaska	Florida	New Orleans	Santa Fe, Taos, Albuquerque
Arizona	Hawaii	New York City	
Boston	Las Vegas, Reno, Tahoe	Pacific North Coast	Seattle & Vancouver
California		Philadelphia & the Pennsylvania Dutch Country	The South
Cape Cod, Martha's Vineyard, Nantucket	Los Angeles		U.S. & British Virgin Islands
	Maine, Vermont, New Hampshire		
The Carolinas & the Georgia Coast	Maui	The Rockies	USA
Chicago	Miami & the Keys	San Diego	Virginia & Maryland
Colorado	New England	San Francisco	Waikiki
			Washington, D.C.

Foreign

Australia & New Zealand	Egypt	Madrid & Barcelona	Provence & the Riviera
Austria	Europe	Mexico	Scandinavia
The Bahamas	Florence, Tuscany & Umbria	Montréal & Québec City	Scotland
Barbados	France	Morocco	Singapore
Bermuda	Germany	Moscow, St. Petersburg, Kiev	South America
Brazil	Great Britain		South Pacific
Budapest	Greece	The Netherlands, Belgium & Luxembourg	Southeast Asia
Canada	Hong Kong		Spain
Cancún, Cozumel, Yucatán Peninsula	India	New Zealand	Sweden
Caribbean	Ireland	Norway	Switzerland
China	Israel	Nova Scotia, New Brunswick, Prince Edward Island	Thailand
Costa Rica, Belize, Guatemala	Italy		Tokyo
	Japan	Paris	Toronto
The Czech Republic & Slovakia	Kenya & Tanzania	Portugal	Turkey
	Korea		Vienna & the Danube
Eastern Europe	London		

Fodor's Special-Interest Guides

Branson	Fodor's London Companion	Kodak Guide to Shooting Great Travel Pictures	Walt Disney World for Adults
Caribbean Ports of Call	France by Train		Where Should We Take the Kids? California
The Complete Guide to America's National Parks	Halliday's New England Food Explorer	Shadow Traffic's New York Shortcuts and Traffic Tips	
		Sunday in New York	Where Should We Take the Kids? Northeast
Condé Nast Traveler Caribbean Resort and Cruise Ship Finder	Healthy Escapes	Sunday in San Francisco	
	Italy by Train		
Cruises and Ports of Call		Walt Disney World, Universal Studios and Orlando	

pecial Series

ffordables

Caribbean

Europe

Florida

France

Germany

Great Britain

Italy

London

Paris

Fodor's Bed & Breakfasts and Country Inns

America's Best B&Bs

California's Best B&Bs

Canada's Great Country Inns

Cottages, B&Bs and Country Inns of England and Wales

The Mid-Atlantic's Best B&Bs

New England's Best B&Bs

The Pacific Northwest's Best B&Bs

The South's Best B&Bs

The Southwest's Best B&Bs

The Upper Great Lakes' Best B&Bs

The Berkeley Guides

California

Central America

Eastern Europe

Europe

France

Germany & Austria

Great Britain & Ireland

Italy

London

Mexico

Pacific Northwest & Alaska

Paris

San Francisco

Compass American Guides

Arizona

Canada

Chicago

Colorado

Hawaii

Hollywood

Las Vegas

Maine

Manhattan

Montana

New Mexico

New Orleans

Oregon

San Francisco

South Carolina

South Dakota

Texas

Utah

Virginia

Washington

Wine Country

Wisconsin

Wyoming

Fodor's Español

California

Caribe Occidental

Caribe Oriental

Gran Bretaña

Londres

Mexico

Nueva York

Paris

Fodor's Exploring Guides

Australia

Boston & New England

Britain

California

Caribbean

China

Florence & Tuscany

Florida

France

Germany

Ireland

Italy

London

Mexico

Moscow & St. Petersburg

New York City

Paris

Prague

Provence

Rome

San Francisco

Scotland

Singapore & Malaysia

Spain

Thailand

Turkey

Venice

Fodor's Flashmaps

Boston

New York

San Francisco

Washington, D.C.

Fodor's Pocket Guides

Acapulco

Atlanta

Barbados

Jamaica

London

New York City

Paris

Prague

Puerto Rico

Rome

San Francisco

Washington, D.C.

Rivages Guides

Bed and Breakfasts of Character and Charm in France

Hotels and Country Inns of Character and Charm in France

Hotels and Country Inns of Character and Charm in Italy

Short Escapes

Country Getaways in Britain

Country Getaways in France

Country Getaways Near New York City

Fodor's Sports

Golf Digest's Best Places to Play

Skiing USA

USA Today The Complete Four Sport Stadium Guide

Fodor's Vacation Planners

Great American Learning Vacations

Great American Sports & Adventure Vacations

Great American Vacations

National Parks and Seashores of the East

National Parks of the West